75
READINGS
PLUS

75
READINGS
PLUS

Santi Buscemi
Middlesex County College

Charlotte Smith
Virginia Polytechnic Institute
and State University

McGRAW-HILL, INC.
New York   St. Louis   San Francisco   Auckland   Bogotá   Caracas
Lisbon   London   Madrid   Mexico   Milan   Montreal
New Delhi   Paris   San Juan   Singapore   Sydney   Tokyo   Toronto

This book was set in Times Roman by The Clarinda Company.
The editors were Lesley Denton and Tom Holton;
the production supervisor was Janelle S. Travers.
The cover was designed by Carol Couch;
cover illustration by Jane Moorman.
R. R. Donnelley & Sons Company was printer and binder.

75 READINGS PLUS

Acknowledgments appear on pages 479–483, and on this page by reference.

2 3 4 5 6 7 8 9 0 DOC DOC 9 0 9 8 7 6 5 4 3 2

ISBN 0-07-009348-2

Library of Congress Cataloging-in-Publication Data

75 readings plus / [edited by] Santi Buscemi, Charlotte Smith.
      p.   cm.
   "Portions of this book have been taken from 75 readings: an anthology"—T.p. verso.
   ISBN 0-07-009348-2
   1. College readers.   2. English language—Rhetoric.   I. Buscemi,
Santi V.   II. Smith, Charlotte.   III. 75 readings.   IV. Title:
Seventy-five readings plus.
PE1417.A14   1992
808'0427—dc20   91-35197

About the Authors

Santi Buscemi teaches reading and writing and chairs the English department at Middlesex County College in Edison, New Jersey.

Charlotte Smith teaches literature and writing at Virginia Polytechnic Institute and State University in Blacksburg, Virginia.

Contents

CHAPTER 1
Narration

CHAPTER 2
Description

CHAPTER 3
Process

CHAPTER 4
Definition

CHAPTER 5
Division and Classification

CHAPTER 6
Comparison and Contrast

Thematic Contents

Perspectives on Existence

Growing Up, Growing Old

Life in America

Canadian Voices

Power and Politics

Problems, Solutions, and Consequences

Territory and Competition

Cultural Rules of Form and Behavior

The Evolution of Science and Technology

Fear and Exhilaration

On Media

On Language and the Writing Process

To the Instructor

When first published in 1987, *75 Readings* responded to a demand by freshman composition instructors for an easy-to-use collection of well-known essays that, over the years, had proven to be effective as springboards for classroom discussion and as rhetorical models. Now in its third edition, *75 Readings* continues to reflect our commitment to offer a wide variety of themes, subjects, writing styles, voices, and cultural perspectives. The notion that the text should be simple and accessible gave rise to the decision that instructional apparatus should be limited and that it should appear only in an ancillary text from which instructors could make copies for students as needed. This accomplished two goals. It reduced the cost of the book, and it allowed faculty to assign instructional apparatus selectively.

Recently, however, conversations with instructors who make frequent and thorough use of the ancillary materials revealed that the text would be even more useful were the essay selections and instructional apparatus combined in one volume. Our response is *75 Readings Plus.*

The table of contents in this text is identical to what appears in the current edition of *75 Readings.* As with other versions of the text, an author biography, a complete set of discussion questions on content and strategy, and at least two fully developed Suggestions for Sustained Writing are provided for each selection.

However, the instructional apparatus in *75 Readings Plus* has been revised and enhanced. Of special interest is a new section called Suggestions for Short Writing, which includes two or three prompts for informal writing following immediately upon and inspired by a reading of each essay selection. These prompts can also be used as journal assignments or as warm-up exercises for longer projects such as those described in Suggestions for Sustained Writing, and in some cases can even be used as prompts for complete essays. Though most of the Suggestions for Short Writing are specific to the essay they follow, they can be altered to generate discussion on other essays as well.

In addition, each chapter now offers students a brief introduction to the selections it contains and an explanation of the rhetorical strategies those selections illustrate. Designed to help students draw important connections among chapter selections in regard to purpose, strategy, and voice, such commentary enhances the students' appreciation of the material and provides inspiration and direction for their own writing.

We are very grateful for the support and suggestions of the many fine instructors who have used *75 Readings* over the past five years, and we hope that those of you whose comments led to the creation of *75 Readings Plus* will find what we have done useful. Special thanks go to Lesley Denton, our editor and good friend, for suggesting this project in the first place, for providing the encouragement we needed to complete it, and especially for being responsive to the needs of students and teachers.

Santi Buscemi
Charlotte Smith

75
READINGS
PLUS

1

Narration

One of the things that defines us as human is the universal desire and ability to create narrative. "Tell me a story," the child implores; and we willingly oblige by reciting an old favorite passed down through the generations or by making up one of our own.

We are naturally curious creatures, wanting to know what happened, when, and to whom—even if none of it is true. Perhaps that is why we feel compelled to create mythologies on one hand and to report the news or write history on the other.

Some narratives contain long evocative descriptions of setting. Others present fascinating characters whose predicaments rivet our attention or whose lives mirror our own. Still others seem more like plays, heavy with dialogue by which writers allow their characters to reveal themselves. Whatever combination of techniques authors use, all stories—from the briefest anecdotes to the longest novels—have a plot. They recount events in a more-or-less chronological order. They reveal what happened, and, in most cases, allow readers or listeners to draw their own conclusions about the significance of those events.

This is perhaps the chief difference between what you will read in Chapter 1 and essays in other parts of this text. While some types of writing are aimed at explaining or persuading, narration dramatizes important human concerns by presenting events that, when taken together, create a world the author wants the reader to share.

Moving from beginning to end by order of time, narration generally relies on a more natural pattern of organization than other types of writing, but it is no less sophisticated or powerful a tool for explaining complex ideas or for changing readers' opinions than, say, analogy, classification, or formal argument. All storytellers, no matter how entertaining their tales, have something to say about human beings and the world they inhabit. If you have already read selections from the chapters that follow, you know that writers often couple narration with other techniques to develop ideas and support opinions which

1

otherwise might have remained abstract, unclear, or unconvincing. A good story may reveal more about a person or a place than physical description, and it can sometimes help readers understand an important problem or issue beyond our most valiant attempts to explain it "logically."

The point is that writers of narrative are not compelled to underscore the connection between the events in a story and the point it makes. Readers can find their own "theses."

Many of the essays you will read in this chapter are autobiographical: Angelou, Hughes, and Kurosawa show how they confronted difficult situations and, in the process, achieved significant insight into themselves and their worlds. The writing of essays like theirs often results from a profound compulsion to find meaning in what once seemed devoid of it, a process that may define the act of narration itself.

In other selections, authors draw inspiration from their life's work to share observations that both comfort and disturb. Zinsser reminds us that writing, like most other important activities, must be intensely private and personal if it is to succeed. Selzer's story is more unsettling. The brief but meticulous history of an illness, it is at once so clear and absorbing that we cannot help recognize the agony of both patient and doctor.

The selections by Orwell and Herrera might be placed in a third category. They point beyond themselves to social and political issues that are universal and perennial. And though Schreiner writes in an intensely personal voice, she too reminds us that "nothing in the Universe is quite alone."

However the pieces in this chapter seem to be related—and you will surely find connections of your own to talk about—remember that each has been included because it has a poignant story to tell. Read each selection carefully, and learn what you can about the techniques of narration. Here's hoping that at least a few will inspire you to narrate a personal vision of the world that will enrich both you and your readers.

A Hanging

George Orwell

George Orwell is the pseudonym of Eric Blair (1903–1950). Born in India, where his father served in the British colonial government, Orwell was educated at Eton. As a young man, he served as a British police officer in Burma, the setting for this selection. Later, he was wounded while fighting for the loyalists in the Spanish Civil War, about which he wrote in Homage to Catalonia. *Orwell despised the "Big Brother" mentalities of both the fascists and the communists, who backed opposing sides in that war. However, he also condemned the crass bureaucracy of the democratic governments of his time. In short, Orwell was an enemy of politics and politicians in general. He is remembered for* Animal Farm *(1946) and* 1984 *(1949), classics of political satire, and for his many essays.*

It was in Burma, a sodden morning of the rains. A sickly light, like yel- 1
low tinfoil, was slanting over the high walls into the jail yard. We were waiting outside the condemned cells, a row of sheds fronted with double bars, like small animal cages. Each cell measured about ten feet by ten and was quite bare within except for a plank bed and a pot of drinking water. In some of them brown silent men were squatting at the inner bars, with their blankets draped round them. These were the condemned men, due to be hanged within the next week or two.

One prisoner had been brought out of his cell. He was a Hindu, a puny 2
wisp of a man, with a shaven head and vague liquid eyes. He had a thick, sprouting moustache, absurdly too big for his body, rather like the moustache of a comic man in the films. Six tall Indian warders were guarding him and getting him ready for the gallows. Two of them stood by with rifles and fixed bayonets, while the others handcuffed him, passed a chain through his handcuffs and fixed it to their belts, and lashed his arms tight to his sides. They crowded very close about him, with their hands always on him in a careful, caressing grip, as though all the while feeling him to make sure he was there. It was like men handling a fish which is still alive and may jump back into the water. But he stood quite unresisting, yielding his arms limply to the ropes, as though he hardly noticed what was happening.

Eight o'clock struck and a bugle call, desolately thin in the wet air, 3
floated from the distant barracks. The superintendent of the jail, who was standing apart from the rest of us, moodily prodding the gravel with his stick, raised his head at the sound. He was an army doctor, with a grey toothbrush moustache and a gruff voice. "For God's sake hurry up, Francis," he said irritably. "The man ought to have been dead by this time. Aren't you ready yet?"

Francis, the head jailer, a fat Dravidian in a white drill suit and gold spec- 4

3

tacles, waved his black hand. "Yes sir, yes sir," he bubbled. "All iss satisfacto-
rily prepared. The hangman iss waiting. We shall proceed."

"Well, quick march, then. The prisoners can't get their breakfast till this   5
job's over."

We set out for the gallows. Two warders marched on either side of the   6
prisoner, with their rifles at the slope; two others marched close against him,
gripping him by arm and shoulder, as though at once pushing and supporting
him. The rest of us, magistrates and the like, followed behind. Suddenly, when
we had gone ten yards, the procession stopped short without any order or warning. A dreadful thing had happened—a dog, come goodness knows whence, had
appeared in the yard. It came bounding among us with a loud volley of barks,
and leapt round us wagging its whole body, wild with glee at finding so many
human beings together. It was a large woolly dog, half Airedale, half pariah.
For a moment it pranced round us, and then, before anyone could stop it, it had
made a dash for the prisoner, and jumping up tried to lick his face. Everyone
stood aghast, too taken aback even to grab at the dog.

"Who let that bloody brute in here?" said the superintendent angrily.   7
"Catch it, someone!"

A warder, detached from the escort, charged clumsily after the dog, but it   8
danced and gambolled just out of his reach, taking everything as part of the
game. A young Eurasian jailer picked up a handful of gravel and tried to stone
the dog away, but it dodged the stones and came after us again. Its yaps echoed
from the jail walls. The prisoner, in the grasp of the two warders, looked on
incuriously, as though this was another formality of the hanging. It was several
minutes before someone managed to catch the dog. Then we put my handkerchief through its collar and moved off once more, with the dog still straining
and whimpering.

It was about forty yards to the gallows. I watched the bare brown back of   9
the prisoner marching in front of me. He walked clumsily with his bound arms,
but quite steadily, with that bobbing gait of the Indian who never straightens his
knees. At each step his muscles slid neatly into place, the lock of hair on his
scalp danced up and down, his feet printed themselves on the wet gravel. And
once, in spite of the men who gripped him by each shoulder, he stepped slightly
aside to avoid a puddle on the path.

It is curious, but till that moment I had never realised what it means to   10
destroy a healthy, conscious man. When I saw the prisoner step aside to avoid
the puddle, I saw the mystery, the unspeakable wrongness, of cutting a life
short when it is in full tide. This man was not dying, he was alive just as we
were alive. All the organs of his body were working—bowels digesting food,
skin renewing itself, nails growing, tissues forming—all toiling away in solemn
foolery. His nails would still be growing when he stood on the drop, when he
was falling through the air with a tenth of a second to live. His eyes saw the
yellow gravel and the grey walls, and his brain still remembered, foresaw, reasoned— reasoned even about puddles. He and we were a party of men walking

together, seeing, hearing, feeling, understanding the same world; and in two minutes, with a sudden snap, one of us would be gone—one mind less, one world less.

The gallows stood in a small yard, separate from the main grounds of the 11 prison, and overgrown with tall prickly weeds. It was a brick erection like three sides of a shed, with planking on top, and above that two beams and a crossbar with the rope dangling. The hangman, a grey-haired convict in the white uniform of the prison, was waiting beside his machine. He greeted us with a servile crouch as we entered. At a word from Francis the two warders, gripping the prisoner more closely than ever, half led, half pushed him to the gallows and helped him clumsily up the ladder. Then the hangman climbed up and fixed the rope round the prisoner's neck.

We stood waiting, five yards away. The warders had formed in a rough cir- 12 cle round the gallows. And then, when the noose was fixed, the prisoner began crying out on his god. It was a high, reiterated cry of "Ram! Ram! Ram! Ram!", not urgent and fearful like a prayer or a cry for help, but steady, rhythmical, almost like the tolling of a bell. The dog answered the sound with a whine. The hangman, still standing on the gallows, produced a small cotton bag like a flour bag and drew it down over the prisoner's face. But the sound, muffled by the cloth, still persisted, over and over again: "Ram! Ram! Ram! Ram! Ram!"

The hangman climbed down and stood ready, holding the lever. Minutes 13 seemed to pass. The steady, muffled crying from the prisoner went on and on, "Ram! Ram! Ram!" never faltering for an instant. The superintendent, his head on his chest, was slowly poking the ground with his stick; perhaps he was counting the cries, allowing the prisoner a fixed number—fifty, perhaps, or a hundred. Everyone had changed colour. The Indians had gone grey like bad coffee, and one or two of the bayonets were wavering. We looked at the lashed, hooded man on the drop, and listened to his cries—each cry another second of life; the same thought was in all our minds: oh, kill him quickly, get it over, stop that abominable noise!

Suddenly the superintendent made up his mind. Throwing up his head he 14 made a swift motion with his stick. "Chalo!" he shouted almost fiercely.

There was a clanking noise, and then dead silence. The prisoner had van- 15 ished, and the rope was twisting on itself. I let go of the dog, and it galloped immediately to the back of the gallows; but when it got there it stopped short, barked, and then retreated into a corner of the yard, where it stood among the weeds, looking timorously out at us. We went round the gallows to inspect the prisoner's body. He was dangling with his toes pointed straight downwards, very slowly revolving, as dead as a stone.

The superintendent reached out with his stick and poked the bare body; it 16 oscillated slightly. "*He's* all right," said the superintendent. He backed out from under the gallows, and blew out a deep breath. The moody look had gone out of his face quite suddenly. He glanced at his wrist-watch. "Eight minutes past eight. Well, that's all for this morning, thank God."

The warders unfixed bayonets and marched away. The dog, sobered and   17
conscious of having misbehaved itself, slipped after them. We walked out of the
gallows yard, past the condemned cells with their waiting prisoners, into the big
central yard of the prison. The convicts, under the command of warders armed
with lathis, were already receiving their breakfast. They squatted in long rows,
each man holding a tin pannikin, while two warders with buckets marched
round ladling out rice; it seemed quite a homely, jolly scene, after the hanging.
An enormous relief had come upon us now that the job was done. One felt an
impulse to sing, to break into a run, to snigger. All at once everyone began
chattering gaily.

The Eurasian boy walking beside me nodded towards the way we had   18
come, with a knowing smile: "Do you know, sir, our friend (he meant the dead
man), when he heard his appeal had been dismissed, he pissed on the floor of
his cell. From fright.— Kindly take one of my cigarettes, sir. Do you not admire my new silver case, sir? From the boxwallah, two rupees eight annas.
Classy European style."

Several people laughed—at what, nobody seemed certain.   19

Francis was walking by the superintendent, talking garrulously: "Well, sir,   20
all hass passed off with the utmost satisfactoriness. It wass all finished—flick!
like that. It iss not always so— oah, no! I have known cases where the doctor
wass obliged to go beneath the gallows and pull the prisoner's legs to ensure
decease. Most disagreeable!"

"Wriggling about, eh? That's bad," said the superintendent.   21

"Ach, sir, it iss worse when they become refractory! One man, I recall,   22
clung to the bars of hiss cage when we went to take him out. You will scarcely
credit, sir, that it took six warders to dislodge him, three pulling at each leg. We
reasoned with him. 'My dear fellow,' we said, 'think of all the pain and trouble
you are causing to us!' But no, he would not listen! Ach, he wass very troublesome!"

I found that I was laughing quite loudly. Everyone was laughing. Even   23
the superintendent grinned in a tolerant way. "You'd better all come out and
have a drink," he said quite genially. "I've got a bottle of whisky in the car. We
could do with it."

We went through the big double gates of the prison, into the road.   24
"Pulling at his legs!" exclaimed a Burmese magistrate suddenly, and burst into
a loud chuckling. We all began laughing again. At that moment Francis's
anecdote seemed extraordinarily funny. We all had a drink together, native
and European alike, quite amicably. The dead man was a hundred yards
away.

1931

QUESTIONS FOR DISCUSSION

Content

a. Does this narrative essay have a "message," or do you think Orwell deliberately avoided one?

b. Orwell avoids saying anything directly about the English presence in Burma—he neither explains it nor states his opinion explicitly. Nevertheless, his opinion is voiced. What is his attitude toward his country's presence in Burma?

c. How would you characterize Orwell's description of the Burmese in this piece? Of the Hindu prisoner? How do these descriptions relate to his attitude toward the British?

d. What details of the hanging does Orwell depict as significant? What are his reasons for including these details? What effect do they have on you?

Strategy and Style

e. In which paragraphs does Orwell use descriptive details most effectively? What other paragraphs do you find effective? Why?

f. Orwell is careful to tell us the dimensions of the prisoners' cells, the time, the number of people, the distance to the gallows, the distance between the officials and the prisoners, etc. Why are these numerical references important?

g. "A Hanging" is a mature writer's recollection of an earlier time in his life. Does Orwell present himself sympathetically, or does he describe himself with a satiric edge? Point to details that support your answer.

h. How does the use of dialogue affect the tone of the essay? In what way would your reaction have been different if Orwell had not used dialogue?

SUGGESTIONS FOR SHORT WRITING

a. Write a letter to Orwell, telling him what you do not understand about his essay. As best you can, tell him why you do not understand it.

b. Ask a question (or questions) about this essay, and then try to answer the question(s) as Orwell might by piecing together phrases drawn from the essay itself. Then write your own answer, or write a response to Orwell's "answer."

SUGGESTIONS FOR SUSTAINED WRITING

a. In paragraph 10, Orwell writes of an epiphany of sorts: "It is curious, but till that moment I had never realised what it means to destroy a healthy, conscious man. When I saw the prisoner step aside to avoid the puddle, I saw the mystery, the unspeakable wrongness, of cutting a life short...." Tell the story of an event during an ordinary day that suddenly and profoundly changed your thinking. What details do you remember? Make those details as significant to your readers as they are to you.

b. Orwell communicates his feelings about capital punishment and other issues in this essay. Use narration to present an issue about which you feel strongly. Present your opinion(s) implicitly by drawing on Orwell's narrative techniques: the use of dialogue, the detailed description of characters, the chronological sequencing of events, and the inclusion of humor, to name a few. In short, imbed your opinion within the framework of a story.

c. Orwell learned a great deal about himself from this rather wrenching experience. Narrate a traumatic experience in your life which revealed to you something important about yourself.

Salvation

Langston Hughes

Among the chief figures of the Harlem Renaissance in the 1920s, Hughes (1902–1967) is one of the best known poets and playwrights in America. A native of Mississippi, he also wrote numerous essays that detail Negro life in the South during the early part of this century. His novels and his autobiography, I Wonder as I Wander, *are still read widely. This selection captures the trauma and disillusion he experienced during a childhood incident.*

I was saved from sin when I was going on thirteen. But not really 1 saved. It happened like this. There was a big revival at my Auntie Reed's church. Every night for weeks there had been much preaching, singing, praying, and shouting, and some very hardened sinners had been brought to Christ, and the membership of the church had grown by leaps and bounds. Then just before the revival ended, they held a special meeting for children, "to bring the young lambs to the fold." My aunt spoke of it for days ahead. That night I was escorted to the front row and placed on the mourners' bench with all the other young sinners, who had not yet been brought to Jesus.

My aunt told me that when you were saved you saw a light, and some- 2 thing happened to you inside! And Jesus came into your life! And God was with you from then on! She said you could see and hear and feel Jesus in your soul. I believed her. I had heard a great many old people say the same thing and it seemed to me they ought to know. So I sat there calmly in the hot, crowded church, waiting for Jesus to come to me.

The preacher preached a wonderful rhythmical sermon, all moans and 3 shouts and lonely cries and dire pictures of hell, and then he sang a song about the ninety and nine safe in the fold, but one little lamb was left out in the cold. Then he said: "Won't you come? Won't you come to Jesus? Young lambs, won't you come?" And he held out his arms to all us young sinners there on the mourners' bench. And the little girls cried. And some of them jumped up and went to Jesus right away. But most of us just sat there.

A great many old people came and knelt around us and prayed, old 4 women with jet-black faces and braided hair, old men with work-gnarled hands. And the church sang a song about the lower lights are burning, some poor sinners to be saved. And the whole building rocked with prayer and song.

Still I kept waiting to *see* Jesus. 5

Finally all the young people had gone to the altar and were saved, but one 6 boy and me. He was a rounder's son named Westley. Westley and I were surrounded by sisters and deacons praying. It was very hot in the church, and getting late now. Finally Westley said to me in a whisper: "God damn! I'm tired o' sitting here. Let's get up and be saved." So he got up and was saved.

Then I was left all alone on the mourners' bench. My aunt came and knelt 7
at my knees and cried, while prayers and songs swirled all around me in the little church. The whole congregation prayed for me alone, in a mighty wail of moans and voices. And I kept waiting serenely for Jesus, waiting, waiting—but he didn't come. I wanted to see him, but nothing happened to me. Nothing! I wanted something to happen to me, but nothing happened.

I heard the songs and the minister saying: "Why don't you come? My 8
dear child, why don't you come to Jesus? Jesus is waiting for you. He wants you. Why don't you come? Sister Reed, what is this child's name?"

"Langston," my aunt sobbed. 9

"Langston, why don't you come? Why don't you come and be saved? Oh, 10
Lamb of God! Why don't you come?"

Now it was really getting late. I began to be ashamed of myself, holding 11
everything up so long. I began to wonder what God thought about Westley, who certainly hadn't seen Jesus either, but who was now sitting proudly on the platform, swinging his knickerbockered legs and grinning down at me, surrounded by deacons and old women on their knees praying. God had not struck Westley dead for taking his name in vain or for lying in the temple. So I decided that maybe to save further trouble, I'd better lie, too, and say that Jesus had come, and get up and be saved.

So I got up. 12

Suddenly the whole room broke into a sea of shouting, as they saw me 13
rise. Waves of rejoicing swept the place. Women leaped in the air. My aunt threw her arms around me. The minister took me by the hand and led me to the platform.

When things quieted down, in a hushed silence, punctuated by a few ec- 14
static "Amens," all the new young lambs were blessed in the name of God. Then joyous singing filled the room.

That night, for the last time in my life but one—for I was a big boy 15
twelve years old—I cried. I cried, in bed alone, and couldn't stop. I buried my head under the quilts, but my aunt heard me. She woke up and told my uncle I was crying because the Holy Ghost had come into my life, and because I had seen Jesus. But I was really crying because I couldn't bear to tell her that I had lied, that I had deceived everybody in the church, that I hadn't seen Jesus, and that now I didn't believe there was a Jesus any more, since he didn't come to help me.

1940

QUESTIONS FOR DISCUSSION

Content

a. What is Hughes' purpose in recalling this event?
b. The author's portrayal of the revival meeting is extremely realistic. What narrative techniques make it so?
c. What exactly is a religious revival?
d. What Biblical metaphor is Hughes alluding to when he tells the reader that this was to be a special meeting "to bring the young lambs to the fold"?
e. Why does Hughes spend time talking about Westley? How is the young Langston different from this boy?
f. Explain why Langston cries so much after coming home. Is there only one reason behind his tears? What does the last paragraph tell you about the young Langston? What does his waiting so long before going up to be "saved" tell you about him?

Strategy and Style

g. The telling of this story is enhanced by the author's description of the church and the members of the congregation. In which paragraphs is Hughes' facility with description most evident?
h. What examples of metaphoric language do you find in this essay? How do such figures of speech help Hughes accomplish his purpose?
i. Hughes often makes use of a childlike perspective to relate the incident at his aunt's church. What details help him create that perspective? Does he use words like those a child might use?
j. What is Hughes' attitude or tone when recalling this incident?

SUGGESTIONS FOR SHORT WRITING

a. Write about one of your religious experiences, comparing it to that of Hughes.
b. Write an advertisement for Salvation (the concept or the essay).

SUGGESTIONS FOR SUSTAINED WRITING

a. Describe a religious ceremony that has or used to have significance for you. As clearly and convincingly as you can, describe the emotional or spiritual benefits you derive or derived from that ceremony. Address your essay to someone you know is skeptical about the value of religious or social ceremonies and observances.
b. At one time or another, we have all been pressured into doing things we did

not want to do. Recount such an incident from your experience; make sure to describe your feelings both during the incident and after it occurred. If appropriate, narrate the incident in a letter addressed to the individual or individuals who did the pressuring.

c. This brief recollection allows us only a peek into the author's personality. But the details are so vibrant that we are tempted to imagine what Langston Hughes was like as a child. Write about an incident from your own childhood that illustrates something about your personality or about the personality of a close friend or relative.

d. Recount a childhood incident that disillusioned you about a belief, an event, or a person. Describe what caused this disillusionment and explain how you coped with it. Please, no essays about the day you found out there was no Santa Claus!

Grandmother's Victory

Maya Angelou

Born Marguerita Johnson (b. 1928), Angelou spent most of her childhood in Stamps, Arkansas, where her family owned the general store that is the setting for this selection. After a difficult youth, Angelou became a dancer, actress, and writer. She has performed all over the world, most notably in the U.S. State Department-sponsored production of Porgy and Bess, *in the television mini-series* Roots, *and in a production of Genet's* The Blacks. *She has also taught dance in Rome and Tel Aviv. Active in the civil rights movement, Angelou was appointed northern director for the Southern Christian Leadership Conference by Dr. Martin Luther King, Jr., in the 1960s. In 1970, she published the first volume of her autobiography,* I Know Why the Caged Bird Sings, *of which this selection is the fifth chapter. Three other volumes followed. Angelou has also written several books of poetry, including* And Still I Rise *(1978) and* I Shall Not Be Moved *(1990). Recent works include two autobiographies:* The Heart of a Woman *(1981) and* All God's Children Need Traveling Shoes *(1986); and* Shaker, Why Don't You Sing? *(1983).*

"Thou shall not be dirty" and "Thou shall not be impudent" were the two 1 commandments of Grandmother Henderson upon which hung our total salvation.

Each night in the bitterest winter we were forced to wash faces, arms, 2 necks, legs and feet before going to bed. She used to add, with a smirk that unprofane people can't control when venturing into profanity, "and wash as far as possible, then wash possible."

We would go to the well and wash in the ice-cold, clear water, grease our 3 legs with the equally cold stiff Vaseline, then tiptoe into the house. We wiped the dust from our toes and settled down for schoolwork, cornbread, clabbered milk, prayers and bed, always in that order. Momma was famous for pulling the quilts off after we had fallen asleep to examine our feet. If they weren't clean enough for her, she took the switch (she kept one behind the bedroom door for emergencies) and woke up the offender with a few aptly placed burning reminders.

The area around the well at night was dark and slick, and boys told about 4 how snakes love water, so that anyone who had to draw water at night and then stand there alone and wash knew that moccasins and rattlers, puff adders and boa constrictors were winding their way to the well and would arrive just as the person washing got soap in her eyes. But Momma convinced us that not only was cleanliness next to Godliness, dirtiness was the inventor of misery.

The impudent child was detested by God and a shame to its parents and 5 could bring destruction to its house and line. All adults had to be addressed as Mister, Missus, Miss, Auntie, Cousin, Unk, Uncle, Buhbah, Sister, Brother and

13

a thousand other appellations indicating familial relationship and the lowliness of the addressor.

Everyone I knew respected these customary laws, except for the 6 powhitetrash children.

Some families of powhitetrash lived on Momma's farm land behind the 7 school. Sometimes a gaggle of them came to the Store, filling the whole room, chasing out the air and even changing the well-known scents. The children crawled over the shelves and into the potato and onion bins, twanging all the time in their sharp voices like cigar-box guitars. They took liberties in my Store that I would never dare. Since Momma told us that the less you say to white-folks (or even powhitetrash) the better, Bailey and I would stand, solemn, quiet, in the displaced air. But if one of the playful apparitions got close to us, I pinched it. Partly out of angry frustration and partly because I didn't believe in its flesh reality.

They called my uncle by his first name and ordered him around the Store. 8 He, to my crying shame, obeyed them in his limping dip-straight-dip fashion.

My grandmother, too, followed their orders, except that she didn't seem 9 to be servile because she anticipated their needs.

"Here's sugar, Miz Potter, and here's baking powder. You didn't buy soda 10 last month, you'll probably be needing some."

Momma always directed her statements to the adults, but sometimes, Oh 11 painful sometimes, the grimy, snotty-nosed girls would answer her.

"Naw, Annie…"—to Momma? Who owned the land they lived on? Who 12 forgot more than they would ever learn? If there was any justice in the world, God should strike them dumb at once!—"Just give us some extra sody crackers, and some more mackerel."

At least they never looked in her face, or I never caught them doing so. 13 Nobody with a smidgen of training, not even the worst roustabout, would look right in a grown person's face. It meant the person was trying to take the words out before they were formed. The dirty little children didn't do that, but they threw their orders around the Store like lashes from a cat-o'-nine-tails.

When I was around ten years old, those scruffy children caused me the 14 most painful and confusing experience I had ever had with my grandmother.

One summer morning, after I had swept the dirt yard of leaves, spear- 15 mint-gum wrappers and Vienna-sausage labels, I raked the yellow-red dirt, and made half-moons carefully, so that the design stood out clearly and mask-like. I put the rake behind the Store and came through the back of the house to find Grandmother on the front porch in her big, wide white apron. The apron was so stiff by virtue of the starch that it could have stood alone. Momma was admir-ing the yard, so I joined her. It truly looked like a flat redhead that had been raked with a big-toothed comb. Momma didn't say anything but I knew she liked it. She looked over toward the school principal's house and to the right at Mr. McElroy's. She was hoping one of those community pillars would see the design before the day's business wiped it out. Then she looked upward to the school. My head had swung with hers, so at just about the same time we saw a troop of powhitetrash kids marching over the hill and down by the side of the school.

I looked to Momma for direction. She did an excellent job of sagging 16 from her waist down, but from the waist up she seemed to be pulling for the top of the oak tree across the road. Then she began to moan a hymn. Maybe not to moan, but the tune was so slow and the meter so strange that she could have been moaning. She didn't look at me again. When the children reached halfway down the hill, halfway to the Store, she said without turning, "Sister, go on inside."

I wanted to beg her, "Momma, don't wait for them. Come on inside with 17 me. If they come in the Store, you go to the bedroom and let me wait on them. They only frighten me if you're around. Alone I know how to handle them." But of course I couldn't say anything, so I went in and stood behind the screen door.

Before the girls got to the porch I heard their laughter crackling and pop- 18 ping like pine logs in a cooking stove. I suppose my lifelong paranoia was born in those cold, molasses-slow minutes. They came finally to stand on the ground in front of Momma. At first they pretended seriousness. Then one of them wrapped her right arm in the crook of her left, pushed out her mouth and started to hum. I realized that she was aping my grandmother. Another said, "Naw, Helen, you ain't standing like her. This here's it." Then she lifted her chest, folded her arms and mocked that strange carriage that was Annie Henderson. Another laughed, "Naw, you can't do it. Your mouth ain't pooched out enough. It's like this."

I thought about the rifle behind the door, but I knew I'd never be able to 19 hold it straight, and the .410, our sawed-off shotgun, which stayed loaded and was fired every New Year's night, was locked in the trunk and Uncle Willie had the key on his chain. Through the fly-specked screen-door, I could see that the arms of Momma's apron jiggled from the vibrations of her humming. But her knees seemed to have locked as if they would never bend again.

She sang on. No louder than before, but no softer either. No slower or 20 faster.

The dirt of the girls' cotton dresses continued on their legs, feet, arms and 21 faces to make them all of a piece. Their greasy uncolored hair hung down, un- combed, with a grim finality. I knelt to see them better, to remember them for all time. The tears that had slipped down my dress left unsurprising dark spots, and made the front yard blurry and even more unreal. The world had taken a deep breath and was having doubts about continuing to revolve.

The girls had tired of mocking Momma and turned to other means of ag- 22 itation. One crossed her eyes, stuck her thumbs in both sides of her mouth and said, "Look here, Annie." Grandmother hummed on and the apron strings trembled. I wanted to throw a handful of black pepper in their faces, to throw lye on them, to scream that they were dirty, scummy peckerwoods, but I knew I was as clearly imprisoned behind the scene as the actors outside were confined to their roles.

One of the smaller girls did a kind of puppet dance while her fellow 23 clowns laughed at her. But the tall one, who was almost a woman, said something very quietly, which I couldn't hear. They all moved backward from the porch, still watching Momma. For an awful second I thought they were going to throw a rock at Momma, who seemed (except for the apron strings) to have turned into stone herself. But the big girl turned her back, bent down and put her hands flat on the ground—she didn't pick up anything. She simply shifted her weight and did a hand stand.

Her dirty bare feet and long legs went straight for the sky. Her dress fell 24 down around her shoulders, and she had on no drawers. The slick pubic hair made a brown triangle where her legs came together. She hung in the vacuum of that lifeless morning for only a few seconds, then wavered and tumbled. The other girls clapped her on the back and slapped their hands.

Momma changed her song to "Bread of Heaven, bread of Heaven, feed 25 me till I want no more."

I found that I was praying too. How long could Momma hold out? What 26 new indignity would they think of to subject her to? Would I be able to stay out of it? What would Momma really like me to do?

Then they were moving out of the yard, on their way to town. They 27 bobbed their heads and shook their slack behinds and turned, one at a time:

"'Bye, Annie."   28

"'Bye, Annie."   29

"'Bye, Annie."   30

Momma never turned her head or unfolded her arms, but she stopped 31 singing and said, "'Bye, Miz Helen, 'bye, Miz Ruth, 'bye, Miz Eloise."

I burst. A firecracker July-the-Fourth burst. How could Momma call them 32 Miz? The mean nasty things. Why couldn't she have come inside the sweet, cool store when we saw them breasting the hill? What did she prove? And then if they were dirty, mean and impudent, why did Momma have to call them Miz?

She stood another whole song through and then opened the screen door to 33 look down on me crying in rage. She looked until I looked up. Her face was a brown moon that shone on me. She was beautiful. Something had happened out there, which I couldn't completely understand, but I could see that she was happy. Then she bent down and touched me as mothers of the church "lay hands on the sick and afflicted" and I quieted.

"Go wash your face, Sister." And she went behind the candy counter and 34 hummed, "Glory, glory, hallelujah, when I lay my burden down."

I threw the well water on my face and used the weekday handkerchief to 35 blow my nose. Whatever the contest had been out front, I knew Momma had won.

I took the rake back to the front yard. The smudged footprints were easy 36
to erase. I worked for a long time on my new design and laid the rake behind
the wash pot. When I came back in the Store, I took Momma's hand and we
both walked outside to look at the pattern.

It was a large heart with lots of hearts growing smaller inside, and pierc- 37
ing from the outside rim to the smallest heart was an arrow. Momma said, "Sister, that's right pretty." Then she turned back to the Store and resumed, "Glory,
glory, hallelujah, when I lay my burden down."

1970

QUESTIONS FOR DISCUSSION

Content

a. Is this simply a story about bad-mannered children and racism? Or is Angelou's intent more complex?
b. Why does the speaker bother to tell us that she made careful patterns when
   she raked the yard? Why did Momma admire these designs?
c. Angelou describes a number of outdated social observances such as never
   looking "right in a grown person's face." What other examples can you find
   in this selection? Why does she make it a point to include them in this recollection of her childhood?
d. The speaker remembers to tell us that Grandmother Henderson addressed the
   white girls as "Miz." How did Momma's doing so contribute to her victory
   over these brats?
e. What details does Angelou use to create this obviously unflattering picture
   of "powhitetrash children"?
f. What does Angelou mean when she describes her uncle's limping in "dip-
   straight-dip fashion"?

Strategy and Style

g. How does Angelou's ability to describe places and people help her enrich
   this narrative?
h. In light of what the speaker says early in the story, is it important for her to
   quote all three of the girls as they leave the store (paragraphs 28 through
   30)? In general, what effect does Angelou's extensive use of dialogue create?
i. This selection begins with two rather odd commandments, which both startle
   and amuse the reader. Why are they important to the rest of the essay?
j. Angelou's use of metaphor is brilliant. In paragraph 18, she tells us that her
   "paranoia was born in those cold, molasses-slow minutes." What other examples of figurative language can you find?

k. How would you describe the speaker's tone at the beginning of this essay? When, exactly, does this tone change?

SUGGESTIONS FOR SHORT WRITING

a. What is victory to Angelou's grandmother?
b. Write your own definition of "victory." What does it mean to you personally?

SUGGESTIONS FOR SUSTAINED WRITING

a. What kind of person is Grandmother Henderson? Based upon the details Angelou provides, jot down a few notes that might help explain her character to other readers. Then, relying on your own experiences, narrate an incident from the life of a close family relative. Through the use of description, dialogue, and action, make sure to include the kind of details that will provide the reader with a fairly vivid picture of the person you're recalling. Address your essay to someone who has never met this person and/or knows very little about him or her.
b. Grandmother Henderson's triumph may well reside in the fact that she has done a far better job of raising children than many of her "powhitetrash" neighbors. Analyze Angelou's essay in order to explain this and other sources of "Momma's" victory.
c. The term "powhitetrash" has many connotations, several of which are apparent in this narrative. Choose a label often used in conversation to describe a type of person or group of persons. Using events from your life as illustrations, explain the kind of person(s) it is used to label. Examples might include:

A Hero/Heroine	A Yuppie
A Creep	A Jock
A Spoiled Brat	A Nerd
A Winner/Loser	A Giver/Taker
An Egg Head	A Witch

Crybaby

Akira Kurosawa

Akira Kurosawa (b. 1910) is a Japanese film director best known for his film The
Seven Samurai, *upon which the American film* The Magnificent Seven *is based.
Kurosawa trained to be a painter but in 1937, finding himself short of money, he took
a "temporary" job as an assistant director to Kajiro Yamamoto, one of Japan's leading
filmmakers. Kurosawa both writes and directs his films, many of which are drawn from
literary classics, such as* The Idiot *from Dostoevsky's novel of the same title;* Throne
of Blood *and* Ran *from Shakespeare's* Macbeth *and* King Lear; *and* Donzoko *from
Maxim Gorki's play* The Lower Depths. *Kurosawa's reputation was at its zenith in
the 1950s. In the 1960s, however, negative criticism of his films made it difficult to
secure funding, and in 1971 he attempted suicide. His career was revived in the 1980s
with the production of critically acclaimed films such as* Kagemusha *(The Shadow
Warrior),* Ran, *and* Dreams. *"Crybaby" is an excerpt from his* Something Like an
Autobiography *(1982).*

It was in the second or third term of my second year in school that I   1
transferred to this school. Here everything was so entirely different from
Morimura Gakuen that I was astounded. The schoolhouse itself was not painted
white, but was an unadorned, humble wooden building rather in the style of a
Meijiera military barracks. At Morimura all the students had worn smart Euro-
pean-style uniforms with lapels; here they wore Japanese clothing with the wide
trousers called hakama. At Morimura they had all worn "Landsel," German-
style leather knapsacks for their books; here they carried canvas bookbags. At
Morimura they had worn leather shoes; here they wore wooden clogs.

Above all, their faces were different. They should have been, because   2
while at Morimura students had all let their hair grow long, here they had their
hair shaved close. And yet I think that the Kuroda students may have been even
more surprised by me than I was by them.

Imagine someone like me suddenly appearing among a group that lives   3
by purely Japanese customs: a haircut like a sheltered little sissy's, a belted,
double-breasted coat over short pants, red socks and low, buckled shoes. What's
more, I was still in a wide-eyed daze and had a face as white as a girl's. I immediately became a laughingstock.

They pulled my long hair, poked at my knapsack, rubbed snot on my   4
clothes and made me cry a lot. I had always been a crybaby, but at this new
school I immediately got a new nickname on account of it. They called me
Konbeto-san ("Mr. Gumdrop") after a popular song that had a verse something
like this:

> Konbeto-san at our house,
> He's so much trouble, so much trouble.

19

He's always in tears, in tears.
Blubber blubber, blubber blubber.

The idea was that the crybaby's tears were as big as gum-drops. Even today I can't recall that name, "Konbeto-san," without a feeling of severe humiliation.

But at the same time I entered the Kuroda Primary School, my older 5 brother also arrived. He conquered them all straightaway with his genius, and there is no doubt in my mind that this "Konbeto-san" cried all the more because his brother did not lend his dignity to back him up. It took a full year for me to find a place for myself. At the end of that year I no longer cried in front of people, and no one called me "Konbeto-san" any more. I was now very respectably known as "Kuro-chan." The changes that occurred during that year were in part natural. My intelligence began to bud and blossom, growing with such speed that I caught up with my peers. Spurring my remarkable progress there were three hidden forces.

One of these hidden forces was my older brother. We lived near Ōmagari, 6 which was the center of the Koishikawa district, and every morning I would walk along the banks of the Edogawa River with my brother on the way to school. Since I was in a lower grade, school ended earlier for me and I would have to make my way back home alone in the afternoon. But every morning I went side by side with him. Every morning my brother would deride me thoroughly. The vast number of different expressions he found to abuse me with was in itself amazing. He did this not in a loud or conspicuous way, but in a very soft voice that was barely audible even to me. None of the passers-by could hear him. If he had been loud, I could have shouted back, or cried and run away, or covered my ears with my hands. But he spoke in a subdued pattern so that I could never retaliate while he was continually showering me with scathing insults.

I thought of complaining to my mother and older sister about the way my 7 brother was treating me, but I couldn't do it. As soon as we got close to the school, my brother would say, "I know you're a dirty little rotten sissy coward, so I know you'll go straight to Mother and our sisters and tell them about me. Well, just you try it. I'll despise you even more." I found myself unable to lift a finger to stop his needling me like this.

Nevertheless, this very same mean and nasty brother of mine always 8 turned up at recess time when I needed him. Whenever I was being teased by the other children, he would appear from somewhere—I don't know how he happened to be watching. He was the center of attention for the entire school, and those pestering me were younger than he, so without exception they would shrink back when he arrived on the scene. Not even bothering to look at them, he would command, "Akira, come here a minute." Relieved, I would happily run up to him and say, "What is it?" but he'd only reply, "Nothing" and walk briskly away.

As this same sequence of events occurred over and over again, my fogged 9 brain began to think a little: My brother's behavior on the way to school was different from his behavior in the schoolyard. Gradually his abuse on the way to school every morning became less hateful to me, and I began to listen in silent appreciation. Looking back on it now, I feel that this was the time when I began to grow from a baby-level intelligence toward the thinking capacity of a normal school-age child.

There is one more incident I would like to relate about my brother. When 10 I was still in my "Konbeto-san" period, my father suddenly decided to start taking us all to the Suifuryū practice pool, which was built out into the Arakawa River. At this time my brother was already wearing a white bathing cap with a black triangle pattern on it and swimming around the practice pool with a first-rate over-arm crawl stroke. I was put in the charge of the Suifuryū teacher, who was apparently a friend of my father.

Because I was the youngest child, my father spoiled me. But how irritated 11 he must have been to see me carrying on like a girl, playing patty-cake and cat's cradle with my older sisters. He said if I learned to swim and got tanned by the sun—even if I just got a suntan without learning to swim—he would give me a reward. But I was afraid of the water, and I never entered the practice pool. It took many days of scolding by the swimming teacher for me even to get wet up to my navel.

My older brother also accompanied me whenever we went to the pool, 12 but as soon as we arrived, he would abandon me. He would swim straightaway to the diving raft out in the deepest part of the river, and he never came back till it was time to go home. I spent many a lonely and frightened day.

Then one day, when I was finally learning how to kick my feet along with 13 the other beginners, holding on to a log floating in the river, my brother appeared. He came rowing up to me in a boat and offered me a ride. Rejoicing, I reached out my hand and let him pull me up into the boat. As soon as I was on board, he began rowing vigorously out toward the middle of the river. Just when the flag and the reed blinds of the poolside hut began to look very small, he suddenly pushed me into the river.

I flailed with all my strength to keep afloat and reach the boat with my 14 brother in it. But as soon as I came close, he rowed away from me. After he repeated this action several times, my strength drained from me. When I could no longer see the boat or my brother and had already sunk below the surface, he grabbed me by my loincloth and pulled me up into the boat.

Shaken and surprised, I found there was nothing wrong with me except 15 that I had swallowed a little water. As I sat gasping and wide-eyed, my brother said, "So you can swim after all, Akira." And sure enough, after that I wasn't afraid of the water any more. I learned to swim, and I learned to love swimming.

On the way home that day my brother bought me some shaved ice with 16 sweet red-bean sauce. As we ate, he said, "Akira, it's true that drowning people die smiling—you were." It made me angry, but it had seemed that way to me,

too. I remembered having felt a strangely peaceful sensation just before I went
under.

A second hidden force that aided my growth was that of the teacher in   17
charge of Kuroda Primary School, Tachikawa Seiji. Some two years after I
transfered to Kuroda, Mr. Tachikawa's progressive educational principles came
into direct conflict with the conservatism of the school principal, and my
teacher resigned. He was subsequently invited to teach at Gyōsei Primary
School, where he was responsible for developing a great number of talented
men.

I will have more to say about Mr. Tachikawa, but I'd like to start with an   18
incident that took place when I was still behind the others of my age in my
intellectual development and very timid about it. Mr. Tachikawa came to my
aid and for the first time in my life enabled me to feel what is called confidence. It happened during art class.

In the old days—in my day, that is—art education was terribly haphazard.   19
Some tasteless picture would be the model, and it was simply a matter of copy-
ing it. The student drawings that most closely resembled the original would always get the highest marks.

But Mr. Tachikawa did nothing so foolish. He just said, "Draw whatever   20
you like." Everyone took out drawing paper and colored pencils and began. I
too started to draw—I don't remember what it was I attempted to draw, but I
drew with all my might. I pressed so hard the pencils broke, and then I put
saliva on my fingertips and smeared the colors around, eventually ending up
with my hands a variety of hues.

When we finished, Mr. Tachikawa took each student's picture and put it   21
up on the blackboard. He asked the class to express opinions freely on each in
turn, and when it came to mine, the only response was raucous laughter. But
Mr. Tachikawa turned a stern gaze on the laughing multitude and proceeded to
praise my picture to the skies. I don't remember exactly what he said. But I do
seem to recall that he called special attention to the places where I had rubbed
my spit-covered fingers on the colors. Then he took my picture and put three
big concentric circles on it in bright red ink: the highest mark. That I remember
perfectly.

From that time on, even though I still hated school, I somehow found my-   22
self hurrying to school in anticipation on the days when we had art classes.
That grade of three circles had led me to enjoy drawing pictures. I drew everything. And I became really good at drawing. At the same time my marks in
other subjects suddenly began to improve. By the time Mr. Tachikawa left
Kuroda, I was the president of my class, wearing a little gold badge with a purple ribbon on my chest.

I have another unforgettable memory of Mr. Tachikawa during my time at   23
Kuroda Primary School. One day—I think it was during handicrafts class—he
came into the classroom carrying a huge roll of thick paper. When he opened it
up and showed it to us, laid out flat, it was a map, with streets drawn on it. He

then instructed us to build our own houses on these streets and make our own town. Everyone started in with great enthusiasm. Many ideas came forth, and we ended with not only each student's own dream house, but with landscaping for tree-lined streets, ancient trees that had always been on the site and living fences of flowering vines. It was a lovely city, and it had been created by cleverly drawing out the individual personality of each child in the class. Upon completion of our project, our eyes shone, our faces glowed and we gazed proudly at our handiwork. I remember the feeling of that moment as if it were yesterday.

In the early Taishō era (1912–1926), when I started school, the word 24 "teacher" was synonymous with "scary person." The fact that at such a time I encountered such free and innovative education with such creative impulse behind it—that I encountered a teacher like Mr. Tachikawa at such a time—I cherish among the rarest of blessings.

There was a third hidden force that helped me grow. In my class at 25 Kuroda there was another crybaby, a child who was worse than I. The very existence of this child was like having a mirror thrust in front of my face. I was forced to see myself objectively. I recognized that he was like me, and watching him and realizing how unacceptable his behavior was made me feel uneasy about myself. The child who resembled me and who afforded me the opportunity of seeing my own reflection, this perfect specimen of a crybaby, was named Uekusa Keinosuke, much later co-scriptwriter with me on several films. (Now, don't get angry, Kei-chan. We're both crybabies, aren't we? Only now you've become a romantic crybaby and I'm a humanist crybaby.)

Through some kind of strange fate, Uekusa and I were joined together 26 from childhood to adolescence. We grew like two wisteria vines, clinging and twining around each other. The details of our life in this era can be found in a novel Uekusa wrote. But Uekusa has his viewpoint and I have mine. And because people want themselves to have been a certain way, they have a disturbing tendency to convince themselves they really were that way. Perhaps if I wrote an account of my childhood with Uekusa to be compared with the account in his novel, we would come very close to the truth. Be that as it may, Uekusa was unable to describe his own childhood without writing about me, just as I can't write about myself without talking about him.

When I try to write about Uekusa and me when we were students at 27 Kuroda Primary School, all I can remember is the two of us like tiny dots of human figures in an Oriental landscape painting. I see us standing beneath the wisteria arbor on the school grounds, the clusters of flowers waving in the wind. I see us walking up the slope of Hattorizaka, or up Kagurazaka hill. I see us under a huge Zelkova tree busily nailing up straw dolls to exorcise evil spirits during a shrine visit at the Hour of the Ox, between two and four a.m. In every instance the landscape comes to mind with glistening clarity, but the two boys remain nothing more than silhouettes.

Whether this lack of distinctness is due to the passage of so much time, or 28 whether it has something to do with my personality, I can't tell. Whatever the cause, it requires a special effort for me to recall the detailed characteristics of these two boys. I have to do something equivalent to removing the wide-angle lens from the camera and replacing it with a telephoto lens, then looking once again through the viewfinder. And even this isn't enough. I need to concentrate all my lights on these two boys and stop down the lens so as to record them clearly.

Well, then, looking at Uekusa Keinosuke through my telephoto lens, I 29 now see that, like me, he was someone who differed from the rest of the students at Kuroda Primary School. Even his clothes were different: he wore some kind of silk-like flowing material, and his hakama trousers weren't the usual duck cloth, but a soft fabric. The overall impression was that of a stage actor's child. He was like a miniature player of lover-boy roles, the kind you can knock over with one punch.

Speaking of knocking him over with one punch, Uekusa the primary- 30 school student was always falling down and crying. I remember him falling once on a stretch of bad road and ruining his fancy clothes. I accompanied him as he cried all the way home. Another time, at a track meet, he fell in a mud puddle and turned his sparkling white athletic outfit pitch black; I had to try to comfort him while he blubbered.

The saying goes that birds of a feather flock together. Cry-baby Uekusa 31 and I felt something in common; we were drawn to each other, and soon we were playing together continually. Gradually I came to treat Uekusa the way my older brother had treated me.

Our relations are very frankly described in the passage about the track 32 meet in Uekusa's novel. Once Uekusa, who always came in last in any race, for some inexplicable reason was running in second place. I rushed up behind and shouted, "Good! Good! Come on, come on!" Together we ran the last stretch and leaped across the finish line into the open arms of the beaming Mr. Tachikawa.

When the meet was over, we took our prizes—colored pencils or paints 33 or whatever—and went to see Uekusa's mother on her sickbed. She cried tears of joy and kept thanking me on her son's behalf. But, looking back on it all now, I am the one who should have been saying "Thank you," because while this weakling Uekusa made me feel protective toward him, I somehow at the same time became someone the school bully could no longer push around.

Mr. Tachikawa seems to have looked favorably on our friendship. He 34 once called me in for consultation as the class president and asked me what I thought of appointing a vice president. Thinking this meant I had been doing a poor job as president, I fell into a dark silence. Mr. Tachikawa studied my expression and asked whom I would recommend. I named one of the best students in the class. Mr. Tachikawa said that he would prefer to try putting a less impressive student in that position. I stared at him in surprise. He went on to say with a big smile that if we put someone who was not very good in the job now, that person would be sure to shape up and prove worthy. Then, addressing me as my classmates did, he said, "So, Kuro-chan, what do you say to making Uekusa vice president?" At this point I became painfully aware of the warmth of Mr. Tachikawa's feeling toward us.

Deeply moved, I stood staring at him. "Fine," he announced, "it's all set- 35 tled, then." He slapped me on the shoulder and with a grin told me to go and tell Uekusa's mother straightaway; he knew she'd be happy. As he walked away, there seemed to be a kind of halo around his head.

From this time on, Uekusa wore a silver badge with a red ribbon on his 36 chest, and in both the classroom and the schoolyard he was always at my side. Recognition of him as vice president of the class was instantaneous. It was as if he had been planted in the flower pot of the class vice presidency and placed in full sun. He began to bloom. Mr. Tachikawa had referred to him as "not very good" in a way that may sound disparaging, but in reality I think he had observed the talent that lay dormant within Uekusa.

1982

QUESTIONS FOR DISCUSSION

Content

a. What was Kurosawa's purpose in including this selection in his autobiography?

b. How did the "three hidden forces" Kurosawa discusses spur his "remarkable progress"? What did each contribute to that progress?

c. Some of the things Kurosawa's brother does to "help" him—for example, pushing him into the river in order to force him to learn to swim—seem cruel. Was his brother being cruel, or did he have Akira's welfare at heart?

d. Why does the attitude of the teacher, Mr. Tachikawa, play such an important role in this memoir? What does Kurosawa learn from Mr. Tachikawa that he would not have learned from another teacher?

e. What does Kurosawa mean in paragraph 26 when he writes that "because people want themselves to have been a certain way, they have a disturbing tendency to convince themselves they really were that way"? What part does Kurosawa's recognition of this tendency play in his writing this selection?

f. Would Kurosawa say that one's intellectual progress is the result of a gradual and inevitable growth from within or that it is a sudden growth occurring only when spurred on by outside influences? How would you answer the same question?

g. In paragraph 31, he writes that he went from empathizing with Uekusa to berating him: "Gradually I came to treat Uekusa the way my older brother had treated me." What accounts for this change?

Strategy and Style

h. Describe the author's plan for organizing this selection. Why does he discuss his friendship with Uekusa last?
i. Kurosawa's writing is simple and direct. What is the relationship between his style and the point(s) he wishes to make? Is his message also simple, or does his style mask a more complex and sophisticated intent?
j. The author refers to himself as a "sissy" and as acting like a "girl": [I] had a face as white as a girl's. I immediately became a laughingstock" (paragraph 3) and "how irritated [my father] must have been to see me carrying on like a girl" (paragraph 11). Are these remarks sexist?
k. In paragraph 27, Kurosawa talks about the difficulty he has remembering Uekusa and himself exactly as they were. Why is he having so much trouble? Why does he place such significance on trying to describe these "silhouettes"?
l. All personal narratives that recall childhood events provide a natural outlet for writers to express their adult voices. Nonetheless, the persona of the adult Kurosawa seems especially strong here, far stronger, say, than what we hear in the selections by Hughes and Angelou. What accounts for this?
m. Is it possible to read this essay as if it had been originally written in English? Or are there cultural differences that might cause a non-Japanese reader to mistake Kurosawa's intent? For example, might some statements, like those that seem sexist or cruel, be interpreted differently depending upon the reader's cultural background?

SUGGESTIONS FOR SHORT WRITING

a. Write about an elementary teacher who had a profound influence (positive or negative) on you.
b. Did you have a descriptive nickname when you were young? Write the story of how you came to get that nickname. If you did not have such a nickname, what nickname would have described you, and why?

SUGGESTIONS FOR SUSTAINED WRITING

a. As uncomfortable as it may be, recall a humiliating experience and tell the story of how you dealt with it. Did you just ignore it and eventually leave it behind? Did you deal with the situation alone? Did you have the help, direct or indirect, of others? To help you focus on a specific audience and purpose, imagine that you are writing this story as a way to help readers who are facing similar experiences.

b. Kurosawa says his "progress" was influenced by "three hidden forces." Many people have been similarly influenced, either positively or negatively, by members of their families or by special people outside their families. Write an essay containing anecdotes that illustrate how the actions of a particular individual have affected your life. Was this person's influence positive or negative?

c. Like Kurosawa, discuss your early education by narrating events that will give the reader a good idea of the people and the factors that determined your intellectual growth.

The Transaction
William Zinsser

A feature writer, editorialist, and film and drama critic, Zinsser (b. 1922) is one of America's best-known nonfiction writers. Born in New York City, he was educated at Princeton University. He taught at Yale for nine years, where he created the extremely popular course in the writing of nonfiction that was to become the basis for On Writing Well *(1976), his most celebrated text. Zinsser's other works include* Seen Any Good Movies Lately? *(1958),* The City Dwellers *(1962),* Pop Goes America *(1966),* Writing With a Word Processor *(1983), and* Willie and Dwike: An American Profile *(1984). He has also been a columnist for* Look, Life, *and* The New York Times, *and he continues to publish in* The New Yorker *and other periodicals. At the heart of his theory of writing is a commitment to infusing even the most direct and precise nonfiction with warmth and clarity. This is the "transaction" Zinsser discusses so eloquently in this essay.*

Five or six years ago a school in Connecticut held "a day devoted to the 1 arts," and I was asked if I would come and talk about writing as a vocation. When I arrived I found that a second speaker had been invited—Dr. Brock (as I'll call him), a surgeon who had recently begun to write and had sold some stories to national magazines. He was going to talk about writing as an avocation. That made us a panel, and we sat down to face a crowd of student newspaper editors and reporters, English teachers and parents, all eager to learn the secrets of our glamorous work.

Dr. Brock was dressed in a bright red jacket, looking vaguely Bohemian, 2 as authors are supposed to look, and the first question went to him. What was it like to be a writer?

He said it was tremendous fun. Coming home from an arduous day at the 3 hospital, he would go straight to his yellow pad and write his tensions away. The words just flowed. It was easy.

I then said that writing wasn't easy and it wasn't fun. It was hard and 4 lonely, and the words seldom just flowed.

Next Dr. Brock was asked if it was important to rewrite. Absolutely not, 5 he said. "Let it all hang out," and whatever form the sentences take will reflect the writer at his most natural.

I then said that rewriting is the essence of writing. I pointed out that pro- 6 fessional writers rewrite their sentences repeatedly and then rewrite what they have rewritten. I mentioned that E. B. White and James Thurber were known to rewrite their pieces eight or nine times.

"What do you do on days when it isn't going well?" Dr. Brock was 7 asked. He said he just stopped writing and put the work aside for a day when it would go better.

28

I then said that the professional writer must establish a daily schedule and 8
stick to it. I said that writing is a craft, not an art, and that the man who runs
away from his craft because he lacks inspiration is fooling himself. He is also
going broke.

"What if you're feeling depressed or unhappy?" a student asked. "Won't 9
that affect your writing?"

Probably it will, Dr. Brock replied. Go fishing. Take a walk.   10

Probably it won't, I said. If your job is to write every day, you learn to do 11
it like any other job.

A student asked if we found it useful to circulate in the literary world. Dr. 12
Brock said that he was greatly enjoying his new life as a man of letters, and he
told several lavish stories of being taken to lunch by his publisher and his agent
at Manhattan restaurants where writers and editors gather. I said that professional writers are solitary drudges who seldom see other writers.

"Do you put symbolism in your writing?" a student asked me.   13

"Not if I can help it," I replied. I have an unbroken record of missing the 14
deeper meaning in any story, play or movie, and as for dance and mime, I have
never had even a remote notion of what is being conveyed.

"I *love* symbols!" Dr. Brock exclaimed, and he described with gusto the 15
joys of weaving them through his work.

So the morning went, and it was a revelation to all of us. At the end Dr. 16
Brock told me he was enormously interested in my answers—it had never occurred to him that writing could be hard. I told him I was just as interested in
his answers—it had never occurred to me that writing could be easy. (Maybe I
should take up surgery on the side.)

As for the students, anyone might think that we left them bewildered. But 17
in fact we probably gave them a broader glimpse of the writing process than if
only one of us had talked. For of course there isn't any "right" way to do such
intensely personal work. There are all kinds of writers and all kinds of methods,
and any method that helps somebody to say what he wants to say is the right
method for him.

Some people write by day, others by night. Some people need silence, 18
others turn on the radio. Some write by hand, some by typewriter, some by talking into a tape recorder. Some people write their first draft in one long burst
and then revise; others can't write the second paragraph until they have fiddled
endlessly with the first.

But all of them are vulnerable and all of them are tense. They are driven 19
by a compulsion to put some part of themselves on paper, and yet they don't
just write what comes naturally. They sit down to commit an act of literature,
and the self who emerges on paper is a far stiffer person than the one who sat
down. The problem is to find the real man or woman behind all the tension.

For ultimately the product that any writer has to sell is not his subject, but 20
who he is. I often find myself reading with interest about a topic that I never
thought would interest me—some unusual scientific quest, for instance. What

holds me is the enthusiasm of the writer for his field. How was he drawn into it? What emotional baggage did he bring along? How did it change his life? It is not necessary to want to spend a year alone at Walden Pond to become deeply involved with a man who did.

This is the personal transaction that is at the heart of good nonfiction 21 writing. Out of it come two of the most important qualities that this book will go in search of: humanity and warmth. Good writing has an aliveness that keeps the reader reading from one paragraph to the next, and it's not a question of gimmicks to "personalize" the author. It's a question of using the English language in a way that will achieve the greatest strength and the least clutter.

Can such principles be taught? Maybe not. But most of them can be 22 learned.

1976

QUESTIONS FOR DISCUSSION

Content

a. In your own words, define "the personal transaction" Zinsser discusses in paragraphs 20 and 21. In what ways does this term contribute to Zinsser's thesis? What is that thesis?
b. Considering what the author tells us in the anecdote about himself and "Dr. Brock," how would you describe Zinsser's theory of writing? Summarize the major points or aspects of that theory as explained in this selection.
c. Contrast Dr. Brock's theory of writing with Zinsser's. What are the most significant differences between the two? How does Zinsser's explanation of these differences help him achieve his purpose?
d. To what is Zinsser alluding when he mentions Walden Pond in paragraph 20? Who are E. B. White and James Thurber?

Strategy and Style

e. Explain what the author means when he calls writing "intensely personal work" in paragraph 17. What is the function of paragraph 18?
f. The essay seems to exhibit a shift in tone about halfway through. Explain. Precisely where does the shift occur? Is the shift appropriate? Why?
g. Zinsser's description of his work as "glamorous" is obviously ironic. What other examples of irony can you identify?
h. Given what we know of Zinsser's theory of writing, is the use of irony appropriate in an essay designed to "inform" or "instruct"?
i. What is Zinsser's attitude toward Dr. Brock? Why does he tell us that he looked "vaguely Bohemian"? Should he have been more objective when describing this individual?

SUGGESTIONS FOR SHORT WRITING

a. Try writing in which you "let it all hang out." Time yourself for five or ten minutes and write whatever and everything that comes to mind, without thinking about grammatical or stylistic correctness. When you are finished, read over what you have written—how formal or informal is it? Were you able really to "let it all hang out"?

b. Now revise what you just wrote. Try to make it a single, coherent, formal paragraph.

SUGGESTIONS FOR SUSTAINED WRITING

a. Do you agree that principles of good writing can't be taught but can be learned? Write an essay explaining how you mastered a skill—any skill at all—through practice and self-application. Develop your essay by narrating appropriate personal experiences you remember vividly.

b. Do you write better when you have an intense personal interest in your subject or when you are coldly detached from it? What role does "enthusiasm" play in your writing process? Reread the last few paragraphs of this essay. Then, think about an important event in your life or about an intensely personal conviction you've recently developed. Discuss this event or belief in a letter to a fellow student or close friend. Explain why it holds such significance for you. No love letters, please!

Testimonies of Guatemalan Women[*]

Luz Alicia Herrera, translated by Maria Alice Jacob

Luz Alicia Herrera is a political activist in Guatemala.

INTRODUCTION

As a contribution to the knowledge of Guatemalan social reality, I offer 1
the following statements as they were told to me by the women themselves.
Each is selected for a reason. Through the statement of the first woman, we
discover thousands of Guatemalan women: poor peasants, agricultural workers,
maids, industrial workers, unmarried mothers, and the women who are active in
the struggle of popular organizations. Through the statement of the second
woman, we see an example of a person from a wealthy background who opts
for the interests of the great oppressed majority of Guatemalans. We present
this second interview, knowing full well that it may generate the common psychological interpretation that this serious process of transformation is actually a
manifestation of "social resentment." With such an explanation the bourgeoisie
tries to dismiss the choice of those who side with the majority of the people.

FIRST WOMAN'S TESTIMONY

I was born in a little village on the southeast coast. I was fifteen when we 2
moved to a parcel of land far away, still on the same south coast. My mother
was a widow. There were four children, three girls and a boy. In the new place
where we went to live, my mother established a little restaurant. We cooked for
thirty people. We also picked cotton. My mother, my thirteen-year-old sister,
and I would get up at one in the morning to do the household chores: cook
corn, make tortillas, prepare food and clean the house. At 6 o'clock all was
ready, and at 7 a.m. we would take the bus to the cotton fields. I used to go
with my sister to a plantation that employed between 150 and 200 cotton pickers, men and women.

On the plantation, an active picker would pick 100 to 150 pounds of cot- 3
ton. My sister and I would pick 100 pounds between us and be paid one cent
per pound. We would take our own food with us. When it rained, we would
work from 8 a.m. in the morning to 3 p.m. in the afternoon. If the weather was
very humid, we would work from 12 noon to 3 p.m. in the afternoon.

It is hard work under the hot sun on a cotton plantation. The women wore 4

[*]Excerpted and abridged from *Latin American Perspectives,* Issues 25 and 26, Spring and Summer 1980, Vol. VII, Nos. 2 and 3.

hats to protect their heads from the sun. There would be many of us women with the sack of cotton tied to our waists. The foreman and the labor contractors made sure that the workers kept their attention on the picking and tried to keep them from establishing contact with their fellow workers.

Sometimes, when we were picking cotton, the airplane would fly over us, 5 spraying insecticide, and the majority of the workers would get poisoned. We had to hide the water and food so that the poison wouldn't get to them.

The foremen were rough and would make the women use the plough by 6 themselves if they left some cotton behind. They treated us badly and humiliated us. The indigenous workers were treated even worse than other workers. They were given only tortillas and beans to eat. Indigenous workers were forced to weigh their cotton on a different scale, undoubtedly to pay them less. The indigenous workers came with their whole families to work—wives and children. The children were only five years old when they began to pick cotton.

Working on the plantation, I was angry about earning so little. Working 7 under the hot sun all day and for so little pay! The foreman and the labor contractors who took advantage of us thought they were kings. A man from the village—a contractor— hired the rest of the workers from the village to do the picking. The foremen were also exploited people but they chose to be on the side of the bosses. We would get home from work at 6 or 7 p.m. and after that feed the other workers—about thirty people outside of our family. Then we would do the dishes and start to cook corn all over again. We would cook 25 pounds of corn a day.

"Serious work. Get up, get up, it's time." That's how my mother would 8 wake us up. So short was the night! We would go to bed at 10 p.m. the evening before and get up at 1 a.m. in the morning. At that time, I was fifteen years old and my sister was thirteen; since we were the eldest, we were made to do the hardest work. We also worked on the little plot of land that was given to my mother. On it, we would plant corn, *maicillo* (millet), and chile for everyday use. Sometimes we would sell the little bit that was left. For us, there were no Sundays, no good times. Only weeks of work.

In 1963, through a friend, I got a job working as a babysitter and maid in 9 Escuintla. I worked there for five years. The first six months they paid me seven *quetzales* a month[1] to take care of a little girl from 7 a.m. in the morning to noon when the woman of the house, who was a secretary in an office, would get home.

After this job I returned to my mother's place in the village. The three of 10 us sisters separated from my mother because she was with a man who didn't like us. We rented a tiny house. With a little money that my mother gave us we started a store, and, there in the house, my sister (since she is a dressmaker) had her sewing machine, and we continued with the little restaurant, just we three.

---

[1]One quetzal is the equivalent of U.S. $1.

There we had thirty mobile military police and the people who passed by on their way to the *fincas* (ranches) for customers. The three of us lived happily. We earned very little, just enough to eat, more or less dress, and shoe ourselves.

After that, I came once again to work in Escuintla, in a soft-drink stand. 11 There I worked only for room and board. During this time I had the stupidity to run off with a boyfriend. He studied in the capital and his parents paid for him to stay in a boarding house. From the soft-drink stand, I went with him to the capital. I lived a year and a half with him. We lived on what his parents sent us in a small room that didn't have a place to cook so we bought our meals. I put up with this difficult situation for a year and a half. I went to work in a clothing factory. I was a seam-gatherer. It was my job to gather and trim. I earned four quetzales and twelve cents weekly. I didn't know how to sew on the electric machines. There were times when I worked extra hours and then I would earn twenty quetzales a month. But I didn't continue in this factory because he didn't like me to work. At the same time, what we had didn't cover anything. I became so desperate that I went home to my mother in the village, once again.

My boyfriend fought with me a lot because I didn't get pregnant. "You'll 12 never have a child; heaven knows what things you do" [he would say]. Well, it was just my bad luck that the month I left him I was already pregnant, but neither of us knew it then. Once when I was with my mother, I noticed how I was, and I told my sister and she told my mother. And my mother caused a big uproar. My mother did not like the boy and she was angry at me. My mother threw me out of the house on my own. I went to a friend's, the one with the soft-drink stand and told her my problem, and I worked with her for room and board.

After two months, my mother arrived to look for me and took me back to 13 the house. I returned to the house and in the state I was in, no one would give me work. An uncle told me, "You can't work in a bar anymore." I told the problem to a neighbor who had a *nixtamal* (the dough used for tortillas) mill. She let me go there and grind for one quetzal a day. I felt very tired and worn-out working there. Everyday my belly grew larger. My friend found some women who would buy tortillas from me each day and she ground my corn without charging me a cent. Daily, I ground twenty pounds of corn, made and sold the corn. After that, I washed clothes for people, did embroidery and needlework, and bought small clothing to sell with the earnings of the needlework. My stepfather would say: "I will not maintain someone else's children," and my mother would get angry with me.

I sent a message to my boyfriend about my pregnancy, and the response 14 he gave was that the child I was about to have was no child of his, and he wouldn't pass me one cent—at least until the child was born. My son was three months old when my boyfriend came to see him with his mother. They came with the idea of taking him away from me but, like the majority of mothers who struggle to keep their children, I wouldn't give him up.

My ex-boyfriend had married another girl and he wanted to keep me as 15 his lover. He only arrived to see his child when he was drunk and never even brought him candy. One time he even arrived with a revolver, threatening us from the window. My sister and I threw him out and punched him. Not until my son was three years old did I manage to convince his father to recognize him. I did it because children need to carry their father's name.

My son didn't like his father. Because he is not with us, he would say. He 16 would notice that other fathers would bring their little children home from school. I've told him everything, and he doesn't like his father. "Because he was bad with us, because of that, I only love you," the child would say to me.

I began working for the revolution some time ago. My stepfather was 17 from a peasant organization. Aside from the fact that he was bad with us, sometimes, when he was in good humor, he gave us advice and we began to collaborate with the organization in the countryside. I, working as a babysitter, already collaborated.

He did not think like me.[2] He is a teacher but he doesn't understand the 18 necessity of organizing the workers. He didn't know that I had those ideas and when he realized it, he told me not to get involved in anything, that this was bad for me. I told him that as long as I lived, I would continue struggling for an organization wherever I was and that there were no limits on where my commitment might take me. "You believe in a struggle that will never triumph, one that won't ever even end," he would say. I went to work in a factory again, and there, convinced that I should stay, joined a union. I have girlfriends who say I am crazy, that I shouldn't get involved in these things, that all I am going to get in return is unemployment or death. But I feel even braver when they tell me that I am going to end up dead. Also, it makes me want to know things I haven't known before.

I have had a lot of serious problems, but I have never been afraid. They 19 have taken away my job....I think about my son. But he tells me: "If my mother dies, I will stay with the *compañeros* (comrades)...." The compañeros are from the *sindicato* (union). Therefore, thinking about the welfare of my child has not kept me from organizing. Sooner or later we all have to die. It might be in some accident. My little boy already is aware of everything and I have taught him how one survives here. He already pays attention to the movements of the police...and advises us of them.

SECOND WOMAN'S TESTIMONY

What motivated you to join the struggle to transform Guatemalan society?

I am going to answer you with what may seem to be a contradiction but it 20 was, precisely, because of my nonproletarian class background. I come from

[2]Here she seems to be referring back to her ex-boyfriend (rather than her stepfather).

what could be called the agro export bourgeoisie. As a child, I customarily spent my end-of-the-year vacation at the *finca*. This vacation coincided with cutting and harvesting. It was there where the answers that were given to my innumerable questions didn't satisfy my childhood curiosity about the conditions I confronted daily.

My father considered the Indian a species half-way between human and animal. I noticed this in a number of incidents. For example, one day, seeing hundreds of men, women, and children descend from the mountains bathed in sweat, carrying enormous loads, I had an enormous feeling of pain and anguish. My father must have noticed it because he explained that Indians were born to do such work, that they were incapable of doing any other, that they were dumb, lazy, drunken, that they had no desire to better themselves, and that they lacked our intelligence—those of us who were descendants of Spaniards. (He never referred to us as *ladinos;* he considered us to be located at the top of the social stratification among whites, and the term *ladino* was applied to the *mestizo* or white who did not possess a powerful name). 21

At harvest time, the labor of *mozos colonos* (resident tenants) or *rancheros* (ranch hands) who live on the finca is not sufficient, and day laborers are contracted from more arid regions where from necessity they migrate to the fincas to supplement their precarious family income. They would arrive in trucks, piled up like animals, dragging along with them their misery and disease. They were put up in enormous *galeras* (sheds) which only had a few posts, a roof, and no walls. There, each family gathered around a fireplace previously placed, was given a *comal* (a piece of clay on which corn tortillas are cooked), an empty tin can of milk or whatever other product in which the corn could be cooked, a grinding stone, and naturally, tools. There wouldn't even be a cloth dividing one family from another. 22

I was strictly prohibited from entering these sheds because the Indians were said to have fleas, were dirty, and some were sick. One night, I remember, a child in one of the sheds began to cough. The next day, there were about five children coughing; the next week, all of the children had whooping cough. The sheds were almost in front of the house of the finca, and during the night you could hear the coughing of the little children as though it were part of a bad dream. A certain fear overcame me and I ran to my father's room to tell my father that these children were going to die, that they were suffocating, and that we had to do something. My father took my hand and walked me back to my room, put me to bed, covered me up and said sweetly, "Don't worry, they're not children, they're Indians." 23

Thus, I later saw, lined up in front of the house, some little caskets, painted white, accompanied only by the fathers, mothers, and others who were most likely relatives. The rest of their fellow workers were missing because the harvest had to continue. At night, much larger groups of people climbed up to the cemetery; many Indians, lighting the way with candles, lanterns of wood 24 and paper, moving in silence or with low voices, speaking in low voices in dialect, carrying out their rituals. My father pointed out to me "these pagans who worship idols and get drunk and weep and wail in the cemetery."

"You see?" he would say, "they don't even care that their children have died; the only thing that interests them is the *guaro* (liquor); they are not like us." 25

My questions were endless. Innocently, I asked why shoes weren't bought for them, why they weren't given food, why the children had inflated stomachs, why they never laughed, why they spoke differently, why doctors weren't called for them. Why? Why? Until one day, my father, tired of so much questioning, said, "Because they are Indians, understand? I don't want to hear another word about the matter again." 26

I began to ask questions again and I received a beating. I learned, then, "not to stick your nose in matters that don't concern you," and I opted for silence. For several years I lived these experiences, always painful. 27

I remember that in order to reach the finca, two jeeps were necessary, one for us and one for the baggage and food. One would suppose that these were marvelous vacations; our friends and my father's friends would arrive at the ranch, I would entertain myself and almost grow accustomed to the situation. But as I grew to adolescence, I began to judge my parents and their friends; now it was no longer necessary to ask questions. I knew by then there was injustice and exploitation; but not at the level of reason. I just felt it. 28

One of the last times I was there at the *finca,* there was a storm, rains that wouldn't stop. The rivers grew and we had to return to the capital. The jeeps couldn't pass to the other side. Up on their shoulders, I saw my mother and brothers and sisters who went ahead. All on the shoulders of Indians, dirty and sweaty. I swore I would never return, and so I never did. 29

I had a turbulent adolescence. I lived in a world of total frivolity. Sex presented itself in a very natural manner. I had a group of friends who often got together to have fun. There were parties with everything—food, alcohol, even drugs. Accustomed as I was to not asking questions, I only observed. Inside me I had a lot of doubts: why was it necessary for us to have stimulants in order to be happy? I saw this decadence, this rottenness, this promiscuity as natural, but I didn't stop thinking. I was always looking for another path, another way out, another life. 30

My parents didn't stop worrying about me. They thought it wasn't normal for me to be worried about such things. To them, it was irrational for me to be sad at seeing a beggar or kids who sleep on the streets covered with newspapers or drunkards lying on the streets. I was crazy! They sent me to a psychologist. Laziness was my problem. They registered me at the university so I would "do something." It wasn't the national university, of course, but the Catholic one (Universidad de Rafael Landiver). I wasn't enthusiastic about it at first, but to my surprise, I met young men and women from the same background as my 31 own, with the same concerns. We started to look together for solutions, read books, make hypotheses, and try to change the world. We were a group of seven people. Five of them have died, victims of repression.

How was your political education after that?

This group of seven who shared the same ideas, not yet clearly defined, **32** fell apart. I returned to being alone. I took a trip to Europe where I met an old militant who lived in political exile. He started telling me his personal experiences, answering my many doubts, lecturing to me, showing me the way. Back in Guatemala, I immediately tried to get involved in practice. That's when I acquired my real education. A new conception of the world and of life. A well-defined objective: contribute to the continuation of the revolution that was stopped in Guatemala in 1954, a revolution that Guatemala still needs.

Studying and practicing Marxism resolved the doubts of my childhood **33** and adolescence. Now I know what the Indian is, what my father and other landlords like him are, what we—myself included—the salaried middle sectors are, what the urban and agricultural proletariat is.

In what way have you been affected by political repression in Guatemala?

Before responding to this question, I'd like to relate what I know of the **34** repression: in the houses of the bourgeoisie, particularly in that of my parents, there is economic aid to repressive groups. Fortunately, at the time when these right-wing paramilitary groups appeared, I already had a political formation, and I knew how to take advantage of all occasions. I knew many people in "La Mano" (National Organized Anti-Communist Movement), made up of groups of assassins who massacred thousands of peasants in the eastern part of the country under the orders of ex-President Arana Osorio. Many times I have had to bite my tongue. I would hear these men speak of us, vainglorious about their exploits, telling how they personally fight against the guerrillas, mentioning forms of tortures that Cuban exiles in Guatemala would provide them. I knew of their assaults and their links. All of this we studied and interpreted with the compañeros; they never said more in my house than what they wanted me to hear, but they always revealed more than they thought they did.

I remember, for example, that in an assault on the Bank of Guatemala, **35** they dressed up as priests. I knew, likewise, that it was the priest of a certain Church who gave them the cassocks. I saw them dressed up as women on one occasion (for purposes of disguise, they said). I saw my mother dye the hair of one of them. In short, I had them very close and what I most remember about them was the death outlined in their eyes. Such hard looks behind friendly smiles. Since they were dealing with paid groups, little by little they began to degenerate into common delinquents, and in doing so entered into conflict with their "papa" Arana who took responsibility for eliminating them one by one after the supposed "pacification" of the eastern part of the country.

These events were clear manifestations of the union between the Church 36 and the dominant classes. "The faithful, above all the poor and the miserable, should be humble and accept the Christian dogma along with exploitation because God knows what he does. Some were born to be poor and some to be rich. It is the law of God."

I, personally, have not been a victim of repression. Nevertheless, many 37 compañeros in the struggle, which is much broader than the popular organization to which I belong, have been its victims. With so many of these Guatemalans (men and women) who have been captured or have died I feel solidarity!

What has been your relation with your compañeros?

I had to pass several difficult tests and demonstrate my loyalty to the rev- 38 olutionary struggle. Revolutionary discipline demands of us a behavior worthy of someone who struggles with the oppressed of Guatemala, our brothers and sisters. In this struggle, men and women have equal rights and obligations such that I can say that my relationship with both is very good.

What has been the historic participation of Guatemalan women in social change?

Definitely the participation of women throughout the long history of Gua- 39 temala is undeniable. At the moment, I can think of the example of Maria Chinchilla who died struggling for changes in the schools and the working conditions of teachers. Women within the dominant classes play a role too; remember, for example, the participation of women in the 1954 campaign to overthrow President Arbenz.

In your opinion, what do women need to do to achieve their liberation?

In this case, let me speak concretely of the revolutionary woman. The 40 fundamental tasks that are necessary to achieve her liberation cannot be separated from the political emancipation of the population. To speak of personal liberation doesn't make sense for us. Men and women linked to the revolutionary struggle work together for the liberation from dependency, underdevelopment, and the ignorance that typifies us as a backward country, by means of a permanent struggle that will allow us to construct a society free of exploitation of man by man. It is only possible to speak of liberation in a society not divided in classes.

Within all of the groups that struggle for the interests of the great major- 41 ity of oppressed people, there are remnants of typical bourgeois *machismo,* and there, fundamentally, the revolutionary woman has a well-defined task. These particular cases have to be eliminated through study, dialogue, criticism and self-criticism.

Is there some particular experience you would like to share?

Yes, there is one. After several years in this struggle—ones dedicated exclusively to the study of Marxism, education of young people and theoretical work—I became anxious to go out to the countryside. One nice day in the month of July, two compañeros and I went out destined for a place in one of the departments (provinces). During the day, we rested a little but at night we walked all the time in order to finally arrive at different little towns, intersections, and fincas where we would meet with agrarian workers to talk about their struggle. There for the first time since I had first seen Indians in the service of my father, we talked together as equals, as comrades.   42

1983

QUESTIONS FOR DISCUSSION

Content

a. What is Herrera's probable motivation to interview these two women in particular? Is the choice of whom she interviews influenced by her politics? How do the two testimonies work together to convey Herrera's message? What is her message?

b. Comment on the use of the word "testimonies" in the title. How are these narratives testimonies?

c. Why did Herrera choose to interview women rather than men?

d. What are each woman's reasons for joining the revolution? Do you agree with their actions?

e. According to each of the interviewees, what is the role of women in revolution?

f. What might the two women say to each other if they met? Would there be instant rapport and comradeship, or would there be uneasy restraint? Would class differences still exist in any form?

Strategy and Style

g. What are the basic similarities between the two narratives? What are the basic differences?

h. How does narrative presented as directly transcribed speech affect the persuasiveness of this "essay"? How does this kind of narrative compare to the personal narratives of the other writers in this chapter?

i. What questions may Herrera have asked the first woman? Why does she include her questions to the second woman but not those to the first woman? Are there rhetorical reasons for doing so?

j. How edited are these testimonies? What things would Herrera most likely have taken out in order to get the results of the interviews into their present form?

k. Comment on the differences between the vocabulary, sentence structure, and grammar of the first woman and those of the second. How is their language indicative of their status and of their attitude toward revolution?

SUGGESTIONS FOR SHORT WRITING

a. Ask a friend or relative to tell you about an important event in his or her life. Record or write what he or she says. At home, relisten to or reread a portion of the text and write a response to it.

b. Write about a government or educational policy or practice, or about any social problem that angers you.

SUGGESTIONS FOR SUSTAINED WRITING

a. Interview one or two people whose life stories you think would be interesting to your readers or would illuminate some aspect of a culture. Tape the interviews. Then, transcribe and edit them into a final form that both retains the immediacy of direct speech and conveys a point you would like to make. Before you interview your subjects, try a practice interview with a friend or classmate, and revise your questions accordingly. After transcribing the interviews, draw up an editorial policy to help you remain consistent and protect the integrity of your subjects.

b. Read any of Studs Terkel's collections of narratives based on interviews. You should be able to find a copy of his *Working,* for example, in your college library or in a local book store. Write an essay in which you compare two or three of the narratives in Terkel's book with those of Herrera. How do they compare in structure, in content, and in the way they are edited?

c. Read more about the political struggles in Guatemala. What is the relationship between these struggles and the more well-known struggles in Nicaragua and El Salvador? Write an essay discussing this relationship.

The Discus Thrower

Richard Selzer

Born in Troy, New York, Richard Selzer (b. 1928) took his M.D. from Albany Medical College. He teaches at Yale University Medical School and maintains a private practice in New Haven, Connecticut. The author of numerous short stories and essays, Selzer has contributed to Harper's, The New England Review *and the* American Review. *In 1975, he won the National Magazine Award for essays published in* Esquire. *Selzer is certainly not the only practicing physician writing for popular audiences. But, as Ana Fels commented in* The New York Times, *he is "one of the few medical writers who take a hard look at the actual subjects of medicine: disease, deformity and the human body with all its frailties." Selzer never shelters readers from the hideousness of mortality. He describes it clearly, sharply, and without apology. While maintaining a degree of accuracy we expect of a scientist, he writes in a language that is lush with emotional significance. Selzer's essays have been collected in* Confessions of a Knife *(1979),* Letters to a Young Doctor *(1982), and* Taking the World in for Repairs *(1986). He has also published an anthology of short stories,* Mortal Lessons *(1982).*

I spy on my patients. Ought not a doctor to observe his patients by any 1
means and from any stance, that he might the more fully assemble evidence? So I stand in the doorways of hospital rooms and gaze. Oh, it is not all that furtive an act. Those in bed need only look up to discover me. But they never do.

From the doorway of Room 542 the man in the bed seems deeply tanned. 2
Blue eyes and close-cropped white hair give him the appearance of vigor and good health. But I know that his skin is not brown from the sun. It is rusted, rather, in the last stage of containing the vile repose within. And the blue eyes are frosted, looking inward like the windows of a snowbound cottage. This man is blind. This man is also legless—the right leg missing from midthigh down, the left from just below the knee. It gives him the look of a bonsai, roots and branches pruned into the dwarfed facsimile of a great tree.

Propped on pillows, he cups his right thigh in both hands. Now and then 3
he shakes his head as though acknowledging the intensity of his suffering. In all of this he makes no sound. Is he mute as well as blind?

The room in which he dwells is empty of all possessions— no get-well 4
cards, small, private caches of food, day-old flowers, slippers, all the usual kickshaws of the sickroom. There is only the bed, a chair, a nightstand, and a tray on wheels that can be swung across his lap for meals.

"What time is it?" he asks. 5

"Three o'clock." 6

"Morning or afternoon?" 7

"Afternoon." 8

He is silent. There is nothing else he wants to know. 9

"How are you?" I say. 10

"Who is it?" he asks. 11

"It's the doctor. How do you feel?" 12

He does not answer right away. 13

"Feel?" he says. 14

"I hope you feel better," I say. 15

I press the button at the side of the bed. 16

"Down you go," I say. 17

"Yes, down," he says. 18

He falls back upon the bed awkwardly. His stumps, unweighted by legs 19
and feet, rise in the air, presenting themselves. I unwrap the bandages from the
stumps, and begin to cut away the black scabs and the dead, glazed fat with
scissors and forceps. A shard of white bone comes loose. I pick it away. I wash
the wounds with disinfectant and redress the stumps. All this while, he does not
speak. What is he thinking behind those lids that do not blink? Is he remembering a time when he was whole? Does he dream of feet? Of when his body was
not a rotting log?

He lies solid and inert. In spite of everything, he remains impressive, as 20
though he were a sailor standing athwart a slanting deck.

"Anything more I can do for you?" I ask. 21

For a long moment he is silent. 22

"Yes," he says at last and without the least irony. "You can bring me a 23
pair of shoes."

In the corridor, the head nurse is waiting for me. 24

"We have to do something about him," she says. "Every morning he or- 25
ders scrambled eggs for breakfast, and, instead of eating them, he picks up the
plate and throws it against the wall."

"Throws his plate?" 26

"Nasty. That's what he is. No wonder his family doesn't come to visit. 27
They probably can't stand him any more than we can."

She is waiting for me to do something. 28

"Well?" 29

"We'll see," I say. 30

The next morning I am waiting in the corridor when the kitchen delivers 31
his breakfast. I watch the aide place the tray on the stand and swing it across
his lap. She presses the button to raise the head of the bed. Then she leaves.

In time the man reaches to find the rim of the tray, then on to find the 32
dome of the covered dish. He lifts off the cover and places it on the stand. He
fingers across the plate until he probes the eggs. He lifts the plate in both
hands, sets it on the palm of his right hand, centers it, balances it. He hefts it up
and down slightly, getting the feel of it. Abruptly, he draws back his right arm
as far as he can.

There is the crack of the plate breaking against the wall at the foot of his 33 bed and the small wet sound of the scrambled eggs dropping to the floor.

And then he laughs. It is a sound you have never heard. It is something **34** new under the sun. It could cure cancer.

Out in the corridor, the eyes of the head nurse narrow. **35**

"Laughed, did he?" **36**

She writes something down on her clipboard. **37**

A second aide arrives, brings a second breakfast tray, puts it on the night- **38** stand, out of his reach. She looks over at me shaking her head and making her mouth go. I see that we are to be accomplices.

"I've got to feed you," she says to the man. **39**

"Oh, no you don't," the man says. **40**

"Oh, yes I do," the aide says, "after the way you just did. Nurse says so." **41**

"Get me my shoes," the man says. **42**

"Here's oatmeal," the aide says. "Open." And she touches the spoon to **43** his lower lip.

"I ordered scrambled eggs," says the man. **44**

"That's right," the aide says. **45**

I step forward. **46**

"Is there anything I can do?" I say. **47**

"Who are you?" the man asks. **48**

In the evening I go once more to that ward to make my rounds. The head **49** nurse reports to me that Room 542 is deceased. She has discovered this quite by accident, she says. No, there had been no sound. Nothing. It's a blessing, she says.

I go into his room, a spy looking for secrets. He is still there in his bed. **50** His face is relaxed, grave, dignified. After a while, I turn to leave. My gaze sweeps the wall at the foot of the bed, and I see the place where it has been repeatedly washed, where the wall looks very clean and very white.

1979

QUESTIONS FOR DISCUSSION

Content

a. Why does the patient hurl his breakfast against the wall every morning, and why does he laugh? What is Selzer's thesis?
b. Selzer's title is obviously ironic. Why does he compare this blind amputee to a robust athlete you might encounter at a track meet? Do they have anything in common?
c. Why does he describe the hospital room so carefully in paragraph 4? Does this information tell us anything about the patient? In what way does this paragraph relate to Selzer's concluding paragraph?

d. Why has the author chosen to use such graphic and disturbing details in paragraph 19? How do they help illuminate what he tells about the patient in paragraph 20?

e. What other details does he use to describe his patient? Reread paragraph 49. What does the way the patient's death is reported tell us about the way this man is viewed by the hospital staff?

f. Does this view differ from the speaker's? If so, how do you account for this difference?

g. Why don't we ever learn the patient's name?

Strategy and Style

h. Isn't it odd for doctors to spy on their patients? Comment upon Selzer's strange introduction.

i. How does Selzer foreshadow the death of the patient in Room 542? Why does he make it a point to do so?

j. This selection is organized around a series of visits to Room 542. What does this fact tell you about the author's point of view?

k. Like many narrative essays, this one makes excellent use of dialogue. Why is the dialogue we experience in this piece so simple, concise, and even curt? What does it tell us about the setting and about the people in it?

l. What do you make of Selzer's comment that the amputation has made his patient look like "the dwarfed facsimile of a great tree" (paragraph 2)? What other examples of figurative language do you find?

m. What irony is implicit in the author's claim that the patient's laugh "could cure cancer" (paragraph 34)?

SUGGESTIONS FOR SHORT WRITING

a. Selzer uses the analogy of a discus thrower to portray his patient. What other analogies could he have used? Try describing the patient using different analogies.

b. To practice dialogue, eavesdrop on a conversation among your family or friends and record what they say, attempting to get every word and other sounds down on paper. Compare the dialogue to the dialogue in this essay. How do they differ in structure? Try rewriting your dialogue to match the structure of Selzer's. What decisions do you find yourself making as you rewrite? What are your reasons for making those decisions?

SUGGESTIONS FOR SUSTAINED WRITING

a. Have you ever spent any length of time in a hospital as a patient or as a frequent visitor to a patient you knew well? If so, narrate that experience in an attempt to explain how difficult a long hospital stay can be.

b. Recalling the death of a relative or a close friend may be difficult, but doing so sometimes helps us come to grips with his or her passing. If you can, write an essay in which you recount such an experience and explain why the person you lost meant so much to you.

c. Selzer implies that the patient was heroic. Write a narrative essay *from the patient's point of view* to prove what Selzer is suggesting. Feel free to speak for the "discus thrower" by explaining what he might have said had he expressed his courage and agony.

Somewhere, Some Time, Some Place
Olive Schreiner

Born in Basutoland, South Africa, to missionary parents, Olive Schreiner (1855–1920) was self-educated and self-supporting. She began her first work, a semiautobiographical novel, The Story of an African Farm *(1883), when she was in her teens. It was published under the pseudonym Ralph Iron when Schreiner was in England. The novel's exotic setting and the unconventional stance of its author made it an immediate success—until it was revealed that "Iron" was a woman; the book's refreshing unconventionality was then seen as dangerous nonconformity. Unable to publish anything else in England, Schreiner returned to South Africa. There she became well known as a critic and essayist, writing primarily on women's and racial issues. Her most important piece of nonfiction is the long essay* Women and Labour *(1911). Schreiner also wrote short stories, which are quite different in style from her realistic, straightforward essays and novel.* Dreams *(1890) and* Stories, Dreams, and Allegories *(1923) are, as their titles suggest, collections of stories that are mystical and poetic in style and tone.*

When a child, not yet nine years old, I walked out one morning along the mountain tops on which my home stood. The sun had not yet risen, and the mountain grass was heavy with dew; as I looked back I could see the marks my feet had made on the long, grassy slope behind me. I walked till I came to a place where a little stream ran, which farther on passed over the precipices into the deep valley below. Here it passed between soft, earthy banks; at one place a large slice of earth had fallen away from the bank on the other side, and it had made a little island a few feet wide with water flowing all round it. It was covered with wild mint and a weed with yellow flowers and long waving grasses. I sat down on the bank at the foot of a dwarfed olive tree, the only tree near. All the plants on the island were dark with the heavy night's dew, and the sun had not yet risen.

I had got up so early because I had been awake much in the night and could not sleep longer. My heart was heavy; my physical heart seemed to have a pain in it, as if small, sharp crystals were cutting into it. All the world seemed wrong to me. It was not only that sense of the small misunderstandings and tiny injustices of daily life, which perhaps all sensitive children feel at some time pressing down on them; but the whole Universe seemed to be weighing on me.

I had grown up in a land where wars were common. From my earliest years I had heard of bloodshed and battles and hairbreadth escapes; I had heard them told of by those who had seen and taken part in them. In my native country dark men were killed and their lands taken from them by white men armed with superior weapons; even near to me such things had happened. I knew also how white men fought white men; the stronger even hanging the weaker on gallows when they did not submit; and I had seen how white men used the dark

47

as beasts of labour, often without any thought for their good or happiness. Three times I had seen an ox striving to pull a heavily loaded wagon up a hill, the blood and foam streaming from its mouth and nostrils as it struggled, and I had seen it fall dead, under the lash. In the bush in the kloof below I had seen bush-bucks and little long-tailed monkeys that I loved so shot dead, not from any necessity but for the pleasure of killing, and the cock-o-veets and the honey- suckers and the wood-doves that made the bush so beautiful to me. And sometimes I had seen bands of convicts going past to work on the roads, and had heard the chains clanking which went round their waists and passed between their legs to the irons on their feet; I had seen the terrible look in their eyes of a wild creature, when every man's hand is against it, and no one loves it, and it only hates and fears. I had got up early in the morning to drop small bits of tobacco at the roadside, hoping they would find them and pick them up. I had wanted to say to them, 'Someone loves you'; but the man with the gun was always there. Once I had seen a pack of dogs set on by men to attack a strange dog, which had come among them and had done no harm to anyone. I had watched it torn to pieces, though I had done all I could to save it. Why did everyone press on everyone and try to make them do what they wanted? Why did the strong always crush the weak? Why did we hate and kill and torture? Why was it all as it was? Why had the world ever been made? Why, oh why, had I ever been born?

The little sharp crystals seemed to cut deeper into my heart.   4

And then, as I sat looking at that little, damp, dark island, the sun began to   5
rise. It shot its lights across the long, grassy slopes of the mountains and struck the little mound of earth in the water. All the leaves and flowers and grasses on it turned bright gold, and the dewdrops hanging from them were like diamonds; and the water in the stream glinted as it ran. And, as I looked at that almost intolerable beauty, a curious feeling came over me. It was not what I *thought* put into exact words, but I seemed to *see* a world in which creatures no more hated and crushed, in which the strong helped the weak, and men understood each other, and forgave each other, and did not try to crush others, but to help. I did not think of it, as something to be in a distant picture; it was there, about me, and I was in it, and a part of it. And there came to me, as I sat there, a joy such as never besides have I experienced, except perhaps once, a joy without limit.

And then, as I sat on there, the sun rose higher and higher, and shone hot   6
on my back, and the morning light was everywhere. And slowly and slowly the vision vanished, and I began to think and question myself.

How could that glory ever really be? In a world where creature preys on   7
creature, and man, the strongest of all, preys more than all, how could this be? And my mind went back to the dark thoughts I had in the night. In a world where the little ant-lion digs his hole in the sand and lies hidden at the bottom for the small ant to fall in and be eaten, and the leopard's eyes gleam yellow through bushes as it watches the little bush-buck coming down to the fountain to drink, and millions and millions of human beings use all they know, and their

wonderful hands, to kill and press down others, what hope could there ever be? The world was as it was! And what was I? A tiny, miserable worm, a speck within a speck, an imperceptible atom, a less than a nothing! What did it matter what *I* did, how *I* lifted my hands, and how *I* cried out? The great world would roll on, and on, just as it had! What if nowhere, at no time, in no place, was there anything else?

The band about my heart seemed to grow tighter and tighter. A helpless, **8** tiny, miserable worm! Could I prevent one man from torturing an animal that was in his power; stop one armed man from going out to kill? In my own heart, was there not bitterness, the anger against those who injured me or others, till my heart was like a burning coal? If the world had been made so, so it was! But, why, oh why, had I ever been born? Why did the Universe exist?

And then, as I sat on there, another thought came to me; and in some **9** form or other it has remained with me ever since, all my life. It was like this: You cannot by willing it alter the vast world outside of you; you cannot, per- haps, cut the lash from one whip; you cannot stop the march of even one armed man going out to kill; you cannot, perhaps, strike the handcuff from one chained hand; you cannot even remake your own soul so that there shall be no tendency to evil in it; the great world rolls on, and *you* cannot reshape it; but this one thing only you can do—in that one, small, minute, almost infinitesimal spot in the Universe, where your will rules, there where alone you are as God, *strive* to make that you hunger for real! No man can prevent you there. In your own heart strive to kill out all hate, all desire to see evil come even to those who have injured you or another; what is weaker than yourself try to help; whatever is in pain or unjustly treated and cries out, say, 'I am here! I, little, weak, feeble, but I will do what I can for you.' This is all you can do; but do it; it is not nothing! And then this feeling came to me, a feeling it is not easy to put into words, but it was like this: You also are a part of the great Universe; what you strive for something strives for; *and nothing in the Universe is quite alone;* you are moving on towards something.

And as I walked back that morning over the grass slopes, I was not sorry **10** I was going back to the old life. I did not wish I was dead and that the Universe had never existed. I, also, had something to live for—and even if I failed to reach it utterly— somewhere, some time, some place, it was! I was not alone.

More than a generation has passed since that day, but it remains to me the **11** most important and unforgettable of my life. In the darkest hour its light has never quite died out.

In the long years which have passed, the adult has seen much of which **12** the young child knew nothing.

In my native land I have seen the horror of a great war. Smoke has risen **13** from burning homesteads; women and children by thousands have been thrown into great camps to perish there; men whom I have known have been tied in chairs and executed for fighting against strangers in the land of their own birth. In the world's great cities I have seen how everywhere the upper stone grinds hard on the nether, and men and women feed upon the toil of their fellow men without any increase of spiritual beauty or joy for themselves, only a heavy congestion; while those who are fed upon grow bitter and narrow from the loss of the life that is sucked from them. Within my own soul I have perceived elements militating against all I hungered for, of which the young child knew nothing; I have watched closely the great, terrible world of public life, of politics, diplomacy, and international relations, where, as under a terrible magnifying glass, the greed, the ambition, the cruelty and falsehood of the individual soul are seen, in so hideously enlarged and wholly unrestrained a form that it might be forgiven to one who cried out to the powers that lie behind life: 'Is it not possible to put out a sponge and wipe up humanity from the earth? It is stain!' I have realised that the struggle against the primitive, self-seeking instincts in human nature, whether in the individual or in the larger social organism, is a life-and-death struggle, to be renewed by the individual till death, by the race through the ages. I have tried to wear no blinkers. I have not held a veil before my eyes, that I might profess that cruelty, injustice, and mental and physical anguish were not. I have tried to look nakedly in the face those facts which make most against all hope—and yet, in the darkest hour, the consciousness which I carried back with me that morning has never wholly deserted me; even as a man who clings with one hand to a rock, though the waves pass over his head, yet knows what his hand touches.

But, in the course of the long years which have passed, something else **14** has happened. That which was for the young child only a vision, a flash of almost blinding light, which it could hardly even to itself translate, has, in the course of a long life's experience, become a hope, which I think the cool reason can find grounds to justify, and which a growing knowledge of human nature and human life does endorse.

Somewhere, some time, some place—even on earth! **15**

1920

QUESTIONS FOR DISCUSSION

Content

a. On the face of it, this essay looks like a narrative, "just" a story of something that happened to the writer. But it is also an argument. What does Schreiner argue? What might have been her reasons for using a narrative structure to make an argument?
b. Does Schreiner answer any of the questions she asks? If so, what is her answer? If not, does it matter that the questions go unanswered? Does she expect her readers to answer them?
c. Is Schreiner too optimistic? Is what she proposes a realistic solution to the misery of the world? What do you think we should do?

d. In paragraph 13, Schreiner writes that "the struggle against the primitive, self-seeking instincts in human nature...is a life-and-death struggle, to be renewed by the individual till death, by the race through the ages." What does she mean? Do you agree with this statement?

e. Schreiner tries to reconcile visualizing with thinking (paragraph 5), and hope with "cool reason" (paragraph 14). Is it necessary to reconcile these in order to find a solution to the world's problems?

Strategy and Style

f. How do changes in the light and the scenery affect the author's thinking? How does she use them to structure her essay? Does this structure help make the essay convincing?

g. In paragraph 3, she writes that the "dark men were killed and their lands taken from them by white men armed with superior weapons." She doesn't say that the white men are superior, just that their weapons are. What does this subtle phrasing tell us? How do comments such as this help Schreiner make her point?

h. The sentence style of this essay is characterized by a frequent use of questions and of sentences that begin with "and." How does this style affect the essay?

i. Find examples of metaphorical language. What images do they evoke? How do they affect your reading of the essay?

j. The author describes a scene from her childhood, ascribing her thoughts and conclusions as an adult to herself as the child narrator. How does she manage to combine the sensations of a child with the intellectualizing of an adult?

k. Would this essay have been different had it been written by a man? Could this essay have been written by a man?

SUGGESTIONS FOR SHORT WRITING

a. What image(s) does this essay evoke in your mind? Think of this essay visually, and draw what you see. Then write a short description or explanation of what you drew. If any of your classmates have followed this suggestion, compare your drawings. How did each of you "see" the essay?

b. Describe what Schreiner calls "somewhere, some time, some place" (paragraph 15).

SUGGESTIONS FOR SUSTAINED WRITING

a. Think of an event from your youth or childhood that still has great significance for you. In what ways does this significance extend to other people?

What do you now realize about the experience that you could not have known as a child? How has it affected your present actions? In a first draft, just describe the event as thoroughly as possible; then, considering your readers' interests and the overall message you want to convey, prune the description of the event so that only the most important details remain, and retell the story. When you revise, continually ask yourself how the story suits your purpose.

b. Try to answer any of the rhetorical questions Schreiner asks in her essay. Focus on one (or more) of the questions, and consider it (them) as a straightforward question. How would you answer?

2

Description

Description makes for diversity. The people, places, and things described in the eight selections that follow vary as widely as the distinctive styles and perspectives of their authors. Nonetheless, each essay is a portrait sketched in details that are at once concrete, specific, and vivid.

Good description is never hurried; it is crafted with carefully chosen details that *show* the reader something. Take "Where the World Began," for example. Not content to tell us that watching the hometown fire company answer an alarm was "exciting, colorful, and noisy," Laurence savors the moment and helps us do the same:

> ...the wooden tower's bronze bell would clonk and toll like a thousand speeded funerals in a time of plague, and in a few minutes the team of giant black horses would cannon forth, pulling the fire wagon like some scarlet chariot of the Goths, while the firemen clung with one hand, adjusting their helmets as they went.

Appealing to the senses—in this case sight and sound—is fundamental to the process of describing. Some writers rely almost solely upon vision and hearing as sources of descriptive detail, but the authors in this chapter teach us that we can use the other senses as well—taste, smell, and touch—to guide readers through our private worlds.

The excerpt from "Where the World Began" also shows that writers of description exploit techniques often associated with narration, especially the use of verbs that are informative and evocative. More important, Laurence's use of figurative language—her comparison of the alarm to the sounds of bells at a "thousand speeded funerals," for example—reminds us that invoking facts and images from the knowledge we share with readers is a good way to show them something new. Flashes of brilliance appear throughout the chapter. Woolf's reference to the "narrow and intricate corridors" of her brain, for example, and Least Heat Moon's reminder that "the twenty-five thousand square miles of Na-

53

vajo reservation" is "nearly equal to West Virginia" testify to the power and clarity with which they invest their writing.

While relying heavily on physical description, none of the essays collected here is a purely sensate record of its subject. More often than not, describing is a means to an end. It is hard to read a narrative, for example, without stumbling over details that reveal setting and character. Even writers of scientific prose use information that appeals to the senses as a way to discuss the lives of plants and animals or to explore the workings of machines and processes.

The authors in this chapter use description to reveal the character or capture the essence of their subjects, though their purpose may not be immediately apparent. Consider Doris Lessing, who transcends physical appearance to expose the psychology of her father by allowing him to speak to us directly and by recalling his memories, his dreams, and his failures.

Anecdotes and bits of dialogue enrich portraits of home turf by Richler and Laurence, allowing us to understand the character of places that nurtured the authors and helped determine their own characters. Similar techniques appear in Least Heat Moon's description of the reservation. And like other writers represented here, Didion reminds us that discussing the people who inhabit a place is a way to reveal its soul.

Though there is little similarity in approach, subject, or style between the description of a dentist's office and the recollection of an insect's demise, both Freundlich and Woolf seem to engage their subjects not simply to describe an exterior reality but to tell us about themselves. Something like this can be said of Schjeldahl, of Richler, and even of Laurence.

As always, you are invited to make your own comparisons and to draw conclusions as you see fit. What makes the selections in this chapter so enjoyable is that each reveals the strong and distinctive voice of its author. Enjoy the artists behind the subjects they describe. They will teach you that your personal commitment to a subject—the "wonder" with which it fills you, Woolf might say—is worth sharing with others.

Where the World Began

Margaret Laurence

Born in Manitoba, Margaret (Wemyss) Laurence (1926–1987) was one of Canada's foremost novelists, essayists, and writers of short fiction and of children's books. She based much of her work on her travels in Africa, and on her life in the small Canadian prairie town where she was born. The former yielded A Tree for Poverty *(1954), a translation of Somali poems and stories she gathered during two years in the harsh Haud desert;* This Side Jordan *(1960), a novel;* The Tomorrow Tamer and Other Stories *(1963); and* The Prophet's Camel Bell *(1963), a travel memoir. Neepawa, the hometown she renamed Manawaka in her novels, figures in* The Stone Angel *(1964);* A Jest of God *(1966), republished as* Rachel, Rachel; Fire Dwellers *(1969); and* A Bird in the House *(1970). It is on the Manawaka books that Laurence's fame chiefly rests. However, she is also noted for her essays, a collection of which she published as* Heart of a Stranger *(1976). In* Book Forum, *John Caldwell cited "the search for the lost Eden, for Jerusalem the Golden, for the promised land of one's own freedom" as an important ingredient in her work. For Laurence, that little prairie town "Where the World Began" might very well have contained the "promised land."*

1   A strange place it was, that place where the world began. A place of incredible happenings, splendors and revelations, despairs like multitudinous pits of isolated hells. A place of shadow-spookiness, inhabited by the unknowable dead. A place of jubilation and of mourning, horrible and beautiful.

2   It was, in fact, a small prairie town.

3   Because that settlement and that land were my first and for many years my only real knowledge of this planet, in some profound way they remain my world, my way of viewing. My eyes were formed there. Towns like ours, set in a sea of land, have been described thousands of times as dull, bleak, flat, uninteresting. I have had it said to me that the railway trip across Canada is spectacular, except for the prairies, when it would be desirable to go to sleep for several days, until the ordeal is over. I am always unable to argue this point effectively. All I can say is—well, you really have to live there to know that country. The town of my childhood could be called bizarre, agonizingly repressive or cruel at times, and the land in which it grew could be called harsh in the violence of its seasonal changes. But never merely flat or uninteresting. Never dull.

4   In winter, we used to hitch rides on the back of the milk sleigh, our moccasins squeaking and slithering on the hard rutted snow of the roads, our hands in ice-bubbled mitts hanging onto the box edge of the sleigh for dear life, while Bert grinned at us through his great frosted mustache and shouted the horse into speed, daring us to stay put. Those mornings, rising, there would be the perpetual fascination of the frost feathers on windows, the ferns and flowers and eerie

faces traced there during the night by unseen artists of the wind. Evenings, coming back from skating, the sky would be black but not dark, for you could see a cold glitter of stars from one side of the earth's rim to the other. And then the sometime astonishment when you saw the Northern Lights flaring across the sky, like the scrawled signature of God. After a blizzard, when the snowplow hadn't yet got through, school would be closed for the day, the assumption being that the town's young could not possibly flounder through five feet of snow in the pursuit of education. We would then gaily don snowshoes and flounder for miles out into the white dazzling deserts, in pursuit of a different kind of knowing. If you came back too close to night, through the woods at the foot of the town hill, the thin black branches of poplar and chokecherry now meringued with frost, sometimes you heard coyotes. Or maybe the banshee wolf-voices were really only inside your head.

Summers were scorching, and when no rain came and the wheat became ⁵ bleached and dried before it headed, the faces of farmers and townsfolk would not smile much, and you took for granted, because it never seemed to have been any different, the frequent knocking at the back door and the young men standing there, mumbling or thrusting defiantly their requests for a drink of water and a sandwich if you could spare it. They were riding the freights, and you never knew where they had come from, or where they might end up, if anywhere. The Drought and Depression were like evil deities which had been there always. You understood and did not understand.

Yet the outside world had its continuing marvels. The poplar bluffs and ⁶ the small river were filled and surrounded with a zillion different grasses, stones, and weed flowers. The meadowlarks sang undaunted from the twanging telephone wires along the gravel highway. Once we found an old flat-bottomed scow, and launched her, poling along the shallow brown waters, mending her with wodges of hastily chewed Spearmint, grounding her among the tangles of yellow marsh marigolds that grew succulently along the banks of the shrunken river, while the sun made our skins smell dusty-warm.

My best friend lived in an apartment above some stores on Main Street ⁷ (its real name was Mountain Avenue, goodness knows why), an elegant apartment with royal-blue velvet curtains. The back roof, scarcely sloping at all, was corrugated tin, of a furnace-like warmth on a July afternoon, and we would sit there drinking lemonade and looking across the back lane at the Fire Hall. Sometimes our vigil would be rewarded. Oh joy! Somebody's house burning down! We had an almost-perfect callousness in some ways. Then the wooden tower's bronze bell would clonk and toll like a thousand speeded funerals in a time of plague, and in a few minutes the team of giant black horses would cannon forth, pulling the fire wagon like some scarlet chariot of the Goths, while the firemen clung with one hand, adjusting their helmets as they went.

The oddities of the place were endless. An elderly lady used to serve, as ⁸ her afternoon tea offering to other ladies, soda biscuits spread with peanut butter and topped with a whole marshmallow. Some considered this slightly eccentric, when compared with chopped egg sandwiches, and admittedly talked about her behind her back, but no one ever refused these delicacies or indicated to her that they thought she had slipped a cog. Another lady dyed her hair a bright and cherry orange, by strangers often mistaken at twenty paces for a feather hat. My own beloved stepmother wore a silver fox neckpiece, a whole pelt, *with the embalmed (?) head still on.* My Ontario Irish grandfather said, "sparrow grass," a more interesting term than asparagus. The town dump was known as "the nuisance grounds," phrase fraught with weird connotations, as though the effluvia of our lives was beneath contempt but at the same time was subtly threatening to the determined and sometimes hysterical propriety of our ways.

Some oddities were, as idiom had it, "funny ha ha"; others were "funny **9** peculiar." Some were not so very funny at all. An old man lived, deranged, in a shack in the valley. Perhaps he wasn't even all that old, but to us he seemed a wild Methuselah figure, shambling among the underbrush and the tall couchgrass, muttering indecipherable curses or blessings, a prophet who had forgotten his prophecies. Everyone in town knew him, but no one knew him. He lived among us as though only occasionally and momentarily visible. The kids called him Andy Gump, and feared him. Some sought to prove their bravery by tormenting him. They were the medieval bear baiters, and he the lumbering bewildered bear, half blind, only rarely turning to snarl. Everything is to be found in a town like mine. Belsen, writ small but with the same ink.

All of us cast stones in one shape or another. In grade school, among the **10** vulnerable and violet girls we were, the feared and despised were those few older girls from what was charmingly termed "the wrong side of the tracks." Tough in talk and tougher in muscle, they were said to be whores already. And may have been, that being about the only profession readily available to them.

The dead lived in that place, too. Not only the grandparents who had, in **11** local parlance, "passed on" and who gloomed, bearded or bonneted, from the sepia photographs in old albums, but also the uncles, forever eighteen or nineteen, whose names were carved on the granite family stones in the cemetery, but whose bones lay in France. My own young mother lay in that graveyard, beside other dead of our kin, and when I was ten, my father, too, only forty, left the living town for the dead dwelling on the hill.

When I was eighteen, I couldn't wait to get out of that town, away from **12** the prairies. I did not know then that I would carry the land and town all my life within my skull, that they would form the mainspring and source of the writing I was to do, wherever and however far away I might live.

This was my territory in the time of my youth, and in a sense my life **13** since then has been an attempt to look at it, to come to terms with it. Stultifying to the mind it certainly could be, and sometimes was, but not to the imagination. It was many things, but it was never dull.

The same, I now see, could be said for Canada in general. Why on earth **14** did generations of Canadians pretend to believe this country dull? We knew perfectly well it wasn't. Yet for so long we did not proclaim what we knew. If our upsurge of so-called nationalism seems odd or irrelevant to outsiders, and even to some of our own people (*what's all the fuss about?*), they might try to understand that for many years we valued ourselves insufficiently, living as we did under the huge shadows of those two dominating figures, Uncle Sam and Britannia. We have only just begun to value ourselves, our land, our abilities. We have only just begun to recognize our legends and to give shape to our myths.

There are, God knows, enough aspects to deplore about this country. When I see the killing of our lakes and rivers with industrial wastes, I feel rage and despair. When I see our industries and natural resources increasingly taken over by America, I feel an overwhelming discouragement, especially as I cannot simply say "damn Yankees." It should never be forgotten that it is ourselves who have sold such a large amount of our birthright for a mess of plastic Progress. When I saw the War Measures Act being invoked in 1970, I lost forever the vestigial remains of the naïve wish-belief that repression could not happen here, or would not. And yet, of course, I had known all along in the deepest and often hidden caves of the heart that anything can happen anywhere, for the seeds of both man's freedom and his captivity are found everywhere, even in the microcosm of a prairie town. But in raging against our injustices, our stupidities, I do so *as family*, as I did, and still do in writing, about those aspects of my town which I hated and which are always in some ways aspects of myself. 15

The land still draws me more than other lands. I have lived in Africa and in England, but splendid as both can be, they do not have the power to move me in the same way as, for example, that part of southern Ontario where I spent four months last summer in a cedar cabin beside a river. "Scratch a Canadian, and you find a phony pioneer," I used to say to myself in warning. But all the same it is true, I think, that we are not yet totally alienated from physical earth, and let us only pray we do not become so. I once thought that my lifelong fear and mistrust of cities made me a kind of old-fashioned freak; now I see it differently. 16

The cabin has a long window across its front western wall, and sitting at the oak table there in the mornings, I used to look out at the river and at the tall trees beyond, green-gold in the early light. The river was bronze; the sun caught it strangely, reflecting upon its surface the near-shore sand ripples underneath. Suddenly, the crescenting of a fish, gone before the eye could clearly give image to it. The old man next door said these leaping fish were carp. Himself, he preferred muskie, for he was a real fisherman and the muskie gave him a fight. The wind most often blew from the south, and the river flowed toward the south, so when the water was wind-riffled, and the current was strong, the river seemed to be flowing both ways. I liked this, and interpreted it as an omen, a natural symbol. 17

A few years ago, when I was back in Winnipeg, I gave a talk at my old college. It was open to the public, and afterward a very old man came up to me 18 and asked me if my maiden name had been Wemyss. I said yes, thinking he might have known my father or my grandfather. But no. "When I was a young lad," he said, "I once worked for your great-grandfather, Robert Wemyss, when he had the sheep ranch at Raeburn." I think that was a moment when I realized all over again something of great importance to me. My long-ago families came from Scotland and Ireland, but in a sense that no longer mattered so much. My true roots were here.

I am not very patriotic, in the usual meaning of that word. I cannot say 19 "My country right or wrong" in any political, social or literary context. But one thing is inalterable, for better or worse, for life.

This is where my world began. A world which includes the ancestors— 20 both my own and other people's ancestors who become mine. A world which formed me, and continues to do so, even while I found it in some of its aspects, and continue to do so. A world which gave me my own lifework to do, because it was here that I learned the sight of my own particular eyes.

1976

QUESTIONS FOR DISCUSSION

Content

a. Do you find Laurence's title intriguing? What exactly does she mean by it? Think about various Biblical allusions that John Caldwell makes in his remarks about Laurence.

b. The author's purpose goes beyond simply describing a prairie town. What is that purpose, and how does her use of descriptive details help her accomplish it?

c. How would you describe the audience to whom Laurence is writing?

d. What important distinction does Laurence draw in paragraph 3? Why is this distinction important? In what other parts of the essay does she allude to it?

e. In what way does her recolleciton of the "almost-perfect callousness" (paragraph 7) she possessed as a girl help develop the thesis? Why does she devote two entire paragraphs to "the oddities of the place" (paragraphs 8 and 9)?

f. What are the "Drought and Depression" mentioned in paragraph 5? In what ways does the author's mention of these "evil deities" help her recapture her childhood?

g. Who were "the young men…thrusting defiantly their requests for a drink of water and a sandwich…." (paragraph 5)? What do they add to Laurence's description of her home?

h. In which of the World Wars did the "uncles…whose bones lay in France" die (paragraph 11)? What are some of the context clues that help us determine the answer?

i. What is the one insidious notion about both Canada and her home town that Laurence wishes to dispel?

j. What does she mean by "plastic Progress" (paragraph 15)?

k. Paragraphs 16 and 17 explain Laurence's belief that she and other Canadians are "not yet totally alienated from physical earth…." Why is it important for her to tell us this? What is the "omen" she describes in paragraph 17?

Strategy and Style

l. To a great degree this selection is really two essays. Where does one end and the other begin? In what way is the little town in which Laurence grew up a microcosm of the whole of Canada?

m. Like all good descriptive pieces, this selection uses details "to show" rather than "to tell." Nowhere is that statement more applicable than in paragraph 4. Explain why this paragraph is so effective in helping Laurence counter the charge that her prairie town was "dull."

n. Comment upon the author's choice of verbs in paragraph 4. In what other paragraphs of the essay is her language (nearly) as vivid and exciting?

o. Laurence's use of metaphors, similes and other kinds of figurative language is superb. In paragraph 7, she compares a fire truck to "some scarlet chariot of the Goths." In paragraph 11, she uses an oxymoron (a rhetorical figure that contains contradictory elements) when she says the "dead lived in that place, too." What other examples of figurative language did you find?

p. Near the end of the essay, Laurence becomes almost rhapsodic in explaining how growing up as a Canadian has influenced her writing. In what way does her chance meeting with one of her great-grandfather's farm workers help her create an appropriate conclusion for this essay?

q. What is the author's attitude toward herself both as the adult who wrote this essay and as the child who is one of its subjects?

SUGGESTIONS FOR SHORT WRITING

a. Choose a passage (a sentence or a paragraph) and relate that passage to your own life.

b. Describe one of the "oddities of the place" (paragraph 8) of your hometown.

SUGGESTIONS FOR SUSTAINED WRITING

a. Describe your hometown or community. In what ways has it helped shape you as an individual and helped determine what you want out of life?

b. In what ways is your hometown a microcosm of your country? Like Laurence, compare both positive and negative aspects.

c. Describe the small town (or big city, for that matter) in which you were raised in such a way as to prove that living there was anything but dull.

d. Everyone's community has its "oddities." Describe some of the people, places, laws, rituals, etc. of your hometown that you find odd.

The Metropolitan Cathedral in San Salvador

Joan Didion

Born in Sacramento, California, Joan Didion (b. 1934) served as associate feature editor for Vogue, *as a columnist for* The Saturday Evening Post, *and as a contributing editor to the* National Review. *Her essays are subtle portraits of the American experience and of those who live it. Her major works include novels:* Play It as It Lays *(1971),* A Book of Common Prayer *(1977), and* Democracy *(1984); collections of essays:* Slouching Towards Bethlehem *(1968) and* The White Album *(1979); and nonfiction:* Salvador *(1983) and* Miami *(1987). She is also coauthor of several screenplays, including* The Panic in Needle Park *(1971),* A Star Is Born *(1976), and* True Confessions *(1981). The following excerpt is from* Salvador, *a book about her experiences in El Salvador.*

During the week before I flew down to El Salvador a Salvadoran woman who works for my husband and me in Los Angeles gave me repeated instructions about what we must and must not do. We must not go out at night. We must stay off the street whenever possible. We must never ride in buses or taxis, never leave the capital, never imagine that our passports would protect us. We must not even consider the hotel a safe place: people were killed in hotels. She spoke with considerable vehemence, because two of her brothers had been killed in Salvador in August of 1981, in their beds. The throats of both brothers had been slashed. Her father had been cut but stayed alive. Her mother had been beaten. Twelve of her other relatives, aunts and uncles and cousins, had been taken from their houses one night the same August, and their bodies had been found some time later, in a ditch. I assured her that we would remember, we would be careful, we would in fact be so careful that we would probably (trying for a light touch) spend all our time in church. 1

She became still more agitated, and I realized that I had spoken as a *norteamericana:* churches had not been to this woman the neutral ground they had been to me. I must remember: Archbishop Romero killed saying mass in the chapel of the Divine Providence Hospital in San Salvador. I must remember: more than thirty people killed at Archbishop Romero's funeral in the Metropolitan Cathedral in San Salvador. I must remember: more than twenty people killed before that on the steps of the Metropolitan Cathedral. CBS had filmed it. It had been on television, the bodies jerking, those still alive crawling over the dead as they tried to get out of range. I must understand: the Church was dangerous. 2

I told her that I understood, that I knew all that, and I did, abstractly, but the specific meaning of the Church she knew eluded me until I was actually there, at the Metropolitan Cathedral in San Salvador, one afternoon when rain sluiced down its corrugated plastic windows and puddled around the supports 3

62

of the Sony and Phillips billboards near the steps. The effect of the Metropolitan Cathedral is immediate, and entirely literary. This is the cathedral that the late Archbishop Oscar Arnulfo Romero refused to finish, on the premise that the work of the Church took precedence over its display, and the high walls of raw concrete bristle with structural rods, rusting now, staining the concrete, sticking out at wrenched and violent angles. The wiring is exposed. Fluorescent tubes hang askew. The great high altar is backed by warped plyboard. The cross on the altar is of bare incandescent bulbs, but the bulbs, that afternoon, were unlit: there was in fact no light at all on the main altar, no light on the cross, no light on the globe of the world that showed the northern American continent in gray and the southern in white; no light on the dove above the globe, *Salvador del Mundo*. In this vast brutalist space that was the cathedral, the unlit altar seemed to offer a single ineluctable message: at this time and in this place the light of the world could be construed as out, off, extinguished.

In many ways the Metropolitan Cathedral is an authentic piece of politi- **4** cal art, a statement for El Salvador as *Guernica* was for Spain. It is quite devoid of sentimental relief. There are no decorative or architectural references to familiar parables, in fact no stories at all, not even the Stations of the Cross. On the afternoon I was there the flowers laid on the altar were dead. There were no traces of normal parish activity. The doors were open to the barricaded main steps, and down the steps there was a spill of red paint, lest anyone forget the blood shed there. Here and there on the cheap linoleum inside the cathedral there was what seemed to be actual blood, dried in spots, the kind of spots dropped by a slow hemorrhage, or by a woman who does not know or does not care that she is menstruating.

There were several women in the cathedral during the hour or so I spent **5** there, a young woman with a baby, an older woman in house slippers, a few others, all in black. One of the women walked the aisles as if by compulsion, up and down, across and back, crooning loudly as she walked. Another knelt without moving at the tomb of Archbishop Romero in the right transept. "Loor a Monsenor Romero," the crude needlepoint tapestry by the tomb read, "Praise to Monsignor Romero from the Mothers of the Imprisoned, the Disappeared, and the Murdered," the *Comité de Madres y Familiares de Presos, Desaparecidos, y Asesinados Politicos de El Salvador*.

The tomb itself was covered with offerings and petitions, notes decorated **6** with motifs cut from greeting cards and cartoons. I recall one with figures cut from a Bugs Bunny strip, and another with a pencil drawing of a baby in a crib. The baby in this drawing seemed to be receiving medication or fluid or blood intravenously, through the IV line shown on its wrist. I studied the notes for a while and then went back and looked again at the unlit altar, and at the red paint on the main steps, from which it was possible to see the guardsmen on the balcony of the National Palace hunching back to avoid the rain. Many Salvadorans are offended by the Metropolitan Cathedral, which is as it should be, because the place remains perhaps the only unambiguous political statement in El Salvador, a metaphorical bomb in the ultimate power station.

1983

QUESTIONS FOR DISCUSSION

Content

a. Is Didion simply describing the Metropolitan Cathedral, or is she using her description as a metaphor for something else? If so, what is the metaphor?
b. Why does she describe the interior of the cathedral in such detail?
c. What senses does Didion appeal to in this description?
d. What does she tell us about the people who worship at the cathedral? How do references to people enrich her description of this place?
e. The author says that the churches in El Salvador are not "neutral ground" (paragraph 2). What does she mean? Does Didion give us any indication about why the Church is involved in Salvadoran politics?
f. What is the "specific meaning of the Church" (paragraph 3) that Didion says eluded her until she came to El Salvador?

Strategy and Style

g. Why does Didion begin by recalling the advice of the Salvadoran woman who works for her?
h. What is *Guernica* (paragraph 4)? How does Didion's comparing the Metropolitan Cathedral to this "piece of political art" help her achieve her purpose?
i. Are Didion's description of the place and the accompanying political commentary convincing? If so, what makes them so?
j. Is your reaction to the cathedral generally positive or negative? What details in the essay account for your reaction?
k. Is Didion justified in saying in paragraph 6 that "many Salvadorans are offended by the Metropolitan Cathedral, which is as it should be..."? Why should Salvadorans be offended by the cathedral?
l. Is she justified in saying that the cathedral is the "only unambiguous political statement in El Salvador..."? What is this statement?
m. How objective is Didion? Is she praising, criticizing, or just describing? How would you describe her tone, and what elements in this essay reveal that tone?

SUGGESTIONS FOR SHORT WRITING

a. Try describing a place that is very familiar to you as if you had never seen it before. You might want to find a place in which you can sit, observe, and write unnoticed. First, sit for a while and try to see the place as a stranger would; then write your description of it.
b. Try rewriting paragraph 4, excising all political language. What do you end up with? What words did you consider to be political?

SUGGESTIONS FOR SUSTAINED WRITING

a. Think of a building that you believe symbolizes a political or social situation. What physical details of this building mirror aspects of the situation? Write a description of the building in which you make the connection clear.
b. Describe the government of the United States, of another country, of your state, or of your hometown through the use of an extended metaphor developed through description. Like Didion, use carefully chosen descriptive details to show how a building or a place mirrors major aspects of that government.
c. Recall a time when you were an outsider—for example, when you traveled to a foreign country or moved to a new community. What were your thoughts about and reactions to this new place? Do you think your outsider status allowed you to see the place more clearly and objectively than the "natives" do? Try describing this place so that these "natives" might see their culture in a new way.

Tuesday Morning
William Least Heat Moon

William Least Heat Moon (b. 1939) was born William Trogdon, of both Sioux and European ancestry. Least Heat Moon earned a doctorate at the University of Missouri in 1973 and taught English in Columbia, Missouri, until he was laid off in 1978. He then took the opportunity to travel around the United States; the record of his trip, Blue Highways: A Journey into America, *which was published in 1982, continues to be a best-selling travelogue. "Tuesday Morning" is taken from that book. Least Heat Moon also contributes to* Esquire, The Atlantic, *and* The New York Times.

Tuesday morning: the country east of Heber was a desert of sagebrush 1
and globe-shaped junipers and shallow washes with signs warning of flash
floods. I turned north at Snowflake, founded by Erastus Snow and Bill Flake,
and headed toward the twenty-five thousand square miles of Navajo reservation
(nearly equal to West Virginia) which occupies most of the northeastern corner
of Arizona. The scrub growth disappeared entirely and only the distant outlines
of red rock mesas interrupted the emptiness. But for the highway, the land was
featureless.

Holbrook used to be a tough town where boys from the Hash Knife cattle 2
outfit cut loose. Now, astride I-44 (once route 66), Holbrook was a tourist stop
for women with Instamatics and men with metal detectors; no longer was the
big business cattle, but rather rocks and gems.

North of the interstate, I entered the reserve. Although the area has been 3
part of the Navajo homeland for five hundred years, settlers of a century before,
led by Kit Carson, drove the Navajo out of Arizona in retribution for their raids
against whites and other Indians alike. A few years later, survivors of the infamous "Long Walk" returned to take up their land again. Now the Navajo possess the largest reservation in the United States and the one hundred fifty thousand descendants of the seven thousand survivors comprise far and away the largest tribe. Their reservation is the only one in the country to get bigger—five times bigger—after it was first set aside; their holdings increased largely because white men had believed Navajo land worthless. But in fact, the reservation contains coal, oil, gas, uranium, helium, and timber; those resources may explain why Navajos did not win total control over their land until 1972.

Liquor bottles, beercans, an occasional stripped car littered the unfenced 4
roadside. Far off the highway, against the mesa bottoms, stood small concrete-block or frame houses, each with a television antenna, pickup, privy, and ceremonial hogan of stone, adobe, and cedar. Always the hogan doors faced east.

In a classic scene, a boy on a pinto pony herded a flock of sheep and 5
goats—descendants of the Spanish breed—across the highway. A few miles

later, a man wearing a straw Stetson and pegleg Levi's guided up a draw a pair of horses tied together at the neck in the Indian manner. With the white man giving up on the economics of cowpunching, it looked as if the old categories of cowboys and Indians had merged; whoever the last true cowboy in America turns out to be, he's likely to be an Indian.

At the center of the reservation lay Hopi territory, a large rectangle with   6
boundaries the tribes cannot agree on because part of the increase of Navajo land has come at the expense of the Hopis. A forbidding sign in Latinate English:

> YOU ARE ENTERING THE EXCLUSIVE
> HOPI RESERVATION AREA. YOUR
> ENTRANCE CONSITITUTES CONSENT
> TO THE JURISDICTION OF THE HOPI
> TRIBE AND ITS COURTS.

Although the Hopi have lived here far longer than any other surviving   7
people and consider their mile-high spread of rock and sand, wind and sun, the center of the universe, they are now, by Anglo decree, surrounded by their old enemies, the Navajo, a people they see as latecomers. In 1880, Hopis held two and one half million acres; today it has decreased to about a half million.

Holding on to their land has been a long struggle for the Hopi. Yet for a   8
tribe whose name means "well behaved," for Indians without war dances, for a group whose first defense against the conquistadors was sprinkled lines of sacred cornmeal, for a people who protested priestly corruption (consorting with Hopi women and whipping men) by quietly pitching a few padres over the cliffs, Hopis have done well. But recently they have fought Navajo expansion in federal courts, and a strange case it is: those who settled first seeking judgment from those who came later through laws of those who arrived last.

Because the Navajo prefer widely dispersed clusters of clans to village   9
life, I'd seen nothing resembling a hamlet for seventy-five miles. But Hopi Polacca almost looked like a Western town in spite of Indian ways here and there: next to a floral-print bedsheet on a clothesline hung a coyote skin, and beside box houses were adobe bread ovens shaped like skep beehives. The Navajo held to his hogan, the Hopi his oven. Those things persisted.

Like bony fingers, three mesas reached down from larger Black Mesa 10
into the middle of Hopi land; not long ago, the only way onto these mesas was by handholds in the steep rock heights. From the tops, the Hopi look out upon a thousand square miles. At the heart of the reservation, topographically and culturally, was Second Mesa. Traditionally, Hopis, as do the eagles they hold sacred, prefer to live on precipices; so it was not far from the edge of Second Mesa that they built the Hopi Cultural Center. In the gallery were drawings of mythic figures by Hopi children who fused centuries and cultures with grotesque Mudhead Kachinas wearing large terra-cotta masks and jackolantern smiles, dancing atop spaceships with Darth Vader and Artoo Deetoo.

At the Center, I ate *nokquivi,* a good hominy stew with baked chile pep- 11
pers, but I had no luck in striking up a conversation. I drove on toward the
western edge of the mesa. Not far from the tribal garage (TRIBAL VEHICLES ONLY)
stood small sandstone houses, their slabs precisely cut and fitted as if by ancient Aztecs, a people related to the Hopi. The solid houses blended with the
tawny land so well they appeared part of the living rock. All were empty. The
residents had moved to prefabs and doublewides.

I couldn't see how anyone could survive a year in this severe land, yet 12
Hopis, like other desert life, are patient and clever and not at all desperate; they
have lasted here for ten centuries by using tiny terraced plots that catch spring
rain and produce a desert-hardy species of blue corn, as well as squash, onions,
beans, peppers, melons, apricots, peaches. The bristlecone pine of American Indians, Hopis live where almost nothing else will, thriving long in adverse conditions: poor soil, drought, temperature extremes, high winds. Those give life to
the bristlecone and the Hopi.

Clinging to the southern lip of Third Mesa was ancient Oraibi, most prob- 13
ably the oldest continuously occupied village in the United States. Somehow
the stone and adobe have been able to hang on to the precipitous edge since the
twelfth century. More than eight hundred Hopis lived at Oraibi in 1901—now
only a few. All across the reservation I'd seen no more than a dozen people,
and on the dusty streets of the old town I saw just one bent woman struggling
against the wind. But somewhere there must have been more.

To this strangest of American villages the Franciscan father, Tomás 14
Garces, came in 1776 from Tucson with gifts and "true religion." Hopis permitted him to stay at Oraibi, looking then as now if you excluded an occasional
television antenna, but they refused his gifts and god, and, on the fourth day of
July, sent him off disheartened. To this time, no other North American tribe has
held closer to its own religion and culture. Although the isolated Hopi had no
knowledge of the importance of religious freedom to the new nation surrounding them, several generations successfully ignored "the code of religious offenses"—laws designed by the Bureau of Indian Affairs to destroy the old rituals and way of life—until greater bureaucratic tolerance came when Herbert
Hoover appointed two Quakers to direct the BIA.

A tribal squadcar checked my speed at Hotevilla, where the highway 15
started a long descent off the mesa. The wind was getting up, and tumbleweed
bounded across the road, and sand hummed against the Ghost. West, east,
north, south—to each a different weather: sandstorm, sun, rain, and bluish snow
on the San Francisco Peaks, that home of the Kachinas who are the spiritual
forces of Hopi life.

Tuba City, founded by Mormon missionaries as an agency and named af- 16
ter a Hopi chieftain although now mostly a Navajo town, caught the sandstorm
full face. As I filled the gas tank, I tried to stay behind the van, but gritty gusts
whipped around the corners and stung me and forced my eyes shut. School was
just out, and children, shirts pulled over their heads, ran for the trading post,
where old Navajo men who had been sitting outside took cover as the sand

changed the air to matter. I ducked in too. The place was like an A&P, TG&Y, and craft center.

In viridescent velveteen blouses and violescent nineteenth-century skirts, 17 Navajo women of ample body, each laden with silver and turquoise bracelets, necklaces, and rings—not the trading post variety but heavy bands gleaming under the patina of long wear—reeled off yards of fabric. The children, like schoolkids anywhere, milled around the candy; they spoke only English. But the old men, now standing at the plate glass windows and looking into the brown wind, popped and puffed out the ancient words. I've read that Navajo, a language related to that of the Indians of Alaska and northwest Canada, has no curse words unless you consider "coyote" cursing. By comparison with other native tongues, it's remarkably free of English and Spanish; a Navajo mechanic, for example, has more than two hundred purely Navajo terms to describe automobile parts. And it might be Navajo that will greet the first extraterrestrial ears to hear from planet Earth: on board each *Voyager* spacecraft traveling toward the edge of the solar system and beyond is a gold-plated, long-playing record; following an aria from Mozart's *Magic Flute* and Chuck Berry's "Johnny B. Goode," is a Navajo night chant, music the conquistadors heard.

Intimidated by my ignorance of Navajo and by fear of the contempt that 18 full-bloods often show lesser bloods, I again failed to stir a conversation. After the storm blew on east, I followed the old men back outside, where they squatted to watch the day take up the weather of an hour earlier. To one with a great round head like an earthen pot, I said, "Is the storm finished now?" He looked at me, then slowly turned his head, while the others examined before them things in the air invisible to me.

I took a highway down the mesa into a valley of the Painted Desert, 19 where wind had textured big drifts of orange sand into rills. U.S. 89 ran north along the Echo Cliffs. Goats grazed in stubble by the roadsides, and to the west a horseman moved his sheep. Hogans here stood alone; they were not ceremonial lodges but homes. For miles at the highway edges sat little cardboard and scrapwood ramadas, each with a windblasted sign advertising jewelry and cedar beads. In another era, white men came in wagons to trade beads to Indians; now they came in stationwagons and bought beads. History may repeat, but sometimes things get turned around in the process.

1982

QUESTIONS FOR DISCUSSION

Content

a. What changes in Indian life does Least Heat Moon describe? Is he upset that things have changed, or does he accept or even applaud the changes?

b. What is Least Heat Moon's purpose? Does it go beyond simply describing what he saw in the reservation? If not, how does description help him achieve that purpose?

c. "History may repeat, but sometimes things get turned around in the process," we are told in the last sentence. What are the implications of this statement? What is Least Heat Moon trying to do by adding this twist to the cliché that "history repeats itself"?

d. What role does comparison/contrast play in this essay? What is the relationship between Navajo and Hopi as Least Heat Moon describes it? Is it analogous to other relationships you can think of?

e. In paragraph 5, the author writes that "it looked as if the old categories of cowboys and Indians had merged...." What are these old categories? Is their merging significant?

f. In paragraph 12, Least Heat Moon uses a metaphor to describe the hardiness of the Hopi: "The bristlecone pine of American Indians, Hopis live where almost nothing else will, thriving long in adverse conditions...." Can this metaphor also be used to describe other aspects of the Hopi? How else can this sentence be read?

g. Reread paragraphs 14 and 17. What is the relationship of religion and politics? Of language and politics?

Strategy and Style

h. What is the significance of including a Navajo night chant on the record sent with the *Voyager* spacecraft? Why does the author remember to tell us that it follows pieces by Mozart and Chuck Berry?

i. While on the Navajo reservation, Least Heat Moon encounters a sandstorm (paragraph 18). When he asks the old men of the village if the storm is "finished now," he gets no answer. Why don't the men answer him? Why does Least Heat Moon include this anecdote?

j. Is Least Heat Moon's description of the place convincing? Pick out passages containing details that are particularly specific and concrete.

k. Least Heat Moon is being ironic in paragraph 8 when he comments on the fact that the Hopi take the Navajo to court: "those who settled first seeking judgment from those who came later through the laws of those who arrived last." Find other examples of irony.

l. In an earlier question, you learned that the author uses an interesting, and perhaps complex, metaphor in paragraph 12. What other examples of figurative language do you find in this piece? What do they add to Least Heat Moon's description?

m. Would you call the author's perspective objective? If not, in what ways is it subjective? Explain your answer by citing passages from the text.

n. How would you characterize the author's tone?

SUGGESTIONS FOR SHORT WRITING

a. Buy a postcard, or draw one in your notebook, and try to convey an accurate impression of a particular place within the confines of the postcard. The place can be the scene on the postcard, a place you have visited, or a place you know well. For a variation, select a few photos of you on vacation and write postcard captions for them.

b. Summarize the argument of Least Heat Moon's descriptive essay.

SUGGESTIONS FOR SUSTAINED WRITING

a. According to the author, the decision to make this trip and its design—traveling around the perimeter of the U.S., for example—were heavily influenced by his reading John Steinbeck's *Travels with Charley*. Read Steinbeck's book or a section of it, and write an essay comparing the two writers. What aspects of the country and culture they describe do they consider important? What are their attitudes toward their subjects? Do you find fundamental differences in the writers' writing style, attitude toward people, values, political philosophies, etc.?

b. Try writing a travelogue of your own. If possible, describe a recent trip day by day. If you kept a diary of a recent trip, use the diary as a source of information or, if possible, as a first draft. In either case, make the record of your experience an extended description of and reflection on the place and the people you visited. Keep in mind what William Least Heat Moon said about writing *Blue Highways*: "It's important to distinguish between the actual journey that I made and the book that came out of that journey." He stressed the writing of several drafts, deleting much of what might seem rambling, uninteresting, or immature to his readers. The finished product was not so much an exact record of what happened as a thoughtful distillation of the meaning of the journey.

Cyclone! Rising to the Fall

Peter Schjeldahl

Born in North Dakota, Peter Schjeldahl (b. 1942) has written art criticism for the Village Voice *and* Art News. *In 1964, he cofounded the poetry magazine* Mother. *His poetical works include* White Country *(1968),* An Adventure of the Thought Police *(1971), and* Dreams *(1973), as well as collections of later poetry. "Cyclone!" was commissioned by* Harper's *magazine in 1988.*

The Cyclone is art, sex, God, the greatest. It is the most fun you can have 1
without risking bad ethics. I rode the Cyclone seven times one afternoon last summer, and I am here to tell everybody that it is fun for fun's sake, the pure abstract heart of the human capacity for getting a kick out of anything. Yes, it may be anguishing initially. (I promise to tell the truth.) Terrifying, even, the first time or two the train is hauled upward with groans and creaks and with you in it. At the top then—where there is sudden strange quiet but for the fluttering of two tattered flags, and you have a poignantly brief view of Brooklyn, and of ships far out on the Atlantic—you may feel very lonely and that you have made a serious mistake, cursing yourself in the last gleam of the reflective consciousness you are about, abruptly, to leave up there between the flags like an abandoned thought-balloon. To keep yourself company by screaming may help, and no one is noticing: try it. After a couple of rides, panic abates, and after four or five you aren't even frightened, exactly, but *stimulated,* blissed, sent. The squirt of adrenaline you will never cease to have at the top as the train lumbers, wobbling slightly, into the plunge, finally fuels just happy wonderment because you can't, and never will, *believe* what is going to happen.

Every roller coaster has that first, immense drop. In practical terms, it 2
provides the oomph for the entire ride, which is of course impelled by nothing but ecologically sound gravity, momentum, and the odd slingshot of centrifugal force. The coaster is basically an ornate means of falling and a poem about physics in parts or stanzas, with jokes. The special quality of the Cyclone is how different, how *articulated,* all the components of its poem are, the whole of which lasts a minute and thirty-some seconds—exactly the right length, composed of distinct and perfect moments. By my fifth ride, my heart was leaping at the onset of each segment as at the approach of a dear old friend, and melting with instantaneous nostalgia for each at its finish.

I think every part of the Cyclone should have a name, the better to be 3
recalled and accurately esteemed. In my mind, the big drop is Kismet—fate, destiny. I can't think of what to call the second, a mystery drop commenced in a jiffy after we have been whipped around, but good, coming out of Kismet. (Someday soon I will devote particular attention to the huge and violent but

elusive second drop.) I do know that the third drop's name can only be Pasha. It is so round and generous, rich and powerful, looking like a killer going in but then actually like a crash landing in feathers that allows, for the first time in the ride, an instant for luxuriating in one's endorphin rush.

This brings me to another important function of the first drop, which (I   4
firmly contend) is to trigger the release of endorphins, natural morphine, into the bloodstream by persuading the organism that it is going to die. I know all about endorphins from reading the *New York Times* science section, and from an accident a few years ago. I broke my elbow, which is something not to do. It hurts. Or let me put it this way: in relation to what I had previously understood of pain, the sensation of breaking an elbow was *a whole new idea,* a new continent suddenly—whole unknown worlds of pain out there over the horizon. I was aghast, when I broke my elbow, at the extent of my naïveté about pain— but only for a second. Then I was somewhere else, pain-free, I think it was a cocktail party, but confusing, I didn't recognize anybody. On some level I knew the party wasn't real, that I was in another, real place which had something unpleasant about it that made me not want to be there, but then I began to be afraid that if I stayed at the party I would be unable ever to be real again, so with an effort of will I returned to my body, which was sitting up with family members leaning over. The pain returned, but muffled and dull, drastically lessened. Endorphins.

Other things than breaking an elbow can give you an endorphin high, and   5
one of them is suddenly falling ninety-some feet, seeing the ground charge directly at you. I think the forebrain, loaded with all sorts of chemical gimmicks we don't suspect, just there for special occasions, registers the situation, and, quick, pours a last-minute, bon voyage endorphin highball: "Hey, name here], this one's for you!" That's why it's important to ride the Cyclone many times, to comb out the distraction of terror—which gradually yields to the accumulating evidence that you are not dead—in order to savor the elixir for its own sake and for the sake of loving God or whatever—Nature—for cunningly secreted kindnesses. But Kismet is such a zonk, and the anonymous second drop is so perplexing and a zonk, too, that it isn't until mid-Pasha, in great fleshy Pasha's lap, that consciousness catches up with physiologic ravishment. Some part of my soul, because of the Cyclone, is still and will remain forever in that state, which I think is a zone of overlap among the heavens of all the world's mystic religions, where transcendent swamis bump around with freaked Spanish women saints. Blitzed in Pasha permanently, I have this lasting glimpse into the beyond that is not beyond, and you know what I'm talking about, or you don't.

Rolling up out of Pasha, we enter the part of the Cyclone that won't quit   6
laughing. First there's the whoop of a whipping hairpin curve, which, if someone is sitting with you, Siamese-twins you. (Having tried different cars in different company, I prefer being alone at the very front—call me a classicist.) The ensuing dips, humps, dives, and shimmies that roar, chortle, cackle, and

snort continue just long enough to suggest that they may go on forever—as worrisome as the thought, when you're laughing hard, that maybe you can never stop—and then it's hello, Irene. Why do I think Irene is the name of the very sharp drop, not deep but savage, that wipes the grin off the laughing part of the Cyclone? (Special about it is a crosspiece, low over the track at the bottom, that you swear is going to fetch you square in the eyebrows.) Irene is always the name—or kind of name, slightly unusual but banal—of the ordinary-seeming girl whom a young man may pursue idly, in a bored time, and then *wham!* fall horribly in love with, blasted in love with this person he never bothered to even particularly look at and now it's too late, she's his universe, Waterloo, *personal* Kismet. This is one good reason I can think of for growing older: learning an aversion reflex for girls named something like Irene. In this smallish but vicious, sobering drop, abstract shapes of my own youthful romantic sorrows do not fail to flash before my inner eye...but then, with a jarring zoom up and around, I am once more grown-up, wised-up me, and the rest of the ride is rejoicing.

The Cyclone differs from other roller coasters in being (a) a work of art 7 and (b) old, and not only old but old-looking, decrepit, rusting in its metal parts and peeling in its more numerous wooden parts, filthy throughout and jammed into a wire (Cyclone!) fence abutting cracked sidewalks of the Third World sinkhole that Coney Island is, intoxicatingly. Nor is it to be denied or concealed that the Cyclone, unlike newer coasters, tends to run *rough,* though each ride is unique and some are inexplicably velvety. One time the vibration, with the wheels shrieking and the cars threatening to explode with strain, made me think, "This is *no fun at all!*" It was an awful moment, with a sickening sense of betrayal and icy-fingered doubt: was my love malign?

That was my worst ride, which left me with a painfully yanked muscle in 8 my shoulder, but I am glad to say it wasn't my last. I got back on like a thrown cowboy and discovered that the secret of handling the rough rides is indeed like riding a horse, at trot or gallop—not tensing against it, as I had, but posting and rolling. It's all in the thighs and rear end, as I especially realized when—what the hell—I joined pimpled teenagers in the arms-raised *no hands!* trick. I should mention that a heavy, cushioned restraining bar locks down snugly into your lap and is very reassuring, although, like everything upholstered in the cars, it may be cracked or slashed and leaking tufts of stuffing from under swatches of gray gaffer's tape. One thing consistently disquieting is how, under stress, a car's wooden sides may *give* a bit. I wish they wouldn't do that, or that my imagination were less vivid. If a side did happen to fail on a curve, one would depart like toothpaste from a stomped-on tube.

I was proud of braving the *no hands!* posture—as trusting in the restrain- 9 ing bar as a devout child in his heavenly Father—particularly the first time I did it, while emerging from the slinging turn that succeeds Irene into the long, long careen that bottoms out at absolute ground level a few feet from the fence where pedestrians invariably gather to watch, transfixed. I call this swift, showy glide Celebrity: the ride's almost over, and afflatus swells the chest. But going *no hands!* soon feels as cheap and callow as it looks, blocking with vulgar self-centeredness   the   wahoo-glimmering-away-of-personality-in-convulsive-Nirvana that is the Cyclone's essence. A righteous ride is hands on, though lightly, like grace. The payoff is intimacy in the sweet diminuendo, the jiggling and chuckling smart little bumps and dandling dips that bring us to a quick, pillowy deceleration in the shed, smelling of dirty machine oil, where we began and will begin again. It is a warm debriefing, this last part: "Wasn't that *great?*" it says. "Want to go again?"

Of course I do, but first there is the final stage of absorption, when you   10 squeeze out (it's easy to bang a knee then, so watch it) to stand wobbly but weightless, euphoric, and then to enjoy the sensation of walking as if it were a neat thing you had just invented. Out on the sidewalk, the object of curious gazes, you see that they see that you see them, earthlings, in a diminishing perspective, through the wrong end of the telescope of your pleasure, and your heart is pitying. You nod, smiling, to convey that yes, they should ride, and no, they won't regret it.

1988

QUESTIONS FOR DISCUSSION

Content

a. What descriptive techniques does Schjeldahl use to make you feel as if you were riding the Cyclone along with him? Mark words and phrases that evoke this empathy.

b. In paragraph 2, the author says a roller coaster "is basically an ornate means of falling and a poem about physics…." What does he mean? Why does he characterize it as a poem and not, say, a short story or play? In what way is the poem about physics?

c. In continuing the sentence above, Schjeldahl says the poem contains "jokes." What are these jokes?

Strategy and Style

d. In what ways did Schjeldahl's training as a poet help him shape the essay? What is poetic about it? Could he have written it as a poem?

e. In paragraph 4, the author mentions that "the release of endorphins" once made him feel as if he were at a cocktail party. Why is this analogy appropriate? What other analogies does he create?

f. The author combines sophisticated vocabulary with slang. What are his reasons for doing so? What effect does the combination have on the description of the Cyclone? What effect does it have on the reader?

g. Look up some of the sophisticated words Schjeldahl uses in an unabridged dictionary to find their etymologies and original meanings. Some possibilities to start with are "articulated" (paragraph 2); "ravishment," "transcendent" (paragraph 5); "chortle" (paragraph 6); and "euphoric" (paragraph 10).
h. Schjeldahl often refers to exotic terms such as "Kismet," "transcendent swamis,", and "nirvana." Why are these references appropriate?
i. Is this essay fundamentally humorous or serious? Would its being considered one or the other affect the way it is interpreted?
j. Read the essay aloud in order to hear distinctive sounds and cadences. Does reading it aloud affect the way you interpret the essay?

SUGGESTIONS FOR SHORT WRITING

a. With a particularly vivid experience in mind, list as many single words or short phrases as you can think of to describe it. Write down everything, even if it sounds silly. Be adventurous and playful with your language.
b. Now try to incorporate some or all of the words and phrases from your list into a paragraph describing that experience. To help you get started, read passages from Schjeldahl's essay aloud and note how his word choice and sentence structure help convey the impression of riding the Cyclone.

SUGGESTIONS FOR SUSTAINED WRITING

a. Schjeldahl names the parts of the roller coaster. Does this division of the ride into named sections help you visualize the Cyclone? Think of an exciting, dangerous, frightening, or frustrating experience you had with a machine (an amusement park ride would work well, but any machine will do). In describing the machine, make sure to name and explain its major parts so that your reader will visualize it. Then relate the experience you had with it. You might want to put your comments in the form of a letter to a friend.
b. Narrate an activity in such a way that it conveys to your reader the same feeling that you had in doing it. To make your essay vivid, include the same kinds of descriptive techniques you see in "Cyclone! Rising to the Fall." In revising your essay, pay special attention to word choice, punctuation, and word order, etc., so as to convey the feeling effectively.
c. Follow up on one of the Questions for Discussion above, and try to rewrite the essay, or a section of the essay, as a poem. On the other hand, convert a favorite poem into an essay. (Make sure the poem is long enough to yield a full-length essay.) How must the language be changed in order to convert a piece from one genre to another? Can you manage to keep the same tone and convey the same message when moving from one genre to another, or must the tone and message necessarily change?

Main Street

Mordecai Richler

Born in Montreal, Mordecai Richler (b. 1931) has received several Canadian and international awards for literature including a Guggenheim Fellowship (1961), a Canada Council Senior Arts Fellowship (1968), the Paris Review *Humor Prize (1969), and two Governor General's Awards for Literature (1969 and 1972). His most important novel,* The Apprenticeship of Duddy Kravitz *(1959), is often compared to Salinger's* A Catcher in the Rye *and has a prominent place in the curricula of many Canadian schools and colleges. Richler wrote the screenplay for the film taken from his novel as well as for* Life at the Top *(1965). Other works include* Joshua Then and Now *(1980), a novel;* Home Sweet Home *(1984), a collection of essays; and* Jacob Two-Two and the Dinosaur *(1987), a children's book. Richler grew up on St. Urbain Street in a Jewish neighborhood of Montreal, with French Canadians on one side and English speakers on the other. This is the environment of much of his work, especially* St. Urbain's Horsemen *(1971) and* The Street *(1969), a collection of essays and stories that form his autobiography. In this excerpt, Richler describes that environment vividly and poignantly.*

Two streets below our own came the Main. Rich in delights, but also 1
squalid, filthy, and hollering with stores whose wares, whether furniture or fruit, were ugly or damaged. The signs still say FANTASTIC DISCOUNTS or FORCED TO SELL PRICES HERE, but the bargains so bitterly sought after are illusory—and perhaps they always were.

The Main, with something for all our appetites, was dedicated to pinching 2
pennies from the poor, but it was there to entertain, educate and comfort us too. Across the street from the synagogue you could see THE PICTURE THEY CLAIMED COULD NEVER BE MADE. A little further down the street there was the Workman's Circle and, if you liked, a strip show. Peaches, Margo, Lili St. Cyr. Around the corner there was the ritual baths, the *shvitz* or *mikva,* where my grandfather and his cronies went before the High Holidays, emerging boiling red from the highest reaches of the steam rooms to happily flog each other with brushes fashioned of pine tree branches. Where supremely orthodox women went once a month to purify themselves.

It was to the Main, once a year before the High Holidays, that I was taken 3
for a new suit (the itch of the cheap tweed was excruciating) and shoes (with a built-in squeak). We also shopped for fruit on the Main, meat and fish, and here the important thing was to watch the man at the scales. On the Main, too, was the Chinese laundry—"Have you ever seen such hard workers?"—the Italian hat-blocker—"Tony's a good goy, you know. Against Mussolini from the very first."—and strolling French Canadian priests—"Some of them speak Hebrew now." "Well, if you ask me, it's none of their business. Enough's enough, you

know." Kids like myself were dragged along on shopping expeditions to carry parcels. Old men gave us snuff, at the delicatessens we were allowed salami butts, card players pushed candies on us for luck, and everywhere we were poked and pinched by the mothers. Absolutely the best that could be said of us was, "He eats well, knock wood," and later, as we went off to school, "He's a rank-one boy."

After the shopping, once our errands had been done, we returned to the 4 Main once more, either for part-time jobs or to study with our *melamud.* Jobs going on the Main included spotting pins in a bowling alley, collecting butcher bills and, best of all, working at a newsstand, where you could devour the *Police Gazette* free and pick up a little extra short-changing strangers during the rush hour. Work was supposed to be good for our character development and the fact that we were paid was incidental. To qualify for a job we were supposed to be "bright, ambitious, and willing to learn." An ad I once saw in a shoe store window read:

PART-TIME BOY WANTED FOR EXPANDING BUSINESS.
EXPERIENCE ABSOLUTELY NECESSARY, BUT NOT ESSENTIAL

Our jobs and lessons finished, we would wander the street in small 5 groups smoking Turret cigarettes and telling jokes.

"Hey, *shmo-hawk,* what's the difference between a mail box and an ele- 6 phant's ass?"

"I dunno." 7

"Well, I wouldn't send *you* to mail my letters." 8

As the French Canadian factory girls passed arm-in-arm we would call 9 out, "I've got the time, if you've got the place."

Shabus it was back to the Main again and the original Young Israel syn- 10 agogue. While our grandfathers and fathers prayed and gossiped and speculated about the war in Europe in the musty room below, we played chin the bar in the upstairs attic and told jokes that began, "Confucius say..." or, "Once there was an Englishman, an Irishman, and a Hebe...."

We would return to the Main once more when we wanted a fight with the 11 pea-soups. Winter, as I recall it, was best for this type of sport. We could throw snowballs packed with ice or frozen horse buns, and with darkness falling early, it was easier to elude pursuers. Soon, however, we developed a technique of battle that served us well even in the spring. Three of us would hide under an outside staircase while the fourth member of our group, a kid named Eddy, would idle provocatively on the sidewalk. Eddy was a good head-and-a-half shorter than the rest of us. (For this, it was rumoured, his mother was to blame. She wouldn't let Eddy have his tonsils removed and that's why he was such a runt. It was not that Eddy's mother feared surgery, but Eddy sang in the choir of a rich synagogue, bringing in some thirty dollars a month, and if his tonsils were removed it was feared that his voice would go too.) Anyway, Eddy would stand out there alone and when the first solitary pea-soup passed he would kick him in the shins. "Your mother fucks," he'd say.

The pea-soup, looking down on little Eddy, would naturally knock him 12
one on the head. Then, and only then, would we emerge from under the staircase.

"Hey, that's my kid brother you just slugged."   13

And before the bewildered pea-soup could protest, we were scrambling 14
all over him.

These and other fights, however, sprang more out of boredom than from 15
racial hatred, not that there were no racial problems on the Main.

If the Main was a poor man's street, it was also a dividing line. Below, 16
the French Canadians. Above, some distance above, the dreaded WASPS. On
the Main itself there were some Italians, Yugoslavs and Ukrainians, but they
did not count as true Gentiles. Even the French Canadians, who were our enemies, were not entirely unloved. Like us, they were poor and coarse with large
families and spoke English badly.

Looking back, it's easy to see that the real trouble was there was no dia- 17
logue between us and the French Canadians, each elbowing the other, striving
for WASP acceptance. We fought the French Canadians stereotype for stereotype. If many of them believed that the St. Urbain Street Jews were secretly
rich, manipulating the black market, then my typical French Canadian was a
moronic gum-chewer. He wore his greasy black hair parted down the middle
and also affected an eyebrow moustache. His zoot trousers were belted just under the breastbone and ended in a peg hugging his ankles. He was the dolt who
held up your uncle endlessly at the liquor commission while he tried unsuccessfully to add three figures or, if he was employed at the customs office, never
knew which form to give you. Furthermore, he only held his liquor commission
or customs or any other government job because he was the second cousin of a
backwoods notary who had delivered the village vote to the *Union Nationale*
for a generation. Other French Canadians were speed cops, and if any of these
ever stopped you on the highway you made sure to hand him a folded two dollar bill with your licence.

Wartime shortages, the admirable Protestant spirit of making-do, bene- 18
fited both Jews and French Canadians. Jews with clean fingernails were allowed to teach within the Protestant School system and French Canadians off
the Atwater League and provincial sandlots broke into the International Baseball League. Jean-Pierre Roy won twenty-five games for the Montreal Royals
one year and a young man named Stan Breard enjoyed a season as a stylish but
no-hit shortstop. Come to think of it, the only French Canadians I heard of were
athletes. Of course there was Maurice Richard, the superb hockey player, but
there was also Dave Castiloux, a cunning welterweight, and, above all, the
wrestler-hero, Yvon Robert, who week after week gave the blond Anglo-Saxon
wrestlers what for at the Forum.

Aside from boyhood street fights and what I read on the sports pages, all 19
I knew of French Canadians was that they were clearly hilarious. Our Scots
schoolmaster would always raise a laugh in class by reading us the atrocious

Uncle Tom-like dialect verse of William Henry Drummond: *Little Baptiste & Co.*

> On wan dark night on Lac St. Pierre,
> De win' she blow, blow, blow,
> An' de crew of de wood scow "Julie Plante"
> Got scar't and run below—
> Bimeby she blow some more,
> An' de scow bus' up on Lac St. Pierre
> Wan arpent from de shore.

Actually, it was only the WASPS who were truly hated and feared. [20] "Among them," I heard it said, "with those porridge faces, who can tell what they're thinking?" It was, we felt, their country, and given sufficient liquor who knew when they would make trouble?

We were a rude, aggressive bunch round the Main. Cocky too. But bring [21] down the most insignificant, pinched WASP fire insurance inspector and even the most arrogant merchant on the street would dip into the drawer for a ten spot or a bottle and bow and say, "Sir."

After school we used to race down to the Main to play snooker at the [22] Rachel or the Mount Royal. Other days, when we chose to avoid school altogether, we would take the No. 55 streetcar as far as St. Catherine Street, where there was a variety of amusements offered. We could play the pinball machines and watch archaic strip-tease movies for a nickel at the Silver Gameland. At the Midway or the Crystal Palace we could see a double feature and a girlie show for as little as thirty-five cents. The Main, at this juncture, was thick with drifters, panhandlers and whores. Available on both sides of the street were "Tourist Rooms by Day and Night," and everywhere there was the smell of french fried potatoes cooking in stale oil. Tough, unshaven men in checked shirts stood in knots outside the taverns and cheap cafés. There was the promise of violence.

As I recall it, we were always being warned about the Main. Our grand- [23] parents and parents had come there by steerage from Rumania or by cattleboat from Poland by way of Liverpool. No sooner had they unpacked their bundles and cardboard suitcases than they were planning a better, brighter life for us, the Canadian-born children. The Main, good enough for them, was not to be for us, and that they told us again and again was what the struggle was for. The Main was for *bummers,* drinkers, and (heaven forbid) failures.

During the years leading up to the war, the ideal of the ghetto, no differ- [24] ent from any other in America, was the doctor. This, mistakenly, was taken to be the very apogee of learning and refinement. In those days there also began the familiar and agonizing process of alienation between immigrant parents and Canadian-born children. Our older brothers and cousins, off to university, came home to realize that our parents spoke with embarrassing accents. Even the younger boys, like myself, were going to "their" schools. According to them, the priests had made a tremendous contribution to the exploration and development of this country. Some were heroes. But our parents had other memories, different ideas, about the priesthood. At school we were taught about the glory of the Crusades and at home we were instructed in the bloodier side of the story. Though we wished Lord Tweedsmuir, the Governor-General, a long life each Saturday morning in the synagogue, there were those among us who knew him as John Buchan. From the very beginning there was their history, and ours. Our heroes, and theirs.

Our parents used to apply a special standard to all men and events. "Is it good for the Jews?" By this test they interpreted the policies of Mackenzie King and the Stanley Cup play-offs and earthquakes in Japan. To take one example—if the Montreal *Canadiens* won the Stanley Cup it would infuriate the WASPS in Toronto, and as long as the English and French were going at each other they left us alone: *ergo,* it was good for the Jews if the *Canadiens* won the Stanley Cup.

We were convinced that we gained from dissension between Canada's two cultures, the English and the French, and we looked neither to England nor France for guidance. We turned to the United States. The real America.

America was Roosevelt, the Yeshiva College, Max Baer, Mickey Katz records, Danny Kaye, a Jew in the Supreme Court, the *Jewish Daily Forward,* Dubinsky, Mrs. Nussbaum of Allen's Alley, and Gregory Peck looking so cute in *Gentleman's Agreement.* Why, in the United States a Jew even wrote speeches for the president. Returning cousins swore they had heard a cop speak Yiddish in Brooklyn. There were the Catskill hotels, Jewish soap operas on the radio and, above all earthly pleasure grounds, Florida. Miami. No manufacturer had quite made it in Montreal until he was able to spend a month each winter in Miami.

We were governed by Ottawa, we were also British subjects, but our true capital was certainly New York. Success was (and still is) acceptance by the United States. For a boxer this meant a main bout at Madison Square Garden, for a writer or an artist, praise from New York critics, for a businessman, a Miami tan and, today, for comics, an appearance on the Ed Sullivan Show or for actors, not an important part at the Stratford Festival, but Broadway, or the lead in a Hollywood TV series (Lorne Green in *Bonanza*). The outside world, "their" Canada, only concerned us insofar as it affected our living conditions. All the same, we liked to impress the *goyim.* A knock on the knuckles from time to time wouldn't hurt them. So, while we secretly believed that the baseball field or the prize-fighting ring was no place for a Jewish boy, we took enormous pleasure in the accomplishments of, say, Kermit Kitman, the Montreal Royals outfielder, and Maxie Berger, the welterweight.

Streets such as ours and Outremont, where the emergent middle-class and the rich lived, comprised an almost self-contained world. Outside of business there was a minimal contact with the Gentiles. This was hardly petulant clannishness or naive fear. In the years leading up to the war neo-fascist groups were extremely active in Canada. In the United States there was Father Coughlin, Lindbergh, and others. We had Adrian Arcand. The upshot was almost the same. So I can recall seeing swastikas and *"A bas les Juifs"* painted on the Laurentian highway. There were suburbs and hotels in the mountains and country clubs where we were not wanted, beaches with signs that read GENTILES ONLY, quotas at the universities, and occasional racial altercations on Park Avenue. The democracy we were being invited to defend was flawed and hostile to us. Without question it was better for us in Canada than in Europe, but this was still their country, not ours.

I was only a boy during the war. I can remember signs in cigar stores that 30 warned us THE WALLS HAVE EARS and THE ENEMY IS EVERYWHERE. I can also recall my parents, uncles and aunts, cracking peanuts on a Friday night and waiting for those two unequalled friends of the Jews, Roosevelt and Walter Winchell, to come off it and get into the war. We admired the British, they were gutsy, but we had more confidence in the United States Marines. Educated by Hollywood, we could see the likes of John Wayne, Gable, and Robert Taylor making minced meat out of the Panzers, while Noel Coward, Laurence Olivier, and others, seen in a spate of British war films, looked all too humanly vulnerable to us. Briefly, then, Pearl Harbour was a day of jubilation, but the war itself made for some confusions. In another country, relatives recalled by my grandparents were being murdered. But on the street in our air cadet uniforms, we F.F.H.S. boys were more interested in seeking out the fabulously wicked V-girls ("They go the limit with guys in uniform, see.") we had read about in the *Herald*. True, we made some sacrifices. American comic books were banned for the duration due, I think, to a shortage of U.S. funds. So we had to put up a quarter on the black market for copies of the *Batman* and *Tip-Top Comics*. But at the same newsstand we bought a page on which four pigs had been printed. When we folded the paper together, as directed, the four pigs' behinds made up Hitler's hateful face. Outside Cooperman's Superior Provisions, where if you were a regular customer you could get sugar without ration coupons, we would chant "Black-market Cooperman! Black-market Cooperman!" until the old man came out, wielding his broom, and sent us flying down the street.

The war in Europe brought about considerable changes within the Jewish 31 community in Montreal. To begin with, there was the coming of the refugees. These men, interned in England as enemy aliens and sent to Canada where they were eventually released, were to make a profound impact on us. I think we had conjured up a picture of the refugees as penurious *hassidim* with packs on their backs. We were eager to be helpful, our gestures were large, but in return we expected more than a little gratitude. As it turned out, the refugees, mostly German and Austrian Jews, were far more sophisticated and better educated than we were. They had not, like our immigrant grandparents, come from *shtetls* in Galicia or Russia. Neither did they despise Europe. On the contrary, they found our culture thin, the city provincial, and the Jews narrow. This bewildered and stung us. But what cut deepest, I suppose, was that the refugees spoke English better than many of us did and, among themselves, had the effrontery to talk in the abhorred German language. Many of them also made it clear that Canada was no more than a frozen place to stop over until a U.S. visa was forthcoming. So for a while we real Canadians were hostile.

For our grandparents who remembered those left behind in Rumania and 32 Poland the war was a time of unspeakable grief. Parents watched their sons grow up too quickly and stood by helplessly as the boys went off to the fighting one by one. They didn't have to go, either, for until the last days of the war Canadians could only be drafted for service within Canada. A boy had to volunteer before he could be sent overseas.

For those of my age the war was something else. I cannot remember it as 33 a black time, and I think it must be so for most boys of my generation. The truth is that for many of us to look back on the war is to recall the first time our fathers earned a good living. Even as the bombs fell and the ships went down, always elsewhere, our country was bursting out of a depression into a period of hitherto unknown prosperity. For my generation the war was hearing of death and sacrifice but seeing with our own eyes the departure from cold-water flats to apartments in Outremont, duplexes and split-levels in the suburbs. It was when we read of the uprising in the Warsaw ghetto and saw, in Montreal, the changeover from poky little *shuls* to big synagogue-cumparochial schools with stained glass windows and mosaics outside. During the war some of us lost brothers and cousins but in Canada we had never had it so good, and we began the run from rented summer shacks with outhouses in Shawbridge to Colonial-style summer houses of our own and speedboats on the lake in Ste. Agathe.

1969

QUESTIONS FOR DISCUSSION

Content

a. What is Richler's purpose in describing the place where he grew up? How does that place help reveal the author?
b. Analyze Richler's use of descriptive details. To which of the five senses does he appeal most often when describing "the Main"?
c. What is Richler's view of the Jewish community in which he grew up (paragraphs 24 through 28)? Explain his reference to the Crusades.
d. Richler recalls several ethnic stereotypes that he knew as a boy. How did the French Canadians view the Jews of Montreal? Discuss the author's comments about a typical French Canadian.
e. The acronym WASP stands for White Anglo-Saxon Protestant. Using details from this selection, describe Richler's stereotypical WASP.

f. What important meaning did young Richler ascribe to "Gentile"? Why didn't Italians, Yugoslavs, Ukrainians and even French Canadians count "as true Gentiles"?

g. Why did the Jewish community in Canada look to the United States as "the real America" (paragraph 26)? What does Richler mean when he says "our true capital was certainly New York" (paragraph 28)?

h. How do the developments the author discusses in paragraph 29 help explain why "Outside of business there was minimal contact with the Gentiles"?

i. To what is the author alluding when in paragraph 30 he tells us that, "In another country, relatives recalled by my grandparents were being murdered"? Why does he call the attack on Pearl Harbor a "day of jubilation"?

Strategy and Style

j. Paragraph 33 describes how World War II changed the lifestyles of the people in Richler's generation. Explain the irony implicit in these changes. Does this paragraph serve as an appropriate way to conclude?

k. In what way does Richler's use of dialogue enhance his description of his neighborhood? Why does he recall what was written on storefront signs? What is the purpose of quoting from the poem by Drummond?

l. What are *Shabus* and the High Holidays? Who are the *hassidim*, and what are *shtetls*? Should the author have defined these terms or used synonyms?

m. What are the "zoot trousers" mentioned in paragraph 17? Who are the "peasoups" in paragraph 11? What does Richler mean by "Uncle Tom-like dialect verse" (paragraph 19)? What other examples of figurative language can you find in this selection, and how do they enrich it?

n. In what way is the author's comment about "the admirable Protestant spirit of making-do" (paragraph 18) ironic? What about the ethnic joke that begins "Once there was..." (paragraph 10)? What other examples of irony can you identify in this piece, and how do they contribute to Richler's distinctive tone?

o. Is Richler's view of himself as a boy flattering? What details reveal important characteristics about the speaker both as a child and as an adult?

SUGGESTIONS FOR SHORT WRITING

a. From memory, write a description of a place in your present community that you think you know well. Write as thorough a description as possible. Then go to that place and compare your description to the real thing. How closely do they match? While there, make a list of the details that differ.

b. Back at home, write a short reflection in which you explain why the details differed. Are those details important to you in some way?

SUGGESTIONS FOR SUSTAINED WRITING

a. Recall the place where you grew up. Was it a teeming city neighborhood like Richler's "Main"? Was it suburban? Or did you spend your childhood in a setting of farms, lakes, and woodlands? What did the place look like, sound like, smell like? How would you describe your friends and neighbors? What did growing up there teach you about life? Did it help make you the person you are today, or did you become what you are despite that environment? Describe the place in as much detail as you can; like Richler, capture its character and the character of its people.

b. To a greater or lesser degree, all of us can claim an ethnic heritage. What are some of the stereotypical characteristics most commonly associated with your own ethnic group or with an ethnic group you know well? Do you believe that they are appropriate? For instance, are all Italians great singers? Are all Jews good business people? Discuss a few commonly accepted notions about the ethnic group you are writing about and, through description and illustration, evaluate the extent to which they reflect that group.

c. Relying mainly on narration and description, recall an anecdote (interesting or humorous story) from childhood that will give your reader insight into the kind of person you were then. Don't be afraid to use dialogue to dramatize events or ideas important to understanding your character. Assume that your reader is a close friend but one whom you've known only for the past two or three years.

The Death of the Moth

Virginia Woolf

The daughter of the British essayist and scholar Leslie Stephen, Virginia Woolf (1882–1941) was at the center of the Bloomsbury Group, a circle that included Lytton Strachey and John Maynard Keynes as well as several other important intellectuals, poets, and artists. With her husband Leonard, Woolf founded the Hogarth Press and published the work of brilliant young writers like T. S. Eliot and E. M. Forster. Her fiction is important because of her experimentation with the stream-of-consciousness technique and her ability to expose the psychology of characters in a way that is at once subtle and vivid. Among her most memorable novels are Mrs. Dalloway *(1925),* To the Lighthouse *(1927),* Orlando *(1928), and* The Waves *(1931). Her nonfiction includes* A Room of One's Own *(1929) and* The Death of the Moth *(1942).*

Moths that fly by day are not properly to be called moths; they do not 1
excite that pleasant sense of dark autumn nights and ivy-blossom which the
commonest yellow-underwing asleep in the shadow of the curtain never fails to
rouse in us. They are hybrid creatures, neither gay like butterflies nor sombre
like their own species. Nevertheless the present specimen, with his narrow hay-
coloured wings, fringed with a tassel of the same colour, seemed to be content
with life. It was a pleasant morning, mid-September, mild, benignant, yet with a
keener breath than that of the summer months. The plough was already scoring
the field opposite the window, and where the share had been, the earth was
pressed flat and gleamed with moisture. Such vigour came rolling in from the
fields and the down beyond that it was difficult to keep the eyes strictly turned
upon the book. The rooks too were keeping one of their annual festivities; soar-
ing round the tree tops until it looked as if a vast net with thousands of black
knots in it had been cast up into the air; which, after a few moments sank
slowly down upon the trees until every twig seemed to have a knot at the end
of it. Then, suddenly, the net would be thrown into the air again in a wider
circle this time, with the utmost clamour and vociferation, as though to be
thrown into the air and settle slowly down upon the tree tops were a tremen-
dously exciting experience.

The same energy which inspired the rooks, the ploughmen, the horses, 2
and even, it seemed, the lean bare-backed downs, sent the moth fluttering from
side to side of his square of the window-pane. One could not help watching
him. One was, indeed, conscious of a queer feeling of pity for him. The possibilities of pleasure seemed that morning so enormous and so various that to
have only a moth's part in life, and a day moth's at that, appeared a hard fate,
and his zest in enjoying his meagre opportunities to the full, pathetic. He flew

vigorously to one corner of his compartment, and, after waiting there a second, flew across to the other. What remained for him but to fly to a third corner and then to a fourth? That was all he could do, in spite of the size of the downs, the width of the sky, the far-off smoke of houses, and the romantic voice, now and then, of a steamer out at sea. What he could do he did. Watching him, it seemed as if a fibre, very thin but pure, of the enormous energy of the world had been thrust into his frail and diminutive body. As often as he crossed the pane, I could fancy that a thread of vital light became visible. He was little or nothing but life.

Yet, because he was so small, and so simple a form of the energy that 3 was rolling in at the open window and driving its way through so many narrow and intricate corridors in my own brain and in those of other human beings, there was something marvellous as well as pathetic about him. It was as if someone had taken a tiny bead of pure life and decking it as lightly as possible with down and feathers, had set it dancing and zig-zagging to show us the true nature of life. Thus displayed one could not get over the strangeness of it. One is apt to forget all about life, seeing it humped and bossed and garnished and cumbered so that it has to move with the greatest circumspection and dignity. Again, the thought of all that life might have been had he been born in any other shape caused one to view his simple activities with a kind of pity.

After a time, tired by his dancing apparently, he settled on the window 4 ledge in the sun, and, the queer spectacle being at an end, I forgot about him. Then, looking up, my eye was caught by him. He was trying to resume his dancing, but seemed either so stiff or so awkward that he could only flutter to the bottom of the windowpane; and when he tried to fly across it he failed. Being intent on other matters I watched these futile attempts for a time without thinking, unconsciously waiting for him to resume his flight, as one waits for a machine, that has stopped momentarily, to start again without considering the reason of its failure. After perhaps a seventh attempt he slipped from the wooden ledge and fell, fluttering his wings, on to his back on the window sill. The helplessness of his attitude roused me. It flashed upon me that he was in difficulties; he could no longer raise himself; his legs struggled vainly. But, as I stretched out a pencil, meaning to help him to right himself, it came over me that the failure and awkwardness were the approach of death. I laid the pencil down again.

The legs agitated themselves once more. I looked as if for the enemy 5 against which he struggled. I looked out of doors. What had happened there? Presumably it was midday, and work in the fields had stopped. Stillness and quiet had replaced the previous animation. The birds had taken themselves off to feed in the brooks. The horses stood still. Yet the power was there all the same, massed outside, indifferent, impersonal, not attending to anything in particular. Somehow it was opposed to the little hay-coloured moth. It was useless to try to do anything. One could only watch the extraordinary efforts made by those tiny legs against an oncoming doom which could, had it chosen, have submerged an entire city, not merely a city, but masses of human beings; nothing, I knew, had any chance against death. Nevertheless after a pause of exhaustion the legs fluttered again. It was superb this last protest, and so frantic that he succeeded at last in righting himself. One's sympathies, of course, were all on the side of life. Also, when there was nobody to care or to know, this gigantic effort on the part of an insignificant little moth, against a power of such magnitude, to retain what no one else valued or desired to keep, moved one strangely. Again, somehow, one saw life, a pure bead. I lifted the pencil again, useless though I knew it to be. But even as I did so, the unmistakable tokens of death showed themselves. The body relaxed, and instantly grew stiff. The struggle was over. The insignificant little creature now knew death. As I looked at the dead moth, this minute wayside triumph of so great a force over so mean an antagonist filled me with wonder. Just as life had been strange a few minutes before, so death was now as strange. The moth having righted himself now lay most decently and uncomplainingly composed. O yes, he seemed to say, death is stronger than I am.

1942

QUESTIONS FOR DISCUSSION

Content

a. Woolf's essay is obviously a serious discussion of the inevitability of death. Why does she rely on the death of so inconsequential a creature to convey her impressions? Why didn't she describe the death of a human being instead?

b. To what is Woolf referring in paragraph 2 when she says, "The same energy which inspired the rooks, the ploughmen, the horses…sent the moth fluttering…"?

c. In the same paragraph, Woolf indicates that the moth was "little or nothing but life." Yet, by paragraph 5, the insect has died. Did the same power that gave him life strike him down?

d. What connection does Woolf draw between the moth and the world of living things outside her window? Why is it appropriate that the moth die at midday?

Strategy and Style

e. Throughout the first three paragraphs, Woolf refers to herself in the third person ("one"). In paragraphs 4 and 5, however, she uses the more familiar first-person pronoun ("I"). Does this change indicate a change in tone? Explain.

f. What other differences do you notice between the first three paragraphs and the last two in regard to both content and rhetorical strategy?

g. At the end of paragraph 1, Woolf uses an extended metaphor. What other interesting examples of figurative language can you identify?

SUGGESTIONS FOR SHORT WRITING

a. Choose a window, or some equally limited area, at home and describe the "world" of that window.

b. Study Woolf's opening paragraph, looking at the way she structures each sentence, the way she uses punctuation, the subject matter of each sentence. Then, with some animal other than a moth, write an opening paragraph of your own in Woolf's style.

SUGGESTIONS FOR SUSTAINED WRITING

a. Woolf's perspective on the death of the moth is, for the most part, subjective. As such, it is a good example of the extent to which our personal vision of the world can color our perceptions of natural objects and events. Spend some time observing the night sky, a field of corn in autumn, a newborn calf, the yard outside your bedroom window, a potted geranium, or some other natural subject. Write two short essays about it. In the first, be objective. Describe things accurately and scientifically. Use factual details only, and make reference to exact sizes, shapes, and colors. In the second, flex the muscles of your imagination by writing a subjective description. Let your emotions color your perceptions. If possible, use metaphors and other figures of speech to convey your personal impressions of the subject.

b. Woolf proves that even a creature as insignificant as a moth is an appropriate subject for an essay that explores significant human questions. Go outside and watch the activity in an anthill for ten or fifteen minutes, observe what a mother bird must go through to keep her babies alive, or recall the birth of a puppy or kitten. What lessons does the natural world teach us about how to live our lives?

The Crime of the Tooth: Dentistry in the Chair

Peter Freundlich

*Peter Freundlich is a former CBS newswriter and is now working on his first novel.
His satirical essays, such as "The Crime of the Tooth," have appeared in* Harper's *and
other magazines.*

If you are anything like me (and you must pray, of course, that you are 1
not, and behave yourself besides, or your prayers will be denied), you will have
experienced this. Just before eye-crack on a sunny day, warm light on the eye-
lids only, and already a trickle of pleasure, a soft worm in the ear, an electric
tingle to which—still asleep—your muscles react, tightening in preparation for
the flinging back of the covers and the springing up from the bed.

And then, awesome quick change of weather, there is a blackness across 2
the sun and a dampness in the soul. You recollect, at the very moment of the
leap from bed, with feet high and arms wide, that this is the day you go to the
dentist.

How well, as Auden wrote, the Old Masters understood suffering. How 3
the calamity happens on a mild golden day, and goes unseen by the happy and
the hard at work. Auden was talking about the fall of Icarus, and so am I, for
what else is the sudden recollection of an appointment with the dentist than a
terrible chuteless fall from hopeful, sleepy midair, a melting—no, a vaporiz-
ing—of the wax wings of dream and a blind drop to the killing ground.

The truth on such a morning is that in half an hour you will be laid out on 4
a morgue slab rigged to look like a reclining chair, with Dr. Kaliper's masked
face filling your entire sky, and all eight of his hands at play in your mouth.

The knowledge that you are going to the dentist changes everything. 5
Where a minute ago the sunlight seemed marmalade, richly spread across your
window, now it is a mockery. It does not beckon, it jeers.

You would have jumped into your clothes before, all eager cinchings and 6
zippings and knottings. Now you drag your leggings on, shrug mournfully into
your shirt, fuss thick-fingered with every button. Your face in the mirror is
smudged with worry.

It is not the local pain that causes dread, but the *greater* pain: the loss of 7
speech, the pinioning, the drool tides coming in and washing out, the maroon-
ing of the brain. For two hours, the brain is Robinson Crusoe alone in the bone
cup of the skull, peering out at faraway chrome implements and rubber-
sheathed fingers and cotton cylinders red with blood, peering out but forbidden
to signal for help.

Pushing open the lobby door, you descend three marble steps into the an- 8

90

teroom of the underworld. In place of Charon, there is only a buzzer to conduct you across this Styx; you are vacuumed into the starched white smile of the receptionist and, behind her, the starched white smile of the hygienist and, behind her, the green-tunic smile of Kaliper himself.

There is perfunctory talk. How are you today? You are fine. (Or would 9 be, if not here.) And how is the practitioner this morning? He too is fine.

Meanwhile you have been settling yourself into Kaliper's astronaut's 10 couch, in preparation for the launching.

Of course, he would not have you go uninformed into that good night. He 11 explains at length his objectives and methods while showing you what looks to be the seating plan of a Greek amphitheater, two opposed semicircles with many Xs along the perimeters. These do not mark reserved seats but the sites of work to be done.

Kaliper continues to hold forth on such matters as roots and canals and 12 crowns and tiaras and diadems. You pretend to follow it all, but in fact have already turned your attention inward, into your mouth, which is independently alive: All the little underskin creatures—the stalks and cones and antlered antennae—are nervously atwit, snuffling, shuffling, pawing, like forest animals before a storm.

You have had the X-rays already. The lead blanket was laid on your chest 13 and you were told to be still while that timid funnel-beaked behemoth with its triple-jointed metal neck poked its snout against your face. Though eyeless, the creature still managed an audible wink wherever it stopped tenderly to nuzzle. All that by which you are everywhere known to be you and not someone else— your entire exterior, your features, hair color, eye color, skin color, marks commemorating your birth and childhood diseases—the funnel-beaked thing sees not at all. It is blind except to your insides.

Now Dr. Kaliper stands by the X-ray lightbox and points to the snap- 14 shots: a valley to be filled, a ridge to be rounded off, a cave in which something rotten lurks. Kaliper will turn spelunker, go into the cave and yank out the rot. You continue to nod sagely; the underskin animals are braying wildly now.

He asks, rhetorically, if you are ready. Then, pressing a button that makes 15 the machinery of the chair moan, he causes your head to be lowered. You turn pink as blood sloshes down from your feet and legs.

They must be taught in school not to let their patients see the needles and 16 the instruments coming. Kaliper manages the sleight of hand nicely. His forearm grazing your nose, he takes the novocaine-filled syringe from the hygienist. Then he brings the thing down along your jawline, too low for your radar to pick up. Finally, he has it under your chin, then up, aimed, and ready. It is now too close for you to focus on; you have only an impression—an orange cylinder and a glint.

Hold on just a bit, he says, *you're going to feel this.* 17

There is a small intrusion into your gum, a cold, sharp pinch, as if a steel 18 no-see-um had landed there. Then the midge grows suddenly much heavier, sinking in. It is Kaliper, of course, his arm behind the work now.

Okay, we'll give that a minute or two to numb you up. 19

It seems that your upper lip is growing not numb but fat and thick, as if 20 swollen with liquid. It is now out beyond the tip of your nose, billowing in a spinnaker curve until finally it is so big and heavy that it hangs down even over your lower lip.

Starting to work? 21

You mutter as much of a *yeah* as you can with your lower lip alone, the 22 upper answering to no authority now.

Kaliper is ready to begin. 23

And your brain, crazy Crusoe, settles in a hunker on a bone ridge. 24

This, unless you ask for fumes, is one of the few things in life from 25 which you cannot turn away. It is an event that happens *on* you, *in* you: a sub-cutaneous circus, a riot under your nose.

And only your brain, that ball bearing in its bone cup, only your brain is 26 free. Under any other circumstances, you would flee before these chrome threats. All your greater muscles would clench and work—legs wildly pumping, arms wildly swinging—and you'd be gone in a flash from a masked mugger like Kaliper. But now all your retreats must be microscopic, tics and twitches and tremors only. All you can do, on a large scale, is think.

And you do. What *don't* you think? 27

This is what a road would feel, if it were sentient, when the yellow trucks 28 of early spring bring burly armed men and pots of tar to repair frost heaves. Just so, you are being worked on: jackhammered, steam-chiseled, bulldozed.

You yourself, having become a structure, are sentient in a different way 29 now. You feel a pounding in your joists, as if the dentist were a carpenter working in your attic. The thudding he causes with his little mallets and mauls is conducted down through your studs, raising a pulse to rival the heart's.

Why was Shakespeare silent on this subject? Hath not a Jew teeth? Does 30 he not cry out to high heaven when, molar-pierced, he feels the iron worm in the velvet hand, and hears the keening of his own resisting bone?

There are no dentists in nature. Animals doctor themselves and each 31 other, probing and licking and tamping on wounds mud- and spittle-bound grass. But no animal puts on rubber gloves and...

Wider. Open wider. 32

Wider? The corners of your mouth have already met at the back of your 33 head, and Dr. Kaliper blandly asks for easier access. To what?

How fine to feel your bronchioles warmed by his lamp, and the fresh 34 breeze from his nostrils rippling your intestines.

Turn toward me. 35

Only lovemaking happens at this range: Arm's length is otherwise the 36 closest we come, but this is finger's length, and finger's width, and less.

What confidence these men must have, to work so very close to hostile 37 observers, offering themselves for microscopic inspection, aware as they must be that their every pore looks like a dreadful hole from this vantage point. Look: the tapioca surface of the skin, the thick upstanding face-hair bristles grown out from that cheesy plain like cacti, like the legs of half-buried scorpions struggling to right themselves.

But then this is the scale at which they work (and tit for tat): they, nose 38 up against your breath, digging with microshovels in the topsoil of your tooth-rot, and you, threatened by their follicles.

Our mouths should be full of horn, sharp wedges of antler or tortoise 39 shell, grinders that grow like fingernails trimmed weekly to a new, fresh edge.

There is music playing, yes. *Music:* old tunes made toothless by accordi- 40 ons and violas and clarinets. Soothing music, Kaliper must think it is. But it is not music enough to catch the ear, or really to engage the brain. It is just a mask for the drill sounds, and ineffective even at that. The drill plays an octave higher than any instrument on the radio.

The body rejects foreign objects and Kaliper is most foreign. You gag 41 and guff and hack, your throat-flap lashed by drill-storm, a minuscule typhoon of spray.

You have down your gullet already air-jets and water-jets and a teeny 42 goddamn bilge pump on a metal hook. Now comes a vacuum cleaner on a stick put in your mouth to slurp up more of your juices.

Hold on now. Be still a moment. 43

You would laugh sardonically, if you could. Snake-fingered Gorgon Kal- 44 iper, who has long since turned you to stone, now commands stillness.

Through your mouth he is drilling holes in your wallet. 45

Last night, you remember now, you had a dream. You were eating 46 money. Your own money, green and fibrous, vegetal. Next to you was an insur-ance-looking man. He threw coins into your mouth, a nickel for every dollar of your own. Looking up beyond him, you saw a vast herd of big-eyed dentists, all of them placidly grazing in a field of rippling sawbucks.

What is the prayer for surcease from dentistry? 47

You remember your daughter's first tooth, and the joy: she in that scoot- 48 ling thing she had, a sling seat hung in a wheeled metal frame with a fore-mounted tray, and one day in the wide smile, a glint of white in the upper pink ridge. A toof! A toof! Lookit, lookit, clap clap clap. The sight made you break into ecstatic Eddie Cantorish dumbshow, palms pushed repeatedly flat together, fingers straight up, just below the chin. A toof, a toof, welcome to toddler's estate.

And welcome to all this. 49

Dentists are our alchemists, transmuting rot into gold. 50

There was an Ancient Dentist, and he drilleth one of three. Then he dril- 51 leth the other two. Then he billeth.

There is no fetish involving teeth. Men secretly adore feet and buttocks 52 and thighs and axillae. But Krafft-Ebing never lapsed into Latin over teeth.

Some aborigines wear teeth around their necks: they ought to wear dentists—
little shriveled sun-dried dentists.

It is high tide in your mouth now. Your nose is Cape Horn, and, God help   53
you, Kaliper means to round it, to point his chrome prow toward the rocky
promontories of your teeth, to find safe passage between them. He means to
land somewhere under your uvula.

Peace, peace. You are here for a reason and you must hug close the prom-   54
ise, which is that you will have a smile of tourist-attraction quality, a smile of such
perfection and brilliance that omnibuses bursting with camera-strewn pilgrims
will pull up at your door, Japanese, Germans, Italians, all with their heads cocked
attentively toward their bull-horned tour-guides who, in their respective languages, will tell the tale of your teeth, will put your teeth in their proper dento-
historical contexts, who will make plain to the milling bell-shaped women and
the big-nosed men that, in your mouth, they will be seeing the dental Sistine
ceiling, the periodontal Pietà, the bridgework winged Victory of Samothrace.

You will feel the long lenses and the moist eyes trained upon you, and   55
you will favor the pilgrims with a glimpse of the fabled teeth. But slowly, gradually, so as not literally to knock them arse over teakettle with the splendor of
the sight. You will be impoverished, yes, but with God's own smile.

The Brits will not come, of course, they of the gnarled yellow choppers,   56
overlapped, jagged. A people of deplorable dental cavalierness, the Brits would
rather invest their money in Savile Row tailoring and Harley Street doctoring
and Bentley motor cars and manor houses. A fine thing. The thirtieth Duke approaches, tall, fair-skinned, as richly veined about the nose and cheeks as Stil-
ton cheese, in balmoral and balmacaan, walking stick at the ready; says hello
and, beneath the grenadier's mustache, shows chiaroscuro smile, some teeth
long and tending toward the spiral, some squat and striated, as rune-covered as
river rocks. Of course he has money, having forsworn dentistry.

Why exactly does Kaliper wear a mask? Is it to hide his own teeth? Do   57
they become, when he's working, black and pointed or blood-red and outward-
curled, like the tips of Turkish slippers?

Kaliper is hot with enthusiasm now. His hands fly about the tray held by   58
his mechanical butler, selecting picks and spears. Inside your mouth, your pulse
must be visible again, a growing and shrinking of the veins. Kaliper construes
this, you suppose, as a readiness to reach a dental climax, in tandem with him.

Nearly there, he says, *nearly there.*   59

How do they endure this, the famous? They must endure it with great reg-   60
ularity, for, as is well known, the teeth of the famous are not teeth at all. They
are wonderful facsimiles, made by master technicians and implanted by master
dentists. If Michelangelo were alive today, he'd be carving teeth in Hollywood.

The drill sounds like a winch now, makes the sound the winch makes   61
when, the mourners having turned to go, the coffin begins to be lowered. You

feel pain, not in your teeth, but everywhere else—the small of your back, your legs, your neck, your shoulders, and especially your face because you've been holding your mouth scream-wide for so long.

Or you *were* holding your mouth open. Now it is stuffed, overstuffed, 62 filled to cracking, with egg-beaters and chrome tricycles and socket wrenches and antique wristwatches, small prams, suits of armor, coffee-makers.

You think you feel the lower end of a ramp being placed on your tongue, 63 and you think you hear, from a distance, the sound of a motor being cranked. Kaliper must be mounting an expedition into your interior, with fresh supplies loaded aboard a Land-Rover.

You gurgle.   64

You alright? Kaliper asks.   65

You gurgle again.   66

Good, he says.   67

Kaliper is maneuvering into position, for a trial fitting, the crown he has 68 had made. It is a bit of porcelain-covered metal, very like a tooth. But it is not a tooth, and your flesh knows it.

You are given a mirror to see what Kaliper has wrought. And of course 69 your eyes, stupid gelatinous organs, are fooled.

Looks good, you mumble.   70

And you mean it: the simulacrum *does* look good. But your tongue wor- 71 ries the thing, frets and pushes at it as would an animal at something dead. Your gum, the flesh most directly intruded upon, pulses, is offended. And there is an undulation in your cheek, a threadwide, millimeters-long surf—your cheek is offended on behalf of your gum.

Kaliper has emptied your mouth of his gear. His work now, a tightly con- 72 trolled scratching, has an air of finality. You think he may be etching his name on the permanently installed crown. You will have *Kaliper fecit* inscribed on the dark side of the not-tooth, a joke to be appreciated someday by the coroner.

All done, he says.   73

And his assistant swings away an arm of the chair on which you have 74 been marooned, so that you may stand.

Which you do, crowned now, and dizzy.   75

1987

QUESTIONS FOR DISCUSSION

Content

a. What is (are) the main point(s) of this essay? *Is* there a point, besides recalling a visit to the dentist? If so, which sentences in the essay reveal it?

b. In structure, the essay is narrative; it presents the chronology of a visit to Dr.

Kaliper's from beginning to agonizing end. In what ways does it qualify as an example of descriptive writing?

c. Is this selection serious or humorous? Cite passages to defend your answer. Remember, satire is not necessarily humorous.

d. What does the statement "If Michelangelo were alive today, he'd be carving teeth in Hollywood" (paragraph 60) reveal about Freundlich's view of American society? What other passages make a similar revelation? Do you agree with these statements?

e. Freundlich makes allusions and comparisons to numerous fields unrelated to dentistry—literature, mythology, the Bible, sports, art, history, and foreign cultures, to name a few. Find several such allusions or comparisons, and explain them. Do they clarify the experience of a visit to the dentist, or do they confuse it?

Strategy and Style

f. Freundlich sometimes asks direct questions such as "What is the prayer for surcease from dentistry?" (paragraph 47); "Why exactly does Kaliper wear a mask?" (paragraph 57); or "How do they endure this, the famous?" (paragraph 60). Does Freundlich intend for you to answer these questions? If so, what would your answer be? If not, why does Freundlich ask them?

g. Many paragraphs in this essay are only one brief sentence. What purpose do such paragraphs serve?

h. Similarly, what purpose does the quoted speech (in italics) of the dentist serve?

i. Why does Freundlich use "you" instead of "I"? In what ways would the essay be different if he used "I" rather than "you"?

j. What is Freundlich's purpose in using a flippant, mocking tone? How does he create and maintain this tone?

SUGGESTIONS FOR SHORT WRITING

a. Write your opinion of Dr. Kaliper. How similar is he to your own dentist?

b. Describe your image of the narrator (not the author) of this essay. Does the narrator differ from your image of the author? If so, how do the two differ? Do you notice a difference between yourself as author and as narrator in your own essays?

SUGGESTIONS FOR SUSTAINED WRITING

a. Describe an experience that horrified you. Determine whether the reasons that it horrified you were purely personal or part of a broader social situation or problem.

b. Freundlich says in paragraph 5 that knowing "you are going to the dentist changes everything." Think of a similar event that radically changed your day for the better or worse and describe that event, making sure that your readers understand the transformation.

c. Write a satirical description of a modern ritual that is usually taken for granted but which you feel is absurd in some way. Write a description that will both entertain your readers and expose the absurdity of the ritual.

My Father

Doris Lessing

Doris Lessing (b. 1919) was born in Persia, the daughter of English parents who had moved there hoping to make a good living at banking. When that venture did not turn out as her father had hoped, the family moved to Rhodesia, where they settled as farmers. In 1949, Lessing moved to London, where her first novel, The Grass Is Singing *(1950), won her instant fame. Soon after, she won the Somerset Maugham Award for* Five Short Novels *(1954).* The Golden Notebook *(1962), a complex autobiographical novel that weaves an exploration of the psychology of women with Lessing's views of social history, is her best-known work. An experimenter with form and subject, she covers a wide range of themes and motifs in her novels. In* Briefing for a Descent into Hell *(1971) and* Memoirs of a Survivor *(1974), for example, she deals with psychological disturbances, engages in dreamlike fantasy, and portrays a pessimistic view of history. In 1979, she began a series of "space fiction" novels beginning with* Shikasta. *Recent nonfiction includes* Prisons We Choose to Live Inside *(1986) and* The Wind Blows Away Our Worlds *(1987).*

1　　We use our parents like recurring dreams, to be entered into when needed; they are always there for love or for hate; but it occurs to me that I was not always there for my father. I've written about him before, but novels, stories, don't have to be "true." Writing this article is difficult because it has to be "true." I knew him when his best years were over.

2　　There are photographs of him. The largest is of an officer in the 1914–18 war. A new uniform—buttoned, badged, strapped, tabbed—confines a handsome, dark young man who holds himself stiffly to confront what he certainly thought of as his duty. His eyes are steady, serious, and responsible, and show no signs of what he became later. A photograph at sixteen is of a dark, introspective youth with the same intent eyes. But it is his mouth you notice—a heavily-jutting upper lip contradicts the rest of a regular face. His moustache was to hide it: "Had to do something—a damned fleshy mouth. Always made me uncomfortable, that mouth of mine."

3　　Earlier a baby (eyes already alert) appears in a lace waterfall that cascades from the pillowy bosom of a fat, plain woman to her feet. It is the face of a head cook. "Lord, but my mother was a practical female—almost as bad as you!" as he used to say, or throw at my mother in moments of exasperation. Beside her stands, or droops, arms dangling, his father, the source of the dark, arresting eyes, but otherwise masked by a long beard.

4　　The birth certificate says: Born 3rd August, 1886, Walton Villa, Creffield Road, S. Mary at the Wall, R.S.D. Name, Alfred Cook. Name and surname of Father: Alfred Cook Tayler. Name and maiden name of Mother: Caroline May Batley. Rank or Profession: Bank Clerk. Colchester, Essex.

98

They were very poor. Clothes and boots were a problem. They "made ₅ their own amusements." Books were mostly the Bible and *The Pilgrim's Progress.* Every Saturday night they bathed in a hipbath in front of the kitchen fire. No servants. Church three times on Sundays. "Lord, when I think of those Sundays! I dreaded them all week, like a nightmare coming at you full tilt and no escape." But he rabbited with ferrets along the lanes and fields, bird-nested, stole fruit, picked nuts and mushrooms, paid visits to the blacksmith and the mill and rode a farmer's carthorse.

They ate economically, but when he got diabetes in his forties and sub- ₆ sisted on lean meat and lettuce leaves, he remembered suet puddings, treacle puddings, raisin and currant puddings, steak and kidney puddings, bread and butter pudding, "batter cooked in the gravy with the meat," potato cake, plum cake, butter cake, porridge with treacle, fruit tarts and pies, brawn, pig's trotters and pig's cheek and home-smoked ham and sausages. And "lashings of fresh butter and cream and eggs." He wondered if this diet had produced the diabetes, but said it was worth it.

There was an elder brother described by my father as: "Too damned ₇ clever by half. One of those quick, clever brains. Now I've always had a slow brain, but I get there in the end, damn it!"

The brothers went to a local school and the elder did well, but my father ₈ was beaten for being slow. They both became bank clerks in, I think, the Westminster Bank, and one must have found it congenial, for he became a manager, the "rich brother," who had cars and even a yacht. But my father did not like it, though he was conscientious. For instance, he changed his writing, letter by letter, because a senior criticised it. I never saw his unregenerate hand, but the one he created was elegant, spiky, careful. Did this mean he created a new personality for himself, hiding one he did not like, as he hid his "damned fleshy mouth"? I don't know.

Nor do I know when he left home to live in Luton, or why. He found ₉ family life too narrow? A safe guess—he found everything too narrow. His mother was too down-to-earth? He had to get away from his clever elder brother?

Being a young man in Luton was the best part of his life. It ended in ₁₀ 1914, so he had a decade of happiness. His reminiscences of it were all of pleasure, the delight of physical movement, of dancing in particular. All his girls were "a beautiful dancer, light as a feather." He played billiards and ping-pong (both for his country); he swam, boated, played cricket and football, went to picnics and horse races, sang at musical evenings. One family of a mother and two daughters treated him "like a son only better. I didn't know whether I was in love with the mother or the daughters, but oh I did love going there; we had such good times." He was engaged to one daughter, then, for a time, to the other. An engagement was broken off because she was rude to a waiter. "I could not marry a woman who allowed herself to insult someone who was defenceless." He used to say to my wryly smiling mother: "Just as well I didn't marry either of *them;* they would never have stuck it out the way you have, old girl."

Just before he died he told me he had dreamed he was standing in a 11 kitchen on a very high mountain holding X in his arms. "Ah, yes, that's what I've missed in my life. Now don't you let yourself be cheated out of life by the old dears. They take all the colour out of everything if you let them."

But in that decade—"I'd walk 10, 15 miles to a dance two or three times 12 a week and think nothing of it. Then I'd dance every dance and walk home again over the fields. Sometimes it was moonlight, but I liked the snow best all crisp and fresh. I loved walking back and getting into my digs just as the sun was rising. My little dog was so happy to see me, and I'd feed her, and make myself porridge and tea, then I'd wash and shave and go off to work."

The boy who was beaten at school, who went too much to church, who 13 carried the fear of poverty all his life, but who nevertheless was filled with the memories of country pleasures; the young bank clerk who worked such long hours for so little money, but who danced, sang, played, flirted—this naturally vigorous, sensuous being was killed in 1914, 1915, 1916. I think the best of my father died in that war, that his spirit was crippled by it. The people I've met, particularly the women, who knew him young, speak of his high spirits, his energy, his enjoyment of life. Also of his kindness, his compassion and—a word that keeps recurring—his wisdom. "Even when he was just a boy he understood things that you'd think even an old man would find it easy to condemn." I do not think these people would have easily recognised the ill, irritable, abstracted, hypochondriac man I knew.

He "joined up" as an ordinary soldier out of a characteristically quirky 14 scruple: it wasn't right to enjoy officers' privileges when the Tommies had such a bad time. But he could not stick the communal latrines, the obligatory drinking, the collective visits to brothels, the jokes about girls. So next time he was offered a commission he took it.

His childhood and young man's memories, kept fluid, were added to, 15 grew, as living memories do. But his war memories were congealed in stories that he told again and again, with the same words and gestures, in stereotyped phrases. They were anonymous, general, as if they had come out of a communal war memoir. He met a German in no-man's-land, but both slowly lowered their rifles and smiled and walked away. The Tommies were the salt of the earth, the British fighting men the best in the world. He had never known such comradeship. A certain brutal officer was shot in a sortie by his men, but the other officers, recognising rough justice, said nothing. He had known men intimately who saw the Angels at Mons. He wished he could force all the generals on both sides into the trenches for just one day, to see what the common soldiers endured—*that* would have ended the war at once.

There was an undercurrent of memories, dreams, and emotions much 16 deeper, more personal. This dark region in him, fate-ruled, where nothing was true but horror, was expressed inarticulately, in brief, bitter exclamations or phrases of rage, incredulity, betrayal. The men who went to fight in that war believed it when they said it was to end war. My father believed it. And he was never able to reconcile his belief in his country with his anger at the cynicism of its leaders. And the anger, the sense of betrayal, strengthened as he grew old and ill.

But in 1914 he was naïve, the German atrocities in Belgium inflamed   17 him, and he enlisted out of idealism, although he knew he would have a hard time. He knew because a fortuneteller told him. (He could be described as un-critically superstitious or as psychically gifted.) He would be in great danger twice, yet not die—he was being protected by a famous soldier who was his ancestor. "And sure enough, later I heard from the Little Aunties that the church records showed we were descended the backstairs way from the Duke of Wellington, or was it Marlborough? Damn it, I forget. But one of them would be beside me all through the war, she said." (He was romantic, not only about this solicitous ghost, but also about being a descendant of the Huguenots, on the strength of the "e" in Tayler; and about "the wild blood" in his veins from a great uncle who, sent unjustly to prison for smuggling, came out of a ten-year sentence and earned it, very efficiently, along the coasts of Cornwall until he died.)

The luckiest thing that ever happened to my father, he said, was getting   18 his leg shattered by shrapnel ten days before Passchendaele. His whole com-pany was killed. He knew he was going to be wounded because of the fortune-teller, who had said he would know. "I did not understand what she meant, but both times in the trenches, first when my appendix burst and I nearly died, and then just before Passchendaele, I felt for some days as if a thick, black velvet pall was settled over me. I can't tell you what it was like. Oh, it was awful, awful, and the second time it was so bad I wrote to the old people and told them I was going to be killed."

His leg was cut off at mid-thigh, he was shell-shocked, he was very ill for   19 many months, with a prolonged depression afterwards. "You should always re-member that sometimes people are all seething underneath. You don't know what terrible things people have to fight against. You should look at a person's eyes, that's how you tell....When I was like that, after I lost my leg, I went to a nice doctor man and said I was going mad, but he said, don't worry, everyone locks up things like that. You don't know—horrible, horrible, awful things. I was afraid of myself, of what I used to dream. I wasn't myself at all."

In the Royal Free Hospital was my mother, Sister McVeagh. He married   20 his nurse which, as they both said often enough (though in different tones of voice), was just as well. That was 1919. He could not face being a bank clerk in England, he said, not after the trenches. Besides, England was too narrow and conventional. Besides, the civilians did not know what the soldiers had suf-fered, they didn't want to know, and now it wasn't done even to remember "The Great Unmentionable." He went off to the Imperial Bank of Persia, in which country I was born.

The house was beautiful, with great stone-floored high-ceilinged rooms 21 whose windows showed ranges of snow-streaked mountains. The gardens were full of roses, jasmine, pomegranates, walnuts. Kermanshah he spoke of with liking, but soon they went to Teheran, populous with "Embassy people," and my gregarious mother created a lively social life about which he was irritable even in recollection.

Irritableness—that note was first struck here, about Persia. He did not 22 like, he said, "the graft and the corruption." But here it is time to try and describe something difficult—how a man's good qualities can also be his bad ones, or if not bad, a danger to him.

My father was honourable—he always knew exactly what that word 23 meant. He had integrity. His "one does not do that sort of thing," his "no, it is *not* right," sounded throughout my childhood and were final for all of us. I am sure it was true he wanted to leave Persia because of "the corruption." But it was also because he was already unconsciously longing for something freer, because as a bank official he could not let go into the dream-logged personality that was waiting for him. And later in Rhodesia, too, what was best in him was also what prevented him from shaking away the shadows: it was always in the name of honesty or decency that he refused to take this step or that out of the slow decay of the family's fortunes.

In 1925 there was leave from Persia. That year in London there was an 24 Empire Exhibition, and on the Southern Rhodesian stand some very fine maize cobs and a poster saying that fortunes could be made on maize at 25/- a bag. So on an impulse, turning his back forever on England, washing his hands of the corruption of the East, my father collected all his capital, £800, I think, while my mother packed curtains from Liberty's, clothes from Harrods, visiting cards, a piano, Persian rugs, a governess and two small children.

Soon, there was my father in a cigar-shaped house of thatch and mud on 25 the top of a kopje that overlooked in all directions a great system of mountains, rivers, valleys, while overhead the sky arched from horizon to empty horizon. This was a couple of hundred miles south from the Zambesi, a hundred or so west from Mozambique, in the district of Banket, so called because certain of its reefs were of the same formation as those called *banket* on the Rand. Lomagundi—gold country, tobacco country, maize country—wild, almost empty. (The Africans had been turned off it into reserves.) Our neighbours were four, five, seven miles off. In front of the house...no neighbours, nothing; no farms, just wild bush with two rivers but no fences to the mountains seven miles away. And beyond these mountains and bush again to the Portuguese border, over which "our boys" used to escape when wanted by the police for pass or other offences.

And then? There was bad luck. For instance, the price of maize dropped 26 from 25/- to 9/- a bag. The seasons were bad, prices bad, crops failed. This was the sort of thing that made it impossible for him ever to "get off the farm," which, he agreed with my mother, was what he most wanted to do.

It was an absurd country, he said. A man could "own" a farm for years 27 that was totally mortgaged to the Government and run from the Land Bank, meanwhile employing half-a-hundred Africans at 12/- a month and none of them knew how to do a day's work. Why, two farm labourers from Europe could do in a day what twenty of these ignorant black savages would take a week to do. (Yet he was proud that he had a name as a just employer, that he gave "a square deal.") Things got worse. A fortuneteller had told him that her heart ached when she saw the misery ahead for my father: this was the misery.

But it was my mother who suffered. After a period of neurotic illness, 28 which was a protest against her situation, she became brave and resourceful. But she never saw that her husband was not living in a real world, that he had made a captive of her common sense. We were always about to "get off the farm." A miracle would do it—a sweepstake, a goldmine, a legacy. And then? What a question! We would go to England where life would be normal with people coming in for musical evenings and nice supper parties at the Trocadero after a show. Poor woman, for the twenty years we were on the farm, she waited for when life would begin for her and for her children, for she never understood that what was a calamity for her was for them a blessing.

Meanwhile my father sank towards his death (at 61). Everything changed 29 in him. He had been a dandy and fastidious, now he hated to change out of shabby khaki. He had been sociable, now he was misanthropic. His body's disorders—soon diabetes and all kinds of stomach ailments—dominated him. He was brave about his wooden leg, and even went down mine shafts and climbed trees with it, but he walked clumsily and it irked him badly. He greyed fast, and slept more in the day, but would be awake half the night pondering about....

It could be gold divining. For ten years he experimented on private theo- 30 ries to do with the attractions and repulsions of metals. His whole soul went into it but his theories were wrong or he was *unlucky*—after all, if he had found a mine he would have had to leave the farm. It could be the relation between the minerals of the earth and of the moon; his decision to make infusions of all the plants on the farm and drink them himself in the interests of science; the criminal folly of the British Government in not realising that the Germans and the Russians were conspiring as Anti-Christ to...the inevitability of war be- cause no one would listen to Churchill, but it would be all right because God (by then he was a British Israelite) had destined Britain to rule the world; a prophecy said 10 million dead would surround Jerusalem—how would the corpses be cleared away?; people who wished to abolish flogging should be flogged; the natives understood nothing but a good beating; hanging must not be abolished because the Old Testament said "an eye for an eye and a tooth for a tooth...."

Yet, as this side of him darkened, so that it seemed all his thoughts were 31 of violence, illness, war, still no one dared to make an unkind comment in his presence or to gossip. Criticism of people, particularly of women, made him more and more uncomfortable till at last he burst out with: "It's all very well, but no one has the right to say that about another person."

In Africa, when the sun goes down, the stars spring up, all of them in 32 their expected places, glittering and moving. In the rainy season, the sky flashed and thundered. In the dry season, the great dark hollow of night was lit by veld fires: the mountains burned through September and October in chains of red fire. Every night my father took out his chair to watch the sky and the mountains, smoking, silent, a thin shabby fly-away figure under the stars. "Makes you think—there are so many worlds up there, wouldn't really matter if we did blow ourselves up—plenty more where we came from."

The Second World War, so long foreseen by him, was a bad time. His 33 son was in the Navy and in danger, and his daughter a sorrow to him. He became very ill. More and more often it was necessary to drive him into Salisbury with him in a coma, or in danger of one, on the back seat. My mother moved him into a pretty little suburban house in town near the hospitals, where he took to his bed and a couple of years later died. For the most part he was unconscious under drugs. When awake he talked obsessively (a tongue licking a nagging sore place) about "the old war." Or he remembered his youth. "I've been dreaming—Lord, to see those horses come lickety-split down the course with their necks stretched out and the sun on their coats and everyone shouting....I've been dreaming how I walked along the river in the mist as the sun was rising....Lord, lord, lord, what a time that was, what good times we all had then, before the old war."

1956

QUESTIONS FOR DISCUSSION

Content

a. What was Lessing's motivation for writing this article? Does she ever reveal her motives?
b. What role does physical description play in this brilliant psychological portrait? To what extent does Lessing combine description with techniques normally associated with narration?
c. Does the overall image Lessing builds of her father satisfy you? Is the behavior of her father accounted for in her description of specific, perhaps isolated, events?
d. What image does Lessing build of her father by contrasting his youth with his old age? By contrasting remembrances of the past with the present?
e. Does the author ever reveal who or what is the main cause of her father's deterioration? What do you think is the main cause?

f. How did World War I change Lessing's father? Why were the changes significant? What are Lessing's feelings about them?

g. Besides showing that her father relied on reminiscences to justify current situations, Lessing shows that he dreamt of future successes as a way to justify current hardships (paragraphs 26 through 28). What do reminiscing and dreaming reveal about the author's father? What do they reveal about the author?

Strategy and Style

h. In the first paragraph, Lessing says that this essay "has to be 'true.'" Why does she tell us this, and how does her insistence that the essay be true affect its content and tone?

i. Why does Lessing put quotation marks around "true"? How do you define this word? How closely does this essay conform to your definition? Must an essay be factual to be true?

j. Lessing uses details of her father's youth to counterbalance those about his old age, yet she must rely on his own reminiscences for information about his youth. In what ways might these reminiscences affect the essay's truthfulness?

k. Lessing distinguishes between types of memories (reminiscences, paragraph 10; living memories, paragraph 15; congealed war stories, paragraph 15; undercurrent of personal memories, paragraph 16; hallucinatory dreaming, paragraph 33). Why does she make these distinctions?

l. How objective is Lessing in recalling her father? Are there any phrases or passages that reveal positive or negative feelings about him?

SUGGESTIONS FOR SHORT WRITING

a. Annotate this essay, writing down, as well as you can remember, what you are thinking as you read. Write your comments in the margins or jot them down in your notebook.

b. Then, choose one of your annotations and write a short explanation to yourself about why you wrote that annotation.

SUGGESTIONS FOR SUSTAINED WRITING

a. Write a history of your father or mother in which you rely on photographs and reminiscences to build a "truthful" image of him or her. Keep in mind your motivation for doing this history.

b. What might a history of yourself, written by your parents, be like? How objective and/or truthful would it be? Write a history of yourself from either parent's point of view.

c. Read other essays in this anthology that use memory and personal reminiscence as a framework (for example, "Salvation," "Grandmother's Victory," "Main Street," "I Remember…"). Write a reflective essay on the significance of memory as a means to create meaning and order out of past events.

3

Process

Often thought of as a way to develop scientific papers, process analysis can be used with a variety of topics and in combination with many of the other methods of development illustrated in this text. It is the type of writing used to convey instructions—how to change a tire, write a research paper, take someone's temperature, cook a carp, or compose a "rotten" poem. Process can also explain how something happens or happened—the destruction of the ozone layer, the writing of a classic horror novel like *Frankenstein*, or even the way you convinced your boss to give you a raise!

Like narratives, essays on such topics generally follow chronological order, with each step in the process likened to events in a well-developed plot. Much is made of transitional words and phrases to keep the reader on the right track. "First," Euell Gibbons tells us, "instead of merely scaling the fish, [my brother] skinned them." And like any good storyteller, the writer of process analysis usually begins at the beginning and follows through to the end, sometimes listing steps by number but always providing sufficient detail to help the reader picture the activity accurately and concretely.

At times, you will find it impossible to follow a strict chronological arrangement, for you will have to explain steps or events that occur simultaneously. In such cases, make sure to cue your reader, as Rachel Carson does when, in "The Grey Beginnings," she explains: "All the while the cloud cover was thinning, the darkness of the nights alternated with palely illumined days...."

Sometimes, writers of process analysis infuse their work with vivid, if not unnerving, description like the kind we find in Mitford's "Behind the Formaldehyde Curtain." More often than not, however, process papers also explain the relationship of causes and effects, as in Petrunkevitch's "The Spider and the Wasp."

Nonetheless, the purpose of process analysis is instructive in the most practical sense: narrative and description may show *what* happens, causal analysis may explain *why* it happens, but process analysis always focuses on *how* it happens. The most important aspect of any process essay, therefore, is clarity. Readers will not follow unless your explanations are complete, your language is familiar, and your organization is simple. Take your lead from Franklin, who lays out important information in lists and easy-to-follow schemas even when explaining how to attain "moral virtue." And whenever you give instructions, pay your readers the courtesy of preparing them for the task by mentioning required tools, materials, and expectations as does Richard Howey: "Have your paper ready. You must first understand that the poem you write here will not be brilliant."

Like selections in other parts of this text, those that appear here represent a variety of subjects, approaches, and styles. But there is a common denominator. As you might expect, the selections that follow are models of clarity, but their authors never seem cold and detached, even when explaining what might first seem recondite or abstract. The committed, sometimes impassioned, voice of the writer always comes through. That is probably why we read these sometimes "technical" pieces with alacrity. Each selection has something important to teach us, but the lesson has little to do with the process its author describes. What we learn here is a need to respect the reader, to understand our attitude toward the subject, and to believe that what we have to say is important.

Attaining Moral Virtue

Benjamin Franklin

Born in Boston, Benjamin Franklin (1706–1790) was at twelve apprenticed to his brother James, a printer. While pursuing this trade, he trained himself as a writer by imitating the essays in The Spectator. *When his brother was jailed for criticizing the authorities in his paper, the* New England Courant, *Benjamin became editor, retaining the position, in name at least, when James was released but forbidden to edit the paper. Never getting along well with his brother, Franklin left for Philadelphia. He arrived penniless but quickly got a job as a printer. Extremely industrious, he soon owned his own printing company. It was during this period that he began* Poor Richard's Almanack, *which was published annually from 1732 to 1764. Franklin was able to "retire" from printing at 42, upon which he turned to civic, scientific, and political pursuits. His legendary experiments with electricity led to the writing of* Experiments and Observations on Electricity *(1751–53); he invented bifocals and the slow combustion engine; and he helped start the University of Pennsylvania as well as a circulating library and a debating society. As if that were not enough, he was also a member of the Pennsylvania Assembly, Postmaster General for the Colonies, a diplomat to France and England, and one of the drafters of the Declaration of Independence. His* Autobiography, *from which "Attaining Moral Virtue" (editors' title) is taken, was begun as a letter to his son in 1771 and expanded throughout Franklin's life.*

It was about this time I conceived the bold and arduous project of arriv- 1
ing at moral perfection. I wished to live without committing any fault any time;
I would conquer all that either natural inclination, custom, or company might
lead me into. As I knew, or thought I knew, what was right and wrong, I did
not see why I might not always do the one and avoid the other. But I soon
found I had undertaken a task of more difficulty than I had imagined. While my
care was employed in guarding against one fault, I was often surprised by another; habit took the advantage of inattention; inclination was sometimes too
strong for reason. I concluded at length, that the mere speculative conviction
that it was our interest to be completely virtuous was not sufficient to prevent
our slipping; and that the contrary habits must be broken, and good ones acquired and established, before we can have any dependence on a steady, uniform rectitude of conduct. For this purpose I therefore contrived the following
method.

In the various enumerations of the moral virtues I had met with in my 2
reading, I found the catalogue more or less numerous, as different writers included more or fewer ideas under the same name. Temperance, for example,
was by some confined to eating and drinking, while by others it was extended
to mean the moderating every other pleasure, appetite, inclination, or passion,
bodily or mental, even to our avarice and ambition. I proposed to myself, for

the sake of clearness, to use rather more names, with fewer ideas annexed to each, than a few names with more ideas; and I included under thirteen names of virtues all that at that time occurred to me as necessary or desirable, and annexed to each a short precept, which fully expressed the extent I gave to its meaning.

These names of virtues, with their precepts, were: 3

1. TEMPERANCE. Eat not to dullness; drink not to elevation.
2. SILENCE. Speak not but what may benefit others or yourself; avoid trifling conversation.
3. ORDER. Let all your things have their places; let each part of your business have its time.
4. RESOLUTION. Resolve to perform what you ought; perform without fail what you resolve.
5. FRUGALITY. Make no expense but to do good to others or yourself; *i.e.*, waste nothing.
6. INDUSTRY. Lose no time; be always employed in something useful; cut off all unnecessary actions.
7. SINCERITY. Use no hurtful deceit; think innocently and justly, and, if you speak, speak accordingly.
8. JUSTICE. Wrong none by doing injuries, or omitting the benefits that are your duty.
9. MODERATION. Avoid extremes; forbear resenting injuries so much as you think they deserve.
10. CLEANLINESS. Tolerate no uncleanliness in body, clothes, or habitation.
11. TRANQUILITY. Be not disturbed at trifles, or at accidents common or unavoidable.
12. CHASTITY. Rarely use venery but for health or offspring, never to dullness, weakness, or the injury of your own or another's peace or reputation.
13. HUMILITY. Imitate Jesus and Socrates.

My intention being to acquire the *habitude* of all these virtues, I judged it   4 would be well not to distract my attention by attempting the whole at once, but to fix it on one of them at a time; and, when I should be master of that, then to proceed to another, and so on, till I should have gone through the thirteen; and, as the previous acquisition of some might facilitate the acquisition of certain others, I arranged them with that view, as they stand above. *Temperance* first, as it tends to procure that coolness and clearness of head, which is so necessary where constant vigilance was to be kept up, and guard maintained against the unremitting attraction of ancient habits, and the force of perpetual temptations. This being acquired and established, *Silence* would be more easy; and my desire being to gain knowledge at the same time that I improved in virtue, and considering that in conversation it was obtained rather by the use of the ears than of the tongue, and therefore wishing to break a habit I was getting into of prattling, punning, and joking, which only made me acceptable to trifling company, I gave *Silence* the second place. This and the next, *Order,* I expected would allow me more time for attending to my project and my studies. *Resolution,* once become habitual, would keep me firm in my endeavors to obtain all the subsequent virtues; *Frugality* and *Industry* freeing me from my remaining debt, and producing affluence and independence, would make more easy the practice of *Sincerity and Justice,* etc., etc. Conceiving then, that, agreeably to the advice of Pythagoras in his Golden Verses, daily examination would be necessary, I contrived the following method for conducting that examination.

The precept of *Order* requiring that *every part of my business should have* **5** *its allotted time,* one page in my little book contained the following scheme of employment for the twenty-four hours of a natural day.

THE MORNING *Question.* What good shall I do this day?	5 6 7	Rise, wash and address *Powerful Goodness!* Contrive day's business, and take the resolution of the day; prosecute the present study, and breakfast.
	8 9 10 11	Work.
NOON	12 1	Read, or overlook my accounts, and dine.
	2 3 4 5	Work.
Question. What good have I done to-day?	6 7 8 9	Put things in their places. Supper. Music or diversion, or conversation. Examination of the day.
NIGHT	10 11 12 1 2 3 4	Sleep.

My list of virtues contained at first but twelve; but a Quaker friend hav- **6** ing kindly informed me that I was generally thought proud; that my pride showed itself frequently in conversation; that I was not content with being in the right when discussing any point, but was overbearing, and rather insolent, of which he convinced me by mentioning several instances; I determined endeavoring to cure myself, if I could, of this vice or folly among the rest, and I added *Humility* to my list, giving an extensive meaning to the word.

I cannot boast of much success in acquiring the *reality* of this virtue, but ⁊
I had a good deal with regard to the *appearance* of it.

1784

QUESTIONS FOR DISCUSSION

Content

a. How does Franklin define "moral perfection" (paragraph 1)? How does he define "virtue"? How do you define these terms?

b. What is the "method" Franklin has "contrived" for "arriving at moral perfection"? Why does he choose to follow a particular sequence in attaining the moral virtues he lists? How successful is he in following the sequence?

c. Initially, why did Franklin contrive such a plan? What was his objective?

d. What flaws do you see in Franklin's plan? Would you try attaining these virtues in the same order Franklin does, or would you follow another plan?

e. What is Franklin's plan for evaluating his attempts at attaining moral virtue? Do you think you could use such a plan to promote self-reflection?

f. Near the end of this selection, he says that a friend told him he was considered proud. Does this essay contain other indications that Franklin may not have been humble?

g. In his conclusion, Franklin tells us, "I cannot boast of much success in acquiring the *reality* of this virtue, but I had a good deal with regard to the *appearance* of it." Is Franklin saying that appearance is all that matters? Or is he actually being humble here?

Strategy and Style

h. Process analysis is the kind of writing used by scientists to explain natural occurrences or to give instructions. In what ways do the organization and style of this selection remind you of the writing in science texts or articles you have read in other courses?

i. Look ahead to the essays by Carson, Mitford and Gibbons. How does the style and sentence structure in this selection compare with theirs?

SUGGESTIONS FOR SHORT WRITING

a. Update—seriously or in jest—Franklin's thirteen moral virtues to fit a 1990s lifestyle. Follow this with a paragraph about whether you think Franklin would be able to live according to your revised list of "virtues."

b. Write a list of moral virtues that you would like to follow, or at least think you should follow. Which of these would be most difficult for you to follow? Why?

SUGGESTIONS FOR SUSTAINED WRITING

a. Explain your own plan for attaining moral virtue. How does your plan differ from Franklin's? Has our morality changed significantly from what people tried to follow two hundred years ago?

Begin your plan by listing the virtues you would like to attain. Then, write reflectively by explaining why you chose those particular virtues. Next, explain how and in what order you will go about attaining each of them. Try to predict the problems you will have putting your plan into action. Finally, like Franklin, make sure to describe a method by which you can evaluate your progress day by day.

b. Write a parody of Franklin's proposal. Your purpose is to show through satire that his plan is not feasible.

c. Write a critique of Franklin's proposal. You might want to base it on his views of moral virtue. Do they differ significantly from your own? How does Franklin define morality? Where in the essay does he come close to your own definition? Where in the essay do you and he part company?

The Spider and the Wasp

Alexander Petrunkevitch

Alexander Petrunkevitch (1875–1964) arrived in the United States around the turn of the century after having studied in Russia, his native country, and in Germany. A world-famous zoologist, Petrunkevitch taught at several American universities including Harvard and Yale. As an expert on spiders, he published what is now a standard reference in the field: Index Catalogue of Spiders of North, Central and South America. *Like Rachel Carson, Isaac Asimov, James Rettie, and Lewis Thomas, whose works also appear in this text, Petrunkevitch writes scientific prose that, while accurate and well documented, is colorful, exciting, and accessible to readers with little scientific training. "The Spider and the Wasp" first appeared in* Scientific American *in 1952.*

1 To hold its own in the struggle for existence, every species of animal must have a regular source of food, and if it happens to live on other animals, its survival may be very delicately balanced. The hunter cannot exist without the hunted; if the latter should perish from the earth, the former would, too. When the hunted also prey on some of the hunters, the matter may become complicated.

2 This is nowhere better illustrated than in the insect world. Think of the complexity of a situation such as the following: There is a certain wasp, *Pimpla inquisitor,* whose larvae feed on the larvae of the tussock moth. *Pimpla* larvae in turn serve as food for the larvae of a second wasp, and the latter in their turn nourish still a third wasp. What subtle balance between fertility and mortality must exist in the case of each of these four species to prevent the extinction of all of them! An excess of mortality over fertility in a single member of the group would ultimately wipe out all four.

3 This is not a unique case. The two great orders of insects, Hymenoptera and Diptera, are full of such examples of interrelationship. And the spiders (which are not insects but members of a separate order of arthropods) also are killers and victims of insects.

4 In the feeding and safeguarding of their progeny the insects and spiders exhibit some interesting analogies to reasoning and some crass examples of blind instinct. The case I propose to describe here is that of the tarantula spiders and their arch-enemy, the digger wasps of the genus Pepsis. It is a classic example of what looks like intelligence pitted against instinct—a strange situation in which the victim, though fully able to defend itself, submits unwittingly to its destruction.

5 A fertilized female tarantula lays from 200 to 400 eggs at a time; thus it is possible for a single tarantula to produce several thousand young. She takes no care of them beyond weaving a cocoon of silk to enclose the eggs. After

they hatch, the young walk away, find convenient places in which to dig their burrows and spend the rest of their lives in solitude. Tarantulas feed mostly on insects and millepedes. Once their appetite is appeased, they digest the food for several days before eating again. Their sight is poor, being limited to sensing a change in the intensity of light and to the perception of moving objects. They apparently have little or no sense of hearing, for a hungry tarantula will pay no attention to a loudly chirping cricket placed in its cage unless the insect happens to touch one of its legs.

But all spiders, and especially hairy ones, have an extremely delicate **6** sense of touch. Laboratory experiments prove that tarantulas can distinguish three types of touch: pressure against the body wall, stroking of the body hair and riffling of certain very fine hairs on the legs called trichobothria. Pressure against the body, by a finger or the end of a pencil, causes the tarantula to move off slowly for a short distance. The touch excites no defensive response unless the approach is from above where the spider can see the motion, in which case it rises on its hind legs, lifts its front legs, opens its fangs and holds this threatening posture as long as the object continues to move. When the motion stops, the spider drops back to the ground, remains quiet for a few seconds and then moves slowly away.

The entire body of a tarantula, especially its legs, is thickly clothed with **7** hair. Some of it is short and woolly, some long and stiff. Touching this body hair produces one of two distinct reactions. When the spider is hungry, it responds with an immediate and swift attack. At the touch of a cricket's antennae the tarantula seizes the insect so swiftly that a motion picture taken at the rate of 64 frames per second shows only the result and not the process of capture. But when the spider is not hungry, the stimulation of its hairs merely causes it to shake the touched limb. An insect can walk under its hairy belly unharmed.

The trichobothria, very fine hairs growing from disklike membranes on **8** the legs, were once thought to be the spider's hearing organs, but we now know that they have nothing to do with sound. They are sensitive only to air movement. A light breeze makes them vibrate slowly without disturbing the common hair. When one blows gently on the trichobothria, the tarantula reacts with a quick jerk of its four front legs. In the front and hind legs are stimulated at the same time, the spider makes a sudden jump. This reaction is quite independent of the state of its appetite.

These three tactile responses—to pressure on the body wall, to moving of **9** the common hair and to flexing of the trichobothria—are so different from one another that there is no possibility of confusing them. They serve the tarantula adequately for most of its needs and enable it to avoid most annoyances and dangers. But they fail the spider completely when it meets its deadly enemy, the digger wasp Pepsis.

These solitary wasps are beautiful and formidable creatures. Most species **10** are either a deep shiny blue all over, or deep blue with rusty wings. The largest have a wing span of about four inches. They live on nectar. When excited, they give off a pungent odor—a warning that they are ready to attack. The sting is much worse than that of a bee or common wasp, and the pain and swelling last longer. In the adult stage the wasp lives only a few months. The female produces but a few eggs, one at a time at intervals of two or three days. For each egg the mother must provide one adult tarantula, alive but paralyzed. The tarantula must be of the correct species to nourish the larva. The mother wasp attaches the egg to the paralyzed spider's abdomen. Upon hatching from the egg, the larva is many hundreds of times smaller than its living but helpless victim. It eats no other food and drinks no water. By the time it has finished its single gargantuan meal and become ready for wasphood, nothing remains of the tarantula but its indigestible chitinous skeleton.

The mother wasp goes tarantula-hunting when the egg in her ovary is almost ready to be laid. Flying low over the ground late on a sunny afternoon, the wasp looks for its victim or for the mouth of a tarantula burrow, a round hole edged by a bit of silk. The sex of the spider makes no difference, but the mother is highly discriminating as to species. Each species of Pepsis requires a certain species of tarantula, and the wasp will not attack the wrong species. In a cage with a tarantula which is not its normal prey the wasp avoids the spider, and is usually killed by it in the night. 11

Yet when a wasp finds the correct species, it is the other way about. To identify the species the wasp apparently must explore the spider with her antennae. The tarantula shows an amazing tolerance to this exploration. The wasp crawls under it and walks over it without evoking any hostile response. The molestation is so great and so persistent that the tarantula often rises on all eight legs, as if it were on stilts. It may stand this way for several minutes. Meanwhile the wasp, having satisfied itself that the victim is of the right species, moves off a few inches to dig the spider's grave. Working vigorously with legs and jaws, it excavates a hole 8 to 10 inches deep with a diameter slightly larger than the spider's girth. Now and again the wasp pops out of the hole to make sure that the spider is still there. 12

When the grave is finished, the wasp returns to the tarantula to complete her ghastly enterprise. First she feels it all over once more with her antennae. Then her behavior becomes more aggressive. She bends her abdomen, protruding her sting, and searches for the soft membrane at the point where the spider's leg joins its body—the only spot where she can penetrate the horny skeleton. From time to time, as the exasperated spider slowly shifts ground, the wasp turns on her back and slides along with the aid of her wings, trying to get under the tarantula for a shot at the vital spot. During all this maneuvering, which can last for several minutes, the tarantula makes no move to save itself. Finally the wasp corners it against some obstruction and grasps one of its legs in her powerful jaws. Now at last the harassed spider tries a desperate but vain defense. The two contestants roll over and over on the ground. It is a terrifying sight and the outcome is always the same. The wasp finally manages to thrust her sting into the soft spot and holds it there for a few seconds while she pumps 13 in the poison. Almost immediately the tarantula falls paralyzed on its back. Its legs stop twitching; its heart stops beating. yet it is not dead, as is shown by the fact that if taken from the wasp it can be restored to some sensitivity by being kept in a moist chamber for several months.

After paralyzing the tarantula, the wasp cleans herself by dragging her 14 body along the ground and rubbing her feet, sucks the drop of blood oozing from the wound in the spider's abdomen, then grabs a leg of the flabby, helpless animal in her jaws and drags it down to the bottom of the grave. She stays there for many minutes, sometimes for several hours, and what she does all that time in the dark we do not know. Eventually she lays her egg and attaches it to the side of the spider's abdomen with a sticky secretion. Then she emerges, fills the grave with soil carried bit by bit in her jaws, and finally tramples the ground all around to hide any trace of the grave from prowlers. Then she flies away, leaving her descendant safely started in life.

In all this the behavior of the wasp evidently is qualitatively different 15 from that of the spider. The wasp acts like an intelligent animal. This is not to say that instinct plays no part or that she reasons as man does. But her actions are to the point; they are not automatic and can be modified to fit the situation. We do not know for certain how she identifies the tarantula—probably it is by some olfactory or chemo-tactile sense—but she does it purposefully and does not blindly tackle a wrong species.

On the other hand, the tarantula's behavior shows only confusion. Evi- 16 dently the wasp's pawing gives it no pleasure, for it tries to move away. That the wasp is not simulating sexual stimulation is certain, because male and female tarantulas react in the same way to its advances. That the spider is not anesthetized by some odorless secretion is easily shown by blowing lightly at the tarantula and making it jump suddenly. What, then, makes the tarantula behave as stupidly as it does?

No clear, simple answer is available. Possibly the stimulation by the 17 wasp's antennae is masked by a heavier pressure on the spider's body, so that it reacts as when prodded by a pencil. But the explanation may be much more complex. Initiative in attack is not in the nature of tarantulas; most species fight only when cornered so that escape is impossible. Their inherited patterns of behavior apparently prompt them to avoid problems rather than attack them. For example, spiders always weave their webs in three dimensions, and when a spider finds that there is insufficient space to attach certain threads in the third dimension, it leaves the place and seeks another, instead of finishing the web in a single plane. This urge to escape seems to arise under all circumstances, in all phases of life and to take the place of reasoning. For a spider to change the pattern of its web is as impossible as for an inexperienced man to build a bridge across a chasm obstructing his way.

In a way the instinctive urge to escape is not only easier but often more 18 efficient than reasoning. The tarantula does exactly what is most efficient in all cases except in an encounter with a ruthless and determined attacker dependent for the existence of her own species on killing as many tarantulas as she can lay eggs. Perhaps in this case the spider follows its usual pattern of trying to escape, instead of seizing and killing the wasp, because it is not aware of its danger. In any case, the survival of the tarantula species as a whole is protected by the fact that the spider is much more fertile than the wasp.

1952

QUESTIONS FOR DISCUSSION

Content

a. In paragraph one, Petrunkevitch claims that, for some species, "survival may be very delicately balanced." How does this statement relate to the rest of the essay?

b. How does the word "complicated" (paragraph 1) prepare the reader for what is to follow?

c. Based on your reading of this essay, in what way(s) is process analysis similar to narration?

d. Petrunkevitch makes it a point to describe a number of significant differences between the spider and the wasp. Identify a few of these. Why are they significant?

e. As you probably inferred from the two questions before this one, a variety of techniques, including narration and contrast, can be used to explain a process. What function does description play in this essay?

f. What, according to Petrunkevitch, may account for the tarantula's unwitting acceptance of its own destruction?

Strategy and Style

g. Outline Petrunkevitch's major points in an attempt to trace the organization of the essay.

h. Given the fact that this selection was first published in *Scientific American*, it is probably safe to assume that Petrunkevitch was writing for a highly educated reader but one who may not have had formal training in zoology. Comment upon his use of technical language. Does the author stop to define unfamiliar words? Why?

i. Petrunkevitch's tone is typically scientific—detached and objective— through most of the selection. At times, however, his language seems highly emotional and charged with excitement. Analyze his choice of words in these instances. What are the connotations of words like "desperate" and "ghastly"? What images does Petrunkevitch evoke with phrases like "she pumps in the poison"?

SUGGESTIONS FOR SHORT WRITING

a. Try to summarize the battle between the spider and the wasp in one short paragraph.

b. Closely observe a pet, if you have one, or an animal in a park or zoo for fifteen or twenty minutes, and describe its behavior.

SUGGESTIONS FOR SUSTAINED WRITING

a. Write an explanation (process analysis) about the way in which an animal undertakes a task necessary to its survival or the survival of its species. Topics to choose from might include how a beaver constructs a dam, how ants build colonies, how deer forage for food, or how birds care for their young. In addition to observing animals firsthand, you might want to research this topic in your college library.

b. In many ways, "The Spider and the Wasp" is a study in contrasts. Choose two animals or types of animals which, while apparently similar, exhibit distinctive differences in "personality" or behavior. For instance, compare two house pets, two kinds of saltwater fish you've caught, a hawk and a crow, or two common insects.

c. As the author shows, nature can be cruel and terrifying. Write a description of a natural process that you find frightening, painful, or unpleasant. Be as specific as you can in conveying an objective picture of the process but, like Petrunkevitch, don't hesitate to allow your emotions to influence your writing.

The Grey Beginnings
Rachel Carson

A marine biologist, scholar, and noted writer of popular scientific literature, Rachel Carson (1907–1964) taught at the University of Maryland and worked for the federal government's Bureau of Fisheries. In 1951, she published The Sea Around Us, *for which she won the National Book Award and from which "The Grey Beginnings" is taken. She is probably best remembered for* Silent Spring (1962), *a landmark work about the destructive effects of pesticides on the environment. Carson is one of those rare people in whom eloquent mastery of the language joins with scientific acumen to produce writing that is at once informative and moving.*

And the earth was without form, and void; and darkness was upon the face of the deep.

Genesis

Beginnings are apt to be shadowy, and so it is with the beginnings of that great mother of life the sea. Many people have debated how and when the earth got its ocean, and it is not surprising that their explanations do not always agree. For the plain and inescapable truth is that no one was there to see, and in the absence of eyewitness accounts there is bound to be a certain amount of disagreement. So if I tell here the story of how the young planet Earth acquired an ocean, it must be a story pieced together from many sources and containing whole chapters the details of which we can only imagine. The story is founded on the testimony of the earth's most ancient rocks, which were young when the earth was young; on other evidence written on the face of the earth's satellite, the moon; and on hints contained in the history of the sun and the whole universe of star-filled space. For although no man was there to witness this cosmic birth, the stars and the moon and the rocks were there, and, indeed, had much to do with the fact that there is an ocean. 1

The events of which I write must have occurred somewhat more than 2 billion years ago. As nearly as science can tell that is the approximate age of the earth, and the ocean must be very nearly as old. It is possible now to discover the age of the rocks that compose the crust of the earth by measuring the rate of decay of the radioactive materials they contain. The oldest rocks found anywhere on earth—in Manitoba—are about 2.3 billion years old. Allowing 100 million years or so for the cooling of the earth's materials to form a rocky crust, we arrive at the supposition that the tempestuous and violent events connected with our planet's birth occurred nearly 2½ billion years ago. But this is only a minimum estimate, for rocks indicating an even greater age may be found at any time. 2

The new earth, freshly torn from its parent sun, was a ball of whirling 3 gases, intensely hot, rushing through the black spaces of the universe on a path and at a speed controlled by immense forces. Gradually the ball of flaming gases cooled. The gases began to liquefy, and Earth became a molten mass. The materials of this mass eventually became sorted out in a definite pattern: the heaviest in the center, the less heavy surrounding them, and the least heavy forming the outer rim. This is the pattern which persists today—a central sphere of molten iron, very nearly as hot as it was 2 billion years ago, an intermediate sphere of semiplastic basalt, and a hard outer shell, relatively quite thin and composed of solid basalt and granite.

The outer shell of the young earth must have been a good many millions   4
of years changing from the liquid to the solid state, and it is believed that, before this change was completed, an event of the greatest importance took place—the formation of the moon. The next time you stand on a beach at night, watching the moon's bright path across the water, and conscious of the moon-drawn tides, remember that the moon itself may have been born of a great tidal wave of earthly substance, torn off into space. And remember that if the moon was formed in this fashion, the event may have had much to do with shaping the ocean basins and the continents as we know them.

There were tides in the new earth, long before there was an ocean. In re-   5
sponse to the pull of the sun the molten liquids of the earth's whole surface rose in tides that rolled unhindered around the globe and only gradually slackened and diminished as the earthly shell cooled, congealed, and hardened. Those who believe that the moon is a child of earth say that during an early stage of the earth's development something happened that caused this rolling, viscid tide to gather speed and momentum and to rise to unimaginable heights. Apparently the force that created these greatest tides the earth has ever known was the force of resonance, for at this time the period of the solar tides had come to approach, then equal, the period of the free oscillation of the liquid earth. And so every sun tide was given increased momentum by the push of the earth's oscillation, and each of the twice-daily tides was larger than the one before it. Physicists have calculated that, after 500 years of such monstrous, steadily increasing tides, those on the side toward the sun became too high for stability, and a great wave was torn away and hurled into space. But immediately, of course, the newly created satellite became subject to physical laws that sent it spinning in an orbit of its own about the earth. This is what we call the moon.

There are reasons for believing that this event took place after the earth's   6
crust had become slightly hardened, instead of during its partly liquid state. There is to this day a great scar on the surface of the globe. This scar or depression holds the Pacific Ocean. According to some geophysicists, the floor of the Pacific is composed of basalt, the substance of the earth's middle layer, while all other oceans are floored with a thin layer of granite, which makes up most of the earth's outer layer. We immediately wonder what became of the Pacific's granite covering and the most convenient assumption is that it was torn away

when the moon was formed. There is supporting evidence. The mean density of the moon is much less than that of the earth (3.3 compared with 5.5), suggesting that the moon took away none of the earth's heavy iron core, but that it is composed only of the granite and some of the basalt of the outer layers.

The birth of the moon probably helped shape other regions of the world 7 ocean besides the Pacific. When part of the crust was torn away, strains must have been set up in the remaining granite envelope. Perhaps the granite mass cracked open on the side opposite the moon scar. Perhaps, as the earth spun on its axis and rushed on its orbit through space, the cracks widened and the masses of granite began to drift apart, moving over a tarry, slowly hardening layer of basalt. Gradually the outer portions of the basalt layer became solid and the wandering continents came to rest, frozen into place with oceans between them. In spite of theories to the contrary, the weight of geologic evidence seems to be that the locations of the major ocean basins and the major continental land masses are today much the same as they have been since a very early period of the earth's history.

But this is to anticipate the story, for when the moon was born there was 8 no ocean. The gradually cooling earth was enveloped in heavy layers of cloud, which contained much of the water of the new planet. For a long time its surface was so hot that no moisture could fall without immediately being reconverted to steam. This dense, perpetually renewed cloud covering must have been thick enough that no rays of sunlight could penetrate it. And so the rough outlines of the continents and the empty ocean basins were sculptured out of the surface of the earth in darkness, in a Stygian world of heated rock and swirling clouds and gloom.

As soon as the earth's crust cooled enough, the rains began to fall. Never 9 have there been such rains since that time. They fell continuously, day and night, days passing into months, into years, into centuries. They poured into the waiting ocean basins, or, falling upon the continental masses, drained away to become sea.

That primeval ocean, growing in bulk as the rains slowly filled its basins, 10 must have been only faintly salt. But the falling rains were the symbol of the dissolution of the continents. From the moment the rains began to fall, the lands began to be worn away and carried to the sea. It is an endless, inexorable process that has never stopped—the dissolving of the rocks, the leaching out of their contained minerals, the carrying of the rock fragments and dissolved minerals to the ocean. And over the eons of time, the sea has grown ever more bitter with the salt of the continents.

In what manner the sea produced the mysterious and wonderful stuff 11 called protoplasm we cannot say. In its warm, dimly lit waters the unknown conditions of temperature and pressure and saltiness must have been the critical ones for the creation of life from nonlife. At any rate they produced the result that neither the alchemists with their crucibles nor modern scientists in their laboratories have been able to achieve.

Before the first living cell was created, there may have been many trials 12
and failures. It seems probable that, within the warm saltiness of the primeval
sea, certain organic substances were fashioned from carbon dioxide, sulphur,
nitrogen, phosphorus, potassium, and calcium. Perhaps these were transition
steps from which the complex molecules of protoplasm arose—molecules that
somehow acquired the ability to reproduce themselves and begin the endless
stream of life. But at present no one is wise enough to be sure.

Those first living things may have been simple microorganisms rather 13
like some of the bacteria we know today—mysterious borderline forms that
were not quite plants, not quite animals, barely over the intangible line that sep-
arates the non-living from the living. It is doubtful that this first life possessed
the substance chlorophyll, with which plants in sunlight transform lifeless
chemicals into the living stuff of their tissues. Little sunshine could enter their
dim world, penetrating the cloud banks from which fell the endless rains. Probably the sea's first children lived on the organic substances then present in the
ocean waters, or, like the iron and sulphur bacteria that exist today, lived directly on inorganic food.

All the while the cloud cover was thinning, the darkness of the nights al- 14
ternated with palely illumined days, and finally the sun for the first time shone
through upon the sea. By this time some of the living things that floated in the
sea must have developed the magic of chlorophyll. Now they were able to take
the carbon dioxide of the air and the water of the sea and of these elements, in
sunlight, build the organic substances they needed. So the first true plants came
into being.

Another group of organisms, lacking the chlorophyll but needing organic 15
food, found they could make a way of life for themselves by devouring the
plants. So the first animals arose, and from that day to this, every animal in the
world has followed the habit it learned in the ancient seas and depends, directly
or through complex food chains, on the plants for food and life.

As the years passed, and the centuries, and the millions of years, the 16
stream of life grew more and more complex. From simple, one-celled creatures,
others that were aggregations of specialized cells arose, and then creatures with
organs for feeding, digesting, breathing, reproducing. Sponges grew on the
rocky bottom of the sea's edge and coral animals built their habitations in
warm, clear waters. Jellyfish swam and drifted in the sea. Worms evolved, and
starfish, and hard-shelled creatures with many-jointed legs, the arthropods. The
plants, too, progressed, from the microscopic algae to branched and curiously
fruiting seaweeds that swayed with the tides and were plucked from the coastal
rocks by the surf and cast adrift.

During all this time the continents had no life. There was little to induce 17
living things to come ashore, forsaking their all-providing, all-embracing
mother sea. The lands must have been bleak and hostile beyond the power of
words to describe. Imagine a whole continent of naked rock, across which no
covering mantle of green had been drawn—a continent without soil, for there

were no land plants to aid in its formation and bind it to the rocks with their roots. Imagine a land of stone, a silent land, except for the sound of the rains and winds that swept across it. For there was no living voice, and no living thing moved over the surface of the rocks.

Meanwhile, the gradual cooling of the planet, which had first given the   18 earth its hard granite crust, was progressing into its deeper layers; and as the interior slowly cooled and contracted, it drew away from the outer shell. This shell, accommodating itself to the shrinking sphere within it, fell into folds and wrinkles—the earth's first mountain ranges.

Geologists tell us that there must have been at least two periods of moun-   19 tain building (often called "revolutions") in that dim period, so long ago that the rocks have no record of it, so long ago that the mountains themselves have long since been worn away. Then there came a third great period of upheaval and readjustment of the earth's crust, about a billion years ago, but of all its majestic mountains the only reminders today are the Laurentian hills of eastern Canada, and a great shield of granite over the flat country around Hudson Bay.

The epochs of mountain building only served to speed up the processes of   20 erosion by which the continents were worn down and their crumbling rock and contained minerals returned to the sea. The uplifted masses of the mountains were prey to the bitter cold of the upper atmosphere and under the attacks of frost and snow and ice the rocks cracked and crumbled away. The rains beat with greater violence upon the slopes of the hills and carried away the sub-stance of the mountains in torrential streams. There was still no plant covering to modify and resist the power of the rains.

And in the sea, life continued to evolve. The earliest forms have left no   21 fossils by which we can identify them. Probably they were soft-bodied, with no hard parts that could be preserved. Then, too, the rock layers formed in those early days have since been so altered by enormous heat and pressure, under the foldings of the earth's crust, that any fossils they might have contained would have been destroyed.

For the past 500 million years, however, the rocks have preserved the fos-   22 sil record. By the dawn of the Cambrian period, when the history of living things was first inscribed on rock pages, life in the sea had progressed so far that all the main groups of backboneless or invertebrate animals had been de-veloped. But there were no animals with backbones, no insects or spiders, and still no plant or animal had been evolved that was capable of venturing on to the forbidding land. So for more than three-fourths of geologic time the conti-nents were desolate and uninhabited, while the sea prepared the life that was later to invade them and make them habitable. Meanwhile, with violent trem-blings of the earth and with the fire and smoke of roaring volcanoes, mountains rose and wore away, glaciers moved to and fro over the earth, and the sea crept over the continents and again receded.

It was not until Silurian time, some 350 million years ago, that the first   23 pioneer of land life crept out on the shore. It was an arthropod, one of the great tribe that later produced crabs and lobsters and insects. It must have been something like a modern scorpion, but, unlike some of its descendants, it never wholly severed the ties that united it to the sea. It lived a strange life, half-terrestrial, half-aquatic, something like that of the ghost crabs that speed along the beaches today, now and then dashing into the surf to moisten their gills.

Fish, tapered of body and stream-molded by the press of running waters, 24 were evolving in Silurian rivers. In times of drought, in the drying pools and lagoons, the shortage of oxygen forced them to develop swim bladders for the storage of air. One form that possessed an air-breathing lung was able to survive the dry period by burying itself in mud, leaving a passage to the surface through which it breathed.

It is very doubtful that the animals alone would have succeeded in colo- 25 nizing the land, for only the plants had the power to bring about the first amelioration of its harsh conditions. They helped make soil of the crumbling rocks, they held back the soil from the rains that would have swept it away, and little by little they softened and subdued the bare rock, the lifeless desert. We know very little about the first land plants, but they must have been closely related to some of the larger seaweeds that had learned to live in the coastal shallows, developing strengthened stems and grasping, rootlike holdfasts to resist the drag and pull of the waves. Perhaps it was in some coastal lowlands, periodically drained and flooded, that some such plants found it possible to survive, though separated from the sea. This also seems to have taken place in the Silurian period.

The mountains that had been thrown up by the Laurentian revolution 26 gradually wore away, and as the sediments were washed from their summits and deposited on the lowlands, great areas of the continents sank under the load. The seas crept out of their basins and spread over the lands. Life fared well and was exceedingly abundant in those shallow, sunlit seas. But with the later retreat of the ocean water into the deeper basins, many creatures must have been left stranded in shallow, landlocked bays. Some of these animals found means to survive on land. The lakes, the shores of the rivers, and the coastal swamps of those days were the testing grounds in which plants and animals either became adapted to the new conditions or perished.

As the lands rose and the seas receded, a strange fishlike creature 27 emerged on the land, and over the thousands of years its fins became legs, and instead of gills it developed lungs. In the Devonian sandstone this first amphibian left its footprint.

On land and sea the stream of life poured on. New forms evolved; some 28 old ones declined and disappeared. On land the mosses and the ferns and the seed plants developed. The reptiles for a time dominated the earth, gigantic, grotesque, and terrifying. Birds learned to live and move in the ocean of air. The first small mammals lurked inconspicuously in hidden crannies of the earth as though in fear of the reptiles.

When they went ashore the animals that took up a land life carried with 29 them part of the sea in their bodies, a heritage which they passed on to their children and which even today links each land animal with its origin in the ancient sea. Fish, amphibian, and reptile, warm-blooded bird and mammal—each of us carries in our veins a salty stream in which the elements sodium, potassium, and calcium are combined in almost the same proportions as in sea water. This is our inheritance from the day untold millions of years ago, when a remote ancestor, having progressed from the one-celled to the many-celled stage, first developed a circulatory system in which the fluid was merely the water of the sea. In the same way, our lime-hardened skeletons are a heritage from the calcium-rich ocean of Cambrian time. Even the protoplasm that streams within each cell of our bodies has the chemical structure impressed upon all living matter when the first simple creatures were brought forth in the ancient sea. And as life itself began in the sea, so each of us begins his individual life in a miniature ocean within his mother's womb, and in the stages of his embryonic development repeats the steps by which his race evolved, from gill-breathing inhabitants of a water world to creatures able to live on land.

Some of the land animals later returned to the ocean. After perhaps 50 **30** million years of land life, a number of reptiles entered the sea about 170 million years ago, in the Triassic period. They were huge and formidable creatures. Some had oarlike limbs by which they rowed through the water; some were web-footed, with long, serpentine necks. These grotesque monsters disappeared millions of years ago, but we remember them when we come upon a large sea turtle swimming many miles at sea, its barnacle-encrusted shell eloquent of its marine life. Much later, perhaps no more than 50 million years ago, some of the mammals, too, abandoned a land life for the ocean. Their descendants are the sea lions, seals, sea elephants, and whales of today.

Among the land mammals there was a race of creatures that took to an **31** arboreal existence. Their hands underwent remarkable development, becoming skilled in manipulating and examining objects, and along with this skill came a superior brain power that compensated for what these comparatively small mammals lacked in strength. At last, perhaps somewhere in the vast interior of Asia, they descended from the trees and became again terrestrial. The past million years have seen their transformation into beings with the body and brain of man.

Eventually man, too, found his way back to the sea. Standing on its **32** shores, he must have looked out upon it with wonder and curiosity, compounded with an unconscious recognition of his lineage. He could not physically re-enter the ocean as the seals and whales had done. But over the centuries, with all the skill and ingenuity and reasoning powers of his mind, he has sought to explore and investigate even its most remote parts, so that he might re-enter it mentally and imaginatively.

He built boats to venture out on its surface. Later he found ways to de- **33** scend to the shallow parts of its floor, carrying with him the air that, as a land mammal long unaccustomed to aquatic life, he needed to breathe. Moving in fascination over the deep sea he could not enter, he found ways to probe its depths, he let down nets to capture its life, he invented mechanical eyes and ears that could re-create for his senses a world long lost, but a world that, in the deepest part of his subconscious mind, he had never wholly forgotten.

And yet he has returned to his mother sea only on her own terms. He **34** cannot control or change the ocean as, in his brief tenancy of earth, he has subdued and plundered the continents. In the artificial world of his cities and towns, he often forgets the true nature of his planet and the long vistas of its history, in which the existence of the race of men has occupied a mere moment of time. The sense of all these things comes to him most clearly in the course of a long ocean voyage, when he watches day after day the receding rim of the horizon, ridged and furrowed by waves; when at night he becomes aware of the earth's rotation as the stars pass overhead; or when, alone in this world of water and sky, he feels the loneliness of his earth in space. And then, as never on land, he knows the truth that his world is a water world, a planet dominated by its covering mantle of ocean, in which the continents are but transient intrusions of land above the surface of the all-encircling sea.

1950

QUESTIONS FOR DISCUSSION

Content

a. Carson traces the birth of the oceans and the beginnings of life in chronological (narrative) order. Summarize, in outline form, what you believe to be the major events in the formation of our earth as revealed in this selection.

b. What role does description play in this essay? Overall, are the descriptive details Carson uses as specific as those in Petrunkevitch's essay? If not, what accounts for this difference?

c. In paragraphs 1 and 2, the author explains how it is possible to draw conclusions about the origins of the earth. Why does she bother to do so? Does she refer to scientific studies and authorities in other parts of the essay?

d. How does Carson account for the formation of the moon, and how does she support the validity of this theory? Why is it important that she offer such proof?

e. In paragraph 22, Carson pauses briefly to define the term "Cambrian." What does this tell you about the audience for whom she is writing? Where else in the essay does the author define technical language?

f. According to Carson, what exactly is our inheritance from the oceans? In what ways has humankind attempted to "re-enter" the sea?

Strategy and Style

g. Why is it appropriate for Carson to introduce her essay with a quote from Genesis?

h. The author uses numerous transitional phrases (connective devices) to indicate the passage of time in this process analysis. Identify a few of them.

i. Carson obviously believes it is important to mention the names of various periods in geological history. How does her doing so help her organize her material? Does it increase the essay's credibility?

j. For the most part, Carson's tone is detached, and her approach to the material is factual and straightforward. At times, however, she reveals her excitement and wonder over the material. For example, in paragraph 8, she describes the earth as "a Stygian world of heated rock and swirling clouds and gloom." What does this metaphor help her convey? In what other passages does her tone reveal an attitude unlike the detachment we have come to associate with scientific writing?

SUGGESTIONS FOR SHORT WRITING

a. Read "'But a Watch in the Night'" in Chapter 9, or at least the last three paragraphs, and compare/contrast the way the two authors treat humankind.

b. Think of a body of water that you know well and describe it as it undergoes a particular change, such as a seasonal change, a change by pollution, or a change in your experience of it from one time of your life to another.

SUGGESTIONS FOR SUSTAINED WRITING

a. Explain a natural process you know well by narrating each of its steps in chronological order. Be complete and accurate, but don't be afraid to use colorful language if you believe doing so will make an emotional impact on your reader and, in that way, increase the effectiveness of your writing. Processes to explain might include the origin of rain clouds; the way bees pollinate flowers; the formation of fossils; the development of oil or natural gas deposits; or the process of digestion or respiration in the human body. If necessary, use your library to gather information, but be sure to explain the process in your own words and to provide appropriate documentation for material taken from texts, journal articles, encyclopedias, etc.

b. Carson refers to the sea as the mother of life on earth. In what ways does the sea still provide for us? Write an essay in which you describe what it is about the sea that we find so enticing. Don't be afraid to include things like the thrill of diving into the pounding surf on a hot July afternoon, the exquisite taste of a broiled lobster dripping with butter, or the tranquillity of a summer sunset at the beach.

How to Cook a Carp

Euell Gibbons

Euell Gibbons (1911-1975) was born and raised in Clarkesville, Texas, but left home when he was fifteen. He worked in Texas and New Mexico as a harvest hand, a cowboy, a carpenter, and a trapper before he joined the army in 1934. After his discharge in 1936, he moved to Washington where he continued working odd jobs. He joined the Communist party but resigned when the Soviet Union attacked Finland in 1939. During World War II, he worked for the U.S. Navy as a civilian boat-builder. After the war, he moved to Hawaii and turned beachcomber, living in a thatched hut for two years and subsisting entirely on wild food. He entered the University of Hawaii as a freshman at the age of 36. Shortly thereafter, he began a career of teaching, writing, and lecturing about wild foods. His books on foraging combine detailed "how-to" instructions and recipes with delightfully entertaining narrative. Among his best-known works are Stalking the Wild Asparagus *(1962), from which "How to Cook a Carp" is taken;* Stalking the Blue-Eyed Scallop *(1964);* Stalking the Healthful Herbs *(1966); and* Euell Gibbons' Beachcomber's Handbook *(1967).*

1   When I was a lad of about eighteen, my brother and I were working on a cattle ranch in New Mexico that bordered on the Rio Grande. Most Americans think of the Rio Grande as a warm southern stream, but it rises among the high mountains of Colorado, and in the spring it is fed by melting snows. At this time of the year, the water that rushed by the ranch was turbulent, icy-cold and so silt-laden as to be semisolid. "A little too thick to drink, and a little too thin to plow" was a common description of the waters of the Rio Grande.

2   A few species of fish inhabited this muddy water. Unfortunately, the most common was great eight- to ten-pound carp, a fish that is considered very poor eating in this country, although the Germans and Asiatics have domesticated this fish, and have developed some varieties that are highly esteemed for the table.

3   On the ranch where we worked, there was a drainage ditch that ran through the lower pasture and emptied its clear waters into the muddy Rio Grande. The carp swimming up the river would strike this clear warmer water and decide they preferred it to the cold mud they had been inhabiting. One spring day, a cowhand who had been riding that way reported that Clear Ditch was becoming crowded with huge carp.

4   On Sunday we decided to go fishing. Four of us armed ourselves with pitchforks, saddled our horses and set out. Near the mouth of the ditch, the water was running about two feet deep and twelve to sixteen feet wide. There is a saying in that part of the country that you can't get a cowboy to do anything unless it can be done from the back of a horse, so we forced our mounts into the ditch and started wading them upstream, four abreast, herding the carp before us.

130

By the time we had ridden a mile upstream, the water was less than a foot $\quad$ 5
deep and so crystal clear that we could see our herd of several hundred carp
still fleeing from the splashing, wading horses. As the water continued to shallow, our fish began to get panicky. A few of the boldest ones attempted to dart
back past us and were impaled on pitchforks. We could see that the whole herd
was getting restless and was about to stampede back downstream, so we piled
off our horses into the shallow water to meet the charge. The water boiled
about us as the huge fish swirled past us and we speared madly in every direction with our pitchforks, throwing each fish we managed to hit over the ditch
bank. This was real fishing—cowhand style. The last of the fish herd was by us
in a few minutes and it was all over, but we had caught a tremendous quantity
of fish.

Back at the ranch house, after we had displayed our trophies, we began $\quad$ 6
wondering what we were going to do with so many fish. This started a series of
typical cowboy tall tales on "how to cook a carp." The best of these yarns was
told by a grizzled old *vaquero,* who claimed he had made his great discovery
when he ran out of food while camping on a tributary of the Rio Grande. He
said that he had found the finest way to cook a carp was to plaster the whole
fish with a thick coating of fresh cow manure and bury it in the hot ashes of a
campfire. In an hour or two, he said, the casing of cow manure had become
black and very hard. He then related how he had removed the fish from the fire,
broken the hard shell with the butt of his Winchester and peeled it off. He said
that as the manure came off the scales and skin adhered to it, leaving the baked
fish, white and clean. He then ended by saying, "Of course, the carp still wasn't
fit to eat, but manure in which it was cooked tasted pretty good."

There were also some serious suggestions and experiments. The chief ob- $\quad$ 7
jection to the carp is that its flesh is full of many forked bones. One man said that
he had enjoyed carp sliced very thin and fried so crisp that one could eat it, bones
and all. He demonstrated, and you really could eat it without the bones bothering
you, but it was still far from being an epicurean dish. One cowboy described the
flavor as "a perfect blend of Rio Grande mud and rancid hog lard."

Another man said that he had eaten carp that had been cooked in a pres- $\quad$ 8
sure cooker until the bones softened and became indistinguishable from the
flesh. A pressure cooker is almost a necessity at that altitude, so we had one at
the ranch house. We tried this method, and the result was barely edible. It
tasted like the poorest possible grade of canned salmon flavored with a bit of
mud. It was, however, highly appreciated by the dogs and cats on the ranch,
and solved the problem of what to do with the bulk of the fish we had caught.

It was my brother who finally devised a method of cooking carp that not $\quad$ 9
only made it fit for human consumption, but actually delicious. First, instead of
merely scaling the fish, he skinned them. Then, taking a large pinch, where the
meat was thickest, he worked his fingers and thumb into the flesh until he
struck the median bones, then he worked his thumb and fingers together and
tore off a handful of meat. Using this tearing method, he could get two or three

goodsized chunks of flesh from each side of the fish. He then heated a pot of bland vegetable shortening, rubbed the pieces of fish with salt and dropped them into the hot fat. He used no flour, meal, crumbs or seasoning other than salt. They cooked to a golden brown in a few minutes, and everyone pronounced them "mighty fine eating." The muddy flavor seemed to have been eliminated by removing the skin and the large bones. The forked bones were still there, but they had not been multiplied by cutting across them, and one only had to remove several bones still intact with the fork from each piece of fish.

For the remainder of that spring, every few days one or another of the cowboys would take a pitchfork and ride over to Clear Ditch and spear a mess of carp. On these evenings, my brother replaced the regular *cocinero* and we enjoyed some delicious fried carp. 10

The flavor of carp varies with the water from which it is caught. Many years after the above incidents I attended a fish fry at my brother's house. The main course was all of his own catching, and consisted of bass, catfish and carp, all from Elephant Butte Lake farther down the Rio Grande. All the fish were prepared exactly alike, except that the carp was pulled apart as described above, while the bass and catfish, being all twelve inches or less in length, were merely cleaned and fried whole. None of his guests knew one fish from another, yet all of them preferred the carp to the other kinds. These experiences have convinced me that the carp is really a fine food fish when properly prepared. 11

Carp can, of course, be caught in many ways besides spearing them with pitchforks from the back of a horse. In my adopted home state, Pennsylvania, they are classed as "trash fish" and one is allowed to take them almost any way. They will sometimes bite on worms, but they are vegetarians by preference and are more easily taken on dough balls. Some states allow the use of gill nets, and other states, because they would like to reduce the population of this unpopular fish, will issue special permits for the use of nets to catch carp. 12

A good forager will take advantage of the lax regulations on carp fishing while they last. When all fishermen realize that the carp is really a good food fish when prepared in the right way, maybe this outsized denizen of our rivers and lakes will no longer be considered a pest and will take his rightful place among our valued food and game fishes. 13

1962

QUESTIONS FOR DISCUSSION

Content

a. What do you think is Gibbons' goal in writing this essay? How successful is he in reaching this goal?

b. How would you describe Gibbons' ideal reader? If you were that reader, of what use would this essay be to you?

c. Is there an argument implied in this essay? If so, how would you phrase the argument? What would the counterargument be?

d. Carp is common throughout North America. Besides the obvious reason that the essay is based on personal experience, why would Gibbons set his narrative in the ranch country along the Rio Grande and not in another locale? How would the essay be different if, for example, it were set in Gibbons' "adopted home state, Pennsylvania"?

Strategy and Style

e. Though Gibbons titles his essay "How to Cook a Carp," he doesn't actually describe that process until paragraph 9. What does he do first, and what are his reasons for providing this long introduction?

f. Gibbons was an expert on foraging for and cooking wild plants and game, and this essay appears in one of his popular books about foraging. Why, then, does he describe so many failed attempts at cooking carp? Do these accounts add to or detract from his authority as an expert?

g. How do anecdotes such as the account of catching carp with pitchforks or the tale of the "old *vaquero*" (paragraphs 5 and 6) affect the essay? What purpose do they serve other than entertaining the reader?

h. What metaphors does Gibbons use to describe carp and the process of catching them? What effect do these metaphors have on the essay? On you?

SUGGESTIONS FOR SHORT WRITING

a. Have some fun and write a recipe for an inedible, or seemingly inedible, product. Include directions on how to capture or collect it, how to prepare it, and how to serve it.

b. Write an anecdote of a time when you tried an unusual food.

SUGGESTIONS FOR SUSTAINED WRITING

a. Write a narrative essay that explains how you accomplished a common but important task. Limit your essay to a simple process that can be explained fully in three or four typewritten pages. For example, explain how you hang wallpaper, cook a Thanksgiving turkey, load software into a home computer, do laundry, set up an aquarium, change the oil in a car, or plant a vegetable patch. Put your comments in the form of a letter to a friend or classmate who has asked for instructions about a process you know well. Assume that your reader knows little about the process.

b. Recall (or create) a personal experience in which you learned by trial and error how to do something well. Write an account of this series of processes.

c. Write an essay in which you convince your readers to change their minds about some process they now consider uninteresting, difficult, or unimportant. Make them see that washing the dog, studying for final exams, or going on a special diet, for instance, might be fun, easy, or beneficial if they only understood the process as well as you do. Choose a limited topic, one that can be covered in three or four typewritten pages. Include an account of the process.

d. Conduct interviews and collect anecdotes and tall tales that relate a process. Include them in an essay in which you explain, record, or satirize the process.

Behind the Formaldehyde Curtain
Jessica Mitford

Born in Great Britain to parents who were members of the nobility, Jessica Mitford (b. 1917) immigrated to the United States in 1939. In 1960, she published the first volume of her autobiography, Daughters and Rebels, *in which she described what it is like to grow up in an aristocratic English household and to receive one's education at home. The title of this book was to prove prophetic, for much of Mitford's later work is social criticism. For instance,* The American Way of Death *(1963), from which this selection is taken, is an indictment of morticians and their profession as well as of American funeral customs in general. In* Kind and Usual Punishment: The Prison Business *(1973), Mitford exposes the scandal of our corrections system. In 1977, she published the second part of her autobiography,* A Fine Old Madness. *Since then, she has published* Faces of Philip: A Memoir of Philip Toynbee *(1984) and* Grace Had an English Heart: The Story of Grace Darling *(1988).*

1   The drama begins to unfold with the arrival of the corpse at the mortuary.

2   Alas, poor Yorick! How surprised he would be to see how his counterpart of today is whisked off to a funeral parlor and is in short order sprayed, sliced, pierced, pickled, trussed, trimmed, creamed, waxed, painted, rouged and neatly dressed— transformed from a common corpse into a Beautiful Memory Picture. This process is known in the trade as embalming and restorative art, and is so universally employed in the United States and Canada that the funeral director does it routinely, without consulting corpse or kin. He regards as eccentric those few who are hardy enough to suggest that it might be dispensed with. Yet no law requires embalming, no religious doctrine commends it, nor is it dictated by considerations of health, sanitation, or even of personal daintiness. In no part of the world but in Northern America is it widely used. The purpose of embalming is to make the corpse presentable for viewing in a suitably costly container; and here too the funeral director routinely, without first consulting the family, prepares the body for public display.

3   Is all this legal? The processes to which a dead body may be subjected are after all to some extent circumscribed by law. In most states, for instance, the signature of next of kin must be obtained before an autopsy may be performed, before the deceased may be cremated, before the body may be turned over to a medical school for research purposes; or such provision must be made in the decedent's will. In the case of embalming, no such permission is required nor is it ever sought. A textbook, *The Principles and Practices of Embalming*, comments on this: "There is some question regarding the legality of much that is done within the preparation room." The author points out that it would be most unusual for a responsible member of a bereaved family to instruct the mortician, in so many words, to *"embalm"* the body of a deceased relative. The

135

very term "embalming" is so seldom used that the mortician must rely upon custom in the matter. The author concludes that unless the family specifies otherwise, the act of entrusting the body to the care of a funeral establishment carries with it an implied permission to go ahead and embalm.

Embalming is indeed a most extraordinary procedure, and one must wonder at the docility of Americans who each year pay hundreds of millions of dollars for its perpetuation, blissfully ignorant of what it is all about, what is done, how it is done. Not one in ten thousand has any idea of what actually takes place. Books on the subject are extremely hard to come by. They are not to be found in most libraries or bookshops.   4

In an era when huge television audiences watch surgical operations in the comfort of their living rooms, when, thanks to the animated cartoon, the geography of the digestive system has become familiar territory even to the nursery school set, in a land where the satisfaction of curiosity about almost all matters is a national pastime, the secrecy surrounding embalming can, surely, hardly be attributed to the inherent gruesomeness of the subject. Custom in this regard has within this century suffered a complete reversal. In the early days of American embalming, when it was performed in the home of the deceased, it was almost mandatory for some relative to stay by the embalmer's side and witness the procedure. Today, family members who might wish to be in attendance would certainly be dissuaded by the funeral director. All others, except apprentices, are excluded by law from the preparation room.   5

A close look at what does actually take place may explain in large measure the undertaker's intractable reticence concerning a procedure that has become his major *raison d'être*. It is possible he fears that public information about embalming might lead patrons to wonder if they really want this service? If the funeral men are loath to discuss the subject outside the trade, the reader may, understandably, be equally loath to go on reading at this point. For those who have the stomach for it, let us part the formaldehyde curtain....   6

The body is first laid out in the undertaker's morgue—or rather, Mr. Jones is reposing in the preparation room—to be readied to bid the world farewell.   7

The preparation room in any of the better funeral establishments has the tiled and sterile look of a surgery, and indeed the embalmer-restorative artist who does his chores there is beginning to adopt the term "dermasurgeon" (appropriately corrupted by some mortician-writers as "demi-surgeon") to describe his calling. His equipment, consisting of scalpels, scissors, augers, forceps, clamps, needles, pumps, tubes, bowls and basins, is crudely imitative of the surgeon's, as is his technique, acquired in a nine- or twelve-month post-high-school course in an embalming school. He is supplied by an advanced chemical industry with a bewildering array of fluids, sprays, pastes, oils, powders, creams, to fix or soften tissue, shrink or distend it as needed, dry it here, restore the moisture there. There are cosmetics, waxes and paints to fill and cover features, even plaster of Paris to replace entire limbs. There are ingenious aids to   8 prop and stabilize the cadaver: a Vari-Pose Head Rest, the Edwards Arm and Hand Positioner, the Repose Block (to support the shoulders during the embalming), and the Throop Foot Positioner, which resembles an old-fashioned stocks.

Mr. John H. Eckels, president of the Eckels College of Mortuary Science, thus describes the first part of the embalming procedure: "In the hands of a skilled practitioner, this work may be done in a comparatively short time and without mutilating the body other than by slight incision—so slight that it scarcely would cause serious inconvenience if made upon a living person. It is necessary to remove the blood, and doing this not only helps in the disinfecting, but removes the principal cause of disfigurements due to discoloration."   9

Another textbook discusses the all-important time element: "The earlier this is done, the better, for every hour that elapses between death and embalming will add to the problems and complications encountered...." Just how soon should one get going on the embalming? The author tells us, "On the basis of such scanty information made available to this profession through its rudimentary and haphazard system of technical research, we must conclude that the best results are to be obtained if the subject is embalmed before life is completely extinct—that is, before cellular death has occurred. In the average case, this would mean within an hour after somatic death." For those who feel that there is something a little rudimentary, not to say haphazard, about this advice, a comforting thought is offered by another writer. Speaking of fears entertained in early days of premature burial, he points out, "One of the effects of embalming by chemical injection, however, has been to dispel fears of live burial." How true; once the blood is removed, chances of live burial are indeed remote.   10

To return to Mr. Jones, the blood is drained out through the veins and replaced by embalming fluid pumped in through the arteries. As noted in *The Principles and Practices of Embalming,* "every operator has a favorite injection and drainage point—a fact which becomes a handicap only if he fails or refuses to forsake his favorites when conditions demand it." Typical favorites are the carotid artery, femoral artery, jugular vein, subclavian vein. There are various choices of embalming fluid. If Flextone is used, it will produce a "mild, flexible rigidity. The skin retains a velvety softness, the tissues are rubbery and pliable. Ideal for women and children." It may be blended with B. and G. Products Company's Lyf-Lyk tint, which is guaranteed to reproduce "nature's own skin texture...the velvety appearance of living tissue." Suntone comes in three separate tints: Suntan; Special Cosmetic Tint, a pink shade "especially indicated for female subjects"; and Regular Cosmetic Tint, moderately pink.   11

About three to six gallons of a dyed and perfumed solution of formaldehyde, glycerin, borax, phenol, alcohol and water is soon circulating through Mr. Jones, whose mouth has been sewn together with a "needle directed upward between the upper lip and gum and brought out through the left nostril," with the corners raised slightly "for a more pleasant expression." If he should be bucktoothed, his teeth are cleaned with Bon Ami and coated with colorless nail pol-   12 ish. His eyes, meanwhile, are closed with flesh-tinted eye caps and eye cement.

The next step is to have at Mr. Jones with a thing called a trocar. This is 13 a long, hollow needle attached to a tube. It is jabbed into the abdomen, poked around the entrails and chest cavity, the contents of which are pumped out and replaced with "cavity fluid." This done, and the hole in the abdomen sewn up, Mr. Jones's face is heavily creamed (to protect the skin from burns which may be caused by leakage of the chemicals), and he is covered with a sheet and left unmolested for a while. But not for long—there is more, much more, in store for him. He has been embalmed, but not yet restored, and the best time to start the restorative work is eight to ten hours after embalming, when the tissues have become firm and dry.

The object of all this attention to the corpse, it must be remembered, is to 14 make it presentable for viewing in an attitude of healthy repose. "Our customs require the presentation of our dead in the semblance of normality…unmarred by the ravages of illness, disease or mutilation," says Mr. J. Sheridan Mayer in his *Restorative Art*. This is rather a large order since few people die in the full bloom of health, unravaged by illness and unmarked by some disfigurement. The funeral industry is equal to the challenge: "In some cases the gruesome appearance of a mutilated or disease-ridden subject may be quite discouraging. The task of restoration may seem impossible and shake the confidence of the embalmer. This is the time for intestinal fortitude and determination. Once the formative work is begun and affected tissues are cleaned or removed, all doubts of success vanish. It is surprising and gratifying to discover the results which may be obtained."

The embalmer, having allowed an appropriate interval to elapse, returns 15 to the attack, but now he brings into play the skill and equipment of sculptor and cosmetician. Is a hand missing? Casting one in plaster of Paris is a simple matter. "For replacement purposes, only a cast of the back of the hand is necessary; this is within the ability of the average operator and is quite adequate." If a lip or two, a nose or an ear should be missing, the embalmer has at hand a variety of restorative waxes with which to model replacements. Pores and skin texture are simulated by stippling with a little brush, and over this cosmetics are laid on. Head off? Decapitation cases are rather routinely handled. Ragged edges are trimmed, and head joined to torso with a series of splints, wires and sutures. It is a good idea to have a little something at the neck—a scarf or a high collar—when time for viewing comes. Swollen mouth? Cut out tissue as needed from inside the lips. If too much is removed, the surface contour can easily be restored by padding with cotton. Swollen necks and cheeks are reduced by removing tissue through vertical incisions made down each side of the neck. "When the deceased is casketed, the pillow will hide the suture incisions…as an extra precaution against leakage, the suture may be painted with liquid sealer."

The opposite condition is more likely to present itself—that of emacia- 16 tion. His hypodermic syringe now loaded with massage cream, the embalmer seeks out and fills the hollowed and sunken areas by injection. In this procedure the backs of the hands and fingers and the under-chin area should not be neglected.

Positioning the lips is a problem that recurrently challenges the ingenuity   17 of the embalmer. Closed too tightly, they tend to give a stern, even disapproving expression. Ideally, embalmers feel, the lips should give the impression of being ever so slightly parted, the upper lip protruding slightly for a more youthful appearance. This takes some engineering, however, as the lips tend to drift apart. Lip drift can sometimes be remedied by pushing one or two straight pins through the inner margin of the lower lip and then inserting them between the two front upper teeth. If Mr. Jones happens to have no teeth, the pins can just as easily be anchored in his Armstrong Face Former and Denture Replacer. Another method to maintain lip closure is to dislocate the lower jaw, which is then held in its new position by a wire run through holes which have been drilled through the upper and lower jaws at the midline. As the French are fond of saying, *il faut souffrir pour être belle.*

If Mr. Jones has died of jaundice, the embalming fluid will very likely   18 turn him green. Does this deter the embalmer? Not if he has intestinal fortitude. Masking pastes and cosmetics are heavily laid on, burial garments and casket interiors are color- correlated with particular care, and Jones is displayed beneath rose-colored lights. Friends will say "How *well* he looks." Death by carbon monoxide, on the other hand, can be rather a good thing from the embalmer's viewpoint: "One advantage is the fact that this type of discoloration is an exaggerated form of a natural pink coloration." This is nice because the healthy glow is already present and needs but little attention.

The patching and filling completed, Mr. Jones is now shaved, washed and   19 dressed. Cream-based cosmetic, available in pink, flesh, suntan, brunette and blond, is applied to his hands and face, his hair is shampooed and combed (and, in the case of Mrs. Jones, set), his hands manicured. For the horny-handed son of toil special care must be taken; cream should be applied to remove ingrained grime, and the nails cleaned. "If he were not in the habit of having them manicured in life, trimming and shaping is advised for better appearance—never questioned by kin."

Jones is now ready for casketing (this is the present participle of the verb   20 "to casket"). In this operation his right shoulder should be depressed slightly "to turn the body a bit to the right and soften the appearance of lying flat on the back." Positioning the hands is a matter of importance, and special rubber positioning blocks may be used. The hands should be cupped slightly for a more lifelike, relaxed appearance. Proper placement of the body requires a delicate sense of balance. It should lie as high as possible in the casket, yet not so high that the lid, when lowered, will hit the nose. On the other hand, we are cautioned, placing the body too low "creates the impression that the body is in a box."

Jones is next wheeled into the appointed slumber room where a few last   21 touches may be added—his favorite pipe placed in his hand or, if he was a great reader, a book propped into position. (In the case of little Master Jones a Teddy bear may be clutched.) Here he will hold open house for a few days, visiting hours 10 A.M. to 9 P.M.

All now being in readiness, the funeral director calls a staff conference to make sure that each assistant knows his precise duties. Mr. Wilber Kriege writes: "This makes your staff feel that they are a part of the team, with a definite assignment that must be properly carried out if the whole plan is to succeed. You never heard of a football coach who failed to talk to his entire team before they go on the field. They have drilled on the plays they are to execute for hours and days, and yet the successful coach knows the importance of making even the bench-warming third-string substitute feel that he is important if the game is to be won." The winning of *this* game is predicated upon glass-smooth handling of the logistics. The funeral director has notified the pallbearers whose names were furnished by the family, has arranged for the presence of clergyman, organist, and soloist, has provided transportation for everybody, has organized and listed the flowers sent by friends. In *Psychology of Funeral Service* Mr. Edward A. Martin points out: "He may not always do as much as the family thinks he is doing, but it is his helpful guidance that they appreciate in knowing they are proceeding as they should.... The important thing is how well his services can be used to make the family believe they are giving unlimited expression to their own sentiment." 22

The religious service may be held in a church or in the chapel of the funeral home; the funeral director vastly prefers the latter arrangement, for not only is it more convenient for him but it affords him the opportunity to show off his beautiful facilities to the gathered mourners. After the clergyman has had his say, the mourners queue up to file past the casket for a last look at the deceased. The family is *never* asked whether they want an open- casket ceremony; in the absence of their instruction to the contrary, this is taken for granted. Consequently well over 90 percent of all American funerals feature the open casket—a custom unknown in other parts of the world. Foreigners are astonished by it. An English woman living in San Francisco described her reaction in a letter to the writer: 23

> I myself have attended only one funeral here—that of an elderly fellow worker of mine. After the service I could not understand why everyone was walking towards the coffin (sorry, I mean casket), but thought I had better follow the crowd. It shook me rigid to get there and find the casket open and poor old Oscar lying there in his brown tweed suit, wearing a suntan makeup and just the wrong shade of lipstick. If I had not been extremely fond of the old boy, I have a horrible feeling that I might have giggled. Then and there I decided that I could never face another American funeral—even dead.

The casket (which has been resting throughout the service on a Classic Beauty Ultra Metal Casket Bier) is now transferred by a hydraulically operated 24 device called Porto-Lift to a balloon-tired, Glide Easy casket carriage which will wheel it to yet another conveyance, the Cadillac Funeral Coach. This may be lavender, cream, light green—anything but black. Interiors, of course, are color-correlated, "for the man who cannot stop short of perfection."

At graveside, the casket is lowered into the earth. This office, once the   25 prerogative of friends of the deceased, is now performed by a patented mechanical lowering device. A "Lifetime Green" artificial grass mat is at the ready to conceal the sere earth, and overhead, to conceal the sky, is a portable Steril Chapel Tent ("resists the intense heat and humidity of summer and the terrific storms of winter…available in Silver Grey, Rose or Evergreen"). Now is the time for the ritual scattering of earth over the coffin, as the solemn words "earth to earth, ashes to ashes, dust to dust" are pronounced by the officiating cleric. This can today be accomplished "with a mere flick of the wrist with the Gordon Leak-Proof Earth Dispenser. No grasping of a handful of dirt, no soiled fingers. Simple, dignified, beautiful, reverent! The modern way!" The Gordon Earth Dispenser (at $5) is of nickel-plated brass construction. It is not only "attractive to the eye and long wearing"; it is also "one of the 'tools' for building better public relations" if presented as "an appropriate non-commercial gift" to the clergyman. It is shaped something like a saltshaker.

Untouched by human hand, the coffin and the earth are now united.   26

It is in the function of directing the participants through this maze of gad-   27 getry that the funeral director has assigned to himself his relatively new role of "grief therapist." He has relieved the family of every detail, he has revamped the corpse to look like a living doll, he has arranged for it to nap for a few days in a slumber room, he has put on a well-oiled performance in which the concept of *death* has played no part whatsoever—unless it was inconsiderately mentioned by the clergyman who conducted the religious service. He has done everything in his power to make the funeral a real pleasure for everybody concerned. He and his team have given their all to score an upset victory over death.

1963

QUESTIONS FOR DISCUSSION

Content

a. What is Mitford's purpose? Do you agree that "public information about embalming might lead patrons to wonder if they really want this service" (paragraph 6)?

b. In what ways does this selection resemble a narrative? What aspects are arranged in chronological order? How does Mitford indicate the passage of time?

c. According to Mitford, why is it odd that embalming remains so secretive a business? What can we infer about the reasons for the persistence of embalming as a widespread practice only in this part of the world?

d. Do you know of any important differences between funeral practices in "Northern America" and those in other parts of the world? Why does Mitford bother to allude to such differences early in this essay?

e. The beginning of paragraph 2 alludes to Shakespeare's *Hamlet*. Who was Yorick, and why has Mitford chosen to include him in her introduction?

f. Why does the author make it a point to mention the brand names of the supplies and equipment used by undertakers?

Strategy and Style

g. Mitford's use of detail seems to be accurate and thorough. Is it too thorough? Could she have achieved her purpose without being so detailed?

h. The author relies heavily on the use of quoted material from embalming textbooks to develop her indictment of morticians. Explain how these citations help her achieve her purpose.

i. In paragraph 6, before parting "the formaldehyde curtain," why does Mitford warn us about what is to follow?

j. What other interesting metaphors does Mitford use? Do they help enliven her prose?

k. What is ironic about her calling the embalming procedure the mortician's *raison d'etre?* Identify other examples of irony in this selection.

l. Look up the roots of the term "dermasurgeon" in a good dictionary. What do their meanings suggest? Now look up "demi"; what does the corruption "demi-surgeon" tell you about Mitford's view of undertakers? What does Mitford mean by "grief therapist" (paragraph 27)? Why does she say that funeral directors have "assigned" themselves this role?

m. How would you describe Mitford's tone? Analyze at least one paragraph closely (paragraph 13, 14, or 15 would be a good choice). How does her choice of language make her attitude about the subject clear?

n. When does irony turn to sarcasm? Reread paragraph 25. What makes Mitford's treatment of graveside ceremonies so caustic?

SUGGESTIONS FOR SHORT WRITING

a. Write a response entirely made up of exclamatory statements.

b. Address a response to Mitford. Tell her what you think of her essay, and why.

SUGGESTIONS FOR SUSTAINED WRITING

a. Do you agree with Mitford's assessment of the undertaker's profession? If not, write an essay in which you refute her by explaining the important role current funeral customs and practices play. Address your comments to Mitford directly, perhaps in the form of a letter.

b. Funeral customs differ from country to country and from culture to culture. Have you ever witnessed or read about funeral rites that are distinctive from those one might consider typically American? If so, write an essay in which you explain how such rites are carried out.

c. Do you believe our funeral customs should be changed? What aspect of the way in which we deal with our dead do you object to most? Write an essay in which you explain the basis for your objection and suggest alternatives to current practices.

d. Mitford focuses on only one method of laying the dead to rest; actually there are many alternatives. One is cremation; another is burial at sea. Explain the process involved in any funeral practice other than the one she discusses.

Introduction to *Frankenstein*
Mary Wollstonecraft Shelley

Mary Wollstonecraft Shelley (1797-1851) was the daughter of two literary celebrities, the philosopher William Godwin and the writer Mary Wollstonecraft. She had no formal schooling but was an avid reader of her father's extensive library and an eager listener to the conversations between her father and his friends. From 1812 to 1814, she lived in Scotland with family friends. After meeting the poet Percy Bysshe Shelley, she returned to London in March of 1814; in July of that year, even though Shelley was married, she eloped with him to France. It was not until December 30, 1816, three weeks after Shelley's first wife died, that they were married. The couple spent the summer of 1816 in Switzerland, where they were the neighbors of Lord Byron and where Mary Shelley thought of the idea for Frankenstein, *a process she relates in the book's introduction.* Frankenstein *was an immediate popular success both as a novel (1818) and as a dramatic production (1823). However, it was only in 1822, after her husband had died and she was faced with supporting herself and a son, that Mary Shelley began writing and publishing regularly. Her other books, including* Valperga *(1823),* The Last Man *(1826), and* The Fortunes of Perkin Warbeck *(1830), were well received, but* Frankenstein *remains her most powerful and popular work. From 1840 to 1843, she traveled in Europe with her son and daughter-in-law, publishing an account of her travels,* Rambles in Germany and Italy, *in 1844.*

1 The publishers of the standard novels, in selecting *Frankenstein* for one of their series, expressed a wish that I should furnish them with some account of the origin of the story. I am the more willing to comply because I shall thus give a general answer to the question so very frequently asked me—how I, then a young girl, came to think of and to dilate upon so very hideous an idea. It is true that I am very averse to bringing myself forward in print, but as my account will only appear as an appendage to a former production, and as it will be confined to such topics as have connection with my authorship alone, I can scarcely accuse myself of a personal intrusion.

2 It is not singular that, as the daughter of two persons of distinguished literary celebrity, I should very early in life have thought of writing. As a child I scribbled, and my favourite pastime during the hours given me for recreation was to "write stories." Still, I had a dearer pleasure than this, which was the formation of castles in the air—the indulging in waking dreams—the following up trains of thought, which had for their subject the formation of a succession of imaginary incidents. My dreams were at once more fantastic and agreeable than my writings. In the latter I was a close imitator—rather doing as others had done than putting down the suggestions of my own mind. What I wrote was intended at least for one other eye—my childhood's companion and friend; but my dreams were all my own; I accounted for them to nobody; they were my refuge when annoyed—my dearest pleasure when free.

I lived principally in the country as a girl and passed a considerable time ₃
in Scotland. I made occasional visits to the more picturesque parts, but my habitual residence was on the blank and dreary northern shores of the Tay, near
Dundee. Blank and dreary on retrospection I call them; they were not so to me
then. They were the aerie of freedom and the pleasant region where unheeded I
could commune with the creatures of my fancy. I wrote then, but in a most
commonplace style. It was beneath the trees of the grounds belonging to our
house, or on the bleak sides of the woodless mountains near, that my true com-
positions, the airy flights of my imagination, were born and fostered. I did not
make myself the heroine of my tales. Life appeared to me too commonplace an
affair as regarded myself. I could not figure to myself that romantic woes or
wonderful events would ever be my lot; but I was not confined to my own
identity, and I could people the hours with creations far more interesting to me
at that age than my own sensations.

After this my life became busier, and reality stood in place of fiction. My ₄
husband, however, was from the first very anxious that I should prove myself
worthy of my parentage and enrol myself on the page of fame. He was forever
inciting me to obtain literary reputation, which even on my own part I cared for
then, though since I have become infinitely indifferent to it. At this time he desired that I should write, not so much with the idea that I could produce anything worthy of notice, but that he might himself judge how far I possessed the
promise of better things hereafter. Still I did nothing. Travelling, and the cares
of a family, occupied my time; and study, in the way of reading or improving
my ideas in communication with his far more cultivated mind was all of literary
employment that engaged my attention.

In the summer of 1816 we visited Switzerland and became the neighbours ₅
of Lord Byron. At first we spent our pleasant hours on the lake or wandering on
its shores; and Lord Byron, who was writing the third canto of *Childe Harold,*
was the only one among us who put his thoughts upon paper. These, as he
brought them successively to us, clothed in all the light and harmony of poetry,
seemed to stamp as divine the glories of heaven and earth, whose influences we
partook with him.

But it proved a wet, ungenial summer, and incessant rain often confined ₆
us for days to the house. Some volumes of ghost stories translated from the
German into French fell into our hands. There was the *History of the Inconstant
Lover,* who, when he thought to clasp the bride to whom he had pledged his
vows, found himself in the arms of the pale ghost of her whom he had deserted.
There was the tale of the sinful founder of his race whose miserable doom it
was to bestow the kiss of death on all the younger sons of his fated house, just
when they reached the age of promise. His gigantic, shadowy form, clothed like
the ghost in *Hamlet,* in complete armour, but with the beaver up, was seen at
midnight, by the moon's fitful beams, to advance slowly along the gloomy avenue. The shape was lost beneath the shadow of the castle walls; but soon a
gate swung back, a step was heard, the door of the chamber opened, and he

advanced to the couch of the blooming youths, cradled in healthy sleep. Eternal sorrow sat upon his face as he bent down and kissed the forehead of the boys, who from that hour withered like flowers snapped upon the stalk. I have not seen these stories since then, but their incidents are as fresh in my mind as if I had read them yesterday.

"We will each write a ghost story," said Lord Byron, and his proposition **7** was acceded to. There were four of us. The noble author began a tale, a fragment of which he printed at the end of his poem of Mazeppa. Shelley, more apt to embody ideas and sentiments in the radiance of brilliant imagery and in the music of the most melodious verse that adorns our language than to invent the machinery of a story, commenced one founded on the experiences of his early life. Poor Polidori had some terrible idea about a skull-headed lady who was so punished for peeping through a key-hole—what to see I forget: something very shocking and wrong of course; but when she was reduced to a worse condition than the renowned Tom of Coventry, he did not know what to do with her and was obliged to dispatch her to the tomb of the Capulets, the only place for which she was fitted. The illustrious poets also, annoyed by the platitude of prose, speedily relinquished their uncongenial task.

I busied myself *to think of a story*—a story to rival those which had ex- **8** cited us to this task. One which would speak to the mysterious fears of our nature and awaken thrilling horror—one to make the reader dread to look round, to curdle the blood, and quicken the beatings of the heart. If I did not accomplish these things, my ghost story would be unworthy of its name. I thought and pondered—vainly. I felt that blank incapability of invention which is the greatest misery of authorship, when dull Nothing replies to our anxious invocations. "Have you thought of a story?" I was asked each morning, and each morning I was forced to reply with a mortifying negative.

Everything must have a beginning, to speak in Sanchean phrase; and that **9** beginning must be linked to something that went before. The Hindus give the world an elephant to support it, but they make the elephant stand upon a tortoise. Invention, it must be humbly admitted, does not consist in creating out of void, but out of chaos; the materials must, in the first place, be afforded: it can give form to dark, shapeless substances but cannot bring into being the substance itself. In all matters of discovery and invention, even of those that appertain to the imagination, we are continually reminded of the story of Columbus and his egg. Invention consists in the capacity of seizing on the capabilities of a subject and in the power of moulding and fashioning ideas suggested by it.

Many and long were the conversations between Lord Byron and Shelley **10** to which I was a devout but nearly silent listener. During one of these, various philosophical doctrines were discussed, and among others the nature of the principle of life, and whether there was any probability of its ever being discovered and communicated. They talked of the experiments of Dr. Darwin (I speak not of what the doctor really did or said that he did, but, as more to my purpose, of what was then spoken of as having been done by him), who preserved a piece of vermicelli in a glass case till by some extraordinary means it began to move with voluntary motion. Not thus, after all, would life be given. Perhaps a corpse would be reanimated; galvanism had given token of such things: perhaps the component parts of a creature might be manufactured, brought together, and endued with vital warmth.

Night waned upon this talk, and even the witching hour had gone by be- 11 fore we retired to rest. When I placed my head on my pillow I did not sleep, nor could I be said to think. My imagination, unbidden, possessed and guided me, gifting the successive images that arose in my mind with a vividness far beyond the usual bounds of reverie. I saw—with shut eyes, but acute mental vision—I saw the pale student of unhallowed arts kneeling beside the thing he had put together. I saw the hideous phantasm of a man stretched out, and then, on the working of some powerful engine, show signs of life and stir with an uneasy, half-vital motion. Frightful must it be, for supremely frightful would be the effect of any human endeavour to mock the stupendous mechanism of the Creator of the world. His success would terrify the artist; he would rush away from his odious handiwork, horror- stricken. He would hope that, left to itself, the slight spark of life which he had communicated would fade, that this thing which had received such imperfect animation would subside into dead matter, and he might sleep in the belief that the silence of the grave would quench forever the transient existence of the hideous corpse which he had looked upon as the cradle of life. He sleeps; but he is awakened; he opens his eyes; behold, the horrid thing stands at his bedside, opening his curtains and looking on him with yellow, watery, but speculative eyes.

I opened mine in terror. The idea so possessed my mind that a thrill of 12 fear ran through me, and I wished to exchange the ghastly image of my fancy for the realities around. I see them still: the very room, the dark parquet, the closed shutters with the moonlight struggling through, and the sense I had that the glassy lake and white high Alps were beyond. I could not so easily get rid of my hideous phantom; still it haunted me. I must try to think of something else. I recurred to my ghost story—my tiresome, unlucky ghost story! Oh! If I could only contrive one which would frighten my reader as I myself had been frightened that night!

Swift as light and as cheering was the idea that broke in upon me. "I have 13 found it! What terrified me will terrify others; and I need only describe the spectre which had haunted my midnight pillow." On the morrow I announced that I had *thought of a story.…*

1819

QUESTIONS FOR DISCUSSION

Content

a. What motivations does the author list for her desire to write, especially to write *Frankenstein*?

b. According to Shelley, in what ways did her childhood affect her later outlook on life? How important was environment on the development of her personality?

c. Why do you think Shelley was motivated to think of a story, even long after her three companions had given up? In what ways is she different from each of them?

d. Mark passages that mention landscape or weather. How did landscape and weather affect Shelley's life? How did they affect the origin and the story of *Frankenstein*?

e. Shelley writes in paragraph 9 that "invention...does not consist in creating out of void, but out of chaos...it can give form to dark, shapeless substances but cannot bring into being the substance itself." What does this statement tell us about Shelley's creation of the Frankenstein story? From your knowledge of *Frankenstein* (the novel or a film version) speculate on the "dark, shapeless substances" with which she built her creature.

f. Go to the library and look up "galvanism" (paragraph 10). What is it, and why was it such a fascinating topic to people in Shelley's time? In your opinion, why is it still fascinating to people today?

g. Read a brief biography of Mary Shelley (the biography above does not count). What discrepancies and/or correlations do you find between the biographer's account of Shelley's life, or the origins of *Frankenstein*, and Shelley's own account? How do you explain any discrepancies?

Strategy and Style

h. How does Shelley's choice of vocabulary enhance the supernatural tone of her introduction?

i. In your opinion, why has the story of Frankenstein remained so popular over the years? What aspects of the story have kept it popular?

j. To what extent does Shelley take responsibility for creating the story of *Frankenstein*? Which passages in the introduction reveal how she feels about her role in its creation and her status as an author?

SUGGESTIONS FOR SHORT WRITING

a. As best you can remember, recount the story of the first time you "encountered" Frankenstein the monster. How did you react? Do you think that

Frankenstein has the same impact on us today as it had on the people of Shelley's time?

b. Write the story of a nightmare, or a prophetic or recurring dream. To what extent does your dream relate to Shelley's reverie, or your telling of it relate to her telling?

SUGGESTIONS FOR SUSTAINED WRITING

a. Write an "introduction" to one of your previous essays or stories, reflecting on your process of writing that essay. You may wish to include past events of your life that have resulted in certain themes in your work.

b. Read Shelley's *Frankenstein* and compare it to or contrast it with other written or film versions of this tale. What significant changes were made in later versions? Do these changes detract from or add to the power of the original story? (A thorough list of film, book, and drama adaptations can be found in *Something About the Author*, vol. 29.)

c. What are the essential elements that make stories like *Frankenstein* so frightening? Try writing your own ghost, monster, or science fiction classic. Take your time to think of this tale. Think of a story that will affect your readers as much as it does you, and tell it by concentrating on the kinds of details that will make it powerful and evocative.

d. Write an analytical essay explaining why *Frankenstein* has been one of the most popular and well-known stories ever since it was written.

How to Write a Rotten Poem with Almost No Effort

Richard Howey

Richard Howey (b. 1945) he is a freelance journalist. He has written for the local pub-lic broadcasting station in Cleveland, Ohio, and he is frequently published in the Cleveland Plain Dealer. *"How to Write a Rotten Poem with Almost No Effort" is his thoroughly delightful explanation of a surefire way to produce poetic drivel. It first appeared in the* Plain Dealer *in 1978.*

1   So you want to write a poem. You've had a rotten day or an astounding thought or a car accident or a squalid love affair and you want to record it for all time. You want to organize those emotions that are pounding through your veins. You have something to communicate via a poem but you don't know where to start.

2   This, of course, is the problem with poetry. Most people find it difficult to write a poem so they don't even try. What's worse, they don't bother reading any poems either. Poetry has become an almost totally foreign art form to many of us. As a result, serious poets either starve or work as account executives. There is no middle ground. Good poets and poems are lost forever simply be-cause there is no market for them, no people who write their own verse and seek out further inspiration from other bards.

3   Fortunately, there is a solution for this problem, as there are for all im-ponderables. The answer is to make it easy for everyone to write at least one poem in his life. Once a person has written a poem, of whatever quality, he will feel comradeship with fellow poets and, hopefully, read their works. Ideally, there would evolve a veritable society of poet-citizens, which would elevate the quality of life worldwide. Not only that, good poets could make a living for a change.

4   So, to begin. Have your paper ready. You must first understand that the poem you write here will not be brilliant. It won't even be mediocre. But it will be better than 50% of all song lyrics and at least equal to one of Rod McKuen's best efforts. You will be instructed how to write a four-line poem but the basic structure can be repeated at will to create works of epic length.

5   The first line of your poem should start and end with these words: "In the _____of my mind." The middle word of this line is optional. Any word will do. It would be best not to use a word that has been overdone, such as "wind-mills" or "gardens" or "playground." Just think of as many nouns as you can and see what fits best. The rule of thumb is to pick a noun that seems totally out of context, such as "filing cabinet" or "radiator" or "parking lot." Just re-member, the more unusual the noun, the more profound the image.

150

The second line should use two or more of the human senses in a con- 6
flicting manner, as per the famous, "listen to the warm." This is a sure way to
conjure up "poetic" feeling and atmosphere. Since there are five different
senses, the possibilities are endless. A couple that come to mind are "see the
noise" and "touch the sound." If more complexity is desired other senses can be
added, as in "taste the color of my hearing," or "I cuddled your sight in the
aroma of the night." Rhyming, of course, is optional.

The third line should be just a simple statement. This is used to break up 7
the insightful images that have been presented in the first two lines. This line
should be as prosaic as possible to give a "down-to-earth" mood to the poem.
An example would be "she gave me juice and toast that morning," or perhaps
"I left for work next day on the 8:30 bus." The content of this line may or may
not relate to what has gone before.

The last line of your poem should deal with the future in some way. This 8
gives the poem a forward thrust that is always helpful. A possibility might be,
"tomorrow will be a better day," or "I'll find someone sometime," or "maybe
we'll meet again in July." This future-oriented ending lends an aura of hope
and yet need not be grossly optimistic.

By following the above structure, anyone can write a poem. For example, 9
if I select one each of my sample lines, I come up with:

> In the parking lot of my mind,
>> I cuddled your sight in the aroma of the night.
> I left for work next day on the 8:30 bus.
>> Maybe we'll meet again in July.

Now that poem (like yours, when you're finished) is rotten. But at least 10
it's a poem and you've written it, which is an accomplishment that relatively
few people can claim.

Now that you're a poet, feel free to read poetry by some of your more 11
accomplished brothers and sisters in verse. Chances are, you'll find their offerings stimulating and refreshing. You might even try writing some more of your
own poems, now that you've broken the ice. Observe others' emotions and experience your own—that's what poetry is all about.

Incidentally, if you find it impossible to sell the poem you write to Bobby 12
Goldsboro or John Denver, burn it. It will look terrible as the first page of your
anthology when it's published.

1978

QUESTIONS FOR DISCUSSION

Content

a. Has Howey written this essay simply to give us a good laugh, or is there a serious purpose behind all this humor? What is Howey's implied thesis?

b. Using illustrations is an effective way to develop a process paper. To what degree does Howey use examples in this selection? What do they help him accomplish?

c. What problem does the author articulate in paragraph 2, and how does that paragraph help him establish his purpose?

d. Is Howey serious when, in paragraph 3, he envisions—"ideally" at least— a "society of poet-citizens"? What is he suggesting in this curious statement?

e. What function do paragraphs 10 and 11 serve? How do they contribute to Howey's purpose?

f. What, according to Howey, are the characteristics of a rotten poem? What makes the sample poem in paragraph 9 so bad?

g. Who is Rod McKuen, and why does his name appear in this essay? What about Bobby Goldsboro and John Denver? If you need help finding information on these folks, consult your college librarians for source materials on popular culture.

Strategy and Style

h. In which ways is the introduction ironic? Is having a "rotten day" in and of itself a good reason to sit down and write poetry?

i. What other examples of irony can you identify in this essay?

j. How does Howey's four-line sample poem serve as the foundation or organizing principle for the essay? Why didn't Howey simply define "rotten poetry" rather than going to all the trouble of explaining how to write bad poetry?

k. Why does Howey use direct address in line 1? Is so familiar a tone appropriate to an introductory paragraph? Is it effective?

l. How does Howey's tone in paragraph 2 differ from the kind he uses in most of the rest of this essay?

SUGGESTIONS FOR SHORT WRITING

a. Using Howey's formula, write a rotten poem of your own.

b. Then, write the opening one or two paragraphs of a "review" of your poem, or of the rotten poem in Howey's essay.

SUGGESTIONS FOR SUSTAINED WRITING

a. Using this selection as a model, write your own essay explaining how to fail at something. For instance, describe how to write an "F" paper for freshman composition, how to bake the world's worst cake, how to throw a party that will surely flop, how to alienate a date.

b. Find a short poem that you suspect might be "rotten." One of the first places to look is between the covers of an expensive greeting card or in the lyrics of a popular song that you've heard on the car radio over and over. And, if your skin is thick enough, you might even find one in a love note you meant to send off to a high school sweetheart. Is the poem really rotten? Discuss the ways it is similar to or different from the kind of poetry Howey describes in this selection.

c. Quite obviously, Howey is complaining that not enough people read or appreciate good poetry these days. Do you agree? If so, try explaining to a friend (preferably someone who does not read poetry unless he/she has to) what reading poetry does for you and how it might "elevate the quality of [one's] life."

4

Definition

Generally speaking, definitions fall into three broad categories: lexical, stipulative, and extended. The dictionary is of course the best place to begin familiarizing yourself with new concepts, but lexical definitions tend to be abstract, for they sometimes explain terms without reference to particular contexts. And stipulative definitions, while practical, are by their very nature limited to special purposes. Say you were writing a paper on the advantages and disadvantages of being a part-time student. You might *stipulate* that, for the purposes of your essay, "a part-timer is someone enrolled for less than 12 credits." Thus, while both lexical and stipulative definitions have their uses, extended definitions are the type used most often to explain complex topics like those discussed in this chapter.

The many practical uses to which extended definition can be applied make it a powerful tool for exposition. In the hands of writers like Epstein, Sontag, and Harrison, it can provide a systematic way to grapple with difficult moral or intellectual questions. It can correct common, sometimes dangerous, misconceptions, as in Bruno Bettelheim's "The Holocaust" or Jo Goodwin Parker's "What Is Poverty?" It can introduce the complexities of new cultural phenomena like the one discussed in Tom Wolfe's "Pornoviolence." It can even serve as a vehicle for social commentary and a source of entertainment, as we see in Dorothy Parker's "Good Souls."

Like process essays, extended definitions can be developed by using a number of methods. Among the most common are analogy and comparison/contrast. Bettelheim is careful to draw the distinction between *victims* and *martyrs;* in comparing *pornography* to *pornoviolence,* Wolfe creates an analogy to violence and gambling; Epstein explains that "As drunks have done to alcohol, the single-minded have done to ambition—given it a bad name"; and Sontag both compares and contrasts notions of beauty in Catholic and Protestant countries.

Indeed, many techniques can be used to develop extended definitions.

154

The illustrations and anecdotal (narrative) evidence by which Jo Goodwin Parker demonstrates the meaning of poverty are powerful and incisive tools for correcting social myopia. Examples and anecdotes, though used for different purposes, also appear in Dorothy Parker's "Good Souls" and Wolfe's "Pornoviolence."

Approaches to the process of defining, then, are as varied as the authors who devise them. Sontag launches her discussion of beauty by tracing its etymology from the Greeks to the present. Wolfe delights us with fantastic headlines from the tabloids, and Harrison addresses the work of a fellow author to help her show that some issues are not amenable to "right-on slogans." Bettelheim, Epstein, Wolfe, and Sontag even make limited use of lexical information to introduce or clarify specific points in a larger context.

You can learn a great deal more about techniques for writing extended definitions by considering the Questions for Discussion—especially those on strategy and style—and by addressing the Suggestions for Writing that follow each of the selections in this chapter. Another good way to learn the skills of definition is to read each of the essays in this chapter twice. On your first pass, simply make sure you understand each selection thoroughly and accurately. The second time around, ask yourself how you might define the term being explained, whether you agree with the author's perception, or what other examples or evidence you might bring to bear to make the definition even more credible.

The method described above might require more time than you had planned to spend on this chapter, but it is the kind of mental exercise that will strengthen your analytical muscles and help you use definition as a powerful tool whenever you need to explain complex ideas.

The Holocaust
Bruno Bettelheim

*Born in Vienna, Bruno Bettelheim (1903–1990) was able to escape the Nazi terror and immigrate to the United States in 1939. A year before, however, shortly after having received his doctorate from the University of Vienna, he had been condemned to Dachau and Buchenwald, where he experienced the horrors of the concentration camps that he describes in this selection. His studies of children's literature and child psychol-*ogy, *including* Love Is Not Enough *(1950) and* The Uses of Enchantment *(1976), are world renowned. Among his other important works are* The Informed Heart *(1960) and* Surviving and Other Essays *(1979), which contains "The Holocaust." His most recent works are* Freud and Man's Soul *(1984);* The Third Reich of Dreams: The Nightmares of a Nation *(1985); and* A Good Enough Parent: A Book on Child-Rearing *(1987).*

To begin with, it was not the hapless victims of the Nazis who named 1 their incomprehensible and totally unmasterable fate the "holocaust." It was the Americans who applied this artificial and highly technical term to the Nazi ex-termination of the European Jews. But while the event when named as mass murder most foul evokes the most immediate, most powerful revulsion, when it is designated by a rare technical term, we must first in our minds translate it back into emotionally meaningful language. Using technical or specially cre-ated terms instead of words from our common vocabulary is one of the best-known and most widely used distancing devices, separating the intellectual from the emotional experience. Talking about "the holocaust" permits us to manage it intellectually where the raw facts, when given their ordinary names, would overwhelm us emotionally—because it was catastrophe beyond compre-hension, beyond the limits of our imagination, unless we force ourselves against our desire to extend it to encompass these terrible events.

This linguistic circumlocution began while it all was only in the planning 2 stage. Even the Nazis—usually given to grossness in language and action—shied away from facing openly what they were up to and called this vile mass murder "the final solution of the Jewish problem." After all, solving a problem can be made to appear like an honorable enterprise, as long as we are not forced to recognize that the solution we are about to embark on consists of the completely unprovoked, vicious murder of millions of helpless men, women, and children. The Nuremberg judges of these Nazi criminals followed their ex-ample of circumlocution by coining a neologism out of one Greek and one Latin root: genocide. These artificially created technical terms fail to connect with our strongest feelings. The horror of murder is part of our most common human heritage. From earliest infancy on, it arouses violent abhorrence in us. Therefore in whatever form it appears we should give such an act its true designation and not hide it behind polite, erudite terms created out of classical words.

To call this vile mass murder "the holocaust" is not to give it a special 3
name emphasizing its uniqueness which would permit, over time, the word becoming invested with feelings germane to the event it refers to. The correct definition of "holocaust" is "burnt offering." As such, it is part of the language of the psalmist, a meaningful word to all who have some acquaintance with the Bible, full of the richest emotional connotations. By using the term "holocaust," entirely false associations are established through conscious and unconscious connotations between the most vicious of mass murders and ancient rituals of a deeply religious nature.

Using a word with such strong unconscious religious connotations when 4
speaking of the murder of millions of Jews robs the victims of this abominable mass murder of the only thing left to them: their uniqueness. Calling the most callous, most brutal, most horrid, most heinous mass murder a burnt offering is a sacrilege, a profanation of God and man.

Martyrdom is part of our religious heritage. A martyr, burned at the stake, 5
is a burnt offering to his god. And it is true that after the Jews were asphyxiated, the victims' corpses were burned. But I believe we fool ourselves if we think we are honoring the victims of systematic murder by using this term, which has the highest moral connotations. By doing so, we connect for our own psychological reasons what happened in the extermination camps with historical events we deeply regret, but also greatly admire. We do so because this makes it easier for us to cope; only in doing so we cope with our distorted image of what happened, not with the events the way they did happen.

By calling the victims of the Nazis "martyrs," we falsify their fate. The 6
true meaning of "martyr" is: "one who voluntarily undergoes the penalty of death for refusing to renounce his faith" (*Oxford English Dictionary*). The Nazis made sure that nobody could mistakenly think that their victims were murdered for their religious beliefs. Renouncing their faith would have saved none of them. Those who had converted to Christianity were gassed, as were those who were atheists, and those who were deeply religious Jews. They did not die for any conviction, and certainly not out of choice.

Millions of Jews were systematically slaughtered, as were untold other 7
"undesirables," not for any convictions of theirs, but only because they stood in the way of the realization of an illusion. They neither died for their convictions, nor were they slaughtered because of their convictions, but only in consequence of the Nazis' delusional belief about what was required to protect the purity of their assumed superior racial endowment, and what they thought necessary to guarantee them the living space they believed they needed and were entitled to. Thus while these millions were slaughtered for an idea, they did not die for one.

Millions—men, women, and children—were processed after they had 8
been utterly brutalized, their humanity destroyed, their clothes torn from their

bodies. Naked, they were sorted into those who were destined to be murdered immediately, and those others who had a short-term usefulness as slave labor. But after a brief interval they, too, were to be herded into the same gas chambers into which the others were immediately piled, there to be asphyxiated so that, in their last moments, they could not prevent themselves from fighting each other in vain for a last breath of air.

To call these most wretched victims of a murderous delusion, of destruc-   9
tive drives run rampant, martyrs or a burnt offering is a distortion invented for our comfort, small as it may be. It pretends that this most vicious of mass murders had some deeper meaning; that in some fashion the victims either offered themselves or at least became sacrifices to a higher cause. It robs them of the last recognition which could be theirs, denies them the last dignity we could accord them: to face and accept what their death was all about, not embellishing it for the small psychological relief this may give us.

We could feel so much better if the victims had acted out of choice. For 10
our emotional relief, therefore, we dwell on the tiny minority who did exercise some choice: the resistance fighters of the Warsaw ghetto, for example, and others like them. We are ready to overlook the fact that these people fought back only at a time when everything was lost, when the overwhelming majority of those who had been forced into the ghettos had already been exterminated without resisting. Certainly those few who finally fought for their survival and their convictions, risking and losing their lives in doing so, deserve our admiration; their deeds give us a moral lift. But the more we dwell on these few, the more unfair are we to the memory of the millions who were slaughtered—who gave in, did not fight back—because we deny them the only thing which up to the very end remained uniquely their own: their fate.

1979

QUESTIONS FOR DISCUSSION

Content

a. Why does Bettelheim object to calling the annihilation of six million Jews "the holocaust"?

b. To what does he attribute the tendency to describe painful experiences in technical language?

c. According to Bettelheim, what terms, other than the "holocaust," should we use to describe what happened in the concentration camps? What terms does he use?

d. What distinction is Bettelheim making when, in paragraph 7, he says: "Thus while these millions were slaughtered for an idea, they did not die for one"?

e. In an encyclopedia or world history textbook, read all you can about the Nazi concentration camps and the era that Bettelheim is discussing. What did the Nazis mean by "the final solution of the Jewish problem" (paragraph 2)?

f. Bettelheim both begins and concludes his essay with references to the "fate" of the Nazis' six million victims. Why does he call their "fate" the only thing that remained "uniquely their own" (paragraph 10)? How does he distinguish these victims from the resistance fighters of the Warsaw ghetto?

Strategy and Style

g. Paragraph 9 seems to summarize the major arguments in the first eight paragraphs of the essay. As such, it could have served as an appropriate conclusion. Why does Bettelheim add paragraph 10?

h. To what end does Bettelheim explain the original and correct definition of "holocaust" (paragraph 3) and the religious significance of "martyr" (paragraph 6)?

i. Look up the word "genocide" in an unabridged dictionary. What are the Latin and Greek roots of this neologism?

j. What is the effect of Bettelheim's using the first person plural ("we") point of view?

k. Bettelheim makes some sophisticated distinctions about a topic that is somber, serious, and complex. Yet this essay is interesting and energetic. What makes it so?

SUGGESTIONS FOR SHORT WRITING

a. Write ten questions about this essay. Then choose one and write an answer to it. Or, if you are doing this suggestion with other students, exchange your lists and answer each other's questions.

b. Find a newspaper or magazine article that includes what you consider to be misleading language. Isolate some of the words and explain what you think is misleading about them.

SUGGESTIONS FOR SUSTAINED WRITING

a. Do you agree with Bettelheim that using technical terms to describe human suffering decreases our emotional involvement? If so, select a few technical terms and distinguish them from synonyms that have emotionally charged connotations. For example, try contrasting medical terms like "coronary thrombosis" and "carcinoma" with their more common names.

b. Select a popular term from the world of politics, economics, sports, popular culture, or entertainment. Write an extended definition of the term, making sure to explain the negative or positive connotations associated with it. (In some cases, you might be able to explore both negative and positive connotations.) Some examples to choose from include "apartheid," "Star Wars," "affirmative action," "feminism," "high technology," "condominiums," "nuclear deterrence," "recycling," "greenpeace," and "segregation."

Beauty

Susan Sontag

Susan Sontag (b. 1933) took her B.A. at the University of Chicago and her M.A. at Radcliffe College. She also studied at Oxford University. She is an accomplished novelist, film director, and writer of screenplays. Through her essays, which have been published in magazines and journals across the country, Sontag has established a reputation as a critic of modern culture. She will probably be best remembered, however, for her contribution to the theory of aesthetics. In her best-known work, Against Interpretation *(1966), she enunciates a theory of art based upon a reliance on the senses and not the intellect. Her place of authority in the contemporary world of art criticism was confirmed when, in 1976, she published* On Photography. *Her novels include* The Benefactor *(1964) and* Death Kit *(1967). Sontag's nonfiction—*Trip to Hanoi *(1969),* Styles of Radical Will *(1969),* Illness as Metaphor *(1978),* Vudu Urbano *(1985), and* AIDS and Its Metaphors *(1989)—demonstrates her ability to address current social and political realities with the same incisiveness with which she approaches questions of art. In "Beauty," which she published in* Vogue *in 1975, Sontag provides us with a feminist interpretation of the uses and misuses of that word throughout history.*

1   For the Greeks, beauty was a virtue: a kind of excellence. Persons then were assumed to be what we now have to call—lamely, enviously—*whole* persons. If it did occur to the Greeks to distinguish between a person's "inside" and "outside," they still expected that inner beauty would be matched by beauty of the other kind. The well-born young Athenians who gathered around Socrates found it quite paradoxical that their hero was so intelligent, so brave, so honorable, so seductive—and so ugly. One of Socrates' main pedagogical acts was to be ugly—and teach those innocent, no doubt splendid-looking disciples of his how full of paradoxes life really was.

2   They may have resisted Socrates' lesson. We do not. Several thousand years later, we are more wary of the enchantments of beauty. We not only split off—with the greatest facility—the "inside" (character, intellect) from the "outside" (looks); but we are actually surprised when someone who is beautiful is also intelligent, talented, good.

3   It was principally the influence of Christianity that deprived beauty of the central place it had in classical ideals of human excellence. By limiting excellence (*virtus* in Latin) to *moral* virtue only, Christianity set beauty adrift—as an alienated, arbitrary, superficial enchantment. And beauty has continued to lose prestige. For close to two centuries it has become a convention to attribute beauty to only one of the two sexes: the sex which, however Fair, is always Second. Associating beauty with women has put beauty even further on the defensive, morally.

161

A beautiful woman, we say in English. But a handsome man. "Hand- 4
some" is the masculine equivalent of—and refusal of—a compliment which has
accumulated certain demeaning overtones, by being reserved for women only.
That one can call a man "beautiful" in French and in Italian suggests that Catholic countries—unlike those countries shaped by the Protestant version of
Christianity—still retain some vestiges of the pagan admiration for beauty. But
the difference, if one exists, is of degree only. In every modern country that is
Christian or post-Christian, women *are* the beautiful sex—to the detriment of
the notion of beauty as well as of women.

To be called beautiful is thought to name something essential to women's 5
character and concerns. (In contrast to men—whose essence is to be strong, or
effective, or competent.) It does not take someone in the throes of advanced
feminist awareness to perceive that the way women are taught to be involved
with beauty encourages narcissism, reinforces dependence and immaturity. Everybody (women and men) knows that. For it is "everybody," a whole society,
that has identified being feminine with caring about how one *looks.* (In contrast
to being masculine—which is identified with caring about what one *is* and *does*
and only secondarily, if at all, about how one looks.) Given these stereotypes, it
is no wonder that beauty enjoys, at best, a rather mixed reputation.

It is not, of course, the desire to be beautiful that is wrong but the obliga- 6
tion to be—or to try. What is accepted by most women as a flattering idealiza-
tion of their sex is a way of making women feel inferior to what they actually
are—or normally grow to be. For the ideal of beauty is administered as a form
of self-oppression. Women are taught to see their bodies in *parts,* and to evaluate each part separately. Breasts, feet, hips, waistline, neck, eyes, nose, com-
plexion, hair, and so on—each in turn is submitted to an anxious, fretful, often
despairing scrutiny. Even if some pass muster, some will always be found wanting. Nothing less than perfection will do.

In men, good looks is a whole, something taken in at a glance. It does not 7
need to be confirmed by giving measurements of different regions of the body,
nobody encourages a man to dissect his appearance, feature by feature. As for
perfection, that is considered trivial—almost unmanly. Indeed, in the ideally
good-looking man a small imperfection or blemish is considered positively desirable. According to one movie critic (a woman) who is a declared Robert
Redford fan, it is having that cluster of skin-colored moles on one cheek that
saves Redford from being merely a "pretty face." Think of the depreciation of
women—as well as of beauty—that is implied in that judgment.

"The privileges of beauty are immense," said Cocteau. To be sure, beauty 8
is a form of power. And deservedly so. What is lamentable is that it is the only
form of power that most women are encouraged to seek. This power is always
conceived in relation to men; it is not the power to do but the power to attract.
It is a power that negates itself. For this power is not one that can be chosen
freely—at least, not by women—or renounced without social censure.

To preen, for a woman, can never be just a pleasure. It is also a duty. It is 9
her work. If a woman does real work—and even if she has clambered up to a

leading position in politics, law, medicine, business, or whatever—she is always under pressure to confess that she still works at being attractive. But in so far as she is keeping up as one of the Fair Sex, she brings under suspicion her very capacity to be objective, professional, authoritative, thoughtful. Damned if they do—women are. And damned if they don't.

One could hardly ask for more important evidence of the dangers of con- 10 sidering persons as split between what is "inside" and what is "outside" than that interminable half-comic half-tragic tale, the oppression of women. How easy it is to start off by defining women as caretakers of their surfaces, and then to disparage them (or find them adorable) for being "superficial." It is a crude trap, and it has worked for too long. But to get out of the trap requires that women get some critical distance from that excellence and privilege which is beauty, enough distance to see how much beauty itself has been abridged in order to prop up the mythology of the "feminine." There should be a way of saving beauty *from* women—and *for* them.

1975

QUESTIONS FOR DISCUSSION

Content

a. What is Sontag's thesis?
b. The author makes it a point to explain differences between the connotations of "handsome" and those of "beautiful." How does this contrast help her develop her thesis? In what other ways does she use contrast as a method of developing her definition?
c. Is Sontag's message aimed at a predominantly female audience? At a predominantly male audience? At a mixed audience?
d. Consult appropriate sources in the reference section of your college library. Who are Socrates and Cocteau? Why does Sontag mention them (paragraphs 1 and 8 respectively)?
e. What was it that caused beauty to "lose prestige" (paragraph 3)? How does our conception of beauty differ from the one the Greeks had?
f. What is Sontag referring to when she talks about countries that are "post-Christian" (paragraph 4)?
g. If beauty is "a form of power" (paragraph 8), what about it is "lamentable"?
h. What does Sontag mean when she claims that women are "Damned if they do.... And damned if they don't" (paragraph 9)?

Strategy and Style

i. Sontag launches the essay by spending considerable time discussing notions of beauty through history. Is such a long introduction justified? Why or why not?

j. Does the essay's conclusion echo its introduction? Explain.

k. In some instances, Sontag seems to be addressing the reader directly. Find a few such instances, and explain their effect on you.

l. Analyze the author's style. What is the effect of her insistence on varying sentence length and structure?

m. Overall, how would you describe Sontag's tone?

SUGGESTIONS FOR SHORT WRITING

a. Rewrite Sontag's essay as song lyrics. An easy way to do this is to use the melody of a well-known song for the structure of your lyrics. Try to remain true to what you believe to be Sontag's meaning.

b. Write a short definition of "ugliness." Is it the antithesis of beauty, or do beauty and ugliness share some of the same characteristics?

SUGGESTIONS FOR SUSTAINED WRITING

a. In paragraph 5, the author claims that "the way women are taught to be involved with beauty encourages narcissism, reinforces dependence and immaturity." Think about some relevant television or magazine advertisements for beauty products. Is Sontag correct? Write an analytical essay in which you explain how such ads define "beauty."

b. Is there such a thing as "inner beauty" as distinguished from one's physical appearance? Establish your own definition of "inner beauty," but make sure to illustrate it with concrete details about a person or persons you know quite well.

c. Sontag seems to have concentrated on the negative effects of our preoccupation with physical beauty. Are there any positive effects? Write an essay from the other side of the issue.

The Virtues of Ambition
Joseph Epstein

Joseph Epstein was born in 1937 in Chicago, where he lives today. He is a professor of English at Northwestern University and editor of The American Scholar, *but he is probably best known for his commentaries on American society. His stories and essays appear in magazines such as* Commentary, Harper's, *and* The New Yorker. *Many of his essays have been anthologized in* Familiar Territory *(1979),* The Middle of My Tether *(1983),* Once More Round the Block *(1987), and other collections. In 1980, he published* Ambition: The Secret Passion, *a close look at what he calls the "fuel of achievement."*

Ambition is one of those Rorschach words: define it and you instantly 1 reveal a great deal about yourself. Even that most neutral of works, *Webster's,* in its Seventh New Collegiate Edition, gives itself away, defining ambition first and foremost as "an ardent desire for rank, fame, or power." Ardent immediately assumes a heat incommensurate with good sense and stability, and rank, fame, and power have come under fairly heavy attack for at least a century. One can, after all, be ambitious for the public good, for the alleviation of suffering, for the enlightenment of mankind, though there are some who say that these are precisely the ambitious people most to be distrusted.

Surely ambition is behind dreams of glory, of wealth, of love, of distinc- 2 tion, of accomplishment, of pleasure, of goodness. What life does with our dreams and expectations cannot, of course, be predicted. Some dreams, begun in selflessness, end in rancor; other dreams, begun in selfishness, end in large-heartedness. The unpredictability of the outcome of dreams is no reason to cease dreaming.

To be sure, ambition, the sheer thing unalloyed by some larger purpose 3 than merely clambering up, is never a pretty prospect to ponder. As drunks have done to alcohol, the single-minded have done to ambition—given it a bad name. Like a taste for alcohol, too, ambition does not always allow for easy satiation. Some people cannot handle it; it has brought grief to others, and not merely the ambitious alone. Still, none of this seems sufficient cause for driving ambition under the counter.

What is the worst that can be said—that has been said—about ambition? 4 Here is a (surely) partial list:

To begin with, it, ambition, is often antisocial, and indeed is now out- 5 moded, belonging to an age when individualism was more valued and useful than it is today. The person strongly imbued with ambition ignores the collectivity; socially detached, he is on his own and out for his own. Individuality and ambition are firmly linked. The ambitious individual, far from identifying himself and his fortunes with the group, wishes to rise above it. The ambitious man or woman sees the world as a battle; rivalrousness is his or her principal emo-

165

tion: the world has limited prizes to offer, and he or she is determined to get his or hers. Ambition is, moreover, jesuitical; it can argue those possessed by it into believing that what they want for themselves is good for everyone—that the satisfaction of their own desires is best for the commonweal. The truly ambitious believe that it is a dog-eat-dog world, and they are distinguished by wanting to be the dogs that do the eating.

From here it is but a short hop to believe that those who have achieved   6
the common goals of ambition—money, fame, power—have achieved them through corruption of a greater or lesser degree, mostly a greater. Thus all politicians in high places, thought to be ambitious, are understood to be, ipso facto, without moral scruples. How could they have such scruples—a weighty burden in a high climb—and still have risen as they have?

If ambition is to be well regarded, the rewards of ambition—wealth, dis-   7
tinction, control over one's destiny—must be deemed worthy of the sacrifices made on ambition's behalf. If the tradition of ambition is to have vitality, it must be widely shared; and it especially must be esteemed by people who are themselves admired, the educated not least among them. The educated not least because, nowadays more than ever before, it is they who have usurped the platforms of public discussion and wield the power of the spoken and written word in newspapers, in magazines, on television. In an odd way, it is the educated who have claimed to have given up on ambition as an ideal. What is odd is that they have perhaps most benefited from ambition—if not always their own then that of their parents and grandparents. There is a heavy note of hypocrisy in this; a case of closing the barn door after the horses have escaped—with the educated themselves astride them.

Certainly people do not seem less interested in success and its accoutre-   8
ments now than formerly. Summer homes, European travel, BMWs—the locations, place names and name brands may change, but such items do not seem less in demand today than a decade or two years ago. What has happened is that people cannot own up to their dreams, as easily and openly as once they could, lest they be thought pushing, acquisitive, vulgar. Instead we are treated to fine pharisaical spectacles, which now more than ever seem in ample supply: the revolutionary lawyer quartered in the $250,000 Manhattan condominium; the critic of American materialism with a Southampton summer home; the publisher of radical books who takes his meals in three-star restaurants; the journalist advocating participatory democracy in all phases of life, whose own children are enrolled in private schools. For such people and many more perhaps not so egregious, the proper formulation is, "Succeed at all costs but refrain from *appearing* ambitious."

The attacks on ambition are many and come from various angles; its pub-   9
lic defenders are few and unimpressive, where they are not extremely unattractive. As a result, the support for ambition as a healthy impulse, a quality to be admired and inculcated in the young, is probably lower than it has ever been in the United States. This does not mean that ambition is at an end, that people no

longer feel its stirrings and promptings, but only that, no longer openly honored, it is less often openly professed. Consequences follow from this, of course, some of which are that ambition is driven underground, or made sly, or perverse. It can also be forced into vulgarity, as witness the blatant pratings of its contemporary promoters. Such, then, is the way things stand: on the left angry critics, on the right obtuse supporters, and in the middle, as usual, the majority of earnest people trying to get on in life.

Many people are naturally distrustful of ambition, feeling that it repre- 10 sents something intractable in human nature. Thus John Dean entitled his book about his involvement in the Watergate affair during the Nixon administration *Blind Ambition,* as if ambition were to blame for his ignoble actions, and not the constellation of qualities that make up his rather shabby character. Ambition, it must once again be underscored, is morally a two-sided street. Place next to John Dean Andrew Carnegie, who, among other philanthropic acts, bought the library of Lord Acton, at a time when Acton was in financial distress, and assigned its custodianship to Acton, who never was told who his benefactor was. Need much more be said on the subject than that, important though ambition is, there are some things that one must not sacrifice to it?

But going at things the other way, sacrificing ambition so as to guard 11 against its potential excesses, is to go at things wrongly. To discourage ambition is to discourage dreams of grandeur and greatness. All men and women are born, live, suffer, and die; what distinguishes us one from another is our dreams, whether they be dreams about worldly or unworldly things, and what we do to make them come about.

It may seem an exaggeration to say that ambition is the linchpin of soci- 12 ety, holding many of its disparate elements together, but it is not an exaggeration by much. Remove ambition and the essential elements of society seem to fly apart. Ambition, as opposed to mere fantasizing about desires, implies work and discipline to achieve goals, personal and social, of a kind society cannot survive without. Ambition is intimately connected with family, for men and women not only work partly for their families; husbands and wives are often ambitious for each other, but harbor some of their most ardent ambitions for their children. Yet to have a family nowadays—with birth control readily available, and inflation a good economic argument against having children—is nearly an expression of ambition in itself. Finally, though ambition was once the domain chiefly of monarchs and aristocrats, it has, in more recent times, increasingly become the domain of the middle classes. Ambition and futurity—a sense of building for tomorrow—are inextricable. Working, saving, planning—these, the daily aspects of ambition—have always been the distinguishing marks of a rising middle class. The attack against ambition is not incidentally an attack on the middle class and what it stands for. Like it or not, the middle class has done much of society's work in America; and it, the middle class, has from the beginning run on ambition.

It is not difficult to imagine a world shorn of ambition. It would probably 13

be a kinder world: without demands, without abrasions, without disappoint-
ments. People would have time for reflection. Such work as they did would not
be for themselves but for the collectivity. Competition would never enter in.
Conflict would be eliminated, tension become a thing of the past. The stress of
creation would be at an end. Art would no longer be troubling, but purely cel-
ebratory in its functions. The family would become superfluous as a social unit,
with all its former power for bringing about neurosis drained away. Longevity
would be increased, for fewer people would die of heart attack or stroke caused
by tumultuous endeavor. Anxiety would be extinct. Time would stretch on and
on, with ambition long departed from the human heart.

    Ah, how unrelievedly boring life would be!   14

    There is a strong view that holds that success is a myth, and ambition   15
therefore a sham. Does this mean that success does not really exist? That
achievement is at bottom empty? That the efforts of men and women are of no
significance alongside the force of movements and events? Now not all success,
obviously, is worth esteeming, nor all ambition worth cultivating. Which are
and which are not is something one soon enough learns on one's own. But even
the most cynical secretly admit that success exists; that achievement counts for
a great deal; and that the true myth is that the actions of men and women are
useless. To believe otherwise is to take on a point of view that is likely to be
deranging. It is, in its implications, to remove all motive for competence, interest in attainment, and regard for posterity.

    We do not choose to be born. We do not choose our parents. We do not   16
choose our historical epoch, the country of our birth or the immediate circumstances of our upbringing. We do not, most of us, choose to die; nor do we
choose the time or conditions of our death. But within all this realm of choice-
lessness, we do choose how we shall live: courageously or in cowardice, hon-
orably or dishonorably, with purpose or in drift. We decide what is important
and what is trivial in life. We decide that what makes us significant is either
what we do or what we refuse to do. But no matter how indifferent the universe
may be to our choices and decisions, these choices and decisions are ours to
make. We decide. We choose. And as we decide and choose, so are our lives
formed. In the end, forming our own destiny is what ambition is about.

1980

QUESTIONS FOR DISCUSSION

Content

a. How does Epstein define "ambition"? How do you define it? How does your
   definition compare to *Webster's?* To Epstein's? Do you consider yourself to
   be ambitious in the sense of any of these definitions?

b. In the first paragraph, Epstein says that people who are "ambitious for the public good" are sometimes the most distrusted. What does he mean?

c. What is Epstein's argument? To whom is he arguing? Do you agree or disagree with him?

d. According to Epstein, how did the change in our opinion of ambition, from positive to negative, come about? Trace the development (or deterioration) as Epstein presents it.

e. In paragraph 10, Epstein asserts that ambition "is morally a two-sided street." What does he consider the two sides to be? Can one walk on both sides?

f. What examples does the author use to illustrate the two sides of ambition? Why does he choose these particular examples?

g. Epstein says in paragraph 12: "Remove ambition and the essential elements of society seem to fly apart." Do you agree? Is there or can there be a society that gets along without ambition as Epstein defines it? What is or would such a society be like?

h. What reasons does the author use to support his belief that ambition is beneficial? What counterarguments do these reasons evoke? How does he deal with these counterarguments?

Strategy and Style

i. Epstein occasionally uses rhetorical questions (see paragraphs 4, 6, 10, and 15). What effect do these questions have on his essay? On his argument?

j. What other subtle devices does Epstein use to persuade his readers? For example, notice that in the last paragraph he often begins sentences, and clauses within sentences, with "we." Compare the length and rhythm of these sentences with sentences in the rest of the essay. What is their effect on you?

k. Similarly, examine Epstein's choice of vocabulary, particularly adjectives that describe people who attack ambition and people who defend it. How do these words help create a positive or negative image of ambition?

l. Describe Epstein's tone. What words and passages create this tone? What does his tone reveal about Epstein's own ambition?

SUGGESTIONS FOR SHORT WRITING

a. Write your own definition of ambition. Epstein says that the definition will "instantly reveal a great deal about yourself" (paragraph 1). What does your definition reveal about you?

b. Choose another concept that has a bad reputation for most people, such as anxiety, anger, fatigue, isolation, loneliness. Point out its virtues.

SUGGESTIONS FOR SUSTAINED WRITING

a. Write a counterargument to this essay, persuading your readers that ambition is ultimately bad for society.

b. Write an essay in which you define a word in order to clear up what you believe to be misconceptions about that word. Here are some topics you might choose from: friendship, pride, competitiveness, self-reliance, wealth, education, loneliness, modesty.

c. What would a "world shorn of ambition" (paragraph 13) be like? Beginning with your own detailed definition of "ambition," describe this world. You may also wish to persuade your readers that this world is (un)desirable and/or (im)possible.

Moral Ambiguity

Barbara Grizzuti Harrison

Barbara Grizzuti Harrison was born in 1931 in Brooklyn, New York, where she still lives. A journalist, she publishes frequently in the Village Voice, New Republic, The Nation, *and* Ms. *Much of her investigative writing grows out of events in her own life; for example,* Unlearning the Lie: Sexism in School *(1969) was based on an incident at her children's school. When she was nine years old, Harrison and her mother became Jehovah's Witnesses; at nineteen, she moved to the Witnesses' world headquarters, a huge working/residential complex in Brooklyn. Her desire to be a writer, however, came into conflict with her religion, and she eventually left, but the experience yielded* Visions of Glory: A History and a Memory of the Jehovah's Witnesses *(1978). Although most of her work is nonfiction, Harrison has also written a novel,* Foreign Bodies *(1984).* Off Center: Essays *(1980), from which "Moral Ambiguity" is taken, is a collection of some of her most controversial articles.*

The main thrust of the feminist movement, in all its historical manifestations, has been to recognize the value and to enhance the dignity of human life. At its best—its most noble and most useful—it has always said *no* to that which degrades and diminishes the quality of life; *no* to the sexual and economic exploitation of women and children in factories, mills, homes, offices; *no* to the slaughter of women, children, sons, lovers, husbands, and fathers in senseless wars; and *yes* to that which enlarges the possibilities of goodness. The main thrust of feminism has always been pro-life. 1

What an irony that feminists now find themselves locked in battle with people who describe themselves as "pro-life"; that we who have so passionately proclaimed, with all the authenticity of suffering, that our minds and bodies are inviolate find ourselves in bitter opposition to those whose rallying cry is the "sanctity of human life." 2

Feminists may protest that the highly organized, well-financed "pro-life" forces have been known to use violence to achieve their "pious" ends. We may say that—inasmuch as "pro-lifers" were remarkably silent when lives were being lost in Indochina and were silent on the issue of capital punishment—they are not pro-life, but merely antiabortion. But to say that is not to address ourselves to a real, heartbreaking question: have we become so brutalized by our struggles that we see abortion only in terms of expediency? 3

Now that our right to legal abortion stands in jeopardy, one is frequently given to understand that it is not expedient to explore moral and emotional ambiguities. Of course that is wrong. Now that we are at the barricades, precisely *because* we are at the barricades, when moral sensitivity tends to crumble in the face of action, I think we need to ask ourselves many questions. The consequence of not discussing the moral ambiguities of abortion is that we allow 4

171

"pro-lifers" to catch the moral ball and run with it. We are afraid to say that abortion is terrible—for the woman whose body undergoes the trauma, and (I think) for the other life involved. Afraid to give our "enemies" ammunition, we whisper these things to one another; we are afraid to say them out loud.

Is it really so awful to admit to confusion and unhappiness over the issue   5
of abortion?

That is what Linda Bird Francke did. In 1973 Francke, the mother of   6
three children, had an abortion. Three years later, under a pseudonym, she published an account of her experience in the *The New York Times,* and she was
roundly denounced, both by Right-to-Lifers and by women she describes as
"pro-abortion zealots." Neither group liked her "line."

The truth is that Francke didn't have a "line." Her brief piece was a mas-   7
terpiece of ambivalence: it spoke implicitly of her relief—and explicitly of her
remorse. Like most pieces written for catharsis (Francke had originally no intention to publish), it had more of sensibility than of sense. In spite of its shortcomings, however—perhaps because of them—Francke's piece struck a nerve.
The *Times* received hundreds of letters in response. *The Ambivalence of Abortion* grew out of those responses.

Like Francke, women spoke of relief; they also spoke of anger (some-   8
times turned inward, sometimes directed toward doctors, clergymen, husbands,
lovers, men in general, mothers, fathers, and the women's movement, and the
fetus); they spoke of anguish, grieving, remorse, physical and emotional es-
trangement from loved ones. Not a few of the women interviewed felt betrayed
by feminists who'd led them to believe that abortion was "as easy as pulling a
tooth."

Francke allows the hundreds of women interviewed—young, old, single,   9
and married women—to speak for themselves. The interviews are revelatory,
painful, vivid. But I would wish for more editorial comment. Francke addresses
herself only to the emotional ambivalence surrounding abortion. She doesn't
deal with moral ambiguity (or she chooses to regard morality and emotion as
synonymous). I think I understand her difficulty. It is this: when one considers
abortion as a moral issue, one is confronted with two absolute positions. *One,*
the fetus is a human life, and abortion is, therefore, immoral. *Two,* women have
the absolute right to control their bodies, and the placing of any limits on that
control is, therefore, immoral. Unhappily, it is perfectly possible to have one's
emotions *and* one's morality colored by both those positions—and the collision
of absolutes throws one into the realm of relative morality, a realm from which
it is next to impossible to write with any degree of clarity.

Francke chose not to wade into this messy territory, though she would un-   10
doubtedly describe herself as "pro-choice":

> Regardless of whether chooses to continue her pregnancy or to terminate
> it…it is her decision alone. So it falls to all of us to support that decision
> with grace, safety, and understanding—and to live with it, and each other, as
> best we can.

Francke takes an "I'm okay/You're okay" approach: she hopes that, as a 11 result of her book, "women who are suffering from guilt will feel comforted that others have suffered like them, and that women who feel guilty because they *don't* feel guilty will also find comfort in the stories of others who have no regrets."

Francke says that many abortions were a "life-style choice." What she 12 means, by that deplorable jargon, is that some women chose to abort because— as they unhesitatingly tell us—they didn't want to be cursed with morning sickness while on a Caribbean vacation; they didn't want their graduate degrees deferred; or, chillingly, because the fetus was the "wrong" sex. I think such "life-style" choices are wasteful, frivolous—immoral.

I was also appalled by the number of women who became pregnant be- 13 cause neither they nor their insensitive lovers took the trouble to use contraceptive devices; I was even more appalled by the women who routinely use abortion as a contraceptive device—and astounded that these same women could righteously mouth clichés about "control of their bodies," when the idea of exercising "control" never seemed to occur to them before having intercourse. (I want to say that the notion that we have, or ought to have, *absolute* control of our bodies is a sloppy one. I have no "right," for example, to place my body in front of a moving car; I have no "right" to perform private bodily functions in public. Civilization—as well as good sense—implies a measure of restraint.)

If all of this sounds like fodder for "pro-lifers," one has only to read the 14 testimony of women who were too young, too old, or simply too worn out by life to bear children without devastating physical and emotional consequences. Most of all, one has to read the testimonies of women who had abortions before abortion was legal. Their experiences were so savage, so degrading, that—at the bottom line—one can only say that this kind of brutality, this carnage, can never be allowed to occur again.

The trouble is that to say this is also to say that one life—the life of the 15 unborn child—must be sacrificed to preserve the life of another. This is a very great trouble: unless one does a moral/intellectual tap dance (such as likening the right to abortion to the concept of the "just" war), there seems to be no morally tenable position one can take, no "pure" position.

As feminists, we tend now to focus our moral indignation on the fact that 16 poor women will not be able to receive Medicaid funds for legal abortions. Here we seem to be standing on morally unambiguous ground: why should poor women be so unjustly penalized? We care about the quality of life; and giving birth to a baby that may be ill-fed, ill-educated, or physically abused does nothing to enhance the quality of anybody's life. But the other side of the moral coin, as amply demonstrated by Francke's interviewees, is that many poor women abort *because* they are poor; many women wanted babies but believed they couldn't afford them. Where should one direct one's anger? Toward the life-isn't-fair people who would *deny* women the right to abort, or toward the economic system (perpetuated, of course, by the same life-isn't-fair people) that allows poverty and affluence to coexist and *forces* women to abort? (One thing I didn't need to be convinced of before I read this book was that abortion does not cure poverty.)

I can imagine no circumstances under which I would have an abortion; I consider the fetus a human life. But I would also consider it immoral to bend my efforts to stop any other human being from having an abortion she deemed necessary. I hate the idea of abortion, but I hate even more the death of a woman by coat hangers or lye. I hate, that is to say, the idea of murder twice done.   17

We live in a secular, pluralistic society. I believe that Heaven is an actual place—as real as the physical headquarters of Planned Parenthood. But the promise of a Heavenly Reward is cold comfort to those who do not so believe—and, even if I wished to, I could not impose my belief on others.   18

Young Bolshevist revolutionaries once said that murder was sometimes necessary, but never justifiable. That thinking informs my thinking about abortion—and makes it no easier to come to a comfortably unambiguous conclusion about it.   19

I have a teenage daughter. If she were to become pregnant, I would consider it a violation of her integrity to tell her that she could not have an abortion if she chose to have one; I would take her to a doctor—and I would thank God that we had legal access to a doctor who would not maim or butcher her. But if she were, of her own free will and without coercion, to choose to give birth to a child, I would consider it sinful not to support her in that decision.   20

To read *The Ambivalence of Abortion* is to be convinced that the problems raised by abortion cannot be satisfied by right-on slogans. What, for example, are the consequences, for the mother, of bearing a child to term and offering it up for adoption? Is this truly a humane solution, or does that mother also grieve and mourn the loss of her child forever? I think the real message of Francke's book is something philosophers and moral logicians have always known: the most painful moral struggles are not those between good and evil, but between the good and the lesser good.   21

1978

QUESTIONS FOR DISCUSSION

Content

a. How does Harrison define "moral ambiguity"? Would you define it similarly? What forms of moral ambiguity do you see in other essays in this section, for instance, in "The Holocaust," "What Is Poverty?" or "Pornoviolence"?

b. Whom do you think Harrison had in mind as her audience when she wrote this? What was her probable intention in writing it?
c. What is the "irony" she refers to in paragraph 2? In your own words, paraphrase what she means by this word.
d. What is Harrison's stance on abortion? Is she "pro-life," "pro-choice," or neither? Find quotes that support your answer.
e. In paragraph 9, Harrison distinguishes "emotional ambivalence" from "moral ambiguity." What is that distinction?
f. In Harrison's opinion, what is morally ambiguous about the abortion issue? Do you agree with her explanation?
g. This article was written more than thirteen years ago. Has the situation changed since then? If so, in what ways? If not, do you think a solution to the conflict is possible?
h. Is Harrison arguing for an absolute morality or for a relative morality? Point to phrases in the article that support your answer.

Strategy and Style

i. In paragraph 19, Harrison tells us "Bolshevist revolutionaries once said that murder was sometimes necessary, but never justifiable." What are her reasons for including this reference? How does it affect her argument? Does it make it less or more convincing?
j. What does Harrison mean by her concluding statement that "the most painful moral struggles are not those between good and evil, but between the good and the lesser good"? Does this statement form part of her definition of moral ambiguity? Does it serve to summarize her essay?
k. Much of this essay addresses the issue articulated by Linda Bird Francke in "The Ambivalence of Abortion." What is Harrison's attitude toward Francke? In what way is this attitude indicative of Harrison's tone?

SUGGESTIONS FOR SHORT WRITING

a. Summarize Harrison's definition of moral ambiguity.
b. Do you agree with this definition? If not, write your own. If you agree with Harrison, relate how you have come to take this stance.

SUGGESTIONS FOR SUSTAINED WRITING

a. Write an essay in which you show the complexity, the ambiguity, of an issue that is frequently treated as if it were a simple either/or issue. Try to convince your readers that neither extreme view is practical for finding a solution. If you can, present a solution that satisfies both sides. Possible issues:

the death penalty; nuclear power plants; the legalization of marijuana, prostitution, or euthanasia. Note: any such issue can be oversimplified—your
task is to find a new or more complex way to discuss it.

b. Write a counterargument to Harrison's essay. Take a stance in direct opposition to her fundamental argument, or reply to her article point by point.

c. Conversely, expand on any point in Harrison's article that you strongly agree
with.

What Is Poverty?

Jo Goodwin Parker

The author has requested that no biographical information be provided.

You ask me what is poverty? Listen to me. Here I am, dirty, smelly, and 1
with no "proper" underwear on and with the stench of my rotting teeth near
you. I will tell you. Listen to me. Listen without pity. I cannot use your pity.
Listen with understanding. Put yourself in my dirty, worn out, ill-fitting shoes,
and hear me.

Poverty is getting up every morning from a dirt- and illness-stained mat- 2
tress. The sheets have long since been used for diapers. Poverty is living in a smell
that never leaves. This is a smell of urine, sour milk, and spoiling food sometimes
joined with the strong smell of long-cooked onions. Onions are cheap. If you have
smelled this smell, you did not know how it came. It is the smell of the outdoor
privy. It is the smell of young children who cannot walk the long dark way in the
night. It is the smell of the mattresses where years of "accidents" have happened.
It is the smell of the milk which has gone sour because the refrigerator long has
not worked, and it costs money to get it fixed. It is the smell of rotting garbage.
I could bury it, but where is the shovel? Shovels cost money.

Poverty is being tired. I have always been tired. They told me at the hos- 3
pital when the last baby came that I had chronic anemia caused from poor diet,
a bad case of worms, and that I needed a corrective operation. I listened po-
litely—the poor are always polite. The poor always listen. They don't say that
there is no money for iron pills, or better food, or worm medicine. The idea of
an operation is frightening and costs so much that, if I had dared, I would have
laughed. Who takes care of my children? Recovery from an operation takes a
long time. I have three children. When I left them with "Granny" the last time I
had a job, I came home to find the baby covered with fly specks, and a diaper
that had not been changed since I left. When the dried diaper came off, bits of
my baby's flesh came with it. My other child was playing with a sharp bit of
broken glass, and my oldest was playing alone at the edge of a lake. I made
twenty-two dollars a week, and a good nursery school costs twenty dollars a
week for three children. I quit my job.

Poverty is dirt. You can say in your clean clothes coming from your clean 4
house, "Anybody can be clean." Let me explain about housekeeping with no
money. For breakfast I give my children grits with no oleo or cornbread without
eggs and oleo. This does not use up many dishes. What dishes there are, I wash
in cold water and with no soap. Even the cheapest soap has to be saved for the
baby's diapers. Look at my hands, so cracked and red. Once I saved for two
months to buy a jar of Vaseline for my hands and the baby's diaper rash. When

177

I had saved enough, I went to buy it and the price had gone up two cents. The baby and I suffered on. I have to decide every day if I can bear to put my cracked sore hands into the cold water and strong soap. But you ask, why not hot water? Fuel costs money. If you have a wood fire it costs money. If you burn electricity, it costs money. Hot water is a luxury. I do not have luxuries. I know you will be surprised when I tell you how young I am. I look so much older. My back has been bent over the wash tubs every day for so long, I cannot remember when I ever did anything else. Every night I wash every stitch my school age child has on and just hope her clothes will be dry by morning.

Poverty is staying up all night on cold nights to watch the fire knowing   5
one spark on the newspaper covering the walls means your sleeping child dies in flames. In summer poverty is watching gnats and flies devour your baby's tears when he cries. The screens are torn and you pay so little rent you know they will never be fixed. Poverty means insects in your food, in your nose, in your eyes, and crawling over you when you sleep. Poverty is hoping it never rains because diapers won't dry when it rains and soon you are using newspapers. Poverty is seeing your children forever with runny noses. Paper handkerchiefs cost money and all your rags you need for other things. Even more costly are antihistamines. Poverty is cooking without food and cleaning without soap.

Poverty is asking for help. Have you ever had to ask for help, knowing   6
your children will suffer unless you get it? Think about asking for a loan from a relative, if this is the only way you can imagine asking for help. I will tell you how it feels. You find out where the office is that you are supposed to visit. You circle that block four or five times. Thinking of your children, you go in. Everyone is very busy. Finally, someone comes out and you tell her that you need help. That never is the person you need to see. You go see another person, and after spilling the whole shame of your poverty all over the desk between you, you find that this isn't the right office after all—you must repeat the whole process, and it never is any easier at the next place.

You have asked for help, and after all it has a cost. You are again told to   7
wait. You are told why, but you don't really hear because of the red cloud of shame and the rising cloud of despair.

Poverty is remembering. It is remembering quitting school in junior high   8
because "nice" children had been so cruel about my clothes and my smell. The attendance officer came. My mother told him I was pregnant. I wasn't, but she thought that I could get a job and help out. I had jobs off and on, but never long enough to learn anything. Mostly I remember being married. I was so young then. I am still young. For a time, we had all the things you have. There was a little house in another town, with hot water and everything. Then my husband lost his job. There was unemployment insurance for a while and what few jobs I could get. Soon, all our nice things were repossessed and we moved back here. I was pregnant then. This house didn't look so bad when we first moved in. Every week it gets worse. Nothing is ever fixed. We now had no money. There were a few odd jobs for my husband, but everything went for food then,

as it does now. I don't know how we lived through three years and three babies, but we did. I'll tell you something, after the last baby I destroyed my marriage. It had been a good one, but could you keep on bringing children in this dirt? Did you ever think how much it costs for any kind of birth control? I knew my husband was leaving the day he left, but there were no goodbys between us. I hope he has been able to climb out of this mess somewhere. He never could hope with us to drag him down.

That's when I asked for help. When I got it, you know how much it was? **9** It was, and is, seventy-eight dollars a month for the four of us; that is all I ever can get. Now you know why there is no soap, no needles and thread, no hot water, no aspirin, no worm medicine, no hand cream, no shampoo. None of these things forever and ever and ever. So that you can see clearly, I pay twenty dollars a month rent, and most of the rest goes for food. For grits and cornmeal, and rice and milk and beans. I try my best to use only the minimum electricity. If I use more, there is that much less for food.

Poverty is looking into a black future. Your children won't play with my **10** boys. They will turn to other boys who steal to get what they want. I can already see them behind the bars of their prison instead of behind the bars of my poverty. Or they will turn to the freedom of alcohol or drugs, and find themselves enslaved. And my daughter? At best, there is for her a life like mine.

But you say to me, there are schools. Yes, there are schools. My children **11** have no extra books, no magazines, no extra pencils, or crayons, or paper and most important of all, they do not have health. They have worms, they have infections, they have pink-eye all summer. They do not sleep well on the floor, or with me in my one bed. They do not suffer from hunger, my seventy-eight dollars keeps us alive, but they do suffer from malnutrition. Oh yes, I do remember what I was taught about health in school. It doesn't do much good. In some places there is a surplus commodities program. Not here. The country said it cost too much. There is a school lunch program. But I have two children who will already be damaged by the time they get to school.

But, you say to me, there are health clinics. Yes, there are health clinics **12** and they are in the towns. I live out here eight miles from town. I can walk that far (even if it is sixteen miles both ways), but can my little children? My neighbor will take me when he goes; but he expects to get paid, *one way or another.* I bet you know my neighbor. He is that large man who spends his time at the gas station, the barbershop, and the corner store complaining about the government spending money on the immoral mothers of illegitimate children.

Poverty is an acid that drips on pride until all pride is worn away. Poverty **13** is a chisel that chips on honor until honor is worn away. Some of you say that you would do *something* in my situation, and maybe you would, for the first week or the first month, but for year after year after year?

Even the poor can dream. A dream of a time when there is money. Money **14** for the right kinds of food, for worm medicine, for iron pills, for toothbrushes, for hand cream, for a hammer and nails and a bit of screening, for a shovel, for a bit of paint, for some sheeting, for needles and thread. Money to pay *in money* for a trip to town. And, oh, money for hot water and money for soap. A dream of when asking for help does not eat away the last bit of pride. When the office you visit is as nice as the offices of other governmental agencies, when there are enough workers to help you quickly, when workers do not quit in defeat and despair. When you have to tell your story to only one person, and that person can send you for other help and you don't have to prove your poverty over and over and over again.

I have come out of my despair to tell you this. Remember I did not come 15 from another place or another time. Others like me are all around you. Look at us with an angry heart, anger that will help you help me. Anger that will let you tell of me. The poor are always silent. Can you be silent too?

1971

QUESTIONS FOR DISCUSSION

Content

a. How would you define the author's purpose? Besides paragraph 15, in what parts of the essay is that purpose most apparent?
b. Why does the speaker address her audience directly, especially in paragraphs 4 and 10? How would you describe that audience?
c. What is the speaker's attitude about her estranged husband? Do you find it curious? What does it tell you about her? What does it tell you about Parker's purpose?
d. In paragraph 8, the speaker seems to describe a cycle of poverty into which the poor are born and in which they remain. Explain. In what other sections of the essay does she allude to this cycle?
e. How does she account for her inability to keep her family clean? Why is it futile for her to seek a job?
f. What is the distinction between "hunger" and "malnutrition" that she makes in paragraph 11? Why does she deny the usefulness of school lunch programs?
g. The speaker relates incidents in which she has had to endure both public and private humiliation in order to obtain help for her family. What is the source of such humiliation? How does Parker's inclusion of these incidents help her define "poverty"?

Strategy and Style

h. Often, the speaker makes sure to anticipate and to discuss opposing arguments. What is the effect of her doing so? How does this practice help illuminate her character?

i. Parker has organized the essay by having her speaker enunciate a series of qualities that define poverty. What is the effect of her beginning several paragraphs with "Poverty is…"?

j. Comment upon the author's use of illustrations. To what physical senses does she appeal most often? What use does she make of metaphor?

k. Parker has created a "persona" or speaker who tells her story by using the first-person pronoun ("I"). How would you describe this persona?

l. What is the purpose of paragraph 15 besides concluding the essay? How would you describe the speaker's tone in this paragraph? Does it differ from the tone she uses in other parts of the essay?

SUGGESTIONS FOR SHORT WRITING

a. Write a dictionary definition of "poverty" without using a dictionary. Then look the word up and compare your definition with the dictionary's. How specific were you or the dictionary able to get?

b. Now write a definition by using examples drawn from life. In your opinion, which of the definitions is clearer?

SUGGESTIONS FOR SUSTAINED WRITING

a. Parker has done an excellent job of defining an abstract term by using concrete illustrations. Think about one abstract term that describes a human reality with which you are thoroughly familiar: power, personal ambition, grief, hunger, physical pain, pride, for example. Explain what that term means to you. Use your own experiences as illustrations.

b. The speaker tells us about material poverty. Are there other kinds of poverty that are less frequently talked about—intellectual, spiritual, or moral poverty, for instance? Try to define one of these less commonly discussed types of poverty by using concrete details and illustrations as Parker does in this selection.

c. Does Parker believe that many of her readers harbor unfair and unrealistic assumptions about the poor? If so, what are these assumptions? Do you agree that they are unfair and unrealistic? Use what you know about poverty and the poor to write an essay that addresses such assumptions.

Pornoviolence

Tom Wolfe

One of America's leading satirists, Tom Wolfe (b. 1931) took a doctorate at Yale University and worked as a reporter for a number of years at various newspapers including The Washington Post. *Wolfe has also written for* New York *magazine,* Rolling Stone, *and* Esquire. *It was he who coined the phrase "The New Journalism," a technique that combines narration with reporting, a style somewhat less objective and detached than had once been thought appropriate for professional reporters. It suited him well. As a social critic, he wielded it like a scythe to expose the worst in American culture and its various subcultures, especially those considered chic in the 1960s and '70s. His most colorful titles include* The Electric Kool-Aid Acid Test *(1965) and* Kandy-Kolored Tangerine-Flake Streamline Baby *(1968). More recently, he published* The Right Stuff *(1979), which was made into a popular motion picture, and* From Bauhaus to Our House *(1981). In 1988 he published his first novel,* Bonfire of the Vanities, *upon which another film was based.*

"*Keeps His Mom-in-law in Chains,* meet *Kills Son and Feeds Corpse to* 1
Pigs."

"Pleased to meet you." 2

"*Teenager Twists Off Corpse's Head…to Get Gold Teeth,* meet *Strangles* 3
Girl Friend, Then Chops Her to Pieces."

"How you doing?" 4

"*Nurse's Aide Sees Fingers Chopped Off in Meat Grinder,* meet *I Left My* 5
Babies in the Deep Freeze."

"It's a pleasure." 6

It's a pleasure! No doubt about that! In all these years of journalism I 7
have covered more conventions than I care to remember. Podiatrists, theosophists, Professional Budget Finance dentists, oyster farmers, mathematicians, truckers, dry cleaners, stamp collectors, Esperantists, nudists, and newspaper editors—I have seen them all, together, in vast assemblies, sloughing through the wall-to-wall of a thousand hotel lobbies (the nudists excepted) in their shimmering gray-metal suits and pajama-stripe shirts with white Plasti-Coat name cards on their chests, and I have sat through their speeches and seminars (the nudists included) and attentively endured ear baths such as you wouldn't believe. And yet none has ever been quite like the convention of the stringers for *The National Enquirer.*

The Enquirer is a weekly newspaper that is probably known by sight to 8
millions more than know it by name. No one who ever came face-to-face with *The Enquirer* on a newsstand in its wildest days is likely to have forgotten the sight: a tabloid with great inky shocks of type all over the front page saying

something on the order of *Gouges Out Wife's Eyes to Make Her Ugly, Dad Hurls Hot Grease in Daughter's Face, Wife Commits Suicide after 2 Years of Poisoning Fails to Kill Husband...*

The stories themselves were supplied largely by stringers, i.e., correspon- 9
dents, from all over the country, the world, for that matter, mostly copy editors and reporters on local newspapers. Every so often they would come upon a story, usually via the police beat, that was so grotesque the local sheet would discard it or run it in a highly glossed form rather than offend or perplex its readers. The stringers would preserve them for *The Enquirer,* which always rewarded them well and respectfully.

One year *The Enquirer* convened and feted them at a hotel in Manhattan. 10
This convention was a success in every way. The only awkward moment was at the outset when the stringers all pulled in. None of them knew each other. Their hosts got around the problem by introducing them by the stories they had supplied. The introductions went like this:

"Harry, I want you to meet Frank here. Frank did that story, you remem- 11
ber that story, *Midget Murderer Throws Girl Off Cliff after She Refuses to Dance with Him.*"

"Pleased to meet you. That was some story."   12

"And Harry did the one about *I Spent Three Days Trapped at Bottom of* 13
Forty-Foot-Deep Mine Shaft and Was Saved by a Swarm of Flies."

"Likewise, I'm sure."   14

And *Midget Murderer Throws Girl Off Cliff* shakes hands with *I Spent* 15
Three Days Trapped at Bottom of Forty-Foot-Deep Mine Shaft, and *Buries Her Baby Alive* shakes hands with *Boy, Twelve, Strangles Two-Year-Old Girl,* and *Kills Son and Feeds Corpse to Pigs* shakes hands with *He Strangles Old Woman and Smears Corpse with Syrup, Ketchup, and Oatmeal*...and...

...There was a great deal of esprit about the whole thing. These men 16
were, in fact, the avant-garde of a new genre that since then has become institutionalized throughout the nation without anyone knowing its proper name. I speak of the new pornography, the pornography of violence.

Pornography comes from the Greek word "*porne,*" meaning harlot, and 17
pornography is literally the depiction of the acts of harlots. In the new pornography, the theme is not sex. The new pornography depicts practitioners acting out another, murkier drive: people staving teeth in, ripping guts open, blowing brains out, and getting even with all those bastards...

The success of *The Enquirer* prompted many imitators to enter the field, 18
Midnight, The Star Chronicle, The National Insider, Inside News, The National Close-up, The National Tattler, The National Examiner. A truly competitive free press evolved, and soon a reader could go to the newspaper of his choice for *Kill the Retarded! (Won't You Join My Movement?)* and *Unfaithful Wife? Burn Her Bed!, Harem Master's Mistress Chops Him with Machete, Babe Bites Off Boy's Tongue,* and *Cuts Buddy's Face to Pieces for Stealing His Business and Fiancée.*

And yet the last time I surveyed the Violence press, I noticed a curious 19
thing. These pioneering journals seem to have pulled back. They seem to be
regressing to what is by now the Redi-Mix staple of literate Americans, mere
sex. *Ecstasy and Me (by Hedy Lamarr),* says *The National Enquirer. I Run a
Sex Art Gallery,* says *The National Insider.* What has happened, I think, is
something that has happened to avant-gardes in many fields, from William
Morris and the Craftsmen to the Bauhaus group. Namely, their discoveries have
been preempted by the Establishment and so thoroughly dissolved into the
mainstream they no longer look original.

Robert Harrison, the former publisher of *Confidential,* and later publisher 20
of the aforementioned *Inside News,* was perhaps the first person to see it coming. I was interviewing Harrison early in January 1964 for a story in *Esquire*
about six weeks after the assassination of President Kennedy, and we were in a
cab in the West Fifties in Manhattan, at a stoplight, by a newsstand, and Harrison suddenly pointed at the newsstand and said, "Look at that. They're doing
the same thing *The Enquirer* does."

There on the stand was a row of slick-paper, magazine-size publications, 21
known in the trade as one-shots, with titles like *Four Days That Shook the
World, Death of a President, An American Tragedy,* or just *John Fitzgerald
Kennedy (1921–1963).* "You want to know why people buy those things?" said
Harrison. "People buy those things to see a man get his head blown off."

And, of course, he was right. Only now the publishers were in many 22
cases the pillars of the American press. Invariably, these "special coverages" of
the assassination bore introductions piously commemorating the fallen President, exhorting the American people to strength and unity in a time of crisis,
urging greater vigilance and safeguards for the new President, and even raising
the nice metaphysical question of collective guilt in "an age of violence."

In the years since then, of course, there has been an incessant replay, with 23
every recoverable clinical detail, of those less than five seconds in which a man
got his head blown off. And throughout this deluge of words, pictures, and film
frames, I have been intrigued with one thing: The point of view, the vantage
point, is almost never that of the victim, riding in the Presidential Lincoln Continental. What you get is…the view from Oswald's rifle. You can step right up
here and look point-blank right through the very hairline cross in Lee Harvey
Oswald's Optics Ordnance in weaponry four-power Japanese telescope sight
and watch, frame by frame by frame by frame, as that man there's head comes
apart. Just a little History there before your very eyes.

The television networks have schooled us in the view from Oswald's rifle 24
and made it seem a normal pastime. The TV viewpoint is nearly always that of
the man who is going to strike. The last time I watched *Gunsmoke,* which was
not known as a very violent Western in TV terms, the action went like this: The
Wellington agents and the stagecoach driver pull guns on the badlands gang
leader's daughter and Kitty, the heart-of-gold saloonkeeper, and kidnap them.
Then the badlands gang shoots two Wellington agents. Then they tie up five

more and talk about shooting them. Then they desist because they might not be able to get a hotel room in the next town if the word got around. Then one badlands gang gunslinger attempts to rape Kitty while the gang leader's younger daughter looks on. Then Kitty resists, so he slugs her one in the jaw. Then the gang leader slugs him. Then the gang leader slugs Kitty. Then Kitty throws hot stew in a gang member's face and hits him over the back of the head with a revolver. Then he knocks her down with a rock. Then the gang sticks up a bank. Here comes the marshal, Matt Dillon. He shoots a gang member and breaks it up. Then the gang leader shoots the guy who was guarding his daughter and the woman. Then the marshal shoots the gang leader. The final exploding bullet signals The End.

It is not the accumulated slayings and bone crushings that make this por- 25 noviolence, however. What makes it pornoviolence is that in almost every case the camera angle, therefore the viewer, is with the gun, the fist, the rock. The pornography of violence has no point of view in the old sense that novels do. You do not live the action through the hero's eyes. You live with the aggressor, whoever he may be. One moment you are the hero. The next you are the villain. No matter whose side you may be on consciously, you are in fact with the muscle, and it is you who disintegrate all comers, villains, lawmen, women, anybody. On the rare occasions in which the gun is emptied into the camera— i.e., into your face—the effect is so startling that the pornography of violence all but loses its fantasy charm. There are not nearly so many masochists as sadists among those little devils whispering into one's ears.

In fact, sex—"sadomasochism"—is only a part of the pornography of vi- 26 olence. Violence is much more wrapped up, simply, with status. Violence is the simple, ultimate solution for problems of status competition, just as gambling is the simple, ultimate solution for economic competition. The old pornography was the fantasy of easy sexual delights in a world where sex was kept unavailable. The new pornography is the fantasy of easy triumph in a world where status competition has become so complicated and frustrating.

Already the old pornography is losing its kick because of over-exposure. 27 In the late thirties, Nathanael West published his last and best-regarded novel, *The Day of the Locust,* and it was a terrible flop commercially, and his publisher said if he ever published another book about Hollywood it would "have to be *My Thirty-nine Ways of Making Love by Hedy Lamarr.*" He thought he was saying something that was funny because it was beyond the realm of possibility. Less than thirty years later, however, Hedy Lamarr's *Ecstasy and Me* was published. Whether she mentions thirty-nine ways, I'm not sure, but she gets off to a flying start: "The men in my life have ranged from a classic case history of impotence, to a whip-brandishing sadist who enjoyed sex only after he tied my arms behind me with the sash of his robe. There was another man who took his pleasure with a girl in my own bed, while he thought I was asleep in it."

Yet she was too late. The book very nearly sank without a trace. The sin 28 itself is wearing out. Pornography cannot exist without certified taboo to violate. And today Lust, like the rest of the Seven Deadly Sins—Pride, Sloth, Envy, Greed, Anger, and Gluttony—is becoming a rather minor vice. The Seven Deadly Sins, after all, are only sins against the self. Theologically, the idea of Lust—well, the idea is that if you seduce some poor girl from Akron, it is not a sin because you are ruining her, but because you are wasting your time and your energies and damaging your own spirit. This goes back to the old work ethic, when the idea was to keep every able-bodied man's shoulder to the wheel. In an age of riches for all, the ethic becomes more nearly: Let him do anything he pleases, as long as he doesn't get in my way. And if he does get in my way, or even if he doesn't...well...we have *new* fantasies for that. *Put hair on the walls.*

"Hair on the walls" is the invisible subtitle of Truman Capote's book *In* 29 *Cold Blood.* The book is neither a who-done-it nor a will-they-be-caught, since the answers to both questions are known from the outset. It does ask why-did-they-do-it, but the answer is soon as clear as it is going to be. Instead, the book's suspense is based largely on a totally new idea in detective stories: the promise of gory details, and the withholding of them until the end. Early in the game one of the two murderers, Dick, starts promising to put "plenty of hair on them-those walls" with a shotgun. So read on, gentle readers, and on and on; you are led up to the moment before the crime on page 60—yet the specifics, what happened, the gory details, are kept out of sight, in grisly dangle, until page 244.

But Dick and Perry, Capote's killers, are only a couple of Low Rent 30 bums. With James Bond the new pornography reached a dead center, the bureaucratic middle class. The appeal of Bond has been explained as the appeal of the lone man who can solve enormously complicated, even world problems through his own bravery and initiative. But Bond is not a lone man at all, of course. He is not the Lone Ranger. He is much easier to identify than that. He is a salaried functionary in a bureaucracy. He is a sport, but a believable one; not a millionaire, but a bureaucrat on an expense account. He is not even a high-level bureaucrat. He is an operative. This point is carefully and repeatedly made by having his superiors dress him down for violations of standard operating procedure. Bond, like the Lone Ranger, solves problems with guns and fists. When it is over, however, the Lone Ranger leaves a silver bullet. Bond, like the rest of us, fills out a report in triplicate.

Marshall McLuhan says we are in a period in which it will become harder 31 and harder to stimulate lust through words and pictures—i.e., the old pornography. In the latest round of pornographic movies the producers have found it necessary to introduce violence, bondage, torture, and aggressive physical destruction to an extraordinary degree. The same sort of bloody escalation may very well happen in the pure pornography of violence. Even such able craftsmen as Truman Capote, Ian Fleming, NBC, and CBS may not suffice. Fortunately, there are historical models to rescue us from this frustration. In the latter days of the Roman Empire, the Emperor Commodus became jealous of the celebrity of the great gladiators. He took to the arena himself, with his sword, and began dispatching suitably screened cripples and hobbled fighters. Audience participation became so popular that soon various *illuminati* of the Commodus set, various boys and girls of the year, were out there, suited up, gaily cutting a sequence of dwarfs and feebles down to short ribs. Ah, swinging generations, what new delights await?

1967

QUESTIONS FOR DISCUSSION

Content

a. According to Wolfe, what is "pornoviolence" and what accounts for its success?

b. Wolfe's decision to use *Gunsmoke, In Cold Blood,* the Lone Ranger, and James Bond as illustrations reveal an awareness of audience. How would you characterize Wolfe's intended reader?

c. How does "pornoviolence" differ from the old pornography? What do Wolfe's references to gambling and to "the old pornography" contribute to his definition of "pornoviolence" (paragraph 26)?

d. In which sections of this extended definition does Wolfe use techniques common to narration?

e. Make use of the reference section of your college library to identify the following: Hedy Lamarr, the Bauhaus, William Morris, and Marshall McLuhan.

f. What are "those little devils whispering into one's ears" (paragraph 25)?

g. What, according to Wolfe, is the difference between the old work ethic and the ethic in "an age of riches for all" (paragraph 28)? Why is Lust becoming a minor vice? What role do the work ethic and the Seven Deadly Sins play in Wolfe's extended definition of "pornoviolence"?

h. What does the author see as the critical difference between James Bond and the Lone Ranger?

i. What does he mean by "point of view"? Why is this term central to the purpose of the essay?

j. Why does Wolfe call *The National Enquirer* and other such newspapers "pioneering journals"?

k. What does his recollection of President Kennedy's assassination and of the period that followed tell us about the nature of "pornoviolence"?

Strategy and Style

l. At first we don't know what to make of Wolfe's unusual introduction. When do we first realize that he is quoting headlines that might appear in the *En-*

quirer? Does this way of beginning an essay work? What dangers might an inexperienced writer encounter if he or she tried to do something similar?

m. In what ways does Wolfe's concluding paragraph echo his introduction?

n. Why does Wolfe bother to provide an etymological definition (definition based on word origins) for "pornography"?

o. Wolfe's choice of words seems to be a masterful blending of the erudite with the familiar to create a distinctive and energetic style. Find passages in which these two levels of language complement each other.

SUGGESTIONS FOR SHORT WRITING

a. Choose one of the pornoviolent headlines Wolfe mentions in this essay and write an introductory paragraph or two of a story that would most likely accompany it. Try to imitate the style of tabloid writers.

b. Try coining other compound terms that describe modern culture. Brainstorm a list of nouns that come to mind; next, combine them in different ways and write a definition of one of them.

SUGGESTIONS FOR SUSTAINED WRITING

a. Think back to a movie or television show you have seen recently or to a book you have read during the last month or so. Could Wolfe have used it to help illustrate his definition of "pornoviolence"? If so, write an essay in which you apply his definition to that book, film, or television show.

b. Do you read any of the tabloids Wolfe mentions in this essay? If so, refute (or support) his contention that they appeal to the worst in us.

c. Is "pornoviolence" on the rise in our society? In a well-developed essay, argue for or against Wolfe's belief that we might experience an "escalation...in the pure pornography of violence."

d. Are people's ethical values changing for the better or for the worse? Write an essay in which you try to define one or two basic principles upon which you base your own ethics. Provide as many concrete illustrations as you can to help your reader understand and relate to what you're explaining.

Good Souls

Dorothy Parker

Dorothy Parker (1893–1967) began her career shortly after graduating from high school by writing essays, sketches, and poetry for Vogue *and* Vanity Fair. *Later, she published in* The New Yorker *and, on occasion, in the* Saturday Evening Post *and* Life. *Parker was one of the "charter members" of the Algonquin Round Table, an informal literary club that included humorist Robert Benchley and Harold Ross, the founder of* The New Yorker. *Versatile as well as witty, Parker published books of poetry, collections of essays and stories, and wrote many plays and screenplays, including* A Star Is Born, *which she coauthored with her husband, Alan Campbell. "Big Blonde," for which she won the O. Henry Award in 1929, is her best-known short story. Parker also helped found the Screen Writers Guild in 1934 and the Anti-Nazi League in 1936. But her life was not all happiness and success. She was often troubled and twice attempted suicide. Her outspoken Marxist politics landed her before the House Un-American Activities Committee in 1952. Yet she always survived, perhaps supported by a sense of humor, the possession of which she felt was essential to living. Her suggestions for an epitaph reveal an ability to chuckle even over her own demise: "Excuse my dust" and "If you can read this, you've come too close." "Good Souls" is an early piece by this brilliant American wit; it appeared in* Vanity Fair *in 1919.*

1   All about us, living in our very families, it may be, there exists a race of curious creatures. Outwardly, they possess no marked peculiarities; in fact, at a hasty glance, they may be readily mistaken for regular human beings. They are built after the popular design; they have the usual number of features, arranged in the conventional manner; they offer no variations on the general run of things in their habits of dressing, eating, and carrying on their business.

2   Yet, between them and the rest of the civilized world, there stretches an impassable barrier. Though they live in the very thick of the human race, they are forever isolated from it. They are fated to go through life, congenital pariahs. They live out their little lives, mingling with the world, yet never a part of it.

3   They are, in short, Good Souls.

4   And the piteous thing about them is that they are wholly unconscious of their condition. A Good Soul thinks he is just like anyone else. Nothing could convince him otherwise. It is heartrending to see him, going cheerfully about, even whistling or humming as he goes, all unconscious of his terrible plight. The utmost he can receive from the world is an attitude of good-humored patience, a perfunctory word of approbation, a praising with faint damns, so to speak—yet he firmly believes that everything is all right with him.

5   There is no accounting for Good Souls.

6   They spring up anywhere. They will suddenly appear in families which,

189

for generations, have had no slightest stigma attached to them. Possibly they are throw-backs. There is scarcely a family without at least one Good Soul somewhere in it at the present moment—maybe in the form of an elderly aunt, an unmarried sister, an unsuccessful brother, an indigent cousin. No household is complete without one.

The Good Soul begins early; he will show signs of his condition in ex-   7
treme youth. Go now to the nearest window, and look out on the little children playing so happily below. Any group of youngsters that you may happen to see will do perfectly. Do you observe the child whom all the other little dears make "it" in their merry games? Do you follow the child from whom the other little ones snatch the cherished candy, to consume it before his streaming eyes? Can you get a good look at the child whose precious toys are borrowed for indefinite periods by the other playful youngsters, and are returned to him in fragments? Do you see the child upon whom all the other kiddies play their complete repertory of childhood's winsome pranks—throwing bags of water on him, running away and hiding from him, shouting his name in quaint rhymes, chalking coarse legends on his unsuspecting back?

Mark that child well. He is going to be a Good Soul when he grows up.   8

Thus does the doomed child go through early youth and adolescence. So   9
does he progress towards the fulfillment of his destiny. And then, some day, when he is under discussion, someone will say of him, "Well, he means well, anyway." That settles it. For him, that is the end. Those words have branded him with the indelible mark of his pariahdom. He has come into his majority; he is a full-fledged Good Soul.

The activities of the adult of the species are familiar to us all. When you   10
are ill, who is it that hastens to your bedside bearing molds of blancmange, which, from infancy, you have hated with unspeakable loathing? As usual, you are way ahead of me, gentle reader—it is indeed the Good Soul. It is the Good Souls who efficiently smooth out your pillow when you have just worked it into the comfortable shape, who creak about the room on noisy tiptoe, who tenderly lay on your fevered brow damp cloths which drip ceaselessly down your neck. It is they who ask, every other minute, if there isn't something that they can do for you. It is they who, at great personal sacrifice, spend long hours sitting beside your bed, reading aloud the continued stories in the *Woman's Home Companion,* or chatting cozily on the increase in the city's death rate.

In health, as in illness, they are always right there, ready to befriend you.   11
No sooner do you sit down, than they exclaim that they can see you aren't comfortable in that chair, and insist on your changing places with them. It is the Good Souls who just *know* that you don't like your tea that way, and who bear it masterfully away from you to alter it with cream and sugar until it is a complete stranger to you. At the table, it is they who always feel that their grapefruit is better than yours and who have to be restrained almost forcibly from exchanging with you. In a restaurant the waiter invariably makes a mistake and brings them something which they did not order—and which they refuse to

have changed, choking it down with a wistful smile. It is they who cause traffic blocks, by standing in subway entrances arguing altruistically as to who is to pay the fare.

At the theater, should they be members of a box-party, it is the Good 12 Souls who insist on occupying the rear chairs; if the seats are in the orchestra, they worry audibly, all through the performance, about their being able to see better than you, until finally in desperation you grant their plea and change seats with them. If, by so doing, they can bring a little discomfort on themselves—sit in a draught, say, or behind a pillar—then their happiness is complete. To feel the genial glow of martyrdom—that is all they ask of life....

The lives of Good Souls are crowded with Occasions, each with its own 13 ritual which must be solemnly followed. On Mother's Day, Good Souls conscientiously wear carnations; on St. Patrick's Day, they faithfully don boutonnieres of shamrocks; on Columbus Day, they carefully pin on miniature Italian flags. Every feast must be celebrated by the sending out of cards—Valentine's Day, Arbor , Groundhog Day, and all the other important festivals, each is duly observed. They have a perfect genius for discovering appropriate cards of greeting for the event. It must take hours of research.

If it's too long a time between holidays, then the Good Soul will send 14 little cards or little mementoes, just by way of surprises. He is strong on surprises, anyway. It delights him to drop in unexpectedly on his friends. Who has not known the joy of those evenings when some Good Soul just runs in, as a surprise? It is particularly effective when a chosen company of other guests happens to be present—enough for two tables of bridge, say. This means that the Good Soul must sit wistfully by, patiently watching the progress of the rubber, or else must cut in at intervals, volubly voicing his desolation at causing so much inconvenience, and apologizing constantly during the evening.

His conversation, admirable though it is, never receives its just due of at- 15 tention and appreciation. He is one of those who believe and frequently quote the exemplary precept that there is good in everybody; hanging in his bedchamber is the whimsically phrased, yet vital, statement, done in burned leather— "There is so much good in the worst of us and so much bad in the best of us that it hardly behooves any of us to talk about the rest of us." This, too, he archly quotes on appropriate occasions. Two or three may be gathered together, intimately discussing some mutual acquaintance. It is just getting really absorbing, when comes the Good Soul, to utter his dutiful, "We mustn't judge harshly—after all, we must always remember that many times our own actions may be misconstrued." Somehow, after several of these little reminders, there seems to be a general waning of interest; the little gathering breaks up, inventing quaint excuses to get away and discuss the thing more fully, adding a few really good details, some place where the Good Soul will not follow. While the Good Soul pitifully ignorant of their evil purpose glows with the warmth of conscious virtue, and settles himself to read the Contributors' Club, in the *Atlantic Monthly,* with a sense of duty well done....

Good Souls are no mean humorists. They have a time-honored formula of 16
fun-making, which must be faithfully followed. Certain words or phrases must
be whimsically distorted every time they are used. "Over the river," they dutifully say, whenever they take their leave. "Don't you cast any asparagus on
me," they warn, archly; and they never fail to speak of "three times in concus-
sion." According to their ritual, these screaming phrases must be repeated several times, for the most telling effect, and are invariably followed by hearty
laughter from the speaker, to whom they seem eternally new.

Perhaps the most congenial role of the Good Soul is that of advice-giver. 17
He loves to take people aside and have serious little personal talks, all for their
own good. He thinks it only right to point out faults or bad habits which are,
perhaps unconsciously, growing on them. He goes home and laboriously writes
long, intricate letters, invariably beginning, "Although you may feel that this is
no affair of mine, I think that you really ought to know," and so on, indefinitely.
In his desire to help, he reminds one irresistibly of Marcelline, who used to try
so pathetically and so fruitlessly to be of some assistance in arranging the circus arena, and who brought such misfortunes on his own innocent person
thereby.

The Good Souls will, doubtless, gain their reward in Heaven; on this 18
earth, certainly, theirs is what is technically known as a rough deal. The most
hideous outrages are perpetrated on them. "Oh, he won't mind," people say.
"He's a Good Soul." And then they proceed to heap the rankest impositions
upon him. When Good Souls give a party, people who have accepted weeks in
advance call up at the last second and refuse, without the shadow of an excuse
save that of a subsequent engagement. Other people are invited to all sorts of
entertaining affairs; the Good Soul, unasked, waves them a cheery good-bye
and hopes wistfully that they will have a good time. His is the uncomfortable
seat in the motor; he is the one to ride backwards in the train; he is the one who
is always chosen to solicit subscriptions and make up deficits. People borrow
his money, steal his servants, lose his golf balls, use him as a sort of errand boy,
leave him flat whenever something more attractive offers—and carry it all off
with their cheerful slogan, "Oh, he won't mind—he's a Good Soul."

And that's just it—Good Souls never do mind. After each fresh atrocity 19
they are more cheerful, forgiving and virtuous, if possible, than they were before. There is simply no keeping them down—back they come, with their little
gifts, and their little words of advice, and their little endeavors to be of service,
always anxious for more.

Yes, there can be no doubt about it—their reward will come to them in 20
the next world.

Would that they were even now enjoying it!   21

1919

QUESTIONS FOR DISCUSSION

Content

a. Parker takes a well-worn phrase and treats it as worthy of thorough definition. How would her definition of "good souls" sound if it were to be defined seriously in a standard dictionary?

b. The many touches of sarcasm aside, do you feel that overall Parker is attempting to be serious or humorous? What specific details do you find to support either answer?

c. What is Parker's opinion of Good Souls? Does she sympathize with them at all? How do you know?

d. Do Good Souls as Parker defines them really exist? If so, suppose that one of them happened to read this essay. What would his or her reaction be? To what extent would he or she agree or disagree with Parker's description?

e. This essay was written more than seventy years ago. Is Parker's definition of Good Souls still relevant? In what way?

Strategy and Style

f. How does the author's use of imagined situations and conversations affect the essay? In what way would the essay have been different had Parker named real people and recalled real conversations?

g. Find examples of irony in this essay.

h. Sometimes, Parker uses language that is affected (archaic, sentimental, or overblown—even for 1919!): for example, "little dears" and "merry games" in paragraph 7; "gentle readers" and "fevered brow" in paragraph 10; and "rankest impositions" in paragraph 18. What were her reasons for using these words? What effect do they have on the tone of the essay?

i. What purpose do the one-sentence paragraphs near the beginning of the essay serve?

j. Why does Parker include the last sentence? Does this sentence clarify the essay's purpose? Does it alter the essay's tone?

SUGGESTIONS FOR SHORT WRITING

a. Write a brief description of any Good Souls of your acquaintance.

b. Drawing from your own experience, write a different introduction for "Good Souls." Use dialogue or an anecdote instead of Parker's more or less straightforward description.

SUGGESTIONS FOR SUSTAINED WRITING

a. In the first paragraph, Parker distinguishes between Good Souls and "regular human beings." Write an essay in which you define and describe these "regular human beings." Could "Regular Human Beings" be the title of your essay? One way to organize and develop your essay is to compare "regular human beings" with Good Souls.

b. Do you know any Good Souls? Write a sequel or extension to Parker's essay in which you show that this person or these persons fit Parker's definition.

5

Division and Classification

Division and classification are attempts to explain the nature and connections between bits of information that may, at first, seem unrelated and confusing. Writers often find it useful to identify like qualities or characteristics among various facts, ideas, people, or things so as to create related categories or classes by which the material can be divided logically and discussed systematically.

If you are a people watcher, you know that public places—a bus station, a sports stadium, or even your college library—offer a wide variety of subjects. Let's say that two days before a math midterm, you resolve to study hard in the library. As you walk into the main reading room, you hear the giggles of young lovers seated in a corner. A few yards beyond, you see one of the college's maintenance workers, who is spending her lunch hour turning the pages of a large newspaper. To your right, you begin to eavesdrop on several students discussing a fraternity party, and you notice that their chatter annoys a woman trying to take notes for a term paper. In a less crowded part of the room, two of your friends kill time by browsing through a few magazines they found lying about. After a while, you decide that the reading room offers too many distractions, so you find a corner in the basement where you can hide. It is no coincidence that other members of your math class had the same idea; you sit down quietly and begin studying.

The decision to join your classmates and not stay in the reading room resulted from dividing the group of people you found at the library into three smaller categories: fun seekers, browsers, and serious students! Your analysis may have been quick and informal, but it was effective. What's more, it revealed something important about the nature and function of classification: you began by observing similarities among various individuals; you created categories based on those similarities and placed each individual you observed into one of those categories; and you made a decision—to study in one place and not another—based upon what your classification revealed.

195

Classification is a versatile tool. It can be used to discuss social problems as in "Struggle for Justice" or to satirize fads and faddists as in Erika Ritter's "Bicycles." William Golding and Susan Allen Toth show that it even makes an effective tool for self-analysis and for shedding light on aspects of our personalities and private lives that might parallel those of our readers.

The success of a classification paper depends upon how logically its author divides the material and how thoroughly and concretely he or she develops each category. Among the most effective methods to develop such an essay is illustration. Specific, well-developed examples like the kind found in James David Barber's "Presidential Character...." and Robert Brustein's "Reflections on Horror Movies" are essential to the writers' purposes. Without such examples, their essays might have remained lists of ill-defined labels and abstractions. But good writers are in the habit of using a variety of techniques to keep readers interested. The essays by Golding, Ludlum, and Toth, though different in style and approach, all contain anecdotes (narration) to support important points; Ritter takes time to describe both bicycles and bicyclists in her essay; and Ludlum contrasts what we know and what we once believed to define "Climythology" and explain its causes and effects.

As you read through the selections that follow, keep in mind that almost any conglomeration of seemingly unrelated information can be classified logically to reveal patterns of meaning that readers will find valuable and interesting. The perspectives from which you view a subject and the choices you make to impose order on the material should be determined only by your purpose. Read the Suggestions for Writing at the end of each selection. They describe activities that may help you use classification to accomplish a well-defined purpose in a full-length paper. But even if you approach a writing assignment without a clear notion of purpose—a phenomenon not uncommon even among experienced writers—you may still want to use classification in the preliminary stages of your project to review the raw information you have gathered, to group facts, ideas, and insights logically, and, ultimately, to improve your understanding both of the material and of your purpose.

Thinking as a Hobby

William Golding

A native of Cornwall, England, Golding (b. 1911) was educated at Oxford University, where he received his B.A. in 1935. Since then, except for service with the Royal Navy, he has spent his life teaching and writing. In 1983 he won the Nobel Prize. His most famous work, Lord of the Flies *(1954), is now a classic in high-school and college curricula around the world. This anti-utopian novel tells of several schoolboys stranded on a desert island and of their ill-fated attempts to govern themselves. Like many of Golding's other works,* Lord of the Flies *is laden with religious symbolism, and it focuses on the conflict between the forces of good and evil in the human soul. Other novels by Golding include* Pincher Martin *(1950);* The Spire *(1964);* The Pyramid *(1967);* Darkness Visible *(1979); and a trilogy:* Rites of Passage *(1980),* Close Quarters *(1987), and* Fire Down Below *(1989). He has also written plays and poetry. "Thinking as a Hobby" was published as a magazine piece in 1961.*

While I was still a boy, I came to the conclusion that there were three grades of thinking; and since I was later to claim thinking as my hobby, I came to an even stranger conclusion—namely, that I myself could not think at all. 1

I must have been an unsatisfactory child for grownups to deal with. I remember how incomprehensible they appeared to me at first, but not, of course, how I appeared to them. It was the headmaster of my grammar school who first brought the subject of thinking before me—though neither in the way, nor with the result he intended. He had some statuettes in his study. They stood on a high cupboard behind his desk. One was a lady wearing nothing but a bath towel. She seemed frozen in an eternal panic lest the bath towel slip down any farther; and since she had no arms, she was in an unfortunate position to pull the towel up again. Next to her, crouched the statuette of a leopard, ready to spring down at the top drawer of a filing cabinet labeled A–AH. My innocence interpreted this as the victim's last, despairing cry. Beyond the leopard was a naked, muscular gentleman, who sat, looking down, with his chin on his fist and his elbow on his knee. He seemed utterly miserable. 2

Some time later, I learned about these statuettes. The headmaster had placed them where they would face delinquent children, because they symbolized to him the whole of life. The naked lady was the Venus of Milo. She was Love. She was not worried about the towel. She was just busy being beautiful. The leopard was Nature, and he was being natural. The naked, muscular gentleman was not miserable. He was Rodin's Thinker, an image of pure thought. It is easy to buy small plaster models of what you think life is like. 3

I had better explain that I was a frequent visitor to the headmaster's study, because of the latest thing I had done or left undone. As we now say, I was not integrated. I was, if anything, disintegrated; and I was puzzled. Grownups never 4

197

made sense. Whenever I found myself in a penal position before the headmaster's desk, with the statuettes glimmering whitely above him, I would sink my head, clasp my hands behind my back and writhe one shoe over the other.

The headmaster would look opaquely at me through flashing spectacles.   5

"What are we going to do with you?"   6

Well, what *were* they going to do with me? I would writhe my shoe some   7
more and stare down at the worn rug.

"Look up, boy! Can't you look up?"   8

Then I would look up at the cupboard, where the naked lady was frozen   9
in her panic and the muscular gentleman contemplated the hindquarters of the leopard in endless gloom. I had nothing to say to the headmaster. His spectacles caught the light so that you could see nothing human behind them. There was no possibility of communication.

"Don't you ever think at all?"   10

No, I didn't think, wasn't thinking, couldn't think—I was simply waiting   11
in anguish for the interview to stop.

"Then you'd better learn—hadn't you?"   12

On one occasion the headmaster leaped to his feet, reached up and   13
plonked Rodin's masterpiece on the desk before me.

"That's what a man looks like when he's really thinking."   14

I surveyed the gentleman without interest or comprehension.   15

"Go back to your class."   16

Clearly there was something missing in me. Nature had endowed the rest   17
of the human race with a sixth sense and left me out. This must be so, I mused, on my way back to the class, since whether I had broken a window, or failed to remember Boyle's Law, or been late for school, my teachers produced me one, adult answer: "Why can't you think?"

As I saw the case, I had broken the window because I had tried to hit   18
Jack Arney with a cricket ball and missed him; I could not remember Boyle's Law because I had never bothered to learn it; and I was late for school because I preferred looking over the bridge into the river. In fact, I was wicked. Were my teachers, perhaps, so good that they could not understand the depths of my depravity? Were they clear, untormented people who could direct their every action by this mysterious business of thinking? The whole thing was incomprehensible. In my earlier years, I found even the statuette of the Thinker confusing. I did not believe any of my teachers were naked, ever. Like someone born deaf, but bitterly determined to find out about sound, I watched my teachers to find out about thought.

There was Mr. Houghton. He was always telling me to think. With a   19
modest satisfaction, he would tell me that he had thought a bit himself. Then why did he spend so much time drinking? Or was there more sense in drinking than there appeared to be? But if not, and if drinking were in fact ruinous to health—and Mr. Houghton was ruined, there was no doubt about that—why was he always talking about the clean life and the virtues of fresh air? He

would spread his arms wide with the action of a man who habitually spent his time striding along mountain ridges.

"Open air does me good, boys—I know it!"   20

Sometimes, exalted by his own oratory, he would leap from his desk and   21 hustle us outside into a hideous wind.

"Now, boys! Deep breaths! Feel it right down inside you—huge draughts   22 of God's good air!"

He would stand before us, rejoicing in his perfect health, an open-air   23 man. He would put his hands on his waist and take a tremendous breath. You could hear the wind, trapped in the cavern of his chest and struggling with all the unnatural impediments. His body would reel with shock and his ruined face go white at the unaccustomed visitation. He would stagger back to his desk and collapse there, useless for the rest of the morning.

Mr. Houghton was given to high-minded monologues about the good life,   24 sexless and full of duty. Yet in the middle of one of these monologues, if a girl passed the window, tapping along on her neat little feet, he would interrupt his discourse, his neck would turn of itself and he would watch her out of sight. In this instance, he seemed to me ruled not by thought but by an invisible and irresistible spring in his nape.

His neck was an object of great interest to me. Normally it bulged a bit   25 over his collar. But Mr. Houghton had fought in the First World War alongside both Americans and French, and had come—by who knows what illogic?—to a settled detestation of both countries. If either happened to be prominent in current affairs, no argument could make Mr. Houghton think well of it. He would bang the desk, his neck would bulge still further and go red. "You can say what you like," he would cry, "but I've thought about this—and I know what I think!"

Mr. Houghton thought with his neck.   26

There was Miss Parsons. She assured us that her dearest wish was our   27 welfare, but I knew even then, with the mysterious clairvoyance of childhood, that what she wanted most was the husband she never got. There was Mr. Hands—and so on.

I have dealt at length with my teachers because this was my introduction   28 to the nature of what is commonly called thought. Through them I discovered that thought is often full of unconscious prejudice, ignorance and hypocrisy. It will lecture on disinterested purity while its neck is being remorselessly twisted toward a skirt. Technically, it is about as proficient as most businessmen's golf, as honest as most politicians' intentions, or—to come near my own preoccupation—as coherent as most books that get written. It is what I came to call grade-three thinking, though more properly, it is feeling, rather than thought.

True, often there is a kind of innocence in prejudices, but in those days I   29 viewed grade-three thinking with an intolerant contempt and an incautious mockery. I delighted to confront a pious lady who hated the Germans with the proposition that we should love our enemies. She taught me a great truth in dealing with grade-three thinkers; because of her, I no longer dismiss lightly a mental process which for nine-tenths of the population is the nearest they will ever get to thought. They have immense solidarity. We had better respect them, for we are outnumbered and surrounded. A crowd of grade-three thinkers, all shouting the same thing, all warming their hands at the fire of their own prejudices, will not thank you for pointing out the contradictions in their beliefs. Man is a gregarious animal, and enjoys agreement as cows will graze all the same way on the side of a hill.

    Grade-two thinking is the detection of contradictions. I reached grade two 30 when I trapped the poor, pious lady. Grade-two thinkers do not stampede easily, though often they fall into the other fault and lag behind. Grade-two thinking is a withdrawal, with eyes and ears open. It became my hobby and brought satisfaction and loneliness in either hand. For grade-two thinking destroys without having the power to create. It set me watching the crowds cheering His Majesty and King and asking myself what all the fuss was about, without giving me anything positive to put in the place of that heady patriotism. But there were compensations. To hear people justify their habit of hunting foxes and tearing them to pieces by claiming that the foxes liked it. To hear our Prime Minister talk about the great benefit we conferred on India by jailing people like Pandit Nehru and Gandhi. To hear American politicians talk about peace in one sentence and refuse to join the League of Nations in the next. Yes, there were moments of delight.

    But I was growing toward adolescence and had to admit that Mr. Hough- 31 ton was not the only one with an irresistible spring in his neck. I, too, felt the compulsive hand of nature and began to find that pointing out contradiction could be costly as well as fun. There was Ruth, for example, a serious and attractive girl. I was an atheist at the time. Grade-two thinking is a menace to religion and knocks down sects like skittles. I put myself in a position to be converted by her with an hypocrisy worthy of grade three. She was a Methodist—or at least, her parents were, and Ruth had to follow suit. But, alas, instead of relying on the Holy Spirit to convert me, Ruth was foolish enough to open her pretty mouth in argument. She claimed that the Bible (King James Version) was literally inspired. I countered by saying that the Catholics believed in the literal inspiration of Saint Jerome's *Vulgate,* and the two books were different. Argument flagged.

    At last she remarked that there were an awful lot of Methodists, and they 32 couldn't be wrong, could they—not all those millions? That was too easy, said I restively (for the nearer you were to Ruth, the nicer she was to be near to) since there were more Roman Catholics than Methodists anyway; and they couldn't be wrong, could they—not all those hundreds of millions? An awful flicker of doubt appeared in her eyes. I slid my arm around her waist and murmured breathlessly that if we were counting heads, the Buddhists were the boys for my money. But Ruth had *really* wanted to do me good, because I was so nice. She fled. The combination of my arm and those countless Buddhists was too much for her.

That night her father visited my father and left, red-cheeked and indig- 33 nant. I was given the third degree to find out what had happened. It was lucky we were both of us only fourteen. I lost Ruth and gained an undeserved reputation as a potential libertine.

So grade-two thinking could be dangerous. It was in this knowledge, at the 34 age of fifteen, that I remember making a comment from the heights of grade two, on the limitations of grade three. One evening I found myself alone in the school hall, preparing it for a party. The door of the headmaster's study was open. I went in. The headmaster had ceased to thump Rodin's Thinker down on the desk as an example to the young. Perhaps he had not found any more candidates, but the statuettes were still there, glimmering and gathering dust on top of the cupboard. I stood on a chair and rearranged them. I stood Venus in her bath towel on the filing cabinet, so that now the top drawer caught its breath in a gasp of sexy excitement. "A-ah!" The portentous Thinker I placed on the edge of the cupboard so that he looked down at the bath towel and waited for it to slip.

Grade-two thinking, though it filled life with fun and excitement, did not 35 make for content. To find out the deficiencies of our elders bolsters the young ego but does not make for personal security. I found that grade two was not only the power to point out contradictions. It took the swimmer some distance from the shore and left him there, out of his depth. I decided that Pontius Pilate was a typical grade-two thinker. "What is truth?" he said, a very common grade-two thought, but one that is used always as the end of an argument instead of the beginning. There is still a higher grade of thought which says, "What is truth?" and sets out to find it.

But these grade-one thinkers were few and far between. They did not visit 36 my grammar school in the flesh though they were there in books. I aspired to them, partly because I was ambitious and partly because I now saw my hobby as an unsatisfactory thing if it went no further. If you set out to climb a mountain, however high you climb, you have failed if you cannot reach the top.

I *did* meet an undeniably grade-one thinker in my first year at Oxford. I 37 was looking over a small bridge in Magdalen Deer Park, and a tiny mustached and hatted figure came and stood by my side. He was a German who had just fled from the Nazis to Oxford as a temporary refuge. His name was Einstein.

But Professor Einstein knew no English at that time and I knew only two 38 words of German. I beamed at him, trying wordlessly to convey by my bearing all the affection and respect that the English felt for him. It is possible—and I have to make the admission—that I felt here were two grade-one thinkers standing side by side; yet I doubt if my face conveyed more than a formless awe. I would have given my Greek and Latin and French and a good slice of my English for enough German to communicate. But we were divided; he was as inscrutable as my headmaster. For perhaps five minutes we stood together on the bridge, undeniable grade-one thinker and breathless aspirant. With true greatness, Professor Einstein realized that my contact was better than none. He pointed to a trout wavering in midstream.

He spoke: *"Fisch."*   39

My brain reeled. Here I was, mingling with the great, and yet helpless as 40
the veriest grade-three thinker. Desperately I sought for some sign by which I
might convey that I, too, revered pure reason. I nodded vehemently. In a brilliant flash I used up half of my German vocabulary.

"Fisch. Ja Ja."   41

For perhaps another five minutes we stood side by side. Then Professor 42
Einstein, his whole figure still conveying good will and amiability, drifted away
out of sight.

I, too, would be a grade-one thinker. I was irreverent at the best of times. 43
Political and religious systems, social customs, loyalties and traditions, they all
came tumbling down like so many rotten apples off a tree. This was a fine
hobby and a sensible substitute for cricket, since you could play it all the year
round. I came up in the end with what must always remain the justification for
grade-one thinking, its sign, seal and charter. I devised a coherent system for
living. It was a moral system, which was wholly logical. Of course, as I readily
admitted, conversion of the world to my way of thinking might be difficult,
since my system did away with a number of trifles, such as big business, centralized government, armies, marriage....

It was Ruth all over again. I had some very good friends who stood by 44
me, and still do. But my acquaintances vanished, taking the girls with them.
Young women seemed oddly contented with the world as it was. They valued
the meaningless ceremony with a ring. Young men, while willing to concede
the chaining sordidness of marriage, were hesitant about abandoning the organizations which they hoped would give them a career. A young man on the first
rung of the Royal Navy, while perfectly agreeable to doing away with big business and marriage, got as rednecked as Mr. Houghton when I proposed a world
without any battleships in it.

Had the game gone too far? Was it a game any longer? In those prewar 45
days, I stood to lose a great deal, for the sake of a hobby.

Now you are expecting me to describe how I saw the folly of my ways 46
and came back to the warm nest, where prejudices are so often called loyalties,
where pointless actions are hallowed into custom by repetition, where we are
content to say we think when all we do is feel.

But you would be wrong. I dropped my hobby and turned professional. 47

If I were to go back to the headmaster's study and find the dusty statu- 48
ettes still there, I would arrange them differently. I would dust Venus and put
her aside, for I have come to love her and know her for the fair thing she is.
But I would put the Thinker, sunk in his desperate thought, where there were
shadows before him—and at his back, I would put the leopard, crouched and
ready to spring.

1961

QUESTIONS FOR DISCUSSION

Content

a. What is the implied meaning of Golding's title?

b. In a few sentences, summarize Golding's three-part classification of "thinking."

c. Do you believe the author is being too critical when, in paragraph 29, he claims that nine-tenths of the population are grade-three thinkers? How is he able to make such a claim without offending his readers?

d. How does grade-three thinking differ from grade-two thinking? Why does Golding's story about rearranging the statuettes (paragraph 34) serve as an example of grade-two thinking?

e. How do Golding's references to Nehru, Gandhi, the League of Nations, and St. Jerome's *Vulgate* (paragraphs 30 and 31) help him define grade-two thinking? Grade-three thinking?

f. Why does Golding call Pontius Pilate "a typical grade-two thinker" (paragraph 35)? What made Einstein a grade-one thinker?

Strategy and Style

g. Why does Golding spend so much time discussing his grade-school teachers? Do his recollections make for an effective introduction?

h. In what ways does the story of Mr. Houghton complement Golding's memories of his relationship with Ruth?

i. Considering the symbolic significance of the statuettes, what do you make of Golding's conclusion? Is this conclusion appropriate in so humorous an essay?

j. Golding is famous for his dry, often ironic, humor. What is ironic about his telling Ruth that the Buddhists are "the boys for [his] money" (paragraph 32)? What other lines do you find funny?

k. Does the anecdote about Golding's encounter with Einstein add to the definition of grade-one thinking, or does this story simply allow the author to poke fun at himself? In what other passages does he become the butt of his own jokes? What function do such passages serve?

l. This selection is full of powerful metaphors and similes that Golding uses to discuss and clarify abstract ideas. Identify a few of these figures of speech, and explain why they are so effective.

SUGGESTIONS FOR SHORT WRITING

a. If this essay were a speech addressed to a graduating class, what would it sound like? Consider what elements such a speech includes and how

"Thinking as a Hobby" would have to be condensed and altered; then write the conclusion of that speech.

b. Write, as rapidly as you can, a series of statements beginning with "Golding thinks that _____...." With which of these statements do you agree? With which do you disagree?

SUGGESTIONS FOR SUSTAINED WRITING

a. What kind of thinker are you? Recall the thoughts you've had or the position you've taken on a recent controversial issue. Explain why your opinions might be described as products of "grade-one," "grade-two," or "grade-three" thinking.

b. Describe three types of teachers, students, drivers, athletes, rock groups, Chinese cooking, movies, lovers, schools of modern art, etc. Include sufficient relevant details and illustrations to make your discussion of each type clear and convincing. Before you begin, however, make sure to limit your topic and write a thesis statement—at least a preliminary thesis statement—that will help you focus your ideas.

c. Have some fun and apply "grade-two" thinking to the "detection of contradictions" in a state law, municipal ordinance, college regulation, or social observance with which you find fault. Then, however, use some "grade-one" thinking to suggest ways in which to correct the problem you have identified. Use as many illustrations as you need to develop your ideas thoroughly. This essay might be written in the form of a letter to the editor of a local or college newspaper.

Bicycles
Erika Ritter

Erika Ritter is a popular Canadian playwright and humorist. Born and raised in Saskatchewan, she has said that there is nothing like a childhood on the prairies to propel a girl toward fantasy as a way of life and a means of creating something to fill up that empty space. A graduate of McGill University in Montreal and The Drama Centre of the University of Toronto, she taught English and drama for three years before writing drama full-time. Her first play, The Splits *(1978), was a great success. This was followed by several others, including* Winter 1671 *in 1979;* Automatic Pilot *in 1980, which won the Chalmers Canadian Play Award; and* The Passing Scene *in 1982. In 1982 she won the ACTRA Award for Best Radio Drama Writer. Since 1981 she has also done freelance broadcasting for the Canadian Broadcasting Corporation, including hosting* Dayshift, *an afternoon talk show. "Bicycles" is reprinted from* Urban Scrawl *(1984), a collection of humorous essays.*

1   It wasn't always like this. There was a time in the life of the world when adults were adults, having firmly put away childish things and thrown away the key.

2   Not any more. The change must have come about innocently enough, I imagine. Modern Man learning to play nicely in the sandbox with the other grown-ups. Very low-tension stuff.

3   Now, in every direction you look, your gaze is met by the risible spectacle of adults postponing adolescence well into senility by means of adult toys: running shoes, baseball bats, roller skates, and—bicycles!

4   But the attitude is no longer the fun-loving approach of a bunch of superannuated kids, and I'm sure you can envision how the evolution occurred. Jogging progressed from a casual encounter with the fresh air to an intensive relationship, attended by sixty-dollar jogging shoes and a designer sweatband. Playing baseball stopped being fun unless you had a Lacoste (as opposed to low-cost) tee-shirt in which to impress your teammates. And where was the thrill in running around a squash court unless it was with a potentially important client?

5   As for bicycles—well, let's not even talk about bicycles. On the other hand, maybe we *should* talk about them, because there's something particularly poignant about how it all went wrong for the bicycle, by what declension this once proud and carefree vehicle sank into the role of beast of burden, to bear the weight of sobersided grown-ups at their supposed sport.

6   First, there was the earliest domestication of the North American bicycle (*cyclus pedalis americanus*) in the late Hippie Scene Era of the 1960s. This was the age of the no-nuke whole-grain cyclist, who saw in the bicycle the possibility of Making a Statement while he rode. A statement about pollution, about

205

materialism, about imperialism, about militarism, about—enough already. You get the picture: two wheels good, four wheels bad.

Thus it was that the basic bicycle gradually evolved into a chunky three-   7
speed number from China, bowed down under a plastic kiddie carrier, army sur-plus knapsacks, and a faded fender-sticker advising Make Tofu, Not War. And a rider clad in a red plaid lumber-jacket, Birkenstock sandals, and an expression of urgent concern for all living things.

Once the very act of bicycle riding had become an act of high moral pur-   8
pose, it was an easy step to the next phase of the bicycle's journey along the path of post-Meanderthal seriousness.

I'm speaking of the era of the high-strung thoroughbred bicycle, whose   9
rider had also made advances, from pedalling peacenik to a hunched and hu-morless habitué of the velodrome, clad in leather-seated shorts, white crash hel-met, and fingerless gloves, whizzing soundlessly, and with no hint of joy, down city streets and along the shoulders of super-highways, aboard a vehicle sculpted in wisps of silver chrome. A vehicle so overbred, in its final evolution-ary stages, that it began to resemble the mere exoskeleton of a conventional cycle, its flesh picked away by birds of carrion.

Having been stripped of any connection with its innocent and leisurely   10
origins, the bicycle now no longer bore the slightest resemblance to the happy creature it once had been. And in the mid-Plastic Scene Era, another crippling blow was struck by the upscale name-brand cyclist, who came along to finish what the fanatical velodromist had refined. Namely, the complete transforma-tion of an ambling and unhurried mode of transit into a fast, nerve-wracking, expensive, and utterly competitive display of high speed, high technology, and high status.

The Upscale Cyclist was looking for a twelve-speed Bottecchia that   11
matches his eyes, something that he'd look trendy upon the seat of, when riding to the office (the office!), and he was ready to pay in four figures for it.

Not only that, he was also prepared to shell out some heavy bread for   12
those status accessories to complete the picture: the backpack designed by the engineers at NASA, the insulated water-bottle to keep his Perrier chilled just right, the sixteen-track Walkman that would virtually assure him the envy of all his friends.

So much for the cyclist. What of his poor debased mount?   13

Not surprisingly, amongst the breed of bicycle, morale is currently low,   14
and personal pride all but a thing of the past. And yet...and yet, there are those who say that *cyclus pedalis americanus* is an indomitable creature, and that it is the bicycle, not its rider, who will make the last evolution of the wheel.

In fact, some theorize that the present high incidence of bicycle thievery,   15
far from being evidence of crime, is actually an indication that the modern bi-cycle has had enough of oppressive exploitation and man's joyless ways, and is in the process of reverting to the wild in greater and greater numbers.

There have always remained a few aboriginal undomesticated bicycles—   16 or so the theory goes—and now it is these free-spirited mavericks, down from the hills at night, who visit urban bikeracks, garages, and back porches to lure tame bicycles away with them.

Costly Kryptonite locks are wrenched asunder, expensive accoutrements 17 are shrugged off, intricate gear systems are torn away, and lo—look what is revealed! Unadorned, undefiled *cyclus* in all his pristine glory, unfettered and unencumbered once more, and free to roam.

A wistful fantasy, you might say? The maundering illusions of someone 18 who's been riding her bicycle too long without a crash helmet? I wonder.

Just the other day, there was that piece in the paper about a bicycle that 19 went berserk in a shopping centre, smashing two display windows before it was subdued. And did you hear about the recent sighting of a whole herd of riderless bicycles, all rolling soundlessly across a park in the night?

It all kind of gets you to thinking. I mean, do *you* know where your ten- 20 speed is tonight?

1984

QUESTIONS FOR DISCUSSION

Content

a. What is Ritter's thesis? Is this essay intended simply to poke fun at the rage over bicycling, or is Ritter aiming at something more fundamental?
b. What can you tell about her attitude toward bicycles in the first two paragraphs? Toward people?
c. Ritter devotes several paragraphs to the evolution of the bicycle. How does her manipulation of this process help to delineate her categories of bicycles and their riders?
d. Why has she chosen to discuss only three categories of bicycles? Why these three in particular? Are there other categories you can add?
e. In the third paragraph, the author calls bicycles "adult toys." What other things fall into this category? Why would these items be considered toys?

Strategy and Style

f. What mood does Ritter create in the first two paragraphs? What expectations do these paragraphs set for the rest of the essay?
g. Personification is the attributing of human characteristics to inanimate objects. What images does Ritter evoke by using this technique? What does it contribute to the tone of the essay?
h. In paragraph 13, Ritter calls the bicycle a "poor debased mount," linking the

bicycle to a horse. What other metaphors does Ritter use to describe the bicycle? What purpose do these metaphors serve?

i. The author enriches her informal, humorous style with puns based on terms from paleontology. What do these puns imply about Ritter's opinions of bicycles and of our obsession with bicycling? About paleontology?

j. Ritter addresses the reader directly (for example, "in every direction *you* look," paragraph 3). How does direct address affect your response?

k. What effect do the many exclamation points, dashes, italicized words, question marks, colons, and parentheses have on the essay's tone? What do they tell you about the author herself?

l. At what point does Ritter switch from sarcasm to fantasy? Does the switch alter the tone with which the essay begins? If so, is the switch effective in helping the author achieve her purpose?

SUGGESTIONS FOR SHORT WRITING

a. Describe your most frequent means of transportation. At what stage is it in the evolution of its "species"?

b. Rewrite a paragraph or two of Ritter's essay, trying to make it as serious and heavy-handed as you can. Is it possible to be serious about the subject matter of this essay?

SUGGESTIONS FOR SUSTAINED WRITING

a. What other products or activities do we seem to be obsessed with these days: VCRs, microwave ovens, playing video games, exercising in expensive gyms, watching sports on TV? Write an essay in which you satirize society's obsession with a particular product or activity you know a great deal about. Categorize the product in such a way that the obsession will become clear to your readers.

b. Write an essay that categorizes and traces the development of another "adult toy." Think of what techniques Ritter uses that can work for your essay as well.

c. Ritter makes fun of bicycle riders as well as bicycles themselves. Write an essay categorizing a segment of society in order to expose its foibles.

Struggle for Justice
American Friends Service Committee

The A.F.S.C. was founded in 1917 by the Society of Friends (the Quakers) to help victims of World War I. In 1947, the A.F.S.C. and the British F.S.C. jointly received the Nobel Peace Prize. The A.F.S.C.'s goals are to promote peace and to search for new ways to attain peace and bring about social change. In particular, the A.F.S.C. conducts relief and education programs in the U.S. and overseas. In the U.S., it often fights for the legal rights of minorities. Among the many reports published by the Committee are Treaties on Trial: The Continuing Controversy over Northwest Indian Fishing Rights *(1986),* South Africa: Challenge and Hope *(1987),* A Compassionate Peace: A Future for Israel, Palestine, the Middle East *(1989), and* Struggle for Justice *(1970), from which this essay is excerpted. The reports are written for the Committee by experts in each field; "Struggle for Justice" was a collaborative effort, written by people familiar with both ends of the law.*

1   A criminal justice system reflects the values of those who hold power in society. In colonial Massachusetts, for example, the most serious crimes were blasphemy, not attending church, and other activities that would appear harmless to us but were heinous to the ruling theocracy. As we examine the contemporary criminal justice system we can expect to find reflected the values and fears of those who hold power in our society. By their control of the legislative, policing, and criminal labeling processes they define what acts are criminal and set the penalties. Thus criminal law, in both content and administration, often becomes a political instrument, formulated and enforced by those with status and power against those who, predominantly, are status-poor and powerless.

2   The Founding Fathers were aware of these problems. With the Constitution, the Bill of Rights, and the Fourteenth Amendment they constructed a legal system to protect the exercise of political freedoms unmatched anywhere in the history of representative government. These procedural safeguards include prohibition of ex post facto laws, guarantees of due process and equal protection under the law, and the outlawing of cruel and unusual punishment. They attempted to create an independent judiciary, protecting judges from political reprisals and temptations by means of high salaries and long (or lifelong) terms. Our federal system, a "government of laws not men," was developed to act as a brake on transitory majority opinion and the growth of governmental power.

3   Yet we see gross inequities in American criminal justice....

4   By and large our prisons are reserved for those with dark skins, little money, or unconventional life-styles. In our view crimes committed by all those now in prison are far less damaging to our society than acts against life and health perpetrated by the powerful. We refer to those who develop and manufacture genocidal weapons, those who perpetuate the arms race or prolong the

Indochina war for their own commercial advantage, those who pollute or destroy this country's natural resources for financial profit, those who manufacture unsafe automobiles and other dangerous products, price fixers, slum landlords, and others.

Not only do the powerful manage, by and large, to escape the sanctions of   5
the criminal justice system, they also manipulate the system for their own political ends. These are the functions of the criminal justice system we will examine here.

ECONOMIC DOMINANCE

Manipulation of the criminal justice system by the powerful is perhaps   6
most evident in the economic sphere. The struggle by labor for the right to organize is one of the bloodiest chapters in American history. Throughout the nineteenth century and into the twentieth, the courts and police repeatedly took the side of industrialists in blocking attempts to form labor unions and in preventing workers from striking. Violence marked many labor struggles, including the 1877 railroad strike, the 1910 Chicago clothing-industry strike, the 1919 strike against U.S. Steel, and the CIO's attempt to organize Little Steel in 1937, when eighteen were killed.

Judicial intervention was also used in labor disputes. When owners were   7
unable to find excuses for court action in the law itself, they obtained court injunctions against strikers. As late as 1921, the United States Supreme Court upheld the position that peaceful picketing could be enjoined on the grounds that it was inherently intimidating and coercive in a strike controversy. Court injunctions against picketing in labor disputes are not uncommon even today.

The prosecution of labor leaders under the Sherman Antitrust Act, origi-   8
nally intended to curb business monopolies, indicates the extent to which the Justice Department and the courts identified themselves with business interests. Although the act is a criminal law, the government is given the option of administrative or criminal proceedings. In the 438 actions initiated by the government between 1890 and 1929 with decisions favorable to the government prosecution, 27 percent of the actions against businesses and business associations were criminal, compared with 71 percent of the actions against labor unions.

The use of the courts and police to hamper the organization of labor con-   9
tinues today. The United Farm Workers are a prime example. Their struggle to gain collective strength has been a bitter one, hampered by court injunctions granted the owners of large grape and lettuce farms. Cesar Chavez and other organizers have been jailed for defying such injunctions. Their organizing successes probably would have been impossible without the support of nationwide consumer boycotts.

In New Jersey and other states where migrant laborers have not yet been   10
able to initiate collective efforts, the local institutions of justice are still used to protect the exploitative economic relationship, subordinating the well-being of

the pickers to the profits of the growers. Predictable abuses occur within the courts and local jails, especially for Spanish-speaking people. Migrants are arrested without real cause or are given a phony reason. A man arrested on a minor charge who does not have a driver's license or other acceptable identification can be held in jail until the court in that municipality meets—and in some places the court meets only once a month! Bail is set beyond the capacity to pay. Loosely worded trespass laws are enforced in an intimidating manner. As one migrant worker complained to a reporter, "It's very bad. If you don't do what the farmer says, if you cause any trouble, he call the police and get you arrested. Don't tell me about justice here. There is no justice for Puerto Ricans here."[1] Legal Services lawyers attempting to remedy this situation have won a series of legal victories. If these decisions are implemented, the migrant worker will have a little more freedom in Cumberland County, New Jersey.

Tax laws are another means whereby the powerful increase their economic dominance. Efforts to plug scandalous tax loopholes have been unsuccessful for years. Today there are dozens of millionaires who pay no income tax at all. Taxes are extracted from salaried workers every payday by means of withholding; those in the upper brackets have considerably more opportunity to avoid taxes, legally, semilegally, or illegally. When violations are detected, the government rarely invokes the criminal process. The tax cheater can usually get off by paying a fine. 11

War tax resisters are particularly aware of the selective enforcement of tax laws. These citizens are convinced of the illegality and the immorality of the war in Vietnam and of the genocidal weapons being developed and manufactured. On grounds of conscience they refuse to pay taxes for these activities. They find that they are sometimes hounded by IRS agents for insignificant sums. Refusers have had automobiles seized and auctioned for tax liabilities of less than $5. Refusers acting publicly have been convicted of income-tax fraud. Rather than securing compliance with the tax laws, government efforts to penalize principaled tax refusers may serve, rather, to build a resistance movement. 12

The government has been extremely reluctant to prosecute business leaders for such widespread and socially harmful crimes as deceptive advertising, pollution, selling dangerous merchandise, and violating antitrust laws. Real-estate agents are almost never prosecuted for blockbusting or for practicing racial discrimination in renting and selling, even though these practices are illegal. Election laws limiting political campaign contributions are violated every two and four years but enforcement policies are lax to the point of not existing. The campaign chests of politicians are regularly enriched by contributions from unions and corporations, even though the Corrupt Practices Act prohibits such institutions from giving money to federal candidates. In its massive *Federal Civil Rights Enforcement Efforts,* the United States Civil Rights Commission recently documented widespread governmental refusal to enforce civil-rights 13

---

[1] *The New York Times,* August 17, 1970.

statutes, particularly in the fields of employment, housing, education, agricultural services, labor programs, public accommodations, and public facilities.

When the government acts at all in such cases, it again usually prefers 14 administrative rather than criminal proceedings. Enforcement statutes for economic regulations regularly provide for a variety of mechanisms for enforcement, with criminal procedure clearly regarded as a last resort. Dealing with violations by written warnings was the course the government took in the vast majority of the 980 white-collar crimes E. H. Sutherland found the top seventy corporations to have committed.[2] Only in 159 of the cases was an adverse decision reached in criminal court; the other 821 adverse decisions were all reached either by an administrative commission or by courts under civil or equity jurisdiction. In those rare instances when criminal procedures are used, penalties are relatively mild, usually including a fine and a short term in a minimum-security prison farm. We do not mean to imply that civil procedures are in themselves unjustified; what must be faulted is the class nature of the law enforcement process. Price-fixing General Electric executives receive a penalty of one month, while a thief who may steal only one item receives a penalty of several years.

Studies indicate that white-collar criminals such as the General Electric 15 executives are far from rare. A 1947 study,[3] for example, revealed that 91 percent of a group of almost seventeen hundred New York City residents, chosen for their resemblance to the general population's socioeconomic characteristics but weighted accidentally toward upper income brackets, had committed at least one felony or serious misdemeanor. Among the forty-nine offenses listed on the questionnaire were robbery, bribery, disorderly conduct, malicious mischief, criminal libel, falsification and fraud, perjury, indecency, and health code violations. Thirteen percent of the males had committed grand larceny, 26 percent auto theft, 17 percent burglary. The mean number of offenses per person was eighteen. Roughly half had committed at least one felony for which he had not been caught. Other studies have also documented the universality of undetected or unreported crime.

These results are confirmed by everyday experience. Many Americans at 16 some time have removed items from a motel room, failed to report income tax accurately, smoked pot, or cashed a check without sufficient funds. Most of these offenses are trivial and injure no one, which explains why we can commit them occasionally or even frequently without regarding ourselves as criminals. But then again, people have been sentenced to long prison terms for offenses equally trivial. The boundary line between harmless middle-class offenses and someone else's harmful violations of the law is a fuzzy one. This prejudice in favor of "our own kind" can be seen at its most blatant in the suggestion made

[2]*White Collar Crime* (New York: Holt, Rinehart and Winston, 1949).
[3]James Wallerstein and C. J. Wyle, "Our Law-abiding Law-breakers," *Probation,* 1947, pp. 107–112.

in standard reference works on criminal procedure that prosecutors wisely refrain from prosecuting in cases of law violation where the offender comes from a "respectable" background. It never occurs to those who write lawbooks, apparently, that people other than professors and white businessmen might be hurt by a trial or a conviction.

SLAVERY AND RACISM

The justice system functions to maintain a racist relationship between the white majority and the black, brown, red and yellow minorities in America. The command-obedience structure of racism has existed in the criminal justice system since the settlement of the country. Possessing the status of real estate or livestock under the cruel system of chattel slavery, black slaves were legal nullities in the eyes of the courts. They were systematically excluded from jury service, holding judgeships, acting in their own defense, and every other provision of criminal law procedure that protected white propertied males. Rendered "three-fifths of a man" by the Constitution, the slave came to know the legal system only as an extension of the rule of the slave system. 17

Before the Civil War the legal status of the freed Negro paralleled the slave's utter legal powerlessness. Criminal sentences often included the provision that freedmen could be sold into slavery as punishment for a criminal offense or in lieu of payment of taxes, fines, or civil judgments. Vaguely worded vagrancy statutes were ideal weapons for intimidating supposedly free black people. Vagrancy and other laws commonly provided for immediate punishment—usually whipping—without trial, enpoweringslave patrols and private citizens to be at one time complainant, judge, jury, and enforcement officer. 18

States outside the South also passed freed Negro laws which, though often less severe than the South's, served the same purpose. The testimony of persons with "one-eighth Negro blood" was declared incompetent by Illinois and Delaware statutes. In Iowa free black persons could not be witnesses in cases involving whites. In Ohio blacks had to post bond as a condition of good behavior to secure residence. In 1853 Illinois made it a misdemeanor for a black to enter the state with the intention of residing. Throughout the country, by law and tradition, blacks were nonpersons in the eyes of the justice system, a status that mirrored their lack of rights of any political, economic, or social consequence in any other area of life. 19

After the Civil War emancipated black people saw the master-slave relationship replaced by a master-servant relationship. Many of the restrictive provisions originally applied to freed Negroes were included in the infamous Black Codes. Several states created separate systems of criminal courts for blacks, who could not testify in white courts, nor could they serve as judges or jurors in either court system. Although such punishments had been abolished for whites, blacks could be confined in public stocks or whipped. 20

As blatantly discriminatory laws were repealed during the era of Radical 21
Reconstruction, more subtly restrictive statutes replaced them. Blacks were allowed to serve as witnesses, but a widely enacted statute provided that "whenever a person of color shall be examined as a witness, the court shall warn the
witness to declare the truth." Whites were not similarly warned. Although the
Black Code of Texas provided that "there shall be no discrimination against
such persons [blacks] in the administration of the criminal laws of this state," it
included the qualifications that the law did not permit blacks to intermarry with
whites, serve on juries, vote, or testify in cases involving whites.

The socially subordinate position of blacks within the criminal justice 22
system has remained practically unchanged. Police brutality and summary violence still characterize the police presence in the black community. Jury service
remains a restricted white privilege, making a mockery of the concept of investigation and judgment by one's peers. With token exceptions, the personnel of
the justice system are white, forcing members of minority groups to face police,
district attorneys, wardens, judges, and parole-board members who represent
historically the oppressor's caste. Other forms of racism are more hidden. A
judge or jury may weigh the credibility of a black witness's testimony differently from a white's. Cultural differences in dress, hairstyle, and speech may
work to the disadvantage of minority men and women. Residual racial practices
surviving from the era of slavery show that discrimination is not simply a matter of intentional policy; it also emerges from deeply ingrained attitudes and
institutional prejudices that still survive.

In prisons racism is manifested in unequal job assignments, with blacks 23
assigned to the most menial tasks. Black nationalist and Black Muslim literature is often banned. Individual guards who are racists or sadists or both have
ample opportunity to abuse prisoners. Blacks who are affirming their cultural
and racial identity are particularly likely targets. Those who show signs of becoming inmate leaders or who challenge institutional practices through lawsuits
commonly suffer administrative punishments (the hole, strip cells, restricted
diet, loss of privileges), or are transferred punitively, often to prisons with notorious reputations for brutal racist environments.

Racism is often consciously encouraged by prison officials who hope to 24
keep black, brown, and white inmates occupied with fighting each other and
hence more easily managed. Their strategy is to divide the races and control the
convicts. A letter smuggled out by a black prisoner in Soledad Prison gives a
picture of the depths of racial oppression and degradation that can occur behind
walls:

> Never more than 6 blacks were allowed on max. row, which houses 24 in-
> mates. Thus the remaining 18 cells were occupied by anti-black Caucasian
> and Mexican inmates who race talk us in shifts so that it's done 24 hours a
> day. On their exercise periods they spit, throw urine and feces in our cells
> while the officials stand by in indifference and approval. They, the officials
> call us HAMMERS and NIGGERS too. (Both expressions mean the same
> thing.) The prison officials here stopped serving the meals and deliberately

selected the Caucasian and Mexican inmates (described throughout this letter) to serve the meals and they immediately proceeded to poison our meals by filling food to be issued to us with cleanser powder, crushed up glass, spit, urine and feces while the officials stood by and laughed.[4]

Another example of officially inspired racism is given by a prisoner at the 25 Federal Youth Center in Ashland, Kentucky, who described an incident in which a black inmate beat up a white guard.

> Notice that this "race trouble" was initiated by a fight between an inmate and a guard, and that the inmate got the better of the guard. Recognizing that the event could readily inspire similar attacks on them, the dormitory guards played up their racist solidarity with white southerners by interpreting the fray as a conflict between black and white instead of as a conflict between guard and prisoner. If they could sell their interpretation, they would at least gain a few white inmate protectors and possibly create enough tension between black and white inmates that the threat to themselves would be removed. The crew bosses' lectures the next day performed the same function of convincing prisoners to fight each other rather than the staff. The racial attack that was successfully instigated in this way set the whole compound on edge and effectively took the heat off the Man.[5]

The experiences of other oppressed minorities within the justice system 26 parallel the treatment of blacks. An an instrument of Anglo domination, the justice apparatus serves to oppress Mexican-Americans in the Southwest. The United States Civil Rights Commission has reported widespread patterns of excessive police violence, discriminatory treatment of Chicano juveniles, biased enforcement of motor vehicle regulations, discourtesies to local Chicano citizens, and excessive use of stop-and-frisk laws to harass and intimidate local communities.[6] The commission found an almost total absence of Mexican-Americans on juries and noted that the "wide disparities" between jury service and population proportion could not be accounted for by language difficulties, educational levels, or other commonly offered excuses. Officials "abused their discretion" in setting excessive bail. In noting an almost total absence of Mexican-Americans among justice system employees, the commission found an almost systematic avoidance of the Spanish language by law enforcement personnel, which meant that routine contacts with police could easily escalate into major conflicts and that Chicanos in criminal courts "cannot plead intelligently, advise their lawyers with respect to the facts, fully understand the testimony of witnesses against them, or otherwise adequately prepare or assist in their own defense." The same pattern extends to probation and parole boards.

The brutality of racism and the indignities of second-class citizenship still 27 characterize much of the administration of criminal justice. The racist ideolo-

---

[4]"Black Caucus Report: Treatment of Prisoners at California Training Facility at Soledad Central," Black Caucus in the California State Legislature, July 1970.
[5]Jim Wessner, "Racism in Federal Prison," *The Peacemaker*, May 2, 1970, pp. 1–2.
[6]"Mexican-Americans and the Administration of Justice in the Southwest," March 1970.

gies of chattel slavery and of "separate but equal" have been declared legally dead, but the funeral continues and the ugly corpse has not yet been buried. The justice system remains an instrument of white Anglo domination and a barrier to the development of full power within communities of oppressed peoples.

JUVENILES

Blacks and Chicanos are not the only groups in our society upon whom 28 cultural assimilation has been forced. The American majority has found all minority races and cultures threatening and has treated many of them ruthlessly. Consider the wholesale slaughter of the American Indian.

In the nineteenth century the waves of European immigrants came in for 29 their share of forced assimilation. Being less different from the majority than Indians and blacks, they were treated less barbarically, but they were still treated as second-class citizens. The criminal justice apparatus was part of the social structure used to repress them. One method of accomplishing this was through the creation of a new category of criminals: juvenile delinquents.

Under the guise of saving children from a debauching environment, juve- 30 nile delinquency laws made into crimes types of youthful behavior that in the past had been handled informally—sexual promiscuity, staying out late at night, drinking, smoking, reading comic books, truancy, running away, and disobedience to parents and teachers.

Of course the child-saving movement was bathed in a sea of self-righ- 31 teousness.[7] Heavy emphasis was placed on "rescuing" victims of unhealthy environments—usually city slums—and "elevating" them to a middle-class style of life. An 1855 report from a New York City agency makes reference to

> large numbers of poor Italian children engaged in street occupations, follow-ing the heart and the hand-organ, selling newspapers, blackening boots, and the like, who were growing up utterly without education or moral discipline...The greatest difficulties were the greed of the parents to get all possible earnings from their children without regard to their education, the bigotry of some of their advisers and the existence amongst them of a species of serf-dom.

This kind of theme runs with monotonous regularity through report after 32 report: Get the Italian children (in Boston it would have been the Irish) away from their "bigoted" advisers (who else but the Catholic priest?) so that they can receive moral and religious treatment from instructors whose denominational neutrality, so the report tells us, runs the gamut from Episcopalian to Uni-

[7]We have drawn on Anthony Platt, *The Child-Savers: The Invention of Delinquency* (Chicago: University of Chicago Press, 1969).

tarian. Save these children from greedy parents and the labor of blackening boots by placing them in child-labor manufacturing establishments or, if female, in domestic service in respectable homes.

To accomplish these ends, new judicial and correctional institutions were 33 created. Since criminal court procedures were thought to be unsuitable to cases involving juveniles—who were, after all, being "helped," not "punished"—procedural guarantees were abolished in favor of an informal approach. Almost every conceivable abuse occurs—the use of unsubstantiated rumor as evidence, coercive imposition of psychiatric or social welfare treatment on the basis of presumed need, confusing procedures that leave parents and child unable to present evidence without the assistance of a lawyer, confusion of child-neglect cases with delinquency, arbitrary sentences, and unnecessary stigmatization through failure to keep records confidential.

Although the juvenile may expect to be rewarded in return for the waiver 34 of so many rights, the rewards are often scanty. The juvenile court system of "Metropolitan City," studied by Abraham Blumberg,[8] convicted juveniles more frequently than adults. Sentences are indeterminate and may be longer than for adults. Perhaps the worst feature of the juvenile court system is that no specific law-violating act has to be committed by a juvenile for him or her to be brought under the "parental" care of the courts. Thus, "growing up in idleness," exhibiting "vicious or immoral behavior," "incorrigibility," or "living with any vicious or disreputable person" can justify judicial intervention.

In addition, the shortcomings of the criminal justice system already de- 35 scribed are inflicted upon juvenile offenders as well. Often, because of their youth, the consequences are worse. In reformatories there is probably more brutality, intimidation, and homosexual coercion than in adult prisons. Educational and vocational programs are probably more outmoded. The juvenile offender probably has less chance than his adult counterpart of breaking away from a life of repeated return to imprisonment.

WOMEN

The law is both the mirror of a biased society and the source of prejudice. 36 Just as the black man was described originally in the Constitution as three-fifths of a man, so under common law "a woman has no legal existence separate from her husband, who was regarded as her head and representative in the social state," according to a United States Supreme Court decision in 1872. Some years later, in 1898, a Virginia court decided that under law a "woman" is not a "person." In 1966 the Supreme Court upheld a Texas law providing that a married woman does not have the capacity to enter into a binding contract. Justice Hugo Black dissented, deploring the fact that the Court "should exalt this ar-

[8]*Criminal Justice* (Chicago): Quadrangle, 1967.

chaic remnant of a primitive caste system...This rule has worked out in reality to mean that though the husband and wife are one, the one is the husband."[9]

A woman under the common-law tradition loses her legal personality [37] when she marries. Issues are raised of "right to a separate domicile; capacity to sue and be sued; change in citizenship upon marriage to an alien."[10] One contemporary example of hardship resulting from a denial of the right to separate domicile is the case of a young woman who tried to enter law school in a Pennsylvania state-supported university. Because her husband, from whom she was separated but not divorced, had his legal residence in another state, the fee would have been doubled and, consequently, she was unable to enroll. In another instance, the woman on welfare has been subjected in recent years to the searching of her home to see if she is having a sexual relationship and if so, cutting off her welfare. Known as the "man in the house" rule, it was not balanced by a "woman in the house" rule.

Gunnar Myrdal, in his classic *An American Dilemma,* comments that the [38] myth of the "contented woman," who does not want suffrage or other civil rights and equal opportunities, has the same social function as the myth of the "contented Negro." Women, black and white, remained unenfranchised until 1920—sixty-five years after the vote had technically at least been granted to males of any race.

Almost one-fourth of the complaints received since passage of Title VII [39] of the 1964 Civil Rights Act, which forbids discrimination, including discrimination on the basis of sex, in employment, have been from women.[11] Approximately half of the women surveyed in a recent study covering all women law-school graduates of the years 1956–1965 stated that they have been discriminated against by employers and that their average income differed sharply, based on sex.[12]

In 1968 the United States Supreme Court considered the case of a girl [40] who was imprisoned for "lascivious carriage" under a Connecticut law authorizing imprisonment of young women if they are "in manifest danger of falling into habits of vice." Laws may provide for different lengths of jail sentences for the same crime, depending on whether the perpetrator is male or female (1968). In many states, dispensing birth-control information is a crime and the struggle of women for legalized and safe abortion is far from won. Thus in the areas of sex and reproduction the law has more direct control over women than men.

One of the most discriminatory areas of criminal law relates to prostitu- [41] tion. "In New York City policemen actively entrap women and then charge them with prostitution...This despite the fact that New York law states that

---

[9]Quoted by Diane B. Schulder, "Does the Law Oppress Women?" in *Sisterhood Is Powerful,* Robin Morgan, ed. (New York: Vintage, 1970), p. 149. This excellent article also contains complete citations of the court decisions mentioned.
[10]Ibid.
[11]"Report of the U.S. Commission on Civil Rights," 1970.
[12]Schulder, op. cit., p. 146.

prostitutes and their customers are guilty of equal violations...The New York District Attorney's office has also chosen not to prosecute the men customers [lest] big business conventions...cancel out of New York City and go elsewhere."[13] This practice is not confined to New York City.

Little has been written about women in prison. The definitive report of 42 the President's Commission on Law Enforcement and the Administration of Justice devotes not even a paragraph to the female "offender." Although only a very small percentage of the crimes committed by women involve violence, alternatives to incarceration are almost nonexistent. "The only advantage women have over men [in America's] penal system is that fewer of them are in it-....But those who are handcuffed and ushered into cells [throughout the nation] face some of the worst conditions available."[14] A special torment for women is separation from their children and the fear that the state may take them away. Often women who are arrested and prohibited from making a phone call have left young children at home and become frantic about their safety. One of the grievances of the inmates of the Tombs was the lack of respect shown by the guards to their wives, mothers, and sisters who came to visit. The wives of prisoners must shoulder responsibility for both parents, often face the scorn and hostility of the community, and are often subjected to insulting treatment from the administrators of prisons.

Jails for women include one federal reformatory, at Alderson, Virginia, 43 which also has the only woman superintendent in the Federal Bureau of Prisons. Some inmates feel that because a woman is its chief officer it is perhaps the "best of the worst" of all the places that incarcerate women. The superintendent has said:

> I don't like jails and I'm not going to defend them. There's no jail in the world that's any good. They're bad places and you're in them against your will. If you're black, poor or a woman in twentieth-century America the dice have been loaded against you.[15]

CULTURAL ASSIMILATION TODAY

As part of treatment and rehabilitation, cultural assimilation is forced 44 upon wayward, threatening, or unconventional groups. Every day criminal justice personnel make hundreds of low-level discretionary decisions that glorify their middle-class life-style. This can be seen in a batch of probation and parole reports involving neglect proceedings against mothers of very young children.

The reports constantly reiterate such factors as the "subject's" "slovenly 45

---

[13]Ibid., pp. 155–156.

[14]Kitsi Burkhart in a prizewinning series on prisons in the Philadelphia *Evening Bulletin,* January 1971.

[15]Kitsi Burkhart, "Women in Prison," *Ramparts,* June 1971.

housekeeping," "sexual promiscuity," "failure to keep her appointments," "frequenting taverns," "allowing older children to loiter on street corners," and "her apparent willingness to let welfare continue supporting her." We will look at the implications of some of these phrases.

The designation of the mother-defendant as a "subject" demeans her, emphasizing her inequality. It also reflects the cold impersonality of a bureaucracy too dehumanized to call her by name.   46

References to "slovenly housekeeping" reveal a Puritanical dust phobia.   47
References to "promiscuity," "taverns," and "loitering" reflect the pervasive middle-class inability to understand why the poor do not unwind in the privacy and quiet of their living rooms instead of in public establishments of dubious propriety. Why don't they take the air on golf courses instead of loitering on street corners? Why don't they conduct their love affairs secretly? Why do they shoot craps in back alleys instead of playing bingo at a neighborhood church? Or why don't they fly to Las Vegas for more elaborate entertainment? References to "welfare" reveal the increasingly outmoded Protestant work ethic.

Complaints about not keeping appointments are frequent in welfare and   48
correctional literature. Woe betide the parolee who misses an appointment! Here we have in microcosm the clash between a life-style where time is relatively unimportant and an establishment whose agencies have long waiting lists, whose courts are smothered by their dockets, whose social workers are bowed down by their case loads, and whose officials exaggerate their own importance. One can imagine Thoreau, who believed in wide margins and had little use for those who voluntarily spent their lives under the crushing weight of a barn and forty acres, siding with the "subjects" and joining in an amused contemplation of the uptight caseworker.

For the prisoner time has a different perspective. It is something to be   49
marked off, endured. He has already learned all too painfully in most contacts with officials that what he really wants or feels or thinks will be ignored. By the time the case worker gets to him, the "subject" will already have experienced an appointed counsel or public defender who gave him the once over lightly; a judge who disposed of his life alternatives in a moment or two of judicial time as part of an assembly-line process, and a whole series of unthinking, unfeeling functionaries within institutions. No wonder the "subjects" keep failing to keep their appointments with those who are trying to "help" them.

One could search the criminal code in vain to find laws prohibiting late-   50
ness to appointments or unconventionality of dress and social habits. Yet these are the standards being enforced. Many prison treatment programs carry this degradation to an extreme. Heavy emphasis is placed on unquestioned obedience to authority, the sanctity of the employer-employee relationship, acquiescence to perform drudgery work or service occupations, and the centrality of money and materialistic goals.

POLITICAL REPRESSION

A fundamental though unacknowledged function of the criminal justice 51 system is political repression. This was the motive for passage of the federal Antiriot and Conspiracy Act of 1968 and for its use in the Chicago and Seattle trials. These trials are in every substantial respect today's counterpart of the prosecution of Communists during the Smith Act trials of the 1950s, the aim in each case being to discredit political opponents. In both instances there were already ample statutes on the books to punish violent disruption and to safeguard society.

The prosecutions of H. Rap Brown, Lee Otis Johnson, John Sinclair, and 52 the Harrisburg 6 are similarly political in motivation. Likewise, a strong element of vindictiveness and persecution for political reasons pervades the treatment of those whose conscience has led them to break the law. We refer, for example, to the Catonsville 9 and the Washington May Day demonstrators. Whatever one may think about the necessity of pressing criminal charges in such cases, the government has responded with overkill tactics in the press and in the courtroom.

The same response to "political" crimes may also be observed on the lo- 53 cal level. The authorities find some offenses more offensive than others. The Philadelphia Police Department swiftly removes and arrests peace demonstrators blocking the Induction Center but has yet to arrest housewives conducting sit-ins in busy intersections to protest the absence of a traffic light.

At times the police have acted as political executioners, as seems to be 54 the case in the alleged murder of Black Panther leaders Mark Clark and Fred Hampton by sheriff's deputies while they slept.

The use of the courts and police against radicals is nothing new in Amer- 55 ican history. Abolitionists and labor organizers came up against these sorts of repression time and time again. In the first decades of this century the Wobblies—Industrial Workers of the World—were persecuted from coast to coast. They were convicted of such crimes as "criminal syndicalism" and their movement was eventually smashed. During the 1960s the full range of repression was used against civil-rights workers in the South.

This country now appears to be entering a new phase of repression 56 against activist forces struggling for change. In addition to the overt political repression already mentioned, there is an ominous expansion of police power that has scarcely been noticed. Police forces, built up after the civil and campus disorders of the late 1960s, have become paramilitary. They have received training from the Department of Defense and are adapting to domestic use weapons developed for Vietnam.

This trend within police departments has led to the emergence of a police/ 57 industrial/educational complex spawned by the Pentagon. The Law Enforcement Assistance Administration (LEAA), a federal agency created in 1968, is budgeted for $1,750,000,000 in 1973 and is slated to continue to expand.[16] LEAA funds police training programs in 880 colleges and universities. It also includes work on counterinsurgency techniques and the development of new weapons and equipment.

Secret police have sprung up like mushrooms in recent years. Not only 58 the FBI, the CIA, and the Intelligence branches of the various armed forces, but dozens of other agencies, national and local, are spying on hundreds of thousands of us. They have at their disposal sophisticated electronic surveillance equipment and computerized storage and retrieval of information. Spying has snowballed and is now out of control. Implications for the future are frightening.

In the face of this strong thrust toward highly centralized, strongly armed, 59 computerized, and professionalized police departments, plus secret police, the traditional concept of the police function in a free society is breaking down. The police are no longer peacekeepers under the control of civilian governments and responsive to the needs and wishes of the people. What can be done to bring the police back under the control of the communities they are supposed to serve? The prospect is not bright.

In a totalitarian society the repressive functions we have enumerated- 60 ...dominate the criminal justice system. In a free society such functions should be minimized or eliminated. We hope that an awareness of the pervasiveness of these functions in the American system can lead to change. We will not be able to do away with these repressive functions until social prejudice and inequality are uprooted and eradicated from society as a whole.

1971

QUESTIONS FOR DISCUSSION

Content

a. To whom is this report most likely addressed? What is the authors' purpose?
b. If you were to update this report, what categories would you add, if any? Would you revise or subdivide any of the categories that the authors make? What other changes would you make to update it?
c. Look up the Bill of Rights and the Fourteenth Amendment (paragraph 2) in a library reference book or a political science textbook to get a more detailed understanding of the protections they provide. Can you think of ways in which these constitutional safeguards are used or violated, other than the ones the authors mention?

[16]Lee Webb, "Back Home: Campus Beat," in *Police on the Homefront* (Philadelphia: National Action/Research on the Military-Industrial Complex, 1971), p. 8.

d. What *are* the functions of the criminal justice system?

e. In paragraph 14, the authors state that "what must be faulted is the class nature of the law enforcement process." What do they mean? Do you agree with this statement?

f. In paragraph 16, they write that "the boundary line between harmless middle-class offenses and someone else's harmful violations of the law is a fuzzy one." Do you agree? If you were to make that boundary clear, how would you define it?

g. Do you agree with the statement in paragraph 17 that "the justice system functions to maintain a racist relationship between the white majority and the black, brown, red and yellow minorities in America"? Either way, support your opinion with reference to the text.

h. Does the section on racism seem outdated? If so, in what ways is it outdated? If not, what do the authors say that still holds true?

i. On whom does this report place the blame for the situation described? What do the authors expect their readers to do about the situation?

Strategy and Style

j. Why did the authors decide to divide the criminal justice system into "functions" (see paragraph 5)? How does this division help (or hinder) the authors in getting their message across?

k. In paragraph 25, the authors quote a prisoner who says that prison guards wanted to "sell their interpretation" of what they called a racial incident. Are the authors also trying to sell their interpretation of history? Explain your answer with reference to the way the authors have structured and presented their material.

l. How does the authors' quoting prisoners' letters affect their credibility?

m. How does the language of the report reflect the authors' political stance? What are their political leanings? Point to specific examples in the text to support your answer.

n. If this were a college research paper, which statements would the author have to support with references to sources and/or with specific data?

SUGGESTIONS FOR SHORT WRITING

a. Randomly choose one passage (a sentence or a paragraph) from the first half of this essay and one passage from the second half. Then write a response to *only* those two passages.

b. At the top of a sheet of paper or a page in your notebook, copy out from the essay a brief passage that strikes you as interesting or confusing. Then divide the rest of the page in half vertically. In the left column write what interests or confuses you about the passage; in the right column ask questions about what you wrote in the left column. Try to answer these questions on the left, ask more questions on the right, and so on.

SUGGESTIONS FOR SUSTAINED WRITING

a. Consider a reference made by the authors to a situation or problem that you think is outdated. Read more about that situation or problem. Then, write a history of its development. Your purpose is to determine whether it *is* outdated, and, if so, to explain what has happened to make it outdated. Remember to cite any secondary sources from which you take information.

b. Find out more about the American Friends Service Committee and the humanitarian projects it has been involved with. One easy way to begin is to look up some of the books it has published under its name. Write a report about one of the projects and reflect on what you think are the positive and/ or negative aspects of it.

c. The report covers a broad topic. Choose one section, passage, or reference in it, and write a research paper in which you deal *specifically* with one issue or event. For example, if you are interested in the labor movement (mentioned in paragraphs 6 through 10), research the history of the labor movement in the U.S. as it developed in or affected one industry, locality, or age, ethnic, or gender group.

Presidential Character and How to Foresee It

James David Barber

Born in Charleston, West Virginia in 1930, James David Barber is a noted political scientist and educator. He received his B.A. and his M.A. from the University of Chicago in 1950 and 1955, and he took a doctorate at Yale in 1960. From 1960 to 1972, he taught at Yale, where he also directed the Office for Advanced Political Studies. He has taught at Stetson and Duke Universities, has been a member of the Board of Directors of Amnesty International since 1981, and has served as a consultant to both the Committee on Economic Development and the Commission on the Year 2000. This selection originally appeared in The Presidential Character: Performance in the White House *(1972), one of Barber's best-known works. Among his other political studies are* Citizen Politics *(1969);* The Pulse of Politics: Electing Presidents in the Media Age *(1980); and* Politics by Humans: Research in American Leadership *(1988).*

When a citizen votes for a Presidential candidate he makes, in effect, a 1 prediction. He chooses from among the contenders the one he thinks (or feels, or guesses) would be the best President. He operates in a situation of immense uncertainty. If he has a long voting history, he can recall time and time again when he guessed wrong. He listens to the commentators, the politicians, and his friends, then adds it all up in some rough way to produce his prediction and his vote. Earlier in the game, his anticipations have been taken into account, either directly in the polls and primaries or indirectly in the minds of politicians who want to nominate someone he will like. But he must choose in the midst of a cloud of confusion, a rain of phony advertising, a storm of sermons, a hail of complex issues, a fog of charisma and boredom, and a thunder of accusation and defense. In the face of this chaos, a great many citizens fall back on the past, vote their old allegiances, and let it go at that. Nevertheless, the citizen's vote says that on balance he expects Mr. X would outshine Mr. Y in the Presidency....

The burden of this book is that the crucial differences can be anticipated 2 by an understanding of a potential President's character, his world view, and his style. This kind of prediction is not easy; well-informed observers often have guessed wrong as they watched a man step toward the White House. One thinks of Woodrow Wilson, the scholar who would bring reason to politics; of Herbert Hoover, the Great Engineer who would organize chaos into progress; of Franklin D. Roosevelt, that champion of the balanced budget; of Harry Truman, whom the office would surely overwhelm; of Dwight D. Eisenhower, militant crusader; of John F. Kennedy, who would lead beyond moralisms to achievements; of Lyndon B. Johnson, the Southern conservative; and of Richard M. Nixon, conciliator. Spotting the errors is easy. Predicting with even approximate

225

accuracy is going to require some sharp tools and close attention in their use. But the experiment is worth it because the question is critical and because it lends itself to correction by evidence.

My argument comes in layers.   3

First, a President's personality is an important shaper of his Presidential   4
behavior on nontrivial matters.

Second, Presidential personality is patterned. His character, world view,   5
and style fit together in a dynamic package understandable in psychological terms.

Third, a President's personality interacts with the power situation he faces   6
and the national "climate of expectations" dominant at the time he serves. The tuning, the resonance—or lack of it—between these external factors and his personality sets in motion the dynamic of his Presidency.

Fourth, the best way to predict a President's character, world view, and   7
style is to see how they were put together in the first place. That happened in his early life, culminating in his first independent political success.

But the core of the argument (which organizes the structure of the book)   8
is that Presidential character—the basic stance a man takes toward his Presidential experience—comes in four varieties. The most important thing to know about a President or candidate is where he fits among these types, defined according to (a) how active he is and (b) whether or not he gives the impression he enjoys his political life.

Let me spell out these concepts briefly before getting down to cases....   9

FOUR TYPES OF PRESIDENTIAL CHARACTER

The five concepts—character, world view, style, power situation, and cli-   10
mate of expectations—run through the accounts of Presidents in the chapters to follow, which cluster the Presidents since Theodore Roosevelt into four types. This is the fundamental scheme of the study. It offers a way to move past the complexities to the main contrasts and comparisons.

The first baseline in defining Presidential types is *activity-passivity*. How   11
much energy does the man invest in his Presidency? Lyndon Johnson went at his day like a human cyclone, coming to rest long after the sun went down. Calvin Coolidge often slept eleven hours a night and still needed a nap in the middle of the day. In between the Presidents array themselves on the high or low side of the activity line.

The second baseline is *positive-negative affect* toward one's activity—   12
that is, how he feels about what he does. Relatively speaking, does he seem to experience his political life as happy or sad, enjoyable or discouraging, positive or negative in its main effect. The feeling I am after here is not grim satisfaction in a job well done, not some philosophical conclusion. The idea is this: is he someone who, on the surfaces we can see, gives forth the feeling that he has

fun in political life? Franklin Roosevelt's Secretary of War, Henry L. Stimson wrote that the Roosevelts "not only understood the *use* of power, they knew the *enjoyment* of power, too....Whether a man is burdened by power or enjoys power; whether he is trapped by responsibility or made free by it; whether he is moved by other people and outer forces or moves them—that is the essence of leadership."

The positive-negative baseline then, is a general symptom of the fit be- 13 tween the man and his experience, a kind of register of *felt* satisfaction.

Why might we expect these two simple dimensions to outline the main 14 character types? Because they stand for two central features of anyone's orientation toward life. In nearly every study of personality, some form of the active-passive contrast is critical; the general tendency to act or be acted upon is evident in such concepts as dominance-submission, extraversion-introversion, aggression-timidity, attack-defense, fight-flight, engagement-withdrawal, approach-avoidance. In everyday life we sense quickly the general energy output of the people we deal with. Similarly we catch on fairly quickly to the affect dimension—whether the person seems to be optimistic or pessimistic, hopeful or skeptical, happy or sad. The two baselines are clear and they are also independent of one another: all of us know people who are very active but seem discouraged, others who are quite passive but seem happy, and so forth. The activity baseline refers to what one does, the affect baseline to how one feels about what he does.

Both are crude clues to character. They are leads into four basic character 15 patterns long familiar in psychological research. In summary form, these are the main configurations:

Active-positive: There is a congruence, a consistency, between much ac- 16 tivity and the enjoyment of it, indicating relatively high self-esteem and relative success in relating to the environment. The man shows an orientation toward productiveness as a value and an ability to use his styles flexibly, adaptively, suiting the dance to the music. He sees himself as developing over time toward relatively well defined personal goals—growing toward his image of himself as he might yet be. There is an emphasis on rational mastery, on using the brain to move the feet. This may get him into trouble; he may fail to take account of the irrational in politics. Not everyone he deals with sees things his way and he may find it hard to understand why.

Active-negative: The contradiction here is between relatively intense ef- 17 fort and low emotional reward for that effort. The activity has a compulsive quality, as if the man were trying to make up for something or to escape from anxiety into hard work. He seems ambitious, striving upward, power-seeking. His stance toward the environment is aggressive and he has a persistent problem in managing his aggressive feelings. His self-image is vague and discontinuous. Life is a hard struggle to achieve and hold power, hampered by the condemnations of a perfectionistic conscience. Active-negative types pour energy into the political system, but it is an energy distorted from within.

Passive-positive: This is the receptive, compliant, other-directed charac- 18
ter whose life is a search for affection as a reward for being agreeable and co-
operative rather than personally assertive. The contradiction is between low
self-esteem (on grounds of being unlovable, unattractive) and a superficial op-
timism. A hopeful attitude helps dispel doubt and elicits encouragement from
others. Passive-positive types help soften the harsh edges of politics. But their
dependence and the fragility of their hopes and enjoyments make disappoint-
ment in politics likely.

Passive-negative: The factors are consistent—but how are we to account 19
for the man's *political* role-taking? Why is someone who does little in politics
and enjoys it less there at all? The answer lies in the passive-negative's charac-
ter-rooted orientation toward doing dutiful service; this compensates for low
self-esteem based on a sense of uselessness. Passive-negative types are in politics because they think they ought to be. They may be well adapted to certain
nonpolitical roles, but they lack the experience and flexibility to perform effectively as political leaders. Their tendency is to withdraw, to escape from the
conflict and uncertainty of politics by emphasizing vague principles (especially
prohibitions) and procedural arrangements. They become guardians of the right
and proper way, above the sordid politicking of lesser men.

Active-positive Presidents want most to achieve results. Active-negatives 20
aim to get and keep power. Passive-positives are after love. Passive-negatives
emphasize their civic virtue. The relation of activity to enjoyment in a President
thus tends to outline a cluster of characteristics, to set apart the adapted from
the compulsive, compliant, and withdrawn types.

The first four Presidents of the United States, conveniently, ran through 21
this gamut of character types. (Remember, we are talking about tendencies,
broad directions; no individual man exactly fits a category.) George Washington—clearly the most important President in the pantheon—established the fundamental legitimacy of an American government at a time when this was a matter in considerable question. Washington's dignity, judiciousness, his aloof air
of reserve and dedication to duty fit the passive-negative or withdrawing type
best. Washington did not seek innovation, he sought stability. He longed to retire to Mount Vernon, but fortunately was persuaded to stay on through a second term, in which, by rising above the political conflict between Hamilton and
Jefferson and inspiring confidence in his own integrity, he gave the nation time
to develop the organized means for peaceful change.

John Adams followed, a dour New England Puritan, much given to work 22
and worry, an impatient and irascible man—an active-negative President, a
compulsive type. Adams was far more partisan than Washington; the survival of
the system through his Presidency demonstrated that the nation could tolerate,
for a time, domination by one of its nascent political parties. As President, an
angry Adams brought the United States to the brink of war with France, and
presided over the new nation's first experiment in political repression: the Alien
and Sedition Acts, forbidding, among other things, unlawful combinations

"with intent to oppose any measure or measures of the government of the United States," or "any false, scandalous, and malicious writing or writings against the United States, or the President of the United States, with intent to defame...or to bring them or either of them, into contempt or disrepute."

Then came Jefferson. He too had his troubles and failures—in the design 23 of national defense, for example. As for his Presidential character (only one element in success or failure), Jefferson was clearly active-positive. A child of the Enlightenment, he applied his reason to organizing connections with Congress aimed at strengthening the more popular forces. A man of catholic interests and delightful humor, Jefferson combined a clear and open vision of what the country could be with a profound political sense, expressed in his famous phrase, "Every difference of opinion is not a difference of principle."

The fourth President was James Madison, "Little Jemmy," the constitu- 24 tional philosopher thrown into the White House at a time of great international turmoil. Madison comes closest to the passive-positive, or compliant, type; he suffered from irresolution, tried to compromise his way out, and gave in too readily to the "warhawks" urging combat with Britain. The nation drifted into war, and Madison wound up ineptly commanding his collection of amateur generals in the streets of Washington. General Jackson's victory at New Orleans saved the Madison administration's historical reputation; but he left the Presidency with the United States close to bankruptcy and secession.

These four Presidents—like all Presidents—were persons trying to cope 25 with the roles they had won by using the equipment they had built over a lifetime. The President is not some shapeless organism in a flood of novelties, but a man with a memory in a system with a history. Like all of us, he draws on his past to shape his future. The pathetic hope that the White House will turn a Caligula into a Marcus Aurelius is as naive as the fear that ultimate power inevitably corrupts. The problem is to understand—and to state understandably—what in the personal past foreshadows the Presidential future.

1972

QUESTIONS FOR DISCUSSION

Content

a. What does Barber mean by the "burden of this book" (paragraph 2)? What function does this selection serve in the book?
b. What is a "baseline" (paragraph 11)?
c. What was "the political conflict between Hamilton and Jefferson" mentioned in paragraph 21? How does Barber's reference to this quarrel help him illustrate something about Washington?

d. Does the quote from the Alien and Sedition Acts (paragraph 22) help eluci- date Adams' character? Explain.
e. Why is Jefferson called a "child of the Enlightenment" (paragraph 23)?
f. Caligula and Marcus Aurelius (paragraph 25) were Roman emperors. Why does Barber mention them?

Strategy and Style

g. What use does the author make of comparison or contrast to develop his es- say? What use does he make of illustration?
h. Barber begins by defining his four personality types. Later, he explains how each of the first four American Presidents fits into one of these categories. Could he have organized this essay differently? What would have been the effect of discussing each President's personality and the classification or type to which it belongs simultaneously, i.e., in the same paragraph?
i. Why are paragraphs 3 and 10 important to the purpose of this selection?
j. In what way does Barber's conclusion help clarify his thesis and purpose?

SUGGESTIONS FOR SHORT WRITING

a. Into which category would you put the current U.S. President or the leader of any other country? Describe one or two things this person has said or done that show him or her to be that type.
b. What other character types might there be outside the passive–active/nega- tive–positive matrix? Coin some new types that you think describe the U.S. President or any other head of state.

SUGGESTIONS FOR SUSTAINED WRITING

a. Write an essay in which you demonstrate how any U.S. President—other than Washington, Adams, Jefferson, or Madison—fits or illustrates one of Barber's four character classifications.
b. Analyze the various personality traits among a few individuals in your fam- ily, athletic team, social club, car pool, neighborhood, or dormitory. Discuss these traits by classifying them into well-defined categories. Use information about people you know well to illustrate your ideas and to develop them ad- equately. *Note:* There's no need to adopt Barber's four categories as the ba- sis for your essay, but don't hesitate to do so if you find them useful and appropriate.

The Climythology of America
David M. Ludlum

An expert on weather history, David Ludlum wrote "Climythology" for Weatherwise, *a magazine founded in 1946.*

History is full of myths, and so is climatology. Every generation of histo- 1 rians gives rise to a revisionist school that reinterprets the past in light of new material and facts. Sometimes the revisions join the body of history; other times they are revised by the next generation. Overall, the process leads to a richer and more truthful history.

The settlement of America produced a series of myths about the climate 2 of different regions of our country. Even before the first British settlements in North America, Europeans held certain concepts concerning the supposed climate of the New World, and those concepts greatly influenced their efforts to establish colonies from Newfoundland to the Carolinas.

Once the seaboard was occupied, new myths arose about the lands west 3 of the Allegheny Mountains. Other unfounded beliefs appeared to influence the occupation of the Mississippi Valley and Great Plains until, in the last decade of the nineteenth century, the land office in Washington officially declared the frontier closed, though much territory remained unsettled. Most of this, however, was thought to be wasteland unsuitable for cultivation. This belief would be dispelled in the next century by the introduction of scientific methods of agriculture and the construction of huge irrigation projects.

THE EQUAL-LATITUDE MYTH

The intellectual content of climatology had made little progress from the 4 time of Ptolemy, the Greek astronomer and geographer of the second century A.D., to the year 1601, which marked the beginning of the century of colonization of North America by the English and the French. The concept of *clima,* or parallel bands around the world which shared comparable temperatures and hence weather conditions, was the generally accepted view of global arrangements. So much so, in fact, that the word clima was used by English writers interchangeably with "latitude." This gave rise to what I shall call the equal-latitude myth.

The planners and backers of the new colonies held to the classical view 5 of the distribution of global temperatures and thus were greatly surprised and chagrined when their environmental expectations were not met by the realities of the New World. The French were perplexed by the harsh winter conditions they met in Nova Scotia and the St. Lawrence Valley because both lay at the same latitudes as northern and central France. The British ultimately gave up constant efforts to settle Newfoundland in the early years of the seventeenth century because of the severe winters, despite the fact that it lay at the same latitude as southernmost England, where winters were usually moderate in temperature.

The history of all the British colonies from Maine to the Carolinas ran 6 much the same. The commercial backers of each colony expressed surprise and dismay that these settlements, though at the latitudes of France and Spain, could not produce the exotic agricultural products of those countries.

Believing Virginia to have a Mediterranean climate, the proprietors tried 7 silk culture until the realities of the winter killed all hopes of producing such a tropical product.

Almost a century passed before the backers of the colonies realized that 8 the American climate differed from the European at the same latitudes. By the beginning of the eighteenth century, a more realistic viewpoint prevailed about the climate of the New World. Facts replaced the equal-latitude myth.

THE CLIMATE CHANGE MYTH

During the first two centuries of settlement of the American seaboard, a 9 popular misconception arose about the observed climate. Where were the record snows of yesteryear? Why did we not have the harsh winters so often mentioned by grandfather and great-grandfather? Many homespun philosophers pondered these questions and suggested answers. Though no actual facts were brought forth, most colonists believed that conditions had grown milder and that the seasons had changed, with spring coming later and autumn lasting longer.

These ideas were expressed in an article by Dr. Hugh Williamson of 10 North Carolina in the first issue of the *Transactions of the American Philosophical Society* in 1771: "An attempt to account for the change observed in the Middle Colonies in North America."

Williamson's thesis was that the cutting down of the forests for farms and 11 settlements had produced a warming of the soil for two reasons. First, the felling of the trees allowed easterly winds to penetrate more deeply into the country, bringing temperate marine influences inland. Second, the bare soil received and stored more solar heat than did forested lands, and snow melted more quickly when exposed to direct sunlight.

In addition, some colonials suggested that the rise of urban communities 12 with heated buildings and smokepots was leading to a milder climate, as they claimed had occurred in Europe. These ideas were the first of many about climate change that were to arise and claim a body of believers among Americans.

THE OHIO COUNTRY MYTH

After almost 200 years of English settlement along the Atlantic seaboard, 13 the vast interior of the North American continent remained a *terra incognita* as far as an exact knowledge of its geography and climate was concerned. The French had sent voyageurs, couriers de bois and missionaries deep into the interior, but their first-hand knowledge of the conditions encountered did not reach the seaboard-bound British. Though the barrier of the Appalachian Mountains was breached during the war years that marked the closing decades of the eighteenth century, few scientific men went westward to observe and report on the physical and atmospheric geography of the interior.

A vigorous controversy as to the nature of the climate of the Ohio Coun- 14 try beyond the Allegheny Mountains arose as the century drew to a close and continued to spark lively arguments well into the next century. The controversy became known as the Ohio Country myth.

Between October 1795 and June 1796, Constantin Francois de Chase- 15 boeuf, Comte de Volney, traveled from Washington, D.C., to Vincennes on the Wabash River in Indiana. He was familiar with Jefferson's view, expressed in his *Notes on the State of Virginia,* that the annual temperature west of the mountains was several degrees warmer than at the same latitude east of the mountains along the Atlantic seaboard. Jefferson based his opinion on the different types of plants thriving on opposite sides of the mountains. Volney's seeming confirmation of Jefferson's opinion received wide dissemination in the *View of the Climate and Soil of the United States,* published in London and Paris in 1804.

The first refutation of the ideas promulgated by Volney came from Dr. 16 Daniel Drake in *Notices concerning Cincinnati,* published in 1810, which produced actual comparative temperature readings. Others soon took up their scientific cudgels. In an address before the Albany Institute in 1823, Dr. Lewis Beck took each of Volney's statements and demolished them with facts from more recent material.

William Darby, in his *View of the United States: Historical, Geographical* 17 *and Statistical* (1828), referred to Volney's "by no means innoxious vulgar error." As late as 1842, Dr. Samuel Forry, in the first climatological survey to employ meteorological observations, felt constrained to criticize Volney's opinions as being "barren of precise data."

In 1857, Lorin Blodget put the Ohio Country myth to final rest in his 18 comprehensive *Climatology of the United States:* "The early distinction between the Atlantic States and the Mississippi has been quite dropped, as the progress of observation has shown them to be essentially the same, or to differ only in unimportant particulars."

THE GREAT AMERICAN DESERT MYTH

"When I was a schoolboy my map of the United States showed between 19 the Missouri River and the Rocky Mountains a long, broad white blotch, upon which was printed in small capitals 'THE GREAT AMERICAN DESERT—UNEXPLORED.'" So wrote Colonel Richard Irving Dodge in 1877 when commencing his revealing survey, *The Great Plains of the Great West.* He concluded: "What was then 'unexplored' is now almost thoroughly known. What was regarded as a desert supports, in some portions, thriving populations. The blotch of thirty years ago is now known as 'The Plains'."

Sergeant John Ordway, who had accompanied Lewis and Clark in 1804, 20 had stated "...this country may with propriety be called the Deserts of North America." Captain Zebulon Pike in exploring the headwaters of the Arkansas River had declared that "...these vast plains of the western hemisphere may become in time as celebrated as the sandy deserts of Africa." And Major Stephen H. Long had written, "...the Great Desert at the Base of the Rocky Mountains...is almost wholly unfit for cultivation, and of course uninhabitable...."

When Lorin Blodget published his comprehensive *Climatology of the* 21 *United States* in 1857, he marked a zone running east of the 100° W meridian on his precipitation chart "the eastern limit of the dry plains," and labeled the area of western Kansas and Nebraska "the Desert Plains."

Following the Civil War, a counterattack was launched on the pessimistic 22 opinion about the future of the plains. The pressure for new lands to settle caused a change of view regarding the farming possibilities of the plains west of the Missouri River. Optimistic projections were penned by enthusiastic travelers, booster-type editors and eager business promoters. Their hopes were bolstered by several years of above-normal rainfall in the late 1860s and early 1870s. The concept that "Rain Follows the Plough" was broadcast in chamber-of-commerce style by agricultural improvement societies and business enterprises. This was the "Garden Myth"—that planting trees and crops on the dry plains would result in increased rainfall in a self-perpetuating manner. The climate pendulum, however, underwent several swings from adequate to inadequate rainfall until a nadir was reached in the late 1880s and early 1890s, resulting in disaster for the many cattle ranchers and the abandonment of farming in much of western Kansas and western Nebraska.

The occupation of the central plains by farmers, the western plains by cat- 23 tlemen, the mountains by miners, and the Pacific Northwest by lumbermen brought more adequate knowledge of the actual climates of these regions. The filling in of the nation's climatological charts was completed about 1890, when the availability of free land ended and the frontier was considered closed.

THE SOUTHERN CALIFORNIA HEALTH MYTH

During the first 30 years of American settlement Southern California re- 24 mained a frontier country with ranching and agriculture dominating the economy. The last two decades of the century, however, brought a change. Promoters and developers exploited the region's prime natural attraction, a beneficent climate, to make it the health frontier of the United States. Its favorable features were widely promoted in a tidal wave of publicity, and hordes of Easterners responded by migrating to the promised land in search of restored health. Thanks to man's ingenuity, the barren outlands had suddenly become habitable and even attractive.

During the decades from 1850 to 1880, native Angelenos might have 25 been forgiven for doubting their climate would turn out to be the most promising feature of the region. Damaging floods occurred in 1862 and 1868, devastating droughts came in 1862–64 and 1876–77 and a long spell of recurrent cold weather in the late 1870s and early 1880s set many still-standing date records for coldness. In addition, a destructive earthquake struck in 1857 and every year there were "tremblos."

Despite the lack of knowledge of the effect of California's climate on dis- 26 ease, publicity for the region's salubrity soon poured forth. A pamphlet entitled, *Southern California: The Italy of America,* claimed for the area the "only perfect climate in the world and the grandest scenery under the sun." The *Los Angeles Star* in 1872 carried an article, "Land of Glorious Sunsets," which was considered by historian Oscar O. Winther (in 1946) as "the opening trumpet blast of a climate promotion campaign that has not ended."

Concerted efforts to attract visitors and settlers became an increasingly 27 active industry in the 1880s. The local Chamber of Commerce was careful to point out that not all parts of California enjoyed the salubrious climate claimed for the southern region. The results soon became apparent. A great boom in real estate and business developed in the mid-1880s, similar to those previously experienced in other sections of the western frontier country.

In the 1890s, climate continued to be the principal pitch of promotion 28 agencies. In 1892, the Southern California Information Bureau asserted: "…we sell the climate at so much an acre and throw in the land." To a complaint that the region had nothing to sell except climate, one enthusiast declared: "That's right, and we sell it, too—$10 for an acre of land, $490 an acre for the climate."

The health angle and longevity prospects were emphasized in the promo- 29 tional publications of the 1890s. Dr. Peter C. Remondino stated the extreme

claim for the region in his book, *The Mediterranean Shores of America: Southern California:* "from my personal observations, I can say that at least an extra
ten years' lease on life is gained by a removal to this coast from the Eastern
States; not ten years to be added with its extra weight of age and infirmity, but
ten years more with additional benefit of feeling ten years younger during the
time."

They came at first by the thousands, and finally by the millions; today   30
more than 15 million people live in Southern California where a century ago
there were only 32,000.

Ironically, the concentration of population with attendant urban sprawl   31
and congested freeways affected the climate in a way none of its promoters of
the late 1800s foresaw. The effusions of millions of combustion engines,
trapped in the area's natural basins by the almost daily inversions in the lower
atmosphere, have created smog conditions detrimental to health.

ALASKAN CLIMYTHOLOGY

The bill for $7,200,000 to pay for Alaska "loosed a storm in the House of   32
Representatives. I shall not attempt to say whether it was a hurricane or tor-
nado, but it was accompanied by a lot of wind, by a great flood—a flood of
oratory and some verbal thunder," declared Senator Ernest Gruening at a meeting of the American Meteorological Society at the University of Alaska on June
27, 1962. The former Russian colony was portrayed as "a frozen waste with a
savage climate, where little or nothing could grow, and where few could or
would live."

Typical of the statements of these pioneer climythologists was that of   33
Benjamin F. Loan of St. Louis, who declared:

"...the acquisition of this inhospitable and barren waste will never add a   34
dollar to the wealth of our country or furnish any homes to our people. It is
utterly worthless....To suppose that anyone would leave the United States...to
seek a home...in the regions of perpetual snow is simply to suppose such a
person insane."

Another climatic pessimist, Representative Orange Ferris of Glens Falls,   35
New York, asserted that Alaska "is a barren and unproductive region covered
with ice and snow" and "will never be populated by an enterprising people."

A representative from New York, Dennis McCarthy of Syracuse, cited   36
"reports that every foot of the soil of Alaska is frozen from five to six feet in
depth" and ventured that his colleagues would soon hear that Greenland was on
the market.

And the minority report of the House Committee on Foreign Relations, in   37
a scathing denunciation, declared Alaska "had no capacity as an agricultural
country...no value as a mineral country....its timber generally of poor quality
and growing upon inaccessible mountains....its fur trade...of insignificant

value, and, will speedily come to an end....the fisheries of doubtful value....in a climate unfit for the habitation of civilized men."

Today, Alaska supports a population of more than one half million people 38 and an annual economy worth more than $9 billion.

1987

QUESTIONS FOR DISCUSSION

Content

a. What is Ludlum's purpose? What do you gain from reading about the history of climate myths?
b. Ludlum has coined a new term with "climythology." How does he define this word?
c. Look up the definition of the word "myth." How does a myth differ from a legend, a history, a folktale? Look up "climate" and "weather." How do the two differ?
d. How does Ludlum's discussion of the Europeans' misconceptions about the climate of North America help explain the colonization of North America? What did European settlers do in order to adapt to the climate?
e. What is a "homespun philosopher" (paragraph 9)? Are the writers whom Ludlum quotes in this paragraph and others examples of homespun philosophers? If not, in what ways do the writers quoted differ from them?
f. Ludlum writes that explorers used words such as "desert" to describe the Great Plains. What effect would the use of such words have on the formation of climate myths?
g. What effect did marketing and advertising have on the formation and maintenance of the "Southern California Health Myth"?
h. Do any myths about climate still exist? Do you recall hearing any from your parents or grandparents? Are there any you believe to be true?
i. Has Ludlum left out any myths? How would climate and weather help to explain other historical events and developments?

Strategy and Style

j. Why does Ludlum provide headings for each of the climate myths? How does dividing his essay in this way affect the essay as a whole? How do you account for the sequence in which the myths appear?
k. Ludlum begins his article with a three-paragraph introduction, yet ends the article abruptly. What might be his reasons for doing this?
l. In the sentence "Others soon took up their scientific cudgels" (paragraph 16), why does Ludlum use the word "cudgel"? What does this reveal about the nature of belief in the climate myths?

m. What is it about the way Ludlum develops this essay that makes it so convincing?

n. Describe the tone and language in this essay by comparing them with what you have read in "Thinking as a Hobby" and "Bicycles." Are they different from the tone and word choice in these other essays? Why and in what way?

SUGGESTIONS FOR SHORT WRITING

a. Write a climate myth of your own. The myth can be regional or global in scope; for example, there has been a lot of talk lately about global warming—are there any myths attached to this issue?

b. Choose one of the climate myths that Ludlum presents and write it as a narrated myth, as if you were telling or hearing it as a story with mythological characters and action.

SUGGESTIONS FOR SUSTAINED WRITING

a. What other misconceptions do people have about climate or weather (for example, that lightning never strikes the same place twice, or that the winters of one's childhood were much worse than recent winters)? Write a sequel or continuation of Ludlum's essay in which you expose these misconceptions.

b. What other bodies of modern mythology can you think of? For example, think about the misconceptions people have about particular ethnic groups, sexes, religions, diseases, professions, cities, states, or parts of the world. Write an essay in which you catalog and explain a set of beliefs about a subject.

c. Write a myth of your own that explains the origin or existence of something. Upon what existing beliefs or knowledge will you base your myth?

Reflections on Horror Movies
Robert Brustein

Robert Brustein was born in New York City in 1927. He began his career acting in summer stock productions and teaching English and drama at Columbia University, and Vassar College. In 1966, Brustein joined the faculty at Yale, where he taught English and served as the dean of the School of Drama and as director of the University's Repertory Theater Company. In 1979 he began teaching at Harvard University and directing the American Repertory Theater Company. Brustein publishes drama criticism and contributes regularly to Harper's *and* The New York Times. *Since 1959 he has been the resident theater critic at* The New Republic. *His important works include* The Theater of Revolt: An Approach to the Modern Drama *(1964);* The Third Theater *(1969), a collection of reviews and articles about nontraditional forms of drama;* Revolution as Theater: Notes on the New Radical Style *(1971); and* Who Needs Theater *(1987). In "Reflections on Horror Movies," which appeared in* The Third Theater, *Brustein uses classification to explain prevailing attitudes toward the scientist and scientific inquiry as reflected in one of the most popular forms of contemporary theater.*

1   Although horror movies have recently been enjoying a vogue, they have always been perennial supporting features among Grade B and C fare. The popularity of the form is no doubt partly explained by its ability to engage the spectator's feelings without making any serious demand on his mind. In addition, however, horror movies covertly embody certain underground assumptions about science which reflect popular opinions.

2   The horror movies I am mainly concerned with I have divided into three major categories: Mad Doctor, Atomic Beast and Interplanetary Monster. They do not exhaust all the types but they each contain two essential characters, the Scientist and the Monster, towards whom the attitudes of the movies are in a revealing state of change.

3   The Mad Doctor series is by far the most long lived of the three. It suffered a temporary decline in the Forties when Frankenstein, Dracula, and the Wolfman (along with their countless offspring) were first loaned out as straight men to Abbott and Costello, and then set out to graze in the parched pastures of the cheap all-night movie houses, but it has recently demonstrated its durability in a group of English remakes and a Teen-age Monster craze. These films find their roots in certain European folk myths. Dracula was inspired by an ancient Balkan superstition about vampires, the Werewolf is a Middle European folk myth recorded, among other places, in the Breton *lais* of Marie de France, and even Frankenstein, though out of Mary Shelley by the Gothic tradition, has a medieval prototype in the Golem, a monster the Jews fashioned from clay and earth to free them from oppression. The spirit of these films is still medieval,

239

combining a vulgar religiosity with folk superstitions. Superstition now, however, has been crudely transferred from magic and alchemy to creative science, itself a form of magic to the untutored mind. The devil of the Vampire and Werewolf myths, who turned human beings into baser animals, today has become a scientist, and the metamorphosis is given a technical name—it is a "regression" into an earlier state of evolution. The alchemist and devil-conjuring scholar, Dr. Faustus, gives way to Dr. Frankenstein, the research physician, while the magic circle, the tetragrammaton, and the full moon are replaced by test tubes, complicated electrical apparatus, and Bunsen burners.

Frankenstein, like Faustus, defies God by exploring areas where humans   4
are not meant to trespass. In Mary Shelley's book (it is subtitled *A Modern Prometheus*), Frankenstein is a latter-day Faustus, a superhuman creature whose aspiration embodies the expansiveness of his age. In the movies, however, Frankenstein loses his heroic quality and becomes a lunatic monomaniac, so obsessed with the value of his work that he no longer cares whether his discovery proves a boon or a curse to mankind. When the mad doctor, his eyes wild and inflamed, bends over his intricate equipment, pouring in a little of this and a little of that, the spectator is confronted with an immoral being whose mental superiority is only a measure of his madness. Like the popular image of the theoretical scientist engaged in basic research ("Basic research," says Charles Wilson, "is science's attempt to prove the grass is green"), he succeeds only in creating something badly which nature has already made well. The Frankenstein monster is a parody of man. Ghastly in appearance, clumsy in movement, criminal in behavior, imbecilic of mind, it is superior only in physical strength and resistance to destruction. The scientist has fashioned it in the face of divine disapproval (the heavens disgorge at its birth)—not to mention the disapproval of friends and frightened townspeople—and it can lead only to trouble.

For Dr. Frankenstein, however, the monster symbolizes the triumph of his   5
intellect over the blind morality of his enemies and it confirms him in the ultimate soundness of his thought ("They thought I was mad, but this proves who is the superior being"). When it becomes clear that his countrymen are unimpressed by his achievement and regard him as a menace to society, the monster becomes the agent of his revenge. As it ravages the countryside and terrorizes the inhabitants, it embodies and expresses the scientist's own lust and violence. It is an extension of his own mad soul, come to life not in a weak and ineffectual body but in a body of formidable physical power. (In a movie like *Dr. Jekyll and Mr. Hyde,* the identity of monster and doctor is even clearer; Mr. Hyde, the monster, is the aggressive and libidinous element in the benevolent Dr. Jekyll's personality.) The rampage of the monster is the rampage of mad, unrestrained science which inevitably turns on the scientist, destroying him too. As the lava bubbles over the sinking head of the monster, the crude moral of the film frees itself from the horror and is asserted. Experimental science (and by extension knowledge itself) is superfluous, dangerous, and unlawful, for in exploring the unknown, it leads man to usurp God's creative power. Each of

these films is a victory for obscurantism, flattering the spectator into believing that his intellectual inferiority is a sign that he is loved by God.

The Teen-age Monster films, a very recent phenomenon, amend the as-   6
sumptions of these horror movies in a startling manner. Their titles—*I Was a Teenage Werewolf, I Was a Teenage Frankenstein, Blood of Dracula,* and *Teen-age Monster*—(some wit awaits one called *I Had a Teenage Monkey on My Back*)—suggest a Hollywood prank, but they are deadly serious, mixing the conventions of early horror movies with the ingredients of adolescent culture. The doctor, significantly enough, is no longer a fringe character whose madness can be inferred from the rings around his eyes and his wild hair but a respected member of society, a high-school chemistry teacher (*Blood of Dracula*) or a psychoanalyst (*Teenage Werewolf*) or a visiting lecturer from Britain (*Teenage Frankenstein*). Although he gives the appearance of benevolence—he pretends to help teen-agers with their problems—behind this facade he hides evil experimental designs. The monster, on the other hand, takes on a more fully developed personality. He is a victim who begins inauspiciously as an average, though emotionally troubled, adolescent and ends, through the influence of the doctor, as a voracious animal. The monster as teen-ager becomes the central character in the film and the teen-age audience is expected to identify and sympathize with him.

In *I Was a Teenage Werewolf,* the hero is characterized as brilliant but   7
erratic in his studies and something of a delinquent. At the suggestion of his principal, he agrees to accept therapy from an analyst helping maladjusted students. The analyst gets the boy under his control and, after injecting him with a secret drug, turns him into a werewolf. Against his will he murders a number of his contemporaries. When the doctor refuses to free him from this curse, he kills him and is himself killed by the police. In death, his features relax into the harmless countenance of an adolescent.

The crimes of the adolescent are invariably committed against other   8
youths (the doctor has it in for teen-agers) and are always connected with those staples of juvenile culture, sex and violence. The advertising displays show the male monsters, dressed in leather jackets and blue jeans, bending ambiguously over the diaphanously draped body of a luscious young girl while the female teen-age vampire of *Blood of Dracula,* her nails long and her fangs dripping, is herself half-dressed and lying on top of a struggling male (whether to rape or murder him is not clear). The identification of sex and violence is further underlined by the promotion blurbs: "In her eyes DESIRE! in her veins—the blood of a MONSTER!" (*Blood of Dracula*); "A Teenage Titan on a Lustful Binge that Paralyzed a Town with Fear" (*Teenage Monster*). It is probable that these crimes are performed less reluctantly than is suggested and that the adolescent spectator is more thrilled than appalled by this "lustful binge" which captures the attention of the adult community. The acquisition of power and prestige through delinquent sexual and aggressive activity is a familiar juvenile fantasy (the same distributors exploit it more openly in films like *Reform School Girl*

and *Drag-Strip Girl*), one which we can see frequently acted out by delinquents in our city schools. In the Teen-age Monster films, however, the hero is absolved of his aggressive and libidinous impulses. Although he both feels and acts on them, he can attribute the responsibility to the mad scientist who controls his behavior. What these films seem to be saying, in their underground manner, is that behind the harmless face of the high-school chemistry teacher and the intellectual countenance of the psychoanalyst lies the warped authority responsible for teen-age violence. The adolescent feels victimized by society— turned into a monster by society—and if he behaves in a delinquent manner, society and not he is to blame. Thus, we can see one direction in which the hostility for experimental research, explicit in the Mad Doctor films, can go—it can be transmuted into hatred of adult authority itself.

Or it can go underground, as in the Atomic Beast movies. The Mad Doc-   9
tor movies, in exploiting the supernatural, usually locate their action in Europe (often a remote Bavarian village) where wild fens, spectral castles, and ominous graveyards provide the proper eerie background. The Atomic Beast movies depend for their effect on the contemporary and familiar and there is a corresponding change in locale. The monster (or "thing" as it is more often called) appears now in a busy American city—usually Los Angeles to save the producer money—where average men walk about in business suits. The thing terrorizes not only the hero, the heroine, and a few anonymous (and expendable) characters in Tyrolean costumes, but the entire world. Furthermore, it has lost all resemblance to anything human. It appears as a giant ant (*Them!*), a prehistoric animal (*Beast from Twenty Thousand Fathoms*), an outsized grasshopper (*Beginning of the End*) or a monstrous spider (*Tarantula*). Although these films, in their deference to science fiction, seem to smile more benignly on scientific endeavor, they are unconsciously closer to the anti-theoretical biases of the Mad Doctor series than would first appear.

All these films are similarly plotted, so the plot of *Beginning of the End*   10
will serve as an example of the whole genre. The scene opens on a pair of adolescents necking in their car off a desert road. Their attention is caught by a weird clicking sound, the boy looks up in horror, the girl screams, the music stings and the scene fades. In the next scene, we learn that the car has been completely demolished and its occupants have disappeared. The police, totally baffled, are conducting fruitless investigations when word comes that a small town nearby has been destroyed in the same mysterious way. Enter the young scientist hero. Examining the wreckage of the town, he discovers a strange fluid which when analyzed proves to have been manufactured by a giant grasshopper. The police ridicule his conclusions and are instantly attacked by a fleet of these grasshoppers, each fifteen feet high, which wipe out the entire local force and a few state troopers. Interrupting a perfunctory romance with the heroine, the scientist flies to Washington to alert the nation. He describes the potential danger to a group of bored politicians and yawning big brass, but they remain skeptical until word comes that the things have reached Chicago and are crush-

ing buildings and eating the occupants. The scientist is then put in charge of the army and air force. Although the military men want to evacuate the city and drop an atomic bomb on it, the scientist devises a safer method of destroying the creatures and proceeds to do so through exemplary physical courage and superior knowledge of their behavior. The movie ends on a note of foreboding: have the things been completely exterminated?

Externally, there seem to be very significant changes indeed, especially in 11 the character of the scientist. No longer fang-toothed, long-haired, and subject to delirious ravings (Bela Lugosi, John Carradine, Basil Rathbone), the doctor is now a highly admired member of society, muscular, handsome, and heroic (John Agar). He is invariably wiser, more reasonable, and more humane than the bone-headed bureaucrats and trigger-happy brass that compose the members of his "team," and he even has sexual appeal, a quality which Hollywood's eggheads have never enjoyed before. The scientist-hero, however, is not a very convincing intellectual. Although he may use technical, polysyllabic language when discussing his findings, he always yields gracefully to the admonition to "tell us in our own words, Doc" and proves that he can speak as simply as you or I; in the crisis, in fact, he is almost monosyllabic. When the chips are down, he loses his glasses (a symbol of his intellectualism) and begins to look like everyone else. The hero's intellect is part of his costume and makeup, easily shed when heroic action is demanded. That he is always called upon not only to outwit the thing but to wrestle with it as well (in order to save the heroine) indicates that he is in constant danger of tripping over the thin boundary between specialist and average Joe.

The fact remains that there is a new separation between the scientist and 12 the monster. Rather than being an extension of the doctor's evil will, the monster functions completely on its own, creating havoc through its predatory nature. We learn through charts, biological film, and the scientist's patient explanations that ants and grasshoppers are not the harmless little beasties they appear but actually voracious insects who need only the excuse of size to prey upon humanity. The doctor, rather than allying himself with the monster in its rampage against our cities, is in strong opposition to it, and reverses the pattern of the Mad Doctor films by destroying it.

And yet, if the individual scientist is absolved of all responsibility for the 13 "thing," science somehow is not. These films suggest an uneasiness about science which, though subtle and unpremeditated, reflects unconscious American attitudes. These attitudes are sharpened when we examine the genesis of the thing for, though it seems to rise out of nowhere, it is invariably caused by a scientific blunder. The giant ants of *Them!,* for example, result from a nuclear explosion which caused a mutation in the species; another fission test has awakened, in *Beast from Twenty Thousand Fathoms,* a dinosaur encrusted in polar icecaps; the spider of *Tarantula* grows in size after having been injected with radioactive isotopes, and escapes during a fight in the lab between two scientists; the grasshoppers of *Beginning of the End* enlarge after crawling into some radioactive dust carelessly left about by a researcher. We are left with a puzzling substatement: science destroys the thing but scientific experimentation has created it.

I think we can explain this equivocal attitude when we acknowledge that 14 the thing "which is too horrible to name," which owes its birth to an atomic or nuclear explosion, which begins in a desert or frozen waste and moves from there to cities, and which promises ultimately to destroy the world, is probably a crude symbol for the bomb itself. The scientists we see represented in these films are unlike the Mad Doctors in another more fundamental respect: they are never engaged in basic research. The scientist uses his knowledge in a purely defensive manner, like a specialist working on rocket interception or a physician trying to cure a disease. The isolated theoretician who tinkers curiously in his lab (and who invented the atomic bomb) is never shown, only the practical working scientist who labors to undo the harm. The thing's destructive rampage against cities, like the rampage of the Frankenstein monster, is the result of too much cleverness, and the consequences for all the world are only too apparent.

These consequences are driven home more powerfully in movies like *The* 15 *Incredible Shrinking Man* and *The Amazing Colossal Man* where the audience gets the opportunity to identify closely with the victims of science's reckless experimentation. The hero of the first movie is an average man who, through contact with fallout while on his honeymoon, begins to shrink away to nothing. As he proceeds to grow smaller, he finds himself in much the same dilemma as the other heroes of the *Atomic Beast* series: he must do battle with (now) gigantic insects in order to survive. Scientists can do nothing to save him—after a while they can't even find him—so as he dwindles into an atomic particle he finally turns to God for whom "there is no zero." The inevitable sequel, *The Amazing Colossal Man,* reverses the dilemma. The hero grows to enormous size through the premature explosion of a plutonium bomb. Size carries with it the luxury of power but the hero cannot enjoy his new stature. He feels like a freak and his body is proceeding to outgrow his brain and heart. Although the scientists labor to help him and even succeed in reducing an elephant to the size of a cat, it is too late; the hero has gone mad, demolished Las Vegas and fallen over Boulder Dam. The victimization of man by theoretical science has become, in these two movies, less of a suggestion and more of a fact.

In the Interplanetary Monster movies, Hollywood handles the public's 16 ambivalence towards science in a more obvious way, by splitting the scientist in two. Most of these movies feature both a practical scientist who wishes to destroy the invader and a theoretical scientist who wants to communicate with it. In *The Thing,* for example, we find billeted among a group of more altruistic average-Joe colleagues with crew cuts an academic long-haired scientist of the Dr. Frankenstein type. When the evil thing (a highly evolved vegetable which, by multiplying itself, threatens to take over the world) descends in a flying saucer, this scientist tries to perpetuate its life in order "to find out what it knows." He is violently opposed in this by the others who take the occasion to tell him that such amoral investigation produced the atomic bomb. But he cannot be reasoned with and almost wrecks the entire party. After both he and the thing are destroyed, the others congratulate themselves on remaining safe, though in the dark. In *Forbidden Planet* (a sophisticated thriller inspired in part by Shakespeare's *Tempest*), the good and evil elements in science are represented, as in *Dr. Jekyll and Mr. Hyde,* by the split personality of the scientist. He is urbane and benevolent (Walter Pidgeon plays the role) and is trying to realize an ideal community on the far-off planet he has discovered. Although he has invented a robot (Ariel) who cheerfully performs man's baser tasks, we learn that he is also responsible, though unwittingly, for a terrible invisible force (Caliban) overwhelming in its destructiveness. While he sleeps, the aggressive forces in his libido activate a dynamo he has been tinkering with which gives them enormous power to kill those the doctor unconsciously resents. Thus, Freudian psychology is evoked to endow the scientist with guilt. At the end, he accepts his guilt and sacrifices his life in order to combat the being he has created.

The Interplanetary Monster series sometimes reverses the central situation 17 of most horror films. We often find the monster controlling the scientist and forcing him to do its evil will. In *It Conquered the World* (the first film to capitalize on Sputnik and Explorer), the projection of a space satellite proves to be a mistake, for it results in the invasion of America by a monster from Venus. The monster takes control of the scientist who, embittered by the indifference of the masses towards his ideas, mistakenly thinks the monster will free men from stupidity. This muddled egghead finally discovers the true intentions of the monster and destroys it, dying himself in the process. In *The Brain from Planet Arous,* a hideous brain inhabits the mind of a nuclear physicist with the intention of controlling the universe. As the physical incarnation of the monster, the scientist is at the mercy of its will until he can free himself of its influence. The monster's intellect, like the intellect of the Mad Doctor, is invariably superior, signified graphically by its large head and small body (in the last film named it is nothing but Brain). Like the Mad Doctor, its superior intelligence is always accompanied by moral depravity and an unconscionable lust for power. If the monster is to be destroyed at all, this will not be done by matching wits with it but by finding some chink in its armor. The chink quite often is a physical imperfection: in *War of the Worlds,* the invading Martians are stopped, at the height of their victory, by their vulnerability to the disease germs of earth. Before this Achilles heel is discovered, however, the scientist is controlled to do evil, and with the monster and the doctor in collaboration again, even in this qualified sense, the wheel has come full circle.

The terror of most of these films, then, stems from the matching of 18 knowledge with power, always a source of fear for Americans—when Nietzsche's Superman enters comic book culture he loses his intellectual and spiritual qualities and becomes a muscle man. The muscle man, even with X-ray vision, poses no threat to the will, but muscle in collaboration with mind is generally thought to have a profound effect on individual destinies. The tendency to attribute everything that happens in the heavens, from flying saucers to Florida's cold wave, to science and the bomb ("Why don't they stop," said an old lady on the bus behind me the other day, "they don't know what they're doing") accounts for the extreme ways in which the scientist is regarded in our culture: either as a protective savior or as a destructive blunderer. It is little wonder that America exalts the physician (and the football player) and ignores the physicist. These issues, the issues of the great debate over scientific education and basic research, assert themselves crudely through the unwieldy monster and the Mad Doctor. The films suggest that the academic scientist, in exploring new areas, has laid the human race open to devastation either by human or interplanetary enemies—the doctor's madness, then, is merely a suitable way of expressing a conviction that the scientist's idle curiosity has shaken itself loose from prudence or principle. There is obviously a sensitive moral problem involved here, one which needs more articulate treatment than the covert and superstitious way it is handled in horror movies. That the problem is touched there at all is evidence of how profoundly it has stirred the American psyche.

1958

QUESTIONS FOR DISCUSSION

Content

a. Paragraph 1 offers two explanations for the popularity of horror films. What are they and how do they help the author introduce the three major categories he discusses in this essay?

b. What common theme do Mad Doctor movies share? How do they define the relationship between the scientist and the monster?

c. What leads Brustein to call this type of film "a victory for obscurantism" (paragraph 5)? Why has he placed Teen-Age Monster movies in the same classification?

d. In what way is the psychoanalyst of *I Was A Teenage Werewolf* analogous to Dr. Frankenstein? In what way is he different?

e. Brustein claims that Atomic Beast movies only "seem to smile more benignly on scientific endeavor" than Mad Doctor movies do (paragraph 9). What is he driving at? Why isn't the scientist-hero of Atomic Beast films a "very convincing intellectual" (paragraph 11)?

f. In what light do Atomic Beast movies portray the role of science itself? What is the common message of these films, and why are they so easy to classify?

g. Explain the "new separation between the scientist and the monster," which Brustein mentions in paragraph 12. How does this separation help distinguish Atomic Beast movies from Mad Doctor films?

h. What role does Freudian psychology play in the character portrayal of the scientists who appear in Interplanetary Monster films? What do such films have in common with the other types Brustein discusses? Do you agree that, in such movies, "the wheel has come full circle" (paragraph 17)? Explain.

i. Who was Nietzsche's "Superman," and how does Brustein's reference to this literary figure help explain that for Americans "the matching of knowledge with power" is "always a source of fear" (paragraph 18)?

j. This essay seems to be focused upon America's ambivalence toward the scientist and scientific research. How would you describe that ambivalence? Is fear part of it? In this connection, what is the "sensitive moral problem" the author mentions in his conclusion?

Strategy and Style

k. As a rule, this selection makes extensive use of plot summary and character analysis as illustrative devices. What do they contribute to Brustein's study of horror films?

l. This essay is long and sophisticated, but it is well organized. What techniques does Brustein use to keep the arrangement of details logical and easy to follow?

m. If you have seen any of the films in which Bela Lugosi, John Carradine, Basil Rathbone, or John Agar appeared, explain how Brustein's allusion to these actors facilitates his classification of horror movies (paragraph 11).

n. The author's presentation is meticulous, authoritative, even erudite. Is this kind of presentation appropriate to so popular an art form?

o. Though Brustein generally uses language that is sophisticated and evocative, he sometimes becomes comfortably familiar, such as when he mentions "bone-headed bureaucrats and trigger-happy brass" in paragraph 11. What effect do such phrases have on your reading of the essay?

SUGGESTIONS FOR SHORT WRITING

a. Write about a recent horror film you have seen and how it fits into one of Brustein's three categories. If it does not fit into any of them, invent a new category and explain why your film fits into it.

b. Write a brief review of a recent horror film, or one of the films mentioned by Brustein, from the point of view of one of the characters in the film.

SUGGESTIONS FOR SUSTAINED WRITING

a. Discuss a horror film you've seen recently. Does it fit one of Brustein's three categories? Draw upon your recollection of the movie to gather concrete illustrations that will make the connection clear. If possible, rent a copy of the film from your local video store and watch it one more time. Doing so will help you gather information for your paper and make writing it even more fun.

b. Brustein has succeeded in analyzing and explaining the significance of a very popular genre. Using classification, do the same with an art form (either popular or traditional) with which you are familiar. For instance, think about the various kinds of comic books you have collected over the years, the types of music videos now being aired, or even your three or four favorite classical composers and the different styles of music they represent.

Cinematypes

Susan Allen Toth

Born in Ames, Iowa in 1940, Susan Allen Toth earned a Ph.D. at the University of Minnesota in 1969. She also holds a B.A. from Smith College (1961) and an M.A. from the University of California at Berkeley (1963). Since 1969, she has been on the faculty of Macalester College in St. Paul, Minnesota, where she teaches courses in the British and American novel, contemporary American literature, and creative writing. Toth's first book, Blooming: A Small-Town Girlhood *(1981), was named by the* New York Times *as one of the "notable books of the year."* Ivy Days: Making My Way Out East *appeared in 1984. Her most recent book is* How to Prepare for Your High-School Reunion: And Other Mid-Life Musings *(1988). Toth's stories, essays, and reviews have appeared in* The New York Times Book Review, Harper's, Ms., McCall's, Vogue, *and other publications. She has also written scholarly essays on late nineteenth-century American local-color literature and is currently working on a fictional memoir about her grandmother. "Cinematypes" first appeared in* Harper's *in May, 1980.*

Aaron takes me only to art films. That's what I call them, anyway: 1
strange movies with vague poetic images I don't always understand, long
dreamy movies about a distant Technicolor past, even longer black-and-white
movies about the general meaninglessness of life. We do not go unless at least
one reputable critic has found the cinematography superb. We went to *The Devil's Eye,* and Aaron turned to me in the middle and said, "My God, this is
funny." I do not think he was pleased.

When Aaron and I go to the movies, we drive our cars separately and 2
meet by the box office. Inside the theater he sits tentatively in his seat, ready to
move if he can't see well, poised to leave if the film is disappointing. He leans
away from me, careful not to touch the bare flesh of his arm against the bare
flesh of mine. Sometimes he leans so far I am afraid he may be touching the
woman on his other side. If the movie is very good, he leans forward, too, peering between the heads of the couple in front of us. The light from the screen
bounces off his glasses; he gleams with intensity, sitting there on the edge of
his seat, watching the screen. Once I tapped him on the arm so I could whisper
a comment in his ear. He jumped.

After *Belle de Jour* Aaron said he wanted to ask me if he could stay over- 3
night. "But I can't," he shook his head mournfully before I had a chance to
answer, "because I know I never sleep well in strange beds." Then he apolo-
gized for asking. "It's just that after a film like that," he said, "I feel the need to
assert myself."

Pete takes me only to movies that he thinks have redeeming social value. 4
He doesn't call them "films." They tend to be about poverty, war, injustice, po-

litical corruption, struggling unions in the 1930s, and the military-industrial complex. Pete doesn't like propaganda movies, though, and he doesn't like to be too depressed, either. We stayed away from *The Sorrow and the Pity;* it would be, he said, just too much. Besides, he assured me, things are never that hopeless. So most of the movies we see are made in Hollywood. Because they are always topical, these movies offer what Pete calls "food for thought." When we saw *Coming Home,* Pete's jaw set so firmly with the first half-hour that I knew we would end up at Poppin' Fresh Pies afterward.

When Pete and I go to the movies, we take turns driving so no one owes 5 anyone else anything. We leave the car far from the theater so we don't have to pay for a parking space. If it's raining or snowing, Pete offers to let me off at the door, but I can tell he'll feel better if I go with him while he finds a spot, so we share the walk too. Inside the theater Pete will hold my hand when I get scared if I ask him. He puts my hand firmly on his knee and covers it completely with his own hand. His knee never twitches. After a while, when the scary part is past, he loosens his hand slightly and I know that is a signal to take mine away. He sits companionably close, letting his jacket just touch my sweater, but he does not infringe. He thinks I ought to know he is there if I need him.

One night, after *The China Syndrome,* I asked Pete if he wouldn't like to 6 stay for a second drink, even though it was past midnight. He thought a while about that, considering my offer from all possible angles, but finally he said no. Relationships today, he said, have a tendency to move too quickly.

Sam likes movies that are entertaining. By that he means movies that Will 7 Jones in the *Minneapolis Tribune* loved and either *Time* or *Newsweek* rather liked; also movies that do not have sappy love stories, are not musicals, do not have subtitles, and will not force him to think. He does not go to movies to think. He liked *California Suite* and *The Seduction of Joe Tynan,* though the plots, he said, could have been zippier. He saw it all coming too far in advance, and that took the fun out. He doesn't like to know what is going to happen. "I just want my brain to be tickled," he says. It is very hard for me to pick out movies for Sam.

When Sam takes me to the movies, he pays for everything. He thinks 8 that's what a man ought to do. But I buy my own popcorn, because he doesn't approve of it; the grease might smear his flannel slacks. Inside the theater, Sam makes himself comfortable. He takes off his jacket, puts one arm around me, and all during the movie he plays with my hand, stroking my palm, beating a small tattoo on my wrist. Although he watches the movie intently, his body operates on instinct. Once I inclined my head and kissed him lightly just behind his ear. He beat a faster tattoo on my wrist, quick and musical, but he didn't look away from the screen.

When Sam takes me home from the movies, he stands outside my door 9 and kisses me long and hard. He would like to come in, he says regretfully, but his steady girlfriend in Duluth wouldn't like it. When the *Tribune* gives a movie four stars, he has to save it to see with her. Otherwise her feelings might be hurt.

I go to some movies by myself. On rainy Sunday afternoons I often sneak 10 into a revival house or a college auditorium for old Technicolor musicals, *Kiss Me Kate, Seven Brides for Seven Brothers, Calamity Jane,* even, once, *The Sound of Music.* Wearing saggy jeans so I can prop my feet on the seat in front, I sit toward the rear where no one can see me. I eat large handfuls of popcorn with double butter. Once the movie starts, I feel completely at home. Howard Keel and I are old friends; I grin back at him on the screen. I know the sound tracks by heart. Sometimes when I get really carried away I hum along with Kathryn Grayson, remembering how I once thought I would fill out a formal like that. I am rather glad now I never did. Skirts whirl, feet tap, acrobatic young men perform impossible feats, and then the camera dissolves into a dream sequence I know I can comfortably follow. It is not, thank God, Bergman.

If I can't find an old musical, I settle for Hepburn and Tracy, vintage 11 Grant or Gable, on adventurous days Claudette Colbert or James Stewart. Before I buy my ticket I make sure it will all end happily. If necessary, I ask the girl at the box office. I have never seen *Stella Dallas* or *Intermezzo.* Over the years I have developed other peccadilloes: I will, for example, see anything that is redeemed by Thelma Ritter. At the end of *Daddy Long Legs* I wait happily for the scene when Fred Clark, no longer angry, at last pours Thelma a convivial drink. They smile at each other, I smile at them, I feel they are smiling at me. In the movies I go to by myself, the men and women always like each other.

1980

QUESTIONS FOR DISCUSSION

Content

a. What does the last sentence in the essay reveal about Toth's experiences with movies and men? How does it reveal Toth's thesis? What is that thesis?
b. Why is it necessary to classify the activity of moviegoing? What benefits are gained from classifying this subject?
c. For whom is Toth writing? What might be their reasons for reading this essay?
d. Into what categories does Toth divide movies and men? Why does she choose these categories?
e. How does she distinguish between "film" and "movie"? Do her definitions of these terms match yours? What words does Toth use to reveal her opinion of them?

f. Into which category do you place yourself and your boyfriend, girlfriend, or spouse? Do you find that you agree or disagree with Toth's opinions of movies and men?

g. Has Toth left any categories out? Has she overgeneralized with the categories she has chosen? If so, what might be her reasons for doing so?

Strategy and Style

h. Each category is structured in the same way: name of boyfriend, type of movie, titles of representative movies, mode of transportation to the movie, behavior during the movie, etc. How do the components of one category relate to those of the others? What effect does this rigid structure have on the essay as a whole?

i. Why does Toth focus her description on her friends in the first three categories, leaving herself out until the fourth category?

j. The author does not use a standard introduction or conclusion. How effective is the essay without a standard beginning and ending? Does the abruptness increase or decrease the essay's effectiveness?

k. Why does Toth title her essay "Cinematypes"? Do you think these types refer to cinemas, movies, or moviegoers? What is the benefit of having an ambiguous title?

l. Describe Toth's tone. Is she being serious or humorous? What words, phrases, or sentences reveal her tone?

SUGGESTIONS FOR SHORT WRITING

a. Write the story of one of your own experiences with a date at a movie. Which cinematype did he or she resemble most closely?

b. Write personals ads for Toth, any of her cinematypes, and/or yourself, seeking to find the perfect movie date. You might find examples of such ads in the classified section of your newspaper.

SUGGESTIONS FOR SUSTAINED WRITING

a. Write an essay classifying a popular activity. Be sure that your reasons for classifying are clear to you and to your readers. Take into account the types of people and the types of behavior associated with each category.

b. Write an essay in which you extend Toth's classification, discussing cinematypes which she did not include.

c. Write "Cinematypes" from a man's point of view. Which aspects will remain the same? Which will differ?

6

Comparison and Contrast

The human tendency to measure one thing against another is so pervasive that it is only natural it be used as a way to explore and explain complex ideas in writing. Comparison reveals similarities; contrast, differences. Both allow the writer to explain and explore new ideas by making reference to what the reader already knows. One way to begin describing a microwave oven to someone who has never seen one is to liken it to the oven in the conventional kitchen stove with which he or she is familiar. Both use energy to heat and cook food. Both are relatively easy to use, and both are no fun to clean! But there the similarities end. A microwave is quicker and more economical. And whoever heard of making popcorn in a conventional oven? Spend enough time explaining similarities and differences, and you are sure to give your reader at least a rudimentary knowledge of this newfangled appliance.

As with all writing, the key to composing effective comparison/contrast papers is to collect important information—and plenty of it—before you begin. Look at your subjects long and hard, take careful notes, and gather the kinds of details that will help you reveal differences and similarities of the most telling kind.

You can use a variety of techniques to develop a comparison or contrast. As suits his purpose, Mark Twain relies heavily on description in "Two Views of the Mississippi" while Murray Ross includes both narrative and descriptive details to reveal fascinating distinctions between two of America's most popular sports. Narration also informs Bruce Catton's brilliant study of Grant and Lee, as it does May Sarton's commentary on loneliness and solitude, which she begins with an anecdote. Ralph Waldo Emerson even makes use of an ancient fable. Marie Winn, on the other hand, analyzes causes and effects as she builds a convincing argument about the hazards of watching television.

One of the major advantages of using comparison/contrast to explain ideas is that it can lend itself quite naturally to two easy-to-arrange and easy-to-follow patterns of organization. In the point-by-point method, the writer compares or contrasts a particular aspect of the subject and discusses it completely before moving to the next point. Essentially, this is how the selections by Winn and Emerson are arranged. In the subject-by-subject method, the writer addresses one subject thoroughly before moving on to the second. You can see good examples of the subject-by-subject method in the essays by Twain and Ross. Cynthia Ozick also uses the subject-by-subject method when she explains differences between herself and another author as a preface to the intricacies of granting oneself "permission to write."

But don't be misled. No writer represented in this chapter is content with following a predetermined schema slavishly. Each has a specific purpose in mind and fashions the essay accordingly.

The selections in this chapter present a variety of subjects and purposes— from analyzing the American psyche through its fascination with sport to describing traditional political philosophies to warning us about the most popular national pastime, watching television. Carefully consider the Questions for Discussion and the Suggestions for Short Writing and for Sustained Writing following each essay. They will lead you to many more insights about using comparison/contrast as a way to explore new ideas and to make your writing more powerful no matter what your topic or purpose.

Grant and Lee: A Study in Contrasts

Bruce Catton

Born in Michigan, Bruce Catton (1899–1978) has come to be regarded as one of the most important historians of the American Civil War. Catton received the Pulitzer Prize and the National Book Award for A Stillness at Appomattox *(1953). Among his other works are* The Hallowed Ground *(1956),* Mr. Lincoln's Army *(1951), and* Gettysburg: The Final Fury *(1974). The piece on Grant and Lee that follows is one of the most frequently anthologized short selections on the subject of the Civil War.*

When Ulysses S. Grant and Robert E. Lee met in the parlor of a modest 1 house at Appomattox Court House, Virginia, on April 9, 1865, to work out the terms for the surrender of Lee's Army of Northern Virginia, a great chapter in American life came to a close, and a great new chapter began.

These men were bringing the Civil War to its virtual finish. To be sure, 2 other armies had yet to surrender, and for a few days the fugitive Confederate government would struggle desperately and vainly, trying to find some way to go on living now that its chief support was gone. But in effect it was all over when Grant and Lee signed the papers. And the little room where they wrote out the terms was the scene of one of the poignant, dramatic contrasts in American history.

They were two strong men, these oddly different generals, and they rep- 3 resented the strengths of two conflicting currents that, through them, had come into final collision.

Back of Robert E. Lee was the notion that the old aristocratic concept 4 might somehow survive and be dominant in American life.

Lee was tidewater Virginia, and in his background were family, culture, 5 and tradition...the age of chivalry transplanted to a New World which was making its own legends and its own myths. He embodied a way of life that had come down through the age of knighthood and the English country squire. America was a land that was beginning all over again, dedicated to nothing much more complicated than the rather hazy belief that all men had equal rights, and should have an equal chance in the world. In such a land Lee stood for the feeling that it was somehow of advantage to human society to have a pronounced inequality in the social structure. There should be a leisure class, backed by ownership of land; in turn, society itself should be keyed to the land as the chief source of wealth and influence. It would bring forth (according to this ideal) a class of men with a strong sense of obligation to the community; men who lived not to gain advantage for themselves, but to meet the solemn obligations which had been laid on them by the very fact that they were privileged. From them the country would get its leadership; to them it could look for

255

the higher values—of thought, of conduct, of personal deportment—to give it strength and virtue.

Lee embodied the noblest elements of this aristocratic ideal. Through **6**
him, the landed nobility justified itself. For four years, the Southern states had fought a desperate war to uphold the ideals for which Lee stood. In the end, it almost seemed as if the Confederacy fought for Lee; as if he himself was the Confederacy...the best thing that the way of life for which the Confederacy stood could ever have to offer. He had passed into legend before Appomattox. Thousands of tired, underfed, poorly clothed Confederate soldiers, long-since past the simple enthusiasm of the early days of the struggle, somehow considered Lee the symbol of everything for which they had been willing to die. But they could not quite put this feeling into words. If the Lost Cause, sanctified by so much heroism and so many deaths, had a living justification, its justification was General Lee.

Grant, the son of a tanner on the Western frontier, was everything Lee **7**
was not. He had come up the hard way, and embodied nothing in particular except the eternal toughness and sinewy fiber of the men who grew up beyond the mountains. He was one of a body of men who owed reverence and obeisance to no one, who were self-reliant to a fault, who cared hardly anything for the past but who had a sharp eye for the future.

These frontier men were the precise opposites of the tidewater aristocrats. **8**
Back of them, in the great surge that had taken people over the Alleghenies and into the opening Western country, there was a deep, implicit dissatisfaction with a past that had settled into grooves. They stood for democracy, not from any reasoned conclusion about the proper ordering of human society, but simply because they had grown up in the middle of democracy and knew how it worked. Their society might have privileges, but they would be privileges each man had won for himself. Forms and patterns meant nothing. No man was born to anything, except perhaps to a chance to show how far he could rise. Life was competition.

Yet along with this feeling had come a deep sense of belonging to a na- **9**
tional community. The Westerner who developed a farm, opened a shop or set up in business as a trader, could hope to prosper only as his own community prospered—and his community ran from the Atlantic to the Pacific and from Canada down to Mexico. If the land was settled, with towns and highways and accessible markets, he could better himself. He saw his fate in terms of the nation's own destiny. As its horizons expanded, so did his. He had, in other words, an acute dollars-and-cents stake in the continued growth and development of his country.

And that, perhaps, is where the contrast between Grant and Lee becomes **10**
most striking. The Virginia aristocrat, inevitably, saw himself in relation to his own region. He lived in a static society which could endure almost anything except change. Instinctively, his first loyalty would go to the locality in which that society existed. He would fight to the limit of endurance to defend it, be-

cause in defending it he was defending everything that gave his own life its deepest meaning.

The Westerner, on the other hand, would fight with an equal tenacity for 11 the broader concept of society. He fought so because everything he lived by was tied to growth, expansion, and a constantly widening horizon. What he lived by would survive or fall with the nation itself. He could not possibly stand by unmoved in the face of an attempt to destroy the Union. He would combat it with everything he had, because he could only see it as an effort to cut the ground out from under his feet.

So Grant and Lee were in complete contrast, representing two diametri- 12 cally opposed elements in American life. Grant was the modern man emerging; beyond him, ready to come on the stage, was the great age of steel and machinery, of crowded cities and a restless, burgeoning vitality. Lee might have ridden down from the old age of chivalry, lance in hand, silken banner fluttering over his head. Each man was the perfect champion of his cause, drawing both his strengths and his weaknesses from the people he led.

Yet it was not all contrast, after all. Different as they were—in back- 13 ground, in personality, in underlying aspiration—these two great soldiers had much in common. Under everything else, they were marvelous fighters. Furthermore, their fighting qualities were really very much alike.

Each man had, to begin with, the great virtue of utter tenacity and fidelity. 14 Grant fought his way down the Mississippi Valley in spite of acute personal discouragement and profound military handicaps. Lee hung on in the trenches at Petersburg after hope itself had died. In each man there was an indomitable quality...the born fighter's refusal to give up as long as he can still remain on his feet and lift his two fists.

Daring and resourcefulness they had, too; the ability to think faster and 15 move faster than the enemy. These were the qualities which gave Lee the dazzling campaigns of Second Manassas and Chancellorsville and won Vicksburg for Grant.

Lastly, and perhaps greatest of all, there was the ability, at the end, to turn 16 quickly from war to peace once the fighting was over. Out of the way these two men behaved at Appomattox came the possibility of a peace of reconciliation. It was a possibility not wholly realized, in the years to come, but which did, in the end, help the two sections to become one nation again...after a war whose bitterness might have seemed to make such a reunion wholly impossible. No part of either man's life became him more than the part he played in their brief meeting in the McLean house at Appomattox. Their behavior there put all succeeding generations of Americans in their debt. Two great Americans, Grant and Lee—very different, yet under everything very much alike. Their encounter at Appomattox was one of the great moments of American history.

1958

QUESTIONS FOR DISCUSSION

Content

a. What does Catton mean in paragraph 5 when he says: "[Lee] embodied a way of life that had come down through the age of knighthood and the English country squire"?
b. Catton groups Grant with men who believed: "Forms and patterns meant nothing. No man was born to anything, except perhaps to a chance to show how far he could rise" (paragraph 8). Explain what he means by that.
c. Catton's thesis is stated rather early in the essay. What is it? How does it signal the pattern of organization to follow?
d. If this selection is a "Study in Contrasts," why does Catton spend the last four paragraphs discussing the similarities between Grant and Lee?
e. What are some of these similarities?
f. Discuss the other characteristics that Catton attributes to frontier men.
g. How would you explain the Westerner's "deep sense of belonging to a national community," which Catton mentions in paragraph 9? How does this idea differ from what tidewater aristocrats like Lee felt?

Strategy and Style

h. What function do paragraphs 10 and 11 play in the structure of this essay?
i. Unlike Twain, Catton organizes his prose by alternating the discussion from point to point rather than completing his discussion of one figure before moving on to the next. Does this method prove effective?

SUGGESTIONS FOR SHORT WRITING

a. Describe what you consider to be the ideal general for today. In your opinion, do generals today share the same qualities as those in Grant and Lee's time?
b. Describe the meeting that might have occurred between Grant and Lee if the Confederacy had won the war.

SUGGESTIONS FOR SUSTAINED WRITING

a. Choose two individuals with whom you have the same kind of relationship: two grandfathers, two aunts, two close friends. How do these individuals differ? List the major differences in their personalities or their outlooks on life. Is one a pessimist, the other an optimist? Is one an introvert, the other an extrovert? Write an essay that makes the contrast clear.
b. Catton characterized Lee as a "living justification" of "the Lost Cause." Do

you see yourself as such an idealist? Do you espouse "lost causes" simply because you think they're right? Or are you more pragmatic and realistic in your approach to life? Whatever your answer, explain it in an essay: cite sufficient examples to be convincing and clear.

c. Select two rival candidates in an upcoming or recent political election (local, state, or national). Isolate and explain the major differences in their ideologies.

d. Catton tells us that both Grant and Lee had "the great virtue of utter tenacity and fidelity." Do you know two individuals who, while otherwise quite different, share one important personality trait or human quality? If so, write an essay that compares the two in that regard. Remember, when comparing you must identify and explain similarities, *not* differences. You may want to choose two people from your close circle of friends or relatives, or you might select two figures from the world of politics, art, science, or business about whom you know a great deal.

On Permission to Write

Cynthia Ozick

Cynthia Ozick was born in 1928 in the Bronx. Her parents were Jewish immigrants from Russia, and Ozick grew up feeling an outsider at school. Reading, and listening to her grandmother tell stories of her childhood in Russia, gave Ozick a way to temporarily escape from her feelings of awkwardness, and this love of stories encouraged her to become a writer and storyteller herself. During a job after graduate school as an advertising copywriter, she wrote and sold her first article to the Boston Globe. *In 1966 she published her first novel,* Trust, *a book she began when she was 22 and which is heavily influenced by the writing of Henry James. Ozick writes fiction, essays, criticism, and translations, and her list of awards and nominations is staggering: her first collection of short stories,* The Pagan Rabbi and Other Stories *(1972) received three awards and a nomination for the National Book Award. Her next two collections,* Bloodshed and Three Novellas *(1976) and* Levitation: Five Fictions *(1982), also got awards. She has received the O. Henry First Prize Award three times, the Pushcart Press Lampart Prize, and the American Academy of Arts Award for Literature, among other awards. She has also received numerous honorary degrees. Her other major works include two novels,* The Cannibal Galaxy *(1983) and* The Messiah of Stockholm *(1987), and two essay collections,* Art and Ardor *(1983) and* Metaphor and Memory *(1988).*

I hate everything that does not relate to literature, conversations bore me (even when they relate to literature), to visit people bores me, the joys and sorrows of my relatives bore me to my soul. Conversation takes the importance, the seriousness, the truth, out of everything I think.

Franz Kafka, from his diary, 1918

In a small and depressing city in a nearby state there lives a young man 1 (I will call him David) whom I have never met and with whom I sometimes correspond. David's letters are voluminous, vehemently bookish, and—in obedience to literary modernism—without capitals. When David says "I," he writes "i." This does not mean that he is insecure in his identity or that he suffers from a weakness of confidence—David cannot be characterized by thumbnail psychologizing. He is like no one else (except maybe Jane Austen). He describes himself mostly as poor and provincial, as in Balzac, and occasionally as poor and black. He lives alone with his forbearing and bewildered mother in a flat "with imaginary paintings on the walls in barren rooms," writes stories and novels, has not yet published, and appears to spend his days hauling heaps of books back and forth from the public library.

He has read, it seems, everything. His pages are masses of flashy literary 2 allusions—nevertheless entirely lucid, witty, learned, and sane. David is not *exactly* a crank who writes to writers, although he is probably a bit of that too. I don't know how he gets his living, or whether his letters romanticize either his poverty (he reports only a hunger for books) or his passion (ditto); still, David is a free intellect, a free imagination. It is possible that he hides his manuscripts under a blotter, Jane-Austenly, when his mother creeps mutely in to collect his discarded socks. (A week's worth, perhaps, curled on the floor next to Faulkner and Updike and Cummings and *Tristram Shandy.* Of the latter he remarks: "a worthy book. dare any man get offspring on less?")

On the other hand, David wants to be noticed. He wants to be paid atten-   3
tion to. Otherwise, why would he address charming letters to writers (I am not the only one) he has never met? Like Joyce in "dirty provincial Dublin," he says, he means to announce his "inevitable arrival on the mainland." A stranger's eyes, even for a letter, is a kind of publication. David, far from insisting on privacy, is a would-be public man. It may be that he pants after fame. And yet in his immediate position—his secret literary life, whether or not he intends it to remain secret—there is something delectable. He thirsts to read, so he reads; he thirsts to write, so he writes. He is in the private cave of his freedom, an eremite, a solitary; he orders his mind as he pleases. In this condition he is prolific. He writes and writes. Ah, he is poor and provincial, in a dim lost corner of the world. But his lonely place (a bare cubicle joyfully tumbling with library books) and his lonely situation (the liberty to be zealous) have given him the permission to write. To be, in fact, prolific.

I am not like David. I am not poor, or provincial (except in the New York   4
way), or unpublished, or black. (David, the sovereign of his life, invents an aloofness from social disabilities, at least in his letters, and I have not heard him mythologize "negritude"; he admires poets for their words and cadences.) But all this is not the essential reason I am not like David. I am not like him because I do not own his permission to write freely, and zealously, and at will, and however I damn please; and abundantly; and always.

There is this difference between the prolific and the non-prolific: the pro-   5
lific have arrogated to themselves the permission to write.

By permission I suppose I ought to mean *inner* permission. Now "inner   6
permission" is a phrase requiring high caution: it was handed to me by a Freudian dogmatist, a writer whose energy and confidence depend on regular visits to his psychoanalyst. In a useful essay called "Art and Neurosis," Lionel Trilling warns against the misapplication of Freud's dictum that "we are all ill, i.e., neurotic," and insists that a writer's productivity derives from "the one part of him that is healthy, by any conceivable definition of health...that which gives him the power to conceive, to plan, to work, and to bring his work to a conclusion." The capacity to write, in short, comes from an uncharted space over which even all-prevailing neurosis can have no jurisdiction or dominion. "The use to which [the artist] puts his power...may be discussed with reference to his particular neurosis," Trilling concedes; yet Trilling's verdict is finally steel: "But its essence is irreducible. It is, as we say, a gift."

If permission to write (and for a writer this is exactly equal to the power   7 to write) is a gift, then what of the lack of permission? Does the missing "Go ahead" mean neurosis? I am at heart one of those hapless pre-moderns who believe that the light bulb is the head of a demon called forth by the light switch, and that Freud is a German word for pleasure; so I am not equipped to speak about principles of electricity or psychoanalysis. All the same, it seems to me that the electrifying idea of inward obstacle—neurosis—is not nearly so often responsible for low productivity as we are told. Writer's permission is not something that is switched off by helpless forces inside the writer, but by social currents—human beings and their ordinary predilections and prejudices—outside. If David writes freely and others don't, the reason might be that, at least for a while, David has kidnapped himself beyond the pinch of society. He is Jane Austen with her hidden manuscript momentarily slipped out from under the blotter; he is Thoreau in his cabin. He is a free man alone in a room with imaginary pictures on the walls, reading and writing in a private rapture.

There are some writers who think of themselves as shamans, dervishes of   **8** inspiration, divinely possessed ecstatics—writers who believe with Emerson that the artist "has cast off the common motives of humanity and has ventured to trust himself for a taskmaster": himself above everyone. Emerson it is who advises writers to aspire, through isolation, to "a simple purpose...as strong as iron necessity is to others," and who—in reply to every contingency—exhorts, "O father, O mother, O wife, O brother, O friend, I have lived with you after appearances hitherto. Henceforward I am the truth's." These shaman-writers, with their cult of individual genius and romantic egoism, may be self-glamorizing holy madmen, but they are not maniacs; they know what is good for them, and what is good for them is fences. You cannot get near them, whatever your need or demand. O father, O mother, O wife, O brother, O friend, they will tell you— *beat it.* They call themselves caviar, and for the general their caviar is a caveat.

Most writers are more modest than this, and more reasonable, and don't   **9** style themselves as unbridled creatures celestially privileged and driven. They know that they are citizens like other citizens, and have simply chosen a profession, as others have. These are the writers who go docilely to gatherings where they are required to marvel at every baby; who yield slavishly to the ukase that sends them out for days at a time to scout a samovar for the birthday of an elderly great-uncle; who pretend to overnight guests that they are capable of sitting at the breakfast table without being consumed by print; who craftily let on to in-laws that they are diligent cooks and sheltering wives, though they would sacrifice a husband to a hurricane to fetch them a typewriter ribbon; and so on. In short, they work at appearances, trust others for taskmasters, and do not insist too rigorously on whose truth they will live after. And they are honorable enough. In company, they do their best to dress like everyone else: if they are women they will tolerate panty hose and high-heeled shoes, if they are men they will show up in a three-piece suit; but in either case they will be concealing the fact that during any ordinary row of days they sleep in their clothes. In the same company they lend themselves, decade after decade, to the expectation that they will not lay claim to unusual passions, that they will believe the average belief, that they will take pleasure in the average pleasure. Dickens, foreseeing the pain of relinquishing his pen at a time not of his choosing, reportedly would not accept an invitation. "Thank God for books," Auden said, "as an alternative to conversation." Good-citizen writers, by contrast, year after year decline no summons, refuse no banquet, turn away from no tedium, willingly enter into every anecdote and brook the assault of any amplified band. They will put down their pens for a noodle pudding.

And with all this sterling obedience, this strenuous courtliness and conge- 10 niality, this anxious flattery of unspoken coercion down to the third generation, something goes wrong. One dinner in twenty years is missed. Or no dinner at all is missed, but an "attitude" is somehow detected. No one is fooled; the cordiality is pronounced insincere, the smile a fake, the goodwill a dud, the talk a fib, the cosseting a cozening. These sweating citizen-writers are in the end always found out and accused. They are accused of elitism. They are accused of snobbery. They are accused of loving books and bookishness more feelingly than flesh and blood.

Edith Wharton, in her cool and bitter way, remarked of the literary life 11 that "in my own family it created a kind of restraint that grew with the years. None of my relations ever spoke to me of my books, either to praise or to blame—they simply ignored them;...the subject was avoided as if it were a kind of family disgrace, which might be condoned but could not be forgotten."

Good-citizen writers are not read by their accusers; perhaps they cannot be. 12 "If I succeed," said Conrad, "you shall find there according to your deserts: encouragement, consolation, fear, charm—all you demand—and, perhaps, also that glimpse of truth for which you have forgotten to ask." But some never demand, or demand less. "If you simplified your style," a strict but kindly aunt will advise, "you might come up to par," and her standard does not exempt Conrad.

The muse-inspired shaman-writers are never called snobs, for the plain 13 reason that no strict but kindly aunt will ever get within a foot of any of them. But the good-citizen writers—by virtue of their very try at citizenship—are suspect and resented. Their work will not be taken for work. They will always be condemned for not being interchangeable with nurses or salesmen or schoolteachers or accountants or brokers. They will always be found out. They will always be seen to turn longingly after a torn peacock's tail left over from a fugitive sighting of paradise. They will always have hanging from a back pocket a telltale shred of idealism, or a cache of a few grains of noble importuning, or, if nothing so grandly quizzical, then a single beautiful word, in Latin or Hebrew; or else they will tip their hand at the wedding feast by complaining meekly of the raging horn that obliterates the human voice; or else they will forget not to fall into Mon- taigne over the morning toast; or else they will embarrass everyone by oafishly banging on the kettle of history; or else, while the room fills up with small talk, they will glaze over and inwardly chant "This Lime-Tree Bower My Prison"; or else—but never mind. What is not understood is not allowed. These citizen-pretenders will never be respectable. They will never come up to par. They will always be blamed for their airs. They will always be charged with superiority, disloyalty, coldness, want of family feeling. They will always be charged with estranging their wives, husbands, children. They will always be called snob.

They will never be granted the permission to write as serious writers are **14** obliged to write: fanatically, obsessively, consumingly, torrentially, above all comically—and for life.

And therefore: enviable blissful provincial prolific lonesome David!   **15**

1984

QUESTIONS FOR DISCUSSION

Content

a. What is Ozick's point? Summarize it in a sentence or two.

b. What does Ozick mean by "permission to write"? Who has permission to write and who does not?

c. At the end of paragraph 8, Ozick says that the shaman-writers "call themselves caviar, and for the general their caviar is a caveat." She is making a play on words using a well-known quote from Shakespeare—in *Hamlet,* Hamlet says of the play put on for the king and queen that it is "caviar to the general." What did Hamlet mean by this? What does Ozick mean?

d. Ozick contrasts two groups of writers, the "shaman-writers" and the "good-citizen writers." How does she define each of these groups? Which group does she prefer?

e. The shaman-writers include Austen, Thoreau, Emerson, Dickens, and Auden; the good-citizen writers include Wharton and Conrad. Into which group does she place David? Herself? Into which group would you place Kafka, who is quoted at the beginning of the essay?

f. In paragraph 6, Ozick paraphrases Lionel Trilling as follows: "The capacity to write, in short, comes from an uncharted space over which even all-prevailing neurosis can have no jurisdiction or dominion." Does this make Trilling any clearer? Can you in turn paraphrase Ozick's paraphrase of Trilling?

g. Ozick says that she is "nonprolific" (paragraph 5) because she cannot give herself permission to write, and that she cannot give herself permission to write because she is not in a situation similar to David's. What is David's situation? How is it different from Ozick's? What advantages does David have over Ozick?

h. In paragraph 3, she explains David's behavior by saying that he "wants to be noticed." Do you agree with this explanation? What other reasons could explain David's behavior?

i. Ozick says in paragraph 2 that David's writings are "masses of flashy literary allusions." Ozick's essay also includes many literary allusions. What purpose do these allusions serve? Trace some of the allusions to their sources and notice how they help illustrate Ozick's essay. The authors and works she refers to are Franz Kafka, Jane Austen, Honore de Balzac, William Faulkner, John Updike, e e cummings, Laurence Sterne's *Tristram Shandy,* James Joyce, Lionel Trilling, Henry David Thoreau, Ralph Waldo Emerson, Charles Dickens, Edith Wharton, Joseph Conrad, Michel de Montaigne, Samuel Taylor Coleridge's "This Lime-Tree Bower My Prison."

j. Is David's race important? Ozick refers to his race twice; would her reaction to David be different if he were not black?

Strategy and Style

k. In the last line Ozick admits to being somewhat envious of David's situation. Would we still sense this envy if she had not come out and told us? What words or phrases convey her envy?

l. In paragraph 14, she says that the good-citizen writers "will never be granted the permission to write as serious writers are obliged to write: fanatically, obsessively, consumingly, torrentially, above all comically—and for life." Do you agree that serious writers are *obliged* to write as she describes? To whom are they obliged?

SUGGESTIONS FOR SHORT WRITING

a. After a first reading, summarize the essay in a paragraph or two, and jot down two or three questions you have about the essay.

b. Reread the essay with your questions in mind. Paraphrase the answers you find in the essay.

SUGGESTIONS FOR SUSTAINED WRITING

a. Do the suggestions above for short writing. Then, from what you have written, write an essay in which you reflect on what Ozick has written. If you are interested in literature, does what Ozick wrote ring true? If you are interested in another field, can people in that field be divided into groups such as the shamans and the good-citizens?

b. Observe the people you work or socialize with, the students in your dormitory, your classmates, etc. Can they be divided into two or more contrasting groups? How would you describe the groups? How do they relate to each other? Write an essay in which you describe, compare, and contrast the groups.

Football Red and Baseball Green

Murray Ross

*Born in Pasadena, California, in 1942, Murray Ross is the Director of Theater at the
University of Colorado in Colorado Springs. He completed his undergraduate studies
at Williams College and took an M.A. and Ph.D. in English at the University of California at Berkeley. "Football Red and Baseball Green," which first appeared in* The
Chicago Review *in 1971, has been anthologized several times during the last decades.
A fascinating study in contrasts, it provides brilliant insight into the complex nature
and appeal of America's most popular and most revered sports.*

The 1970 Superbowl, the final game of the professional football season, 1
drew a larger television audience than either the moonwalk or Tiny Tim's wedding. This revelation is one way of indicating just how popular spectator sports
are in this country. Americans, or American men anyway, seem to care about
the games they watch as much as the Elizabethans cared about their plays, and
I suspect for some of the same reasons. There is, in sport, some of the rudimentary drama found in popular theater: familiar plots, type characters, heroic and
comic action spiced with new and unpredictable variations. And common to
watching both activities is the sense of participation in a shared tradition and in
shared fantasies. If it is true that sport exploits these fantasies without significantly transcending them, it seems no less satisfying for all that.

It is my guess that sport spectating involves something more than the vi- 2
carious pleasures of identifying with athletic prowess. I suspect that each sport
contains a fundamental myth which it elaborates for its fans, and that our pleasure in watching such games derives in part from belonging briefly to the
mythic world which the game and its players bring to life. I am especially interested in baseball and football because they are so popular and so uniquely
American; they began here and unlike basketball they have not been widely ex-
ported. Thus whatever can be said, mythically, about these games would seem
to apply directly and particularly to our own culture.

Baseball's myth may be the easier to identify since we have a greater his- 3
torical perspective on the game. It was an instant success during the Industrial-
ization, and most probably it was a reaction to the squalor, the faster pace and
the dreariness of the new conditions. Baseball was old fashioned right from the
start; it seems conceived in nostalgia, in the resuscitation of the Jeffersonian
dream. It established an artificial rural environment, one removed from the toil
of an urban life, which spectators could be admitted to and temporarily breathe
in. Baseball is a *pastoral* sport, and I think the game can be best understood as
this kind of art. For baseball does what all good pastoral does—it creates an
atmosphere in which everything exists in harmony.

266

Consider, for instance, the spatial organization of the game. A kind of 4 controlled openness is created by having everything fan out from home plate, and the crowd sees the game through an arranged perspective that is rarely violated. Visually this means that the game is always seen as a constant, rather calm whole, and that the players and the playing field are viewed in relationship to each other. Each player has a certain position, a special area to tend, and the game often seems to be as much a dialogue between the fielders and the field as it is a contest between the players themselves: will that ball get through the hole? Can that outfielder run under that fly? As a moral genre pastoral asserts the virtue of communion with nature. As a competitive game, baseball asserts that the team which best relates to the playing field (by hitting the ball in the right places) will be the team which wins.

I suspect baseball's space has a subliminal function too, for topographi- 5 cally it is a sentimental mirror of older America. Most of the game is played between the pitcher and the hitter in the extreme corner of the playing area. This is the busiest, most sophisticated part of the ball park, where something is always happening, and from which all subsequent action depends. From this urban corner we move to a supporting infield, active but a little less crowded, and from there we come to the vast stretches of the outfield. As is traditional in American lore danger increases with distance, and the outfield action is often the most spectacular in the game. The long throw, the double off the wall, the leaping catch—these plays take place in remote territory, and they belong, like most legendary feats, to the frontier.

Having established its landscape, pastoral art operates to eliminate any 6 references to that bigger, more disturbing, more real world it has left behind. All games are to some extent insulated from the outside by having their own rules, but baseball has a circular structure as well which furthers its comfortable feeling of self-sufficiency. By this I mean that every motion of extension is also one of return—a ball hit outside is a *home* run, a full circle. Home—familiar, peaceful, secure—it is the beginning and end of everything. You must go out and you must come back, for only the completed movement is registered.

Time is a serious threat to any form of pastoral. The genre poses a time- 7 less world of perpetual spring, and it does its best to silence the ticking of clocks which remind us that in time the green world fades into winter. One's sense of time is directly related to what happens in it, and baseball is so structured as to stretch out and ritualize whatever action it contains. Dramatic moments are few, and they are almost always isolated by the routine texture of normal play. It is certainly a game of climax and drama, but it is perhaps more a game of repeated and predictable action: the foul balls, the walks, the pitcher fussing around on the mound, the lazy fly ball to centerfield. This is, I think, as it should be, for baseball exists as an alternative to a world of too much action, struggle and change. It is a merciful release from a more grinding and insistent tempo, and its time, as William Carlos Williams suggests, makes a virtue out of idleness simply by providing it:

The crowd at the ball game

is moved uniformly

by a spirit of uselessness

which delights them...

Within this expanded and idle time the baseball fan is at liberty to be- **8** come a ceremonial participant and a lover of style. Because the action is normalized, how something is done becomes as important as the action itself. Thus baseball's most delicate and detailed aspects are often, to the spectator, the most interesting. The pitcher's windup, the anticipatory crouch of the infielders, the quick waggle of the bat as it poises for the pitch—these subtle miniature movements are as meaningful as the home runs and the strikeouts. It somehow matters in baseball that all the tiny rituals are observed: the shortstop must kick the dirt and the umpire must brush the plate with his pocket broom. In a sense baseball is largely a continuous series of small gestures, and I think it characteristic that the game's most treasured moment came when Babe Ruth pointed to the place where he subsequently hit a home run.

Baseball is a game where the little things mean a lot, and this, together **9** with its clean serenity, its open space, and its ritualized action is enough to place it in a world of yesterday. Baseball evokes for us a past which may never have been ours, but which we believe was, and certainly that is enough. In the Second World War, supposedly, we fought for "Baseball, Mom and Apple Pie," and considering what baseball means that phrase is a good one. We fought then for the right to believe in a green world of tranquillity and uninterrupted contentment, where the little things would count. But now the possibilities of such a world are more remote, and it seems that while the entertainment of such a dream has an enduring appeal, it is no longer sufficient for our fantasies. I think this may be why baseball is no longer our preeminent national pastime, and why its myth is being replaced by another more appropriate to the new realities (and fantasies) of our time.

Football, especially professional football, is the embodiment of a newer **10** myth, one which in many respects is opposed to baseball's. The fundamental difference is that football is not a pastoral game; it is a heroic one. One way of seeing the difference between the two is by the juxtaposition of Babe Ruth and Jim Brown, both legendary players in their separate genres. Ruth, baseball's most powerful hitter, was a hero maternalized (his name), an epic figure destined for a second immortality as a candy bar. His image was impressive but comfortable and altogether human: round, dressed in a baggy uniform, with a schoolboy's cap and a bat which looked tiny next to him. His spindly legs supported a Santa sized torso, and this comic disproportion would increase when he was in motion. He ran delicately, with quick, very short steps, since he felt that stretching your stride slowed you down. This sort of superstition is typical of baseball players, and typical too is the way in which a personal quirk or mannerism mitigates their awesome skill and makes them poignant and vulnerable.

There was nothing funny about Jim Brown. His muscular and almost perfect physique was emphasized further by the uniform which armored him. Babe Ruth had a tough face, but boyish and innocent; Brown was an expressionless mask under the helmet. In action he seemed invincible, the embodiment of speed and power in an inflated human shape. One can describe Brown accurately only with superlatives, for as a player he was a kind of Superman, undisguised. 11

Brown and Ruth are caricatures, yet they represent their games. Baseball is part of a comic tradition which insists that its participants be humans, while football, in the heroic mode, asks that its players be more than that. Football converts men into gods, and suggests that magnificence and glory are as desirable as happiness. Football is designed, therefore, to impress its audience rather differently than baseball, as I think comparison will show. 12

As a pastoral game, baseball attempts to close the gap between the players and the crowd. It creates the illusion, for instance, that with a lot of hard work, a little luck, and possibly some extra talent, the average spectator might well be playing; not watching. For most of us can do a few of the things the ballplayers do: catch a pop-up, field a ground ball, and maybe get a hit once in a while. Chance is allotted a good deal of play in the game. There is no guarantee, for instance, that a good pitch will not be looped over the infield, or that a solidly batted ball will turn into a double play. In addition to all of this, almost every fan feels he can make the manager's decision for him, and not entirely without reason. Baseball's statistics are easily calculated and rather meaningful; and the game itself, though a subtle one, is relatively lucid and comprehensible. 13

As a heroic game football is not concerned with a shared community of near-equals. It seeks almost the opposite relationship between its spectators and players, one which stresses the distance between them. We are not allowed to identify directly with Jim Brown any more than we are with Zeus, because to do so would undercut his stature as something more than human. The players do much of the distancing themselves by their own excesses of speed, size and strength. When Bob Brown, the giant all pro tackle says that he could "block King Kong all day," we look at him and believe. But the game itself contributes to the players' heroic isolation. As George Plimpton has graphically illustrated in *Paper Lion,* it is almost impossible to imagine yourself in a professional football game without also considering your imminent humiliation and possible injury. There is scarcely a single play that the average spectator could hope to perform adequately, and there is even a difficulty in really understanding what is going on. In baseball what happens is what meets the eye, but in football 14 each action is the result of eleven men acting simultaneously against eleven other men, and clearly this is too much for the eye to totally comprehend. Football has become a game of staggering complexity, and coaches are now wired in to several "spotters" during the games so that they too can find out what is happening.

If football is distanced from its fans by its intricacy and its "superhuman" 15 play, it nonetheless remains an intense spectacle. Baseball, as I have implied, dissolves time and urgency in a green expanse, thereby creating a luxurious and peaceful sense of leisure. As is appropriate to a heroic enterprise, football reverses this procedure and converts space into time. The game is ideally played in an oval stadium, not in a "park," and the difference is the elimination of perspective. This makes football a perfect television game, because even at first hand it offers a flat, perpetually moving foreground (wherever the ball is). The eye in baseball viewing opens up; in football it zeroes in. There is no democratic vista in football, and spectators are not asked to relax, but to concentrate. You are encouraged to watch the drama, not a medley of ubiquitous gestures, and you are constantly reminded that this event is taking place in time. The third element in baseball is the field; in football this element is the clock. Traditionally heroes do reckon with time, and football players are no exceptions. Time in football is wound up inexorably until it reaches the breaking point in the last minutes of a close game. More often than not it is the clock which emerges as the real enemy, and it is the sense of time running out that regularly produces a pitch of tension uncommon in baseball.

A further reason for football's intensity, surely, is that the game is played 16 like a war. The idea is to win by going through, around or over the opposing team and the battle lines, quite literally, are drawn on every play. Violence is somewhere at the heart of the game, and the combat quality is reflected in football's army language ("blitz," "trap," "zone," "bomb," "trenches," etc.). Coaches often sound like generals when they discuss their strategy. Woody Hayes of Ohio State, for instance, explains his quarterback option play as if it had been conceived in the Pentagon: "You know," he says, "the most effective kind of warfare is siege. You have to attack on broad fronts. And that's all the option is—attacking on a broad front. You know General Sherman ran an option right through the South."

Football like war is an arena for action, and like war football leaves little 17 room for personal style. It seems to be a game which projects "character" more than personality, and for the most part football heroes, publicly, are a rather similar lot. They tend to become personifications rather than individuals, and, with certain exceptions, they are easily read emblematically as embodiments of heroic qualities such as "strength," "confidence," "perfection," etc.—cliches really, but forceful enough when represented by the play of a Dick Butkus, a Johnny Unitas or a Bart Starr. Perhaps this simplification of personality results in part from the heroes' total identification with their mission, to the extent that they become more characterized by their work than by what they intrinsically "are." At any rate football does not make allowances for the idiosyncrasies that baseball actually seems to encourage, and as a result there have been few football players as uniquely crazy or human as, say, Casey Stengel or Dizzy Dean.

A further reason for the underdeveloped qualities of football personalities, 18 and one which gets us to the heart of the game's modernity, is that football is very much a game of modern technology. Football's action is largely interaction, and the game's complexity requires that its players mold themselves into a perfectly coordinated unit. Jerry Kramer, the veteran guard and author of *Instant Replay,* writes how Lombardi would work to develop such integration:

> He makes us execute the same plays over and over, a hundred times, two hundred times, until we do every little thing automatically. He works to make the kickoff team perfect, the punt-return team perfect, the field-goal team perfect. He ignores nothing. Technique, technique, technique, over and over and over, until we feel like we're going crazy. But we win.

Mike Garratt, the halfback, gives the player's version: 19

> After a while you train your mind like a computer—put the ideas in, digest it, and the body acts accordingly.

As the quotations imply, pro football is insatiably preoccupied with the 20 smoothness and precision of play execution, and most coaches believe that the team which makes the fewest mistakes will be the team that wins. Individual identity thus comes to be associated with the team or unit that one plays for to a much greater extent than in baseball. To use a reductive analogy, it is the difference between *Bonanza* and *Mission Impossible.* Ted Williams is mostly Ted Williams, but Bart Starr is mostly the Green Bay Packers. The latter metaphor is a precise one, since football heroes stand out not because of purely individual acts, but because they epitomize the action and style of the groups they are connected to. Kramer cites the obvious if somewhat self-glorifying historical precedent: "Perhaps," he writes, "we're living in Camelot." Ideally a football team should be what Camelot was supposed to have been, a group of men who function as equal parts of a larger whole, entirely dependent on each other for their total meaning....

Football's collective pattern is only one aspect of the way in which it 21 seems to echo our contemporary environment. The game, like our society, can be thought of as a cluster of people living under great tension in a state of perpetual flux. The potential for sudden disaster or triumph is as great in football as it is in our own age, and although there is something ludicrous in equating interceptions with assassinations and long passes with moonshots, there is also something valid and appealing in the analogies. It seems to me that football does successfully reflect those salient and common conditions which affect us all, and it does so with the end of making us feel better about them and our lot. For one thing, it makes us feel that something can be connected in all this chaos; out of the accumulated pile of bodies something can emerge—a runner breaks into the clear or a pass finds its way to a receiver. To the spectator plays such as these are human and dazzling. They suggest to the audience what it has hoped for (and been told) all along, that technology is still a tool and not a master. Fans get living proof of this every time a long pass is completed; they see at once that it is the result of careful planning, perfect integration and an effective "pattern," but they see too that it is human and that what counts as well is man, his desire, his natural skill and his "grace under pressure." Football metaphysically yokes heroic action and technology together by violence to suggest that they are mutually supportive. It's a doubtful proposition, but given how we live it has its attractions.

Football, like the space program, is a game in the grand manner, yet it is 22 a rather sober sport and often seems to lack that positive, comic vision of which baseball's pastoral is a part. It is a winter game, as those fans who saw the Minnesota Vikings play the Detroit Lions last Thanksgiving were graphically reminded. The two teams played in a blinding snowstorm, and except for the small flags in the corners of the end zones, and a patch of mud wherever the ball was downed, the field was totally obscured. Even through the magnified television lenses the players were difficult to identify; you saw only huge shapes come out of the gloom, thump against each other and fall in a heap. The movement was repeated endlessly and silently in a muffled stadium, interrupted once or twice by a shot of a bare-legged girl who fluttered her pom-poms in the cold. The spectacle was by turns pathetic, compelling and absurd; a kind of theater of oblivion....

A final note. It is interesting that the heroic and pastoral conventions 23 which underlie our most popular sports are almost classically opposed. The contrasts are familiar: city vs. country, aspiration vs. contentment, activity vs. peace and so on. Judging from the rise of professional football we seem to be slowly relinquishing that unfettered rural vision of ourselves that baseball so beautifully mirrors, and we have come to cast ourselves in a genre more reflective of a nation confronted by constant and unavoidable challenges. Right now, like the Elizabethans, we seem to share both heroic and pastoral yearnings, and we reach out to both. Perhaps these divided needs account in part for the enormous attention we as a nation now give to spectator sports. For sport provides one place, at least, where we can have our football and our baseball too.

1971

QUESTIONS FOR DISCUSSION

Content

a. How would you interpret Ross's title? Why does he associate football with red and baseball with green?

b. Why is baseball "no longer sufficient for our fantasies" (paragraph 9)?

c. How would you describe the audience to which this selection is addressed? What do the references to Tiny Tim, William Carlos Williams, Casey Stengel, and Vince Lombardi tell about Ross's reader?

d. After reading this essay, are you in agreement with Ross's statement that sport "exploits [our] fantasies without significantly transcending them" (paragraph 1)?

e. Who were the Elizabethans and what analogy does Ross draw between them and modern Americans?

f. In what ways are baseball and football uniquely American? Why do they make such good subjects for comparison and contrast?

g. On what basis does he compare baseball with the pastoral "as a moral genre" (paragraph 4)?

h. Is Ross's analogy of football to a war convincing? What evidence does he provide to support this comparison?

i. What, according to Ross, is "the fundamental myth which [baseball] elaborates for its fans" (paragraph 2)? What is the "mythic world" that football evokes?

j. In his conclusion, Ross tells us that the "heroic and pastoral conventions which underlie our most popular sports are almost classically opposed." Should he have explained this in his introduction?

k. How has the shape of the baseball field helped to determine the nature of that sport as well as the myth that surrounds it?

l. In paragraph 13, Ross claims that baseball is "relatively lucid and comprehensible." Is this also true of football?

m. How does baseball encourage idiosyncrasies? How does football discourage them?

Strategy and Style

n. What evidence does Ross provide to prove that baseball is a "pastoral sport"? How does his treatment of this evidence help him organize his essay?

o. Pay close attention to the vocabulary he uses and the allusions he makes in paragraphs 10 and 11. How does his treatment of Ruth and Brown help him explain his vision of the two sports?

p. What does Ross mean when he defines football as a "heroic" game (paragraph 14)?

SUGGESTIONS FOR SHORT WRITING

a. In your opinion, what is Ross's assumption about American sport? Choose several sentences in his essay that you think reveal this assumption; write a short response.

b. Write about the relationship of paragraph 7 to the rest of the essay. Why does Ross talk about time? Why does he quote from a poem by William Carlos Williams?

SUGGESTIONS FOR SUSTAINED WRITING

a. Following Ross's lead, write an essay in which you compare (point out similarities between) one of your favorite team sports and either baseball or football as described in this selection. If you're comparing your subject with baseball, remember to identify its "pastoral" qualities. If you're comparing it to football, try to explain in what ways it is "heroic."

b. Can you identify one or two "uniquely crazy or human" professional athletes as Ross does in paragraph 17? If so, describe these individuals as fully as you can and contrast them to other athletes who are less colorful and more predictable both on and off the playing field.

c. Ross begins his essay claiming that "there is, in sport, some of the rudimentary drama found in popular theater." Do you agree? Explain the similarities between watching a football game and going to a movie, or spending an afternoon at the ballpark and seeing a play.

Two Views of the Mississippi

Mark Twain

Mark Twain (1835–1910) was, of course, the pen name of Samuel Langhorne Clemens, the Missourian who learned to pilot Mississippi riverboats and who grew to become one of America's leading humorists, social critics, and men of letters. Twain recorded his experiences in numerous newspaper features and columns and in several books, including Life on the Mississippi *(1883),* The Adventures of Tom Sawyer *(1876), and his masterpiece,* The Adventures of Huckleberry Finn *(1885). Indeed, for some literary historians, the true American novel has its beginnings in the work of Twain. In the selection that follows, Twain contrasts his views of the Mississippi first as a novice and then as an experienced river pilot.*

Now when I had mastered the language of this water, and had come to know every trifling feature that bordered the great river as familiarly as I knew the letters of the alphabet, I had made a valuable acquisition. But I had lost something, too. I had lost something which could never be restored to me while I lived. All the grace, the beauty, the poetry, had gone out of the majestic river! I still keep in mind a certain wonderful sunset which I witnessed when steamboating was new to me. A broad expanse of the river was turned to blood; in the middle distance the red hue brightened into gold, through which a solitary log came floating black and conspicuous; in one place a long, slanting mark lay sparkling upon the water; in another the surface was broken by boiling, tumbling rings, that were as many-tinted as an opal; where the ruddy flush was faintest, was a smooth spot that was covered with graceful circles and radiating lines, ever so delicately traced; the shore on our left was densely wooded, and the somber shadow that fell from this forest was broken in one place by a long, ruffled trail that shone like silver; and high above the forest wall a clean-stemmed dead tree waved a single leafy bough that glowed like a flame in the unobstructed splendor that was flowing from the sun. There were graceful curves, reflected images, woody heights, soft distances; and over the whole scene, far and near, the dissolving lights drifted steadily, enriching it every passing moment with new marvels of coloring. 1

I stood like one bewitched. I drank it in, in a speechless rapture. The world was new to me, and I had never seen anything like this at home. But as I have said, a day came when I began to cease from noting the glories and the charms which the moon and the sun and the twilight wrought upon the river's face; another day came when I ceased altogether to note them. Then, if that sunset scene had been repeated, I should have looked upon it without rapture, and should have commented upon it, inwardly, after this fashion: "This sun means that we are going to have wind to-morrow; that floating log means that the river is rising, small thanks to it; that slanting mark on the water refers to a 2 bluff reef which is going to kill somebody's steamboat one of these nights, if it keeps on stretching out like that; those tumbling 'boils' show a dissolving bar and a changing channel there; the lines and circles in the slick water over yonder are a warning that that troublesome place is shoaling up dangerously; that silver streak in the shadow of the forest is the 'break' from a new snag, and he has located himself in the very best place he could have found to fish for steamboats; that tall dead tree, with a single living branch, is not going to last long, and then how is a body ever going to get through this blind place at night without the friendly old landmark?"

No, the romance and beauty were all gone from the river. All the value   3
any feature of it had for me now was the amount of usefulness it could furnish toward compassing the safe piloting of a steamboat. Since those days, I have pitied doctors from my heart. What does the lovely flush in a beauty's cheek mean to a doctor but a "break" that ripples above some deadly disease? Are not all her visible charms sown thick with what are to him the signs and symbols of hidden decay? Does he ever see her beauty at all, or doesn't he simply view her professionally, and comment upon her unwholesome condition all to himself? And doesn't he sometimes wonder whether he has gained most or lost most by learning his trade?

1883

QUESTIONS FOR DISCUSSION

Content

a. Why does Twain pity doctors?
b. What purpose does paragraph 3 serve? Why does Twain compare the work of a steamboat pilot to that of a doctor? In what way is the conduct of their work similar?
c. Twain fully describes his view of the river as a novice, then goes on to talk about his perception of it as a trained pilot. Does this pattern serve him better than discussing various aspects of the river point by point?
d. What details does Twain offer to prove that at one time in his life the river held grace, beauty, and poetry for him?

Strategy and Style

e. Twain's thesis, which appears in paragraph 1, is presented in an obvious and straightforward manner. How does it help determine the organization of the rest of the piece?
f. The first paragraph is filled with descriptive language that captures a subjective, almost rhapsodic, view of the river. How would you characterize the language found in paragraph 2?

g. What use does paragraph 2 make of the details Twain has already introduced in paragraph 1?

SUGGESTIONS FOR SHORT WRITING

a. Brainstorm a list of metaphors and similes that Twain might have used to describe the Mississippi River. For example, "the Mississippi River is a _____," or "the Mississippi River is like a _____."
b. Write the copy for a travel brochure for a steamboat holiday on the Mississippi.

SUGGESTIONS FOR SUSTAINED WRITING

a. Select a person or place you have known for a long time. Have your views on this individual or place changed significantly over the years? For better or worse? Explain.
b. As children, we become excited, enraptured, and even mystified by the rituals and customs associated with important religious or national holidays: Christmas, Yom Kippur, Thanksgiving, Halloween, the Fourth of July. Think about the holiday you found most exciting as a child. Has your view of it changed? Explain.
c. Twain's training as a pilot seems to have had a negative effect in that it took the romance out of his view of the river. However, learning more about a subject may enhance one's appreciation of it. Can you relate an instance from your own experience to illustrate this notion? For example, mastering the fundamentals of swimming may have given you the confidence you needed to try skin diving. Tuning your first engine may have motivated you to learn more about auto mechanics in general.
d. In a sense, Twain may be hinting at his disillusionment over his life as a pilot. Have you ever become disillusioned with a job? What were the causes of this disillusionment? Explain.

The Rewards of Living a Solitary Life
May Sarton

May Sarton was born in Belgium in 1912, the daughter of a Belgian father and an English mother, but moved to the United States with her parents when she was four, becoming a U.S. citizen in 1924. She very early began writing poetry, fiction, and drama. When she was only twenty-one, she founded the Apprentice Theatre at the New School for Social Research in New York and acted as its director from 1933 to 1936. During World War II, she was a scriptwriter of documentary films for the U.S. Office of War Information. She has taught creative and dramatic writing at Harvard University, Wellesley College, and the Stuart School in Boston, and has lectured throughout the country. Sarton is a prolific writer, having published eleven volumes of poetry, thirteen novels, and two autobiographies. "Rewards" was written for The New York Times *in 1946.*

1 The other day an acquaintance of mine, a gregarious and charming man, told me he had found himself unexpectedly alone in New York for an hour or two between appointments. He went to the Whitney and spent the "empty" time looking at things in solitary bliss. For him it proved to be a shock nearly as great as falling in love to discover that he could enjoy himself so much alone.

2 What had he been afraid of, I asked myself? That, suddenly alone, he would discover that he bored himself, or that there was, quite simply, no self there to meet? But having taken the plunge, he is now on the brink of adventure; he is about to be launched into his own inner space, space as immense, unexplored and sometimes frightening as outer space to the astronaut. His every perception will come to him with a new freshness and, for a time, seem startlingly original. For anyone who can see things for himself with a naked eye becomes, for a moment or two, something of a genius. With another human being present vision becomes double vision, inevitably. We are busy wondering, what does my companion see or think of this, and what do I think of it? The original impact gets lost, or diffused.

3 "Music I heard with you was more than music." Exactly. And therefore music *itself* can only be heard alone. Solitude is the salt of personhood. It brings out the authentic flavor of every experience.

4 "Alone one is never lonely: the spirit adventures, walking/ In a quiet garden, in a cool house, abiding single there."

5 Loneliness is most acutely felt with other people, for with others, even with a lover sometimes, we suffer from our differences of taste, temperament, mood. Human intercourse often demands that we soften the edge of perception, or withdraw at the very instant of personal truth for fear of hurting, or of being inappropriately present, which is to say naked, in a social situation. Alone we

278

can afford to be wholly whatever we are, and to feel whatever we feel absolutely. That is a great luxury!

For me the most interesting thing about a solitary life, and mine has been that for the last twenty years, is that it becomes increasingly rewarding. When I can wake up and watch the sun rise over the ocean, as I do most days, and know that I have an entire day ahead, uninterrupted, in which to write a few pages, take a walk with my dog, lie down in the afternoon for a long think (why does one think better in a horizontal position?), read and listen to music, I am flooded with happiness.

I am lonely only when I am overtired, when I have worked too long without a break, when for the time being I feel empty and need filling up. And I am lonely sometimes when I come back home after a lecture trip, when I have seen a lot of people and talked a lot, and am full to the brim with experience that needs to be sorted out.

Then for a little while the house feels huge and empty, and I wonder where my self is hiding. It has to be recaptured slowly by watering the plants, perhaps, and looking again at each one as though it were a person, by feeding the two cats, by cooking a meal.

It takes a while, as I watch the surf blowing up in fountains at the end of the field, but the moment comes when the world falls away, and the self emerges again from the deep unconscious, bringing back all I have recently experienced to be explored and slowly understood, when I can converse again with my hidden powers, and so grow, and so be renewed, till death do us part.

1946

QUESTIONS FOR DISCUSSION

Content

a. What does Sarton mean by her sentence in paragraph 3, "Solitude is the salt of personhood"? What is the metaphor here?
b. Do you agree or disagree with Sarton's assessment of solitude?
c. To what does Sarton allude with the last phrase of the essay? What is her implication here?
d. What does Sarton use as examples to support her thesis that solitude is better than constant society? How effective are these examples?
e. What might be Sarton's purpose in including a passage of poetry as an entire paragraph (paragraph 4)?
f. Exactly what does Sarton compare and contrast in her essay?
g. Is this an argumentative essay? If so, what is her argument and to whom is she arguing? What does she hope to persuade them to do?

h. How does Sarton define "loneliness"? Do you agree with her definition? How would her definition differ from standard definitions?
i. Have you ever found yourself in the same situation as Sarton's gregarious acquaintance? If so, were your reactions similar to his?

Strategy and Style

j. Sarton begins her essay with an anecdote. What effect does this opening have on you? Does it draw you into the essay? Would the essay be better, or worse, without it?
k. How do you account for the brevity of this essay? Would it be a better essay if it were longer?
l. What allusions or metaphors does Sarton include?

SUGGESTIONS FOR SHORT WRITING

a. Write your definitions of loneliness and of solitude. How do they compare to what Sarton says of loneliness and solitude?
b. What is your own experience of solitude? Describe a time you were completely solitary.

SUGGESTIONS FOR SUSTAINED WRITING

a. Write an essay justifying your lifestyle. Decide whether you want to persuade your readers to adopt a similar lifestyle.
b. Write an essay comparing and/or contrasting two or more lifestyles, habits, hobbies, etc.
c. Trying to keep it as short as possible, write an essay that captures the essential aspects of a way of life. You may wish to begin with a longer essay, making it more and more compact with each revision.

Viewing vs. Reading

Marie Winn

Marie Winn was born in Prague, Czechoslovakia, in 1936 and immigrated to the United States in 1939. She was educated at Radcliffe College and Columbia University. Winn is the author of more than a dozen books for and about children and has written numerous articles on the effects of the media for The New York Times Magazine *and other periodicals. For* The Plug-In Drug *(1977), she won an award from the American Library Association. In her most recent book, she proposes a solution to the problem posed by "Viewing vs. Reading." The book is aptly titled,* Unplugging the Plug-In Drug *(1987).*

Until the television era a young child's access to symbolic representations of reality was limited. Unable to read, he entered the world of fantasy primarily by way of stories told to him or read to him from a book. But rarely did such "literary" experiences take up a significant proportion of a child's waking time; even when a willing reader or storyteller was available, an hour or so a day was more time than most children spent ensconced in the imagination of others. And when the pretelevision child *did* enter those imaginary worlds, he always had a grown-up escort along to interpret, explain, and comfort, if need be. Before he learned to read, it was difficult for the child to enter the fantasy world alone. 1

For this reason the impact of television was undoubtedly greater on pre-schoolers and pre-readers than on any other group. By means of television, very young children were able to enter and spend sizable portions of their waking time in a secondary world of incorporeal people and intangible things, unaccompanied, in too many cases, by an adult guide or comforter. School-age children fell into a different category. Because they could read, they had other opportunities to leave reality behind. For these children television was merely *another* imaginary world. 2

But since reading, once the school child's major imaginative experience, has now been virtually eclipsed by television, the television experience must be compared with the reading experience to try to discover whether they are, indeed, similar activities fulfilling similar needs in a child's life. 3

WHAT HAPPENS WHEN YOU READ

It is not enough to compare television watching and reading from the viewpoint of quality. Although the quality of the material available in each medium varies enormously, from junky books and shoddy programs to literary masterpieces and fine, thoughtful television shows, the *nature* of the two expe- 4 riences is different and that difference significantly affects the impact of the material taken in.

Few people besides linguistics students and teachers of reading are aware 5 of the complex mental manipulations involved in the reading process. Shortly after learning to read, a person assimilates the process into his life so completely that the words in books seem to acquire an existence almost equal to the objects or acts they represent. It requires a fresh look at a printed page to recognize that those symbols that we call letters of the alphabet are completely abstract shapes bearing no inherent "meaning" of their own. Look at an "o," for instance, or a "k." The "o" is a curved figure; the "k" is an intersection of three straight lines. Yet it is hard to divorce their familiar figures from their sounds, though there is nothing "o-ish" about an "o" or "k-ish" about a "k." A reader unfamiliar with the Russian alphabet will find it easy to look at the symbol " щ " and see it as an abstract shape; a Russian reader will find it harder to detach that symbol from its sound, *shch.* And even when trying to consider "k" as an abstract symbol, we cannot see it without the feeling of a "k" sound somewhere between the throat and the ears, a silent pronunciation of "k" that occurs the instant we see the letter.

That is the beginning of reading: we learn to transform abstract figures 6 into sounds, and groups of symbols into the combined sounds that make up the words of our language. As the mind transforms the abstract symbols into sounds and the sounds into words, it "hears" the words, as it were, and thereby invests them with meanings previously learned in the spoken language. Invariably, as the skill of reading develops, the meaning of each word begins to seem to dwell within those symbols that make up the word. The word "dog," for instance, comes to bear some relationship with the real animal. Indeed, the word "dog" seems to *be* dog in a certain sense, to possess some of the qualities of a dog. But it is only as a result of a swift and complex series of mental activities that the word "dog" is transformed from a series of meaningless squiggles into an idea of something real. This process goes on smoothly and continuously as we read, and yet it becomes no less complex. The brain must carry out all the steps of decoding and investing with meaning each time we read; but it becomes more adept at it as the skill develops, so that we lose the sense of struggling with symbols and meanings that children have when they first learn to read.

But not merely does the mind *hear* words in the process of reading; it is 7 important to remember that reading involves images as well. For when the reader sees the word "dog" and understands the idea of "dog," an image representing a dog is conjured up as well. The precise nature of this "reading image" is little understood, nor is there agreement about what relation it bears to visual images taken in directly by the eyes. Nevertheless images necessarily color our reading, else we would perceive no meaning, merely empty words. The great difference between these "reading images" and the images we take in when viewing television is this: we *create* our own images when reading, based upon our own life experiences and reflecting our own individual needs, while we must accept what we receive when watching television images. This aspect of reading, which might be called "creative" in the narrow sense of the word, is present during all reading experiences, regardless of *what* is being read. The reader "creates" his own images as he reads, almost as if he were creating his own, small, inner television program. The result is a nourishing experience for the imagination. As Bruno Bettelheim notes, "Television captures the imagination but does not liberate it. A good book at once stimulates and frees the mind."

Television images do not go through a complex symbolic transformation. 8 The mind does not have to decode and manipulate during the television experience. Perhaps this is a reason why the visual images received directly from a television set are strong, stronger, it appears, than the images conjured up mentally while reading. But ultimately they satisfy less. A ten-year-old child reports on the effects of seeing television dramatizations of books he has previously read: "The TV people leave a stronger impression. Once you've seen a character on TV, he'll always look like that in your mind, even if you made a different picture of him in your mind before, when you read the book yourself." And yet, as the same child reports, "the thing about a book is that you have so much freedom. You can make each character look exactly the way you want him to look. You're more in control of things when you read a book than when you see something on TV."

It may be that television-bred children's reduced opportunities to indulge 9 in this "inner picture-making" accounts for the curious inability of so many children today to adjust to nonvisual experiences. This is commonly reported by experienced teachers who bridge the gap between the pretelevision and the television eras.

"When I read them a story without showing them pictures, the children 10 always complain—'I can't see.' Their attention flags," reports a first-grade teacher. "They'll begin to talk or wander off. I have to really work to develop their visualizing skills. I tell them that there's nothing to see, that the story is coming out of my mouth, and that they can make their own pictures in their 'mind's eye.' They get better at visualizing, with practice. But children never needed to learn how to visualize before television, it seems to me."

VIEWING VS. READING: CONCENTRATION

Because reading demands complex mental manipulations, a reader is re- 11 quired to concentrate far more than a television viewer. An audio expert notes that "with the electronic media it is openness [that counts]. Openness permits auditory and visual stimuli more direct access to the brain...someone who is taught to concentrate will fail to perceive many patterns of information conveyed by the electronic stimuli."

It may be that a predisposition toward concentration, acquired, perhaps, 12
through one's reading experiences, makes one an inadequate television watcher.
But it seems far more likely that the reverse situation obtains: that a predisposition toward "openness" (which may be understood to mean the opposite of
focal concentration), acquired through years and years of television viewing,
has influenced adversely viewers' ability to concentrate, to read, to write
clearly—in short, to demonstrate any of the verbal skills a literate society requires.

PACE

A comparison between reading and viewing may be made in respect to 13
the pace of each experience, and the relative control a person has over that
pace, for the pace may influence the ways one uses the material received in
each experience. In addition, the pace of each experience may determine how
much it intrudes upon other aspects of one's life.

The pace of reading, clearly, depends entirely upon the reader. He may 14
read as slowly or as rapidly as he can or wishes to read. If he does not understand something, he may stop and reread it, or go in search of elucidation before continuing. The reader can accelerate his pace when the material is easy or
less than interesting, and slow down when it is difficult or enthralling. If what
he reads is moving, he can put down the book for a few moments and cope
with his emotions without fear of losing anything.

The pace of the television experience cannot be controlled by the viewer; 15
only its beginning and end are within his control as he clicks the knob on and
off. He cannot slow down a delightful program or speed up a dreary one. He
cannot "turn back" if a word or phrase is not understood. The program moves
inexorably forward, and what is lost or misunderstood remains so.

Nor can the television viewer readily transform the material he receives 16
into a form that might suit his particular emotional needs, as he invariably does
with material he reads. The images move too quickly. He cannot use his own
imagination to invest the people and events portrayed on television with the
personal meanings that would help him understand and resolve relationships
and conflicts in his own life; he is under the power of the imagination of the
show's creators. In the television experience the eyes and ears are overwhelmed
with the immediacy of sights and sounds. They flash from the television set just
fast enough for the eyes and ears to take them in before moving on quickly to
the new pictures and sounds...so as *not to lose the thread.*

Not to lose the thread...it is this need, occasioned by the irreversible di- 17
rection and relentless velocity of the television experience, that not only limits
the workings of the viewer's imagination, but also causes television to intrude
into human affairs far more than reading experiences can ever do. If someone
enters the room while one is watching television—a friend, a relative, a child,

someone, perhaps, one has not seen for some time—one must continue to watch or one will lose the thread. The greetings must wait, for the television program will not. A book, of course, can be set aside, with a pang of regret, perhaps, but with no sense of permanent loss.

A grandparent describes a situation that is, by all reports, not uncommon: 18

"Sometimes when I come to visit the girls, I'll walk into their room and   19 they're watching a TV program. Well, I know they love me, but it makes me feel *bad* when I tell them hello, and they say, without even looking up, 'Wait a minute...we have to see the end of this program.' It hurts me to have them care more about that machine and those little pictures than about being glad to see me. I know that they probably can't help it, but still...."

Can they help it? Ultimately the power of a television viewer to release   20 himself from his viewing in order to attend to human demands arising in the course of his viewing is not altogether a function of the pace of the program. After all, the viewer might *choose* to operate according to human priorities rather than electronic dictatorship. He might quickly decide "to hell with this program" and simply stop watching when a friend entered the room or a child needed attention.

He might...but the hypnotic power of television makes it difficult to shift   21 one's attention away, makes one desperate not to lose the thread of the program....

THE BASIC BUILDING BLOCKS

There is another difference between reading and television viewing that   22 must affect the response to each experience. This is the relative acquaintance of readers and viewers with the fundamental elements of each medium. While the reader is familiar with the basic building blocks of the reading medium, the television viewer has little acquaintance with those of the television medium.

As a person reads, he has his own writing experience to fall back upon.   23 His understanding of what he reads, and his feelings about it, are necessarily affected, and deepened, by his possession of writing as a means of communicating. As a child begins to learn reading, he begins to acquire the rudiments of writing. That these two skills are always acquired together is important and not coincidental. As the child learns to read words, he needs to understand that a word is something he can write himself, though his muscle control may temporarily prevent him from writing it clearly. That he wields such power over the words he is struggling to decipher makes the reading experience a satisfying one right from the start.

A young child watching television enters a realm of materials completely   24 beyond his control—and understanding. Though the images that appear on the screen may be reflections of familiar people and things, they appear as if by magic. The child cannot create similar images, nor even begin to understand how those flickering, electronic shapes and forms come into being. He takes on a far more powerless and ignorant role in front of the television set than in front of a book.

There is no doubt that many young children have a confused relationship 25 to the television medium. When a group of preschool children were asked, "How do kids get to be on your TV?" only 22 percent of them showed any real comprehension of the nature of the television images. When asked, "Where do the people and kids and things go when your TV is turned off?" only 20 percent of the three-year-olds showed the smallest glimmer of understanding. Although there was an increase in comprehension among the four-year-olds, the authors of the study note that "even among the older children the vast majority still did not grasp the nature of television pictures."

The child's feelings of power and competence are nourished by another 26 feature of the reading experience that does not obtain for television: the nonmechanical, easily accessible, and easily transportable nature of reading matter. The child can always count on a book for pleasure, though the television set may break down at a crucial moment. The child may take a book with him wherever he goes, to his room, to the park, to his friend's house, to school to read under his desk: he can *control* his use of books and reading materials. The television set is stuck in a certain place; it cannot be moved easily. It certainly cannot be casually transported from place to place by a child. The child must not only watch television wherever the set is located, but he must watch certain programs at certain times, and is powerless to change what comes out of the set and when it comes out.

In this comparison of reading and television experiences a picture begins 27 to emerge that quite confirms the commonly held notion that reading is somehow "better" than television viewing. Reading involves a complex form of mental activity, trains the mind in concentration skills, develops the powers of imagination and inner visualization; the flexibility of its pace lends itself to a better and deeper comprehension of the material communicated. Reading engrosses, but does not hypnotize or seduce the reader from his human responsibilities. Reading is a two-way process: the reader can also write; television viewing is a one-way street: the viewer cannot create television images. And books are ever available, ever controllable. Television controls.

1977

QUESTIONS FOR DISCUSSION

Content

a. Winn states her purpose early in the essay. Why does she believe it important to compare television viewing with reading?

b. Winn's thesis is not made explicit until the last paragraph. Is it implied at any time before that?

c. What does Winn say about the relationship between learning to read and learning to write?

d. Why does she spend a great deal of time explaining the complex processes involved in reading (paragraphs 4, 5, 6, and 7) and comparatively little time explaining what happens when we watch television (paragraph 8)?

e. In addition to using comparison/contrast as the dominant method of developing her essay, Winn makes effective use of process analysis, which allows her to explain how various complex mental processes work. In which paragraphs is this method of development most apparent?

f. In regard to pace, what are the most significant differences between watching television and reading?

g. What advantages, other than those mentioned by Winn, does reading have over watching television?

h. Could Winn make the same case against radio? If not, explain why some of her arguments would not apply.

Strategy and Style

i. How do the subheads of this essay affect you as you read? What might have been Winn's purpose for including them?

j. Winn makes extensive use of dialogue and anecdotes to clarify and emphasize important points. Where can you find examples of such devices?

k. How would you describe Winn's tone in paragraph 27?

SUGGESTIONS FOR SHORT WRITING

a. Complete the following sentence in various ways, using quotes from Winn's writing to fill in the first blank: I believe that "_____" is true, except when _____.

b. If Winn and Joyce Maynard ("I Remember…," Chapter 7) were to discuss the pros and cons of television watching, what might each of them say to the other? List the main points each of the two writers would make.

SUGGESTIONS FOR SUSTAINED WRITING

a. Are there advantages to reading a daily newspaper or a weekly news magazine over watching television news broadcasts? List each advantage and provide appropriate examples dealing with current news stories to support your thesis.

b. Is television a totally useless and, indeed, harmful invention, or does it have some redeeming qualities? If so, make a case for watching television on a selective and limited basis. Advise your reader to stay away from certain types of shows but to make time for others.

c. Can you think of any activity you would rather watch on television than read about in a newspaper or book? Take a sporting event, for instance. Explain why it is better to watch the Super Bowl on Sunday afternoon than to read about it on Monday morning.

d. Are there significant differences between watching a sporting event on television and being in the stadium? Write an essay in which you compare and contrast these two experiences. If you're not a sports fan, compare the watching of a ballet, opera, or play on television to seeing a live performance in person.

Conservatives and Liberals

Ralph Waldo Emerson

Raised in Boston and educated at Harvard University, Ralph Waldo Emerson (1803–1882) became a Unitarian minister in 1829. He left his first and only assignment three years later, however, in a dispute over questions of doctrine. Upon resigning his pastorate, Emerson began traveling through Europe, where he met several important Romantic thinkers, including Coleridge and Wordsworth. When he returned to the United States, he relocated in Concord, Massachusetts, and worked closely with Margaret Fuller and Henry David Thoreau to establish American transcendentalism, a philosophical and literary movement based, to a great degree, upon the tenets of European Romanticism. For instance, Emerson argued against the old Calvinist notion that human beings are inherently evil, and he proclaimed the presence of God both in the natural world and in humankind. Like their European counterparts, Emerson and the other transcendentalists also believed that the true path to wisdom was through human intuition and not through pure reason. Perhaps the most important statement of the transcendentalist credo appears in Nature, *which Emerson published in 1836. He continued to develop his philosophy in* The Dial, *a journal of transcendentalist thought, and in the many essays upon which his fame chiefly rests. Perhaps the most important of these are "The American Scholar," in which he advocates intellectual independence from Europe, and "Self-Reliance," from which this selection on conservatives and liberals is excerpted.*

1. The two parties which divide the state, the party of Conservatism and that of Innovation, are very old, and have disputed the possession of the world ever since it was made. This quarrel is the subject of civil history. The conservative party established the reverend hierarchies and monarchies of the most ancient world. The battle of patrician and plebeian, of parent state and colony, of old usage and accommodation to new facts, of the rich and the poor, reappears in all countries and times. The war rages not only in battle-fields, in national councils, and ecclesiastical synods, but agitates every man's bosom with opposing advantages every hour. On rolls the old world meantime, and now one, now the other gets the day, and still the fight renews itself as if for the first time, under new names and hot personalities.

2. Such an irreconcilable antagonism, of course, must have a correspondent depth of seat in the human constitution. It is the opposition of Past and Future, of Memory and Hope, of the Understanding and the Reason. It is the primal antagonism, the appearance in trifles of the two poles of nature.

3. There is a fragment of old fable which seems somehow to have been dropped from the current mythologies, which may deserve attention, as it appears to relate to this subject.

4. Saturn grew weary of sitting alone, or with none but the great Uranus or Heaven beholding him, and he created an oyster. Then he would act again, but

he made nothing more, but went on creating the race of oysters. Then Uranus cried, "a new work, O Saturn! the old is not good again."

Saturn replied, "I fear. There is not only the alternative of making and not making, but also of unmaking. Seest thou the great sea, how it ebbs and flows? So is it with me; my power ebbs; and if I put forth my hands, I shall not do, but undo. Therefore I do what I have done; I hold what I have got; and so I resist Night and Chaos." 5

"O Saturn," replied Uranus. "Thou canst not hold thine own, but by making more. Thy oysters are barnacles and cockles, and with the next flowing of the tide, they will be pebbles and sea foam." 6

"I see," rejoins Saturn, "thou art in league with Night, thou art become an evil eye: thou spakest from love; now thy words smite me with hatred. I appeal to Fate, must there not be rest?"—"I appeal to Fate also," said Uranus, "must there not be motion?"—But Saturn was silent and went on making oysters for a thousand years. 7

After that, the word of Uranus came into his mind like a ray of the sun, and he made Jupiter; and then he feared again; and nature froze, the things that were made went backward, and to save the world, Jupiter slew his father Saturn. 8

This may stand for the earliest account of a conversation on politics between a Conservative and a Radical, which has come down to us. It is ever thus. It is the counteraction of the centripetal and the centrifugal forces. Innovation is the salient energy; Conservatism the pause on the last movement. "That which is was made by God," saith Conservatism. "He is leaving that, he is entering this other;" rejoins Innovation. 9

There is always a certain meanness in the argument of conservatism, joined with a certain superiority in its fact. It affirms because it holds. Its fingers clutch the fact, and it will not open its eyes to see a better fact. The castle, which conservatism is set to defend, is the actual state of things, good and bad. The project of innovation is the best possible state of things. Of course, conservatism always has the worst of the argument, is always apologizing, pleading a necessity, pleading that to change would be to deteriorate; it must saddle itself with the mountainous load of all the violence and vice of society, must deny the possibility of good, deny ideas, and suspect and stone the prophet; whilst innovation is always in the right, triumphant, attacking, and sure of final success. Conservatism stands on man's incontestable limitations; reform on his indisputable infinitude; conservatism on circumstance; liberalism on power; one goes to make an adroit member of the social frame; the other to postpone all things to the man himself; conservatism is debonair and social; reform is individual and imperious. We are reformers in spring and summer, in autumn and winter we stand by the old; reformers in the morning, conservers at night. Reform is affirmative, conservatism negative; conservatism goes for comfort, reform for truth. Conservatism is more candid to behold another's worth; reform more disposed to maintain and increase its own. Conservatism makes no poetry, breathes no 10 prayer, has no invention; it is all memory. Reform has no gratitude, no prudence, no husbandry. It makes a great difference to your figure and to your thought, whether your foot is advancing or receding. Conservatism never puts the foot forward; in the hour when it does that, it is not establishment, but reform. Conservatism tends to universal seeming and treachery, believes in a negative fate; believes that men's temper governs them; that for me, it avails not to trust in principles; they will fail me; I must bend a little; it distrusts nature; it thinks there is a general law without a particular application,—law for all that does not include any one. Reform in its antagonism inclines to asinine resistance, to kick with hoofs; it runs to egotism and bloated self-conceit; it runs to a bodiless pretension, to unnatural refining and elevation, which ends in hypocrisy and sensual reaction.

And so whilst we do not go beyond general statements, it may be safely   11
affirmed of these two metaphysical antagonists, that each is a good half, but an impossible whole. Each exposes the abuses of the other, but in a true society, in a true man, both must combine. Nature does not give the crown of its approbation, namely, Beauty, to any action or emblem or actor but to one which combines both these elements; not to the rock which resists the waves from age to age, nor to the wave which lashes incessantly the rock, but the superior beauty is with the oak which stands with its hundred arms against the storms of a century and grows every year like a sapling; or the river which ever flowing, yet is found in the same bed from age to age; or, greatest of all, the man who has subsisted for years amid the changes of nature, yet has distanced himself, so that when you remember what he was, and see what he is, you say, what strides! what a disparity is here!

1841

QUESTIONS FOR DISCUSSION

Content

a. What is Emerson driving at when he tells us that "Conservatism…has no invention," while "Reform has…no husbandry" (paragraph 10)?
b. What is Emerson's thesis? Why does he withhold it until the very last paragraph?
c. What analogies does Emerson create to help describe the relationship between "Conservatism" and "Innovation"?
d. What are some of the positive aspects of conservatism? What are its shortcomings? What are the positive aspects and shortcomings of liberalism?
e. How would you define the "two poles of nature" to which Emerson makes reference in paragraph 2?

Strategy and Style

f. Analyze Emerson's method of organizing this selection. Why does he wait until paragraph 3 to begin the contrast between conservatism and liberalism in earnest? What functions do paragraphs 1 and 2 serve?

g. Emerson discusses these two "metaphysical antagonists" by contrasting them point by point. What does this method of development help him achieve that would have been impossible had he fully described conservatism first and then liberalism? In what ways does the method Emerson choose contribute to the essay?

h. What synonyms does Emerson use for liberalism? Are these synonyms appropriate? Do they color his definition in any way?

i. What use does Emerson make of personification?

SUGGESTIONS FOR SHORT WRITING

a. Write a dialogue between a conservative and a liberal in which they discuss a current issue.

b. What is the difference between conservative and liberal thinking as Emerson presents it? Write a brief definition of each kind of thinking.

SUGGESTIONS FOR SUSTAINED WRITING

a. Provide your own definitions of the words "conservative" and "liberal" and illustrate or explain the difference by making reference to well-known conservatives and liberals, past and/or present. Try to be consistent, and remember not to compare "apples with oranges," as the old saying goes. In other words, contrast politicians with politicians, religious leaders with religious leaders, etc.

b. Do you agree with Emerson's thesis? If so, write an essay addressed to your classmates in which you explain in what ways the life of a student requires you to be conservative and in what ways it requires you to be liberal. Make reference to Emerson and quote passages from his essay as appropriate.

7

Example and Illustration

Illustration is a natural habit of mind. How often have we offered a "for example" or "for instance" when, as we try to make a point, our listeners respond quizzically or simply shake their heads in disbelief? "What's so unhealthy about my diet?" demands a good friend whose eating habits you have just impugned. "For starters," you respond, "you are a French-fry fanatic, stuffing your face with the greasy, salt-laden sticks at nearly every meal. You eat so much red meat, butter, ice cream, and candy that the *New England Journal of Medicine* ought to report your intake of cholesterol, calories, and fat. And you probably don't even remember what fruits and vegetables look like."

The three examples that explain what you meant by *unhealthy* are products of a powerful and effective technique common to all types of expository or persuasive prose. Good writers are rarely content to tell their readers what they mean; they want to show it. One way to do this is to fill your work with relevant, well-developed illustrations—concrete representations of abstract ideas.

Effective illustrations make possible the explanation of ideas that might otherwise remain vague because they enable the reader to grasp particular realities behind the abstraction, to see specific and pertinent instances of the generality. "My Aunt Tillie is the most unselfish person in town," you may well exclaim. But consider how much more convincing your claim would become if you recalled the times she opened her home to a homeless family, donated her savings to the hospital building fund, and took time off from work to help sick friends and relatives.

The clarity and strength that illustration brings to your writing does not depend on the number of examples you include—although sheer volume can be convincing—but on the degree to which each example is clear, well developed, and appropriate to your thesis. William Buckley recalls only four or five brief anecdotes to explain why we don't complain more often—and why we should. Each situation is narrated in such detail, however, that readers can picture themselves in his place, and they share both his anger and "mortification."

293

Depending on your purpose, you can choose from several kinds of examples to give your writing variety and power. Ann Hodgman creates a vivid picture of regional cooking by describing a minor smorgasbord of less-than-appetizing "backwater" dishes. Developments in the history of eating, each analyzed thoroughly, provide Peter Farb and George Armelagos with a trove of examples to show how changes in table manners "reflect fundamental changes in human relationships." Joyce Maynard's close analysis of *Leave It to Beaver* and her references to other vintage television programs help her explain how dramatically the electronic media influenced a generation. Richard Rodriguez combines the sights, sounds, and smells of the city, memories of his Mexican-American childhood, and reflections on the civil rights movement to illustrate the complexity of the American identity.

Like most other methods of development, illustration is rarely used to the exclusion of other rhetorical techniques. In the selections by Robertson Davies and Stephen Jay Gould, for instance, well-chosen examples develop categories (classification) through which the authors shed new and interesting light on their subjects.

Enjoy the selections in this chapter. They vary significantly in purpose, tone, and subject. Each is effective, however, because it explains an abstract idea in terms that will allow the reader to experience the concrete realities for which that abstraction stands. Each shows us ways to grapple with even the most unwieldy notions in language that is clear, powerful, and convincing.

Backwater Cuisine

Ann Hodgman

Ann Hodgman is a freelance writer whose articles have appeared in many magazines, including Spy, *in which "Backwater Cuisine" first appeared. Many of her published writings, however, are books for children and young adults. Hodgman writes for all ages, from* Galaxy High School *(1987) for high schoolers, to a Lunchroom Series for elementary students, including such appetizing titles as* Night of a Thousand Pizzas, Frog Punch, French Fried Aliens, *and* The Flying Popcorn Experiment, *all published in 1990.*

1   I realize that she's dead and that there are some toes you just don't step on in this culture, but the fact remains: Janis Joplin wasn't really a good singer. If she were to come back today as a food, she'd be some kind of awful regional dish. *So earthy!* the foodies would bellow. *So quirkily honest, so down-home! Such a powerful antidote to our synthetic, overcivilized lives!*

2   "Like white hot dogs?" pipes up a little boy from my hometown, Rochester, New York. Yes, sonny, exactly like them. White hots—which taste like ordinary dogs and look even nastier—are a perfect example of *real* regional cuisine. Not the kind of regional dish Paul Prudhomme makes for Craig Claiborne's birthday, but the kind that arrivistes like me pretend they've never tasted.

3   No, really, I'm happy to be from Rochester, birthplace of Zab's Backyard Hots. We're very proud of Zab's. We think they make a lovely present for the folks downstate.

4   White hots are made from ham, pork, beef, veal, mustard, paprika and other spices. At the same time, say their creators mysteriously, they contain *no seasonings.* What are spices if not seasoning? And anyway, why brag about selling unseasoned food? "We wanted to make sure that three hours later you're not belching," explains company president Don Zabkar helpfully. (Maybe *seasonings* is a Rochester euphemism for *garlic,* the way *sick* is a traveler's euphemism for—well, you know.) There's an advertising slogan in there somewhere, I feel sure. *"Three hours after Zab's White Hots, you're still not belching!"*

5   But why should I feel ashamed? At least white hots contain no variety meats, whereas the most famous regional protein from Pennsylvania—scrapple—seems to be made of little else. It's silly to be concerned about this, of course. Meat is meat, whether it's tucked demurely away under a rib or right out there next to the eye. In any case, Ingredient Concern seems a little starry-eyed in these days of ozone depletion. Still, it gives me some pleasure to realize that some of the ingredients in dog food are considered a little too...chichi to be used in scrapple.

6   My decade-old memory of opening a can of dog food to find an unproc-

295

essed pig's snout still makes me fly into the air, but according to the *Times,* things like snouts give scrapple a false elegance. Some scrapple makers, the paper says, "break further with tradition by enriching their scrapple with such parts as snouts, ears and tails, parts that would formerly have been served on their own." It seems that all real scrapple needs is "useless pork parts, neckbones, backs, skins and livers." And, of course, buckwheat, which is what makes the mixture so nice and gray.

O-*kay!* Let's fry some up! I have a plastic-wrapped block of Parks scrapple here that my husband has forbidden me to cook or even open in front of him. I can hardly blame him; this is perhaps the ugliest food I've ever seen, despite the fact that it does contain those fancy pig snouts. Sidewalk-colored, it's flecked with white blobs and translucent bits of gristle that bounce back when palpated through the plastic. If you look closely, you can see tiny yellow dots throughout, and those pink things....I'm sorry, but I can't bring myself to cut the package open. (I'm treading close enough to Mystery Meat jokes as it is.)   7

Parks scrapple is made not in Pennsylvania but in Baltimore, which is   8
home to some pretty repellent regional dishes itself. One of these is roast turkey with sauerkraut. I don't object to sauerkraut, but am I alone in thinking it's supposed to go with things like white hots? I guess so. "I just couldn't live without my sauerkraut on Thanksgiving," claims a Baltimore woman who—like other Baltimoreans that I've spoken to—obstinately refuses to admit there's anything disgusting about holiday kraut. "It's no worse than cranberry sauce," says a friend of mine, probably crossing her fingers as she speaks.

I hear you're supposed to start with canned sauerkraut. (This part is fine   9
with me. The recipe for fresh sauerkraut in *The Joy of Cooking* tells you to remove the scum daily.) You add some water and a ham hock and cook it for, I swear, ten hours. "It stinks up the house," my friend says proudly. But doesn't sauerkraut get soggy—soggier, I mean—when it's cooked that long? "But it doesn't get *tangy* enough unless you cook it for a long time!"

They don't stop there, though: Baltimore Thanksgivings also include 10
hominy, starch's uncanny imitation of large-curd cottage cheese. But I don't mean to talk only about Thanksgiving—not when another Baltimore specialty is beef kidney stew on waffles.

Speaking of waffles, how about some breakfast? Let's switch to my 11
hometown-in-law, Kansas City, which has few culinary lapses except when it tries to get European. True, it sometimes takes blood-and-guts cooking too far—the Hen House sells chicken hearts in cardboard vats the size of those stupefyingly large tubs of movie popcorn—but I think we've all had enough variety protein for today. For the most part, Kansas City's food mistakes are rare.

There's one exception: T. J. Cinnamons Bakery rolls and sticky buns.   12

It's not only that T. J. Cinnamons sounds like the name of a rascally li'l 13
cartoon character soon to be licensed to Hallmark. It's not only that the rolls are individually packed in Styrofoam containers so that you keep thinking, *A Big Mac is in there,* despite yourself. It's not only that T. J. Cinnamons franchises

sell soft drinks, forcing you to imagine what it would be like to wash down a pecan sticky bun with Sprite.

It's the rolls themselves. Although the top half is like a dry, raisinless raisin bread, the bottom half is drenched, squishy, literally oozing melted butter and sugar. (Maybe things would even out if you turned the rolls upside down for a few days.) When you order a cinnamon roll, they ask, "Do you want icing with that?" and when you say yes, they squeeze big lines of it all over the top. When you order a pecan sticky bun, they scrape up extra stickum from the bottom of the pan and spread it on the pecans. I know, I know—it sounds great. But bear in mind that the rolls weigh something like *half a pound apiece*. These people want us to die. **14**

Well, I'm full—how 'bout you? Let's talk about huevos rancheros and fried pies and chili with spaghetti and jelly omelets another time. Meanwhile, I'll just be glad that I don't live in a region. **15**

1987

QUESTIONS FOR DISCUSSION

Content

a. What is Hodgman's main point in this essay? What examples does she use to illustrate this point?

b. Why did Hodgman capitalize the words "Ingredient Concern" in paragraph 5? What is she implying in this sentence?

c. What might be Hodgman's purpose for making fun of regional foods? Is she just trying to entertain her readers, or is she trying to convince them to stop eating these foods?

d. Hodgman includes quotes from food critics, friends, and cookbooks. How do these quotes help support her dim view of regional foods? Do you find anything suspicious in her choice of quoted material?

e. Hodgman frequently uses questions, sometimes even supplying an answer. (See paragraphs 2, 4, 5, 8, 9, 11, and 15.) To whom is she addressing these questions? Why does she answer some of them herself? What is the nature of these questions and answers?

f. What is the correlation between Janis Joplin and regional food? Do you feel that this is an appropriate correlation?

g. Are you personally familiar with any of the regional foods Hodgman describes? How accurate is Hodgman's description? Does she exaggerate or use understatement? If so, what might be her reasons for distorting her description?

h. In the second paragraph, Hodgman makes a distinction between "real regional cuisine" and "the kind of regional dish Paul Prudhomme makes for

Craig Claiborne's birthday." What distinction is she making here? Why is this distinction important in understanding the rest of the essay?

i. What does Hodgman mean with her last sentence ("Meanwhile, I'll just be glad that I don't live in a region.")? In what ways and for what reasons does this statement contradict a statement she made earlier in the essay?

j. Do you know of any regional foods that Hodgman has left out of her essay? How might Hodgman describe those other regional foods?

k. Read the food reviews in a few newspapers or magazines. What aspect of these reviews does Hodgman make fun of in her article?

Strategy and Style

l. In paragraph 4, Hodgman suggests that the word "seasonings" might be "a Rochester euphemism for garlic." What other names of food can be considered euphemisms?

m. How would you describe Hodgman's tone? What is her attitude toward regional foods as revealed by this tone? Do you think the attitude she adopts in the article is how she really feels about regional foods?

n. Look up the word "irony" in a dictionary of literary terms. In what ways does Hodgman use irony in her essay? What effect does irony have on the essay?

SUGGESTIONS FOR SHORT WRITING

a. List and briefly describe any/all of the "*real* regional cuisine" of *your* region. Describe the process of preparing one such regional dish. Make your description as appetizing or as nauseating as you wish.

b. Using one of your region's dishes, or one that Hodgman describes, write a list comparing and contrasting the positive and negative aspects of your regional dish to a "national dish" such as the hamburger.

SUGGESTIONS FOR SUSTAINED WRITING

a. Write an essay describing the foods from the area in which you grew up or now live that might be considered "regional" using Hodgman's definition. Be aware of the tone you want to project to your readers and the point you want to make; i.e., don't just describe the foods, describe the foods in order to make a point.

b. What other regionalisms besides foods exist in this country? Using examples to support your claim, write an essay describing other regional quirks.

c. Using Hodgman's culinary examples or other regionalisms, trace the regionalisms back to their origins. Show how the regionalisms have evolved from their origins, and give an account of the changes.

Why Don't We Complain?

William F. Buckley, Jr.

Perhaps the best-known and wittiest spokesman for political conservatism in the United States, William F. Buckley was born in New York City in 1925 and is the editor-in-chief of The National Review, *which he founded in 1955. Since 1966, he has hosted* Firing Line, *a weekly television forum for the discussion of important political, social, and moral issues. A prolific writer, he publishes three syndicated newspaper columns each week and contributes regularly to magazines like* Harper's *and* Esquire, *wherein "Why Don't We Complain?" first appeared in 1961. In 1965, he even found time to mount a campaign, albeit unsuccessfully, as a candidate for mayor of New York. He is a graduate of Yale University, which found its way into the title of his first full-length work,* God and Man at Yale, *in 1951. Since then, Buckley has published (among many others)* United Nations Journal *(1974);* Stained Glass *(1978);* Marco Polo, If You Can *(1982), a spy novel; and* Atlantic High *(1982), which recounts his transoceanic adventure in a sailing vessel. His most recent books are* On the Firing Line *(1989) and* Tucker's Last Stand *(1990).*

It was the very last coach and the only empty seat on the entire train, so 1 there was no turning back. The problem was to breathe. Outside, the temperature was below freezing. Inside the railroad car the temperature must have been about 85 degrees. I took off my overcoat, and a few minutes later my jacket, and noticed that the car was flecked with the white shirts of the passengers. I soon found my hand moving to loosen my tie. From one end of the car to the other, as we rattled through Westchester County, we sweated; but we did not moan.

I watched the train conductor appear at the head of the car. "Tickets, all 2 tickets, please!" In a more virile age, I thought, the passengers would seize the conductor and strap him down on a seat over the radiator to share the fate of his patrons. He shuffled down the aisle, picking up tickets, punching commutation cards. *No one addressed a word to him.* He approached my seat, and I drew a deep breath of resolution. "Conductor," I began with a considerable edge to my voice....Instantly the doleful eyes of my seatmate turned tiredly from his newspaper to fix me with a resentful stare: what question could be so important as to justify my sibilant intrusion into his stupor? I was shaken by those eyes. I am incapable of making a discreet fuss, so I mumbled a question about what time we were due in Stamford (I didn't even ask whether it would be before or after dehydration could be expected to set in), got my reply, and went back to my newspaper and to wiping my brow.

The conductor had nonchalantly walked down the gauntlet of eighty 3 sweating American freemen, and not one of them had asked him to explain why the passengers in that car had been consigned to suffer. There is nothing to be

299

done when the temperature *outdoors* is 85 degrees, and indoors the air conditioner has broken down; obviously when that happens there is nothing to do, except perhaps curse the day that one was born. But when the temperature outdoors is below freezing, it takes a positive act of will on somebody's part to set the temperature *indoors* at 85. Somewhere a valve was turned too far, a furnace overstocked, a thermostat maladjusted: something that could easily be remedied by turning off the heat and allowing the great outdoors to come indoors. All this is so obvious. What is not obvious is what has happened to the American people.

It isn't just the commuters, whom we have come to visualize as a supine   4
breed who have got on to the trick of suspending their sensory faculties twice a day while they submit to the creeping dissolution of the railroad industry. It isn't just they who have given up trying to rectify irrational vexations. It is the American people everywhere.

A few weeks ago at a large movie theatre I turned to my wife and said,   5
"The picture is out of focus." "Be quiet," she answered. I obeyed. But a few minutes later I raised the point again, with mounting impatience. "It will be all right in a minute," she said apprehensively. (She would rather lose her eyesight than be around when I make one of my infrequent scenes.) I waited. It was *just* out of focus—not glaringly out, but out. My vision is 20-20, and I assume that is the vision, adjusted, of most people in the movie house. So, after hectoring my wife throughout the first reel, I finally prevailed upon her to admit that it *was* off, and very annoying. We then settled down, coming to rest on the presumption that: a) someone connected with the management of the theatre must soon notice the blur and make the correction; or b) that someone seated near the rear of the house would make the complaint in behalf of those of us up front; or c) that—any minute now—the entire house would explode into catcalls and foot stamping, calling dramatic attention to the irksome distortion.

What happened was nothing. The movie ended, as it had begun *just* out of   6
focus, and as we trooped out, we stretched our faces in a variety of contortions to accustom the eye to the shock of normal focus.

I think it is safe to say that everybody suffered on that occasion. And I   7
think it is safe to assume that everyone was expecting someone else to take the initiative in going back to speak to the manager. And it is probably true even that if we had supposed the movie would run right through the blurred image, someone surely would have summoned up the purposive indignation to get up out of his seat and file his complaint.

But notice that no one did. And the reason no one did is because we are   8
all increasingly anxious in America to be unobtrusive, we are reluctant to make our voices heard, hesitant about claiming our rights; we are afraid that our cause is unjust, or that if it is not unjust, that it is ambiguous; or if not even that, that it is too trivial to justify the horrors of a confrontation with Authority; we will sit in an oven or endure a racking headache before undertaking a head-on, I'm-here-to-tell-you complaint. That tendency to passive compliance, to a heedless endurance, is something to keep one's eyes on—in sharp focus.

I myself can occasionally summon the courage to complain, but I cannot, 9
as I have intimated, complain softly. My own instinct is so strong to let the
thing ride, to forget about it—to expect that someone will take the matter up,
when the grievance is collective, in my behalf—that it is only when the provo-
cation is at a very special key, whose vibrations touch simultaneously a com-
plexus of nerves, allergies, and passions, that I catch fire and find the reserves
of courage and assertiveness to speak up. When that happens, I get quite carried
away. My blood gets hot, my brow wet, I become unbearably and unconsciona-
bly sarcastic and bellicose; I am girded for a total showdown.

Why should that be? Why could not I (or anyone else) on that railroad 10
coach have said simply to the conductor, "Sir"—I take that back: that sounds
sarcastic—"Conductor, would you be good enough to turn down the heat? I am
extremely hot. In fact, I tend to get hot every time the temperature reaches 85
degr—" Strike that last sentence. Just end it with the simple statement that you
are extremely hot, and let the conductor infer the cause.

Every New Year's Eve I resolve to do something about the Milquetoast in 11
me and vow to speak up, calmly, for my rights, and for the betterment of our
society, on every appropriate occasion. Entering last New Year's Eve I was for-
tified in my resolve because that morning at breakfast I had had to ask the wait-
ress three times for a glass of milk. She finally brought it—after I had finished
my eggs, which is when I don't want it any more. I did not have the manliness
to order her to take the milk back, but settled instead for a cowardly sulk, and
ostentatiously refused to drink the milk—though I later paid for it—rather than
state plainly to the hostess, as I should have, why I had not drunk it, and would
not pay for it.

So by the time the New Year ushered out the Old, riding in on my morn- 12
ing's indignation and stimulated by the gastric juices of resolution that flow so
faithfully on New Year's Eve, I rendered my vow. Henceforward I would conquer my shyness, my despicable disposition to supineness. I would speak out
like a man against the unnecessary annoyances of our time.

Forty-eight hours later, I was standing in line at the ski repair store in 13
Pico Peak, Vermont. All I needed, to get on with my skiing, was the loan, for
one minute, of a small screwdriver, to tighten a loose binding. Behind the
counter in the workshop were two men. One was industriously engaged in ser-
vicing the complicated requirements of a young lady at the head of the line, and
obviously he would be tied up for quite a while. The other—"Jiggs," his work-
mate called him—was a middle-aged man, who sat in a chair puffing a pipe,
exchanging small talk with his working partner. My pulse began its telltale ac-
celeration. The minutes ticked on. I stared at the idle shopkeeper, hoping to
shame him into action, but he was impervious to my telepathic reproof and continued his small talk with his friend, brazenly insensitive to the nervous demands of six good men who were raring to ski.

Suddenly my New Year's Eve resolution struck me. It was now or never. 14
I broke from my place in line and marched to the counter. I was going to con-

trol myself. I dug my nails into my palms. My effort was only partially successful.

"If you are not too busy," I said icily, "would you mind handing me a 15 screwdriver?"

Work stopped and everyone turned his eyes on me, and I experienced that 16 mortification I always feel when I am the center of centripetal shafts of curiosity, resentment, perplexity.

But the worst was yet to come. "I am sorry, sir," said Jiggs deferentially, 17 moving the pipe from his mouth. "I am not supposed to move. I have just had a heart attack." That was the signal for a great whirring noise that descended from heaven. We looked, stricken, out the window, and it appeared as though a cyclone had suddenly focused on the snowy courtyard between the shop and the ski lift. Suddenly a gigantic army helicopter materialized, and hovered down to a landing. Two men jumped out of the plane carrying a stretcher, tore into the ski shop, and lifted the shopkeeper onto the stretcher. Jiggs bade his companion goodby, was whisked out the door, into the plane, up to the heavens, down—we learned—to a near-by army hospital. I looked up manfully—into a score of man-eating eyes. I put the experience down as a reversal.

As I write this, on an airplane, I have run out of paper and need to reach 18 into my briefcase under my legs for more. I cannot do this until my empty lunch tray is removed from my lap. I arrested the stewardess as she passed empty-handed down the aisle on the way to the kitchen to fetch the lunch trays for the passengers up forward who haven't been served yet. "Would you please take my tray?" "Just a *moment, sir!*" she said, and marched on sternly. Shall I tell her that since she is headed for the kitchen *anyway,* it could not delay the feeding of the other passengers by more than two seconds necessary to stash away my empty tray? Or remind her that not fifteen minutes ago she spoke unctuously into the loudspeaker the words undoubtedly devised by the airline's highly paid public relations counselor: "If there is anything I or Miss French can do for you to make your trip more enjoyable, *please* let us—" I have run out of paper.

I think the observable reluctance of the majority of Americans to assert 19 themselves in minor matters is related to our increased sense of helplessness in an age of technology and centralized political and economic power. For generations, Americans who were too hot, or too cold, got up and did something about it. Now we call the plumber, or the electrician, or the furnace man. The habit of looking after our own needs obviously had something to do with the assertiveness that characterized the American family familiar to readers of American literature. With the technification of life goes our direct responsibility for our material environment, and we are conditioned to adopt a position of helplessness not only as regards the broken air conditioner, but as regards the overheated train. It takes an expert to fix the former, but not the latter; yet these distinctions, as we withdraw into helplessness, tend to fade away.

Our notorious political apathy is a related phenomenon. Every year, 20 whether the Republican or the Democratic Party is in office, more and more power drains away from the individual to feed vast reservoirs in far-off places; and we have less and less say about the shape of events which shape our future. From this alienation of personal power comes the sense of resignation with which we accept the political dispensations of a powerful government whose hold upon us continues to increase.

An editor of a national weekly news magazine told me a few years ago 21 that as few as a dozen letters of protest against an editorial stance of his magazine was enough to convene a plenipotentiary meeting of the board of editors to review policy. "So few people complain, or make their voices heard," he explained to me, "that we assume a dozen letters represent the inarticulated views of thousands of readers." In the past ten years, he said, the volume of mail has noticeably decreased, even though the circulation of his magazine has risen.

When our voices are finally mute, when we have finally suppressed the 22 natural instinct to complain, whether the vexation is trivial or grave, we shall have become automatons, incapable of feeling. When Premier Khrushchev first came to this country late in 1959 he was primed, we are informed, to experience the bitter resentment of the American people against his tyranny, against his persecutions, against the movement which is responsible for the great number of American deaths in Korea, for billions in taxes every year, and for life everlasting on the brink of disaster; but Khrushchev was pleasantly surprised, and reported back to the Russian people that he had been met with overwhelming cordiality (read: apathy), except, to be sure, for "a few fascists who followed me around with their wretched posters, and should be horsewhipped."

I may be crazy, but I say there would have been lots more posters in a 23 society where train temperatures in the dead of winter are not allowed to climb to 85 degrees without complaint.

1961

QUESTIONS FOR DISCUSSION

Content

a. Relatively speaking, riding in an overheated railroad car and watching a film that is out of focus are minor "vexations." However, what disturbing tendency in the American people does our willingness to endure such discomfort illustrate? Why does Buckley describe that tendency as "something to keep one's eyes on" (paragraph 8)?

b. How would you paraphrase Buckley's thesis? What is his purpose in writing this essay?

c. What are some of the reasons Buckley cites to explain our reluctance to complain? Why, in paragraph 8, does he capitalize "Authority"?

d. What does he mean by "the technification of life" (paragraph 19)? Do you agree that we are being "conditioned to adopt a position of helplessness"? What, according to Buckley, "accounts for this conditioning"?

e. What is the point of paragraph 20? How does it relate to Buckley's discussion of overheated trains and surly airline stewardesses?

f. The author draws upon his own experiences and upon world events for examples. Which of these supports his thesis most effectively?

g. What important events is he alluding to in paragraph 22? What is the function of Buckley's inserting an editorial comment, "read: apathy," when he quotes Khrushchev? In what way does this paragraph serve to emphasize his thesis?

h. Reread paragraphs 9 and 12. How do they help develop the thesis? Why is there so much of Buckley himself in this essay?

i. What does the story of "Jiggs" tell us about Buckley's resolve "to speak out like a man"?

Strategy and Style

j. Is the author's tone at the end of this piece significantly different from what it was at the outset? In what way? Is such a shift important to Buckley's purpose? Why?

k. Can you find examples in this selection of the sarcasm and wit for which the author has become famous? At whom are they aimed? Are they used effectively and, if so, for what purposes?

l. "Why Don't We Complain?" was first published in *Esquire*. Have a look at a recent issue of this periodical. Are Buckley's content, tone, and vocabulary appropriate to the kind of audience that currently reads *Esquire?*

SUGGESTIONS FOR SHORT WRITING

a. Try rewriting paragraph 5 without using any personal narrative (for example, no "I," no dialogue, no storytelling). How does your version compare to Buckley's? What effect does each of the paragraphs create when you read it?

b. Take a paragraph or so of this essay and rewrite it as if it were a speech. How does the tone, structure, and word choice change in order to become spoken rather than written language?

SUGGESTIONS FOR SUSTAINED WRITING

a. Are we becoming a nation of people who are willing to suffer the intolerable rather than to stand up and fight for our rights? If you agree, write an essay in which you support Buckley's thesis with illustrations from your own experience.

b. Do you differ with Buckley on this point? If so, provide illustrations taken from your personal experiences or from events recently in the news that demonstrate our willingness to complain vigorously when conditions call for such action.

c. Is the rail system in this country still deteriorating as Buckley suggests in paragraph 4? What about airlines and bus companies? Are they serving the public as well as they should? Write a letter to the editor of your local newspaper in which you criticize or applaud a specific airline, railroad, or bus company. Look back upon recent trips you have taken on this carrier and recall as many convincing facts as you can to use as illustrations of the service you received.

Does America Still Exist?

Richard Rodriguez

The son of Mexican immigrants, Richard Rodriguez was born in San Francisco in 1944. He took a B.A. and an M.A. at Stanford University, and he completed a doctorate in English at the University of California at Berkeley. In 1982, Rodriguez published Hunger of Memory, *a collection of autobiographical essays in which he describes the challenges of growing up in an immigrant household and of enduring the process of assimilation that eventually led him into the American mainstream. Articles by Rodriguez appear regularly in* The American Scholar, Saturday Review, *and other widely read periodicals. "Does America Still Exist?" first appeared in* Harper's *magazine in 1984. In it Rodriguez explains, among other things, what it means "to perch on a hyphen between two countries."*

1   For the children of immigrant parents the knowledge comes easier. America exists everywhere in the city—on billboards, frankly in the smell of French fries and popcorn. It exists in the pace: traffic lights, the assertions of neon, the mysterious bong-bong-bong through the atriums of department stores. America exists as the voice of the crowd, a menacing sound—the high nasal accent of American English.

2   When I was a boy in Sacramento (California, the fifties), people would ask me, "Where you from?" I was born in this country, but I knew the question meant to decipher my darkness, my looks.

3   My mother once instructed me to say, "I am an American of American descent." By the time I was nine or ten, I wanted to say, but dared not reply, "I am an American."

4   Immigrants come to America and, against hostility or mere loneliness, they recreate a homeland in the parlor, tacking up postcards or calendars of some impossible blue—lake or sea or sky. Children of immigrant parents are supposed to perch on a hyphen between two countries. Relatives assume the achievement as much as anyone. Relatives are, in any case, surprised when the child begins losing old ways. One day at the family picnic the boy wanders away from their spiced food and faceless stories to watch other boys play baseball in the distance.

5   There is sorrow in the American memory, guilty sorrow for having left something behind—Portugal, China, Norway. The American story is the story of immigrant children and of their children—children no longer able to speak to grandparents. The memory of exile becomes inarticulate as it passes from generation to generation, along with wedding rings and pocket watches—like some mute stone in a wad of old lace. Europe. Asia. Eden.

6   But, it needs to be said, if this is a country where one stops being Vietnamese or Italian, this is a country where one begins to be an American. Amer-

306

ica exists as a culture and a grin, a faith and a shrug. It is clasped in a handshake, called by a first name.

As much as the country is joined in a common culture, however, Americans are reluctant to celebrate the process of assimilation. We pledge allegiance to diversity. America was born Protestant and bred Puritan, and the notion of community we share is derived from a seventeenth-century faith. Presidents and the pages of ninth-grade civics readers yet proclaim the orthodoxy: We are gathered together—but as individuals, with separate pasts, distinct destinies. Our society is as paradoxical as a Puritan congregation: We stand together, alone. 7

Americans have traditionally defined themselves by what they refused to include. As often, however, Americans have struggled, turned in good conscience at last to assert the great Protestant virtue of tolerance. Despite outbreaks of nativist frenzy, America has remained an immigrant country, open and true to itself. 8

Against pious emblems of rural America—soda fountain, Elks hall, Protestant church, and now shopping mall—stands the cold-hearted city, crowded with races and ambitions, curious laughter, much that is odd. Nevertheless, it is the city that has most truly represented America. In the city, however, the millions of singular lives have had no richer notion of wholeness to describe them than the idea of pluralism. 9

"Where you from?" the American asks the immigrant child. "Mexico," the boy learns to say. 10

Mexico, the country of my blood ancestors, offers formal contrast to the American achievement. If the United States was formed by Protestant individualism, Mexico was shaped by a medieval Catholic dream of one world. The Spanish journeyed to Mexico to plunder, and they may have gone, in God's name, with an arrogance peculiar to those who intend to convert. But through the conversion, the Indian converted the Spaniard. A new race was born, the *mestizo,* wedding European to Indian. José Vasconcelos, the Mexican philosopher, has celebrated this New World creation, proclaiming it the "cosmic race." 11

Centuries later, in a San Francisco restaurant, a Mexican-American lawyer of my acquaintance says, in English, over *salade niçoise,* that he does not intend to assimilate into gringo society. His claim is echoed by a chorus of others (Italian-Americans, Greeks, Asians) in this era of ethnic pride. The melting pot has been retired, clanking, into the museum of quaint disgrace, alongside Aunt Jemima and the Katzenjammer Kids. But resistance to assimilation is characteristically American. It only makes clear how inevitable the process of assimilation actually is. 12

For generations, this has been the pattern. Immigrant parents have sent their children to school (simply, they thought) to acquire the "skills" to survive in the city. The child returned home with a voice his parents barely recognized or understood, couldn't trust, and didn't like. 13

In Eastern cities—Philadelphia, New York, Boston, Baltimore—class af- 14 ter class gathered immigrant children to women (usually women) who stood in front of rooms full of children, changing children. So also for me in the 1950s. Irish-Catholic nuns. California. The old story. The hyphen tipped to the right, away from Mexico and toward a confusing but true American identity.

I speak now in the chromium American accent of my grammar school 15 classmates—Billy Reckers, Mike Bradley, Carol Schmidt, Kathy O'Grady....I believe I became like my classmates, became German, Polish, and (like my teachers) Irish. And because assimilation is always reciprocal, my classmates got something of me. (I mean sad eyes; belief in the Indian Virgin; a taste for sugar skulls on the Feast of the Dead.) In the blending, we became what our parents could never have been, and we carried America one revolution further.

"Does America still exist?" Americans have been asking the question for 16 so long that to ask it again only proves our continuous link. But perhaps the question deserves to be asked with urgency—now. Since the black civil rights movement of the 1960s, our tenuous notion of a shared public life has deteriorated notably.

The struggle of black men and women did not eradicate racism, but it be- 17 came the great moment in the life of America's conscience. Water hoses, bulldogs, blood—the images, rendered black, white, rectangular, passed into living rooms.

It is hard to look at a photograph of a crowd taken, say, in 1890 or in 18 1930 and not notice the absence of blacks. (It becomes an impertinence to wonder if America *still* exists.)

In the sixties, other groups of Americans learned to champion their rights 19 by analogy to the black civil rights movement. But the heroic vision faded. Dr. Martin Luther King Jr. had spoken with Pauline eloquence of a nation that would unite Christian and Jew, old and young, rich and poor. Within a decade, the struggles of the 1960s were reduced to a bureaucratic competition for little more than pieces of a representational pie. The quest for a portion of power became an end in itself. The metaphor for the American city of the 1970s was a committee: one black, one woman, one person under thirty....

If the small town had sinned against America by too neatly defining who 20 could be an American, the city's sin was a romantic secession. One noticed the romanticism in the antiwar movement—certain demonstrators who demonstrated a lack of tact or desire to persuade and seemed content to play secular protestants. One noticed the romanticism in the competition among members of "minority groups" to claim the status of Primary Victim. To Americans unconfident of their common identity, minority standing became a way of asserting individuality. Middle-class Americans—men and women clearly not the primary victims of social oppression—brandished their suffering with exuberance.

The dream of a single society probably died with *The Ed Sullivan Show.* 21 The reality of America persists. Teenagers pass through big-city high schools banded in racial groups, their collars turned up to a uniform shrug. But then they graduate to jobs at the phone company or in banks, where they end up working alongside people unlike themselves. Typists and tellers walk out together at lunchtime.

It is easier for us as Americans to believe the obvious fact of our sepa- 22 rateness—easier to imagine the black and white Americas prophesied by the Kerner report (broken glass, street fires)—than to recognize the reality of a city street at lunchtime. Americans are wedded by proximity to a common culture. The panhandler at one corner is related to the pamphleteer at the next who is related to the banker who is kin to the Chinese old man wearing an MIT sweatshirt. In any true national history, Thomas Jefferson begets Martin Luther King Jr. who begets the Gray Panthers. It is because we lack a vision of ourselves entire—the city street is crowded and we are each preoccupied with finding our own way home—that we lack an appropriate hymn.

Under my window now passes a little white girl softly rehearsing to her- 23 self a Motown obbligato.

1984

QUESTIONS FOR DISCUSSION

Content

a. How would you define the term "pluralism"? Why is it so important to Rodriguez's thesis?

b. What is Rodriguez's point in telling us that the United States "was formed by Protestant individualism" while Mexico "was shaped by a medieval Catholic dream of one world"? In what way does his discussion of the *mestizo* and Aunt Jemima support this idea?

c. In paragraph 21, Rodriguez tells us that "the reality of America persists." What illustrations does he use to describe that reality, and how does he distinguish it from the "dream of a single society [that] probably died with *The Ed Sullivan Show*"?

d. Was America "born Protestant and bred Puritan"? Explain the significance of this statement.

e. Explain the "orthodoxy" that "Presidents and...ninth-grade civics readers yet proclaim." Who are the "we" Rodriguez refers to in paragraph 7, and how can "we" possibly "stand together, alone"?

f. How does the author's vision of "the city" in paragraph 9 differ from the "metaphor for the American city of the 1970s" that he explains in paragraph 19? Does that contrast help illustrate his concept of American pluralism?

g. Explain what Rodriguez means by assimilation. How does he illustrate the fact that this is a "reciprocal" process, and why is this concept so important to our understanding of the essay?

h. Why does Rodriguez term the civil rights movement of the 1960s "the great moment in the life of America's conscience" (paragraph 17)? Explain what his discussion of this development and of Dr. Martin Luther King, Jr., contribute to the essay.

i. In what ways do paragraphs 13, 14, and 15 help illustrate the statement that "children of immigrant parents are supposed to perch on a hyphen between two countries"?

j. What does Rodriguez say is the essential difference between Mexican and American identities?

Strategy and Style

k. How does paragraph 10 function in the overall structure of the essay? What effect did it have on you when you first read it?

l. What image of America does Rodriguez project in this essay? How does his choice of words create that image?

m. What do you make of the curious term, "Motown obbligato," with which Rodriguez closes? Is it important to understanding his essay?

n. What, if anything, is ironic about the author's Mexican-American friend eating *salade niçoise* and claiming that he will never "assimilate into gringo society"?

SUGGESTIONS FOR SHORT WRITING

a. What things, for Rodriguez, represent American culture? Make a list and write about how they represent American culture.

b. Write a short description of your family's culture. Base your description on particular objects or behaviors that you think represent your family culture.

SUGGESTIONS FOR SUSTAINED WRITING

a. Rodriguez provides several good illustrations to prove that cultural assimilation is, in fact, reciprocal in nature. Can you provide additional examples? Explain how the assimilation of a specific ethnic group into mainstream American culture has affected your community, your college, or you personally.

b. Is there a "sorrow in the American memory…for having left something behind" as the author claims in paragraph 5? Reflect a bit on your own ethnic heritage. What about it seems most valuable to you? In what ways has it determined the kind of person you've become? Using illustration as your primary method of development, explain the effects your cultural inheritance has had upon you.

I Remember...

Joyce Maynard

Joyce Maynard (b. 1953) made her debut as a professional writer when The New York Times *Sunday magazine published "An Eighteen-Year-Old Looks Back at Life." In 1973, Maynard expanded this attack on television and the materialism it promotes in* Looking Back: A Chronicle of Growing-Up in the Sixties. Baby Love, *a novel about teenage motherhood, appeared in 1981. Her recent works include* Camp-Out *(1985), a children's book; and* Domestic Affairs *(1987), a nonfiction work about motherhood. "I Remember..." written for* TV Guide, *is typical of Maynard's ability to create irony that is both hilarious and frightening. Like her other works, it attempts to define the seductiveness with which the media draw us away from the search for meaning and substance in our lives.*

We got our TV set in 1959, when I was 5. So I can barely remember life 1
without television. I have spent 20,000 hours of my life in front of the set. Not
all of my contemporaries watched so much, but many did, and what's more, we
watched the same programs, heard the same commercials, were exposed to the
same end-of-show lessons. So there is, among this generation of television children, a shared history, a tremendous fund of common experience. These massive doses of TV have not affected all of us in an identical way, and it would be
risky to draw broad conclusions. But if a sociologist were—rashly—to try to
uncover some single most important influence on this generation, which has
produced Patty Hearst and Alice Cooper and the Jesus movement and the peace
movement; if he were searching for the roots of 1960s psychedelia and 1970s
apathy, he would do well to look first at television.

My own motives are less ambitious. I know, simply, that a rerun of *I Love* 2
Lucy or *Father Knows Best,* the theme music from *Dr. Kildare* or the sad, whistling refrain from *Lassie* can make me stand, frozen, before the set. It is as if I,
and not Timmy Martin, had been stuck in an abandoned mine shaft during a
thunderstorm, as if I, and not Lucy Ricardo, had dropped a diamond ring somewhere in the batter of a seven-layer cake. I didn't so much *watch* those shows
when I was little; I let them wash over me. Now I study them like a psychiatrist
on his own couch, looking hungrily for some clue inside the TV set to explain
the person I have become.

I was not a dull or energyless child, or neglected by my parents. Our 3
house was full of books and paints, and sometimes I did choose to draw or ride
my bike. But the picture of my childhood that comes to mind is one of a dimly
lit room in a small New Hampshire town and a girl listening, leaden-eyed, to
some talk-show rendition of "I Left My Heart in San Francisco." It is a picture
of myself at age 8, wise to the ways of "Vegas," the timing of standup comics,
the marriages of Zsa Zsa Gabor, the advertising slogans of Bufferin and Fab.

311

And what did all this television watching teach me? Well, I rarely swallowed the little pellets of end-of-show morals presented in the television shows I watched (that crime does not pay, that one must always obey one's parents). But I observed something of the way the world works: that life is easier if one fits in with the established conventions; that everything is easier if one has a pretty face.

And in the process of acquiring those melancholy truths I picked up an embarrassingly large fund of knowledge that is totally unusable (except, perhaps, ironically, on some television game show). I can hum Perry Mason's theme song or give the name of the actress who played Donna Reed's best friend. I would happily trade that knowledge for the facility with piano or ballet I might have had if I'd spent those television hours practicing music and dance instead. But something else I gained from television should be less lightly dismissed. I guess it is a sense of knowing America, not simply its vulgarities but its strengths as well: the rubber face of Lucille Ball, the lovableness of Americans on *Candid Camera,* an athlete's slow-motion grace in an instant replay on *Monday Night Football.*

So many hours of television I watched—hundreds of bank robberies, touch-and-go operations and barroom fights, millions of dollars' worth of refrigerators awarded to thousands of housewives who kissed dozens of game-show moderators—and yet the list of individual programs I remember is very short. One is the Beatles' appearance, the winter I was 10, on *The Ed Sullivan Show.* I remember the on-camera shooting of Lee Oswald, and the face of Jacqueline Kennedy at her husband's funeral. A few particularly marvelous episodes of the old *Dick Van Dyke Show* stand out: Laura Petrie getting her toe stuck in the bathroom faucet; Rob imagining that he's going bald. One or two *I Love Lucy, Andy Griffith* shows, a Miss America contestant who sang a number from "The Sound of Music"—dressed like a nun—and then whipped off her habit to reveal a spangled bathing suit. I remember a special five-part *Dr. Kildare* segment in which a team of doctors had to choose five patients for a life-saving kidney machine out of eight candidates. I remember getting up at midnight to watch Neil Armstrong land on the moon—expecting to be awed, but falling asleep instead.

My strongest memories are of one series and one character. Not the best, but the one that formed me more than any other, that haunts me still, and left its mark on a good-sized part of a generation: *Leave It to Beaver.* I watched that show every day after school (fresh from my own failures) and studied it, like homework, because the Cleaver family was so steady and normal—and my own was not—and because the boys had so many friends, played basketball, drank sodas, *fit in.* Watching that series and other family situation comedies was almost like taking a course in how to be an American.

I loved my father, but I longed secretly for a "Dad" like Ward Cleaver, who puttered in a work shed, building bookcases and oiling hinges, one who spent his Saturday afternoons playing golf or mowing the lawn or dipping his finger into cake batter whipped up by a mother in a frilly apron who spent her time going to PTA meetings and playing bridge with "the girls." Wally Cleaver, the older brother, was one of those boys destined to be captain of every team he plays on. But Beaver had his problems—often he was uncoordinated, gullible, less than perfectly honest, tricked by his older brother's friends, made fun of. He lost library books and haircut money. Once he sent away for a "free" accordion and suddenly found himself wildly in debt. Of course he got caught—he always did. I remember him so clearly, as familiar to me as a brother.

Occasionally I go to college campuses. Some student in the audience always mentions Beaver Cleaver, and when the name is spoken, a satisfied murmur can be heard in the crowd. Somebody—a stranger, in his 20s now—wrote to say he watches *Beaver* reruns every morning. He just wanted to share memories of the show with me and recall favorite episodes. We were not readers, after all, this stranger and I. We have no great literary tradition behind us. Our heritage is television. Wally and Beaver Cleaver were our Tom Sawyer and Huck Finn. **9**

There's something terribly sad about this need to reminisce, and the lack of real stories, true experiences, to reminisce about. Partly it is that we grew up in the '60s, when life was soft, and partly that we grew up with television, which made life softer. We had Vietnam, of course, and civil-rights battles, and a brief threat of nuclear attack that led neighbors, down the block, to talk of building a fallout shelter. But I remember the large events, like the Kennedy and King assassinations, the space launches and the war, as I experienced them through television. I watched it all from a goose-down-filled easy chair with a plate of oatmeal cookies on my lap—on television. **10**

We grew up to be observers, not participants, to respond to action, not initiate it. And I think finally, it was this lack of real hardship (when we lacked for nothing else) that was our greatest hardship and that led so many among this television generation to seek out some kind of artificial pain. Some of us, for a time at least, gave up matching skirt-and-sweater sets for saffron-colored Hare Krishna robes; some gave up parents and clean-cut fiances for the romance of poverty and the excitement of crime. Rebellion like that is not so much inspired by television violence as it is brought about by television banality: it is a response not to *The Man from U.N.C.L.E.* but to *Father Knows Best*. One hears it said that hatred of an idea is closer to love than to indifference. Large and angry rejections of the bourgeois, the conventional—the Beaver Cleaver life—aren't so surprising, coming from a generation that grew up admiring those things so much. **11**

Television smartened us up, expanded our minds, and then proceeded to fill them with the only kinds of knowledge it had to offer: names of Las Vegas nightclubs, brands of detergent, players of bit parts. And knowledge—accurate or not—about life: marriage as we learned about it from Ozzie and Harriet. Justice as practiced by Matt Dillon. Politics as revealed to us on the 6 o'clock news. **12**

Anguished, frustrated and enraged by a decade of war in Vietnam as we   13
saw it on the news, we became part of the news ourselves—with peace
marches, rallies in the streets. But only briefly; we were easily discouraged,
quick to abandon hope for change and to lose interest. That, also, comes from a
television-watching childhood, I think: a short attention span, and a limpness,
an inertia, acquired from too many hours spent in the easy chair, never getting
up except to change the channels.

1975

QUESTIONS FOR DISCUSSION

Content

a. Why does Maynard remember the Cleavers so vividly? What was so attractive about Ward Cleaver, and why does she remain so fond of the Beaver?
b. Maynard makes a number of curious statements in this selection. What does
   she mean by each of the following:

   · "Wally and Beaver Cleaver were our Tom Sawyer and Huck Finn."
   · "…it was this lack of real hardship (when we lacked for nothing else)
     that was our greatest hardship…."
   · "…hatred of an idea is closer to love than to indifference."
   · "Some [of us] gave up…clean-cut fiances for the romance of poverty
     and the excitement of crime."

c. What are some of the illustrations or examples that you find most vivid and
   effective? What can you infer about *I Love Lucy* and *Lassie* from the illustrations Maynard uses to discuss these shows in paragraph 2?
d. What does Maynard set out to do in her introduction? Who are Patty Hearst
   and Alice Cooper? How would you define "1960s psychedelia"?
e. What regrets does Maynard have about spending so much time in front of
   the television?
f. Did TV-watching teach Maynard anything worth learning?
g. What ironic relationship does Maynard draw between these shows and
   TV coverage of events such as the Vietnam War and the Kennedy assassination?
h. Do you find anything ironic about Maynard's pairing of Neil Armstrong's
   landing on the moon with shows like *Dr. Kildare* and with that bizarre episode from a Miss America pageant? What does her falling asleep while
   watching the NASA mission say about the effects of TV?
i. Why is it important for Maynard to reveal her age at various points in this

essay? How does doing so help her organize her ideas? In what ways does this information help us appreciate the role television played in her childhood and adolescence?

Strategy and Style

j. What is the effect of Maynard's informal style—for example, her frequent use of dashes and colons, sentence fragments, and sentences that begin with "so," "but," and "and"? Do you think this informal style is the result of watching so much television?

k. Why might Maynard have used the term "little pellets" to describe the "end-of-show morals presented in the television shows" (paragraph 4)? Did she learn anything of importance from these little pellets?

l. How would you describe Maynard's tone? Is she being too hard on herself and her generation? Why does she tell us that she watched political assassinations, civil-rights battles, and the war in Vietnam "from a goose-down-filled easy chair..." (paragraph 10)?

SUGGESTIONS FOR SHORT WRITING

a. Do the author's childhood television experiences match those of your childhood? Describe their similarities or differences.

b. Make a list of all your favorite television shows from your childhood. Then, next to the list, write one thing you learned about life from each show.

SUGGESTIONS FOR SUSTAINED WRITING

a. Reruns of many of the shows Maynard discusses in this selection appear regularly on local TV channels. If you've seen any of them recently, write an essay in which you define and evaluate their portrayal of the American way of life.

b. Analyze an episode of your favorite current TV show. What does it say about the concerns and values of today's typical viewing audience? Express your views in the form of a letter to the entertainment editor of your favorite magazine or newspaper; don't be afraid to mail it to him/her for inclusion in a forthcoming issue.

c. Do you disagree with the author's assessment that we are becoming a nation of watchers and not "doers"? Address a rebuttal directly to Maynard. Point out that many members of your generation will have no need to "reminisce" over TV experiences because they are creating experiences of their own.

A Few Kind Words for Superstition

Robertson Davies

One of Canada's best-known satirists, novelists, and playwrights, Robertson Davies (b. 1913) was educated at Upper Canada College in Toronto, at Queen's University in Kingston, and at Oxford University in England. He began his career as a London actor and then worked as an editor for Saturday Night *in Toronto and for the* Examiner *in Petersborough, Ontario. He has taught English at the University of Toronto and at Massey College, and has served as Governor of the Stratford Shakespearean Festival in Stratford, Ontario. He is a fellow of the Royal Society of Canada and is a recipient of the Stephen Leacock Medal for Humor. Davies has published numerous plays and critical studies on drama and stagecraft, and he is known throughout Canada for the delightful satires he has written under the colorful pseudonym "Samuel Marchbanks." However, his reputation rests chiefly on his novels. The Salterton trilogy, which includes* Tempest-Tost *(1951),* Leaven of Malice *(1954), and* A Mixture of Frailties *(1958), is a study of a fictional university town in Canada and of its middle-class inhabitants. The Deptford Trilogy, which is made up of* Fifth Business *(1970),* The Manticore *(1972), and* World of Wonders *(1976), affirms the important part that the irrational plays in an individual's search for spiritual identity. Davies' most recent books are* What's Bred in the Bone *(1985),* The Papers of Samuel Marchbanks *(1986), and* The Lyre of Orpheus *(1989).*

1   In grave discussions of "the renaissance of the irrational" in our time, superstition does not figure largely as a serious challenge to reason or science. Parapsychology, UFO's, miracle cures, transcendental meditation and all the paths to instant enlightenment are condemned, but superstition is merely deplored. Is it because it has an unacknowledged hold on so many of us?

2   Few people will admit to being superstitious; it implies naïveté or ignorance. But I live in the middle of a large university, and I see superstition in its four manifestations, alive and flourishing among people who are indisputably rational and learned.

3   You did not know that superstition takes four forms? Theologians assure us that it does. First is what they call Vain Observances, such as not walking under a ladder, and that kind of thing. Yet I saw a deeply learned professor of anthropology, who had spilled some salt, throwing a pinch of it over his left shoulder; when I asked him why, he replied, with a wink, that it was "to hit the Devil in the eye." I did not question him further about his belief in the Devil: but I noticed that he did not smile until I asked him what he was doing.

4   The second form is Divination, or consulting oracles. Another learned professor I know, who would scorn to settle a problem by tossing a coin (which is a humble appeal to Fate to declare itself), told me quite seriously that he had resolved a matter related to university affairs by consulting the *I Ching.* And

why not? There are thousands of people on this continent who appeal to the *I Ching,* and their general level of education seems to absolve them of superstition. Almost, but not quite. The *I Ching,* to the embarrassment of rationalists, often gives excellent advice.

The third form is Idolatry, and universities can show plenty of that. If you 5 have ever supervised a large examination room, you know how many jujus, lucky coins and other bringers of luck are placed on the desks of the candidates. Modest idolatry, but what else can you call it?

The fourth form is Improper Worship of the True God. A while ago, I 6 learned that every day, for several days, a $2 bill (in Canada we have $2 bills, regarded by some people as unlucky) had been tucked under a candlestick on the altar of a college chapel. Investigation revealed that an engineering student, worried about a girl, thought that bribery of the Deity might help. When I talked with him, he did not think he was pricing God cheap, because he could afford no more. A reasonable argument, but perhaps God was proud that week, for the scientific oracle went against him.

Superstition seems to run, a submerged river of crude religion, below the 7 surface of human consciousness. It has done so for as long as we have any chronicle of human behavior, and although I cannot prove it, I doubt if it is more prevalent today than it has always been. Superstition, the theologians tell us, comes from the Latin *supersisto,* meaning to stand in terror of the Deity. Most people keep their terror within bounds, but they cannot root it out, nor do they seem to want to do so.

The more the teaching of formal religion declines, or takes a sociological 8 form, the less God appears to great numbers of people as a God of Love, resuming his older form of a watchful, minatory power, to be placated and cajoled. Superstition makes its appearance, apparently unbidden, very early in life, when children fear that stepping on cracks in the sidewalk will bring ill fortune. It may persist even among the greatly learned and devout, as in the case of Dr. Samuel Johnson, who felt it necessary to touch posts that he passed in the street. The psychoanalysts have their explanation, but calling a superstition a compulsion neurosis does not banish it.

Many superstitions are so widespread and so old that they must have 9 risen from a depth of the human mind that is indifferent to race or creed. Orthodox Jews place a charm on their doorposts; so do (or did) the Chinese. Some peoples of Middle Europe believe that when a man sneezes, his soul, for that moment, is absent from his body, and they hasten to bless him, lest the soul be seized by the Devil. How did the Melanesians come by the same idea? Superstition seems to have a link with some body of belief that far antedates the religions we know—religions which have no place for such comforting little ceremonies and charities.

People who like disagreeable historical comparisons recall that when 10 Rome was in decline, superstition proliferated wildly, and that something of the same sort is happening in our Western world today. They point to the popularity of astrology, and it is true that sober newspapers that would scorn to deal in love philters carry astrology columns and the fashion magazines count them among their most popular features. But when has astrology not been popular? No use saying science discredits it. When has the heart of man given a damn for science?

Superstition in general is linked to man's yearning to know his fate, and   11
to have some hand in deciding it. When my mother was a child, she innocently joined her Roman Catholic friends in killing spiders on July 11, until she learned that this was done to ensure heavy rain the day following, the anniversary of the Battle of Boyne, when the Orangemen would hold their parade. I knew an Italian, a good scientist, who watched every morning before leaving his house, so that the first person he met would not be a priest or a nun, as this would certainly bring bad luck.

I am not one to stand aloof from the rest of humanity in this matter, for   12
when I was a university student, a gypsy woman with a child in her arms used to appear every year at examination time, and ask a shilling of anyone who touched the Lucky Baby; that swarthy infant cost me four shillings altogether, and I never failed an examination. Of course, I did it merely for the joke—or so I thought then. Now, I am humbler.

1978

QUESTIONS FOR DISCUSSION

Content

a. What is Davies' thesis? Which paragraphs supply examples supporting this thesis?
b. Davies asserts in paragraph 11 that "superstition in general is linked to man's yearning to know his fate, and to have some hand in deciding it." Do you agree with this assertion? Is this a generalization?
c. What examples of superstitions does Davies include? What were his probable reasons for including them?
d. Are the examples of superstitions used as persuasive devices? If so, of what are the readers being persuaded?
e. To what does the phrase "'the renaissance of the irrational'" in the first sentence refer? What examples does Davies use? What examples can you add to the list?
f. What is Davies' answer to the last question in the first paragraph? How do you know? Why might Davies have used a question rather than a statement?
g. What are the four kinds of superstition? Do you agree with Davies that these types of superstition are still prevalent today?
h. Do you believe in any of the superstitions that Davies describes? Do you

know of people who do? How do you account for belief in superstitions?

i. In the last paragraph Davies admits that what he did jokingly as a college student to ensure passing his examinations was actually done in earnest. Have you had any similar experiences?

j. According to Davies, what is the relationship between superstition and religion? Between superstition and science? Between superstition and history?

Strategy and Style

k. Why might Davies have first listed the four forms of superstitions and then gone on to a discussion of superstition in general? How do the four forms of superstitions establish expectations for the rest of the essay?

l. The author traces the word "superstition" to its Latin origin, "supersisto" (paragraph 7). Look up the origin of the words "divination," "idolatry," or any of the superstitions his lists. How do the origins of these words and superstitions help to illustrate his thesis?

m. What is Davies' attitude toward superstition? How is his attitude revealed through the tone of the piece?

SUGGESTIONS FOR SHORT WRITING

a. Describe the superstitions you or someone you know adheres to. Into which of Davies' categories do they fall?

b. Are the several questions Davies asks merely rhetorical? Try writing an answer to one or more of them.

SUGGESTIONS FOR SUSTAINED WRITING

a. Trace a popular superstition to its origins and write an essay explaining the relationship of the current superstition to its earlier forms. Try to account for the perseverance of the superstition.

b. Interview friends and fellow students, asking them what superstitions they have and how strongly they believe in them. Using these examples as the raw material for your essay, analyze these superstitions, putting forth your theory of why people believe in them.

c. Write a few *un*kind words for superstition. In what ways does belief in superstition harm society? Why should people try to divest themselves of superstitious beliefs?

Were Dinosaurs Dumb?

Stephen Jay Gould

Since 1967, Stephen Jay Gould (b. 1941) has served on the faculty of Harvard University, where he teaches biology, geology, and the history of science. A native of New York City, he attended Antioch College and earned his Ph.D. at Columbia University. Gould is a prolific writer; he has published a monthly column in Natural History *magazine for over a decade and has contributed more than one hundred scholarly articles to important scientific journals across the United States. Among his full-length works are four collections of essays first published in* Natural History: Ever Since Darwin *(1978),* The Panda's Thumb *(1980),* Hens' Teeth and Horses' Toes *(1983), and* The Flamingo's Smile *(1985). He also wrote* The Mismeasure of Man *(1981), in which he argues against the theory of biological determinism and discusses science's attempts to measure human intelligence. His most recent book is* Time's Arrow, Time's Cycle: Myth and Metaphor in the Discovery of Geological Time *(1987). "Were Dinosaurs Dumb?" which first appeared in* Natural History, *is typical of Gould's style and approach when addressing the lay reader. Like Rettie, Thomas, and Asimov, he makes scientific fact and theory both appetizing and accessible even to readers with no special training.*

1   When Muhammad Ali flunked his army intelligence test, he quipped (with a wit that belied his performance on the exam): "I only said I was the greatest; I never said I was the smartest." In our metaphors and fairy tales, size and power are almost always balanced by a want of intelligence. Cunning is the refuge of the little guy. Think of Br'er Rabbit and Br'er Bear; David smiting Goliath with a slingshot; Jack chopping down the beanstalk. Slow wit is the tragic flaw of a giant.

2   The discovery of dinosaurs in the nineteenth century provided, or so it appeared, a quintessential case for the negative correlation of size and smarts. With their pea brains and giant bodies, dinosaurs became a symbol of lumbering stupidity. Their extinction seemed only to confirm their flawed design.

3   Dinosaurs were not even granted the usual solace of a giant—great physical prowess. God maintained a discreet silence about the brains of behemoth, but he certainly marveled at its strength: "Lo, now, his strength is in his loins, and his force is in the navel of his belly. He moveth his tail like a cedar....His bones are as strong pieces of brass; his bones are like bars of iron [Job 40:16-18]." Dinosaurs, on the other hand, have usually been reconstructed as slow and clumsy. In the standard illustration, *Brontosaurus* wades in a murky pond because he cannot hold up his own weight on land.

4   Popularizations for grade school curricula provide a good illustration of prevailing orthodoxy. I still have my third grade copy (1948 edition) of Bertha

320

Morris Parker's *Animals of Yesterday,* stolen, I am forced to suppose, from P.S. 26, Queens (sorry Mrs. McInerney). In it, boy (teleported back to the Jurassic) meets brontosaur:

> It is huge, and you can tell from the size of its head that it must be stu-pid....This giant animal moves about very slowly as it eats. No wonder it moves slowly! Its huge feet are very heavy, and its great tail is not easy to pull around. You are not surprised that the thunder lizard likes to stay in the water so that the water will help it hold up its huge body....Giant dinosaurs were once the lords of the earth. Why did they disappear? You can probably guess part of the answer—their bodies were too large for their brains. If their bodies had been smaller, and their brains larger, they might have lived on.

Dinosaurs have been making a strong comeback of late, in this age of "I'm OK, you're OK." Most paleontologists are now willing to view them as energetic, active, and capable animals. The *Brontosaurus* that wallowed in its pond a generation ago is now running on land, while pairs of males have been seen twining their necks about each other in elaborate sexual combat for access to females (much like the neck wrestling of giraffes). Modern anatomical re-constructions indicate strength and agility, and many paleontologists now be-lieve that dinosaurs were warmblooded.... **5**

The idea of warmblooded dinosaurs has captured the public imagination and received a torrent of press coverage. Yet another vindication of dinosaurian capability has received very little attention, although I regard it as equally sig-nificant. I refer to the issue of stupidity and its correlation with size. The revi-sionist interpretation, which I support in this column, does not enshrine dino-saurs as paragons of intellect, but it does maintain that they were not small brained after all. They had the "right-sized" brains for reptiles of their body size. **6**

I don't wish to deny that the flattened, minuscule head of large-bodied *Stegosaurus* houses little brain from our subjective, top-heavy perspective, but I do wish to assert that we should not expect more of the beast. First of all, large animals have relatively smaller brains than related, small animals. The correla-tion of brain size with body size among kindred animals (all reptiles, all mam-mals, for example) is remarkably regular. As we move from small to large ani-mals, from mice to elephants or small lizards to Komodo dragons, brain size increases, but not so fast as body size. In other words, bodies grow faster than brains, and large animals have low ratios of brain weight to body weight. In fact, brains grow only about two-thirds as fast as bodies. Since we have no rea-son to believe that large animals are consistently stupider than their smaller rela-tives, we must conclude that large animals require relatively less brain to do as well as smaller animals. If we do not recognize this relationship, we are likely to underestimate the mental power of very large animals, dinosaurs in particular. **7**

Second, the relationship between brain and body size is not identical in all groups of vertebrates. All share the same rate of relative decrease in brain **8**

size, but small mammals have much larger brains than small reptiles of the same
body weight. This discrepancy is maintained at all larger body weights, since brain
size increases at the same rate in both groups—two-thirds as fast as body size.

Put these two facts together—all large animals have relatively small 9
brains, and reptiles have much smaller brains than mammals at any common
body weight—and what should we expect from a normal, large reptile? The answer, of course, is a brain of very modest size. No living reptile even approaches a middle-sized dinosaur in bulk, so we have no modern standard to
serve as a model for dinosaurs.

Fortunately, our imperfect fossil record has, for once, not severely disap- 10
pointed us in providing data about fossil brains. Superbly preserved skulls have
been found for many species of dinosaurs, and cranial capacities can be measured. (Since brains do not fill craniums in reptiles, some creative, although not
unreasonable, manipulation must be applied to estimate brain size from the hole
within a skull.) With these data, we have a clear test for the conventional hy-
pothesis of dinosaurian stupidity. We should agree, at the outset, that a reptilian
standard is the only proper one—it is surely irrelevant that dinosaurs had
smaller brains than people or whales. We have abundant data on the relationship of brain and body size in modern reptiles. Since we know that brains increase two-thirds as fast as bodies as we move from small to large living species, we can extrapolate this rate to dinosaurian sizes and ask whether dinosaur
brains match what we would expect of living reptiles if they grew so large.

Harry Jerison studied the brain sizes of ten dinosaurs and found that they 11
fell right on the extrapolated reptilian curve. Dinosaurs did not have small
brains; they maintained just the right-sized brains for reptiles of their dimensions. So much for Ms. Parker's explanation of their demise.

Jerison made no attempt to distinguish among various kinds of dinosaurs; 12
ten species distributed over six major groups scarcely provide a proper basis for
comparison. Recently, James A. Hopson of the University of Chicago gathered
more data and made a remarkable and satisfying discovery.

Hopson needed a common scale for all dinosaurs. He therefore compared 13
each dinosaur brain with the average reptilian brain we would expect at its
body weight. If the dinosaur falls on the standard reptilian curve, its brain receives a value of 1.0 (called an encephalization quotient, or EQ—the ratio of
actual brain to expected brain for a standard reptile of the same body weight).
Dinosaurs lying above the curve (more brain than expected in a standard reptile
of the same body weight) receive values in excess of 1.0, while those below the
curve measure less than 1.0.

Hopson found that the major groups of dinosaurs can be ranked by in- 14
creasing values of average EQ. This ranking corresponds perfectly with inferred
speed, agility and behavioral complexity in feeding (or avoiding the prospect of
becoming a meal). The giant sauropods, *Brontosaurus* and its allies, have the
lowest EQ's—0.20 to 0.35. They must have moved fairly slowly and without
great maneuverability. They probably escaped predation by virtue of their bulk

alone, much as elephants do today. The armored ankylosaurs and stegosaurs come next with EQ's of 0.52 to 0.56. These animals, with their heavy armor, probably relied largely upon passive defense, but the clubbed tail of ankylosaurs and the spiked tail of stegosaurs imply some active fighting and increased behavioral complexity.

The ceratopsians rank next at about 0.7 to 0.9. Hopson remarks: "The 15 larger ceratopsians, with their great horned heads, relied on active defensive strategies and presumably required somewhat greater agility than the tail-weaponed forms, both in fending off predators and in intraspecific combat bouts. The smaller ceratopsians, lacking true horns, would have relied on sensory acuity and speed to escape from predators." The ornithopods (duckbills and their allies) were the brainiest herbivores, with EQ's from 0.85 to 1.5. They relied upon "acute senses and relatively fast speeds" to elude carnivores. Flight seems to require more acuity and agility than standing defense. Among ceratopsians, small, hornless, and presumably fleeing *Protoceratops* had a higher EQ than great three-horned *Triceratops.*

Carnivores have higher EQ's than herbivores, as in modern vertebrates. 16 Catching a rapidly moving or stoutly fighting prey demands a good deal more upstairs than plucking the right kind of plant. The giant theropods (*Tyrannosaurus* and its allies) vary from 1.0 to nearly 2.0. Atop the heap, quite appropriately at its small size, rests the little coelurosaur *Stenonychosaurus* with an EQ well above 5.0. Its actively moving quarry, small mammals and birds perhaps, probably posed a greater challenge in discovery and capture than *Triceratops* afforded *Tyrannosaurus.*

I do not wish to make a naive claim that brain size equals intelligence or, 17 in this case, behavioral range and agility (I don't know what intelligence means in humans, much less in a group of extinct reptiles). Variation in brain size within a species has precious little to do with brain power (humans do equally well with 900 or 2,500 cubic centimeters of brain). But comparison across species, when the differences are large, seems reasonable. I do not regard it as irrelevant to our achievements that we so greatly exceed koala bears—much as I love them—in EQ. The sensible ordering among dinosaurs also indicates that even so coarse a measure as brain size counts for something.

If behavioral complexity is one consequence of mental power, then we 18 might expect to uncover among dinosaurs some signs of social behavior that demand coordination, cohesiveness, and recognition. Indeed we do, and it cannot be accidental that these signs were overlooked when dinosaurs labored under the burden of a falsely imposed obtuseness. Multiple trackways have been uncovered, with evidence for more than twenty animals traveling together in parallel movement. Did some dinosaurs live in herds? At the Davenport Ranch sauropod trackway, small footprints lie in the center and larger ones at the periphery. Could it be that some dinosaurs traveled much as some advanced herbivorous mammals do today, with large adults at the borders sheltering juveniles in the center?

In addition, the very structures that seemed most bizarre and useless to **19**
older paleontologists—the elaborate crests of hadrosaurs, the frills and horns of
ceratopsians, and the nine inches of solid bone above the brain of *Pachyceph-
alosaurus*—now appear to gain a coordinated explanation as devices for sexual
display and combat. Pachycephalosaurs may have engaged in head-butting con-
tests much as mountain sheep do today. The crests of some hadrosaurs are well
designed as resonating chambers; did they engage in bellowing matches? The
ceratopsian horn and frill may have acted as sword and shield in the battle for
mates. Since such behavior is not only intrinsically complex, but also implies
an elaborate social system, we would scarcely expect to find it in a group of
animals barely muddling through at a moronic level.

But the best illustration of dinosaurian capability may well be the fact **20**
most often cited against them—their demise. Extinction, for most people, carries many of the connotations attributed to sex not so long ago—a rather disreputable business, frequent in occurrence, but not to anyone's credit, and certainly not to be discussed in proper circles. But, like sex, extinction is an ineluctable part of life. It is the ultimate fate of all species, not the lot of unfortunate and ill-designed creatures. It is no sign of failure.

The remarkable thing about dinosaurs is not that they became extinct, but **21**
that they dominated the earth for so long. Dinosaurs held sway for 100 million
years while mammals, all the while, lived as small animals in the interstices of
their world. After 70 million years on top, we mammals have an excellent track
record and good prospects for the future, but we have yet to display the staying
power of dinosaurs.

People, on this criterion, are scarcely worth mentioning—5 million years **22**
perhaps since *Australopithecus,* a mere 50,000 for our own species, *Homo sapiens.* Try the ultimate test within our system of values: Do you know anyone
who would wager a substantial sum, even at favorable odds, on the proposition
that *Homo sapiens* will last longer than *Brontosaurus?*

1980

QUESTIONS FOR DISCUSSION

Content

a. On what basis does Gould conclude that "large animals require relatively
   less brain to do as well as small animals" (paragraph 7)? Why is this statement central to the argument that dinosaurs were not "dumb"?
b. Summarize other evidence that Gould has collected to prove that these extinct reptiles were more intelligent than scientists once believed.
c. How does the author account for the extinction of dinosaurs? In what way
   does this explanation relate to his thesis?
d. While they may not have been trained specifically in the scientific discipline

this selection addresses, Gould's readers are surely learned, sophisticated, and intellectually curious. How do we know this?

e. Are the illustrations Gould uses to explain EQ convincing? What proof does he offer to support his belief that carnivores were smarter than herbivores?

f. In many instances, Gould draws upon the contemporary world of animals as a source of information and illustrations. How do such illustrations help him explain his theory of dinosaur intelligence?

g. In paragraph 1, Gould alludes to some well-known tales and myths. Identify them. What do these stories help illustrate? Why does he mention Muhammad Ali?

h. Summarize the "revisionist interpretation" (paragraph 6) that the author advocates in this piece.

i. Reread the quote in paragraph 4. Why is it a good example of what Gould terms "prevailing orthodoxy"?

j. How would you define "encephalization quotient"? In what way was James A. Hopson able to determine EQ's for creatures that lived millions of years ago?

k. Gould seems to be having a great deal of fun in this essay. What parts of it do you find most amusing? What is the joke he makes in paragraph 22? Is this a good way to conclude?

Strategy and Style

l. What is the "behemoth" to which Gould refers in paragraph 3? What is the "extrapolated reptilian curve" mentioned in paragraph 11?

m. What does the author mean by "behavioral complexity," and how does it relate to measuring animal intelligence? What illustrations does Gould use to define this phenomenon? Why are they so convincing?

n. Describe Gould's tone. What do you make of statements such as "Dinosaurs have been making a strong comeback...."? Is this the kind of language you are used to reading in textbooks and articles about science?

SUGGESTIONS FOR SHORT WRITING

a. Describe the impression you get of dinosaurs' intelligence from the first four paragraphs. Then describe your impression at the end of the essay. How do the two impressions differ?

b. If the dinosaurs of Gould's essay could talk to us, what might they have to say in their defense?

SUGGESTIONS FOR SUSTAINED WRITING

a. Using this selection as a source of inspiration, write an essay in which you illustrate your belief that dogs, cats, horses (or any other animals you are familiar with) are smarter than most people believe. Address your essay to someone who might, at first, be skeptical about your opinion.

b. Explain why you believe humankind will (or will not) "last longer than *Brontosaurus.*" Rely on your knowledge of human nature and of world events as a source of examples.

c. Identify a popularly held theory that you believe is untrue. For instance, examine the notion that intelligence is hereditary or that most criminals cannot be rehabilitated or that women as a group are more "sensitive" and caring than men. Then, using illustrations drawn from your own observations, write an essay in which you invalidate that theory.

The Patterns of Eating

Peter Farb and George Armelagos

An anthropologist, naturalist, and acknowledged expert on the American Indian, Peter Farb (1929–1980) wrote numerous studies on the natural history of North America and of its original inhabitants. He also published several introductions to scientific subjects for young readers. Farb was educated at Vanderbilt and Columbia Universities. He worked as feature editor for Argosy *from 1950–52 and as curator for the Riverside Museum in New York City from 1964–71. He also held teaching positions at Yale University and at Calhoun College and served as a consultant to the Smithsonian Institution in Washington, D.C. From 1959–63, Farb wrote a column for* Better Homes and Gardens *and contributed numerous articles on science and nature to many other popular American magazines. Some of his best-known, full-length works include* Living Earth *(1959),* The Forest *(1961),* Face of North America: The Natural History of a Continent *(1963), and* Man's Rise to Civilization as Shown by the Indians of North America from Primeval Times to the Coming of the Industrial State (1968).*

George Armelagos (b. 1936) received his Ph.D. in anthropology from the University of Colorado and is now professor of anthropology at the University of Massachusetts at Amherst. He has completed extensive research on the relationship between nutrition and human evolution.

Consuming Passions (1980), the book from which this selection was taken, is a well-documented look at the development of eating habits through the centuries. In it, Farb and Armelagos explain how the rituals we have come to associate with food preparation, table manners, and dietary practices in general have helped both reveal and define our cultural identity. "The interrelation of men and menus," wrote one Time *book reviewer, "has filled hundreds of texts. But none of them has digested so many facts so well."*

      Among the important societal rules that represent one component of cuisine are table manners. As a socially instilled form of conduct, they reveal the attitudes typical of a society. Changes in table manners through time, as they have been documented for western Europe, likewise reflect fundamental changes in human relationships. Medieval courtiers saw their table manners as distinguishing them from crude peasants; but by modern standards, the manners were not exactly refined. Feudal lords used their unwashed hands to scoop food from a common bowl and they passed around a single goblet from which all drank. A finger or two would be extended while eating, so as to be kept free of grease and thus available for the next course, or for dipping into spices and condiments—possibly accounting for today's "polite" custom of extending the finger while holding a spoon or small fork. Soups and sauces were commonly drunk by lifting the bowl to the mouth; several diners frequently ate from the

1

same bread trencher. Even lords and nobles would toss gnawed bones back into the common dish, wolf down their food, spit onto the table (preferred conduct called for spitting under it), and blew their noses into the tablecloth.

By about the beginning of the sixteenth century, table manners began to move in the direction of today's standards. The importance attached to them is indicated by the phenomenal success of a treatise, *On Civility in Children,* by the philosopher Erasmus, which appeared in 1530; reprinted more than thirty times in the next six years, it also appeared in numerous translations. Erasmus' idea of good table manners was far from modern, but it did represent an advance. He believed, for example, that an upper class diner was distinguished by putting only three fingers of one hand into the bowl, instead of the entire hand in the manner of the lower class. Wait a few moments after being seated before you dip into it, he advises. Do not poke around in your dish, but take the first piece you touch. Do not put chewed food from the mouth back on your plate; instead, throw it under the table or behind your chair.

By the time of Erasmus, the changing table manners reveal a fundamental shift in society. People no longer ate from the same dish or drank from the same goblet, but were divided from one another by a new wall of constraint. Once the spontaneous, direct, and informal manners of the Middle Ages had been repressed, people began to feel shame. Defecation and urination were now regarded as private activities; handkerchiefs came into use for blowing the nose; nightclothes were now worn, and bedrooms were set apart as private areas. Before the sixteenth century, even nobles ate in their vast kitchens; only then did a special room designated for eating come into use away from the bloody sides of meat, the animals about to be slaughtered, and the bustling servants. These new inhibitions became the essence of "civilized" behavior, distinguishing adults from children, the upper classes from the lower, and Europeans from the "savages" then being discovered around the world. Restraint in eating habits became more marked in the centuries that followed. By about 1800, napkins were in common use, and before long they were placed on the thighs rather than wrapped around the neck; coffee and tea were no longer slurped out of the saucer; bread was genteelly broken into small pieces with the fingers rather than cut into large chunks with a knife.

Numerous paintings that depict meals—with subjects such as the Last Supper, the wedding at Cana, or Herod's feast—show what dining tables looked like before the seventeenth century. Forks were not depicted until about 1600 (when Jacopo Bassano painted one in a Last Supper), and very few spoons were shown. At least one knife is always depicted—an especially large one when it is the only one available for all the guests—but small individual knives were often at each place. Tin disks or oval pieces of wood had already replaced the bread trenchers. This change in eating utensils typified the new table manners in Europe. (In many other parts of the world, no utensils at all were used. In the Near East, for example, it was traditional to bring food to the mouth with the fingers of the right hand, the left being unacceptable because it was reserved for wiping the buttocks.) Utensils were employed in part because of a change in the attitude toward meat. During the Middle Ages, whole sides of meat, or even an entire dead animal, had been brought to the table and then carved in view of the diners. Beginning in the seventeenth century, at first in France but later elsewhere, the practice began to go out of fashion. One reason was that the family was ceasing to be a production unit that did its own slaughtering; as that function was transferred to specialists outside the home, the family became essentially a consumption unit. In addition, the size of the family was decreasing, and consequently whole animals, or even large parts of them, were uneconomical. The cuisines of Europe reflected these social and economic changes. The animal origin of meat dishes was concealed by the arts of preparation. Meat itself became distasteful to look upon, and carving was moved out of sight to the kitchen. Comparable changes had already taken place in Chinese cuisine, with meat being cut up beforehand, unobserved by the diners. England was an exception to the change in Europe, and in its former colonies—the United States, Canada, Australia, and South Africa—the custom has persisted of bringing a joint of meat to the table to be carved.

Once carving was no longer considered a necessary skill among the well- 5 bred, changes inevitably took place in the use of the knife, unquestionably the earliest utensil used for manipulating food. (In fact, the earliest English cookbooks were not so much guides to recipes as guides to carving meat.) The attitude of diners toward the knife, going back to the Middle Ages and the Renaissance, had always been ambivalent. The knife served as a utensil, but it offered a potential threat because it was also a weapon. Thus taboos were increasingly placed upon its use: It was to be held by the point with the blunt handle presented; it was not to be placed anywhere near the face; and most important, the uses to which it was put were sharply restricted. It was not to be used for cutting soft foods such as boiled eggs or fish, or round ones such as potatoes, or to be lifted from the table for courses that did not need it. In short, good table manners in Europe gradually removed the threatening aspect of the knife from social occasions. A similar change had taken place much earlier in China when the warrior was supplanted by the scholar as a cultural model. The knife was banished completely from the table in favor of chopsticks, which is why the Chinese came to regard Europeans as barbarians at their table who "eat with swords."

The fork in particular enabled Europeans to separate themselves from the 6 eating process, even avoiding manual contact with their food. When the fork first appeared in Europe, toward the end of the Middle Ages, it was used solely as an instrument for lifting chunks from the common bowl. Beginning in the sixteenth century, the fork was increasingly used by members of the upper classes—first in Italy, then in France, and finally in Germany and England. By then, social relations in western Europe had so changed that a utensil was

needed to spare diners from the "uncivilized" and distasteful necessity of picking up food and putting it into the mouth with the fingers. The addition of the
fork to the table was once said to be for reasons of hygiene, but this cannot be
true. By the sixteenth century people were no longer eating from a common
bowl but from their own plates, and since they also washed their hands before
meals, their fingers were now every bit as hygienic as a fork would have been.
Nor can the reason for the adoption of the fork be connected with the wish not
to soil the long ruff that was worn on the sleeve at the time, since the fork was
also adopted in various countries where ruffs were not then in fashion.

Along with the appearance of the fork, all table utensils began to change   7
and proliferate from the sixteenth century onward. Soup was no longer eaten
directly from the dish, but each diner used an individual spoon for that purpose.
When a diner wanted a second helping from the serving dish, a ladle or a fresh
spoon was used. More and more special utensils were developed for each kind
of food: soup spoons, oyster forks, salad forks, two-tined fondue forks, blunt
butter knives, special utensils for various desserts and kinds of fruit, each one
differently shaped, of a different size, with differently numbered prongs and
with blunt or serrated edges. The present European pattern eventually emerged,
in which each person is provided with a table setting of as many as a dozen
utensils at a full-course meal. With that, the separation of the human body from
the taking of food became virtually complete. Good table manners dictated that
even the cobs of maize were to be held by prongs inserted in each end, and the
bones of lamb chops covered by ruffled paper panta- lettes. Only under special
conditions—as when Western people consciously imitate an earlier stage in culture at a picnic, fish fry, cookout, or campfire—do they still tear food apart with
their fingers and their teeth, in a nostalgic reenactment of eating behaviors long
vanished.

Today's neighborhood barbecue recreates a world of sharing and hospital-   8
ity that becomes rarer each year. We regard as a curiosity the behavior of hunters in exotic regions. But every year millions of North Americans take to the
woods and lakes to kill a wide variety of animals—with a difference, of course:
What hunters do for survival we do for sport (and also for proof of masculinity,
for male bonding, and for various psychological rewards). Like hunters, too, we
stuff ourselves almost whenever food is available. Nibbling on a roasted ear of
maize gives us, in addition to nutrients, the satisfaction of participating in culturally simpler ways. A festive meal, however, is still thought of in Victorian
terms, with the dominant male officiating over the roast, the dominant female
apportioning vegetables, the extended family gathered around the table, with
everything in its proper place—a revered picture, as indeed it was so painted by
Norman Rockwell, yet one that becomes less accurate with each year that
passes.

1980

QUESTIONS FOR DISCUSSION

Content

a. What were the Last Supper, the wedding at Cana, and Herod's feast? How do references to paintings of these events help illustrate important points about the history of table manners?

b. Summarize the illustrations Farb and Armelagos use to distinguish manners in the Renaissance from those of earlier eras. Does their treatment of the subject need to be as graphic as it is?

c. What illustrations do Farb and Armelagos use to explain the European's "ambivalent" attitude toward knives?

d. Who was Erasmus, and how did his ideas help advance table manners?

e. To what are Farb and Armelagos alluding when they tell us that the new table manners adopted by Europeans during the Renaissance distinguished them "from the 'savages' then being discovered around the world" (paragraph 3)? Why is the word "savages" in quotes?

f. This essay attempts to trace various developments that led to the separation of "the human body from the taking of food." How would you interpret this statement?

g. The authors claim that, early in the seventeenth century, the family "was ceasing to be a production unit." What did this development have to do with the profound changes in the way Europeans prepared and served meat?

h. Explain the Chinese's opinion of European eating habits. Why did the Chinese banish knives from their tables, and how did their doing so affect the development of their cuisine?

i. Why did forks come into use? What other "special utensils" and instruments have since become common in table settings?

j. What accounts for the fact that, in the United States and other English-speaking countries, people still carve large cuts of meat at the table? Why do Farb and Armelagos consider this custom as well as the contemporary American cookout "a nostalgic reenactment of eating behaviors long vanished"?

k. How would you describe the work of Norman Rockwell, and why is one of his "revered pictures" mentioned in the conclusion?

Strategy and Style

l. How would you define the terms "Middle Ages" and "Renaissance"? Why does this essay begin with the former? Should the authors have begun with an earlier period of history?

m. What are the "Victorian terms" to which the authors allude in the concluding paragraph?

n. To what extent are Farb and Armelagos making fun of people's eating habits? Point out instances where the tone becomes humorous.

SUGGESTIONS FOR SHORT WRITING

a. Write about what you thought of eating etiquette before you read this essay. In what ways did the essay corroborate or challenge your thinking? Did it change your mind about what is proper etiquette?
b. Describe the eating habits of your family, your roommates, or the patrons of the campus cafeteria. At which stage of the evolution of eating patterns would you say they belonged?

SUGGESTIONS FOR SUSTAINED WRITING

a. Describe and evaluate the table manners people use in your college's dining hall or cafeteria. Like Farb and Armelagos, use as many concrete illustrations as you can to make your writing vivid and convincing. You might want to submit this essay for publication in your college newspaper or literary magazine, so keep your audience in mind!
b. What makes a meal "festive"? Using illustration as your dominant method of development, discuss how this term might apply to your favorite holiday dinner. You need not focus on table manners exclusively. Describing place settings and table decorations or explaining the elaborate rituals that go into preparing traditional family dishes might also help illustrate your idea of "festive."
c. Describe one or more eating or cooking rituals from another culture that you find interesting. You might be able to gather many details about this topic from personal experience, from conversations with the foreign students you meet in your classes, or from chats with people who have immigrated to this country but still follow the traditional culinary practices of their homelands. Address this essay to someone who knows very little about the culture you're discussing, and be sure to include a sufficient number of examples and explanatory details.

8

Cause and Effect

If you read Chapter 3, you know that explaining causes and effects is similar to analyzing a process. While the latter explains how something happens, however, the former seeks to reveal why it happens. Causal analysis is often used to explore questions in science, history, economics, and the social sciences. If you have taken courses in these subjects you may have written papers or essay exams that discuss the major causes of World War I; explain revisions in the U.S. banking system brought on by the Great Depression; or, like the selection by Isaac Asimov, predict the long-term effects of pumping carbon dioxide into the atmosphere.

Causal analysis is so natural an activity that it appears in the earliest of stages of mental awareness. It is a tool by which we reflect upon and learn from our past: the child who burns her hand knows why she should stay away from the stove. But it is also a common way to anticipate the future. Peering into metaphorical crystal balls, we create elaborate plans, theorize about the consequences of our actions, and make appropriate changes in the way we live. "If I graduate in four years and get a fellowship to law school," dreams the ambitious college freshman, "I might land a job with Biddle and Biddle and even run for city council by the time I'm thirty. But, first, I'd better improve my grades, which will mean studying harder and spending less time socializing."

The student's thinking illustrates an important point about the connection between causes and effects: it is often more complex than we imagine. In "The Villain in the Atmosphere," for example, Asimov cannot explain the burning of fossil fuels and the decimating of forests as *ultimate* causes behind the steady rise in sea levels unless he deals with several *proximate* causes as well: the increase in atmospheric carbon dioxide, which creates the greenhouse effect, which, in turn, raises the planet's temperature and melts the polar caps.

Keep this example in mind as you begin to use causal analysis as a way to develop ideas. More often than not, each cause and effect you discuss will require thorough explanation in detail that is carefully chosen and appropriate

333

to your purpose. Remember, too, that you can call on a variety of skills and techniques to help you develop your analysis. In one part of "Nuclear Holocaust," for example, Jonathan Schell uses both narration and description in the form of eyewitness accounts to convey the tragedy of Hiroshima; in another, he compares what happened in Japan to what might occur if even larger bombs were dropped on New York City, thereby theorizing an even more horrible hell. Ellen Goodman joins illustration with cause and effect, a brilliant combination that reveals the irony behind why planners and nonplanners reap the same rewards.

An important question anytime you use cause and effect is where to place your emphasis. Will you discuss what caused a particular phenomenon or will you focus on its consequences? E. M. Forster deals almost exclusively with the effects of owning property, Jonathan Schell with the outcomes of nuclear war. Marya Mannes, on the other hand, spends most of her time explaining what causes so many people to "deny the existence of any valid criteria" for judging the arts. Of course, you may decide to strike a balance, as does Norman Cousins when he discusses both the reasons for and the consequences of our "becoming a nation of pill-grabbers and hypochondriacs."

As with the other kinds of writing in this text, purpose determines content and strategy. You read earlier that causal analysis is used frequently to explain historical or scientific phenomena. Such writing is often objective and dispassionate, but causal analysis has many applications. Because it is an especially powerful tool for persuasion, you might even want to use it to express a strong voice over issues to which you are firmly committed. Take your lead from Mannes, for example, who addresses her readers directly and encourages them to adopt aesthetic standards "timeless as the universe itself." Like Asimov or Cousins, warn your readers about an ecological or medical danger. Express concern over threats to human rights—here or in other parts of the world—as Nadine Gordimer does in "Art and the State in South Africa." You might even want to do a bit of soul-searching *à la* E. M. Forster. What do your reactions to the world around you tell you about yourself?

How Do You Know It's Good?

Marya Mannes

Marya Mannes (1904–1990) was born in New York City into a family of musicians. Her father, David Mannes, conducted the New York Symphony from 1898 to 1912 and was the founder of the Mannes College of Music. Her mother, Clara Mannes, was a professional pianist. Her brother, Leopold, was both a musician and a chemist; along with another musician/chemist, he invented Kodachrome. Marya, however, became a professional writer, editor, and television commentator. She was the feature editor at Vogue; *a columnist for* McCall's, The New York Times, *and* United Features Syndicate; *and a commentator for Channel 13, a public broadcasting station in New York. She also contributed frequently to several national magazines and was the author of two novels,* Message from a Stranger *(1948) and* They *(1968), and an autobiography,* Out of My Time *(1971). She was best known, however, for her essays, which have been collected in several books, including* But Will It Sell? *(1964), in which "How Do You Know It's Good?" appears.*

Suppose there were no critics to tell us how to react to a picture, a play, 1
or a new composition of music. Suppose we wandered innocent as the dawn
into an art exhibition of unsigned paintings. By what standards, by what values
would we decide whether they were good or bad, talented or untalented, successes or failures? How can we ever know that what we think is right?

For the last fifteen or twenty years the fashion in criticism or appreciation 2
of the arts has been to deny the existence of any valid criteria and to make the
words "good" or "bad" irrelevant, immaterial, and inapplicable. There is no
such thing, we are told, as a set of standards, first acquired through experience
and knowledge and later imposed on the subject under discussion. This has
been a popular approach, for it relieves the critic of the responsibility of judgment and the public of the necessity of knowledge. It pleases those resentful of
disciplines, it flatters the empty-minded by calling them open-minded, it comforts the confused. Under the banner of democracy and the kind of equality
which our forefathers did *not* mean, it says, in effect, "Who are you to tell us
what *is* good or bad?" This is the same cry used so long and so effectively by
the producers of mass media who insist that it is the public, not they, who decides what it wants to hear and see, and that for a critic to say that *this* program
is bad and *this* program is good is purely a reflection of personal taste. Nobody
recently has expressed this philosophy more succinctly than Dr. Frank Stanton,
the highly intelligent president of CBS television. At a hearing before the Federal Communications Commission, this phrase escaped him under questioning:
"One man's mediocrity is another man's good program."

There is no better way of saying "No values are absolute." There is an- 3
other important aspect to this philosophy of *laissez faire:* It is the fear, in all

335

observers of all forms of art, of guessing wrong. This fear is well come by, for who has not heard of the contemporary outcries against artists who later were called great? Every age has its arbiters who do not grow with their times, who cannot tell evolution from revolution or the difference between frivolous faddism, amateurish experimentation, and profound and necessary change. Who wants to be caught *flagrante delicto* with an error of judgment as serious as this? It is far safer, and certainly easier, to look at a picture or a play or a poem and to say "This is hard to understand, but it may be good," or simply to welcome it as a new form. The word "new"—in our country especially—has magical connotations. What is new must be good; what is old is probably bad. And if a critic can describe the new in language that nobody can understand, he's safer still. If he has mastered the art of saying nothing with exquisite complexity, nobody can quote him later as saying anything.

But all these, I maintain, are forms of abdication from the responsibility   4
of judgment. In creating, the artist commits himself; in appreciating, you have a commitment of your own. For after all, it is the audience which makes the arts. A climate of appreciation is essential to its flowering, and the higher the expectations of the public, the better the performance of the artist. Conversely, only a public ill-served by its critics could have accepted as art and as literature so much in these last years that has been neither. If anything goes, everything goes; and at the bottom of the junkpile lie the discarded standards too.

But what are these standards? How do you get them? How do you know   5
they're the right ones? How can you make a clear pattern out of so many intangibles, including that greatest one, the very private I?

Well for one thing, it's fairly obvious that the more you read and see and   6
hear, the more equipped you'll be to practice that art of association which is at the basis of all understanding and judgment. The more you live and the more you look, the more aware you are of a consistent pattern—as universal as the stars, as the tides, as breathing, as night and day—underlying everything. I would call this pattern and this rhythm an order. Not order—*an* order. Within it exists an incredible diversity of forms. Without it lies chaos—the wild cells of destruction—sickness. It is in the end up to you to distinguish between the diversity that is health and the chaos that is sickness, and you can't do this without a process of association that can link a bar of Mozart with the corner of a Vermeer painting, or a Stravinsky score with a Picasso abstraction; or that can relate an aggressive act with a Franz Kline painting and a fit of coughing with a John Cage composition.

There is no accident in the fact that certain expressions of art live for all   7
time and that others die with the moment, and although you may not always define the reasons, you can ask the questions. What does an artist say that is timeless; how does he say it? How much is fashion, how much is merely reflection? Why is Sir Walter Scott so hard to read now, and Jane Austen not? Why is baroque right for one age and too effulgent for another?

Can a standard of craftsmanship apply to art of all ages, or does each   8 have its own, and different, definitions? You may have been aware, inadvertently, that craftsmanship has become a dirty word these years because, again, it implies standards—something done well or done badly. The result of this convenient avoidance is a plenitude of actors who can't project their voices, singers who can't phrase their songs, poets who can't communicate emotion, and writers who have no vocabulary—not to speak of painters who can't draw. The dogma now is that craftsmanship gets in the way of expression. You can do better if you don't know *how* you do it, let alone *what* you're doing.

I think it is time you helped reverse this trend by trying to rediscover   9
craft: the command of the chosen instrument, whether it is a brush, a word, or a voice. When you begin to detect the difference between freedom and sloppiness, between serious experimentation and egotherapy, between skill and slickness, between strength and violence, you are on your way to separating the sheep from the goats, a form of segregation denied us for quite a while. All you need to restore it is a small bundle of standards and a Geiger counter that detects fraud, and we might begin our tour of the arts in an area where both are urgently needed: contemporary painting.

I don't know what's worse: to have to look at acres of bad art to find the   10
little good, or to read what the critics say about it all. In no other field of expression has so much double-talk flourished, so much confusion prevailed, and so much nonsense been circulated: further evidence of the close interdependence between the arts and the critical climate they inhabit. It will be my pleasure to share with you some of this double-talk so typical of our times.

Item one: preface for a catalogue of an abstract painter: 11

"Time-bound meditation experiencing a life; sincere with plastic piety at   12
the threshold of hallowed arcana; a striving for pure ideation giving shape to inner drive; formalized patterns where neural balances reach a fiction." End of quote. Know what this artist paints like now?

Item two: a review in the *Art News:*   13

"...a weird and disparate assortment of material, but the monstrosity   14
which bloomed into his most recent cancer of aggregations is present in some form everywhere...." Then, later, "A gluttony of things and processes terminated by a glorious constipation."

Item three, same magazine, review of an artist who welds automobile   15
fragments into abstract shapes:

"Each fragment...is made an extreme of human exasperation, torn at and   16
fought all the way, and has its rightness of form as if by accident. *Any technique that requires order or discipline would just be the human ego.* No, these must be egoless, uncontrolled, undesigned and different enough to give you a bang—fifty miles an hour around a telephone pole...."

"Any technique that requires order or discipline would just be the human   17
ego." What does he mean—"just be"? What are they really talking about? Is this journalism? Is it criticism? Or is it that other convenient abdication from standards of performance and judgment practiced by so many artists and critics

that they, like certain writers who deal only in sickness and depravity, "reflect the chaos about them"? Again, whose chaos? Whose depravity?

I had always thought that the prime function of art was to create order *out* **18** of chaos—again, not the order of neatness or rigidity or convention or artifice, but the order of clarity by which one will and one vision could draw the essential truth out of apparent confusion. I still do. It is not enough to use parts of a car to convey the brutality of the machine. This is as slavishly representative, and just as easy, as arranging dried flowers under glass to convey nature.

Speaking of which, i.e., the use of real materials (burlap, old gloves, bot- **19** tletops) in lieu of pigment, this is what one critic had to say about an exhibition of Assemblage at the Museum of Modern Art last year:

> Spotted throughout the show are indisputable works of art, accounting for a quarter or even a half of the total display. But the remainder are works of non-art, anti-art, and art substitutes that are the aesthetic counterparts of the social deficiencies that land people in the clink on charges of vagrancy. These aesthetic bankrupts...have no legitimate ideological roof over their heads and not the price of a square intellectual meal, much less a spiritual sandwich, in their pockets.

I quote these words of John Canaday of *The New York Times* as an exam- **20** ple of the kind of criticism which puts responsibility to an intelligent public above popularity with an intellectual coterie. Canaday has the courage to say what he thinks and the capacity to say it clearly: two qualities notably absent from his profession.

Next to art, I would say that appreciation and evaluation in the field of **21** music is the most difficult. For it is rarely possible to judge a new composition at one hearing only. What seems confusing or fragmented at first might well become clear and organic a third time. Or it might not. The only salvation here for the listener is, again, an instinct born of experience and association which allows him to separate intent from accident, design from experimentation, and pretense from conviction. Much of contemporary music is, like its sister art, merely a reflection of the composer's own fragmentation: an absorption in self and symbols at the expense of communication with others. The artist, in short, says to the public: If you don't understand this, it's because you're dumb. I maintain that you are not. You may have to go part way or even halfway to meet the artist, but if you must go the whole way, it's his fault, not yours. Hold fast to that. And remember it too when you read new poetry, that estranged sister of music.

> A multitude of causes, unknown to former times, are now acting with a combined force to blunt the discriminating powers of the mind, and, unfitting it for all voluntary exertion, to reduce it to a state of almost savage torpor. The most effective of these causes are the great national events which are daily taking place and the increasing accumulation of men in cities, where the uniformity of their occupations produces a craving for extraordinary incident, which the rapid communication of intelligence hourly gratifies. To this ten-

dency of life and manners, the literature and theatrical exhibitions of the
country have conformed themselves.

This startlingly applicable comment was written in the year 1800 by Wil-   22
liam Wordsworth in the preface to his "Lyrical Ballads"; and it has been cited
by Edwin Muir in his recently published book "The Estate of Poetry." Muir
states that poetry's effective range and influence have diminished alarmingly in
the modern world. He believes in the inherent and indestructible qualities of the
human mind and the great and permanent objects that act upon it, and suggests
that the audience will increase when "poetry loses what obscurity is left in it by
attempting greater themes, for great themes have to be stated clearly." If you
keep that firmly in mind and resist, in Muir's words, "the vast dissemination of
secondary objects that isolate us from the natural world," you have gone a long
way toward equipping yourself for the examination of any work of art.

When you come to theatre, in this extremely hasty tour of the arts, you   23
can approach it on two different levels. You can bring to it anticipation and innocence, giving yourself up, as it were, to the life on the stage and reacting to it
emotionally, if the play is good, or listlessly, if the play is boring; a part of the
audience organism that expresses its favor by silence or laughter and its disfa-
vor by coughing and rustling. Or you can bring to it certain critical faculties
that may heighten, rather than diminish, your enjoyment.

You can ask yourselves whether the actors are truly in their parts or   24
merely projecting themselves; whether the scenery helps or hurts the mood;
whether the playwright is honest with himself, his characters, and you. Somewhere along the line you can learn to distinguish between the true creative act
and the false arbitrary gesture; between fresh observation and stale cliché; between the avant-garde play that is pretentious drivel and the avant-garde play
that finds new ways to say old truths.

Purpose and craftsmanship—end and means—these are the keys to your   25
judgment in all the arts. What is this painter trying to say when he slashes a
broad band of black across a white canvas and lets the edges dribble down? Is
it a statement of violence? Is it a self-portrait? If it is *one* of these, has he made
you believe it? Or is this a gesture of the ego or a form of therapy? If it shocks
you, what does it shock you into?

And what of this tight little painting of bright flowers in a vase? Is the   26
painter saying anything new about flowers? Is it different from a million other
canvases of flowers? Has it any life, any meaning, beyond its statement? Is
there any pleasure in its forms or texture? The question is not whether a thing is
abstract or representational, whether it is "modern" or conventional. The question, inexorably, is whether it is good. And this is a decision which only you, on
the basis of instinct, experience, and association, can make for yourself. It takes
independence and courage. It involves, moreover, the risk of wrong decision
and the humility, after the passage of time, of recognizing it as such. As we
grow and change and learn, our attitudes can change too, and what we once
thought obscure or "difficult" can later emerge as coherent and illuminating.

Entrenched prejudices, obdurate opinions are as sterile as no opinions at all.

Yet standards there are, timeless as the universe itself. And when you 27 have committed yourself to them, you have acquired a passport to that elusive but immutable realm of truth. Keep it with you in the forests of bewilderment. And never be afraid to speak up.

1962

QUESTIONS FOR DISCUSSION

Content

a. What are the responsibilities of the audience? Do you feel qualified (based on Mannes' idea of responsibility) to "make the arts"? Do you think Mannes is asking too much or not enough of the audience?

b. Mannes addresses the reader as "you," and her tone is quite authoritative. (See for example lines such as this in paragraph 9: "I think it is time you helped reverse this trend...") To whom is she speaking, and why might she want to sound authoritative? What does she want "you" to do?

c. Mannes bemoans what she considers to be a lack of quality, craftsmanship, etc., in the contemporary arts and gives reasons for this lack. But what other causes might explain the state of recent art? What reasons might Mannes have overlooked or conveniently left out of her essay?

d. In paragraph 8 Mannes implies that recent art is in the poor state it is because people no longer care about craftsmanship. Do you agree with Mannes' explanation of this cause-and-effect relationship? Do you think she

e. Can you infer from the first paragraph what Mannes thinks of critics? Where else in her essay does she reveal her opinion of them?

f. Does she believe that "good" and "bad" can be defined? Does she define those terms? How do you define those terms? *Can* those terms be defined?

g. In paragraph 2, Mannes uses television programming as an example of the difficulty of defining good and bad. Which television programs do you consider good, and which bad? What are your criteria for judgment?

h. In paragraph 4, Mannes states that "it is the audience which makes the arts," an opinion that is implied repeatedly in the essay. Do you agree with this opinion? What effects do you feel an audience has on the arts or on other products?

i. What are the steps Mannes recommends to acquire the standards necessary to determine what is good and what is bad?

j. Mannes focuses her discussion on literature, fine arts, music, and the performing arts. Would her essay apply to other things just as well (for example, architecture, fashion, furniture, even products such as appliances)? If not, do these things require entirely different standards of judgment?

k. Mannes wrote this essay in 1962. Do you think that what she says holds true for today as well?

l. How would you answer the question posed by the title?

Strategy and Style

m. How effective are the examples of critical "double-talk" that Mannes includes in paragraphs 11 through 17? Have you ever come across similar double-talk in magazines, newspapers, or textbooks?

n. Mannes coins a new term in paragraph 9: "egotherapy." What is her implied definition of this word?

SUGGESTIONS FOR SHORT WRITING

a. Go through Mannes' essay and make a list of her suggestions for answering the question posed by the title.

b. Select a work of art in a museum or gallery and write your responses to the questions Mannes suggests in paragraphs 25 and 26. Rephrase her questions to fit the work you have chosen; for example, "What is this artist trying to say when she/he _____?" "Is this a statement of _____?" etc.

SUGGESTIONS FOR SUSTAINED WRITING

a. Using Mannes' suggestions for evaluating the arts, write a review of an art exhibit, play, novel, etc.

b. Write an essay in which you extend Mannes' suggestions for creating one's own standards of bad and good to student essays. Do the same standards fit? Does the audience determine the standards?

c. Write a review in which you deliberately try to imitate the critical double-talk that Mannes criticizes. Keep in mind your possible reasons for writing in this style and the effect your words will have on your readers.

d. Find a professional review that you find especially full of meaningless double-talk and rewrite it in ordinary English. What happens to the authority and to the meaning of the review when it is "translated"?

The Villain in the Atmosphere

Isaac Asimov

Born in 1920 in Russia, Isaac Asimov arrived in the United States when he was three. Besides earning his Ph.D. in biochemistry from Columbia University, this incredibly prolific scientist has written more than 200 books and over 2000 articles and short stories. He is especially well known for scientific texts for lay audiences, like The New Intelligent Man's Guide to Science, *which he published in 1965. Among his most important works of science fiction are* The Foundation Trilogy, The Currents of Space, *and* I, Robot. *He claims to write day in and day out, often on several works at one time.*

The villain in the atmosphere is carbon dioxide.   1

It does not seem to be a villain. It is not very poisonous and it is present   2
in the atmosphere in so small a quantity that it does us no harm. For every
1,000,000 cubic feet of air there are only 340 cubic feet of carbon dioxide—
only 0.034 percent.

What's more, that small quantity of carbon dioxide in the air is essential   3
to life. Plants absorb carbon dioxide and convert it into their own tissues, which
serve as the basic food supply for all of animal life (including human beings, of
course). In the process, they liberate oxygen, which is also necessary for all animal life.

But here is what this apparently harmless and certainly essential gas is   4
doing to us:

The sea level is rising very slowly from year to year. The high tides tend   5
to be progressively higher, even in quiet weather, and storms batter at breakwa-
ters more and more effectively, erode the beaches more savagely, batter houses
farther inland.

In all likelihood, the sea level will continue to rise and do so at a greater   6
rate in the course of the next hundred years. This means that the line separating
ocean from land will retreat inland everywhere. It will do so only slightly
where high land abuts the ocean. In those places, however, where there are
low-lying coastal areas (where a large fraction of humanity lives) the water
will advance steadily and inexorably and people will have to retreat inland.

Virtually all of Long Island will become part of the shallow offshore sea   7
bottom, leaving only a line of small islands running east to west, marking off
what had been the island's highest points. Eventually the sea will reach a maximum of two hundred feet above the present water level, and will be splashing
against the windows along the twentieth floors of Manhattan's skyscrapers.
Naturally the Manhattan streets will be deep under water, as will the New Jersey shoreline and all of Delaware. Florida, too, will be gone, as will much of

342

the British Isles, the northwestern European coast, the crowded Nile valley, and the low-lying areas of China, India, and the Soviet Union.

It is not only that people will be forced to retreat by the millions and that many cities will be drowned, but much of the most productive farming areas of the world will be lost. Although the change will not be overnight, and though people will have time to leave and carry with them such of their belongings as they can, there will not be room in the continental interiors for all of them. As the food supply plummets with the ruin of farming areas, starvation will be rampant and the structure of society may collapse under the unbearable pressures. 8

And all because of carbon dioxide. But how does that come about? What is the connection? 9

It begins with sunlight, to which the various gases of the atmosphere (including carbon dioxide) are transparent. Sunlight, striking the top of the atmosphere, travels right through miles of it to reach the Earth's surface, where it is absorbed. In this way, the Earth is warmed. 10

The Earth's surface doesn't get too hot, because at night the Earth's heat radiates into space in the form of infrared radiation. As the Earth gains heat by day and loses it by night, it maintains an overall temperature balance to which Earthly life is well-adapted. 11

However, the atmosphere is not quite as transparent to infrared radiation as it is to visible light. Carbon dioxide in particular tends to be opaque to that radiation. Less heat is lost at night, for that reason, than would be lost if carbon dioxide were not present in the atmosphere. Without the small quantity of that gas present, the Earth would be distinctly cooler on the whole, perhaps a bit uncomfortably cool. 12

This is called the "greenhouse effect" of carbon dioxide. It is so called because the glass of greenhouses lets sunshine in but prevents the loss of heat. For that reason it is warm inside a greenhouse on sunny days even when the temperature is low. 13

We can be thankful that carbon dioxide is keeping us comfortably warm, but the concentration of carbon dioxide in the atmosphere is going up steadily and that is where the villainy comes in. In 1958, when the carbon dioxide of the atmosphere first began to be measured carefully, it made up only 0.0316 percent of the atmosphere. Each year since, the concentration has crept upward and it now stands at 0.0340 percent. It is estimated that by 2020 the concentration will be about 0.0660 percent, or nearly twice what it is now. 14

This means that in the coming decades, Earth's average temperature will go up slightly. Winters will grow a bit milder on the average and summers a bit hotter. That may not seem frightening. Milder winters don't seem bad, and as for hotter summers, we can just run our air-conditioners a bit more. 15

But consider this: If winters in general grow milder, less snow will fall during the cold season. If summers in general grow hotter, more snow will melt during the warm season. That means that, little by little, the snow line will 16 move away from the equator and toward the poles. The glaciers will retreat, the mountain tops will grow more bare, and the polar ice caps will begin to melt.

That might be annoying to skiers and to other devotees of winter sports, 17 but would it necessarily bother the rest of us? After all, if the snow line moves north, it might be possible to grow more food in Canada, Scandinavia, the Soviet Union, and Patagonia.

Still, if the cold weather moves poleward, then so do the storm belts. The 18 desert regions that now exist in subtropical areas will greatly expand, and fertile land gained in the north will be lost in the south. More may be lost than gained.

It is the melting of the ice caps, though, that is the worst change. It is this 19 which demonstrates the villainy of carbon dioxide.

Something like 90 percent of the ice in the world is to be found in the 20 huge Antarctica ice cap, and another 8 percent is in the Greenland ice cap. In both places the ice is piled miles high. If these ice caps begin to melt, the water that forms won't stay in place. It will drip down into the ocean and slowly the sea level will rise, with the results that I have already described.

Even worse might be in store, for a rising temperature would manage to 21 release a little of the carbon dioxide that is tied up in vast quantities of limestone that exist in the Earth's crust. It will also liberate some of the carbon dioxide dissolved in the ocean. With still more carbon dioxide, the temperature of the Earth will creep upward a little more and release still more carbon dioxide.

All this is called the "runaway greenhouse effect," and it may eventually 22 make Earth an uninhabitable planet.

But, as you can see, it is not carbon dioxide in itself that is the source of 23 the trouble; it is the fact that the carbon dioxide concentration in the atmosphere is steadily rising and seems to be doomed to continue rising. Why is that?

To blame are two factors. First of all, in the last few centuries, first coal, 24 then oil and natural gas, have been burned for energy at a rapidly increasing rate. The carbon contained in these fuels, which has been safely buried underground for many millions of years, is now being burned to carbon dioxide and poured into the atmosphere at a rate of many tons per day.

Some of that additional carbon dioxide may be absorbed by the soil or by 25 the ocean, and some might be consumed by plant life, but the fact is that a considerable fraction of it remains in the atmosphere. It must, for the carbon dioxide content of the atmosphere is going up year by year.

To make matters worse, Earth's forests have been disappearing, slowly at 26 first, but in the last couple of centuries quite rapidly. Right now it is disappearing at the rate of sixty-four acres per minute.

Whatever replaces the forest—grasslands or farms or scrub—produces 27 plants that do not consume carbon dioxide at a rate equal to that of forest. Thus, not only is more carbon dioxide being added to the atmosphere through the burning of fuel, but as the forests disappear, less carbon dioxide is being subtracted from the atmosphere by plants.

But this gives us a new perspective on the matter. The carbon dioxide is 28 not rising by itself. It is people who are burning the coal, oil, and gas, because of their need for energy. It is people who are cutting down the forests, because of their need for farmland. And the two are connected, for the burning of coal and oil is producing acid rain which helps destroy the forests. It is *people,* then, who are the villains.

What is to be done?   29

First, we must save our forests, and even replant them. From forests, 30 properly conserved, we get wood, chemicals, soil retention, ecological health— and a slowdown of carbon dioxide increase.

Second, we must have new sources of fuel. There are, after all, fuels that 31 do not involve the production of carbon dioxide. Nuclear fission is one of them, and if that is deemed too dangerous for other reasons, there is the forthcoming nuclear fusion, which may be safer. There is also the energy of waves, tides, wind, and the Earth's interior heat. Most of all, there is the direct use of solar energy.

All of this will take time, work, and money, to be sure, but all that time, 32 work, and money will be invested in order to save our civilization and our planet itself.

After all, humanity seems to be willing to spend *more* time, work, and 33 money in order to support competing military machines that can only destroy us all. Should we begrudge *less* time, work, and money in order to save us all?

1986

QUESTIONS FOR DISCUSSION

Content

a. Asimov's essay seems so simple and direct that it is difficult not to believe everything he says. Should we believe him unconditionally?

b. What is Asimov's thesis? Does it match the simplicity of the language of this essay?

c. What solutions does Asimov provide? How workable do they seem to you? How might you personally begin to put them into practice?

d. Summarize the chain of events as Asimov describes them. Do the events all trace their origins back to carbon dioxide, or is Asimov oversimplifying the situation?

e. What imaginative, and perhaps fanciful, details does Asimov use in order to create a clear image of what the world will be like in the future?

Strategy and Style

f. Who is the real villain? How does Asimov structure his essay so as to be able, in paragraph 28, to add a twist to his original statement that carbon dioxide is the villain? How would the impact of the essay have been altered if Asimov had begun his essay with "the villains are the people"?

g. As a scientist, Asimov obviously could use technical language to discuss global warming. Why doesn't he? Does he have a purpose for using simple language other than to make his writing accessible to the general public?

h. In this essay, Asimov uses many short paragraphs (in particular, 1, 9, 22, 29, and 32). What is the effect of so many short paragraphs?

i. Similarly, what is the effect of the rhetorical question as a concluding sentence? What does a rhetorical question do that a direct statement cannot?

j. Asimov refers to "us" and "we," not "one," "you," or "they." How does this affect the tone and the persuasiveness of the piece?

SUGGESTIONS FOR SHORT WRITING

a. Asimov, like Schell ("Nuclear Holocaust"), makes a pessimistic prediction about the future of the world. What is your opinion of his prediction?

b. Describe your home community as you envision it a hundred years from now.

SUGGESTIONS FOR SUSTAINED WRITING

a. Write an essay in which you analyze Asimov's style, persuasive techniques, and argument.

b. Although it may not be very popular to do so at present, write a counterargument to Asimov's essay, persuading your readers that they need not worry about the greenhouse effect. Keep in mind that you are arguing against a scientist who carries a lot of authority, so try to make your essay as rational and as convincing as his is.

c. Write an argument in which you show the cause and effect relationship between a current situation and a probable, long-range future situation. For example, what might happen as a result of giving aid to countries whose governments shelter terrorists? As a result of changing the abortion laws?

Pain Is Not the Ultimate Enemy
Norman Cousins

Norman Cousins (1915–1990) served as editor of the prestigious Saturday Review *for more than four decades. From 1978, he was chairman of the editorial board of this journal and senior lecturer at the Medical School of the University of California at Los Angeles. Always interested in international affairs, Cousins was twice president of the World Association of Federalists and of the World Federalist Association. In 1963, he won the Eleanor Roosevelt Peace Award. Shortly thereafter, Cousins was stricken with a disease that left him almost totally paralyzed. His doctors advised him that there was no chance of recovery and that he would remain an invalid the rest of his life. Despite their gloomy predictions, he fought back, often prescribing his own treatment, the foundation of which was an unswerving conviction that he could beat the disease. He wrote two books about his experience,* The Celebration of Life *(1974) and* The Anatomy of an Illness *(1979), in which this selection first appeared. Among Cousins' other well-known works are* Talks with Nehru *(1951),* Who Speaks for Man? *(1953),* Present Tense *(1967), and, recently,* Albert Schweitzer's Mission *(1985),* The Pathology of Power *(1987), and* Head First *(1990).*

1   Americans are probably the most pain-conscious people on the face of the earth. For years we have had it drummed into us—in print, on radio, over television, in everyday conversation—that any hint of pain is to be banished as though it were the ultimate evil. As a result, we are becoming a nation of pill-grabbers and hypochondriacs, escalating the slightest ache into a searing ordeal.

2   We know very little about pain and what we don't know makes it hurt all the more. Indeed, no form of illiteracy in the United States is so widespread or costly as ignorance about pain—what it is, what causes it, how to deal with it without panic. Almost everyone can rattle off the names of at least a dozen drugs that can deaden pain from every conceivable cause—all the way from headaches to hemorrhoids. There is far less knowledge about the fact that about 90 percent of pain is self-limiting, that it is not always an indication of poor health, and that, most frequently, it is the result of tension, stress, worry, idleness, boredom, frustration, suppressed rage, insufficient sleep, overeating, poorly balanced diet, smoking, excessive drinking, inadequate exercise, stale air, or any of the other abuses encountered by the human body in modern society.

3   The most ignored fact of all about pain is that the best way to eliminate it is to eliminate the abuse. Instead, many people reach almost instinctively for the painkillers—aspirins, barbiturates, codeines, tranquilizers, sleeping pills, and dozens of other analgesics or desensitizing drugs.

4   Most doctors are profoundly troubled over the extent to which the medical profession today is taking on the trappings of a pain-killing industry. Their

offices are overloaded with people who are morbidly but mistakenly convinced that something dreadful is about to happen to them. It is all too evident that the campaign to get people to run to a doctor at the first sign of pain has boomeranged. Physicians find it difficult to give adequate attention to patients genuinely in need of expert diagnosis and treatment because their time is soaked up by people who have nothing wrong with them except a temporary indisposition or a psychogenic ache.

Patients tend to feel indignant and insulted if the physician tells them he   5
can find no organic cause for the pain. They tend to interpret the term "psychogenic" to mean that they are complaining of nonexistent symptoms. They need to be educated about the fact that many forms of pain have no underlying physical cause but are the result, as mentioned earlier, of tension, stress, or hostile factors in the general environment. Sometimes a pain may be a manifestation of "conversion hysteria"…the name given by Jean Charcot to physical symptoms that have their origins in emotional disturbances.

Obviously, it is folly for an individual to ignore symptoms that could be a   6
warning of a potentially serious illness. Some people are so terrified of getting bad news from a doctor that they allow their malaise to worsen, sometimes past the point of no return. Total neglect is not the answer to hypochondria. The only answer has to be increased education about the way the human body works, so that more people will be able to steer an intelligent course between promiscuous pill-popping and irresponsible disregard of genuine symptoms.

Of all forms of pain, none is more important for the individual to under-   7
stand than the "threshold" variety. Almost everyone has a telltale ache that is triggered whenever tension or fatigue reaches a certain point. It can take the form of a migraine-type headache or a squeezing pain deep in the abdomen or cramps or a pain in the lower back or even pain in the joints. The individual who has learned how to make the correlation between such threshold pains and their cause doesn't panic when they occur; he or she does something about relieving the stress and tension. Then, if the pain persists despite the absence of apparent cause, the individual will telephone the doctor.

If ignorance about the nature of pain is widespread, ignorance about the   8
way pain-killing drugs work is even more so. What is not generally understood is that many of the vaunted pain-killing drugs conceal the pain without correcting the underlying condition. They deaden the mechanism in the body that alerts the brain to the fact that something may be wrong. The body can pay a high price for suppression of pain without regard to its basic cause.

Professional athletes are sometimes severely disadvantaged by trainers   9
whose job it is to keep them in action. The more famous the athlete, the greater the risk that he or she may be subjected to extreme medical measures when injury strikes. The star baseball pitcher whose arm is sore because of a torn muscle or tissue damage may need sustained rest more than anything else. But his team is battling for a place in the World Series; so the trainer or team doctor, called upon to work his magic, reaches for a strong dose of Butazolidine or

other powerful pain suppressants. Presto, the pain disappears! The pitcher takes his place on the mound and does superbly. That could be the last game, however, in which he is able to throw a ball with full strength. The drugs didn't repair the torn muscle or cause the damaged tissue to heal. What they did was to mask the pain, enabling the pitcher to throw hard, further damaging the torn muscle. Little wonder that so many star athletes are cut down in their prime, more the victims of overzealous treatment of their injuries than of the injuries themselves.

The king of all painkillers, of course, is aspirin. The U.S. Food and Drug 10 Administration permits aspirin to be sold without prescription, but the drug, contrary to popular belief, can be dangerous and, in sustained doses, potentially lethal. Aspirin is self-administered by more people than any other drug in the world. Some people are aspirin-poppers, taking ten or more a day. What they don't know is that the smallest dose can cause internal bleeding. Even more serious perhaps is the fact that aspirin is antagonistic to collagen, which has a key role in the formation of connective tissue. Since many forms of arthritis involve disintegration of the connective tissue, the steady use of aspirin can actually intensify the underlying arthritic condition.

Aspirin is not the only pain-killing drug, of course, that is known to have 11 dangerous side effects. Dr. Daphne A. Roe, of Cornell University, at a medical meeting in New York City in 1974, presented startling evidence of a wide range of hazards associated with sedatives and other pain suppressants. Some of these drugs seriously interfere with the ability of the body to metabolize food properly, producing malnutrition. In some instances, there is also the danger of bone-marrow depression, interfering with the ability of the body to replenish its blood supply.

Pain-killing drugs are among the greatest advances in the history of med- 12 icine. Properly used, they can be a boon in alleviating suffering and in treating disease. But their indiscriminate and promiscuous use is making psychological cripples and chronic ailers out of millions of people. The unremitting barrage of advertising for pain-killing drugs, especially over television, has set the stage for a mass anxiety neurosis. Almost from the moment children are old enough to sit upright in front of a television screen, they are being indoctrinated into the hypochondriac's clamorous and morbid world. Little wonder so many people fear pain more than death itself.

It might be a good idea if concerned physicians and educators could get 13 together to make knowledge about pain an important part of the regular school curriculum. As for the populace at large, perhaps some of the same techniques used by public-service agencies to make people cancer-conscious can be used to counteract the growing terror of pain and illness in general. People ought to know that nothing is more remarkable about the human body than its recuperative drive, given a modicum of respect. If our broadcasting stations cannot provide equal time for responses to the pain-killing advertisements, they might at least set aside a few minutes each day for common-sense remarks on the subject of pain. As for the Food and Drug Administration, it might be interesting to know why an agency that has energetically warned the American people against taking vitamins without prescriptions is doing so little to control over-the-counter sales each year of billions of pain-killing pills, some of which can do more harm than the pain they are supposed to suppress.

1979

QUESTIONS FOR DISCUSSION

Content

a. Why does Cousins believe that aspirin is a dangerous drug? How does his use of aspirin act as an illustration of his thesis?
b. Paragraph 8 may very well be the most important paragraph in this selection. Why?
c. Cousins sometimes refers to medical authorities. What purpose do such references serve? Are they effective?
d. How would you describe the audience Cousins is addressing in this selection? Analyze the details, vocabulary, and illustration he uses as clues.
e. What can you infer about Cousins' opinions of the medical profession, the pharmaceutical industry, and the FDA?
f. Who or what does Cousins imply is mainly at fault for causing or worsening pain?
g. According to Cousins, what are some typical causes of pain? What does he mean when he claims that "90 percent of pain is self-limiting"?
h. What are some of the indications that the "medical profession...is taking on the trappings of the pain-killing industry"?

Strategy and Style

i. What are the solutions Cousins suggests for remedying ignorance about pain and painkillers? Why might he have decided to end rather than to begin his essay with them?
j. How does Cousins define "threshold" pain?
k. Describe Cousins' tone in this essay. What is his attitude toward painkillers, and how is that attitude conveyed by his language?

SUGGESTIONS FOR SHORT WRITING

a. Write about a time when you overcame pain of some sort. How did you overcome it?

b. Consider the current state of your health. Write a letter to yourself, proposing some ways in which to improve it.

SUGGESTIONS FOR SUSTAINED WRITING

a. You may know a hypochondriac—someone who has convinced himself/herself that he/she is, has been, or will be afflicted by a variety of serious illnesses. Describe such a person and explain his/her thinking. In doing so, try to demonstrate the fact that hypochondria is itself a dangerous disease. Illustrate some of its more adverse effects, whether physical or emotional, on the "patient." Assume that your reader knows very little about the subject, and provide sufficient explanatory detail to make your point clear.

b. Cousins is obviously warning us about our overreliance on medication to relieve pain. What other methods of trying to cope with pain have you found effective? Illustrate these methods as completely as you can. It would be wise to remember that some readers of your paper might be skeptical of pain-relieving methods that do not require the taking of medication, so be as convincing as you can without exaggerating.

c. Write a counterargument to Cousins' essay in which you try to convince him, or readers who would agree with him, that painkillers are not as dangerous as he says they are.

My Wood

E. M. Forster

Born in London, Edward Morgan Forster (1879–1970) took a degree at, King's College, Cambridge, and he traveled extensively through the Mediterranean during his early years. Serving as the private secretary of the maharajah of an Indian state provided Forster with materials for his most famous novel, A Passage to India *(1952), which he mentions in paragraph 1 of "My Wood." Among his other novels are* The Longest Journey *(1922),* Howard's End *(1921),* A Room with a View *(1943), and* Maurice *(1971). He also wrote a number of nonfiction works, including* Aspects of the Novel *(1927) and* Abinger Harvest, *in which "My Wood" appeared.*

A few years ago I wrote a book which dealt in part with the difficulties of the English in India. Feeling that they would have had no difficulties in India themselves, the Americans read the book freely. The more they read it the better it made them feel, and a cheque to the author was the result. I bought a wood with the cheque. It is not a large wood—it contains scarcely any trees, and it is intersected, blast it, by a public footpath. Still, it is the first property that I have owned, so it is right that other people should participate in my shame, and should ask themselves, in accents that will vary in horror, this very important question: What is the effect of property upon the character? Don't let's touch economics; the effect of private ownership upon the community as a whole is another question—a more important question, perhaps, but another one. Let's keep to psychology. If you own things, what's their effect on you? What's the effect on me of my wood?

In the first place, it makes me feel heavy. Property does have this effect. Property produces men of weight, and it was a man of weight who failed to get into the Kingdom of Heaven. He was not wicked, that unfortunate millionaire in the parable, he was only stout; he stuck out in front, not to mention behind, and as he wedged himself this way and that in the crystalline entrance and bruised his well-fed flanks, he saw beneath him a comparatively slim camel passing through the eye of a needle and being woven into the robe of God. The Gospels all through couple stoutness and slowness. They point out what is perfectly obvious, yet seldom realized: that if you have a lot of things you cannot move about a lot, that furniture requires dusting, dusters require servants, servants require insurance stamps, and the whole tangle of them makes you think twice before you accept an invitation to dinner or go for a bathe in the Jordan. Sometimes the Gospels proceed further and say with Tolstoy that property is sinful; they approach the difficult ground of asceticism here, where I cannot follow them. But as to the immediate effects of property on people, they just show straightforward logic. It produces men of weight. Men of weight cannot, by definition, move like the lightning from the East unto the West, and the as-

cent of a fourteen-stone bishop into a pulpit is thus the exact antithesis of the
coming of the Son of Man. My wood makes me feel heavy.

In the second place, it makes me feel it ought to be larger.   3

The other day I heard a twig snap in it. I was annoyed at first, for I   4
thought that someone was blackberrying, and depreciating the value of the un-
dergrowth. On coming nearer, I saw it was not a man who had trodden on the
twig and snapped it, but a bird, and I felt pleased. My bird. The bird was not
equally pleased. Ignoring the relation between us, it took fright as soon as it
saw the shape of my face, and flew straight over the boundary hedge into a
field, the property of Mrs. Henessy, where it sat down with a loud squawk. It
had become Mrs. Henessy's bird. Something seemed grossly amiss here, something that would not have occurred had the wood been larger. I could not afford
to buy Mrs. Henessy out, I dared not murder her, and limitations of this sort
beset me on every side. Ahab did not want that vineyard—he only needed it to
round off his property, preparatory to plotting a new curve—and all the land
around my wood has become necessary to me in order to round off the wood. A
boundary protects. But—poor little thing—the boundary ought in its turn to be
protected. Noises on the edge of it. Children throw stones. A little more, and
then a little more, until we reach the sea. Happy Canute! Happier Alexander!
And after all, why should even the world be the limit of possession? A rocket
containing a Union Jack, will, it is hoped, be shortly fired at the moon. Mars.
Sirius. Beyond which...But these immensities ended by saddening me. I could
not suppose that my wood was the destined nucleus of universal dominion—it
is so very small and contains no mineral wealth beyond the blackberries. Nor
was I comforted when Mrs. Henessy's bird took alarm for the second time and
flew clean away from us all, under the belief that it belonged to itself.

In the third place, property makes its owner feel that he ought to do   5
something to it. Yet he isn't sure what. A restlessness comes over him, a vague
sense that he has a personality to express—the same sense which, without any
vagueness, leads the artist to an act of creation. Sometimes I think I will cut
down such trees as remain in the wood, at other times I want to fill up the gaps
between them with new trees. Both impulses are pretentious and empty. They
are not honest movements towards money-making or beauty. They spring from
a foolish desire to express myself and from an inability to enjoy what I have
got. Creation, property, enjoyment form a sinister trinity in the human mind.
Creation and enjoyment are both very very good, yet they are often unattainable
without a material basis, and at such moments property pushes itself in as a
substitute, saying, "Accept me instead—I'm good enough for all three." It is
not enough. It is, as Shakespeare said of lust, "The expense of spirit in a waste
of shame": it is "Before, a joy proposed; behind, a dream." Yet we don't know
how to shun it. It is forced on us by our economic system as the alternative to
starvation. It is also forced on us by an internal defect in the soul, by the feeling
that in property may lie the germs of self-development and of exquisite or heroic deeds. Our life on earth is, and ought to be, material and carnal. But we

have not yet learned to manage our materialism and carnality properly; they are still entangled with the desire for ownership, where (in the words of Dante) "Possession is one with loss."

And this brings us to our fourth and final point: the blackberries.   **6**

Blackberries are not plentiful in this meagre grove, but they are easily   **7** seen from the public footpath which traverses it, and all too easily gathered. Foxgloves, too—people will pull up the foxgloves, and ladies of an educational tendency even grub for toadstools to show them on the Monday in class. Other ladies, less educated, roll down the bracken in the arms of their gentlemen friends. There is paper, there are tins. Pray, does my wood belong to me or doesn't it? And, if it does, should I not own it best by allowing no one else to walk there? There is a wood near Lyme Regis, also cursed by a public footpath, where the owner has not hesitated on this point. He has built high stone walls each side of the path, and has spanned it by bridges, so that the public circulate like termites while he gorges on the blackberries unseen. He really does own his wood, this able chap. Dives in Hell did pretty well, but the gulf dividing him from Lazarus could be traversed by vision, and nothing traverses it here. And perhaps I shall come to this in time. I shall wall in and fence out until I really taste the sweets of property. Enormously stout, endlessly avaricious, pseudo-creative, intensely selfish, I shall weave upon my forehead the quadruple crown of possession until those nasty Bolshies come and take it off again and thrust me aside into the outer darkness.

1936

QUESTIONS FOR DISCUSSION

Content

a. Early in the essay, Forster makes an emphatic distinction between the economic and the psychological effects of owning property. Why? Does his doing so make his arguments more effective?

b. Summarize the four effects that, according to Forster, owning property has on people.

c. What does Forster mean in paragraph 5 when he says that "Creation, property, enjoyment form a sinister trinity in the human mind"?

d. What is the biblical parable to which Forster is alluding in paragraph 2? Who is the "Son of Man"?

e. Forster seems to combine allusions to the Bible and literature with personal observations and anecdotes to develop paragraphs 2 through 7. Explain by pointing to examples of each type of allusion.

f. Do you find Forster's characterization of the public (paragraph 7) offensive, or is it an accurate portrayal of the way people treat natural surroundings?

Strategy and Style

g. The organization of this essay is rather simple and straightforward. Trace Forster's pattern of organization. What transitions does he use?
h. Who are the "Bolshies"? Why does their mention in the last paragraph provide for an especially ironic twist?
i. Though Forster's intent is serious, his tone is somewhat ironic, indeed often humorous. What examples of humor or irony can you find in this selection?

SUGGESTIONS FOR SHORT WRITING

a. Forster says that ownership of his wood "makes [him] feel heavy" (paragraph 2). Describe your emotional relationship to something you own that has some significance for you—a piece of property, a car, an heirloom, etc.
b. Define "ownership" in the context of your community. In other words, what does ownership mean to the people of your neighborhood or hometown?

SUGGESTIONS FOR SUSTAINED WRITING

a. Do you agree totally with Forster's argument that owning property has negative effects? If not, write an essay in which you point out some benefits of land ownership, or ownership of anything for that matter.
b. Focus on an important but specific environmental issue in your community or on campus. Describe what effects (negative or positive) environmental changes might have on people living in that community.
c. Do you have a friend who has recently landed a high-paying job, has won the lottery, or has otherwise become richer? Has his/her personality, lifestyle or attitude changed because of this development? Describe the effects that this new affluence has had on your friend.

Watching the Grasshopper Get the Goodies

Ellen Goodman

Ellen Goodman was born in Boston in 1941. She received her bachelor's degree from Radcliffe College and attended Harvard University on a Nieman Fellowship. Goodman began her journalistic career with Newsweek, *then moved to the* Detroit Free Press, *and is now writing for the* Boston Globe. *Her syndicated column, "At Large," has appeared in more than 200 newspapers across the country. She has won several awards for her commentary, including a Pulitzer Prize in 1980. Many of her columns have been collected into* Close to Home *(1979) and* At Large *(1981), in which "Watching the Grasshopper" appears. Her recent works include* Keeping in Touch *(1986) and* Making Sense *(1989).*

1　I don't usually play the great American game called Categories. There are already too many ways to divide us into opposing teams, according to age, race, sex and favorite flavors. Every time we turn around, someone is telling us that the whole country is made up of those who drive pick-up trucks and those who do not, and then analyzing what this means in terms of the Middle East.

2　Still, it occurs to me that if we want to figure out why people are angry right now, it's not a bad idea to see ourselves as a nation of planners and nonplanners. It's the planners these days who are feeling penalized, right down to their box score at the bank.

3　The part of us which is most visibly and vocally infuriated by inflation, for example, isn't our liberal or conservative side but, rather, our planning side. Inflation devastates our attempts to control our futures—to budget and predict and expect. It particularly makes fools out of the people who saved then to buy now. To a certain extent, it rewards instant gratification and makes a joke out of our traditional notions of preparation.

4　It is no news bulletin that the people who dove over their heads into the real-estate market a few years ago are now generally better off than those who dutifully decided to save up for a larger down payment. With that "larger down payment" they can now buy two double-thick rib lambchops and a partridge in a pear tree.

5　But inflation isn't the only thing that leaves the planners feeling betrayed. There are other issues that find them actively pitched against the nonplanners.

6　We all know families who saved for a decade to send their kids to college. A college diploma these days costs about the same amount as a Mercedes-Benz. Of course, the Mercedes lasts longer and has a higher trade-in value. But the most devoted parent can be infuriated to discover that a neighboring couple who spent its income instead of saving is now eligible for college financial aid, while they are not. To the profligate go the spoils.

7　This can happen anywhere on the economic spectrum. There is probably

356

only one mother in the annals of the New York welfare rolls to save up a few thousand dollars in hopes of getting off aid. But she would have been better off spending it. When she was discovered this year, the welfare department took the money back. She, too, was penalized for planning.

In these crimped times, the Planned Parents of the Purse are increasingly **8** annoyed at other parents—whether they are unwed or on welfare or just prolific. For the first time in my own town, you can hear families with few children complaining out loud at the tax bill for the public schooling of families with many children.

One man I heard even suggesting charging tuition for the third child. He **9** admitted, "It's not a very generous attitude, I know. But I'm not feeling very generous these days." He is suffering from planner's warts.

At the same time I've talked with friends whose parents prepared, often **10** with financial difficulty, for their "old age" and illness. They feel sad when this money goes down a nursing home drain, but furious when other people who didn't save get this same care for free.

Now we are all aware that if many people don't plan their economic **11** lives, it may be because they can't. It does no one any good to keep the cashless out of college, to stash the old and poor into elderly warehouses, to leave the "extra" children illiterate. We do want to help others, but we also want our own efforts to make a difference.

There is nothing that grates a planner more than seeing a nonplanner **12** profit. It's as if the ant had to watch the grasshopper get the goodies.

Our two notions about what's fair end up on opposite sides. It isn't fair if **13** the poor get treated badly, and it isn't fair if those who work and save, plan and postpone aren't given a better shake. We want the winners to be the deserving. Only there is no divining rod for the deserving.

The hard part is to create policies that are neither unkind nor insane. It is, **14** after all, madness not to reward the kind of behavior we want to encourage. If we want the ranks of the planners to increase in this massive behavior-modification program called society, we have to give them the rewards, instead of the outrage.

1981

QUESTIONS FOR DISCUSSION

Content

a. What purpose might Goodman have had in starting her essay with a criticism of categorizing and then turning around and categorizing people into "planners and nonplanners"? Into which category does she place herself?

b. According to the author, what happens when you make long-range plans? Is she suggesting that people should never plan?

c. What might be her motives for writing this essay?

d. To whom is Goodman probably writing? How would you describe the ideal reader of this essay (age, occupation, level of education, opinions, etc.)?

e. What or whom does she specify as the cause of people's anger? Just what are people angry about?

f. To what does the title allude? Why is the title appropriate?

g. Do you think that Goodman paints an overly pessimistic picture of what happens as a result of planning?

h. What type of person is Goodman criticizing in the first paragraph? What harmful effects could "the great American game called Categories" have? Would this criticism also apply to those essays in Chapter 5?

Strategy and Style

i. What rhetorical devices does Goodman use to protect herself from counter-arguments?

j. What statements in this essay are sarcastic? What does this sarcasm reveal about Goodman? Does it help to place her in one of her two categories?

k. What action is Goodman proposing in the last paragraph? Is the tone of this paragraph different from the rest of the essay?

SUGGESTIONS FOR SHORT WRITING

a. Create another fable that would make the same point that Goodman makes in her essay. Write an outline for the fable or briefly describe the characters.

b. Are you a planner or a nonplanner? Write an anecdote that illustrates that you are one or the other.

SUGGESTIONS FOR SUSTAINED WRITING

a. In this essay, Goodman focuses on excessive concerns about money as the cause of unhappiness among planners. Could there be other causes as well? Write an essay in which you show that other things may have caused this unhappiness.

b. Write an essay about a practice, law, or situation that you feel is unfair, not only to you but to a large segment of society. Show the harmful effects this has on people and suggest what might be done to correct the situation.

c. Find another fable with a real-life equivalent. Using this fable as a starting point, describe the real-life situation, explain what is wrong with the situation and what has caused it, and suggest ways to correct the problem.

Nuclear Holocaust

Jonathan Schell

Born in 1943 in New York City, Jonathan Schell is a staff writer at The New Yorker. *Articles for this publication served as the basis for books he has written about the Vietnam conflict—*The Village of Ben Suc *(1967) and* The Military Half *(1968)—and about nuclear war—*The Fate of the Earth *(1982), from which this essay is excerpted, and* The Abolition *(1984).*

Part of the horror of thinking about a holocaust lies in the fact that it 1
leads us to supplant the human world with a statistical world; we seek a human
truth and come up with a handful of figures. The only source that gives us a
glimpse of that human truth is the testimony of the survivors of the Hiroshima
and Nagasaki bombings. Because the bombing of Hiroshima has been more
thoroughly investigated than the bombing of Nagasaki, and therefore more information about it is available, I shall restrict myself to a brief description of
that catastrophe.

On August 6, 1945, at 8:16 A.M., a fission bomb with a yield of twelve 2
and a half kilotons was detonated about nineteen hundred feet above the central
section of Hiroshima. By present-day standards, the bomb was a small one, and
in today's arsenals it would be classed among the merely tactical weapons.
Nevertheless, it was large enough to transform a city of some three hundred and
forty thousand people into hell in the space of a few seconds. "It is no exaggeration," the authors of "Hiroshima and Nagasaki" tell us, "to say that the whole
city was ruined instantaneously." In that instant, tens of thousands of people
were burned, blasted, and crushed to death. Other tens of thousands suffered
injuries of every description or were doomed to die of radiation sickness. The
center of the city was flattened, and every part of the city was damaged. The
trunks of bamboo trees as far away as five miles from ground zero—the point
on the ground directly under the center of the explosion—were charred. Almost
half the trees within a mile and a quarter were knocked down. Windows nearly
seventeen miles away were broken. Half an hour after the blast, fires set by the
thermal pulse and by the collapse of the buildings began to coalesce into a firestorm, which lasted for six hours. Starting about 9 A.M. and lasting until late
afternoon, a "black rain" generated by the bomb (otherwise, the day was fair)
fell on the western portions of the city, carrying radioactive fallout from the
blast to the ground. For four hours at midday, a violent whirlwind, born of the
strange meteorological conditions produced by the explosion, further devastated
the city. The number of people who were killed outright or who died of their
injuries over the next three months is estimated to be a hundred and thirty thousand. Sixty-eight percent of the buildings in the city were either completely de-

359

stroyed or damaged beyond repair, and the center of the city was turned into a flat, rubble-strewn plain dotted with the ruins of a few of the sturdier buildings.

In the minutes after the detonation, the day grew dark, as heavy clouds of 3 dust and smoke filled the air. A whole city had fallen in a moment, and in and under its ruins were its people. Among those still living, most were injured, and of these most were burned or had in some way been battered or had suffered both kinds of injury. Those within a mile and a quarter of ground zero had also been subjected to intense nuclear radiation, often in lethal doses. When people revived enough from their unconsciousness or shock to see what was happening around them, they found that where a second before there had been a city get- ting ready to go about its daily business on a peaceful, warm August morning, now there was a heap of debris and corpses and a stunned mass of injured hu- manity. But at first, as they awakened and tried to find their bearings in the gathering darkness, many felt cut off and alone. In a recent volume of recollec- tions by survivors called "Unforgettable Fire," in which the effects of the bombing are rendered in drawings as well as in words, Mrs. Haruko Oga- sawara, a young girl on that August morning, recalls that she was at first knocked unconscious. She goes on to write:

> How many seconds or minutes had passed I could not tell, but, regaining consciousness, I found myself lying on the ground covered with pieces of wood. When I stood up in a frantic effort to look around, there was darkness. Terribly frightened, I thought I was alone in a world of death, and groped for any light. My fear was so great I did not think anyone would truly under- stand. When I came to my senses, I found my clothes in shreds, and I was without my wooden sandals.

Soon cries of pain and cries for help from the wounded filled the air. Sur- 4 vivors heard the voices of their families and their friends calling out in the gloom. Mrs. Ogasawara writes:

> Suddenly, I wondered what had happened to my mother and sister. My mother was then forty-five, and my sister five years old. When the darkness began to fade, I found that there was nothing around me. My house, the next door neighbor's house, and the next had all vanished. I was standing amid the ruins of my house. No one was around. It was quiet, very quiet— an eerie moment. I discovered my mother in a water tank. She had fainted. Crying out, "Mama, Mama," I shook her to bring her back to her senses. After coming to, my mother began to shout madly for my sister: "Eiko! Eiko!"

> I wondered how much time had passed when there were cries of searchers. Children were calling their parents' names, and parents were calling the names of their children. We were calling desperately for my sister and lis- tening for her voice and looking to see her. Suddenly, Mother cried "Oh Eiko!" Four or five meters away, my sister's head was sticking out and was calling my mother....Mother and I worked desperately to remove the plas-

ter and pillars and pulled her out with great effort. Her body had turned
purple from the bruises, and her arm was so badly wounded that we could
have placed two fingers in the wound.

Others were less fortunate in their searches and rescue attempts. In "Un-   5
forgettable Fire," a housewife describes a scene she saw:

> A mother, driven half-mad while looking for her child, was calling his name.
> At last she found him. His head looked like a boiled octopus. His eyes were
> half-closed, and his mouth was white, pursed, and swollen.

Throughout the city, parents were discovering their wounded or dead chil-   6
dren, and children were discovering their wounded or dead parents. Kikuno
Segawa recalls seeing a little girl with her dead mother:

> A woman who looked like an expectant mother was dead. At her side, a girl
> of about three years of age brought some water in an empty can she had
> found. She was trying to let her mother drink from it.

The sight of people in extremities of suffering was ubiquitous. Kinzo   7
Nishida recalls:

> While taking my severely wounded wife out to the riverbank by the side of
> the hill of Nakahiro-machi, I was horrified, indeed, at the sight of a stark
> naked man standing in the rain with his eyeball in his palm. He looked to be
> in great pain, but there was nothing that I could do for him.

Many people were astonished by the sheer sudden absence of the known   8
world. The writer Yoko Ota later wrote:

> I just could not understand why our surroundings had changed so greatly
> in one instant....I thought it might have been something which had nothing
> to do with the war—the collapse of the earth, which it was said would
> take place at the end of the world, and which I had read about as a
> child.

And a history professor who looked back at the city after the explosion   9
remarked later, "I saw that Hiroshima had disappeared."

As the fires sprang up in the ruins, many people, having found injured   10
family members and friends, were now forced to abandon them to the flames or
to lose their own lives in the firestorm. Those who left children, husbands,
wives, friends, and strangers to burn often found these experiences the most
awful of the entire ordeal. Mikio Inoue describes how one man, a professor,
came to abandon his wife:

> It was when I crossed Miyuki Bridge that I saw Professor Takenaka, standing
> at the foot of the bridge. He was almost naked, wearing nothing but shorts,
> and he had a ball of rice in his right hand. Beyond the streetcar line, the
> northern area was covered by red fire burning against the sky. Far away from
> the line, Ote-machi was also a sea of fire.

That day, Professor Takenaka had not gone to Hiroshima University, and the A-bomb exploded when he was at home. He tried to rescue his wife, who was trapped under a roofbeam, but all his efforts were in vain. The fire was threatening him also. His wife pleaded, "Run away, dear!" He was forced to desert his wife and escape from the fire. He was now at the foot of Miyuki Bridge.

But I wonder how he came to hold that ball of rice in his hand. His naked figure, standing there before the flames with that ball of rice, looked to me as a symbol of the modest hopes of human beings.

In "Hiroshima," John Hersey describes the flight of a group of German 11 priests and their Japanese colleagues through a burning section of the city:

The street was cluttered with parts of houses that had slid into it, and with fallen telephone poles and wires. From every second or third house came the voices of people buried and abandoned, who invariably screamed, with formal politeness, *"Tasukete kure!* Help, if you please!" The priests recognized several ruins from which these cries came as the homes of friends, but because of the fire it was too late to help.

And thus it happened that throughout Hiroshima all the ties of affection 12 and respect that join human beings to one another were being pulled and rent by the spreading firestorm. Soon processions of the injured—processions of a kind that had never been seen before in history—began to file away from the center of the city toward its outskirts. Most of the people suffered from burns, which had often blackened their skin or caused it to sag off them. A grocer who joined one of these processions has described them in an interview with Robert Jay Lifton which appears in his book "Death in Life":

They held their arms bent [forward] ...and their skin—not only on their hands but on their faces and bodies, too—hung down....If there had been only one or two such people...perhaps I would not have had such a strong impression. But wherever I walked, I met these people....Many of them died along the road. I can still picture them in my mind—like walking ghosts. They didn't look like people of this world.

The grocer also recalls that because of people's injuries "you couldn't tell 13 whether you were looking at them from in front or in back." People found it impossible to recognize one another. A woman who at the time was a girl of thirteen, and suffered disfiguring burns on her face, has recalled, "My face was so distorted and changed that people couldn't tell who I was. After a while I could call others' names but they couldn't recognize me." In addition to being injured, many people were vomiting—an early symptom of radiation sickness. For many, horrifying and unreal events occurred in a chaotic jumble. In "Unforgettable Fire," Torako Hironaka enumerates some of the things that she remembers:

1. Some burned work-clothes.
2. People crying for help with their heads, shoulders, or the soles of their feet injured by fragments of broken window glass. Glass fragments were scattered everywhere.
3. [A woman] crying, saying "Aigo! Aigo!" (a Korean expression of sorrow).
4. A burning pine tree.
5. A naked woman.
6. Naked girls crying, "Stupid America!"
7. I was crouching in a puddle, for fear of being shot by a machine gun. My breasts were torn.
8. Burned down electric power lines.
9. A telephone pole had burned and fallen down.
10. A field of watermelons.
11. A dead horse.
12. What with dead cats, pigs, and people, it was just a hell on earth.

Physical collapse brought emotional and spiritual collapse with it. The 14 survivors were, on the whole, listless and stupefied. After the escapes, and the failures to escape, from the firestorm, a silence fell over the city and its remaining population. People suffered and died without speaking or otherwise making a sound. The processions of the injured, too, were soundless. Dr. Michihiko Hachiya has written in his book, "Hiroshima Diary":

> Those who were able walked silently toward the suburbs in the distant hills, their spirits broken, their initiative gone. When asked whence they had come, they pointed to the city and said, "That way," and when asked where they were going, pointed away from the city and said, "This way." They were so broken and confused that they moved and behaved like automatons.

> Their reactions had astonished outsiders, who reported with amazement the spectacle of long files of people holding stolidly to a narrow, rough path when close by was a smooth, easy road going in the same direction. The outsiders could not grasp the fact that they were witnessing the exodus of a people who walked in the realm of dreams.

Those who were still capable of action often acted in an absurd or an in- 15 sane way. Some of them energetically pursued tasks that had made sense in the intact Hiroshima of a few minutes before but were now utterly inappropriate. Hersey relates that the German priests were bent on bringing to safety a suitcase, containing diocesan accounts and a sum of money, that they had rescued from the fire and were carrying around with them through the burning city. And Dr. Lifton describes a young soldier's punctilious efforts to find and preserve the ashes of a burned military code book while people around him were screaming for help. Other people simply lost their minds. For example, when the German priests were escaping from the firestorm, one of them, Father

Wilhelm Kleinsorge, carried on his back a Mr. Fukai, who kept saying that he wanted to remain where he was. When Father Kleinsorge finally put Mr. Fukai down, he started running. Hersey writes:

> Father Kleinsorge shouted to a dozen soldiers, who were standing by the bridge, to stop him. As Father Kleinsorge started back to get Mr. Fukai, Father LaSalle called out, "Hurry! Don't waste time!" So Father Kleinsorge just requested the soldiers to take care of Mr. Fukai. They said they would, but the little, broken man got away from them, and the last the priests could see of him, he was running back toward the fire.

In the weeks after the bombing, many survivors began to notice the appearance of petechiae—small spots caused by hemorrhages—on their skin. These usually signalled the onset of the critical stage of radiation sickness. In the first stage, the victims characteristically vomited repeatedly, ran a fever, and developed an abnormal thirst. (The cry "Water! Water!" was one of the few sounds often heard in Hiroshima on the day of the bombing.) Then, after a few hours or days, there was a deceptively hopeful period of remission of symptoms, called the latency period, which lasted from about a week to about four weeks. Radiation attacks the reproductive function of cells, and those that reproduce most frequently are therefore the most vulnerable. Among these are the bone-marrow cells, which are responsible for the production of blood cells. During the latency period, the count of white blood cells, which are instrumental in fighting infections, and the count of platelets, which are instrumental in clotting, drop precipitously, so the body is poorly defended against infection and is liable to hemorrhaging. In the third, and final, stage, which may last for several weeks, the victim's hair may fall out and he may suffer from diarrhea and may bleed from the intestines, the mouth, or other parts of the body, and in the end he will either recover or die. Because the fireball of the Hiroshima bomb did not touch the ground, very little ground material was mixed with the fission products of the bomb, and therefore very little local fallout was generated. (What fallout there was descended in the black rain.) Therefore, the fatalities from radiation sickness were probably all caused by the initial nuclear radiation, and since this affected only people within a radius of a mile and a quarter of ground zero, most of the people who received lethal doses were killed more quickly by the thermal pulse and the blast wave. Thus, Hiroshima did not experience the mass radiation sickness that can be expected if a weapon is ground-burst. Since the Nagasaki bomb was also burst in the air, the effect of widespread lethal fallout on large areas, causing the death by radiation sickness of whole populations in the hours, days, and weeks after the blast, is a form of nuclear horror that the world has not experienced. **16**

In the months and years following the bombing of Hiroshima, after radiation sickness had run its course and most of the injured had either died of their wounds or recovered from them, the inhabitants of the city began to learn that the exposure to radiation they had experienced would bring about a wide vari- **17** ety of illnesses, many of them lethal, throughout the lifetimes of those who had been exposed. An early sign that the harm from radiation was not restricted to radiation sickness came in the months immediately following the bombing, when people found that their reproductive organs had been temporarily harmed, with men experiencing sterility and women experiencing abnormalities in their menstrual cycles. Then, over the years, other illnesses, including cataracts of the eye and leukemia and other forms of cancer, began to appear in larger than normally expected numbers among the exposed population. In all these illnesses, correlations have been found between nearness to the explosion and incidence of the disease. Also, fetuses exposed to the bomb's radiation in utero exhibited abnormalities and developmental retardation. Those exposed within the mile-and-a-quarter radius were seven times as likely as unexposed fetuses to die in utero, and were also seven times as likely to die at birth or in infancy. Surviving children who were exposed in utero tended to be shorter and lighter than other children, and were more often mentally retarded. One of the most serious abnormalities caused by exposure to the bomb's radiation was microcephaly—abnormal smallness of the head, which is often accompanied by mental retardation. In one study, thirty-three cases of microcephaly were found among a hundred and sixty-nine children exposed in utero.

What happened at Hiroshima was less than a millionth part of a holocaust 18 at present levels of world nuclear armament. The more than millionfold difference amounts to more than a difference in magnitude; it is also a difference in kind. The authors of "Hiroshima and Nagasaki" observe that "an atomic bomb's massive destruction and indiscriminate slaughter involves the sweeping breakdown of all order and existence—in a word, the collapse of society itself," and that therefore "the essence of atomic destruction lies in the totality of its impact on man and society." This is true also of a holocaust, of course, except that the totalities in question are now not single cities but nations, ecosystems, and the earth's ecosphere. Yet with the exception of fallout, which was relatively light at Hiroshima and Nagasaki (because both the bombs were air-burst), the immediate devastation caused by today's bombs would be of a sort similar to the devastation in those cities. The immediate effects of a twenty-megaton bomb are not different in kind from those of a twelve-and-a-half-kiloton bomb; they are only more extensive.... Therefore, while the total effect of a holocaust is qualitatively different from the total effect of a single bomb, the experience of individual people in a holocaust would be, in the short term (and again excepting the presence of lethal fallout wherever the bombs were ground-burst), very much like the experience of individual people in Hiroshima. The Hiroshima people's experience, accordingly, is of much more than historical interest. It is a picture of what our whole world is always poised to become—a backdrop of scarcely imaginable horror lying just behind the surface of our normal life, and capable of breaking through into that normal life at any second. Whether we choose to think about it or not, it is an omnipresent, inescapable truth about our lives today that at every single moment each one of us may suddenly become the deranged mother looking for her burned child; the professor with the ball of rice in his hand whose wife has just told him "Run away, dear!" and died in the fires; Mr. Fukai running back into the firestorm; the naked man standing on the blasted plain that was his city, holding his eyeball in his hand; or, more likely, one of millions of corpses. For whatever our "modest hopes" as human beings may be, every one of them can be nullified by a nuclear holocaust.

One way to begin to grasp the destructive power of present-day nuclear **19** weapons is to describe the consequences of the detonation of a one-megaton bomb, which possesses eighty times the explosive power of the Hiroshima bomb, on a large city, such as New York. Burst some eighty-five hundred feet above the Empire State Building, a one-megaton bomb would gut or flatten almost every building between Battery Park and 125th Street, or within a radius of four and four-tenths miles, or in an area of sixty-one square miles, and would heavily damage buildings between the northern tip of Staten Island and the George Washington Bridge, or within a radius of about eight miles, or in an area of about two hundred square miles. A conventional explosive delivers a swift shock, like a slap, to whatever it hits, but the blast wave of a sizable nuclear weapon endures for several seconds and "can surround and destroy whole buildings."...People, of course, would be picked up and hurled away from the blast along with the rest of the debris. Within the sixty-one square miles, the walls, roofs, and floors of any buildings that had not been flattened would be collapsed, and the people and furniture inside would be swept down onto the street. (Technically, this zone would be hit by various overpressures of at least five pounds per square inch. Overpressure is defined as the pressure in excess of normal atmospheric pressure.) As far away as ten miles from ground zero, pieces of glass and other sharp objects would be hurled about by the blast wave at lethal velocities. In Hiroshima, where buildings were low and, outside the center of the city, were often constructed of light materials, injuries from falling buildings were often minor. But in New York, where the buildings are tall and are constructed of heavy materials, the physical collapse of the city would certainly kill millions of people. The streets of New York are narrow ravines running between the high walls of the city's buildings. In a nuclear attack, the walls would fall and the ravines would fill up. The people in the buildings would fall to the street with the debris of the buildings, and the people in the street would be crushed by this avalanche of people and buildings. At a distance of two miles or so from ground zero, winds would reach four hundred miles an hour, and another two miles away they would reach a hundred and eighty miles an hour. Meanwhile, the fireball would be growing, until it was more than a mile wide, and rocketing upward, to a height of over six miles. For ten seconds, it would broil the city below. Anyone caught in the open within nine miles of ground zero would receive third-degree burns and would probably be killed; closer to the explosion, people would be charred and killed instantly....

If it were possible (as it would not be) for someone to stand at Fifth Av- **20** enue and Seventy-second Street (about two miles from ground zero) without being instantly killed, he would see the following sequence of events. A dazzling white light from the fireball would illumine the scene, continuing for perhaps thirty seconds. Simultaneously, searing heat would ignite everything flammable and start to melt windows, cars, buses, lampposts, and everything else made of metal or glass. People in the street would immediately catch fire, and would shortly be reduced to heavily charred corpses. About five seconds after the light appeared, the blast wave would strike, laden with the debris of a now nonexistent midtown. Some buildings might be crushed, as though a giant fist had squeezed them on all sides, and others might be picked up off their foundations and whirled uptown with the other debris. On the far side of Central Park, the West Side skyline would fall from south to north. The four-hundred-mile-an-hour wind would blow from south to north, die down after a few seconds, and then blow in the reverse direction with diminished intensity. While these things were happening, the fireball would be burning in the sky for the ten seconds of the thermal pulse. Soon huge, thick clouds of dust and smoke would envelop the scene, and as the mushroom cloud rushed overhead (it would have a diameter of about twelve miles) the light from the sun would be blotted out, and day would turn to night. Within minutes, fires, ignited both by the thermal pulse and by broken gas mains, tanks of gas and oil, and the like, would begin to spread in the darkness, and a strong, steady wind would begin to blow in the direction of the blast. As at Hiroshima, a whirl-wind might be produced, which would sweep through the ruins, and radioactive rain, generated under the meteorological conditions created by the blast, might fall. Before long, the individual fires would coalesce into a mass fire, which, depending largely on the winds, would become either a conflagration or a firestorm. In a conflagration, prevailing winds spread a wall of fire as far as there is any combustible material to sustain it; in a firestorm, a vertical updraft caused by the fire itself sucks the surrounding air in toward a central point, and the fires therefore converge in a single fire of extreme heat. A mass fire of either kind renders shelters useless by burning up all the oxygen in the air and creating toxic gases, so that anyone inside the shelters is asphyxiated, and also by heating the ground to such high temperatures that the shelters turn, in effect, into ovens, cremating the people inside them. In Dresden, several days after the firestorm raised there by Allied conventional bombing, the interiors of some bomb shelters were still so hot that when they were opened the inrushing air caused the contents to burst into flame. Only those who had fled their shelters when the bombing started had any chance of surviving. (It is difficult to predict in a particular situation which form the fires will take. In actual experience, Hiroshima suffered a firestorm and Nagasaki suffered a conflagration.)

In this vast theatre of physical effects, all the scenes of agony and death that took place at Hiroshima would again take place, but now involving millions of people rather than hundreds of thousands. Like the people of Hiroshima, the people of New York would be burned, battered, crushed, and irradiated in every con-   21 ceivable way. The city and its people would be mingled in a smoldering heap. And then, as the fires started, the survivors (most of whom would be on the periphery of the explosion) would be driven to abandon to the flames those family members and other people who were unable to flee, or else to die with them. Before long, while the ruins burned, the processions of injured, mute people would begin their slow progress out of the outskirts of the devastated zone....

If instead of being burst in the air the bomb were burst on or near the ground in the vicinity of the Empire State Building, the overpressure would be very much greater near the center of the blast area but the range hit by a minimum of five pounds per square inch of overpressure would be less. The range of the thermal pulse would be about the same as that of the air burst. The fireball would be almost two miles across, and would engulf midtown Manhattan from Greenwich Village nearly to Central Park. Very little is known about what would happen to a city that was inside a fireball, but one would expect a good deal of what was there to be first pulverized and then melted or vaporized. Any human beings in the area would be reduced to smoke and ashes; they would simply disappear. A crater roughly three blocks in diameter and two hundred feet deep would open up. In addition, heavy radioactive fallout would be created as dust and debris from the city rose with the mushroom cloud and then fell back to the ground....Exposure to radioactivity in human beings is measured in units called rems—an acronym for "roentgen equivalent in man." The roentgen is a standard measurement of gamma- and X-ray radiation, and the expression "equivalent in man" indicates that an adjustment has been made to take into account the differences in the degree of biological damage that is caused by radiation of different types. Many of the kinds of harm done to human beings by radiation—for example, the incidence of cancer and of genetic damage—depend on the dose accumulated over many years; but radiation sickness, capable of causing death, results from an "acute" dose, received in a period of anything from a few seconds to several days. Because almost ninety percent of the so-called "infinite-time dose" of radiation from fallout—that is, the dose from a given quantity of fallout that one would receive if one lived for many thousands of years—is emitted in the first week, the one-week accumulated dose is often used as a convenient measure for calculating the immediate harm from fallout. Doses in the thousands of rems, which could be expected throughout the city, would attack the central nervous system and would bring about death within a few hours. Doses of around a thousand rems, which would be delivered some tens of miles downwind from the blast, would kill within two weeks everyone who was exposed to them. Doses of around five hundred rems, which would be delivered as far as a hundred and fifty miles downwind (given a wind speed of fifteen miles per hour), would kill half of all exposed able-bodied young adults. At this level of exposure, radiation sickness proceeds in the three stages observed at Hiroshima. The plume of lethal fallout could descend, depending on the direction of the wind, on other parts of New York State

22

and parts of New Jersey, Pennsylvania, Delaware, Maryland, Connecticut, Massachusetts, Rhode Island, Vermont, and New Hampshire, killing additional millions of people. The circumstances in heavily contaminated areas, in which millions of people were all declining together, over a period of weeks, toward painful deaths, are ones that, like so many of the consequences of nuclear explosions, have never been experienced.

A description of the effects of a one-megaton bomb on New York City [23] gives some notion of the meaning in human terms of a megaton of nuclear explosive power, but a weapon that is more likely to be used against New York is the twenty-megaton bomb, which has one thousand six hundred times the yield of the Hiroshima bomb. The Soviet Union is estimated to have at least a hundred and thirteen twenty-megaton bombs in its nuclear arsenal, carried by Bear intercontinental bombers. In addition, some of the Soviet SS-18 missiles are capable of carrying bombs of this size, although the actual yields are not known. Since the explosive power of the twenty-megaton bombs greatly exceeds the amount necessary to destroy most military targets, it is reasonable to suppose that they are meant for use against large cities. If a twenty-megaton bomb were air-burst over the Empire State Building at an altitude of thirty thousand feet, the zone gutted or flattened by the blast wave would have a radius of twelve miles...reaching from the middle of Staten Island to the northern edge of the Bronx, the eastern edge of Queens, and well into New Jersey, and the zone of heavy damage from the blast wave (the zone hit by a minimum of two pounds of overpressure per square inch) would have a radius of twenty-one and a half miles...reaching to the southernmost tip of Staten Island, north as far as southern Rockland County, east into Nassau County, and west to Morris County, New Jersey. The fireball would be about four and a half miles in diameter and would radiate the thermal pulse for some twenty seconds. People caught in the open twenty-three miles away from ground zero, in Long Island, New Jersey, and southern New York State, would be burned to death....People hundreds of miles away who looked at the burst would be temporarily blinded and would risk permanent eye injury....The mushroom cloud would be seventy miles in diameter. New York City and its suburbs would be transformed into a lifeless, flat, scorched desert in a few seconds.

If a twenty-megaton bomb were ground-burst on the Empire State Build- [24] ing, the range of severe blast damage would, as with the one-megaton ground blast, be reduced, but the fireball...would cover Manhattan from Wall Street to northern Central Park and also parts of New Jersey, Brooklyn, and Queens, and everyone within it would be instantly killed, with most of them physically disappearing. Fallout would again be generated, this time covering thousands of square miles with lethal intensities of radiation. A fair portion of New York City and its incinerated population, now radioactive dust, would have risen into the mushroom cloud and would now be descending on the surrounding territory....[I]f the wind carried the fallout onto populated areas, then this one bomb would probably doom upward of twenty million people, or almost ten percent of the population of the United States.

1982

QUESTIONS FOR DISCUSSION

Content

a. His argument, or one of his arguments, is that we cannot base our idea of the effects of nuclear war on the examples of Hiroshima and Nagasaki, for several reasons. What are these reasons?

b. Do you think Schell has overloaded us with information, particularly horrifying information? What might be his purpose in describing consequences in such detail and at such length?

c. How effective is this essay as an argument? Has Schell left any room for counterarguments?

d. How does the account of the bombing of Hiroshima affect your response to the report? In what ways does it influence the way you read the rest of the report?

e. Schell says that "throughout Hiroshima all the ties…that join human beings to one another were being pulled and rent…" (paragraph 12). What are these ties? What ties does he mention or imply in the several paragraphs that follow this sentence?

f. What are the short-term and the long-term effects of the dropping of a nuclear bomb on a city? Which type of effect is the most devastating?

g. What is the difference between the effects of a single bomb and the effects of a nuclear holocaust?

h. Technology has changed since Hiroshima. Has society? Have politics?

Strategy and Style

i. Schell begins the eyewitness accounts of the bombing with a family who survived, then moves on to the "less fortunate," and finally on to the most horrific examples of suffering. How would the emotional impact of the essay have been altered had he reversed the order? What is his purpose in sequencing them in the way he did?

j. Beginning with paragraph 16, Schell shifts his tone and subject matter to a technical description of the effects of radiation; the next major shift is in paragraph 18 where he moves from the specific discussion of Hiroshima to the general discussion of possible future nuclear war. Where else does he make shifts in tone and subject matter? Try making an outline of his report. What pattern do you see in the structure of his report?

k. In the beginning of paragraph 12, Schell uses language reminiscent of the

language in fairy tales: "And thus it happened that throughout Hiroshima…"
What is Schell implying by using this language?

SUGGESTIONS FOR SHORT WRITING

a. Summarize this essay as if it were a synopsis for a documentary.
b. Describe your feelings as you read this essay. Alternatively, choose one paragraph and describe your emotional reaction to it.

SUGGESTIONS FOR SUSTAINED WRITING

a. Schell combines several rhetorical approaches. He uses narrative, with plenty of examples to illustrate the effects of an action, in order to make an argument. He also contrasts the actual bombings at Hiroshima and Nagasaki with the hypothetical bombing of New York City. Try combining some or all of these approaches in an essay of your own. Begin with thinking of the point you want to make in your argument, then consider how the various approaches can be used to make the argument most convincing.

b. Research the events that led up to the dropping of bombs on Hiroshima and Nagasaki. In what ways was the political situation then different from the political situation now between any two antagonistic countries? In what ways similar? Write a report in which you either predict what will happen between the two countries, or propose a way to resolve the situation.

c. Do you agree completely with Schell's version of nuclear holocaust as portrayed in his hypothetical case of New York City? Read up on current literature about the effects of nuclear war and write a rebuttal, an update, or a continuation of Schell's report.

The Iks

Lewis Thomas

*Lewis Thomas (b. 1915) attended Princeton University as an undergraduate and re-
ceived his M.A. from Harvard University in 1937. He has served as a professor of
medicine and dean of the medical school at Yale University and as professor of medicine and pathology at Cornell University. He now directs the Memorial Sloan-
Kettering Cancer Institute in New York City. Perhaps the best-known and most highly
respected physician in the United States, Thomas, both as scientist and as writer, has
amassed a collection of awards and honors too large to include in this short biographical sketch. He has published "Notes of a Biology Watcher" in* The New England
Journal of Medicine *since 1971. Many of these monthly columns have been collected
in his full-length works, which include* Lives of a Cell *(1974), from which "The Iks"
is taken;* The Medusa and the Snail *(1979); and* The Youngest Scientist *(1983).
Thomas' strength lies in his ability to make scientific subjects interesting to and easily
understood by lay readers. In "The Iks" Thomas uses an anthropologist's study of this
mountain tribe (*The Mountain People, *1972, by Colin M. Turnbull) as a base from
which to propose his own theory for the strange behavior of the Iks.*

The small tribe of Iks, formerly nomadic hunters and gatherers in the 1
mountain valleys of northern Uganda, have become celebrities, literary symbols
for the ultimate fate of disheartened, heartless mankind at large. Two disas-
trously conclusive things happened to them: the government decided to have a
national park, so they were compelled by law to give up hunting in the valleys
and become farmers on poor hillside soil, and then they were visited for two
years by an anthropologist who detested them and wrote a book about them.

The message of the book is that the Iks have transformed themselves into 2
an irreversibly disagreeable collection of unattached, brutish creatures, totally
selfish and loveless, in response to the dismantling of their traditional culture.
Moreover, this is what the rest of us are like in our inner selves, and we will all
turn into Iks when the structure of our society comes all unhinged.

The argument rests, of course, on certain assumptions about the core of 3
human beings, and is necessarily speculative. You have to agree in advance that
man is fundamentally a bad lot, out for himself alone, displaying such graces as
affection and compassion only as learned habits. If you take this view, the story
of the Iks can be used to confirm it. These people seem to be living together,
clustered in small, dense villages, but they are really solitary, unrelated individuals with no evident use for each other. They talk, but only to make ill-tem-
pered demands and cold refusals. They share nothing. They never sing. They
turn the children out to forage as soon as they can walk, and desert the elders to
starve whenever they can, and the foraging children snatch food from the
mouths of the helpless elders. It is a mean society.

372

They breed without love or even casual regard. They defecate on each 4
other's doorsteps. They watch their neighbors for signs of misfortune, and only
then do they laugh. In the book they do a lot of laughing, having so much bad
luck. Several times they even laughed at the anthropologist, who found this especially repellent (one senses, between the lines, that the scholar is not himself
the world's luckiest man). Worse, they took him into the family, snatched his
food, defecated on his doorstep, and hooted dislike at him. They gave him two
bad years.

It is a depressing book. If, as he suggests, there is only Ikness at the cen- 5
ter of each of us, our sole hope for hanging onto the name of humanity will be
in endlessly mending the structure of our society, and it is changing so quickly
and completely that we may never find the threads in time. Meanwhile, left to
ourselves alone, solitary, we will become the same joyless, zestless, untouching
lone animals.

But this may be too narrow a view. For one thing, the Iks are extraordi- 6
nary. They are absolutely astonishing, in fact. The anthropologist has never seen
people like them anywhere, nor have I. You'd think, if they were simply examples of the common essence of mankind, they'd seem more recognizable. Instead, they are bizarre, anomalous. I have known my share of peculiar, difficult,
nervous, grabby people, but I've never encountered any genuinely, consistently
detestable human beings in all my life. The Iks sound more like abnormalities,
maladies.

I cannot accept it. I do not believe that the Iks are representative of iso- 7
lated, revealed man, unobscured by social habits. I believe their behavior is
something extra, something laid on. This unremitting, compulsive repellence is
a kind of complicated ritual. They must have learned to act this way; they cop-
ied it, somehow.

I have a theory, then. The Iks have gone crazy.   8

The solitary Ik, isolated in the ruins of an exploded culture, has built a 9
new defense for himself. If you live in an unworkable society you can make up
one of your own, and this is what the Iks have done. Each Ik has become a
group, a one-man tribe on its own, a constituency.

Now everything falls into place. This is why they do seem, after all, 10
vaguely familiar to all of us. We've seen them before. This is precisely the way
groups of one size or another, ranging from committees to nations, behave. It is,
of course, this aspect of humanity that has lagged behind the rest of evolution,
and this is why the Ik seems so primitive. In his absolute selfishness, his inca-
pacity to give anything away, no matter what, he is a successful committee.
When he stands at the door of his hut, shouting insults at his neighbors in a
loud harangue, he is a city addressing another city.

Cities have all the Ik characteristics. They defecate on doorsteps, in rivers 11
and lakes, their own or anyone else's. They leave rubbish. They detest all
neighboring cities, give nothing away. They even build institutions for deserting
elders out of sight.

Nations are the most Iklike of all. No wonder the Iks seem familiar. For 12 total greed, rapacity, heartlessness, and irresponsibility there is nothing to match a nation. Nations, by law, are solitary, self-centered, withdrawn into themselves. There is no such thing as affection between nations, and certainly no nation ever loved another. They bawl insults from their doorsteps, defecate into whole oceans, snatch all the food, survive by detestation, take joy in the bad luck of others, celebrate the death of others, live for the death of others.

That's it, and I shall stop worrying about the book. It does not signify that 13 man is a sparse, inhuman thing at his center. He's all right. It only says what we've always known and never had enough time to worry about, that we haven't yet learned how to stay human when assembled in masses. The Ik, in his despair, is acting out this failure, and perhaps we should pay closer attention. Nations have themselves become too frightening to think about, but we might learn some things by watching these people.

1974

QUESTIONS FOR DISCUSSION

Content

a. How does Thomas build his argument against the theory of the anthropologist who studied the Iks for two years? What is the basic difference between the two theories?

b. What are the causes given by the anthropologist and by Thomas for the Iks' current situation? What other causes might explain the Iks' extreme behavior?

c. How accurate do you think the anthropologist's description of the Iks is? What details does Thomas include that might make you think the anthropologist's description is tainted?

d. What is the anthropologist's opinion of human nature? What is Thomas' opinion? What might be the Iks' opinion? With whom do you side?

e. In the last line Thomas writes that "nations have themselves become too frightening to think about, but we might learn some things by watching these people." Who is "we"? What is it that "we" may learn from the Iks?

f. Do you feel that the anthropologist and Thomas have accurately assessed the Iks? What problems exist that could hinder both of them from being objective?

g. How do you account for the laughter of the Iks (described in paragraph 4)? Do you think the anthropologist may have misinterpreted their laughter?

Stategy and Style

h. What metaphors does Thomas use to explain the Iks? Are these effective choices? Do they help to persuade you to accept Thomas' theory?

i. What words and short phrases does Thomas use to help him subtly persuade his readers? For example, what effect do the words "of course" in paragraph 3 have?

SUGGESTIONS FOR SHORT WRITING

a. Write your opinion of Thomas' assertion that "we will all turn into Iks when the structure of our society comes all unhinged" (paragraph 2).
b. Write a review, or the beginnings of a review, of Thomas' essay just as he has reviewed the anthropologist's book. You might want to start with the phrase, "The message of the essay is..."

SUGGESTIONS FOR SUSTAINED WRITING

a. Go to the library and find some background material on the Iks and/or read the anthropologist's book (*The Mountain People* by Colin M. Turnbull). Write an essay in which you put forth your own explanation of the Iks' behavior or in which you agree with the theory of either the anthropologist or Thomas.
b. Write an essay from the Iks' point of view, describing and explaining the behavior of the anthropologist or other outsiders. Again, you may want to find some background material on the Iks to give you a more objective picture.
c. What is the essential core of human beings? Thomas says that any theory is "necessarily speculative." Do some speculating of your own and describe what you consider to be humanity's core characteristics.

Art and the State in South Africa

Nadine Gordimer

Nadine Gordimer was born in 1923 in South Africa, and lives in Johannesburg. She is well known internationally as both a lecturer and a writer, and is outspoken in her views of political and social issues. She is a member of International P.E.N., and an honorable member of the American Academy of Arts and Sciences and of the American Academy of Art and Literature. She has won several awards for her literary work, including the Booker Prize in 1974 and the Grand Aigle d'Or in 1975 for The Conservationist. *Her stories appear frequently in* The New Yorker, The Atlantic, *and* Harper's. *Among her best-known novels are* A Guest of Honor *(1970),* Burger's Daughter *(1979), and* July's People *(1981). Two recent works of nonfiction are* Lifetimes: Under Apartheid *(1986) and* My Son's Song *(1990). "Art and the State" was first given as a speech at a conference on human rights in Toronto in 1981. In 1983 it was published in* The Writer and Human Rights, *a collection of essays and speeches by various writers on the subject of human rights. The proceeds from this book go to Amnesty International.*

1   I once wrote that the best way to write was to do so as if one were already dead: afraid of no one's reactions, answerable to no one for one's views. I still think that is the way to write. Insofar as no one forces a writer to visualize an "audience" (unless he has one eye on the bank), to imagine who it is who is going to be moved, shocked, delighted, incensed or perhaps illuminated by the piece of work in hand, it is possible to keep to this ideal of a writer's freedom. But in the circumstances of political and social pressure applicable to writers under consideration at our conference, this basis of the writer's basic freedom is beleaguered from without and psychologically threatened from within.

2   In the society in which I live and work—apartheid South Africa—the legal framework of censorship affects the work even of dead writers, so there's no freedom to be gained there, in my dictum of writing as if from beyond the grave. A banned work remains banned, even if the writer is no longer living, just as it does in the case of the exiled writer, who is alive but civically "dead" in his own country.

3   Censorship of literature is procured chiefly by two statutes, the Internal Security Act of 1950 and the Publications Act No. 42 of 1974. Together those statutes aim to insure that the South African reader is deprived not only of sexually titillating magazines, books and films but also of serious works that question, radically, the institutions and practices of a society based on racial discrimination. Together those statutes are designed to preserve political orthodoxy according to the ruling color and class by isolating the public from radical political thought and contemporary literary trends.

376

The Internal Security Act is aimed at suppressing overtly political writing,   4
but its legislative tentacles have also strangled a substantial body of creative
writing, since in the words of Thomas Mann, in some eras and some countries,
"politics is fate," and imaginative writing has always been occupied, in one interpretation or another, with human fate. The Internal Security Act functions as
a censor by providing for the banning of both publications *and* writers. In the
first instance, the act authorizes the banning of any publication that expresses
views "calculated to further the achievement of any of the objects of communism." That "any" means that the precepts of human rights common to the
spectrum of progressive thought, from liberalism to communism, are lumped
together, along with the actual advocacy of violent overthrow of the state, under
the general heading of subversion.

It was under this act that the moderate, wide-circulation black daily news-   5
paper the *World* was banned in 1977. The relevant clause invoked stated that
the newspaper had served "as a means for expressing views or conveying information the publication of which is calculated to endanger the security of the
State or the maintenance of public order." What the *World* had indeed been
publishing was an accurate account of the actions and state of mind of the black
population of South Africa, and of Soweto in particular, in the year of school
boycotts that followed the black children's and students' uprising against second-class education in 1976, and in the labor unrest which gathered momentum
in 1977.

Other provisions of the act have the power to impose a ban not merely on   6
a single publication such as the *World* but on *all* the utterances as well as the
writings of certain individuals. Persons whose views may not be quoted at all in
South Africa in terms of Section II of the act fall into several categories. First,
members of organizations outlawed under the Internal Security Act; second,
persons banned by the Minister of Justice, under Section 9, from attending
gatherings, on the ground that they have engaged in activities that further the
achievement of any of the objects of communism. In the 1960s, a whole generation of black South African writers living abroad were listed under a third category, which bans former residents of South Africa who, again in the opinion of
the Minister of Justice, "advocate or engage in activities abroad calculated to
further the achievement of any of the objects of communism." The writers include Alex La Guma, Dennis Brutus, Ezekiel Mphahlele and the late Can
Themba. Of them, only the works of Mphahlele, with the passage of time and
his return to South Africa under a restricted academic dispensation, have been
released from this ban. A few white writers in exile, notably Albie Sachs and
Mary Benson, are prevented from being read in South Africa by a similar type
of ban.

With the rise, during the 1970s, of the Black Consciousness movement,   7
with its emphasis on the cultural arm of the black struggle for human rights, a
number of young black writers and aspiring writers have been prevented from
publishing their work because they are banned under Section 9, which forbids

their attendance at gatherings. A ban of this nature would seem to have little to do with writers, since they don't do their writing at public gatherings. But these young writers see their literary activity as an integral part of their political activity. Most are active as speakers at political meetings and as poets or short-story writers at home. If the ban that prevents them from attending gatherings usually is imposed not because of anything they have written but because of their platform or organizational activity, or the part they have played in boycotts or strikes, nevertheless that ban falls upon their writings, since it implies that nothing they say or write may be quoted or published. Thus, a fairy tale or a love poem by one of these writers may not be published any more than a political statement one of them may have made.

Other writers are silenced by a ban in the first category of Section II be- **8** cause they are or are alleged to be members of organizations outlawed under the Internal Security Act. Since 1976, this has meant the Christian Institute, a non-racial radical church organization, as well as the various Black Consciousness movements and, of course, the mass liberatory movements of the 1950s and 1960s—the A.N.C. (African National Congress) and P.A.C. (Pan-African Congress). Among individuals recently banned are Zwelakhe Sisulu (prominent journalist and son of Walter Sisulu, a great A.N.C. leader imprisoned with Nelson Mandela on Robben Island), Phil Mtimkulu, Joe Thloloe, Charles Ngakula, Mathatha Tsedu, Mari Subramoney, Vuyisile Mdleleni, all journalists and/or writers. Amanda Kwadi was detained for some weeks and released just before I left South Africa a month ago.

Needless to say, South Africa's infamous practice of detention without **9** trial has effectively silenced various black writers, sometimes for long periods. Of those who have been brought to trial, few have been charged on the evidence of their writings, with the notable exception of the famous SASO (South African Students Organization) trial in the 1970s, when the chief evidence was plays and poems written by some of the accused. Yet all detained writers without exception are prevented from writing; some, released without ever having been charged with any offense, are nevertheless served with bans upon their release, which then silence them outside prison as well. All prohibitions under the Internal Security Act are characterized by the absoluteness of their terms and by the arbitrary nature of their imposition.

The Publications Act of 1974 replaces the Publications and Entertain- **10** ments Act of 1963, which banned not only books by South African writers but also books by Edmund Wilson, Mary McCarthy, Philip Roth and John Updike, in addition to those by writers one might expect, such as Eldridge Cleaver and Franz Fanon. Under the old legislation, writers were banned by a Publications Control Board, but they had a right to appeal to South Africa's Supreme Court. Although relatively few appeals against the board's decisions were brought into court, a number of its decisions were reversed by the Supreme Court. This led to the present Publications Act, which excludes the right of appeal to the court.

Under this act, Kurt Vonnegut is one of the most recent American writers to join the list of foreign writers banned in South Africa.

The 1974 act established a government-appointed Directorate of Publica- 11 tions, which is responsible for the overall administration of the act. The directorate appoints committees which are given the task of deciding whether publications, objects, films and public entertainment referred to them by the directorate are "undesirable" within the meaning of the act. Appeals can be made only to the Appeal Board set up by the directorate itself.

"Undesirability" is defined thus: 12

A publication, object, film or public entertainment is deemed undesirable 13 if it:

is indecent or obscene or is offensive or harmful to public morals;   14

is blasphemous or is offensive to the religious convictions or feelings of 15 any section of the inhabitants of the Republic;

if it is harmful to the relations between any sections of the inhabitants of 16 the Republic;

if it is prejudicial to the safety of the State, the general welfare or the 17 peace and good order of the State.

In the application of the act, it is laid down that "particular regard" is to 18 be paid to "the constant endeavor of the population of the Republic of South Africa to uphold a Christian view of life"—this in a population where there exist the claims of traditional African, Moslem, Hindu and Jewish religious and secular moralities. Moreover, for the purpose of determining undesirability, the motive of the author is irrelevant. A work may be found undesirable if *any part of it* is undesirable—a principle that reached its apogee when a Gore Vidal novel was banned on the ground that one passage compared the Holy Trinity to male genitalia.

The production and distribution of works declared undesirable is a crimi- 19 nal offense. Sexual candor aside, the most dangerous ground the writer treads is in the area of open or implied criticism of the institutions of state (in particular the police and defense), the administration of justice and the politico-legal apparatus of so-called separate development for people of different colors; in the sympathetic treatment of black liberation movements and radical opponents of the status quo; and in explicit accounts of interracial sexual relations. More and more in the last five years, sympathetic or even simply honest treatment of black liberation movements and the activities of all other radical opponents, of all colors, of the union between capitalism and racial oppression in South Africa have increasingly become the areas to which censorship reacts most strongly.

Under the strictures of these repressive acts, how does a writer work? 20

In the twenty years since censorship was introduced in South Africa, writ- 21
ers' attitudes have changed to meet it in different ways, and in relation to the
different contexts of their lives in a grossly unequal society.

At the beginning, black writers were little interested in censorship. White 22
writers were concerned with the one area where apartheid limited the lives of
black and white alike, but black writers saw the suppression of freedom of expression as the least tangible and therefore the least of the different aspects of
oppression experienced in their daily lives. Without freedom to sell their labor,
without freedom of movement, without freedom of association—in a phrase,
"with the passbook in their pockets"—the risk of having a book banned seemed
trivial. At the beginning of the 1960s, it was difficult to get black intellectuals
to sign protests against censorship. But after the banning of the black mass
movements with their populist appeal, the renaissance of the black spirit of liberation was cupped in the hands of young blacks who saw, in a police state
situation where overt political consciousness-raising was impossible, the importance of cultural consciencization. They looked to writers to imbue the new
generation with a sense of identity and pride in that identity through song and
story rather than taboo political doctrine. They saw those writers, as I have already said, as the cultural fist of liberation. It was then that censorship no
longer seemed irrelevant. This coincided, roughly, with a hardening in the attitude of progressive white writers, who changed their tactic of, in a sense, coop-
erating with the hated censorship by appealing when a book was banned to the
tactic of noncooperation with any functions of censorship. The principle of
"publish and be damned" ran up its flag.

That principle has been implemented, to a surprising extent, by the for- 23
mation of small publishing houses, mainly by people who are themselves writers. These publishers, unlike the rich British publishers operating as a fossilized
colonial outpost in South Africa, were prepared to lose the little money they
had if a book should be banned from sale, in the hope that at least some copies
would be circulated before the ax fell. That is the way many books reach readers in South Africa today, and the way in which writers tread the dangerous
ground of subjects I have referred to.

Conscious and unconscious self-censorship and stylistic defenses are 24
questions with which I have already dealt. There remains to be said that as the
situation in South Africa has become more and more crisis-ridden, painful and
dangerous, the fear that prompted self-censorship has been cast out. And so
something of the writer's innate freedom has been regained.

1983

QUESTIONS FOR DISCUSSION

Content

a. How do the examples Gordimer uses to illustrate her speech also serve to support her argument and to persuade her listeners and readers?
b. What effects does Gordimer mention that the South African government has had on writers?
c. According to Gordimer, what is the relationship between art and the government in South Africa?
d. What does she say is the result of laws that do not distinguish clearly between sexual and political works, between political and creative writing, between progressive thought and subversion (paragraphs 3 and 4)?
e. In what ways do the reasons the South African government gives for its actions (such as closing the *World,* paragraph 5) differ from the reasons that Gordimer gives?
f. In paragraph 7 Gordimer says that the young black writers in South Africa "see their literary activity as an integral part of their political activity." Do you think this is true of writers in other countries as well? What does Gordimer say the relationship between writing and politics is?
g. How do security laws affect white writers and black writers differently?
h. What measures does Gordimer say are being taken by writers as a result of the security laws? What, in turn, may happen as a result of these measures?

Strategy and Style

i. How would you characterize the basic structure of Gordimer's essay? Which paragraphs serve as transitions from one part of the essay to another?
j. Overall, is Gordimer optimistic or pessimistic about the situation in South Africa?

SUGGESTIONS FOR SHORT WRITING

a. Using only or mostly questions, annotate this essay.
b. Read through your annotations, and select one or two questions to which you would like a response. Exchange questions with a classmate, and write a response to each other's questions.

SUGGESTIONS FOR SUSTAINED WRITING

a. Do some library research on your own on South Africa. Write an essay in which you agree or disagree with Gordimer. Be sure to provide credible causes for the current situation.

b. Does censorship in South Africa have an equivalent in the United States? Again, do some research and find cases of the international writers banned in the United States.

c. Write an essay in which you argue for or against the necessity of censorship in general.

9

Analogy

Have you ever taken a test that requires you to evaluate relationships between pairs of items or ideas? A typical question might go something like this:

Truck is to driver as horse is to ——————.

Like other forms of comparison, analogy introduces new subjects or ideas by referencing and drawing parallels to information with which the reader is already familiar. Writers often use analogy to create unexpected and quite startling comparisons between items from very different classes. Consider Loren Eiseley's discussion of our earthly environment as a kind of cosmic prison and his startling revelation that our perspective on this planet may be as limited as that of a white blood cell traveling through the body of a cat. Nonetheless, the beauty of analogy is that it can be used effectively to shed new light even on items from the same class. For example, in the hands of Barry Lopez, the simple comparison of the horse and the truck—two means of transportation—blossoms into a cluster of implications that illuminate the cultures they represent and reveal something about the writer himself.

Analogies, then, bring to light important relationships that can help define a term, describe a person, place, or object, or even argue an important point. Scientific writers rely on analogy to make their descriptions of complex mechanisms or obscure phenomena both interesting and accessible to lay readers. Farley Mowat's "The Perfect House" explains that clothing can act as shelter and, in the process, accounts for the mystery behind how Arctic inhabitants can survive in so severe an environment. But analogy is also a good way to make an abstract idea concrete and vivid, thereby emphasizing its significance. The fact that human beings evolved only relatively recently in the history of the planet will not be news to readers of James C. Rettie's "'But a Watch in the Night.'" Nonetheless, charting the history of the Earth on a twelve-month clock helps the author underscore the fact that "We have just arrived...."

Philosophical concepts, by their very nature abstract, also benefit from

383

explanation through analogy. Plato's "The Myth of the Cave" is a cornerstone in the history of ideas; Camus' recounting the Sisyphus myth illuminates his definition of the absurd and explains why fate is a "human matter." Analogy is indeed a versatile tool. Consider the ironic social commentary Horace Miner is able to pull off in "Body Ritual among the Nacirema" or the personal portrait of a writer's anguish Annie Dillard paints in "Transfiguration."

The Suggestions for Short Writing and Sustained Writing that follow each selection should help you create and develop interesting analogies of your own. But the essays themselves are so provocative they might even help you come to grips with problems, issues, or concerns that play a significant role in your daily life. Can you compare your current social environment to a prison? Is taking fifteen credits and working twenty hours a week like trying to roll a boulder uphill? Do the ways modern college students date resemble courtship rituals among "primitive" peoples (real or fictitious)? If questions like these pop into your mind as you read through the chapter, write them down and show them to your instructor; they might make good topics for an essay. At the very least, they will help you begin using analogy as a tool for thinking and for writing.

The Myth of the Cave
Plato

The great Athenian philosopher of the Fourth Century B.C., Plato was the student of Socrates, whom he made the principal speaker in his dialogues. "The Myth of the Cave" appears in book VII of The Republic. *In it, Socrates addresses a series of questions to Glaucon in an attempt to explain that the world in which we live is a world of illusions and shadows—a mere reflection of the "real world" of the intellect. He explains that the "idea of good" is the "universal author of all things beautiful and right, parent of light...in this visible world, and the immediate source of reason and truth in the intellectual...."*

And now, I said, let me show in a figure how far our nature is enlightened 1
or unenlightened:—Behold! human beings living in an underground den, which has a mouth open toward the light and reaching all along the den; here they have been from their childhood, and have their legs and necks chained so that they cannot move, and can only see before them, being prevented by the chains from turning round their heads. Above and behind them a fire is blazing at a distance, and between the fire and the prisoners there is a raised way; and you will see, if you look, a low wall built along the way, like the screen which marionette players have in front of them, over which they show the puppets.

I see. 2

And do you see, I said, men passing along the wall carrying all sorts of 3
vessels, and statues and figures of animals made of wood and stone and various materials, which appear over the wall? Some of them are talking, others silent.

You have shown me a strange image, and they are strange prisoners. 4

Like ourselves, I replied; and they see only their own shadows, or the 5
shadows of one another, which the fire throws on the opposite wall of the cave?

True, he said; how could they see anything but the shadows if they were 6
never allowed to move their heads?

And of the objects which are being carried in like manner they would 7
only see the shadows?

Yes, he said. 8

And if they were able to converse with one another, would they not sup- 9
pose that they were naming what was actually before them?

Very true. 10

And suppose further that the prison had an echo which came from the 11
other side, would they not be sure to fancy when one of the passers-by spoke that the voice which they heard came from the passing shadow?

No question, he replied. 12

To them, I said, the truth would be literally nothing but the shadows of 13
the images.

385

That is certain. **14**

And now look again, and see what will naturally follow if the prisoners **15** are released and disabused of their error. At first, when any of them is liberated and compelled suddenly to stand up and turn his neck round and walk and look toward the light, he will suffer sharp pains; the glare will distress him, and he will be unable to see the realities of which in his former state he had seen the shadows; and then conceive some one saying to him, that what he saw before was an illusion, but that now, when he is approaching nearer to being and his eye is turned toward more real existence, he has a clearer vision—what will be his reply? And you may further imagine that his instructor is pointing to the objects as they pass and requiring him to name them—will he not be per-plexed? Will he not fancy that the shadows which he formerly saw are truer than the objects which are now shown to him?

Far truer. **16**

And if he is compelled to look straight at the light, will he not have a pain **17** in his eyes which will make him turn away to take refuge in the objects of vi-sion which he can see, and which he will conceive to be in reality clearer than the things which are now being shown to him?

True, he said. **18**

And suppose once more, that he is reluctantly dragged up a steep and rug- **19** ged ascent, and held fast until he is forced into the presence of the sun himself, is he not likely to be pained and irritated? When he approaches the light his eyes will be dazzled, and he will not be able to see anything at all of what are now called realities.

Not all in a moment, he said. **20**

He will require to grow accustomed to the sight of the upper world. And **21** first he will see the shadows best, next the reflections of men and other objects in the water, and then the objects themselves; then he will gaze upon the light of the moon and the stars and the spangled heaven; and he will see the sky and the stars by night better than the sun or the light of the sun by day?

Certainly. **22**

Last of all he will be able to see the sun, and not mere reflections of him **23** in the water, but he will see him in his own proper place, and not in another; and he will contemplate him as he is.

Certainly. **24**

He will then proceed to argue that this is he who gives the season and the **25** years, and is the guardian of all that is in the visible world, and in a certain way the cause of all things which he and his fellows have been accustomed to behold?

Clearly, he said, he would first see the sun and then reason about him. **26**

And when he remembered his old habitation, and the wisdom of the den **27** and his fellow-prisoners, do you not suppose that he would felicitate himself on the change, and pity them?

Certainly, he would. **28**

And if they were in the habit of conferring honors among themselves on **29** those who were quickest to observe the passing shadows and to remark which of them went before, and which followed after, and which were together; and who were therefore best able to draw conclusions as to the future, do you think that he would care for such honors and glories, or envy the possessors of them? Would he not say with Homer,

> Better to be the poor servant of a poor master,

and to endure anything, rather than think as they do and live after their manner?

Yes, he said, I think that he would rather suffer anything than entertain these false notions and live in this miserable manner.   30

Imagine once more, I said, such a one coming suddenly out of the sun to be replaced in his old situation; would he not be certain to have his eyes full of darkness?   31

To be sure, he said.   32

And if there were a contest, and he had to compete in measuring the shadows with the prisoners who had never moved out of the den, while his sight was still weak, and before his eyes had become steady (and the time which would be needed to acquire this new habit of sight might be very considerable), would he not be ridiculous? Men would say of him that up he went and down he came without his eyes; and that it was better not even to think of ascending; and if any one tried to loose another and lead him up to the light, let them only catch the offender, and they would put him to death.   33

No question, he said.   34

This entire allegory, I said, you may now append, dear Glaucon, to the previous argument; the prison-house is the world of sight, the light of the fire is the sun, and you will not misapprehend me if you interpret the journey upwards to be the ascent of the soul into the intellectual world according to my poor belief, which, at your desire, I have expressed—whether rightly or wrongly God knows. But, whether true or false, my opinion is that in the world of knowledge the idea of good appears last of all, and is seen only with an effort; and, when seen, is also inferred to be the universal author of all things beautiful and right, parent of light and of the lord of light in this visible world, and the immediate source of reason and truth in the intellectual; and that this is the power upon which he who would act rationally either in public or private life must have his eye fixed.   35

I agree, he said, as far as I am able to understand you.   36

Moreover, I said, you must not wonder that those who attain to this beatific vision are unwilling to descend to human affairs; for their souls are ever hastening into the upper world where they desire to dwell; which desire of theirs is very natural, if our allegory may be trusted.   37

Yes, very natural.   38

And is there anything surprising in one who passes from divine contemplations to the evil state of man, misbehaving himself in a ridiculous manner; if, while his eyes are blinking and before he has become accustomed to the sur-   39 rounding darkness, he is compelled to fight in courts of law, or in other places, about the images or the shadows of images of justice, and is endeavoring to meet the conceptions of those who have never yet seen absolute justice?

Anything but surprising, he replied.   **40**

Any one who has common sense will remember that the bewilderments **41** of the eyes are of two kinds, and arise from two causes, either from coming out of the light or from going into the light, which is true of the mind's eye, quite as much as of the bodily eye; and he who remembers this when he sees any one whose vision is perplexed and weak, will not be too ready to laugh; he will first ask whether that soul of man has come out of the brighter life, and is unable to see because unaccustomed to the dark, or having turned from darkness to the day is dazzled by excess of light. And he will count the one happy in his condition and state of being, and he will pity the other; or, if he have a mind to laugh at the soul which comes from below into the light, there will be more reason in this than in the laugh which greets him who returns from above out of the light into the den.

That, he said, is a very just distinction.   **42**

ca. 373 b.c.

QUESTIONS FOR DISCUSSION

Content

a. Why does Plato refer to "the world of sight" as a "prison-house"?
b. Does the fact that Plato has cast this extended analogy into a dialogue make it more effective than if he had written in conventional essay form?
c. What does the sun represent in Plato's analogy?
d. Consult an unabridged dictionary, encyclopedia, or reference book on ancient literature or civilization. Who was Homer? Why does Plato allude to him?
e. What is the "beatific" vision that Socrates describes to Glaucon? Why is it important that one "who would act rationally" experience this vision?
f. How does Plato account for the fact that honorable people, who are able to see the truth and to relate it to others, often experience scorn and ridicule?
g. What has Glaucon learned by the end of the dialogue?

Strategy and Style

h. How effective is the dialogue form used in this selection? What is the function of Glaucon's brief responses? Of Socrates' questions?
i. How do Socrates' questions help determine the organization?
j. What is Plato's role in this selection? Is he invisible, a mere transcriber of the dialogue, or is his voice heard in some way?

SUGGESTIONS FOR SHORT WRITING

a. Write a short dialogue between yourself and Plato or between yourself and one of the dwellers in the cave.
b. This is an especially difficult selection. Try to capture the essence of Plato's ideas in a summary of one or two paragraphs

SUGGESTIONS FOR SUSTAINED WRITING

a. Try describing the human condition using another analogy besides the cave.
b. Do you believe that we are prisoners of the material world as Plato suggests? If so, write an essay in which you illustrate how people let their appetites (for food, money, sex, material possessions, for example) determine the course of their lives.
c. Do you believe that whatever is spiritual in a person can prevail? Write an essay in which you illustrate (from your own experiences, from those of people you know well, or from those you have read about) that people will deny themselves physical or material gratification in order to preserve the ethical principles or moral codes they believe in.
d. Create your own analogy by talking about the place where you work, live, or attend school in terms more usually associated with a prison, playground, resort, etc. Or you may want to describe the personality of someone you know well and create an analogy between him/her and an animal, either wild or domesticated, with which your readers might be familiar. Some personalities that you choose to describe will be so complex that you may need to include more than one animal in the analogy.

Body Ritual among the Nacirema

Horace Miner

Horace Miner (b. 1912) is a social anthropologist. He studied at the University of Kentucky and at the University of Chicago, where he took his Ph.D. in 1937. In 1953 he wrote a seminal study of primitive urban culture, The Primitive City of Timbuctoo. *He is a recognized authority on African cultures and has received many awards for his work. "Body Ritual," a parodic departure from his usual scientific writing style, appeared as a "serious" article in* The American Anthropologist.

The anthropologist has become so familiar with the diversity of ways in 1
which different peoples behave in similar situations that he is not apt to be surprised by even the most exotic customs. In fact, if all of the logically possible combinations of behavior have not been found somewhere in the world, he is apt to suspect that they must be present in some yet undescribed tribe. This point has, in fact, been expressed with respect to clan organization by Murdock.[1] In this light, the magical beliefs and practices of the Nacirema present such unusual aspects that it seems desirable to describe them as an example of the extremes to which human behavior can go.

Professor Linton first brought the ritual of the Nacirema to the attention 2
of anthropologists twenty years ago, but the culture of this people is still very poorly understood. They are a North American group living in the territory between the Canadian Cree, the Yaqui and Tarahumare of Mexico, and the Carib and Arawak of the Antilles.[2] Little is known of their origin, although tradition states that they came from the east....

Nacirema culture is characterized by a highly developed market economy 3
which has evolved in a rich natural habitat. While much of the people's time is devoted to economic pursuits, a large part of the fruits of these labors and a considerable portion of the day are spent in ritual activity. The focus of this activity is the human body, the appearance and health of which loom as a dominant concern in the ethos of the people. While such a concern is certainly not unusual, its ceremonial aspects and associated philosophy are unique.

The fundamental belief underlying the whole system appears to be that 4
the human body is ugly and that its natural tendency is to debility and disease. Incarcerated in such a body, man's only hope is to avert these characteristics through the use of the powerful influences of ritual and ceremony. Every household has one or more shrines devoted to this purpose. The more powerful indi-

---

[1] American anthropologist George Peter Murdock authority on primitive cultures.
[2] Native American tribes formerly inhabiting the Saskatchewan region of Canada, the Sonora region of Mexico, and the West Indies.

viduals in the society have several shrines in their houses and, in fact, the opulence of a house is often referred to in terms of the number of such ritual centers it possesses. Most houses are of wattle and daub construction, but the shrine rooms of the more wealthy are walled with stone. Poorer families imitate the rich by applying pottery plaques to their shrine walls.

While each family has at least one such shrine, the rituals associated with 5
it are not family ceremonies but are private and secret. The rites are normally only discussed with children, and then only during the period when they are being initiated into these mysteries. I was able, however, to establish sufficient rapport with the natives to examine these shrines and to have the rituals described to me.

The focal point of the shrine is a box or chest which is built into the wall. 6
In this chest are kept the many charms and magical potions without which no native believes he could live. These preparations are secured from a variety of specialized practitioners. The most powerful of these are the medicine men, whose assistance must be rewarded with substantial gifts. However, the medicine men do not provide the curative potions for their clients, but decide what the ingredients should be and then write them down in an ancient and secret language. This writing is understood only by the medicine men and by the herbalists who, for another gift, provide the required charm.

The charm is not disposed of after it has served its purpose, but is placed 7
in the charm-box of the household shrine. As these magical materials are specific for certain ills, and the real or imagined maladies of the people are many, the charm-box is usually full to overflowing. The magical packets are so numerous that people forget what their purposes were and fear to use them again. While the natives are very vague on this point, we can only assume that the idea in retaining all the old magical materials is that their presence in the charm-box, before which the body rituals are conducted, will in some way protect the worshipper.

Beneath the charm-box is a small font. Each day every member of the 8
family, in succession, enters the shrine room, bows his head before the charm-box, mingles different sorts of holy water in the font, and proceeds with a brief rite of ablution. The holy waters are secured from the Water Temple of the community, where the priests conduct elaborate ceremonies to make the liquid ritually pure.

In the hierarchy of magical practitioners, and below the medicine men in 9
prestige, are specialists whose designation is best translated "holy-mouth-men." The Nacirema have an almost pathological horror of and fascination with the mouth, the condition of which is believed to have a supernatural influence on all social relationships. Were it not for the rituals of the mouth, they believe that their teeth would fall out, their gums bleed, their jaws shrink, their friends desert them, and their lovers reject them. They also believe that a strong relationship exists between oral and moral characteristics. For example, there is a ritual ablution of the mouth for children which is supposed to improve their

moral fiber.

The daily body ritual performed by everyone includes a mouth-rite. Despite the fact that these people are so punctilious about care of the mouth, this rite involves a practice which strikes the uninitiated stranger as revolting. It was reported to me that the ritual consists of inserting a small bundle of hog hairs into the mouth, along with certain magical powders, and then moving the bundle in a highly formalized series of gestures. **10**

In addition to the private mouth-rite, the people seek out a holy-mouth-man once or twice a year. These practitioners have an impressive set of paraphernalia, consisting of a variety of augers, awls, probes, and prods. The use of these objects in the exorcism of the evils of the mouth involves almost unbelievable ritual torture of the client. The holy-mouth-man opens the client's mouth and, using the above mentioned tools, enlarges any holes which decay may have created in the teeth. Magical materials are put into these holes. If there are not naturally occurring holes in the teeth, large sections of one or more teeth are gouged out so that the supernatural substance can be applied. In the client's view, the purpose of these ministrations is to arrest decay and to draw friends. The extremely sacred and traditional character of the rite is evident in the fact that the natives return to the holy-mouth-men year after year, despite the fact that their teeth continue to decay. **11**

It is to be hoped that, when a thorough study of the Nacirema is made, there will be careful inquiry into the personality structure of these people. One has but to watch the gleam in the eye of a holy-mouth-man, as he jabs an awl into an exposed nerve, to suspect that a certain amount of sadism is involved. If this can be established, a very interesting pattern emerges, for most of the population shows definite masochistic tendencies. It was to these that Professor Linton referred in discussing a distinctive part of the daily body ritual which is performed only by men. This part of the rite involves scraping and lacerating the surface of the face with a sharp instrument. Special women's rites are performed only four times during each lunar month, but what they lack in frequency is made up in barbarity. As part of this ceremony, women bake their heads in small ovens for about an hour. The theoretically interesting point is that what seems to be a preponderantly masochistic people have developed sadistic specialists. **12**

The medicine men have an imposing temple, or latipso, in every community of any size. The more elaborate ceremonies required to treat very sick patients can only be performed at this temple. These ceremonies involve not only the thaumaturge but a permanent group of vestal maidens who move sedately about the temple chambers in distinctive costume and headdress. **13**

The latipso ceremonies are so harsh that it is phenomenal that a fair proportion of the really sick natives who enter the temple ever recover. Small children whose indoctrination is still incomplete have been known to resist attempts to take them to the temple because "that is where you go to die." Despite this fact, sick adults are not only willing but eager to undergo the pro- **14** tracted ritual purification, if they can afford to do so. No matter how ill the supplicant or how grave the emergency, the guardians of many temples will not admit a client if he cannot give a rich gift to the custodian. Even after one has gained admission and survived the ceremonies, the guardians will not permit the neophyte to leave until he makes still another gift.

The supplicant entering the temple is first stripped of all his or her 15 clothes. In everyday life the Nacirema avoids exposure of his body and its natural functions. Bathing and excretory acts are performed only in the secrecy of the household shrine, where they are ritualized as part of the body-rites. Psychological shock results from the fact that body secrecy is suddenly lost upon entry into the latipso. A man, whose own wife has never seen him in an excretory act, suddenly finds himself naked and assisted by a vestal maiden while he performs his natural functions into a sacred vessel. This sort of ceremonial treatment is necessitated by the fact that the excreta are used by a diviner to ascertain the course and nature of the client's sickness. Female clients, on the other hand, find their naked bodies are subjected to the scrutiny, manipulation and prodding of the medicine men.

Few supplicants in the temple are well enough to do anything but lie on their 16 hard beds. The daily ceremonies, like the rites of the holy-mouth-men, involve discomfort and torture. With ritual precision, the vestals awaken their miserable charges each dawn and roll them about on their beds of pain while performing ablutions, in the formal movements of which the maidens are highly trained. At other times they insert magic wands in the supplicant's mouth or force him to eat substances which are supposed to be healing. From time to time the medicine men come to their clients and jab magically treated needles into their flesh. The fact that these temple ceremonies may not cure, and may even kill the neophyte, in no way decreases the people's faith in the medicine men.

There remains one other kind of practitioner, known as a "listener." This 17 witchdoctor has the power to exorcise the devils that lodge in the heads of people who have been bewitched. The Nacirema believe that parents bewitch their own children. Mothers are particularly suspected of putting a curse on children while teaching them the secret body rituals. The counter-magic of the witchdoctor is unusual in its lack of ritual. The patient simply tells the "listener" all his troubles and fears, beginning with the earliest difficulties he can remember. The memory displayed by the Nacirema in these exorcism sessions is truly remarkable. It is not uncommon for the patient to bemoan the rejection he felt upon being weaned as a babe, and a few individuals even see their troubles going back to the traumatic effects of their own birth.

In conclusion, mention must be made of certain practices which have 18 their base in native esthetics but which depend upon the pervasive aversion to the natural body and its functions. There are ritual fasts to make fat people thin and ceremonial feasts to make thin people fat. Still other rites are used to make women's breasts larger if they are small, and smaller if they are large. General dissatisfaction with breast shape is symbolized in the fact that the ideal form is virtually outside the range of human variation. A few women afflicted with almost inhuman hyper-mammary development are so idolized that they make a handsome living by simply going from village to village and permitting the natives to stare at them for a fee.

Reference has already been made to the fact that excretory functions are 19 ritualized, routinized, and relegated to secrecy. Natural reproductive functions are similarly distorted. Intercourse is taboo as a topic and scheduled as an act. Efforts are made to avoid pregnancy by the use of magical materials or by limiting intercourse to certain phases of the moon. Conception is actually very infrequent. When pregnant, women dress so as to hide their condition. Parturition takes place in secret, without friends or relatives to assist, and the majority of women do not nurse their infants.

Our review of the ritual life of the Nacirema has certainly shown them to 20 be a magic-ridden people. It is hard to understand how they have managed to exist so long under the burdens which they have imposed upon themselves. But even such exotic customs as these take on real meaning when they are viewed with the insight provided by Malinowski when he wrote:

"Looking from far and above, from our high places of safety in the devel- 21 oped civilization, it is easy to see all the crudity and irrelevance of magic. But without its power and guidance early man could not have mastered his practical difficulties as he has done, nor could man have advanced to the higher stages of civilization."

1956

QUESTIONS FOR DISCUSSION

Content

a. What might be Miner's purpose for writing this essay?
b. To whom is he writing? What reaction would these readers have to this essay?
c. What is Miner's thesis? What is his opinion of the behavior of the Nacirema? What is his relationship to them?
d. At which point in the essay do you begin to realize who the Nacirema really are? What clues does Miner provide to their identity?
e. What do you learn about the Nacirema that you never knew before? Was it necessary for Miner to use an analogy to tell you this? Is it fair of him to present his observations in the form of such an analogy?
f. In paragraph 4 Miner says that "The fundamental belief underlying the whole system appears to be that the human body is ugly...," and in paragraph 20 he says that the Nacirema are "magic-ridden people." Do you agree with his assessment of the Nacirema?

Strategy and Style

g. Look up the word "parody" in a dictionary of literary terms. In what ways is this essay a parody? What does it parody? Do you think it is a good parody?

h. What is the effect of including references to actual anthropologists and tribes?

i. Choose any paragraph and paraphrase it in ordinary language. What patterns does Miner use in transforming terms for bathroom activities into "body rituals"? Do you think that anthropologists (and other scientists as well) follow similar patterns in describing their observations?

j. Describe Miner's tone at the different levels of meaning in this essay. How do the tones reflect his attitude toward the Nacirema?

SUGGESTIONS FOR SHORT WRITING

a. Describe one of the Nacirema. You can describe her/him physically, intellectually, emotionally, behaviorally, etc. In what ways is this Nacireman different from yourself?

b. Describe a "ritual" of your own in the style of Miner.

SUGGESTIONS FOR SUSTAINED WRITING

a. Write an anthropological report of some aspect of society from the point of view of an animal anthropologist. For instance, what might a cat or dog think of a human family's behavior if it were sent to study its members as an anthropologist?

b. Closely observe a particular group of people and write an anthropological analysis of those people. You may wish to become an anthropologist studying the "tribe" on your floor of the dorm, or to observe the "culture" of a park or street.

c. Miner makes an analogy between Americans and a typical tribe studied by anthropologists. What other analogies can be made to describe Americans? Write an essay based on such an analogy.

Transfiguration

Annie Dillard

Born in Pittsburgh in 1945, Annie Dillard made her mark early as contributing editor to Harper's *from 1973 to 1981. Before she was thirty, she had won a Pulitzer Prize for* Pilgrim at Tinker Creek *(1974), a narrative about Virginia's Roanoke Valley, where Dillard once resided. She has served on the U.S. Cultural Delegation to the People's Republic of China and on the National Commission of U.S.-China Relations. From these experiences came* Encounters with Chinese Writers *(1984). She has published anthologies of narrative essays, including* Teaching a Stone to Talk *(1982) and* Holy the Firm *(1977) from which this selection is taken. She has also published a book of poetry entitled* Tickets for a Prayer Wheel *(1974). From 1979 to 1983, Dillard taught at Wesleyan University as a visiting professor and writer in residence.*

1   I live on northern Puget Sound, in Washington State, alone. I have a gold cat, who sleeps on my legs, named Small. In the morning I joke to her blank face, Do you remember last night? Do you remember? I throw her out before breakfast, so I can eat.

2   There is a spider, too, in the bathroom, with whom I keep a sort of company. Her little outfit always reminds me of a certain moth I helped to kill. The spider herself is of uncertain lineage, bulbous at the abdomen and drab. Her six-inch mess of a web works, works somehow, works miraculously, to keep her alive and me amazed. The web itself is in a corner behind the toilet, connecting tile wall to tile wall and floor, in a place where there is, I would have thought, scant traffic. Yet under the web are sixteen or so corpses she has tossed to the floor.

3   The corpses appear to be mostly sow bugs, those little armadillo creatures who live to travel flat out in houses, and die round. There is also a new shred of earwig, three old spider skins crinkled and clenched, and two moth bodies, wingless and huge and empty, moth bodies I drop to my knees to see.

4   Today the earwig shines darkly and gleams, what there is of him: a dorsal curve of thorax and abdomen, and a smooth pair of cerci by which I knew his name. Next week, if the other bodies are any indication, he will be shrunken and gray, webbed to the floor with dust. The sow bugs beside him are hollow and empty of color, fragile, a breath away from brittle fluff. The spider skins lie on their sides, translucent and ragged, their legs drying in knots. And the moths, the empty moths, stagger against each other, headless, in a confusion of arching strips of chitin like peeling varnish, like a jumble of buttresses for cathedral domes, like nothing resembling moths, so that I should hesitate to call them moths, except that I have had some experience with the figure Moth reduced to a nub.

396

Two summers ago I was camping alone in the Blue Ridge Mountains in 5 Virginia. I had hauled myself and gear up there to read, among other things, James Ramsey Ullman's *The Day on Fire,* a novel about Rimbaud that had made me want to be a writer when I was sixteen; I was hoping it would do it again. So I read, lost, every day sitting under a tree by my tent, while warblers swung in the leaves overhead and bristle worms trailed their inches over the twiggy dirt at my feet; and I read every night by candlelight, while barred owls called in the forest and pale moths massed round my head in the clearing, where my light made a ring.

Moths kept flying into the candle. They would hiss and recoil, lost upside 6 down in the shadows among my cooking pans. Or they would singe their wings and fall, and their hot wings, as if melted, would stick to the first thing they touched—a pan, a lid, a spoon—so that the snagged moths could flutter only in tiny arcs, unable to struggle free. These I could release by a quick flip with a stick; in the morning I would find my cooking stuff gilded with torn flecks of moth wings, triangles of shiny dust here and there on the aluminum. So I read, and boiled water, and replenished candles, and read on.

One night a moth flew into the candle, was caught, burnt dry, and held. I 7 must have been staring at the candle, or maybe I looked up when a shadow crossed my page; at any rate, I saw it all. A golden female moth, a biggish one with a two-inch wingspan, flapped into the fire, dropped her abdomen into the wet wax, stuck, flamed, frazzled and fried in a second. Her moving wings ignited like tissue paper, enlarging the circle of light in the clearing and creating out of the darkness the sudden blue sleeves of my sweater, the green leaves of jewelweed by my side, the ragged red trunk of a pine. At once the light contracted again and the moth's wings vanished in a fine, foul smoke. At the same time her six legs clawed, curled, blackened, and ceased, disappearing utterly. And her head jerked in spasms, making a spattering noise; her antennae crisped and burned away and her heaving mouth parts crackled like pistol fire. When it was all over, her head was, so far as I could determine, gone, gone the long way of her wings and legs. Had she been new, or old? Had she mated and laid her eggs, had she done her work? All that was left was the glowing horn shell of her abdomen and thorax—a fraying, partially collapsed gold tube jammed upright in the candle's round pool.

And then this moth-essence, this spectacular skeleton, began to act as a 8 wick. She kept burning. The wax rose in the moth's body from her soaking abdomen to her thorax to the jagged hole where her head should be, and widened into flame, a saffron-yellow flame that robed her to the ground like any immolating monk. That candle had two wicks, two flames of identical height, side by side. The moth's head was fire. She burned for two hours, until I blew her out.

She burned for two hours without changing, without bending or leaning— 9 only glowing within, like a building fire glimpsed through silhouetted walls, like a hollow saint, like a flame-faced virgin gone to God, while I read by her light, kindled, while Rimbaud in Paris burnt out his brains in a thousand poems, while night pooled wetly at my feet.

And that is why I believe those hollow crisps on the bathroom floor are 10 moths. I think I know moths, and fragments of moths, and chips and tatters of utterly empty moths, in any state. How many of you, I asked the people in my class, which of you want to give your lives and be writers? I was trembling from coffee, or cigarettes, or the closeness of faces all around me. (Is this what we live for? I thought; is this the only final beauty: the color of any skin in any light, and living, human eyes?) All hands rose to the question. (You, Nick? Will you? Margaret? Randy? Why do I want them to mean it?) And then I tried to tell them what the choice must mean: you can't be anything else. You must go at your life with a broadax.... They had no idea what I was saying. (I have two hands, don't I? And all this energy, for as long as I can remember. I'll do it in the evenings, after skiing, or on the way home from the bank, or after the children are asleep....) They thought I was raving again. It's just as well.

I have three candles here on the table which I disentangle from the plants 11 and light when visitors come. Small usually avoids them, although once she came too close and her tail caught fire; I rubbed it out before she noticed. The flames move light over everyone's skin, draw light to the surface of the faces of my friends. When the people leave I never blow the candles out, and after I'm asleep they flame and burn.

1977

QUESTIONS FOR DISCUSSION

Content

a. Who was Arthur Rimbaud, and why is he so important to this essay? Why does Dillard mention the title of Ullman's novel about this French poet?

b. What is the significance of Dillard's statement in paragraph 9 that she "read by [the moth's] light, kindled, while Rimbaud in Paris burnt out his brains in a thousand poems..."?

c. What is Dillard driving at when, in paragraph 10, she tells would-be writers that they "must go at life with a broadax...."? What exactly does she do "after skiing, or on the way home from the bank..."?

d. In paragraph 7, Dillard explains that, when the moth's wings ignited, they enlarged "the circle of light in the clearing...." Why does she use the phrase "creating out of the darkness" to explain that the light of the flame revealed "the sudden blue sleeves of [her] sweater..."? How does this image relate to what she is saying in paragraph 10?

e. Why, in paragraph 7, does Dillard recall that, "At once the light contracted again and the moth's wings vanished in a fine, foul smoke"?

f. Explain the primary or controlling analogy upon which this selection is based. What can writers possibly have in common with moths? What other examples of analogy can you identify in this selection?

g. Why does Dillard spend so much time describing the dead insects in her home? Do her comments about them serve as a source of contrast to the moth that was immolated in the candle flame?

h. This essay employs a great deal of religious imagery. Identify such images and discuss why the author has chosen to use them.

i. Name the three locations in which the author sets this essay. Why is each important? Why does she have to take the reader into the wilderness to describe the burning of the moth?

Strategy and Style

j. Paragraphs 6, 7, and 8 demonstrate Dillard's genius for description. What makes these paragraphs so effective? Analyze her choice of vocabulary, her use of alliteration, and her reliance on figurative language to make her prose vivid and powerful.

k. What does she mean by "the only final beauty"? What might have been her reasons for choosing that phrase to describe it?

l. Describe Dillard's tone. Is it consistent throughout the essay, or is there a shift in tone in the conclusion? How does Small help Dillard effect that change?

SUGGESTIONS FOR SHORT WRITING

a. Try, in as much detail as Dillard uses, to describe the world of a creature, however small, that shares your living space.

b. List the metaphors that Dillard uses in her essay. Taking one or two of those metaphors, explain why you think she chose to use them.

SUGGESTIONS FOR SUSTAINED WRITING

a. Dillard's essay is both subtle and complex. Read it a second time. Then, in an attempt to understand and appreciate more fully the brilliant analogy she has created, summarize and explain Dillard's thesis and the major ideas she uses to develop it.

b. Create an extended analogy through which you compare a human event or activity with a phenomenon in the natural world. For instance, you might liken Christmas shopping at a local department store to what goes on in a nest of angry hornets, or you could draw parallels between the way in which certain animals and certain people court their mates.

c. Recall your favorite novel, short story, play, poem, or movie. Why is it your favorite? Do you identify with its characters? Does its theme hold special meaning for you? If so, write an extended analogy between this work and your own life or the way in which you look at life.

"But a Watch in the Night": A Scientific Fable

James C. Rettie

James C. Rettie was educated at the University of Oregon, Yale University, and the University of London, where he studied economics. Employed by the United States Forest Service for many years, Rettie was able to indulge his love for the outdoors and his interest in conservation. During the Kennedy and Johnson administrations, he served as an advisor to Secretary of the Interior Stuart Udall. Rettie published often in his field, but this is the only essay for which he is widely remembered. It first appeared in 1948 in a publication of the Department of Agriculture. Rettie wrote it while serving at a Forest Service station in Pennsylvania.

Out beyond our solar system there is a planet called Copernicus. It came 1
into existence some four or five billion years before the birth of our Earth. In due course of time it became inhabited by a race of intelligent men.

About 750 million years ago the Copernicans had developed the motion 2
picture machine to a point well in advance of the stage that we have reached. Most of the cameras that we now use in motion picture work are geared to take twenty-four pictures per second on a continuous strip of film. When such film is run through a projector, it throws a series of images on the screen and these change with a rapidity that gives the visual impression of normal movement. If a motion is too swift for the human eye to see it in detail, it can be captured and artificially slowed down by means of the slow-motion camera. This one is geared to take many more shots per second—ninety-six or even more than that. When the slow motion film is projected at the normal speed of twenty-four pictures per second, we can see just how the jumping horse goes over a hurdle.

What about motion that is too slow to be seen by the human eye? That 3
problem has been solved by the use of the time-lapse camera. In this one, the shutter is geared to take only one shot per second, or one per minute, or even one per hour—depending upon the kind of movement that is being photographed. When the time-lapse film is projected at the normal speed of twenty-four pictures per second, it is possible to see a bean sprout growing up out of the ground. Time-lapse films are useful in the study of many types of motion too slow to be observed by the unaided, human eye.

The Copernicans, it seems, had time-lapse cameras some 757 million 4
years ago and they also had superpowered telescopes that gave them a clear view of what was happening upon this Earth. They decided to make a film record of the life history of Earth and to make it on the scale of one picture per year. The photography has been in progress during the last 757 million years.

401

In the near future, a Copernican interstellar expedition will arrive upon ₅
our Earth and bring with it a copy of the time-lapse film. Arrangements will be
made for showing the entire film in one continuous run. This will begin at
midnight of New Year's Eve and continue day and night without a single stop
until midnight of December 31. The rate of projection will be twenty-four
pictures per second. Time on the screen will thus seem to move at the rate of
twenty-four years per second; 1440 years per minute; 86,400 years per hour;
approximately two million years per day; and sixty-two million years per
month. The normal life-span of individual man will occupy about three seconds. The full period of earth history that will be unfolded on the screen (some
757 million years) will extend from what the geologists call Pre-Cambrian
times up to the present. This will, by no means, cover the full time-span of the
earth's geological history but it will embrace the period since the advent of living organisms.

During the months of January, February, and March the picture will be ₆
desolate and dreary. The shape of the land masses and the oceans will bear little
or no resemblance to those that we know. The violence of geological erosion
will be much in evidence. Rains will pour down on the land and promptly go
booming down to the seas. There will be no clear streams anywhere except
where the rains fall upon hard rock. Everywhere on the steeper ground the
stream channels will be filled with boulders hurled down by rushing waters.
Raging torrents and dry stream beds will keep alternating in quick succession.
High mountains will seem to melt like so much butter in the sun. The shifting
of land into the seas, later to be thrust up as new mountains, will be going on at
a grand scale.

Early in April there will be some indication of the presence of single- ₇
celled living organisms in some of the warmer and sheltered coastal waters. By
the end of the month it will be noticed that some of these organisms have become multicellular. A few of them, including the Trilobites, will be encased in
hard shells.

Toward the end of May, the first vertebrates will appear, but they will still ₈
be aquatic creatures. In June about 60 per cent of the land area that we know as
North America will be under water. One broad channel will occupy the space
where the Rocky Mountains now stand. Great deposits of limestone will be
forming under some of the shallower seas. Oil and gas deposits will be in process of formation—also under shallow seas. On land there will still be no sign
of vegetation. Erosion will be rampant, tearing loose particles and chunks of
rock and grinding them into sand and silt to be spewed out by the streams into
bays and estuaries.

About the middle of July the first land plants will appear and take up the ₉
tremendous job of soil building. Slowly, very slowly, the mat of vegetation will
spread, always battling for its life against the power of erosion. Almost foot by
foot, the plant life will advance, lacing down with its root structures whatever
pulverized rock material it can find. Leaves and stems will be giving added pro-

tection against the loss of the soil foothold. The increasing vegetation will pave the way for the land animals that will live upon it.

Early in August the seas will be teeming with fish. This will be what geologists call the Devonian period. Some of the races of these fish will be breathing by means of lung tissue instead of through gill tissues. Before the month is over, some of the lung fish will go ashore and take on a crude lizard-like appearance. Here are the first amphibians.

In early September the insects will put in their appearance. Some will look like huge dragonflies and will have a wing spread of 24 inches. Large portions of the land masses will now be covered with heavy vegetation that will include the primitive spore-propagating trees. Layer upon layer of this plant growth will build up, later to appear as the coal deposits. About the middle of this month, there will be evidence of the first seed-bearing plants and the first reptiles. Heretofore, the land animals will have been amphibians that could reproduce their kind only by depositing a soft egg mass in quiet waters. The reptiles will be shown to be freed from the aquatic bond because they can reproduce by means of a shelled egg in which the embryo and its nurturing liquids are sealed and thus protected from destructive evaporation. Before September is over, the first dinosaurs will be seen—creatures destined to dominate the animal realm for about 140 million years and then to disappear.

In October there will be series of mountain uplifts along what is now the eastern coast of the United States. A creature with feathered limbs—half bird and half reptile in appearance—will take itself into the air. Some small and rather unpretentious animals will be seen to bring forth their young in a form that is a miniature replica of the parents and to feed these young on milk secreted by mammary glands in the female parent. The emergence of this mammalian form of animal life will be recognized as one of the great events in geologic time. October will also witness the high water mark of the dinosaurs—creatures ranging in size from that of the modern goat to monsters like Brontosaurus that weighed some 40 tons. Most of them will be placid vegetarians, but a few will be hideous-looking carnivores, like Allosaurus and Tyrannosaurus. Some of the herbivorous dinosaurs will be clad in bony armor for protection against their flesh-eating comrades.

November will bring pictures of a sea extending from the Gulf of Mexico to the Arctic in space now occupied by the Rocky Mountains. A few of the reptiles will take to the air on bat-like wings. One of these, called Pteranodon, will have a wingspread of 15 feet. There will be a rapid development of the modern flowering plants, modern trees, and modern insects. The dinosaurs will disappear. Toward the end of the month there will be a tremendous land disturbance in which the Rocky Mountains will rise out of the sea to assume a dominating place in the North American landscape.

As the picture runs on into December it will show the mammals in command of the animal life. Seed-bearing trees and grasses will have covered most of the land with a heavy mantle of vegetation. Only the areas newly thrust up from the sea will be barren. Most of the streams will be crystal clear. The turmoil of geologic erosion will be confined to localized areas. About December 25 will begin the cutting of the Grand Canyon of the Colorado River. Grinding down through layer after layer of sedimentary strata, this stream will finally expose deposits laid down in Pre-Cambrian times. Thus in the walls of that canyon will appear geological formations dating from recent times to the period when the Earth had no living organisms upon it.

The picture will run on through the latter days of December and even up 15 to its final day with still no sign of mankind. The spectators will become alarmed in the fear that man has somehow been left out. But not so; sometimes about noon on December 31 (one million years ago) will appear a stooped, massive creature of man-like proportions. This will be Pithecanthropus, the Java ape man. For tools and weapons he will have nothing but crude stone and wooden clubs. His children will live a precarious existence threatened on the one side by hostile animals and on the other by tremendous climatic changes. Ice sheets—in places 4000 feet deep—will form in the northern parts of North America and Eurasia. Four times this glacial ice will push southward to cover half the continents. With each advance the plant and animal life will be swept under or pushed southward. With each recession of the ice, life will struggle to reestablish itself in the wake of the retreating glaciers. The woolly mammoth, the musk ox, and the caribou all will fight to maintain themselves near the ice line. Sometimes they will be caught and put into cold storage—skin, flesh, blood, bones and all.

The picture will run on through supper time with still very little evidence 16 of man's presence on the earth. It will be about 11 o'clock when Neanderthal man appears. Another half hour will go by before the appearance of Cro-Magnon man living in caves and painting crude animal pictures on the walls of his dwelling. Fifteen minutes more will bring Neolithic man, knowing how to chip stone and thus produce sharp cutting edges for spears and tools. In a few minutes more it will appear that man has domesticated the dog, the sheep and, possibly, other animals. He will then begin the use of milk. He will also learn the arts of basket weaving and the making of pottery and dugout canoes.

The dawn of civilization will not come until about five or six minutes 17 before the end of the picture. The story of the Egyptians, the Babylonians, the Greeks, and the Romans will unroll during the fourth, the third, and the second minute before the end. At 58 minutes and 43 seconds past 11:00 PM (just 1 minute and 17 seconds before the end) will come the beginning of the Christian era. Columbus will discover the new world 20 seconds before the end. The Declaration of Independence will be signed just 7 seconds before the final curtain comes down.

In those few moments of geologic time will be the story of all that has 18 happened since we became a nation. And what a story it will be! A human swarm will sweep across the face of the continent and take it away from the...red men. They will change it far more radically than it has ever been changed before in a comparable time. The great virgin forests will be seen going down before ax and fire. The soil, covered for eons by its protective mantle of trees and grasses, will be laid bare to the ravages of water and wind erosion. Streams that had been flowing clear will, once again, take up a load of silt and push it toward the seas. Humus and mineral salts, both vital elements of productive soil, will be seen to vanish at a terrifying rate. The railroads and highways and cities that will spring up may divert attention, but they cannot cover up the blight of man's recent activities. In great sections of Asia, it will be seen that man must utilize cow dung and every scrap of available straw or grass for fuel to cook his food. The forests that once provided wood for this purpose will be gone without a trace. The use of these agricultural wastes for fuel, in place of returning them to the land, will be leading to increasing soil impoverishment. Here and there will be seen a dust storm darkening the landscape over an area a thousand miles across. Man-creatures will be shown counting their wealth in terms of bits of printed paper representing other bits of a scarce but comparatively useless yellow metal that is kept buried in strong vaults. Meanwhile, the soil, the only real wealth that can keep mankind alive on the face of this earth is savagely being cut loose from its ancient moorings and washed into the seven seas.

We have just arrived upon this earth. How long will we stay?   19

1950

QUESTIONS FOR DISCUSSION

Content

a. What is the moral of this "scientific fable"?

b. Why does Rettie label this essay a fable? In what ways is it similar to other fables you may have read?

c. Given the fact that this essay was written in the 1940s, is it appropriate for Rettie to spend so much time introducing it with the story of the Copernicans and of their invention of an advanced movie camera? Why does he go to such great lengths to explain time-lapse photography?

d. What is the obvious basis upon which Rettie constructs his analogy?

e. Rettie takes his title from Psalm 90:4 of the King James Version of the Bible. What do you make of this title? Does the last line of the essay shed any light on it? Look up Psalm 90. How does it relate to this selection?

Strategy and Style

f. Does using an analogy aid Rettie in structuring his essay? Explain how Rettie has organized this piece and describe his use of transitions.

g. Consult an unabridged dictionary or encyclopedia in order to identify the following:

Copernicus	Pre-Cambrian	Devonian
Babylonians	Cro-Magnon Man	Neanderthal Man
Java Ape Man	Mammoth	

h. Rettie makes use of scientific language and allusions to develop his essay. Are such terms and references bothersome to a reader without scientific training? Explain. Why does Rettie make it a point to include them?

i. Rettie writes in the future tense. What effect does that have on the narrative?

j. Is there a difference in tone between Rettie's treatment of human history and his discussion of geological events? Where does he think we are heading?

SUGGESTIONS FOR SHORT WRITING

a. Write a brief review of Rettie's "film."

b. Continue Rettie's film into the future, writing an extra paragraph that describes, depending on how you foresee it, either the Earth's destruction or preservation.

SUGGESTIONS FOR SUSTAINED WRITING

a. Rettie's essay is essentially a listing of a number of important events in the history of the Earth and its inhabitants. He singles out several developments as particularly important, including the rise of the mammals, the development of the Rocky Mountains, and the appearance of Java man. Discuss an event or development within the last fifteen years that you believe will have an enormous effect on the history of the world. Explain the consequences of that event or development as fully as you can.

b. How would you answer the question Rettie asks at the very end of the essay? What evidence do you see in the world around you that humanity will continue to build, grow, and flourish—that it will prevail over the forces of doom? What evidence points to the opposite conclusion? Try to be as detailed as you can and to focus on only one or two major developments.

c. Analogy helps us grasp and order difficult concepts by enabling us to compare them to objects, processes, events, or other ideas with which we are more familiar. Compare an experience you are now going through or a problem you are now facing with something that most readers might already be familiar with. Some examples of such analogies are:

- Working at XYZ Company is very much like living in a zoo.
- Driving Route 1 every morning is like playing Russian Roulette.
- By the end of my day, I feel as if I've just run a marathon.
- Having dinner at Aunt Tessie's is like eating at an Italian gourmet restaurant.

The Cosmic Prison

Loren Eiseley

An anthropologist, educator, and poet, Loren Eiseley (1907–1977) was one of the most highly respected and prolific scientific writers of this century. Born in Lincoln, Nebraska, Eiseley was educated at the University of Pennsylvania, where he later became professor of anthropology and of the history of science. His other teaching assignments included appointments to the faculties of the Univeristy of Kansas and of Oberlin College. The recipient of numerous honors and awards for public service, Eiseley is also known for his work as a conservationist and nature lover. He contributed scores of scientific studies and articles to scholarly journals but also wrote two books of poetry, a genre he found difficult to escape even when writing highly technical prose. Eiseley will probably be best remembered for the unique, eloquent, and sometimes verse-like style with which he treats subject matter that would otherwise seem cold, abstract, and esoteric. In short, his work represents the best of both the worlds of poetry and of science: perceptiveness, accuracy, insight, and, above all, an ability to make profound contact with the reader. Eiseley's major works include: The Immense Journey *(1957),* Darwin's Century *(1959),* The Firmament of Time *(1960),* The Unexpected Universe *(1969) and* The Invisible Pyramid *(1970), from which this selection is taken.*

"A name is a prison, God is free," once observed the Greek poet Nikos 1
Kazantzakis. He meant, I think, that valuable though language is to man, it is by very necessity limiting, and creates for man an invisible prison. Language implies boundaries. A word spoken creates a dog, a rabbit, a man. It fixes their nature before our eyes; henceforth their shapes are, in a sense, our own creation. They are no longer part of the unnamed shifting architecture of the universe. They have been transfixed as if by sorcery, frozen into a concept, a word. Powerful though the spell of human language has proven itself to be, it has laid boundaries upon the cosmos.

No matter how far-ranging some of the mental probes that man has philo- 2
sophically devised, by his own created nature he is forced to hold the specious and emerging present and transform it into words. The words are startling in their immediate effectiveness, but at the same time they are always finally imprisoning because man has constituted himself a prison keeper. He does so out of no conscious intention, but because for immediate purposes he has created an unnatural world of his own, which he calls the cultural world, and in which he feels at home. It defines his needs and allows him to lay a small immobilizing spell upon the nearer portions of his universe. Nevertheless, it transforms that universe into a cosmic prison house which is no sooner mapped than man feels its inadequacy and his own.

He seeks then to escape, and the theory of escape involves bodily flight. 3
Scarcely had the first moon landing been achieved before one U.S. senator

408

boldly announced: "We are the masters of the universe. We can go anywhere we choose." This statement was widely and editorially acclaimed. It is a striking example of the comfort of words, also of the covert substitutions and mental projections to which they are subject. The cosmic prison is not made less so by a successful journey of some two hundred and forty thousand miles in a cramped and primitive vehicle.

To escape the cosmic prison man is poorly equipped. He has to drag portions of his environment with him, and his life span is that of a mayfly in terms of the distances he seeks to penetrate. There is no possible way to master such a universe by flight alone. Indeed such a dream is a dangerous illusion. This may seem a heretical statement, but its truth is self-evident if we try seriously to comprehend the nature of time and space that I sought to grasp when held up to view the fiery messenger that flared across the zenith in 1910. "Seventy-five years," my father had whispered in my ear, "seventy-five years and it will be racing homeward. Perhaps you will live to see it again. Try to remember." **4**

And so I remembered. I had gained a faint glimpse of the size of our prison house. Somewhere out there beyond a billion miles in space, an entity known as a comet had rounded on its track in the black darkness of the void. It was surging homeward toward the sun because it was an eccentric satellite of this solar system. If I lived to see it it would be but barely, and with the dimmed eyes of age. Yet it, too, in its long traverse, was but a flitting mayfly in terms of the universe the night sky revealed. **5**

So relative is the cosmos we inhabit that, as we gaze upon the outer galaxies available to the reach of our telescopes, we are placed in about the position that a single white blood cell in our bodies would occupy, if it were intelligently capable of seeking to understand the nature of its own universe, the body it inhabits. The cell would encounter rivers ramifying into miles of distance seemingly leading nowhere. It would pass through gigantic structures whose meaning it could never grasp—the brain, for example. It could never know there was an outside, a vast being on a scale it could not conceive of and of which it formed an infinitesimal part. It would know only the pouring tumult of the creation it inhabited, but of the nature of that great beast, or even indeed that it was a beast, it could have no conception whatever. It might examine the liquid in which it floated and decide, as in the case of the fall of Lucretius's atoms, that the pouring of obscure torrents had created its world. **6**

It might discover that creatures other than itself swam in the torrent. But that its universe was alive, had been born and was destined to perish, its own ephemeral existence would never allow it to perceive. It would never know the sun; it would explore only through dim tactile sensations and react to chemical stimuli that were borne to it along the mysterious conduits of the arteries and veins. Its universe would be centered upon a great arborescent tree of spouting blood. This, at best, generations of white blood cells by enormous labor and continuity might succeed, like astronomers, in charting. **7**

They could never, by any conceivable stretch of the imagination, be **8** aware that their so-called universe was, in actuality, the prowling body of a cat or the more time-enduring body of a philosopher, himself engaged upon the same quest in a more gigantic world and perhaps deceived proportionately by greater vistas. What if, for example, the far galaxies man observes make up, across void spaces of which even we are atomically composed, some kind of enormous creature or cosmic snowflake whose exterior we will never see? We will know more than the phagocyte in our bodies, but no more than that limited creature can we climb out of our universe, or successfully enhance our size or longevity sufficiently to thrust our heads through the confines of the universe that terminates our vision.

Some further "outside" will hover elusively in our thought, but upon its   9
nature, or even its reality, we can do no more than speculate. The phagocyte might observe the salty turbulence of an eternal river system, Lucretius the fall of atoms creating momentary living shapes. We suspiciously sense, in the concept of the expanding universe derived from the primordial atom—the monobloc—some kind of oscillating universal heart. At the instant of its contraction we will vanish. It is not given us, nor can our science recapture, the state beyond the monobloc, nor whether we exist in the diastole of some inconceivable being. We know only a little more extended reality than the hypothetical creature below us. Above us may lie realms it is beyond our power to grasp.

1970

QUESTIONS FOR DISCUSSION

Content

a. What is Eiseley saying in the last two sentences of this essay and how do they relate to the analogy he has created? Would it be accurate to say that these ideas comprise his thesis?
b. What is the "fiery messenger" to which Eiseley alludes in paragraph 4? How does it and the analogy of man's life span to that of a mayfly help him convey the immensity of time and space?
c. How would you explain the analogy between man and the white blood cell that forms the basis of this essay? Is the analogy logical and consistent? What makes it so?
d. Who was Lucretius, and what was his "atomic theory"? How does mentioning this theory help Eiseley develop the central analogy of his essay?
e. What does Eiseley mean when he says that "some further 'outside' will hover elusively in our thought" (paragraph 9)? Why can we only "speculate" on "its nature, or even its reality"?
f. In paragraph 4, the author tells us that the dream of escaping from the "cosmic prison" is a "dangerous illusion." What does he mean by this curious

statement, and why would someone like the U.S. senator quoted in paragraph 3 find it "heretical"?

g. What is "the oscillating universal heart" (paragraph 9) that we can only "suspiciously sense"? How would you define a "monobloc"?

h. Do you believe that the quote from Nikos Kazantzakis and the explanation that proceeds from it serve as an appropriate introduction to this selection?

Strategy and Style

i. Define "the cosmic prison" that Eiseley describes in this selection. Why does he call it a prison?

j. How would you characterize Eiseley's tone in this piece? What image of Eiseley himself does the tone project?

SUGGESTIONS FOR SHORT WRITING

a. Find a passage (a sentence or a paragraph) that has meaning for your own life, and write about the connections you see between Eiseley's words and your life.

b. Eiseley writes of humankind's condition from an earthbound position; writing from a position outside the Earth, describe what you see as humankind's relation to the rest of the cosmos. You might try writing from the point of view of Halley's Comet.

SUGGESTIONS FOR SUSTAINED WRITING

a. Write a short essay in which you make clear what Eiseley means by "the cosmic prison." Use analogies of your own making to get your point across.

b. Eiseley has created a startling comparison between the existence of a human being in the universe with the life of a white blood cell in the human body. Create your own analogy by comparing yourself or someone you know well to a fictional character, to a famous historical figure or even, for that matter, to an animal whose habits would be easily recognized by your audience. Incidentally, the analogy you develop need not be complimentary.

My Horse

Barry Lopez

Barry Lopez (b. 1945) received an A.B. and an M.A.T. from the University of Notre Dame and pursued additional graduate work at the University of Oregon. Since completing his education, Lopez has made freelance writing and photography his career. He writes regularly about the elements of landscape—a physical region, for example, or a particular animal—and the human imagination. Most of his work is grounded in natural history, anthropology, geography, and archaeology. He has contributed several pieces of fiction and numerous articles on natural history and the environment (especially in connection with the American West) to important periodicals, including the North American Review *and* Harper's, *two publications for which he has served as a contributing editor. His best-known, full-length work is* Of Wolves and Men *(1978), which became a best seller and for which Lopez won the John Burroughs Medal for Distinguished Natural History Writing. He has also published several collections of fiction including* The Dance of the Herons *(1979),* Winter Count *(1981), and* Arctic Dreams *(1986). A collection of essays,* Crossing Open Ground *(1989), and a children's book,* Crow and Weasel *(1990), are his most recent works. Lopez wrote "My Horse" for* The North American Review *in 1975.*

It is curious that Indian warriors on the northern plains in the nineteenth 1 century, who were almost entirely dependent on the horse for mobility and status, never gave their horses names. If you borrowed a man's horse and went off raiding for other horses, however, or if you lost your mount in battle and then jumped on mine and counted coup on an enemy—well, those horses would have to be shared with the man whose horse you borrowed, and that coup would be mine, not yours. Because even if I gave him no name, he was my horse.

If you were a Crow warrior and I a young Teton Sioux out after a war- 2 rior's identity and we came over a small hill somewhere in the Montana prairie and surprised each other, I could tell a lot about you by looking at your horse.

Your horse might have feathers tied in his mane, or in his tail, or a med- 3 icine bag tied around his neck. If I knew enough about the Crow, and had looked at you closely, I might make some sense of the decoration, even guess who you were if you were well-known. If you had painted your horse I could tell even more, because we both decorated our horses with signs that meant the same things. Your white handprints high on his flanks would tell me you had killed an enemy in a hand-to-hand fight. Small horizontal lines stacked on your horse's foreleg, or across his nose, would tell me how many times you had counted coup. Horse hoof marks on your horse's rump, or three-sided boxes,

412

would tell me how many times you had stolen horses. If there was a bright red square on your horse's neck I would know you were leading a war party and that there were probably others out there in the coulees behind you.

You might be painted all over as blue as the sky and covered with white   4
dots, with your horse painted the same way. Maybe hailstorms were your power—or if I chased you a hailstorm might come down and hide you. There might be lightning bolts on the horse's legs and flanks, and I would wonder if you had lightning power, or a slow horse. There might be white circles around your horse's eyes to help him see better.

Or you might be like Crazy Horse, with no decoration, no marks on your   5
horse to tell me anything, only a small lightning bolt on your cheek, a piece of turquoise tied behind your ear.

You might have scalps dangling from your rein.   6

I could tell something about you by your horse. All this would come to   7
me in a few seconds. I might decide this was my moment and shout my war cry—*Hoka hey!* Or I might decide you were like the grizzly bear: I would raise my weapon to you in salute and go my way, to see you again when I was older.

I do not own a horse. I am attached to a truck, however, and I have come   8
to think of it in a similar way. It has no name; it never occurred to me to give it a name. It has little decoration; neither of us is partial to decoration. I have a piece of turquoise in the truck because I had heard once that some of the southwestern tribes tied a small piece of turquoise in a horse's hock to keep him from stumbling. I like the idea. I also hang sage in the truck when I go on a long trip. But inside, the truck doesn't look much different from others that look just like it on the outside. I like it that way. Because I like my privacy.

For two years in Wyoming I worked on a ranch wrangling horses. The   9
horse I rode when I had to have a good horse was a quarter horse and his name was Coke High. The name came with him. At first I thought he'd been named for the soft drink. I'd known stranger names given to horses by whites. Years later I wondered if some deviate Wyoming cowboy wise to cocaine had not named him. Now I think he was probably named after a rancher, an historical figure of the region. I never asked the people who owned him for fear of spoiling the spirit of my inquiry.

We were running over a hundred horses on this ranch. They all had   10
names. After a few weeks I knew all the horses and the names too. You had to. No one knew how to talk about the animals or put them in order or tell the wranglers what to do unless they were using the names—Princess, Big Red, Shoshone, Clay.

My truck is named Dodge. The name came with it. I don't know if it was   11
named after the town or the verb or the man who invented it. I like it for a name. Perfectly anonymous, like Rex for a dog, or Old Paint. You can't tell anything with a name like that.

The truck is a van. I call it a truck because it's not a car and because 12
"van" is a suburban sort of consumer word, like "oxford loafer," and I don't

like the sound of it. On the outside it looks like any other Dodge Sportsman 300. It's a dirty tan color. There are a few body dents, but it's never been in a wreck. I tore the antenna off against a tree on a pinched mountain road. A boy in Midland, Texas, rocked one of my rear view mirrors off. A logging truck in Oregon squeeze-fired a piece of debris off the road and shattered my windshield. The oil pan and gas tank are pug-faced from high-centering on bad roads. (I remember a horse I rode for a while named Targhee whose hocks were scarred from tangles in barbed wire when he was a colt and who spooked a lot in high grass, but these were not like "dents." They were more like bad tires.)

I like to travel. I go mostly in the winter and mostly on two-lane roads. 13 I've driven the truck from Key West to Vancouver, British Columbia, and from Yuma to Long Island over the past four years. I used to ride Coke High only about five miles every morning when we were rounding up horses. Hard miles of twisting and turning. About six hundred miles a year. Then I'd turn him out and ride another horse for the rest of the day. That's what was nice about having a remuda. You could do all you had to do and not take it all out on your best horse. Three car family.

My truck came with a lot of seats in it and I've never really known what 14 to do with them. Sometimes I put the seats in and go somewhere with a lot of people, but most of the time I leave them out. I like riding around with that empty cavern of space behind my head. I know it's something with a history to it, that there's truth in it, because I always rode a horse the same way—with empty saddle bags. In case I found something. The possibility of finding something is half the reason for being on the road.

The value of anything comes to me in its use. If I am not using something 15 it is of no value to me and I give it away. I wasn't always that way. I used to keep everything I owned—just in case. I feel good about the truck because it gets used. A lot. To haul hay and firewood and lumber and rocks and garbage and animals. Other people have used it to haul furniture and freezers and dirt and recycled newspapers. And to move from one house to another. When I lend it for things like that I don't look to get anything back but some gas (if we're going to be friends). But if you go way out in the country to a dump and pick up the things you can still find out there (once a load of cedar shingles we sold for $175 to an architect) I expect you to leave some of those things around my place when you come back—if I need them.

When I think back, maybe the nicest thing I ever put in that truck was 16 timber wolves. It was a long night's drive from Oregon up into British Columbia. We were all very quiet about it; it was like moving clouds across the desert.

Sometimes something won't fit in the truck and I think about improving 17 it—building a different door system, for example. I am forever going to add better gauges on the dash and a pair of driving lamps and a sunroof, but I never get around to doing any of it. I remember I wanted to improve Coke High once too, especially the way he bolted like a greyhound through patches of cottonwood on a river flat. But all I could do with him was to try to rein him out of it.

Or hug his back.

Sometimes, road-stoned in a blur of country like southwestern Wyoming 18
or North Dakota, I talk to the truck. It's like wandering on the high plains under
a summer sun, on plains where, George Catlin wrote, you were "out of sight of
land." I say what I am thinking out loud, or point at things along the road. It's
a crazy, sun-stroked sort of activity, a sure sign it's time to pull over, to go for a
walk, to make a fire and have some tea, to lie in the shade of the truck.

I've always wanted to pat the truck. It's basic to the relationship. But it 19
never works.

I remember when I was on the ranch, just at sunrise, after I'd saddled 20
Coke High, I'd be huddled down in my jacket smoking a cigarette and looking
down into the valley, along the river where the other horses had spent the night.
I'd turn to Coke and run my hand down his neck and slap-pat him on the shoulder to say I was coming up. It made a bond, an agreement we started the day
with.

I've thought about that a lot with the truck, because we've gone out to- 21
gether at sunrise on so many mornings. I've even fumbled around trying to do
it. But metal won't give.

The truck's personality is mostly an expression of two ideas: "with-you" 22
and "alone." When Coke High was "with-you" he and I were the same animal.
We could have cut a rooster out of a flock of chickens, we were so in tune. It's
the same with the truck: rolling through Kentucky on a hilly two-lane road,
three in the morning under a full moon and no traffic. Picture it. You roll like
water.

There are other times when you are with each other but there's no con- 23
nection at all. Coke got that way when he was bored and we'd fight each other
about which way to go around a tree. When the truck gets like that—"alone"—
it's because it feels its Detroit fat-ass design dragging at its heart and making a
fool out of it.

I can think back over more than a hundred nights I've slept in the truck, 24
sat in it with a lamp burning, bundled up in a parka, reading a book. It was
always comfortable. A good place to wait out a storm. Like sleeping inside a
buffalo.

The truck will go past 100,000 miles soon. I'll rebuild the engine and put 25
a different transmission in it. I can tell from magazine advertisements that I'll
never get another one like it. Because every year they take more of the heart
out of them. One thing that makes a farmer or a rancher go sour is a truck that
isn't worth a shit. The reason you see so many old pickups in ranch country is
because these are the only ones with any heart. You can count on them. The
weekend rancher runs around in a new pickup with too much engine and not
enough transmission and with the wrong sort of tires because he can afford anything, even the worst. A lot of them have names for their pickups too.

My truck has broken down, in out of the way places at the worst of times. 26
I've walked away and screamed the foulness out of my system and gotten the

tools out. I had to fix a water pump in a blizzard in the Panamint Mountains in California once. It took all day with the Coleman stove burning under the engine block to keep my hands from freezing. We drifted into Beatty, Nevada, that night with it jury-rigged together with—I swear—baling wire, and we were melting snow as we went and pouring it in to compensate for the leaks.

There is a dent next to the door on the driver's side I put there one swel- 27 tering night in Miami. I had gone to the airport to meet my wife, whom I hadn't seen in a month. My hands were so swollen with poison ivy blisters I had to drive with my wrists. I had shut the door and was locking it when the window fell off its runners and slid down inside the door. I couldn't leave the truck unlocked because I had too much inside I didn't want to lose. So I just kicked the truck a blow in the side and went to work on the window. I hate to admit kicking the truck. It's like kicking a dog, which I've never done.

Coke High and I had an accident once. We hit a badger hole at a full 28 gallop. I landed on my back and blacked out. When I came to, Coke High was about a hundred yards away. He stayed a hundred yards away for six miles, all the way back to the ranch.

I want to tell you about carrying those wolves, because it was a fine 29 thing. There were ten of them. We had four in the truck with us in crates and six in a trailer. It was a five hundred mile trip. We went at night for the cool air and because there wouldn't be as much traffic. I could feel from the way the truck rolled along that its heart was in the trip. It liked the wolves inside it, the sweet odor that came from the crates. I could feel that same tireless wolf-lope developing in its wheels; it was like you might never have to stop for gas, ever again.

The truck gets very self-focused when it works like this; its heart is 30 strong and it's good to be around it. It's good to be *with* it. You get the same feeling when you pull someone out of a ditch. Coke High and I pulled a Volkswagen out of the mud once, but Coke didn't like doing it very much. Speed, not strength, was his center. When the guy who owned the car thanked us and tried to pat Coke, the horse snorted and swung away, trying to preserve his distance, which is something a horse spends a lot of time on.

So does the truck.   31

Being distant lets the truck get its heart up. The truck has been cold and 32 alone in Montana at 38 below zero. It's climbed horrible, eroded roads in Idaho. It's been burdened beyond overloading, and made it anyway. I've asked it to do these things because they build heart, and without heart all you have is a machine. You have nothing. I don't think people in Detroit know anything at all about heart. That's why everything they build dies so young.

One time in Arizona the truck and I came through one of the worst storms 33 I've ever been in, an outrageous, angry blizzard. But we went down the road, right through it. You couldn't explain our getting through by the sort of tires I had on the truck, or the fact that I had chains on, or was a good driver, or had a lot of weight over my drive wheels or a good engine, because it was more than this. It was a contest between the truck and the blizzard—and the truck wouldn't quit. I could have gone to sleep and the truck would have just torn a road down Interstate 40 on its own. It scared the hell out of me; but it gave me heart, too.

We came off the Mogollon Rim that night and out of the storm and 34 headed south for Phoenix. I pulled off the road to sleep for a few hours, but before I did I got out of the truck. It was raining. Warm rain. I tied a short piece of red avalanche cord into the grill. I left it there for a long time, like an eagle feather on a horse's tail. It flapped and spun in the wind. I could hear it ticking against the grill when I drove.

When I have to leave that truck I will just raise up my left arm—*Hoka* 35 *hey!*—and walk away.

1975

QUESTIONS FOR DISCUSSION

Content

a. What do you make of Lopez's claim that "the value of anything comes to [him] in its use" (paragraph 15)? Why does he focus exclusively on the truck to illustrate this statement?

b. What function does the story about the timber wolves serve? Why does Lopez mention it briefly in paragraph 16 only to return to it later in the essay?

c. The most prominent analogy in this selection is between Coke High and Dodge. What major similarities does Lopez identify in his comparison of the two? In what ways are the truck and the horse both reliable? In what ways are they temperamental?

d. The author also attempts to create a secondary, but no less significant, analogy between himself and the Indian warriors who once inhabited the American West. Is this analogy successful?

e. How does Lopez's hanging a piece of turquoise in his truck serve to strengthen the analogy between Dodge and Coke High? Between him and Sioux warriors he mentions earlier? What do you make of his tying a "red avalanche cord" on Dodge's grill after coming through a snowstorm?

f. Why does the absence of decoration in the truck enable Lopez to maintain his "privacy"? How does telling us that help him strengthen the analogies he has created?

g. What important comparisons is he making in paragraph 13? Why does he tell us in paragraph 14 that he takes the seats out of the truck when he is not transporting passengers?

h. Lopez makes a number of allusions to American Indian culture in this essay. What does the term "counted coup" mean? Who were the Crow and the Teton Sioux? What image does Lopez hope to evoke by mentioning Crazy Horse?

i. In paragraph 9, he claims that he never asked Coke High's owners how the horse got his name. Why would doing so have spoiled the "spirit of [his] inquiry"? What is the obvious irony Lopez creates by calling the truck Dodge? Why does he like that name so much?

j. In paragraph 32, he tells us that he has asked the truck to do things that "build heart." Are there other indications in this essay that Lopez considers his truck more than a machine?

k. Explain what Lopez means when he says that "the truck's personality is mostly an expression of two ideas: 'with-you' and 'alone.' " In what ways is this description applicable to Coke High as well?

Strategy and Style

l. How would you describe the structure of this essay? Why does the author spend so much time in the first seven paragraphs on Indian lore? Do these paragraphs form an effective introduction?

m. The speaker refuses to call his truck a van. How does this refusal relate to his dislike for Detroit automakers and "weekend ranchers," whom we read about later in the essay?

n. Throughout this selection, Lopez uses phrases such as "road-stoned" (paragraph 18) and "jury-rigged" (paragraph 26). What other colloquial expressions can you find in this piece? What tone do they help Lopez establish?

SUGGESTIONS FOR SHORT WRITING

a. Describe Lopez's truck or a vehicle of your own using various analogies—for example, my rocket, my friend, my house, etc.

b. Lopez writes that an "[Indian warrior] could tell a lot about you by looking at your horse" (paragraph 2). Would you be able to tell a lot about other people by looking at their means of transportation? Using one example of a means of transportation that you have recently seen, describe the person who typically uses it.

SUGGESTIONS FOR SUSTAINED WRITING

a. Draw an analogy between your car (or some other machine you own) and an animal or person. What qualities or characteristics make that machine seem alive?

b. Lopez tells us that a great deal could be determined about an Indian warrior's identity from the decorations with which he adorned his horse or the way in which he painted his face. What do the clothes people wear, their physical appearance, or their homes tell us about them? Write an essay in which you create an analogy that compares a good friend's appearance or lifestyle with his/her personality, moral values, and/or outlook on life. In this case, your purpose will be to identify similarities. However, another way to approach this assignment is to create a "negative analogy." In other words, you might find it more appropriate to demonstrate that what your friend looks like or what he/she owns has little or no relation to what the person really is.

The Perfect House

Farley Mowat

Farley Mowat, born in Ontario in 1921, is one of the world's most famous nature writers. His more than twenty-five books have been translated into more than twenty languages and are published in more than forty countries. He is probably most readily known from the 1982 movie Never Cry Wolf, *which was based on his 1963 book of the same name, which recounts his experiences studying wolves in northern Canada. After serving in the Canadian army from 1940–46, Mowat spent two years in the Arctic. His experiences during the summer and fall of 1947 are recounted in* People of the Deer *(1952), from which "The Perfect House" is excerpted. In this book, Mowat describes the Ihalmiut, a branch of the Innuit. The Ihalmiut, which literally translated means "people of the little hills," were once quite populous and lived in an area northwest of Hudson Bay. When Mowat visited the area in 1947, they had almost died out as a result of disease and starvation, a situation that was caused and aggravated by the "benevolent" intervention of white men. Mowat ends his book with a plea against this exploitative intervention, but for the Ihalmiut, it was too late. The tribe died out in the 1950s.*

As I grew to know the People, so my respect for their intelligence 1
and ingenuity increased. Yet it was a long time before I could reconcile my
feelings of respect with the poor, shoddy dwelling places that they constructed.
As with most Eskimos, the winter homes of the Ihalmiut are the snow-built
domes we call igloos. (Igloo in Eskimo means simply "house" and thus an
igloo can be built of wood or stone, as well as of snow.) But unlike most other
Innuit, the Ihalmiut make snow houses which are cramped, miserable shelters.
I think the People acquired the art of igloo construction quite recently in their
history and from the coast Eskimos. Certainly they have no love for their
igloos, and prefer the skin tents. This preference is related to the problem of
fuel.

Any home in the arctic, in winter, requires some fuel if only for cooking. 2
The coast peoples make use of fat lamps, for they have an abundance of fat
from the sea mammals they kill, and so they are able to cook in the igloo, and
to heat it as well. But the Ihalmiut can ill afford to squander the precious fat of
the deer, and they dare to burn only one tiny lamp for light. Willow must serve
as fuel, and while willow burns well enough in a tent open at the peak to allow
the smoke to escape, when it is burned in a snow igloo, the choking smoke
leaves no place for human occupants.

So snow houses replace the skin tents of the Ihalmiut only when winter 3
has already grown old and the cold has reached the seemingly unbearable extremes of sixty or even seventy degrees below zero. Then the tents are grudgingly abandoned and snow huts built. From that time until spring no fires may

burn inside the homes of the People, and such cooking as is attempted must be done outside, in the face of the blizzards and gales.

Yet though tents are preferred to igloos, it is still rather hard to understand **4** why....Great, gaping slits outline each hide on the frame of a tent. Such a home offers hardly more shelter than a thicket of trees, for on the unbroken sweep of the plains the winds blow with such violence that they drive the hard snow through the tents as if the skin walls did not really exist. But the People spend many days and dark nights in these feeble excuses for houses, while the wind rises like a demon of hatred and the cold comes as if it meant to destroy all life in the land.

In these tents there may be a fire; but consider this fire, this smoldering **5** handful of green twigs, dug with infinite labor from under the drifts. It gives heat only for a few inches out from its sullen coals so that it barely suffices to boil a pot of water in an hour or two. The eternal winds pour into the tent and dissipate what little heat the fire can spare from the cook-pots. The fire gives comfort to the Ihalmiut only through its appeal to the eyes.

However, the tent with its wan little fire is a more desirable place than the **6** snow house with no fire at all. At least the man in the tent can have a hot bowl of soup once in a while, but after life in the igloos begins, almost all food must be eaten while it is frozen to the hardness of rocks. Men sometimes take skin bags full of ice into the beds so that they can have water to drink, melted by the heat of their bodies. It is true that some of the People build cook shelters outside the igloos but these snow hearths burn very badly, and then only when it is calm. For the most part the winds prevent any outside cooking at all, and anyway by late winter the willow supply is so deeply buried under the drifts, it is almost impossible for men to procure it.

So you see that the homes of the Ihalmiut in winter are hardly models of **7** comfort. Even when spring comes to the land the improvement in housing conditions is not great. After the tents go up in the spring, the rains begin. During daylight it rains with gray fury and the tents soak up the chill water until the hides hang slackly on their poles while rivulets pour through the tent to drench everything inside. At night, very likely, there will be frost and by dawn everything not under the robes with the sleepers will be frozen stiff.

With the end of the spring rains, the hot sun dries and shrinks the hides **8** until they are drum-taut, but the ordeal is not yet over. Out of the steaming muskegs come the hordes of bloodsucking and flesh-eating flies and these find that the Ihalmiut tents offer no barrier to their invasion. The tents belong equally to the People and to the flies, until midsummer brings an end to the plague, and the hordes vanish.

My high opinion of the People was often clouded when I looked at their **9** homes. I sometimes wondered if the Ihalmiut were as clever and as resourceful as I thought them to be. I had been too long conditioned to think of home as four walls and a roof, and so the obvious solution of the Ihalmiut housing problem escaped me for nearly a year. It took me that long to realize that the People not only have good homes, but that they have devised the one perfect house.

The tent and the igloo are really only auxiliary shelters. The real home of 10 the Ihalmio is much like that of the turtle, for it is what he carries about on his back. In truth it is the only house that can enable men to survive on the merciless plains of the Barrens. It has central heating from the fat furnace of the body, its walls are insulated to a degree of perfection that we white men have not been able to surpass, or even emulate. It is complete, light in weight, easy to make and easy to keep in repair. It costs nothing, for it is a gift of the land, through the deer. When I consider that house, my opinion of the astuteness of the Ihalmiut is no longer clouded.

Primarily the house consists of two suits of fur, worn one over the other, 11 and each carefully tailored to the owner's dimensions. The inner suit is worn with the hair of the hides facing inward and touching the skin while the outer suit has its hair turned out to the weather. Each suit consists of a pullover parka with a hood, a pair of fur trousers, fur gloves and fur boots. The double motif is extended to the tips of the fingers, to the top of the head, and to the soles of the feet where soft slippers of harehide are worn next to the skin.

The high winter boots may be tied just above the knee so that they leave 12 no entry for the cold blasts of the wind. But full ventilation is provided by the design of the parka. Both inner and outer parkas hang slackly to at least the knees of the wearer, and they are not belted in winter. Cold air does not rise, so that no drafts can move up under the parkas to reach the bare flesh, but the heavy, moisture-laden air from close to the body sinks through the gap between parka and trousers and is carried away. Even in times of great physical exertion, when the Ihalmio sweats freely, he is never in any danger of soaking his clothing and so inviting quick death from frost afterwards. The hides are not in contact with the body at all but are held away from the flesh by the soft resiliency of the deer hairs that line them, and in the space between the tips of the hair and the hide of the parka there is a constantly moving layer of warm air which absorbs all the sweat and carries it off.

Dressed for a day in the winter, the Ihalmio has this protection over all 13 parts of his body, except for a narrow oval in front of his face—and even this is well protected by a long silken fringe of wolverine fur, the one fur to which the moisture of breathing will not adhere and freeze.

In the summer rain, the hide may grow wet, but the layer of air between 14 deerhide and skin does not conduct the water, and so it runs off and is lost while the body stays dry. Then there is the question of weight. Most white men trying to live in the winter arctic load their bodies with at least twenty-five pounds of clothing, while the complete deerskin home of the Innuit weighs about seven pounds. This, of course, makes a great difference in the mobility of the wearers. A man wearing tight-fitting and too bulky clothes is almost as helpless as a man in a diver's suit. But besides their light weight, the Ihalmiut clothes are tailored so that they are slack wherever muscles must work freely beneath them. There is ample space in this house for the occupant to move and to breathe, for there are no partitions and walls to limit his motions, and the man is almost as free in his movements as if he were naked. If he must sleep out, without shelter, and it is fifty below, he has but to draw his arms into his parka, and he sleeps nearly as well as he would in a double-weight eiderdown bag.

This is in winter, but what about summer? I have explained how the po- 15 rous hide nevertheless acts as a raincoat. Well, it does much more than that. In summer the outer suit is discarded and all clothing pared down to one layer. The house then offers effective insulation against heat entry. It remains surprisingly cool, for it is efficiently ventilated. Also, and not least of its many advantages, it offers the nearest thing to perfect protection against the flies. The hood is pulled up so that it covers the neck and the ears, and the flies find it nearly impossible to get at the skin underneath. But of course the Ihalmiut have long since learned to live with the flies, and they feel none of the hysterical and frustrating rage against them so common with us.

In the case of women's clothing, home has two rooms. The back of the 16 parka has an enlargement, as if it were made to fit a hunchback, and in this space, called the *amaut,* lives the unweaned child of the family. A bundle of remarkably absorbent sphagnum moss goes under his backside and the child sits stark naked, in unrestricted delight, where he can look out on the world and very early in life become familiar with the sights and the moods of his land. He needs no clothing of his own, and as for the moss—in that land there is an unlimited supply of soft sphagnum and it can be replaced in an instant.

When the child is at length forced to vacate this pleasant apartment, prob- 17 ably by the arrival of competition, he is equipped with a one-piece suit of hides which looks not unlike the snow suits our children wear in the winter. Only it is much lighter, more efficient, and much less restricting. This first home of his own is a fine home for the Ihalmio child, and one that his white relatives would envy if they could appreciate its real worth.

This then is the home of the People. It is the gift of the land, but mainly it 18 is the gift of Tuktu.*

1952

QUESTIONS FOR DISCUSSION

Content

a. Wht is Mowat's thesis? Is he implying more than he says directly?
b. What is the perfect house? Where does Mowat's analogy begin?
c. Besides making an analogy between the Ihalmiut's clothing and our own

* the caribou

ideas of a house, what other analogies does Mowat make?

d. What comparisons does Mowat make between the Ihalmiut and us? How are the comparisons chosen so as to be favorable to the Ihalmiut?

e. Likewise, how does the choice of the house analogy help to shed favorable light on the Ihalmiut? What other analogy could have been used to describe the Ihalmiut's clothing, and with what positive or negative effects?

f. Would what Mowat calls the "obvious solution of the Ihalmiut housing problem" (paragraph 9) be applicable for other people as well?

g. Do you think Mowat knew that the Ihalmiut would die out? If so, in what ways might that knowledge have influenced his decision to write about them?

Strategy and Style

h. How does the structure of the essay help create trust in Mowat's authority as an expert observer? How does the first part of the essay set the readers up for the description of the perfect house in the second part of the essay?

i. How effective is the great amount of detail that Mowat provides in his descriptions of the Ihalmiut's tents, igloos, and clothing? Why does he use so much detail?

j. Mowat says that he has great respect for the Ihalmiut. Point to places in the text where this respect is apparent.

SUGGESTIONS FOR SHORT WRITING

a. If there were no such things as houses as we know them, what would be the perfect shelter for the people of your community? Describe this shelter.

b. What implied question or questions does Mowat answer in his essay? For one such question, summarize Mowat's answer to it.

SUGGESTIONS FOR SUSTAINED WRITING

a. Make an analogy between two objects (clothes, appliances, furniture, etc.) which sheds light on the function of one of the objects. Write an essay making the analogy and the function clear.

b. "The Perfect House" is an excerpt from a longer work. As mentioned in the biography above, Mowat provides in this book his reasons for the decay and inevitable disappearance of this tribe. Read more of this book, particularly the last two chapters, and write an essay agreeing or disagreeing with Mowat's reasons. You may also wish to analyze Mowat's impassioned rhetoric.

The Myth of Sisyphus

Albert Camus

*Born in what was the French colony of Algeria, Albert Camus (1913–1966) was edu-
cated at the University of Algeria. He began his career as an actor and playwright, but
he soon gave up the theater for journalism and began writing for* Alger Republican
and for Paris-Soir *in France. During World War II, Camus was very active in the
French resistance and contributed regularly to* Combat, *an important underground
newspaper. He is remembered as a leading existentialist, a proponent of the modern
philosophical movement (if it can be so termed) that defines the individual as utterly
free and totally responsible for his own destiny. For many existentialists, God does not
exist, and the world is devoid of meaning except for that which the individual is able
to create for him/herself. Unlike the literature of many of his contemporaries, however,
the works of Camus expose a view of life that, while hardly optimistic, encourages a
belief in the inherent nobility and courageousness of the human character even in the
face of a hostile universe. Though clearly evident in his famous novels,* The Stranger
(1942), The Plague *(1947), and* The Rebel *(1951), nowhere is this belief expressed
more poignantly and eloquently than in "The Myth of Sisyphus."*

1   The gods had condemned Sisyphus to ceaselessly rolling a rock to the top
of a mountain, whence the stone would fall back of its own weight. They had
thought with some reason that there is no more dreadful punishment than futile
and hopeless labor.

2   If one believes Homer, Sisyphus was the wisest and most prudent of mortals. According to another tradition, however, he was disposed to practice the profession of highwayman. I see no contradiction in this. Opinions differ as to the reasons why he became the futile laborer of the underworld. To begin with, he is accused of a certain levity in regard to the gods. He stole their secrets. Aegina, the
daughter of Aesopus, was carried off by Jupiter. The father was shocked by that
disappearance and complained to Sisyphus. He, who knew of the abduction, offered to tell about it on condition that Aesopus would give water to the citadel of
Corinth. To the celestial thunderbolts he preferred the benediction of water. He
was punished for this in the underworld. Homer tells us also that Sisyphus had put
Death in chains. Pluto could not endure the sight of his deserted, silent empire. He
dispatched the god of war, who liberated Death from the hands of her conqueror.

3   It is said also that Sisyphus, being near to death, rashly wanted to test his
wife's love. He ordered her to cast his unburied body into the middle of the
public square. Sisyphus woke up in the underworld. And there, annoyed by an
obedience so contrary to human love, he obtained from Pluto permission to return to earth in order to chastise his wife. But when he had seen again the face
of this world, enjoyed water and sun, warm stones and the sea, he no longer
wanted to go back to the infernal darkness. Recalls, signs of anger, warnings were

425

of no avail. Many years more he lived facing the curve of the gulf, the sparkling sea, and the smiles of earth. A decree of the gods was necessary. Mercury came and seized the impudent man by the collar and, snatching him from his joys, led him forcibly back to the underworld, where his rock was ready for him.

You have already grasped that Sisyphus is the absurd hero. He *is*, as **4** much through his passions as through his torture. His scorn of the gods, his hatred of death, and his passion for life won him that unspeakable penalty in which the whole being is exerted toward accomplishing nothing. This is the price that must be paid for the passions of this earth. Nothing is told us about Sisyphus in the underworld. Myths are made for the imagination to breathe life into them. As for this myth, one sees merely the whole effort of a body straining to raise the huge stone, to roll it and push it up a slope a hundred times over; one sees the face screwed up, the cheek tight against the stone, the shoulder bracing the clay-covered mass, the foot wedging it, the fresh start with arms outstretched, the wholly human security of two earth-clotted hands. At the very end of his long effort measured by skyless space and time without depth, the purpose is achieved. Then Sisyphus watches the stone rush down in a few moments toward that lower world whence he will have to push it up again toward the summit. He goes back down to the plain.

It is during that return, that pause, that Sisyphus interests me. A face that **5** toils so close to stones is already stone itself! I see that man going back down with a heavy yet measured step toward the torment of which he will never know the end. That hour like a breathing-space which returns as surely as his suffering, that is the hour of consciousness. At each of those moments when he leaves the heights and gradually sinks toward the lairs of the gods, he is superior to his fate. He is stronger than his rock.

If this myth is tragic, that is because its hero is conscious. Where would **6** his torture be, indeed, if at every step the hope of succeeding upheld him? The workman of today works every day in his life at the same tasks, and this fate is no less absurd. But it is tragic only at the rare moments when it becomes conscious. Sisyphus, proletarian of the gods, powerless and rebellious, knows the whole extent of his wretched condition: it is what he thinks of during his descent. The lucidity that was to constitute his torture at the same time crowns his victory. There is no fate that cannot be surmounted by scorn.

If the descent is thus sometimes performed in sorrow, it can also take **7** place in joy. This word is not too much. Again I fancy Sisyphus returning toward his rock, and the sorrow was in the beginning. When the images of earth cling too tightly to memory, when the call of happiness becomes too insistent, it happens that melancholy rises in man's heart: this is the rock's victory, this is the rock itself. The boundless grief is too heavy to bear. These are our nights of Gethsemane. But crushing truths perish from being acknowledged. Thus, Oedipus at the outset obeys fate without knowing it. But from the moment he knows, his tragedy begins. Yet at the same moment, blind and desperate, he realizes that the only bond linking him to the world is the cool hand of a girl. Then a tremendous remark rings out: "Despite so many ordeals, my advanced age and the nobility of my soul make me conclude that all is well." Sophocles' Oedipus, like Dostoevsky's Kirilov, thus gives the recipe for the absurd victory. Ancient wisdom confirms modern heroism.

One does not discover the absurd without being tempted to write a man- **8** ual of happiness. "What! by such narrow ways—?" There is but one world, however. Happiness and the absurd are two sons of the same earth. They are inseparable. It would be a mistake to say that happiness necessarily springs from the absurd discovery. It happens as well that the feeling of the absurd springs from happiness. "I conclude that all is well," says Oedipus, and that remark is sacred. It echoes in the wild and limited universe of man. It teaches that all is not, has not been, exhausted. It drives out of this world a god who had come into it with dissatisfaction and a preference for futile sufferings. It makes of fate a human matter, which must be settled among men.

All Sisyphus' silent joy is contained therein. His fate belongs to him. His **9** rock is his thing. Likewise, the absurd man, when he contemplates his torment, silences all the idols. In the universe suddenly restored to its silence, the myriad wondering little voices of the earth rise up. Unconscious, secret calls, invitations from all the faces, they are the necessary reverse and price of victory. There is no sun without shadow, and it is essential to know the night. The absurd man says yes and his effort will henceforth be unceasing. If there is a personal fate, there is no higher destiny, or at least there is but one which he concludes is inevitable and despicable. For the rest, he knows himself to be the master of his days. At that subtle moment when man glances backward over his life, Sisyphus returning toward his rock, in that slight pivoting he contemplates that series of unrelated actions which becomes his fate, created by him, combined under his memory's eye and soon sealed by his death. Thus, convinced of the wholly human origin of all that is human, a blind man eager to see who knows that the night has no end, he is still on the go. The rock is still rolling.

I leave Sisyphus at the foot of the mountain! One always finds one's bur- **10** den again. But Sisyphus teaches the higher fidelity that negates the gods and raises rocks. He too concludes that all is well. This universe henceforth without a master seems to him neither sterile nor futile. Each atom of that stone, each mineral flake of that night-filled mountain, in itself forms a world. The struggle itself toward the heights is enough to fill a man's heart. One must imagine Sisyphus happy.

1955

QUESTIONS FOR DISCUSSION

Content

a. Who exactly was Sisyphus, and what does Camus mean when he calls him an "absurd hero"?

b. Who was Pluto, and what does Camus mean by the "underworld"? Why are Sisyphus' efforts in this place "measured by skyless space and time without depth"?

c. What is Camus driving at when he tells us that "There is no fate that cannot be surmounted by scorn" (paragraph 6) and that we "must imagine Sisyphus happy" (paragraph 10)?

d. How do the various explanations behind his condemnation contribute to his portrayal as an "absurd hero"? In what way does the nature of Sisyphus' punishment help define that term?

e. Does Camus succeed in comparing Sisyphus with a modern human being? Discuss this analogy, and explain in what way a modern human might also be called absurd.

f. In order for Sisyphus to qualify as a "tragic hero," the author tells us, he must know the "whole extent of his wretched condition." In what way does this "lucidity" ennoble Sisyphus?

g. In what works do the famous literary characters Oedipus and Kirilov appear? How do their stories help illustrate "the recipe for the absurd victory"? What is "Gethsemane," which Camus mentions in paragraph 7?

h. What, for Camus, is "sacred" about Oedipus' conclusion that "'all is well'"? In what way does this remark make "of fate a human matter, which must be settled among men" (paragraph 9)?

i. Discuss the "higher fidelity that negates the gods and raises rocks" (paragraph 10).

Strategy and Style

j. Camus uses the pronouns "you," "I," "one," and "he." To whom does each of these pronouns refer? In what ways do they create a persona for Camus?

k. What does Camus, or at least the persona of the essay, think of Sisyphus?

SUGGESTIONS FOR SHORT WRITING

a. Write a job description for what Sisyphus does.

b. What image does this essay call to mind? Try drawing that image and then writing a short description of it.

SUGGESTIONS FOR SUSTAINED WRITING

a. Through a skillful use of analogy, Camus reveals the relevance of a classical myth to the modern world. Recall an ancient myth, parable from the *Bible,* folktale, or children's story that has special significance for you. Why is it still meaningful, and what does it tell us about life and people today? In short, what lesson(s) does it offer the modern reader?

b. In paragraph 6, Camus tells us that "The workman of today works every day in his life at the same tasks, and this fate is no less absurd [than that of Sisyphus]." Do you agree? If so, develop your own analogy of the fate of Sisyphus with that of a modern factory worker, storekeeper, or civil servant. In what way is the latter's "fate" similar to that of Camus' mythical hero? Would it be accurate to describe this person as a "tragic hero"? In what way is he or she "tragic"? In what way a "hero"?

10

Argument

Strictly speaking, argument is a rhetorical technique used to support or deny a proposition by offering detailed evidence for or against it in a logically connected fashion. Classical argument relies on deductive and inductive reasoning; it appeals to reason and reason alone. Deduction proceeds from a general truth or principle to a more specific instance based on that principle. You would be using deduction if you argued:

1. All full-time students are permitted to use the college weight room free of charge;
2. I am a full-time student;
3. I am permitted to use the weight room free of charge.

Inductive reasoning, on the other hand, proceeds from several specific occurrences to one general truth. Let's say you come down with a bad case of food poisoning—fever, cramps, vomiting, the works! When you feel better, you call up the five people with whom you had dinner; each of them claims to have suffered the same symptoms. It is probably safe to infer that all six of you ate contaminated food.

Sometimes, of course, one's purpose may go beyond simply proving a point. The writer may feel a need to persuade, to convert the audience, or even to convey a sense of urgency that will convince readers to act and act quickly. In such cases, pure logic may not suffice. Thus, while grounding the paper in logic and well-developed evidence, a writer may also wish to appeal to the emotions.

Both methods are legitimate forms of argumentation, and both are represented, to varying degrees, in the essays that follow. Indeed it is often hard to draw a line. Jonathan Swift's "A Modest Proposal," a model of deductive reasoning expressed in language that is cool, clear, and eminently logical, is couched in a bitter irony that expresses the author's rage over Britain's treatment of the Irish. Lindsy Van Gelder makes no attempt to hide her impatience

430

with the "well-meaning" defenders of sexist language as she systematically dismantles their arguments. In fact, a case can be made that the Declaration of Independence, perhaps the finest example of Thomas Jefferson's command of formal logic, is as impassioned a document as one will read in this chapter.

Argumentation lends itself naturally to debate on matters moral, political, and social and especially to the defense of human rights. Note the essays by H. L. Mencken, Walter Murdoch, and Alan Paton and the powerful, enduring speech by Martin Luther King, Jr. Of course, all four make strong appeals to reason, but each remains unique, varying in tone and urgency according to the proximity from which its author views his subject.

The selection you might find most relevant to your work as a student is Arthur E. Lean's plea to abolish grading. Some of the evidence here derives from the author's experience as a teacher, but Lean is a skilled debater who finds support for his arguments by quoting other authorities, who presents opinions in an impeccable logic, and who offers alternatives to the present system.

Still, there may be chinks in his armor, and you may wish to take issue with Lean or with any of the other writers in this chapter or, indeed, in this text. Keep in mind, however, that the essential ingredient in building an effective argument is a thorough knowledge of your subject. Without it, your readers will remain unconvinced despite your ability to stir their emotions. Think of yourself as an attorney. You will have difficulty defending your client unless you know all the facts. Anything less will jeopardize your credibility with the jury. The idea applies to your role as a writer. Good readers will approach your thesis with a healthy skepticism. They may be open to persuasion—some may even want to be convinced—but most will insist that you provide reasonable, well-developed, and convincing evidence before they give you their trust!

A Modest Proposal

Jonathan Swift

Swift (1667–1745) was born in Dublin, Ireland, studied at Trinity College, Dublin, and took an M.A. at Oxford. Ordained an Anglican priest, eventually he was made Dean of St. Patrick's Cathedral in Dublin. He is remembered chiefly for his satires, the most famous of which are A Tale of a Tub *(1704), a vicious satire on government abuses in education and religion, and* Gulliver's Travels *(1726). After the death of Queen Anne in 1714, Swift remained almost the rest of his life in Ireland. There he wrote many essays defending the Irish against English oppression. "A Modest Proposal" is one of a series of satirical essays that exposed English cruelties in Ireland. It demonstrates Swift's keen sensitivity to the problems of the poor in his native country as well as his ability to create satire that is both ironic and incisive.*

1   It is a melancholy object to those who walk through this great town or travel in the country, when they see the streets, the roads, and cabin doors, crowded with beggars of the female sex, followed by three, four, or six children, all in rags and importuning every passenger for an alms. These mothers, instead of being able to work for their honest livelihood, are forced to employ all their time in strolling to beg sustenance for their helpless infants: who as they grow up either turn thieves for want of work, or leave their dear native country to fight for the pretender in Spain, or sell themselves to the Barbadoes.

2   I think it is agreed by all parties that this prodigious number of children in the arms, or on the backs, or at the heels of their mothers, and frequently of their fathers, is in the present deplorable state of the kingdom a very great additional grievance; and, therefore, whoever could find out a fair, cheap, and easy method of making these children sound, useful members of the commonwealth, would deserve so well of the public as to have his statue set up for a preserver of the nation.

3   But my intention is very far from being confined to provide only for the children of professed beggars; it is of a much greater extent, and shall take in the whole number of infants at a certain age who are born of parents in effect as little able to support them as those who demand our charity in the streets.

4   As to my own part, having turned my thoughts for many years upon this important subject, and maturely weighed the several schemes of our projectors, I have always found them grossly mistaken in their computation. It is true, a child just dropped from its dam may be supported by her milk for a solar year, with little other nourishment; at most not above the value of 2s., which the mother may certainly get, or the value in scraps, by her lawful occupation of begging; and it is exactly at one year old that I propose to provide for them in such a manner as instead of being a charge upon their parents or the parish, or

wanting food and raiment for the rest of their lives, they shall on the contrary contribute to the feeding, and partly to the clothing, of many thousands.

There is likewise another great advantage in my scheme, that it will pre- 5 vent those voluntary abortions, and that horrid practice of women murdering their bastard children, alas! too frequent among us! sacrificing the poor innocent babes I doubt more to avoid the expense than the shame, which would move tears and pity in the most savage and inhuman breast.

The number of souls in this kingdom being usually reckoned one million 6 and a half, of these I calculate there may be about 200,000 couple whose wives are breeders; from which number I subtract 30,000 couple who are able to maintain their own children (although I apprehend there cannot be so many, under the present distress of the kingdom); but this being granted, there will remain 170,000 breeders. I again subtract 50,000 for those women who miscarry, or whose children die by accident or disease within the year. There only remain 120,000 children of poor parents annually born. The question therefore is, how this number shall be reared and provided for? which, as I have already said, under the present situation of affairs, is utterly impossible by all the methods hitherto proposed. For we can neither employ them in handicraft or agriculture; we neither build houses (I mean live in the country) nor cultivate land; they can very seldom pick up a livelihood by stealing, till they arrive at six years old, except where they are of towardly parts; although I confess they learn the rudiments much earlier; during which time they can, however, be properly looked upon only as probationers; as I have been informed by a principal gentleman in the county of Cavan, who protested to me that he never knew above one or two instances under the age of six, even in a part of the kingdom so renowned for the quickest proficiency in that art.

I am assured by our merchants, that a boy or a girl before twelve years 7 old is no saleable commodity; and even when they come to this age they will not yield above 3l. or 3l.2s. 6d. at most on the exchange; which cannot turn to account either to the parents or kingdom, the charge of nutriment and rags having been at least four times that value.

I shall now therefore humbly propose my own thoughts, which I hope 8 will not be liable to the least objection.

I have been assured by a very knowing American of my acquaintance in 9 London, that a young healthy child well nursed is at a year old a most delicious, nourishing, and wholesome food, whether stewed, roasted, baked, or broiled; and I make no doubt that it will equally serve in a fricassee or a ragout.

I do therefore humbly offer it to public consideration that of the 120,000 10 children already computed, 20,000 may be reserved for breed, whereof only one-fourth part to be males; which is more than we allow to sheep, black cattle, or swine; and my reason is, that these children are seldom the fruits of marriage, a circumstance not much regarded by our savages; therefore one male will be sufficient to serve four females. That the remaining 100,000 may, at a year old, be offered in sale to the persons of quality and fortune through the kingdom; always advising the mother to let them suck plentifully in the last month, so as to render them plump and fat for a good table. A child will make two dishes at an entertainment for friends; and when the family dines alone, the fore or hind quarter will make a reasonable dish, and seasoned with a little pepper or salt will be very good boiled on the fourth day, especially in winter.

I have reckoned upon a medium that a child just born will weigh 12 pounds, and in a solar year, if tolerably nursed, will increase to 28 pounds. 11

I grant this food will be somewhat dear, and therefore very proper for landlords, who, as they have already devoured most of the parents, seem to have the best title to the children. 12

Infant's flesh will be in season throughout the year, but more plentiful in March, and a little before and after: for we are told by a grave author, an eminent French physician, that fish being a prolific diet, there are more children born in Roman Catholic countries about nine months after Lent than at any other season; therefore, reckoning a year after Lent, the markets will be more glutted than usual, because the number of popish infants is at least three to one in this kingdom: and therefore it will have one other collateral advantage, by lessening the number of papists among us. 13

I have already computed the charge of nursing a beggar's child (in which list I reckon all cottagers, laborers, and four-fifths of the farmers) to be about 2s. per annum, rags included; and I believe no gentleman would repine to give 10s. for the carcass of a good fat child, which, as I have said, will make four dishes of excellent nutritive meat, when he has only some particular friend or his own family to dine with him. Thus the squire will learn to be a good landlord, and grow popular among the tenants; the mother will have 8s. net profit, and be fit for work till she produces another child. 14

Those who are more thrifty (as I must confess the times require) may flay the carcass; the skin of which artificially dressed will make admirable gloves for ladies, and summer boots for fine gentlemen. 15

As to our city of Dublin, shambles may be appointed for this purpose in the most convenient parts of it, and butchers we may be assured will not be wanting: although I rather recommend buying the children alive, and dressing them hot from the knife as we do roasting pigs. 16

A very worthy person, a true lover of his country, and whose virtues I highly esteem, was lately pleased in discoursing on this matter to offer a refinement upon my scheme. He said that many gentlemen of this kingdom, having of late destroyed their deer, he conceived that the want of venison might be well supplied by the bodies of young lads and maidens, not exceeding fourteen years of age nor under twelve; so great a number of both sexes in every country being now ready to starve for want of work and service; and these to be disposed of by their parents, if alive, or otherwise by their nearest relations. But with due deference to so excellent a friend and so deserving a patriot, I cannot be altogether in his sentiments; for as to the males, my American acquaintance assured me from frequent experience that their flesh was generally tough and 17 lean, like that of our schoolboys by continual exercise, and their taste disagreeable; and to fatten them would not answer the charge. Then as to the females, it would, I think, with humble submission be a loss to the public, because they soon would become breeders themselves: and besides, it is not improbable that some scrupulous people might be apt to censure such a practice (although indeed very unjustly), as a little bordering upon cruelty; which, I confess, has always been with me the strongest objection against any project, how well soever intended.

But in order to justify my friend, he confessed that this expedient was put 18 into his head by the famous Psalmanazar, a native of the island Formosa, who came from thence to London about twenty years ago: and in conversation told my friend, that in his country when any young person happened to be put to death, the executioner sold the carcass to persons of quality as a prime dainty; and that in his time the body of a plump girl of fifteen, who was crucified for an attempt to poison the emperor, was sold to his imperial majesty's prime minister of state, and other great mandarins of the court, in joints from the gibbet, at 400 crowns. Neither indeed can I deny, that if the same use were made of several plump young girls in this town, who without one single groat to their fortunes cannot stir without a chair, and appear at the playhouse and assemblies in foreign fineries which they never will pay for, the kingdom would not be the worse.

Some persons of a desponding spirit are in great concern about that vast 19 number of poor people, who are aged, diseased, or maimed, and I have been desired to employ my thoughts what course may be taken to ease the nation of so grievous an encumbrance. But I am not in the least pain upon that matter, because it is very well known that they are every day dying and rotting by cold and famine, and filth and vermin, as fast as can be reasonably expected. And as to the young laborers, they are now in as hopeful a condition: they cannot get work, and consequently pine away for want of nourishment, to a degree that if at any time they are accidentally hired to common labor, they have not strength to perform it; and thus the country and themselves are happily delivered from the evils to come.

I have too long digressed, and therefore shall return to my subject. I think 20 the advantages by the proposal which I have made are obvious and many, as well as of the highest importance.

For first, as I have already observed, it would greatly lessen the number 21 of papists, with whom we are yearly overrun, being the principal breeders of the nation as well as our most dangerous enemies; and who stay at home on purpose to deliver the kingdom to the Pretender, hoping to take their advantage by the absence of so many good Protestants, who have chosen rather to leave their country than stay at home and pay tithes against their conscience to an Episcopal curate.

Secondly, The poor tenants will have something valuable of their own, 22 which by law may be made liable to distress and help to pay their landlord's rent, their corn and cattle being already seized, and money a thing unknown.

Thirdly, Whereas the maintenance of 100,000 children from two years old 23 and upward, cannot be computed at less than 10s. a-piece per annum, the nation's stock will be thereby increased £50,000 per annum, beside the profit of a new dish introduced to the tables of all gentlemen of fortune in the kingdom who have any refinement in taste. And the money will circulate among ourselves, the goods being entirely of our own growth and manufacture.

Fourthly, The constant breeders beside the gain of 8s. sterling per annum 24 by the sale of their children, will be rid of the charge of maintaining them after the first year.

Fifthly, This food would likewise bring great custom to taverns, where the 25 vintners will certainly be so prudent as to procure the best receipts for dressing it to perfection, and consequently have their houses frequented by all the fine gentlemen, who justly value themselves upon their knowledge in good eating; and a skilful cook who understands how to oblige his guests, will contrive to make it as expensive as they please.

Sixthly, This would be a great inducement to marriage, which all wise 26 nations have either encouraged by rewards or enforced by laws and penalties. It would increase the care and tenderness of mothers toward their children, when they were sure of a settlement for life to the poor babes, provided in some sort by the public, to their annual profit instead of expense. We should see an honest emulation among the married women, which of them would bring the fattest child to the market. Men would become as fond of their wives during the time of their pregnancy as they are now of their mares in foal, their cows in calf, their sows when they are ready to farrow; nor offer to beat or kick them (as is too frequent a practice) for fear of a miscarriage.

Many other advantages might be enumerated. For instance, the addition 27 of some thousand carcasses in our exportation of barreled beef, the propagation of swine's flesh, and improvement in the art of making good bacon, so much wanted among us by the great destruction of pigs, too frequent at our table; which are no way comparable in taste or magnificence to a well-grown, fat, yearling child, which roasted whole will make a considerable figure at a lord mayor's feast or any other public entertainment. But this and many others I omit, being studious of brevity.

Supposing that 1,000 families in this city would be constant customers for 28 infants' flesh, besides others who might have it at merry-meetings, particularly at weddings and christenings, I compute that Dublin would take off annually about 20,000 carcasses; and the rest of the kingdom (where probably they will be sold somewhat cheaper) the remaining 80,000.

I can think of no one objection that will possibly be raised against this 29 proposal, unless it should be urged that the number of people will be thereby much lessened in the kingdom. This I freely own, and it was indeed one principal design in offering it to the world. I desire the reader will observe, that I calculate my remedy for this one individual kingdom of Ireland and for no other that ever was, is, or I think ever can be upon earth. Therefore let no man talk to me of other expedients: of taxing our absentees at 5s. a pound: of using neither clothes nor household furniture except what is of our own growth and manufacture: of utterly rejecting the materials and instruments that promote foreign luxury: of curing the expensiveness of pride, vanity, idleness, and gaming in our women: of introducing a vein of parsimony, prudence, and temperance: of learning to love our country, in the want of which we differ even from Laplanders and the inhabitants of Topinamboo: of quitting our animosities and factions, nor acting any longer like the Jews, who were murdering one another at the very moment their city was taken: of being a little cautious not to sell our country and conscience for nothing: of teaching landlords to have at least one degree of mercy toward their tenants: lastly, of putting a spirit of honesty, industry, and skill into our shopkeepers; who, if a resolution could now be taken to buy only our native goods, would immediately unite to cheat and exact upon us in the price, the measure, and the goodness, nor could ever yet be brought to make one fair proposal of just dealing, though often and earnestly invited to it.

Therefore I repeat, let no man talk to me of these and the like expedients, 30 till he has at least some glimpse of hope that there will be ever some hearty and sincere attempt to put them in practice.

But as to myself, having been wearied out for many years with offering 31 vain, idle, visionary thoughts, and at length utterly despairing of success, I fortunately fell upon this proposal; which, as it is wholly new, so it has something solid and real, of no expense and little trouble, full in our own power, and whereby we can incur no danger in disobliging England. For this kind of commodity will not bear exportation, the flesh being of too tender a consistence to admit a long continuance in salt, although perhaps I could name a country which would be glad to eat up our whole nation without it.

After all, I am not so violently bent upon my own opinion as to reject any 32 offer proposed by wise men, which shall be found equally innocent, cheap, easy, and effectual. But before something of that kind shall be advanced in contradiction to my scheme, and offering a better, I desire the author or authors will be pleased maturely to consider two points. First, as things now stand, how they will be able to find food and raiment for 100,000 useless mouths and backs. And secondly, there being a round million of creatures in human figure throughout this kingdom, whose subsistence put into a common stock would leave them in debt 2,000,000*l.* sterling, adding those who are beggars by profession to the bulk of farmers, cottagers, and laborers, with the wives and children who are beggars in effect; I desire those politicians who dislike my overture, and may perhaps be so bold as to attempt an answer, that they will first ask the parents of these mortals, whether they would not at this day think it a great happiness to have been sold for food at a year old in the manner I prescribe, and thereby have avoided such a perpetual scene of misfortunes as they have since gone through by the oppression of landlords, the impossibility of paying rent without money or trade, the want of common sustenance, with neither house nor clothes to cover them from the inclemencies of the weather, and the most inevitable prospect of entailing the like or greater miseries upon their breed for ever.

I profess, in the sincerity of my heart, that I have not the least personal 33 interest in endeavoring to promote this necessary work, having no other motive than the public good of my country, by advancing our trade, providing for infants, relieving the poor, and giving some pleasure to the rich. I have no children by which I can propose to get a single penny; the youngest being nine years old, and my wife past childbearing.

1714

QUESTIONS FOR DISCUSSION

Content

a. What is Swift's purpose in writing this seemingly absurd "proposal"? Just what is he proposing?
b. At which point in the essay do you begin to suspect that Swift is being satirical?
c. Indirectly, "A Modest Proposal" provides a clear indication of Swift's attitudes toward the poor and the ruling classes. Recalling information from the text, explain his attitude toward each of these segments of society.
d. Swift makes a number of interesting allusions to the politics and history of his time. Consult an encyclopedia or other appropriate reference work in your college library and brush up on the history of Ireland during the early 1700s. In particular, make sure you understand the following:

   · The Pretender
   · Papists
   · Roman Catholic Countries
   · Cottagers
   · Episcopal Curate
   · Psalmanazar, a Native of the Island of Formosa
   · Mandarins

e. Near the end of the essay, we come upon a list of "expedients." Although the speaker claims otherwise, they represent the kinds of solutions to Ireland's problems that Swift actually believes in. What are these solutions? Why does Swift wait until late in his essay to mention them? Why does he mention them at all?

Strategy and Style

f. Swift the speaker in "A Modest Proposal" is quite different from Swift the author. Describe the speaker. What function does Swift's use of a persona serve?

g. Swift's mention of Psalmanazar serves a particularly ironic purpose. What is it?

h. Swift's solutions to Ireland's problems, though ironic, are explained in a no-nonsense, businesslike tone. Point to specific passages in which this tone is most apparent.

i. Swift's irony is especially biting when he says: "I grant this food will be somewhat dear, and therefore very proper for landlords, who, as they have already devoured most of the parents, seem to have the best title to the children" (paragraph 12). What other passages reveal his anger toward the ruling class?

SUGGESTIONS FOR SHORT WRITING

a. How did you respond on an emotional level when you read this essay? Write a response in which you describe your "gut reaction" to "A Modest Proposal."

b. Write a paragraph response to this essay from the point of view of one of the poor of Ireland; then write a paragraph from the point of view of a member of the ruling class. Compare the two responses.

SUGGESTIONS FOR SUSTAINED WRITING

a. Like Swift, approach a serious subject in tongue-in-cheek fashion and write your own "modest proposal." For instance, discuss a controversial government policy and, while pretending to defend it, describe those aspects of it that you find most offensive. Or, you might simply try to convince your classmates that there really are "advantages" to becoming a chain smoker, to walking into class unprepared day after day, or to cramming for exams rather than studying for them systematically.

b. One of Swift's *real* solutions to Ireland's problems is that its inhabitants use "neither clothes nor household furniture except what is of [their] own growth and manufacture." This seems to be the same idea behind the current "Buy American" movement. Do you believe that buying only goods manufactured at home will improve our economy? Explain.

c. One aspect of Swift's proposal focuses on the relationship between tenants and landlords. This is still an important issue. Using your own experiences as sources of information, write an essay that argues for the enactment of:

- Laws that keep rents at reasonable levels and protect tenants from unscrupulous landlords
- Laws that help landlords make a fair profit and protect their properties from irresponsible tenants.

The Great Person-Hole Cover Debate:
A Modest Proposal for Anyone Who Thinks the Word "He" Is Just Plain Easier...

Lindsy Van Gelder

Lindsy Van Gelder (b. 1944) attended Northwestern University and Sarah Lawrence College, where she took a B.A. in 1966. Van Gelder, who describes herself as a "feminist anarchist," has worked as a reporter for The New York Post *and as a staff writer for* Ms. *magazine. She has also been a columnist for the United Feature Syndicate in New York. While a TV news commentator for WNEW in New York, Van Gelder reported on the massage-parlor scandal in Times Square and covered Anita Bryant's campaign against gays in Miami. In 1970, she won the Page One Award from the New York Newspaper Guild for her expose of the New York City high school system. Van Gelder is the author of* Sisterhood Is Powerful *(1970) and has contributed numerous articles to the* Village Voice, New York *magazine,* Rolling Stone, Esquire *and* Redbook. *"The Great Person-Hole Cover Debate" is a compelling example of Van Gelder's ability to define clearly the disconcerting effects of our reliance on sexist language—language whose exclusiveness and arrogance were once accepted as "the way of the world."*

1   I wasn't looking for trouble. What I was looking for, actually, was a little tourist information to help me plan a camping trip to New England.

2   But there it was, on the first page of the 1979 edition of the State of Vermont *Digest of Fish and Game Laws and Regulations:* a special message of welcome from one Edward F. Kehoe, commissioner of the Vermont Fish and Game Department, to the reader and would-be camper, *i.e.,* me.

3   This person (*i.e.,* me) is called "the sportsman."

4   "We have no 'sportswomen, sportspersons, sportsboys, or sportsgirls,' " Commissioner Kehoe hastened to explain, obviously anticipating that some of us sportsfeminists might feel a bit overlooked. "But," he added, "we are pleased to report that we do have many great sportsmen who are women, as well as young people of both sexes."

5   It's just that the Fish and Game Department is trying to keep things "simple and forthright" and to respect "long-standing tradition." And anyway, we really ought to be flattered, "sportsman" being "a meaningful title being earned by a special kind of dedicated man, woman, or young person, as opposed to just any hunter, fisherman, or trapper."

6   I have heard this particular line of reasoning before. In fact, I've heard it so often that I've come to think of it as The Great Person-Hole Cover Debate, since gender-neutral manholes are invariably brought into the argument as evi-

441

dence of the lengths to which humorless, Newspeak-spouting feminists will go to destroy their mother tongue.

Consternation about woman-handling the language comes from all sides. 7 Sexual conservatives who see the feminist movement as a unisex plot and who long for the good olde days of *vive la différence,* when men were men and women were women, nonetheless do not rally behind the notion that the term "mankind" excludes women.

But most of the people who choke on expressions like "spokesperson" 8 aren't right-wing misogynists, and this is what troubles me. Like the undoubt-edly well-meaning folks at the Vermont Fish and Game Department, they tend to reassure you right up front that they're only trying to keep things "simple" and to follow "tradition," and that some of their best men are women, anyway.

Usually they wind up warning you, with great sincerity, that you're jeop- 9 ardizing the worthy cause of women's rights by focusing on "trivial" side is-sues. I would like to know how anything that gets people so defensive and re-sistant can possibly be called "trivial," whatever else it might be.

The English language is alive and constantly changing. Progress—both 10 scientific and social—is reflected in our language, or should be.

Not too long ago, there was a product called "flesh-colored" Band-Aids. 11 The flesh in question was colored Caucasian. Once the civil rights movement pointed out the racism inherent in the name, it was dropped. I cannot imagine reading a thoughtful, well-intentioned company policy statement explaining that while the Band-Aids would continue to be called "flesh-colored" for old time's sake, black and brown people would now be considered honorary whites and were perfectly welcome to use them.

Most sensitive people manage to describe our national religious tradi- 12 tions as "Judeo-Christian," even though it takes a few seconds longer to say than "Christian." So why is it such a hardship to say "he or she" instead of "he"?

I have a modest proposal for anyone who maintains that "he" is just plain 13 easier: since "he" has been the style for several centuries now—and since it really includes everybody anyway, right?—it seems only fair to give "she" a turn. Instead of having to ponder over the intricacies of, say, "Congressman" versus "Congress person" versus "Representative," we can simplify things by calling them all "Congresswoman."

Other clarifications will follow: "a woman's home is her castle..." "a gi- 14 ant step for all womankind".... "all women are created equal".... "Fisherwom-an's Wharf."...

And don't be upset by the business letter that begins "Dear Madam," 15 fellas. It means you, too.

1980

QUESTIONS FOR DISCUSSION

Content

a. What is the "modest proposal" that Van Gelder makes in this essay? How does it relate to Swift's "modest proposal"?

b. What is the effect Van Gelder wishes to produce by offering such a proposal? How would Commissioner Kehoe react to it?

c. Why are paragraphs 9 and 10 central to her purpose?

d. How would you describe the author's treatment of Commissioner Kehoe? Is it fair and objective? Does what she says about this man cast light upon her comments in paragraph 8?

e. What two important illustrations about language does Van Gelder use to prove that adjustments can and should be made to exclude sexism from our vocabulary?

f. What, according to the author, are some of the arguments that "well-meaning folks" use to explain why they continue to use sexist language? Why does she bother to make these arguments before introducing her "modest proposal"?

g. What is "The Great Person-Hole Cover Debate"? In what ways have critics of the feminist movement used it to try to trivialize concerns about sexist language?

h. "Newspeak" is an allusion to Orwell's *1984*. What does the term mean, and why are feminists sometimes accused of "spouting" it?

i. What does the phrase *vive la différence* mean, and how does it help characterize the "sexual conservatives" described in paragraph 7?

Strategy and Style

j. What do you make of Van Gelder's introduction? Why is it effective in capturing the reader's attention?

k. How would you describe Van Gelder's tone in the last few paragraphs? Is it appreciably different from the tone she employs earlier? In what way does she prepare her readers for this shift?

l. Why does the use of the term "modest proposal," in and of itself, tell us that the author is being ironic?

SUGGESTIONS FOR SHORT WRITING

a. Read, or at least scan, "The Cosmic Prison" (Chapter 9) and rewrite paragraphs 1 and 2, replacing all the masculine pronouns with feminine ones. Then rewrite the paragraphs with nongender-specific usage. In what ways does the tone or meaning differ from version to version?

b. Write your opinion of "he" as a universal pronoun.

SUGGESTIONS FOR SUSTAINED WRITING

a. Van Gelder makes a good case for being aware of the effects of language that is sexist, racist, or otherwise biased. What words and phrases in common use today continue to betray such biases? Are there alternatives with which we can replace them? Suggest some and explain why using such alternatives would be a welcome change.

b. The effects of using language that demeans someone because of his/her gender, race, religion, sexual orientation, politics, or ethnic heritage can be devastating. Using your own experience as a source of illustrations, explain how harmful those effects can be.

c. Do you agree with Van Gelder that language can have a profound effect upon the way we view others, and that sexist language can be devastating? If not, write a rebuttal to this essay. Address your remarks to an audience of your classmates, both male and female.

d. In a letter to your former high-school principal or school board, suggest a number of ways in which the educational system in this country should be revised in order to eliminate sexism (or any other bias, for that matter) from the curriculum and from the language.

The Farce Called "Grading"

Arthur E. Lean

Arthur E. Lean (b. 1909) is a educational philosopher who has taught, written about, and lectured on social and philosophical aspects of education. He is an expert on international education and was consultant to the South Vietnamese Ministry of Education. He is the author of many articles and reviews, and was editor/contributor on John Dewey and the World View *(1964). "The Farce Called 'Grading'" is included in* And Merely Teach: Irreverent Essays on the Mythology of Education *(1968, 1976).*

A sustained effort should be made to throw out false inducements to learning. In one way or another most of these refer to our obsession with grades. A few colleges that have ended the grading system, like those truly brave ones that have thrown out faculty ranks, have shown what can be done. It is possible to interest students in intrinsic learning, once we rid ourselves of the ancient hobby of making book on each performance. Grades may be useful for checking the memory of items of fact or the solving of pat mathematical problems. As a system for evaluating attainment of broad educational aims, it remains a failure. Few teachers have any systematic idea of how to grade fairly. Grading is also the chief villain behind the scandal of college cheating.

Louis T. Benezet

I have long ago reached the conclusion that the marking system itself is damaging in its impact on the education of our children and youth, and that it should go the way of the hickory stick and dunce caps. It should be abandoned at all levels of education.

Ernest O. Melby

Of all the common practices in our schools, doubtless the most tyrannical and indefensible is our insistence on attempting to evaluate students' performance through a system of grades or "marks." The harm done by this practice is incalculable, but we persistently cling to it in spite of its obvious unworkability. Every person who has ever gone to school can cite numerous instances of unfairness and injustice caused by grading systems and practices, but for some strange reason we seem to assume it to be necessary and intrinsic to the process of formal education. 1

Some years ago, when numerical grading on a percentage basis was more common than today, several experiments were conducted in an attempt to determine how precisely teachers could evaluate students' written work. In one well-known study, in order to "prejudice the garden to roses," an *exact* subject was chosen—mathematics, of course, because in that field, as everybody knows, things are either right or wrong—and a panel of experienced mathematics teachers, recognized by their peers for their competence, was assembled to do the evaluating. Student papers in plane geometry were graded by these expert 2

445

teachers, each using an identical copy so as to eliminate any persuasive effect of extraneous factors such as neatness. The result was, of course, that the grades assigned to exactly the same paper ranged all the way from the 90s down to the 40s and 50s. And this in an *exact* subject where answers are "either right or wrong"! Similar results were obtained in other comparable studies.

The shift to letter-grading with fewer distinctions (the familiar A, B, C, D,   3 with either E or F to designate failure) has not really solved the problem; it has merely reduced the number of categories (whereupon, of course, we promptly proceed recidivistically to attach plus and minus signs—multiple ones if single ones will not suffice). And of course we *must* have an equivalency table to indicate that A includes the range 93–100 or 90– 100, B 85–92 or 80–89, and so on down, refusing in our obstinacy to recognize the fatal inconsistency involved: is A 93 or 100 or something in between? How about 95? 98? 96.123456789?

During the hectic post–World War II days I was pressed into service to   4 teach Freshman Composition (Expository Writing) at a large university. There were more than a hundred sections of this course, each with a maximum of twenty-five students. We used a book of readings as a basis for class discussion and weekly themes. In addition to class sessions, each student had a short fortnightly conference with his instructor to go over his work and discuss ways of improving his written expression.

One of the "full" professors in the English department was in charge of   5 all the teaching in this course, and he regularly convened the instructors—some seventy or eighty of us—for purposes of coordination and standardization of instruction. Usually at these sessions we were given identical copies of an actual student theme which had been selected at random and duplicated exactly as originally submitted. We took thirty to forty minutes to read and evaluate this short theme, whereupon we wrote on it a grade and an evaluative comment. Having listed our names alphabetically on the blackboard, the professor in charge then called them one by one, and each instructor responded to his name by stating the grade he had assigned to that theme. This grade was inscribed after his name on the blackboard.

Invariably the assigned grades on the same theme ranged all the way   6 from A (excellent) to E (failure). Those instructors who judged that theme to be in either of those extreme categories were then called upon to stand up and justify their grades. This they usually did with great earnestness and sincerity, albeit with increasing reluctance, for in the process their own personal biases, prejudices, and confusions were soon revealed for all to see. (It quickly became obvious to many neophyte instructors that C-minus was an inconspicuous, colorless grade which would not require them to expose themselves to the public justification-humiliation process.) Most of the assigned grades tended, of course, to cluster in the middle of the scale, but there were almost always some on the extremes. But not once did we stop to consider the *student* who must maintain a certain minimum grade-average to stay in school, and whose mark on that theme might be A or E depending on which instructor he has!

All of us are familiar with the classic examples of students' submitting   7
the same paper to different instructors (or even to the same instructor at different times!) and getting widely varying grades, of handing in obscure works of famous authors and getting them back marked "failure," and so on.

Grading tends to stigmatize and punish the less able student, who may be   8
trying very hard but, through no fault of his own, simply did not inherit much in the way of native intelligence.

In spite of the staggering amount of incontrovertible evidence that grad-   9
ing not only does not accomplish its purpose but in reality inhibits and injures the educative process, we obstinately continue with this perverted practice.

After all, what is a "grade" supposed to be and do? Perhaps we could get   10
general agreement on the statement that it is a symbol purporting to express a measurement of academic achievement—an evaluation of the quality and quantity of learning. Now, in order to measure anything, we need a standard such as a ruler or tapeline for linear measurement, a scale for measuring weight, and so on. By using such standards I can determine that the desk at which I sit is thirty inches high, and that its surface measures twenty-eight inches by twenty inches. I put my portable typewriter on a scale and determine its weight to be nine pounds. I look at the thermometer on the wall and discover that room temperature is sixty-eight degrees Fahrenheit. Other people using the same standards would arrive at the same results; any variations would be infinitesimal and certainly negligible for practical purposes.

If all this be so, then what sense does it make for us to speak of "giving"   11
a grade to a student, or of his "earning" or "deserving" it? Do I "give" my desk a height of thirty inches? Does my typewriter "earn" a weight of nine pounds? Does this room "deserve" a temperature of sixty-eight degrees? Arrant nonsense, of course, but this ridiculous absurdity is exactly what we constantly do with our grading systems.

Compounding our criminal practices, we use grades for reward and pun-   12
ishment. Recently a coed sued her university because she claimed that her failing grade in one course was "unfair" and resulted from an attempt "to discipline and punish her" for alleged wrongful conduct. She asserted that she had been found innocent by the university's disciplinary committee, but that the instructor and administrative superiors to whom she had appealed had refused to "raise the grade" to the B which she said she had "merited." And this occurred in an institution of what we fancifully call "higher learning"!

When students disobey instructions or otherwise transgress (often unin-   13
tentionally) we say to them, "Because of this, I am lowering your grade five points (or one letter)." Such behavior is surely the epitome of cynicism, and if our students display disquieting evidence of becoming increasingly cynical, we have ourselves and our indefensible practices largely to blame. With grades we

teach them cynicism, to say nothing of lying, cheating, competitive throat-cutting, and other reprehensible practices.

"But," objects somebody, "after all, a grade is just a sort of *estimate,* and most teachers try to be fair and accurate in their estimates." Yes; most teachers try to be fair and accurate, but all the time they know—at least, those who are honest with themselves know—that they are attempting the impossible. No self-respecting teacher ever rests peacefully the night after turning in a set of grades, for he knows that the "system" has made a charlatan of him and he goes to bed hating himself for it. And as for the estimate, let us not disregard the fact that an *absolute* pass-or-fail system has no place for estimates. Is that 87 on your test paper an estimate? If it is, then mightn't it really be 88, or 86, or something else? Is that B-minus an estimate? No, indeed; when the reports come out, when the averages and grade-points are computed, when the failures are determined, when you are called in and told that you've flunked out of school, there is no room for estimates—this is a very *absolute* decision. **14**

Incidentally, no teacher I know—myself included, God wot—can explain the precise difference between a B-minus and a C-plus, to say nothing of 60 and 59—or, for that matter, 60 and 59.999999999999. **15**

"But," objects somebody else, "if grades are eliminated, what can we substitute for them?" This inevitable question reminds me of the books that have been written on the subject of how to stop smoking. Such a book can be written in one word: Quit! **16**

We have had this asinine practice of grading in schools for so long that we unconsciously assume it to be necessary to the learning process, but this is a manifestly false assumption. Grades are one aspect of the artificial paraphernalia which we have deliberately superimposed upon education—along with courses, academic credit, "promotion," degrees, diplomas, certificates, commencement exercises, graduation, faculty rank, and so on *ad infinitum, ad nauseam.* **17**

We hold these minatory requirements over the students because we assume that most of them are naturally lazy, stupid dolts who must somehow be coerced, cajoled, persuaded, threatened, strong-armed into learning what we have decided is "good for them." Much of this required material is dull, boring, meaningless, and will be forgotten almost immediately; and the way it is taught is even worse, but students realize that they must perforce jump through the hoops in order to emerge finally with that coveted degree, that beribboned diploma upon which our society places such high value. What we invariably seem to forget is that this superimposed academic apparatus is not at all intrinsic to learning—not at all a *sine qua non* of education, formal or informal. *It is there because we put it there.* Just because we're accustomed to it, let us not delude ourselves into assuming that it is essential, organic or integral; it isn't. But once it becomes an established system, students often shift their motivations and values and begin to "work for grades." And when we talk to them about "earning" and "deserving" marks, we are only compounding this felony. **18**

There have been successful attempts to eliminate marks. The Danish Folk 19
High Schools and other brave experimental schools have gotten along very
well without them. In place of report cards or transcripts covered with
cabalistic symbols, written reports and parent-teacher (or parent-teacher-
student) conferences are sometimes used to facilitate communication and
understanding. For example, employers of young people find descriptive
comments about such traits as dependability, resourcefulness, intelligence,
honesty, ability to get along with others, and so on, much more meaningful than the conventional academic transcripts of prospective employees.
If you were such an employer, would you prefer, on the one hand, a thoughtful evaluation from adults who have observed the young people closely over
a period of time, or, on the other hand, an official piece of paper informing
you about a C-minus in English history and a B-plus in college al-
gebra?

Students themselves are so conditioned to grading that they soon become 20
willing dupes of the system. They go to their instructors and ask, "How am I
doing in this course?" But in most cases they already *know* how they are doing—better than the instructor does—and the fact that they ask the question
demonstrates the unreliability of the system.

Some years ago I found a small midwestern town in which the editor of 21
the local weekly newspaper regularly printed on its front pages the complete
names and marks of all the children in that town's schools each time report
cards were issued. This editor was obviously a sick man who needed immediate
confinement in an institution, but his problem is illustrative of the pathology
endemic to the practice of grading. Its elimination is more than I dare hope for
in my lifetime.* But until the cancer is rooted out and destroyed we can hope
for little real improvement in American education.

1976

QUESTIONS FOR DISCUSSION

Content

a. Paraphrase Lean's argument. Do you agree with him? If you do, what points
   in his argument are most strongly convincing to you? What makes them so
   convincing?

*As William Clark Trow observes, "Marks. . . deserve to be abolished. Anyone who has not lived
his life in the ivory tower, however, knows that trying to abolish them would be like trying to abolish money."

Thomas J. Fleming notes that "the colossal confusion currently reigning in American education
in regard to what teachers call 'evaluating pupil performance' and what more down-to-earth parents
and kids call *marks* is our number-one school scandal."

b. If you disagree with Lean, what parts of his argument do you think are weakest? Why?

c. In paragraph 1, Lean says "The harm done by [grading] is incalculable...." What, in Lean's opinion, is the harm done?

d. Who is Lean's audience? He refers to "us" and "we" at times, and seems to be addressing teachers or university directors, but his strong language against grading seems to be aimed more at students.

e. In paragraph 12, Lean cites an example of a student who sued her university over a grade. What is Lean's probable purpose in citing this example? Does he side with the student, with the university, or both/neither?

f. In paragraph 11, Lean makes an analogy between students and inanimate entities such as desks, typewriters, and temperature. Is this a convincing analogy? What makes it convincing? If you disagree with Lean, what would you say about this analogy to show that it is an unfair rhetorical trick?

g. What have been your own experiences with grades? Do you feel that they have been fair in general? What would be a better way of evaluating students?

h. In paragraph 8, Lean says that "Grading tends to stigmatize and punish the less able student...." Some people might argue that grading reflects the competitive world which the student will soon be entering, and that colleges must maintain a certain standard; therefore, "stigmatize and punish" should actually read "challenge and assess." What is your opinion?

i. Discuss the issue of grading with your teachers. What are their rationales for their grading systems? How do they explain the difference between a B− and a C+?

j. How would you answer the question asked at the end of paragraph 19?

Strategy and Style

k. Why is the word "farce" an appropriate word for Lean's title, considering his feelings toward grading?

l. In paragraph 18, Lean calls grading a felony. Why does he assign it to this degree of crime? What is the punishment for a felony? How would that punishment be translated into punishment for using the grading system?

m. Look up "pathology" (paragraph 21). Why is it such a strong, but appropriate, word to express Lean's attitude toward grading?

SUGGESTIONS FOR SHORT WRITING

a. Write a letter to Lean, stating why you agree or disagree with him. Refer to specific places in his essay to support your points.

b. If you were Lean's teacher, what grade would you give his essay? Write an end comment to Lean to justify the grade.

SUGGESTIONS FOR SUSTAINED WRITING

a. Should grades be abolished? If your answer is yes, what should replace grades as a mark, or grading as a system? Describe a hypothetical case of a school operating without grades.

b. If your answer to the above is no, how do you address the arguments against grading that Lean puts forward? Write a counterargument to Lean's essay.

c. Write a detailed proposal for a grading system that you feel would be acceptable to students, teachers, and your college or university administration. Be as specific, thorough, and practical as possible, and be sure to include a rationale for your suggestions. Then, apply your system to some of your own work, preferable to some of your writing for this class.

The Penalty of Death

H. L. Mencken

A native of Baltimore, Henry Lewis Mencken (1880–1956) is one of the premier liter-ary and social critics of this century. His caustic attacks on the middle class, published throughout the 1920s, became models for the kind of intellectual and aesthetic cynicism many young writers would emulate in the decades to follow. Mencken rose quickly in his career as a journalist, becoming editor of the Baltimore Herald *at the age of 23, moving on to the editorship of the* Baltimore Sun *at age 26. During World War I, he began writing* The American Language, *an immense work that traces the develop-ment of the vocabulary unique to North America. The* American Language *was first published in 1919, though Mencken continued to revise and publish it throughout his life, and it is still being revised and published today. Mencken founded* The American Mercury, *an important vehicle for social and political commentary, to which he con-tributed regularly. He also published several essay collections, including his six-volume* Prejudices *and* A Mencken Chrestomathy *(1949), from which "The Penalty of Death" is taken. This was to be his last book; in 1948 he had a stroke that left him cogent but unable to read or write.*

Of the arguments against capital punishment that issue from uplifters, two 1
are commonly heard most often, to wit:

1. That hanging a man (or frying him or gassing him) is a dreadful business, degrading to those who have to do it and revolting to those who have to witness it.
2. That it is useless, for it does not deter others from the same crime.

The first of these arguments, it seems to me, is plainly too weak to need 2
serious refutation. All it says, in brief, is that the work of the hangman is un-pleasant. Granted. But suppose it is? It may be quite necessary to society for all that. There are, indeed, many other jobs that are unpleasant, and yet no one thinks of abolishing them—that of the plumber, that of the soldier, that of the garbage-man, that of the priest hearing confessions, that of the sand-hog, and so on. Moreover, what evidence is there that any actual hangman complains of his work? I have heard none. On the contrary, I have known many who delighted in their ancient art, and practiced it proudly.

In the second argument of the abolitionists there is rather more force, but 3
even here, I believe, the ground under them is shaky. Their fundamental error consists in assuming that the whole aim of punishing criminals is to deter other (potential) criminals—that we hang or electrocute A simply in order to so alarm B that he will not kill C. This, I believe, is an assumption which confuses a part with the whole. Deterrence, obviously, is *one* of the aims of punishment, but it is surely not the only one. On the contrary, there are at least a half dozen, and

452

some are probably quite as important. At least one of them, practically considered, is *more* important. Commonly, it is described as revenge, but revenge is
really not the word for it. I borrow a better term from the late Aristotle: *katharsis. Katharsis,* so used, means a salubrious discharge of emotions, a healthy letting off of steam. A school-boy, disliking his teacher, deposits a tack upon the
pedagogical chair; the teacher jumps and the boy laughs. This is *katharsis.*
What I contend is that one of the prime objects of all judicial punishments is to
afford the same grateful relief (*a*) to the immediate victims of the criminal punished, and (*b*) to the general body of moral and timorous men.

These persons, and particularly the first group, are concerned only indi-   4
rectly with deterring other criminals. The thing they crave primarily is the satisfaction of seeing the criminal actually before them suffer as he made them
suffer. What they want is the peace of mind that goes with the feeling that accounts are squared. Until they get that satisfaction they are in a state of emotional tension, and hence unhappy. The instant they get it they are comfortable.
I do not argue that this yearning is noble; I simply argue that it is almost universal among human beings. In the face of injuries that are unimportant and can
be borne without damage it may yield to higher impulses; that is to say, it may
yield to what is called Christian charity. But when the injury is serious Christianity is adjourned, and even saints reach for their sidearms. It is plainly asking
too much of human nature to expect it to conquer so natural an impulse. A
keeps a store and has a bookkeeper, B. B steals $700, employs it in playing at
dice or bingo, and is cleaned out. What is A to do? Let B go? If he does so he
will be unable to sleep at night. The sense of injury, of injustice, of frustration
will haunt him like pruritus. So he turns B over to the police, and they hustle B
to prison. Thereafter A can sleep. More, he has pleasant dreams. He pictures B
chained to the wall of a dungeon a hundred feet underground, devoured by rats
and scorpions. It is so agreeable that it makes him forget his $700. He has got
his *katharsis.*

The same thing precisely takes place on a larger scale when there is a   5
crime which destroys a whole community's sense of security. Every law-abiding citizen feels menaced and frustrated until the criminals have been struck
down—until the communal capacity to get even with them, and more than
even, has been dramatically demonstrated. Here, manifestly, the business of deterring others is no more than an afterthought. The main thing is to destroy the
concrete scoundrels whose act has alarmed everyone, and thus made everyone
unhappy. Until they are brought to book that unhappiness continues; when the
law has been executed upon them there is a sigh of relief. In other words, there
is *katharsis.*

I know of no public demand for the death penalty for ordinary crimes,   6
even for ordinary homicides. Its infliction would shock all men of normal decency of feeling. But for crimes involving the deliberate and inexcusable taking
of human life, by men openly defiant of all civilized order—for such crimes it
seems, to nine men out of ten, a just and proper punishment. Any lesser penalty

leaves them feeling that the criminal has got the better of society—that he is free to add insult to injury by laughing. That feeling can be dissipated only by a recourse to *katharsis,* the invention of the aforesaid Aristotle. It is more effectively and economically achieved, as human nature now is, by wafting the criminal to realms of bliss.

The real objection to capital punishment doesn't lie against the actual ex-   7
termination of the condemned, but against our brutal American habit of putting it off so long. After all, every one of us must die soon or late, and a murderer, it must be assumed, is one who makes that sad fact the cornerstone of his metaphysic. But it is one thing to die, and quite another thing to lie for long months and even years under the shadow of death. No sane man would choose such a finish. All of us, despite the Prayer Book, long for a swift and unexpected end. Unhappily, a murderer, under the irrational American system, is tortured for what, to him, must seem a whole series of eternities. For months on end he sits in prison while his lawyers carry on their idiotic buffoonery with writs, injunctions, mandamuses, and appeals. In order to get his money (or that of his friends) they have to feed him with hope. Now and then, by the imbecility of a judge or some trick of juridic science, they actually justify it. But let us say that, his money all gone, they finally throw up their hands. Their client is now ready for the rope or the chair. But he must still wait for months before it fetches him.

That wait, I believe, is horribly cruel. I have seen more than one man sit-   8
ting in the death-house, and I don't want to see any more. Worse, it is wholly useless. Why should he wait at all? Why not hang him the day after the last court dissipates his last hope? Why torture him as not even cannibals would torture their victims? The common answer is that he must have time to make his peace with God. But how long does that take? It may be accomplished, I believe, in two hours quite as comfortably as in two years. There are, indeed, no temporal limitations upon God. He could forgive a whole herd of murderers in a millionth of a second. More, it has been done.

1926

QUESTIONS FOR DISCUSSION

Content

a. In the first paragraph Mencken lists what he considers to be the two most common arguments against capital punishment. Is this list too brief? Are there other arguments that he conveniently overlooks?

b. What flaws of fallacies, if any, do you find in Mencken's argument?

c. What rhetorical devices does Mencken use to make his essay convincing? (You may wish to start with the "unpleasant job" analogies he makes in paragraph 2.)

d. In paragraph 3 Mencken says that there are "at least a half dozen" aims of punishment, though he names only two of these aims in his essay—deterrence and *katharsis*. What might be the other aims of punishment, capital or otherwise?

e. What does Mencken consider to be worse punishment than the death penalty? Do you agree with him?

Strategy and Style

f. Mencken begins the essay with two arguments against capital punishment, and then systematically refutes each one. Why is this systematic approach effective in making the argument persuasive?

g. Why is the word "pruritus" in paragraph 4 a good word for this example? What connotations does pruritus have that make this word a better choice than its synonyms?

h. What examples of humor do you find in the essay? Why does Mencken use humor in an essay on such a serious subject? Does the humor strengthen or weaken his argument?

i. Mencken adopts a rather condescending tone. What might be his reasons for adopting such a tone? To whom is he condescending—to his readers or to a third party?

j. How can you tell that Mencken's tone is condescending? What language does he use that reveals his tone?

SUGGESTIONS FOR SHORT WRITING

a. Take an opposing stance to Mencken and jot down a list of counterarguments to what you consider to be his main points. Does Mencken address your counterarguments?

b. Using Mencken's argument, write a letter to your governor urging the government either to institute the death penalty or to strengthen the existing one.

SUGGESTIONS FOR SUSTAINED WRITING

a. Do you agree or disagree with Mencken's argument? Dissect his argument and write an essay in which you prove that his argument is sound or is full of holes.

b. Mencken takes a common topic (some would say an overused topic) and makes it fresh by using sarcastic humor and by attacking the issue from an uncommon angle. Write an essay for or against capital punishment from a new angle. As an alternative, find another, less common but equally controversial, issue and reduce the arguments on one side or the other to two main points. Then, write an essay refuting those points.

c. Describe an occasion during which you felt *katharsis*. Do you think getting this revenge was necessary or morally justified?

The Declaration of Independence

Thomas Jefferson

Born to the Virginia aristocracy, Thomas Jefferson (1743–1825) is best remembered as the drafter of the Declaration of Independence and as the third President of the United States. He also served as governor of Virginia during the Revolution, as minister to France, as Secretary of State, and as Vice-President. One of Jefferson's greatest accomplishments was the Louisiana Purchase from France, which more than doubled the land mass of the United States. Upon his retirement from politics, he returned to Monticello, the magnificent home he had designed himself, where he continued to pursue numerous scientific studies. Jefferson is also remembered as the founder of the University of Virginia and of the Democratic Party. He died exactly fifty years to the day after the signing of the Declaration, which remains one of the most eloquent, powerful, and often-quoted political documents.

In CONGRESS, July 4, 1776. The Unanimous Declaration of the Thirteen United States of America.

1   When in the Course of human events, it becomes necessary for one people to dissolve the political bands which have connected them with another, and to assume among the powers of the earth, the separate and equal station to which the Laws of Nature and of Nature's God entitle them, a decent respect to the opinions of mankind requires that they should declare the causes which impel them to the separation.

2   We hold these truths to be self-evident, that all men are created equal, that they are endowed by their Creator with certain unalienable Rights, that among these are Life, Liberty and the pursuit of Happiness.

3   That to secure these rights, Governments are instituted among Men, deriving their just powers from the consent of the governed.

4   That whenever any Form of Government becomes destructive of these ends, it is the Right of the People to alter or to abolish it, and to institute new Government, laying its foundation on such principles and organizing its powers in such form, as to them shall seem most likely to effect their Safety and Happiness. Prudence, indeed, will dictate that Governments long established should not be changed for light and transient causes; and accordingly all experience hath shewn, that mankind are more disposed to suffer, while evils are sufferable, than to right themselves by abolishing the forms to which they are accustomed. But when a long train of abuses and usurpations, pursuing invariably the same Object evinces a design to reduce them under absolute Despotism, it is their right, it is their duty, to throw off such Government, and to provide new Guards for their future security.

5   Such has been the patient sufferance of these Colonies; and such is now

457

the necessity which constrains them to alter their former Systems of Government. The history of the present King of Great Britain is a history of repeated injuries and usurpations, all having in direct object the establishment of an absolute Tyranny over these States. To prove this, let Facts be submitted to a candid world.

He has refused his Assent to Laws, the most wholesome and necessary 6 for the public good.

He has forbidden his Governors to pass Laws of immediate and pressing 7 importance, unless suspended in their operation till his Assent should be obtained; and when so suspended, he has utterly neglected to attend to them.

He has refused to pass other Laws for the accommodation of large dis- 8 tricts of people, unless those people would relinquish the right of Representation in the Legislature, a right inestimable to them and formidable to tyrants only.

He has called together legislative bodies at places unusual, uncomfort- 9 able, and distant from the depository of their public Records, for the sole purpose of fatiguing them into compliance with his measures.

He has dissolved Representative Houses repeatedly, for opposing with 10 manly firmness his invasions on the rights of people.

He has refused for a long time, after such dissolutions, to cause others to 11 be elected; whereby the Legislative powers, incapable of Annihilation, have returned to the People at large for their exercise; the State remaining in the mean time exposed to all the dangers of invasion from without, and convulsions within.

He has endeavoured to prevent the population of these States; for that 12 purpose obstructing the Laws for Naturalization of Foreigners; refusing to pass others to encourage their migrations hither, and raising the conditions of new Appropriations of Lands.

He has obstructed the Administration of Justice, by refusing his Assent to 13 Laws for establishing Judiciary powers.

He has made Judges dependent on his Will alone, for the tenure of their 14 offices, and the amount and payment of their salaries.

He has erected a multitude of New Offices, and sent hither swarms of 15 Officers to harass our people, and eat out their substance.

He has kept among us, in times of peace, Standing Armies without the 16 Consent of our legislatures.

He has affected to render the Military independent of and superior to the 17 Civil power.

He has combined with others to subject us to a jurisdiction foreign to our 18 constitution, and unacknowledged by our laws; giving his Assent to their Acts of pretended Legislation:

For Quartering large bodies of armed troops among us: 19

For Protecting them, by a mock Trial, from punishment for any Murders 20 which they should commit on the Inhabitants of these States:

For cutting off our Trade with all parts of the world: 21

For imposing Taxes on us without our Consent: 22

For depriving us in many cases, of the benefits of Trial by Jury: 23

For transporting us beyond Seas to be tried for pretended offenses: 24

For abolishing the free System of English Laws in a neighbouring Prov- 25 ince, establishing therein an Arbitrary government, and enlarging its Boundaries so as to render it at once an example and fit instrument for introducing the same absolute rule into these Colonies:

For taking away our Charters, abolishing our most valuable Laws, and al- 26 tering fundamentally the Forms of our Governments:

For suspending our own Legislatures, and declaring themselves invested 27 with power to legislate for us in all cases whatsoever.

He has abdicated Government here, by declaring us out of his Protection 28 and waging War against us:

He has plundered our seas, ravaged our Coasts, burnt our towns, and de- 29 stroyed the lives of our people.

He is at this time transporting large Armies of foreign Mercenaries to 30 compleat the works of death, desolation and tyranny, already begun with circumstances of Cruelty & perfidy scarcely paralleled in the most barbarous ages, and totally unworthy the Head of a civilized nation.

He has constrained our fellow Citizens taken Captive on the high Seas to 31 bear Arms against their Country, to become the executioners of their friends and Brethren, or to fall themselves by their Hands.

He has excited domestic insurrections amongst us, and has endeavoured 32 to bring on the inhabitants of our frontiers, the merciless Indian Savages, whose known rule of warfare, is an undistinguished destruction of all ages, sexes and conditions. In every stage of these Oppressions We have Petitioned for Redress in the most humble terms: Our repeated Petitions have been answered only by repeated injury. A Prince, whose character is thus marked by every act which may define a Tyrant, is unfit to be the ruler of a free people. Nor have We been wanting in attentions to our British brethren. We have warned them from time to time of attempts by their legislature to extend an unwarrantable jurisdiction over us. We have reminded them of the circumstances of our emigration and settlement here. We have appealed to their native justice and magnanimity, and we have conjured them by the ties of our common kindred to disavow these usurpations, which, would inevitably interrupt our connections and correspondence. They too have been deaf to the voice of justice and of consanguinity. We must, therefore, acquiesce in the necessity, which denounces our Separation, and hold them, as we hold the rest of mankind, Enemies in War, in Peace Friends.

We, THEREFORE the Representatives of the UNITED STATES OF AMERICA, in 33 General Congress Assembled, appealing to the Supreme Judge of the world for the rectitude of our intentions, do, in the Name and by Authority of the good People of these Colonies, solemnly publish and declare, That these United Colonies are, and of Right ought to be FREE AND INDEPENDENT STATES: that they are Absolved from all Allegiance to the British Crown, and that all political connection between them and the State of Great Britain, is and ought to be totally dissolved; and that as Free and Independent States, they have full Power to levy War, conclude Peace, contract Alliances, establish Commerce, and to do all other Acts and Things which Independent States may of right do.

And for the support of this Declaration, with a firm reliance on the pro- 34 tection of divine Providence, we mutually pledge to each other our Lives, our Fortunes and our sacred Honor.

1776

QUESTIONS FOR DISCUSSION

Content

a. In two or three sentences, summarize the major premises around which Jefferson builds his argument.
b. What function does paragraph 2 serve in the Declaration?
c. Why does Jefferson devote so much of the Declaration to an attack upon George III, the British king? Is this attack effective?
d. To what end does he mention the Americans' appeal to their "British brethren"?
e. In paragraph 32, Jefferson anticipates and tries to fend off counterarguments. Does anticipating counterarguments strengthen or weaken his position?
f. Some of Jefferson's arguments seem to be derived entirely from a calculated and logical analysis of the issues. As such, they are representative of the "Age of Reason," a term often used to describe Jefferson's era. Which of Jefferson's statements do you find most "reasonable"? Why?

Strategy and Style

g. Jefferson's use of parallel constructions (for example: "He has refused/He has forbidden/He has dissolved") is typical of the essayists of his age. Indicate those passages in which Jefferson employs parallelism as a rhetorical device. Does parallelism make his writing more persuasive?
h. Why does Jefferson call the truths "self-evident"? Why does he call them "truths"?
i. Some arguments in the Declaration are charged with emotion. Identify these statements and explain how his appeal to the emotions strengthens Jefferson's ability to convince his reader.

SUGGESTIONS FOR SHORT WRITING

a. Think of a person in government or some other position of authority and make a list of that person's wrongs, employing parallel constructions as Jefferson does in paragraphs 6 through 32.

b. Write the introduction to a Declaration of Independence (or Dependence) addressed to your parents.

SUGGESTIONS FOR SUSTAINED WRITING

a. Jefferson argues that life, liberty, and the pursuit of happiness are among the "unalienable Rights" we are endowed with by the Creator. What other human or civil rights do you believe we have? Name one, and argue for its inalienability. Among those you might consider are:

   · the "right" to adequate nutrition
   · the "right" to proper housing
   · the "right" to an education
   · the "right" to appropriate health care

   Send the final draft of your essay to the editor of your local or college newspaper. He/she might decide that it warrants publishing as an opinion column the next time Independence Day or some other appropriate national holiday rolls around.

b. Jefferson believes that the people have the right to overthrow governments when those governments seek to "reduce them under absolute Despotism." Identify a policy of our own government or of any other government in the world that you believe is despotic, i.e., that violates human rights. Write a convincing argument for the abolition or discontinuance of such a policy. Perhaps a letter to the editor of your local newspaper might be the best format for this assignment.

c. In essence, Jefferson is advocating the creation of a situation in which violence is sure to result. Do you agree that violence in the pursuit of liberty is justified? Or should peace be maintained at all costs? Assume that among your readers are those who favor avoiding the use of force under any circumstances and those who believe it is absolutely necessary in order to effect meaningful political changes.

I Have a Dream
Martin Luther King, Jr.

Martin Luther King, Jr. (1929–1968) had at first planned to become a doctor or a law-yer, but when he graduated from Morehouse College in Atlanta at the age of nineteen, he abandoned these ambitions and went into the seminary. After seminary, he went to Boston University, where he received his Ph.D. in 1955. He was ordained as a Baptist minister in the Ebenezer Baptist Church in Atlanta, a church he copastored with his father from 1960–68. He was also founder and director of the Southern Christian Lead-ership Conference from 1957–68, and a member of the Montgomery Improvement As-sociation, an activist group protesting racial segregation. Inspired by Mahatma Gan-dhi's principles of nonviolent protest, King led this group in several demonstrations. In May of 1963, he was arrested and imprisoned in Birmingham for demonstrating against segregation in hotels and restaurants. It was while in jail that he wrote his famous "Letter from Birmingham Jail," a work that was published in 1963 and ex-panded and republished in 1968. It was also in 1963 that King made the speech enti-tled "I Have a Dream" to over 200,000 people at the March on Washington. King re-ceived numerous awards for his work for human rights, including the Nobel Prize for Peace in 1964. On April 4, 1968, while talking with other human rights activists on a motel balcony in Memphis, King was assassinated.

Five score years ago, a great American, in whose symbolic shadow we 1
stand, signed the Emancipation Proclamation. This momentous decree came as a great beacon light of hope to millions of Negro slaves who had been seared in the flames of withering injustice. It came as a joyous daybreak to end the long night of captivity.

But one hundred years later, we must face the tragic fact that the Negro is 2
still not free. One hundred years later, the life of the Negro is still sadly crip-pled by the manacles of segregation and the chains of discrimination. One hun-dred years later, the Negro lives on a lonely island of poverty in the midst of a vast ocean of material prosperity. One hundred years later, the Negro is still languishing in the corners of American society and finds himself an exile in his own land. So we have come here today to dramatize an appalling condition.

In a sense we have come to our nation's capital to cash a check. When 3
the architects of our republic wrote the magnificent words of the Constitution and the Declaration of Independence, they were signing a promissory note to which every American was to fall heir. This note was a promise that all men would be guaranteed the unalienable rights of life, liberty, and the pursuit of happiness.

It is obvious today that America has defaulted on this promissory note 4
insofar as her citizens of color are concerned. Instead of honoring this sacred

462

obligation, America has given the Negro people a bad check; a check which has come back marked "insufficient funds." But we refuse to believe that the bank of justice is bankrupt. We refuse to believe that there are insufficient funds in the great vaults of opportunity of this nation. So we have come to cash this check—a check that will give us upon demand the riches of freedom and the security of justice. We have also come to this hallowed spot to remind America of the fierce urgency of *now*. This is no time to engage in the luxury of cooling off or to take the tranquilizing drugs of gradualism. *Now* is the time to make real the promises of Democracy. *Now* is the time to rise from the dark and desolate valley of segregation to the sunlit path of racial justice. *Now* is the time to open the doors of opportunity to all of God's children. *Now* is the time to lift our nation from the quicksands of racial injustice to the solid rock of brotherhood.

It would be fatal for the nation to overlook the urgency of the moment 5 and to underestimate the determination of the Negro. This sweltering summer of the Negro's legitimate discontent will not pass until there is an invigorating autumn of freedom and equality. 1963 is not an end, but a beginning. Those who hope that the Negro needed to blow off steam and will now be content will have a rude awakening if the nation returns to business as usual. There will be neither rest nor tranquillity in America until the Negro is granted his citizenship rights. The whirlwinds of revolt will continue to shake the foundations of our nation until the bright day of justice emerges.

But there is something that I must say to my people who stand on the 6 warm threshold which leads into the palace of justice. In the process of gaining our rightful place we must not be guilty of wrongful deeds. Let us not seek to satisfy our thirst for freedom by drinking from the cup of bitterness and hatred. We must forever conduct our struggle on the high plane of dignity and discipline. We must not allow our creative protest to degenerate into physical violence. Again and again we must rise to the majestic heights of meeting physical force with soul force. The marvelous new militancy which has engulfed the Negro community must not lead us to a distrust of all white people, for many of our white brothers, as evidenced by their presence here today, have come to realize that their destiny is tied up with our destiny and their freedom is inextricably bound to our freedom. We cannot walk alone.

And as we walk, we must make the pledge that we shall march ahead. We 7 cannot turn back. There are those who are asking the devotees of civil rights, "When will you be satisfied?" We can never be satisfied as long as the Negro is the victim of the unspeakable horrors of police brutality. We can never be satisfied as long as our bodies, heavy with the fatigue of travel, cannot gain lodging in the motels of the highways and the hotels of the cities. We cannot be satisfied as long as the Negro's basic mobility is from a smaller ghetto to a larger one. We can never be satisfied as long as a Negro in Mississippi cannot vote and a Negro in New York believes he has nothing for which to vote. No, no, we are not satisfied, and we will not be satisfied until justice rolls down like waters and righteousness like a mighty stream.

I am not unmindful that some of you have come here out of great trials **8** and tribulations. Some of you have come fresh from narrow jail cells. Some of you have come from areas where your quest for freedom left you battered by the storms of persecution and staggered by the winds of police brutality. You have been the veterans of creative suffering. Continue to work with the faith that unearned suffering is redemptive.

Go back to Mississippi, go back to Alabama, go back to South Carolina, **9** go back to Georgia, go back to Louisiana, go back to the slums and ghettos of our northern cities, knowing that somehow this situation can and will be changed. Let us not wallow in the valley of despair.

I say to you today, my friends, that in spite of the difficulties and frustra- **10** tions of the moment I still have a dream. It is a dream deeply rooted in the American dream.

I have a dream that one day this nation will rise up and live out the true **11** meaning of its creed: "We hold these truths to be self-evident; that all men are created equal."

I have a dream that one day on the red hills of Georgia the sons of former **12** slaves and the sons of former slaveowners will be able to sit down together at the table of brotherhood.

I have a dream that one day even the state of Mississippi, a desert state **13** sweltering with the heat of injustice and oppression, will be transformed into an oasis of freedom and justice.

I have a dream that my four little children will one day live in a nation **14** where they will not be judged by the color of their skin but by the content of their character.

I have a dream today.   **15**

I have a dream that one day the state of Alabama, whose governor's lips **16** are presently dripping with the words of interposition and nullification, will be transformed into a situation where little black boys and black girls will be able to join hands with little white boys and white girls and walk together as sisters and brothers.

I have a dream today.   **17**

I have a dream that one day every valley shall be exalted, every hill and **18** mountain shall be made low, the rough places will be made plain, and the crooked places will be made straight, and the glory of the Lord shall be revealed, and all flesh shall see it together.

This is our hope. This is the faith with which I return to the South. **19** With this faith we will be able to hew out of the mountain of despair a stone of hope. With this faith we will be able to transform the jangling discords of our nation into a beautiful symphony of brotherhood. With this faith we will be able to work together, to pray together, to struggle together, to go to jail together, to stand up for freedom together, knowing that we will be free one day.

This will be the day when all of God's children will be able to sing with 20 new meaning

> My country, 'tis of thee,
> Sweet land of liberty,
>   Of thee I sing:
> Land where my fathers died,
> Land of the pilgrims' pride,
> From every mountain-side
>   Let freedom ring.

And if America is to be a great nation this must become true. So let free- 21 dom ring from the prodigious hilltops of New Hampshire. Let freedom ring from the mighty mountains of New York. Let freedom ring from the heightening Alleghenies of Pennsylvania!

Let freedom ring from the snowcapped Rockies of Colorado! 22

Let freedom ring from the curvaceous peaks of California! 23

But not only that; let freedom ring from Stone Mountain of Georgia! 24

Let freedom ring from Lookout Mountain of Tennessee! 25

Let freedom ring from every hill and molehill of Mississippi. From every 26 mountainside, let freedom ring.

When we let freedom ring, when we let it ring from every village and 27 every hamlet, from every state and every city, we will be able to speed up that day when all of God's children, black men and white men, Jews and Gentiles, Protestants and Catholics, will be able to join hands and sing in the words of the old Negro spiritual, "Free at last! free at last! thank God almighty, we are free at last!"

1963

QUESTIONS FOR DISCUSSION

Content

a. What does King hope to evoke in his audience by mentioning various historical documents (the Emancipation Proclamation, the Declaration of Independence, the Constitution)?

b. King makes it a point to address issues that are of particular interest to white listeners and readers. What might have been his reasons for this?

c. Why might King have decided to quote all of the first seven lines of "My Country 'tis of Thee"? Why did he not stop at "Of thee I sing"?

d. What effect does King create when he makes reference to specific places, events, and public figures?

e. King makes reference to the Bible and to the faith that has sustained him throughout his struggle for civil rights. What effect is created with such references?

Strategy and Style

f. King's speech is especially moving because he succeeds in creating emphasis through parallelism. Find a few examples of parallelism.
g. Does his use of parallelism bring to mind Jefferson's use of this rhetorical device? In what other ways are the Declaration of Independence and "I Have a Dream" similar?
h. What does King mean when he says: "America has given the Negro people a bad check" (paragraph 4)? Identify other metaphors that he uses effectively, and explain why they work so well.
i. Why does King use the term "marvelous" to describe the "new militancy which has engulfed the Negro community"?
j. How would you describe King's tone? Controlled? Angry? Impassioned?

SUGGESTIONS FOR SHORT WRITING

a. In your opinion, has the situation of black Americans changed, or not changed, since King gave this speech?
b. Briefly describe your own dream for a better world.

SUGGESTIONS FOR SUSTAINED WRITING

a. Do some research in your college library by reading several newspaper or magazine articles that chronicle the events leading up to King's address at the Lincoln Memorial. Summarize these events and try to comment on their significance to the civil rights movement of the 1960s. Be certain to footnote or in some way cite the authorship of material you quote or paraphrase.
b. Do you have a "dream" that in the future some social or political injustice will be eliminated, that a cure will be found for a disease, that war and famine will cease? Describe your "dream" and propose ways in which to make it a reality.
c. Has King's dream of equality and opportunity for American blacks been fulfilled in the decades since he spoke at the Lincoln Memorial? Explain by using as much specific detail as possible.

Eight Signposts to Salvation

Alan Paton

Alan Paton (1903–1988) acquired an international reputation as the champion of the rights of all South Africans with the publication of Cry, The Beloved Country *(1948), a novel in which he envisions, symbolically at least, the equality and coopera- tion of the races in his troubled homeland. Paton served as principal of the Diepkloof Reformatory in Johannesburg from 1935 to 1948, an experience that convinced him of the need for an enlightened and humanistic approach to criminal justice and that had a profound influence on his writing. Paton was also the founder and president of the South African Liberal Party until it was dissolved in 1968. His writing and his politi- cal activities helped to a great degree to inform the world of the frightening and tragic consequences of South Africa's policy of apartheid. His second novel,* Too Late the Phalarope *(1953), while not as celebrated as his first, is an even more effective treat- ment of the problem. In this work, Paton analyzes the social and psychological forces that cause the demise of a white South African policeman who sleeps with a young black woman. Paton published a third novel,* Ah, But Your Land Is Beautiful *(1982); a collection of short stories,* Debbie Go Home *(1961); and several works of nonfiction including* Knocking at the Door: Shorter Writings *(1975), from which "Eight Sign- posts to Salvation" is taken. In 1988, his autobiography,* Journey Continued, *was published.*

1 Does a ruling group change towards those it rules because of consider- ations of justice? The answer is, almost certainly, no. Does it change because of internal and external pressures? Possibly, yes.

2 This second answer is not wholly encouraging. If the internal and external pressures become really dangerous, it may be too late to change. The people exerting the pressures may no longer care if you change. The time has come to destroy you. But the answer is not wholly discouraging. A ruling group may consent to change while it can still influence the sit- uation. It may realise that the way to survival no longer lies in resistance to change. It may see the clouds on the horizon and know what they mean.

3 There is a not very nice picture that comes often to my mind. A man lives in a house full of possessions. The poor and the angry and the dispossessed keep knocking at the door. Inside some members of his family urge him to open the door and others tell him that he must never open the door. Then comes the final imperious knock, and he knows at last that he must open. And when he opens, it is Death who is waiting for him.

4 And the man is me, my wife, our children; he is the White man; above all he is the Afrikaner.

But I am not writing to spread gloom. I am writing especially for those **6** inside the house who are telling the man to open the door. I am writing for White students and priests and newspapermen and trade unionists, for the young people of the United Party and the National Party and the Progressive Party, for all those who are working for change in this implacable land.

Why on earth do they do it?   **7**

They do it because of those strange unweighable and immeasurable **8** things like hope and faith. And I admire them for it in this faithless world where for many nothing exists that cannot be weighed and measured, a world that believes in so little.

What a strange thing, to have been away from South Africa for some **9** months, from its threats and bannings and denial of passports, and its implacability, and then to want to get back to it again!

Some people would say: Of course, you want to get back to your White **10** comforts and privileges. Whatever truth there is in this it's not true enough. You want to get back because it's there that your life has meaning. You want to get back to those stubborn things which are the very stuff of your life. You want to get back to the students and the priests and the newspapermen. They make you feel you are alive more than all the sights of Paris and London and even Copenhagen.

These young White people, the Young Turks, the young UPs and Progs **11** and Nats, what do they want?

Well, at least it is clear what a great many of them want. They want noth- **12** ing less than a new country. They have realised that White leadership and Anglo-Afrikaner solidarity and Afrikaner supremacy don't mean anything anymore. Nothing means anything at all if its architects and planners are all White.

I am no longer a party man, and I must confess my impatience with those **13** who think that any existing political party can possibly hold the best, wisest, most practicable solution for our problems, or can possibly know the best, wisest, most practicable way towards such a solution. Some of the computer-like arguments between party and party are exasperating. The house is burning down and the would-be saviours are arguing about what colour to choose for the buckets.

I don't expect younger White people to rush into a new party. But **14** I do expect them to drop these useless recriminations. They must not shun one another. One thing binds them together that is greater than any loyalty to any party, and that is loyalty to their country and all its people.

Are there any things they might all agree about? I believe so and here **15** they are. But I do not dogmatise about them.

1. The days of White domination are over.
2. The days of unilateral White political decisions are over.

3. The progress of the homelands to political independence—however much may be left to be desired—is irreversible.
4. The possibility that all or most of the homelands will eventually form a Black Federation must be recognised.
5. The possibility that the Black Federation may itself offer to federate with 'White' South Africa must be recognised.
6. If it does not make this offer, or if the offer is refused, then the final extinction of 'White' South Africa will be assured.
7. The offer will not be made if 'White' South Africa is not prepared to begin the dismantling of the machinery of apartheid.
8. It is the political constitution of the future 'White' South Africa that is the supreme political question facing all White people, especially young White people. When I say 'young', I don't mean only students. I mean all who are young enough to know that we must change or die.

The problem of 'White' South Africa is that there are:	15
Some four million Whites.	16
Some two million Coloured people.	17
Some 750,000 Asians.	18
Some eight million Africans.	19

According to Nationalist theory these eight million Africans are 'temporary sojourners'. They really belong somewhere else. But at least six million are permanent residents, *except for the fact that no urban African has any real sense of permanence:* [20]

Four million Whites therefore constitute a third of the population of 'White' South Africa. The days of their domination are over. They are faced with the problem—the magnitude of which cannot be exaggerated—of constructing a social order in which justice will be done to all. And they cannot construct it unilaterally. Better wages, the quality of education, the quality of housing, the preservation of family life, all are important. But they are no longer gifts to be given by Whites to Blacks. [21]

I beg to close with three questions to all White people who understand that we change or die. Is there any future for apartheid in 'White' South Africa? Is Afrikaner-English co-operation good enough, and is Afrikaner-English-Coloured-Asian co-operation not only unattainable, but downright dangerous? Is there any place for the qualified franchise in 'White' South Africa, or is it only another of these unilateral gifts? [22]

Change is in the air. It will come whether we White people like it or not. It won't—it cannot—be completely safe, completely sure, completely satisfying. But it will be safer and surer and more satisfying if we take our share in bringing it about in the company of all our fellow South Africans. [23]

1975

QUESTIONS FOR DISCUSSION

Content

a. In paragraph 21, the author tells us that White South Africa cannot construct a new social order "unilaterally." Does this statement qualify as his thesis? If so, why does he not reveal it earlier in the essay?

b. Why does Paton make sure to define his audience so specifically? Who is that audience?

c. The analogy he creates in paragraphs 3 and 4 helps him impart a sense of urgency to his work. Given what we know of his audience, why is it so important for him to do so? What is his purpose?

d. Visit the reference room of your college or community library and do a little background reading on South Africa and on the political and social problems so prominent in that country. Make sure you can answer the following questions:

   · What is apartheid?
   · Who are the Afrikaners, and what is meant by Anglo-Afrikaner solidarity?
   · What are the "homelands"?
   · How does the labeling of eight million Africans as "temporary sojourners" (paragraph 20) relate to the Afrikaner's justification of apartheid?

e. Summarize the assumptions that must be accepted if South Africa is to experience a peaceful transition to a new social order. What changes in the attitudes of young White South Africans does Paton call for?

f. What is the significance of the title of this selection?

g. Is there any place in the future of South Africa for "the qualified franchise" (paragraph 22)?

h. What are the obvious answers to the two other questions Paton asks in this paragraph, and what does asking such rhetorical questions help him accomplish at this point in the essay?

i. What does Paton mean by "Nationalist theory" (paragraph 20)?

j. What do terms such as "Young Turks," "UPs," "Progs," and "Nats" (paragraph 11) refer to?

Strategy and Style

k. Paton lists the terms that the South African government uses to distinguish the various races in his country (paragraph 16 through 19). What is the effect of listing the races?

l. Is paragraph 1 an effective introduction? In what way does it help establish the tone and direction of the rest of the essay? How would you define that tone?

SUGGESTIONS FOR SHORT WRITING

a. Continue Paton's list of "signposts."
b. Think of a current unjust situation and list the signposts that indicate its unjustness.

SUGGESTIONS FOR SUSTAINED WRITING

a. Apartheid is a political policy of separation based upon race. Think of another governmental, religious, or social policy or practice that fosters separation based upon class, age, sex, mental capacity, or social adaptability. Defend or condemn this policy.
b. "Eight Signposts to Salvation" offers a solution to an extremely difficult political and social situation. Think of a problem in this country that you believe demands immediate attention—the plight of the homeless, for instance, or the difficulties of disposing of toxic wastes. Write a letter to the editor of your local or college newspaper and argue for significant political, economic, and/or social changes in response to this serious problem.

On Rabbits, Morality, Etc.

Walter Murdoch

Born in Aberdeenshire, Scotland, Sir Walter Murdoch (1874–1970) was one of Austra-lia's leading educators and writers of nonfiction. He earned an M.A. from Scotch Col-lege in Melbourne and later lectured at the University of Melbourne. For more than thirty-five years, Murdoch was Professor of English Literature at the University of Western Australia, the institution for which he served as Chancellor from 1943 to 1947. His major works include two histories, The Making of Australia *and* Stead-fast, *as well as* A New Primer of English Literature. *Murdoch also edited the* Ox-ford Book of Australasian Verse *(1918) and published numerous essay collections, including* Loose Leaves, Speaking Personally, Saturday Mornings, The Wild Planet, Lucid Intervals, *and* The Spur of the Moment. *One of these essays, "On Rabbits, Morality, Etc.," from* 72 Essays *(1970), makes a cogent argument for the no-tion that the morality of an action can be determined only by the effects of that action and not by the intentions (good or evil) behind it.*

1   I hope the compositor will be especially careful over the title of this es-say, and that the linotype will play no unseemly tricks. To guard against any accident, I must ask you to take notice that the word 'rabbits' is, or ought to be, followed by a comma, not an apostrophe. It would be most distressing if any innocent person were cheated into reading the article in the hope of learning something about rabbits' morality—a subject on which my ignorance is pro-found....When you come to think of it, it would not be a bad subject. The rab-bit might be taken as a fine example of what we call race patriotism. His su-preme ethical motive is the expansion of the race. He dreams of the day when the rabbit family shall inherit the earth from pole to pole. If we could imagine a rabbit singing, we may suppose his song would be something like 'Rule, Britannia', or 'Deutschland uber Alles'. He is careless of the single life; the individual is nothing to him, the race is all. 'Do what you will with me,' he says; 'trap me, poison me, skin me, pack me tight in tins, make my fur into a hat and my carcass into a pie—what does it matter so long as my race endures and spreads and burrows its way across kingdoms until all the earth is one huge rabbit-warren?' He is the perfect Imperialist—that, however, is not my subject today; nor any other day. It deserves to be treated, not in my halting prose, but in Homeric verse. It is a matter for an epic. Mine is a humbler theme.

2   A little while ago you may have noticed on the cable page of your morn-ing paper the following item: 'The death is reported from London of Mr John R. Collison of Maidstone, Kent, who claimed to be the first person to introduce rabbits into Australia. He was 85 years of age.' A few days later the cables in-formed us that Mr Collison's claim to this distinction was disputed. 'Mr C. J.

Thatcher contends that his father was responsible for having introduced rabbits into Australia.'

Now, to begin with, this conflict of claims is surely a somewhat curious 3 and diverting spectacle. The idea of two men each 'claiming' to have been the first to introduce a deadly pest into a country hitherto free from it, has the charm of novelty. Mr C. J. Thatcher, ready to die in the last ditch defending his father's claim to have done more harm to Australia than anybody else, presents a singular example of filial devotion. It is as if a man went about boasting that one of his ancestors had the honour of bringing malaria into Europe. It is as if a man gave himself airs because his Uncle Henry, and nobody else, had started the recent bush-fires in Victoria. It is as if a statesman were to write a large book to prove that he, and he alone, had had the honour of starting the Great War.

As to the historic fact, I have no doubt that Mr C. J. Thatcher is in the 4 right. In 1863, or thereabout, some Victoria sportsmen, sighing like Alexander for more worlds to conquer, bethought them that the coursing of hares and rabbits was a luxury no civilized country ought to be without. So they applied to the Acclimatization Society; and the Society, thinking it rather a bright idea, wrote to its travelling agent in Great Britain, Mr Manning Thatcher, who soon got together a sufficient herd of rabbits and started for Australia in the sailing-ship *Relief.* Ship life seems to have disagreed with the rabbits; when Mr Thatcher reached Australia, not a single one of his rabbits was alive. But he, indomitable man, went straight back to England to get some more rabbits. His next attempt was again unsuccessful; and the next. Three times he started for Australia with a cargo of rabbits; three times he failed to bring a rabbit alive to port. Three times the gods strove to save Australia; but against determination like Mr Thatcher's the very gods do battle in vain. On his third journey he had kept a close watch on his charges and found out the cause of their extraordinary death-rate; he provided a remedy, and his fourth voyage was entirely successful. It was as if the gods had given up the struggle in disgust; Mr Thatcher landed without the loss of a rabbit.

Meanwhile, owing to the long delay, the aforesaid sportsmen seem to 5 have lost interest. Mr Thatcher found that nobody wanted his rabbits. With a companion, he went about the country offering baskets of live rabbits for sale, but he did not sell enough to pay expenses. His stock of rabbits increased faster than he could sell them. One hot summer afternoon the two men decided that they had had enough of the tedious and unprofitable business; so they took all their rabbits out into the bush—and opened the baskets.

I happen to have in my possession an old newspaper containing a portrait 6 of Mr Thatcher—and a thoroughly benevolent old gentleman he looks—also a picture of the medal presented by the Acclimatization Society to Mr Thatcher in recognition of his splendid achievement in the matter of rabbits. I presume Mr C. J. Thatcher possesses the original medal; probably it hangs in a conspicuous place in his drawing-room. It is a perfect example of the irony of history.

Why have I kept that old newspaper? Well, primarily, I suppose, because 7
I am interested in ethics, as we all are whether we know it or not. Every one of
us, every day, is passing moral judgments, though not in the technical terms of
the moralist. We do not, in our daily conversation, talk much about virtue, or
the *summum bonum,* or the moral sense, or the categorical imperative, or the
hedonistic calculus, or our ethical ideals; at least, we do talk about them continually, but not under those names. We don't say of a man that he is a highly
virtuous character; we say he's a pretty decent sort of chap. We don't say that
certain conduct is ethically indefensible; we say it's a bit over the fence. We
mean just the same. We are passing moral judgments.

And our underlying assumption is that it is quite easy to tell a good action 8
from a bad one, right conduct from wrong conduct. And this common assumption is favoured by popular preachers and writers, who tell us that we ought not
to split straws about a plain question, and that it is a simple thing to obey conscience, that divinely-given faculty which tells us, infallibly, what we ought to
do and what we ought not to do. They speak as if this conscience were a kind
of moral sense of smell, by which we can tell a good action from a bad one just
as certainly as we can, in the dark, tell a violet from a polecat. Well, I want to
ask those who hold such a comfortable doctrine a question which puzzles me.
Was Mr Thatcher's action, in introducing the rabbit into Australia, a good action or a bad one?

Mere common sense will not give us the answer. It would be hard to per- 9
suade common sense that an action which ruined thousands of innocent people
and made desolate vast tracts of country, which struck a terrific blow at the agricultural and pastoral industries of a continent, can be described as a good action. Neither will common sense blame Mr Thatcher for obeying orders. He is
unquestionably to be praised for his zeal, his enthusiasm, his unconquerable
persistence in what he thought to be an admirable project. We have only to look
at his portrait to see that he was a man of high character, a man actuated by the
best intentions. If intentions, as common sense tells us, are what really distinguish right conduct from wrong, Mr Thatcher beyond doubt acted rightly. What
then?—will common sense admit that a man may act rightly in doing a bad
action? It sounds like a paradox. It is certainly a puzzle; and if you never, in the
course of your practical life, feel that you are puzzled by it, that can only be
because you never think.

We make a mistake, of course, when we think of 'an action' as if it 10
were a simple separate whole. Merely to open a basket, as Mr Thatcher did,
is a thing neither right nor wrong in itself; all depends on what is inside
the basket—depends, that is, on the *consequence* of the basket's being opened.
The immediate consequence, in this instance, was that the rabbits jumped
out, happy in their freedom; so far, the act had added to the sum of happiness in the sentient world; so far, it was a good action. Ten years later, it
began to be of a darker colour, for its consequences had begun to develop.

Surely there never was a more fallacious saying than Tennyson's: 11

And, because right is right, to follow right
Were wisdom in the scorn of consequence.

Half the disasters endured by the long-suffering human race have been produced by good men who acted in the scorn of consequence. To do a thing without considering what the result of your action will be is mere imbecility. The truth is with that other poet who tells us that

...Of waves
Our life is, and our deeds are pregnant graves
Blown rolling from the sunset to the dawn.

An action must be considered with its consequences; with the sum-total   12 of its consequences. And as no human being will live long enough to see the sum-total of the consequences of any of his actions—for the ultimate consequence cannot be known until time comes to an end—we can never say that a given action is absolutely good or absolutely bad.

How then are we to choose between right and wrong conduct? Choose we   13 must, somehow; 'life's business', as Browning says, 'being just the terrible choice.' Some years ago, certain persons wished to introduce into Western Australia a certain kind of deer. It was pointed out, however, that this very species had been introduced into South Africa, had eaten farmers out of house and home, and had been in fact a greater plague than ever the rabbit was in Australia. The persons who were preparing to do this thing without inquiry into the consequence of similar procedure in other countries would have been guilty, had they had their way, not merely of a bad action, but of a wrong action. It would be of no use to plead that their intentions were good—we know what road is paved with good intentions. It would be of no use to tell us that their consciences had commended the act; it is a common and deadly fallacy, that a mysterious faculty called the conscience absolves us from the duty of finding out, to the best of our ability, the probable consequences of our action....Consideration of Mr Thatcher and his basket of rabbits thus brings us round to the conclusion reached so many centuries ago by Socrates. Virtue is knowledge.

1970

QUESTIONS FOR DISCUSSION

Content

a. Who was Socrates, and in what way does his claim that "virtue is knowledge" serve as Murdoch's thesis? Why did he withhold this statement until the very end of the essay?

b. Why does Murdoch believe that the quote from Tennyson in paragraph 11 is an example of fallacious thinking?

c. Why is the medal awarded to Mr. Thatcher by the Acclimatization Society a "perfect example of the irony of history"? How does this statement relate to Murdoch's thesis?

d. What does the author mean when he claims that "An action must be considered with...the sum-total of its consequences" (paragraph 12)?

e. What can we infer from this selection about the eventual results of Thatcher's introduction of rabbits into Australia? Why does Murdoch call them "deadly pests"?

f. Why, in paragraph 13, does Murdoch tell us of an attempt to introduce deer into Western Australia? Is this illustration necessary? What purpose does it serve?

g. Why is Thatcher's eagerness to defend his father's claim a "singular example of filial devotion" (paragraph 3)? What is the effect of Murdoch's comparing it to someone's attempts at proving "that he, and he alone, had had the honour of starting the Great War"?

h. What is the paradox that Murdoch discusses in paragraph 9? What do you make of his assertion that "if you never...feel that you are puzzled by it, that can only be because you never think"? Does this statment help prepare you for his conclusion?

Strategy and Style

i. What function do paragraphs 7 and 8 serve? Why are they essential to the structure of Murdoch's argument?

j. Why does Murdoch spend so much time telling the Thatcher-Collison story (paragraphs 2 through 6)? Would his argument have been less persuasive had he condensed this anecdote?

k. Paragraph 4 is heavily ironic. Explain the effect of Murdoch's calling Thatcher an Alexander "sighing...for more worlds to conquer." What other examples of irony can you identify in this paragraph?

l. The author's tone at the end of the first paragraph is almost self-effacing. How would you describe the tone of the conclusion? What accounts for the difference in tone?

SUGGESTIONS FOR SHORT WRITING

a. Write a response to this essay using only questions.

b. Do you agree with Murdoch's last sentence, "Virtue is knowledge"? Write an explanation of your opinion. You may want to include your definition of virtue, knowledge, or both, to support your opinion.

SUGGESTIONS FOR SUSTAINED WRITING

a. Using your own experience and Murdoch's essay as sources of information and ideas, argue that "good intentions" don't always guarantee "good actions."

b. In paragraph 11, Murdoch reminds us that "half the disasters endured by the long-suffering human race have been produced by good men who acted in the scorn of consequence." Do you agree that many of the world's ills can be traced to good people who refused to anticipate the consequences of their actions? Explain and defend this notion by providing examples from history or from current events.

c. Do you believe that "we can never say that a given action is absolutely good or absolutely bad"? Write an essay in which you refute or defend Murdoch in response to this question.

ACKNOWLEDGMENTS

American Friends Service Committee, "Struggle for Justice." From *Struggle for Justice, A Report on Crime and Punishment in America,* prepared for the American Friends Service Committee. Copyright © 1971 by Hill and Wang, Inc. Reprinted by permission of Hill & Wang, a division of Farrar, Straus & Giroux, Inc.

Maya Angelou, "Grandmother's Victory." From *I Know Why the Caged Bird Sings.* Copyright © 1969 by Maya Angelou. Reprinted by permission of Random House, Inc.

Isaac Asimov, "The Villain in the Atmosphere." From *Past, Present and Future.* Copyright © 1968 by Isaac Asimov. Reprinted by permission of the author.

James David Barber, "Presidential Character and How to Foresee It." From *The Presidential Character.* Copyright © 1972. Reprinted by permission of the author.

Bruno Bettelheim, "The Holocaust." From *Surviving and Other Essays.* Copyright © 1979 by Bruno Bettelheim. Reprinted by permission of Alfred A. Knopf, Inc.

Robert Brustein, "Reflections on Horror Movies." From *The Third Theatre.* Copyright © 1958 by Robert Brustein. Reprinted by permission of Alfred A. Knopf, Inc.

William F. Buckley, Jr., "Why Don't We Complain?" First appeared in *Esquire,* January 1961. Copyright © 1961 by William F. Buckley, Jr. Reprinted by permission of Wallace Literary Agency, Inc.

Albert Camus, "The Myth of Sisyphus." From *The Myth of Sisyphus,* trans. by Justin O'Brien. Copyright © 1955 by Alfred A. Knopf, Inc. Reprinted by permission of Alfred A. Knopf, Inc.

Rachel Carson, "The Grey Beginnings." From *The Sea Around Us,* Revised Edition, by Rachel L. Carson. Copyright © 1950, 1951, 1961 by Rachel L. Carson; renewed 1979 by Roger Christie. Reprinted by permission of Oxford University Press, Inc.

Bruce Catton, "Grant and Lee: A Study in Contrasts." From *The American Story.* Copyright U.S. Capitol Historical Society. Reprinted by their permission.

Norman Cousins, "Pain Is Not the Ultimate Enemy." From *Anatomy of an Illness, As Perceived by the Patient,* by Norman Cousins, by permission of W. W. Norton & Company, Inc. Copyright © 1979 by W. W. Norton & Company, Inc.

Robertson Davies, "A Few Kind Words for Superstition." From *Newsweek,* November 20, 1978. Copyright © by Robertson Davies. Reprinted by permission of the author.

479

Joan Didion, "The Metropolitan Cathedral." From *Salvador.* Copyright © 1983 by Joan Didion. Reprinted by permission of Simon & Schuster, Inc.

Annie Dillard, "Transfiguration." From *Holy the Firm.* Copyright © 1977 by Annie Dillard. Reprinted by permission of Harper Collins Publishers Inc.

Loren Eiseley, "The Cosmic Prison," Section I. Reprinted with permission of Charles Scribner's Sons, an imprint of Macmillan Publishing Company, from *The Invisible Pyramid* by Loren Eiseley. Copyright © 1970 Loren Eiseley.

Joseph Epstein, "The Virtues of Ambition." From *Ambition: The Secret Passion.* Copyright © 1980 by Joseph Epstein. Reprinted by permission of Georges Borchardt, Inc., for Joseph Epstein.

Peter Farb and George Armelagos, "The Patterns of Eating." From *Consuming Passions.* Copyright © 1980 by the Estate of Peter Farb. Reprinted by permission of Houghton Mifflin Company. All rights reserved.

E. M. Forster, "My Wood." From *Abinger Harvest.* Copyright © 1936; renewed 1964 by Edward Morgan Forster. Reprinted by permission of Harcourt Brace Jovanovich, Inc., and by Edward Arnold Publishers Ltd.

William Freundlich, "The Crime of the Tooth: Dentistry in the Chair." Copyright © 1987 by Harper's Magazine. All rights reserved. Reprinted from the September issue by special permission.

Euell Gibbons, "How to Cook a Carp." From *Stalking the Wild Asparagus.* Copyright © 1962, used by permission of Alan C. Hood & Co., Inc., Brattleboro, VT 05301.

William Golding, "Thinking as a Hobby." From *Holiday,* August 1961. Copyright © 1961 by William Golding. Renewed. Reprinted by permission of Curtis Brown, Ltd.

Ellen Goodman, "Watching the Grasshopper Get the Goodies." From *At Large.* Copyright © 1981 by The Washington Post Company. Reprinted by permission of Summit Books, a division of Simon & Schuster, Inc.

Nadine Gordimer, "Procrustean Bedfellows: Art and the State in South Africa." From the December 24, 1983, issue of *The Nation.* Reprinted by permission of *The Nation* magazine/The Nation Co., Inc., © 1983.

Stephen Jay Gould, "Were Dinosaurs Dumb?" From *The Panda's Thumb: More Reflections in Natural History,* by Stephen Jay Gould, by permission of W. W. Norton & Company, Inc. Copyright © 1980 by Stephen Jay Gould.

Barbara Grizzuti Harrison, "Moral Ambiguity." From *Off Center.* Copyright © 1980 by Barbara Grizzuti Harrison. Used by permission of Doubleday, a division of Bantam Doubleday Dell Publishing Group, Inc.

Luz Alicia Herrara, "Testimonies of Guatemalan Women." From *Latin American Perspectives,* vol. 7, nos. 2 and 3, 1980. Copyright © 1980. Reprinted by permission of Sage Publications, Inc.

Ann Hodgman, "Backwater Cuisine." From *Spy* magazine, September 1987. Copyright © 1987 Spy magazine. Reprinted by permission of Spy magazine.

Richard Howey, "How to Write a Rotten Poem with Almost No Effort." First appeared in *The Plain Dealer.* Reprinted by permission of the author.

Langston Hughes, "Salvation." From *The Big Sea.* Copyright © 1940 by Langston Hughes. Renewal copyright © 1968 by Arna Bontemps and George Houston Bass. Reprinted by permission of Hill and Wang, a division of Farrar, Straus and Giroux, Inc.

Martin Luther King, Jr., "I Have a Dream." Copyright © 1963 by Martin Luther King, Jr. Reprinted by permission of Joan Daves Agency.

Akira Kurosawa, "Crybaby." From *Something Like an Autobiography.* Copyright © 1982 by Akira Kurosawa. Reprinted by permission of Alfred A. Knopf, Inc.

Margaret Laurence, "Where the World Began." From *Heart of a Stranger.* Copyright © 1976. Used by permission of the Canadian publishers, McClelland & Steward, Toronto, and the Lucinda Vardey Agency, Toronto.

Arthur E. Lean, "The Farce Called 'Grading.'" From *And Merely Teach: Irreverent Essays on the Mythology of Education.* Copyright © 1968, 1976. Reprinted by permission of Southern Illinois University Press.

William Least Heat Moon, "Tuesday Morning." From *Blue Highways: A Journey into America.* Copyright © 1982 by William Least Heat Moon. Reprinted by permission of Little, Brown & Company.

Doris Lessing, "My Father." From *A Small Personal Voice.* Copyright © 1956, 1957, 1959, 1963, 1966, 1968, 1971, 1972, 1974 by Doris Lessing. Reprinted by permission of Jonathan Clowes Ltd.

Barry Lopez, "My Horse." From *The North American Review,* Summer 1975. Copyright © 1975 by Barry Lopez. Reprinted by permission of Sterling Lord Literistic, Inc.

David M. Ludlum, "The Climythology of America." From *Weatherwise* magazine, vol. 40, no. 5, October 1987. Reprinted by permission of the Helen Dwight Reid Educational Foundation. Published by Heldref Publications, 4000 Albemarle St., N.W., Washington, DC 20016. Copyright © 1987.

Marya Mannes, "How Do You Know It's Good?" From *Glamour,* November 1962. Copyright © 1962 by Marya Mannes. Reprint permission actively sought.

Joyce Maynard, "I Remember. . . ." First appeared in *TV Guide.* Copyright © 1975 by Joyce Maynard. Reprinted by permission of Robert Cornfield Literary Agency.

H. L. Mencken, "The Penalty of Death." From *A Mencken Chrestomathy.* Copyright 1926 by Alfred A. Knopf, Inc., and renewed 1954 by H. L. Mencken. Reprinted by permission of Alfred A. Knopf, Inc.

Horace Miner, "Body Ritual Among the Nacirema." Reproduced by permission of the American Anthropological Association from *American Anthropologist* 68:3, June 1956. Not for further reproduction.

Jessica Mitford, "Behind the Formaldehyde Curtain." From *The American Way of Death,* Simon & Schuster. Copyright © 1963, 1978 by Jessica Mitford. Reprinted by permission of Jessica Mitford. All rights reserved.

Farley Mowat, "The Perfect House." From *People of the Deer.* Copyright © 1952 Farley Mowat Ltd. Used by permission of the author.

Walter Murdoch, "On Rabbits, Morality, Etc." From *The Best of Walter Murdoch: 72 Essays.* Copyright © 1947, Barbara Murdoch. Reprinted by permission of Collins Angus & Robertson Publishers Pty Limited (Australia).

George Orwell, "A Hanging." From *Shooting an Elephant and Other Essays.* Copyright © 1950 by Sonia Brownell Orwell; renewed 1978 by Sonia Pitt-Rivers. Reprinted by permission of Harcourt Brace Jovanovich, Inc., the estate of the late Sonia Brownell Orwell and Martin Secker & Warburg Ltd.

Cynthia Ozick, "On Permission to Write." From *Metaphor and Memory.* Copyright © 1984 by Cynthia Ozick. Reprinted by permission of Alfred A. Knopf, Inc. Originally appeared in *The New York Times Magazine.*

Jo Goodwin Parker, "What Is Poverty." From *America's Other Children: Public Schools Outside Suburbs* by George Henderson. Copyright © 1971 by the University of Oklahoma Press. Used by permission of George Henderson.

Alan Paton, "Eight Signposts to Salvation." Reprinted with permission of Charles Scribner's Sons, an imprint of Macmillan Publishing Company from *Knocking on the Door* by Alan Paton. Copyright © 1975 Alan Paton.

Alexander Petrunkevitch, "The Spider and the Wasp." From *Scientific American,* August 1952. Reprinted with permission. Copyright © 1952 by Scientific American, Inc. All rights reserved.

James C. Rettie, "'But a Watch in the Night': A Scientific Fable." From *Forever the Land,* edited by Russell and Kate Lord. Copyright 1950 by Harper & Row, Publishers, Inc. Renewed 1978 by Russell and Kate Lord. Reprinted by permission of Harper Collins Publishers.

Mordecai Richler, "Main Street." From *The Street: A Memoir.* Copyright © 1969 by Mordecai Richler. Reprinted by permission of International Creative Management, Inc.

Erika Ritter, "Bicycles." From *Urban Scrawl* © 1984, by Erika Ritter. Used by permission of Macmillan Canada.

Richard Rodriguez, "Does America Still Exist?" First appeared in *Harper's,* March 1984. Copyright © 1984 by Richard Rodriguez. Reprinted by permission of Georges Borchardt, Inc., for Richard Rodriguez.

Murray Ross, "Football Red and Baseball Green." First appeared in *Chicago Review.* Copyright © 1971. Reprinted by permission of the author.

May Sarton, "The Rewards of Living a Solitary Life." From *The New York Times,* April 8, 1974. Copyright © 1974 by The New York Times Company. Reprinted by permission.

Jonathan Schell, "Nuclear Holocaust." From *The Fate of the Earth.* Copyright © 1982 by Jonathan Schell. Reprinted by permission of Alfred A. Knopf, Inc. Originally appeared in *The New Yorker.*

Richard Selzer, "The Discus Thrower." From *Confessions of a Knife.* Copyright © 1979 by David Goldman and Janet Selzer, trustees. Reprinted by permission of William Morrow and Company, Inc., Publishers, New York.

Susan Sontag, "Women's Beauty: Put Down or Power Source." Copyright © 1975 by Susan Sontag. Reprinted by permission of Farrar, Straus and Giroux, Inc.

Lewis Thomas, "The Iks." Copyright © 1973 by The Massachusetts Medical Society. From *The Lives of a Cell* by Lewis Thomas. Used by permission of Viking Penguin, a division of Penguin Books USA Inc.

Susan Allen Toth, "Cinematypes." From *Harper's* magazine, May 1980. Copyright © 1980. Reprinted by permission of the author.

Lindsy Van Gelder, "The Great Person-Hole Cover Debate: A Modest Proposal for Anyone Who Thinks the Word 'He' Is Just Plain Easier. . . ." First appeared in *Ms.* magazine, April 1980. Reprinted by permission of the author.

William Carlos Williams, "At the Ball Game." From *The Collected Poems of William Carlos Williams, 1909–1939, vol. I.* Copyright 1938 by New Directions Publishing Corporation. Reprinted by permission of New Directions Publishing Corporation.

Marie Winn, "Viewing vs. Reading." From *The Plug-in Drug* by Marie Winn. Copyright © 1977, 1985 by Marie Winn Miller. Used by permission of Viking Penguin, a division of Penguin Books USA Inc.

Tom Wolfe, "Pornoviolence." From *Mauve Gloves and Madmen, Clutter and Vine.* Copyright © 1967, 1968, 1973, 1974, 1975, 1976 by Tom Wolfe. Reprinted by permission of Farrar, Straus and Giroux, Inc.